THE COLLECTED WORKS OF
ABRAHAM LINCOLN

THE COLLECTED WORKS OF
ABRAHAM LINCOLN

THE ABRAHAM LINCOLN ASSOCIATION
SPRINGFIELD, ILLINOIS

ROY P. BASLER, *EDITOR*

MARION DOLORES PRATT AND LLOYD A. DUNLAP
ASSISTANT EDITORS

INDEX

RUTGERS UNIVERSITY PRESS
NEW BRUNSWICK, NEW JERSEY

FOREWORD

IN ADDITION to the index of names, places, and subjects of the documents and notes in volumes I through VIII, two supplementary sections (in small type) are included in this volume: an index of appendix II, volume VIII, and a list of the institutions in which Lincoln documents are located. Appendix II, volume VIII, a chronological listing of forgeries, spurious documents, and other Lincoln items as described in the headnote to the appendix (and repeated on page 321 of this volume) will be of primary interest to the specialist. For general use, therefore, where interest is focussed on the extant writings and public utterances of Lincoln actually reproduced in these volumes, attention can be confined to the main index.

From its very nature, the diverse subject matter in a collection of primary source material cannot easily be interpreted and analyzed into a complete set of subject headings which might answer the particular interest of every reader. Therefore, to give the reader a set of subject-matter clues, the following system has been employed: When references to text could be grouped under a head which one might expect to find, a main subject entry has been inserted in its alphabetical position. Then, under a series of LINCOLN, ABRAHAM, entries, the entire text of the eight volumes has been covered either by subentries or cross reference.

These eleven main entries under LINCOLN, ABRAHAM, represent the following division of subject matter in terms of Lincoln's life and career:

LINCOLN, ABRAHAM, autobiographical references: (Subentries indicate location of Lincoln autobiographical data and biographical data in notes.)

LINCOLN, ABRAHAM, his comments on: (Subentries indicate location of a selected list of Lincoln quotations; cross references indicate main entries through which other quotations may be located.)

LINCOLN, ABRAHAM, lawyer:

LINCOLN, ABRAHAM, postmaster:

LINCOLN, ABRAHAM, storekeeper:

LINCOLN, ABRAHAM, surveyor:

LINCOLN, ABRAHAM, political career of: (Subentries and cross references locate all references to Lincoln's political life up to his nomination as President of the United States.)

LINCOLN, ABRAHAM, Presidential nominee:

LINCOLN, ABRAHAM, President-elect:

LINCOLN, ABRAHAM, President: (Subentries and cross references locate references to Lincoln's functioning as Chief Executive, *excluding* references concerning the conduct of the Civil War.)

LINCOLN, ABRAHAM, Commander-in-Chief (Civil War): (Subentries and cross references locate references to Lincoln's functioning as Commander-in-Chief in the Civil War.)

Throughout the index, the order of subentries is chronological; the first page reference to each subentry determines that subentry's chronological position. A page reference without a volume number must be assumed to pertain to the last volume number mentioned in preceding references. Hyphenated page references do not necessarily indicate continuous text; they more frequently indicate that pertaining references are located on each of the included pages.

In compiling the index, certain practical considerations caused a transfer of the work of compilation to the Rutgers University Press, and, specifically, to Ruth M. Field, Associate Editor of the Press. To her the Abraham Lincoln Association expresses its gratitude for bringing to successful completion an interminably detailed task. The section on Troops and much of the research work concerning the identification of names was done by James N. Adams of the Illinois Historical Society. The two supplementary indexes were compiled by Marion D. Pratt, Assistant Editor of the *Collected Works*. From a reading of proof Mrs. Pratt also contributed many helpful suggestions which were incorporated in the finished work. To them also the Association is deeply grateful.

THE COLLECTED WORKS OF
ABRAHAM LINCOLN

Washington, June 12. 1848—

My dear wife:

On my return from Philadelphia yesterday, where, in my anxiety I had been led to attend the whig convention, I found your last letter— I was so tired and sleepy, having ridden all night, that I could not answer it till to-day; and now I have to do so in the H.R. The leading matter in your letter, is your wish to return to this side of the Mountains— Will you be a good girl in all things, if I consent? Then come along, and that as soon as possible— Having got the idea in my head, I shall be impatient till I see you— You will not have money enough to bring you; but I presume your uncle will supply you, and I will refund him here— By the way you do not mention whether you have received the fifty dollars I sent you— I do not much fear but that you got it; because the want of it would have induced you say something in relation to it— If your uncle is already at Lexington, you might induce him to start on earlier than the first of July; he could stay in Kentucky longer on his return, and so make up for lost time— Since I began this letter, the H.R. has passed a resolution for adjourning on the 17th July, which probably will pass the Senate— I hope this letter will not be disagreeable to you, which, together with the circumstances under which I write, I hope will excuse me for not writing a

longer one— Come on just as soon as you can— I want to see you, and our dear dear boys very much— Every body here wants to see our dear Bobby—
                              Affectionately
                                   A. Lincoln

INDEX TO

THE COLLECTED WORKS OF

ABRAHAM LINCOLN

A

Abbot, Mrs. Stephen, II: 307n

Abbott, George, VI: 198

Abbott, John H., VII: 447-48

Abbott, Joseph Carter, IV: 68

Abbott, Titus H., II: 182

Abdul Aziz Khan, Padischah of the Ottoman Empire, IV: 546

Abdul Mejid Khan, Padischah of the Ottoman Empire, IV: 546

Abeel, D. K., VII: 197n

Abel, Oramel H., II: 424-25

Abell, Bennett, I: 55, 86, 93; IV: 310n

Abell, Mrs. Bennett, *see* Abell, Elizabeth (Owens)

Abell, Elizabeth (Owens), I: 55, 79, 117-18

Abell, Oliver Greene, IV: 310

Abercrombie, Daniel P., V: 9

Abercrombie, John Joseph, VI: 211n

Abert, John James, II: 23

Abingdon (Va.), VI: 534; VIII: 302n

Abiqun Indian Agency, IV: 307

Ables, J. Christopher, VIII: 68

Abolition of slavery, *see* Emancipation; Declaration of Independence; *and* Constitution, (U. S.)

Abolitionism: increases evils of slavery, I: 74-76, 113; L. and Whigs charged with, 347, 458, II: 157, 228-29, 322-23, 492, III: 206; and "all men are created free and equal," II: 130-31, 323

L. and Republicans charged with: in 1854 political campaign, 229, 234, 239-40, 273, 288n; in 1856 political campaign, 344-45, 365-66, 368-73; in 1858 political campaign, 459, 497-98, III: 1-326 *passim* (inc. L.-Douglas debates), 388, 396, 440-41, IV: 2

L. "not an abolitionist," II: 323; L. on definition of abolitionist, 365; mention of Abolitionist Club, 524n; Comte de Gasparin on, V: 356n; Weed on Greeley's attitude toward, VI: 83n, 514n; Lowell on the war and, VII: 132n

Abraham Lincoln: A History (Nicolay and Hay), II: 32n, 35n; IV: 63n; V: 337n, 404n; VI:

499n; VII: 234n, 329n, 346n, 420n, 451n, 518n, 531n; VIII: 254n, 326n

Abraham Lincoln: A New Portrait (Hertz), cited in footnotes on the ff. pages: I: 367, 477; II: 53, 118, 191, 201, 208, 225, 376, 382, 410, 412, 458, 460, 473, 482; III: 471; IV: 53, 55, 76, 95, 131, 133, 156, 177, 286, 314, 321, 342, 345, 349, 363, 366, 444, 523, 531, 539

    V: 25, 68, 158, 200, 213, 229, 260, 303, 306, 335, 386, 391, 484, 517; VI: 9, 37, 143, 209, 274, 310, 324, 346, 364, 368, 485; VII: 87, 130, 240, 254, 266, 321, 334-35, 343, 372, 383, 485, 505, 510, 512, 549

    VIII: 42, 98, 236, 241, 337, 387

Abraham Lincoln, Defendant (Townsend), II: 195n

Abraham Lincoln, 1809-1858 (Beveridge), I: 244n

Abraham Lincoln: The People's Leader (Putnam), IV: 59n, 119n

Abraham Lincoln: The War Years (Sandburg), VII: 348n

Abraham Lincoln and His Presidency (Barrett), II: 54n; VII: 280n

Abraham Lincoln and the Jews (Markens), V: 69n; VII: 323n; VIII: 213n

Abraham Lincoln and the Widow Bixby (Bullard), VIII: 117n

"Abraham Lincoln as a Receiving Attorney: Kelly *vs.* Blackledge" (art.), II: 316n

"Abraham Lincoln as Seen by a Life-Long Democrat, After Going through Baltimore" (art.), IV: 544n

Abraham Lincoln Association, I: vii-xv

"Abraham Lincoln at Tremont Temple in 1848" (art.), I: 519n; III: 555n

Abraham Lincoln Association Papers, II: 431n

Abraham Lincoln Book Shop (Chicago), I: xiv

Abraham Lincoln Quarterly, II: 148n

Abraham Lincoln Tributes . . . , IV: 544n

Abrahams, Richard M., VI: 460-61

Abrams, Gordon, II: 149-50

Abrams, R. M., *see* Abrahams, Richard M.

Abshier, John T., VII: 252

Absterdam, John, and his invention of a projectile, VII: 127, 216n, 229, 236-37

Acapulco (Mexico), IV: 536n; V: 257n

Accomac County (Va.), V: 50, 502n; VI: 29, 186-87, 401

Accotink River (Va.), V: 121n

Account of the Private Life and Public Services of Salmon Portland Chase (Warden), IV: 11n, 168n; V: 88n, 219n, 508n; VI: 122n, 202n, 209n, 213n, 294n, 538n; VII: 120n, 182n, 184n, 195n, 376n, 392n

Accounting Office, General, IV: 407n, 528n; V: 394n

Achá, José María de, VI: 45

Acker, William Henry, IV: 446

Ackerman, George B., VII: 257

Ackerman, James, VII: 195n

Acquia, *see* Aquia Creek

Acuff, Anderson, VIII: 68

Adams, Mrs., VII: 544

Adams, Adam, II: 72n, 133-34, 190, 199-201, 206-208, 285; VIII: 592-93

Adams, Augustus, II: 296, 480

Adams, Charles, IV: 181n

Adams, Charles Francis, minister to Great Britain, IV: 161, 281n, 292-93, 376-80; V: 115; VI: 9-10, 65n, 89n, 160; VIII: 140n, 286-87

Adams, Christopher, IV: 361

Adams, Daniel W., VI: 39n, 480

Adams, Miss E. L., VI: 432n

Adams, George Franklin, VII: 155n

Adams, Green, IV: 294; V: 94, 142; VI: 42, 144n, 229, 401-402; VII: 169

Adams, Henry A., IV: 465n

Adams, Mrs. Henry C., VI: 42n

Adams, Henry J., IV: 476

Adams, Jacob, II: 208

Adams, James, I: 89-106; II: 70-71

Adams, John (1735-1826), I: 172; III: 162, 375, 484; IV: 89, 115; VI: 319-20

Adams, John Quincy, I: 172, 175, 450n, 474-75, 482, 485; II: 124, 351; III: 162; IV: 81n, 420

Adams, John S., Sr., V: 142n; VI: 402n; VII: 169n

Adams, Lucien Bonaparte, I: 91n, 95-96, 98-99, 102-103, 105; II: 329

Adams, Miss S. M., VI: 432n

Adams, Stephen M., V: 89n

Adams, Thomas, VIII: 273

Adams, William, VIII: 68

Adams Express Company, V: 364n; VI: 125n; VII: 337n; VIII: 266n

Addams, John Huy, II: 296, 303, 480

Addison, John, II: 59, 65, 67, 91-93

Additional Regulations Concerning Commercial Intercourse with and in States Declared in Insurrection (pamphlet), VII: 152n, 166n, 354n

Address of the Hon. Abraham Lincoln . . . at Cooper Institute . . . (pamphlet), III: 522-50

Address to His Law Students . . . , An (Edmonds), VII: 133n

Adela (ship), VI: 79n

Admiral P. Tordenskiold (ship), V: 520

Advertisements: for a lost horse, I: 47; for sale of town lots; II: 317

A-e-cha-ga (Indian), V: 543

Aesop fable, I: 315

Africa (ship), V: 547

African slave trade, *see* Slave trade

Afton (steamboat), see *Effie Afton*

Agnew, Eliza, V: 279n

Agriculture: L. claims no experience with farming, I: 282, III: 473; agricultural wealth of Ill., I: 135, 402-403; Jefferson, Calhoun, and Jackson on, 310; effect of tariff on, 310, 334, 407-16; importance of Indian corn abroad, 397; advantage of railroad construction to, 397, 402-405; the beginnings of, II: 440; mention of state agricultural societies, III: 471, IV: 166, V: 406; importance of capacity production, III: 473-76; use of machines and steam power, 474-77; importance of free labor to, 478-81; and London World's Fair, IV: 551, V: 98n; establishment of U. S. Department of, V: 46, 526-27, VI: 343, 367-68; foreign purchase of seeds, VI: 50n; international exhibition (Germany), 51, 206, VII: 140; dismissal of U. S. Department chemist, VII: 3-4

Agricultural and Statistical Bureau, V: 46

Agricultural College of Pennsylvania, *see* Pennsylvania State College

Agua Nueva (Mexico), II: 86

Aguirre, Atanasio Cruz, VII: 493-94

Ahotonna (Indian), VII: 325

Aigner, Godfrey, IV: 469

Aiken, ———, VI: 153

Aiken, Frederick A., IV: 504n

Aitkin, William F., II: 188

Alabama, I: 75n; II: 231; V: 122n, 298; VI: 471n; VII: 15; VIII: 112

Alabama (steamboat), VIII: 134-35

Albany (Ill.), survey of, I: facing 49

Albany (N.Y.), I: 209; II: 349, 354; IV: 224-26; V: 300, 433n; VI: 235, 260-69, 302-305; *see also* Albany Penitentiary

Albany Journal, IV: 57n; VI: 83

Albany Penitentiary, V: 430n; VI: 551n; VII: 92n, 176n, 256n; VIII: 119n, 240n, 251n, 300, 326n

Albee, George Emerson, VIII: 32

Albemarle (steamboat), VII: 360; VIII: 94, 134

Albert, Anselme, V: 272n

Albert Edward, Prince of Wales (Edward VII), V: 117-18; VI: 182, 222; VII: 231

Albert of Saxe-Coburg-Gotha, Prince Consort of Great Britain, V: 117-18

Albin, William M., VII: 78

Albrecht, Archduke of Austria, VII: 476

Albright, Charles Jefferson, VII: 131n, 393-94

Alden, George C., V: 228

Alden, James, V: 215

Alderman, David, VI: 544

Alderson, ———, VIII: 76

Aldie (Va.), V: 234, 461

Aldie's Gap (Va.), VI: 289

Aldis, A. O., VIII: 303n

Aldrich, Cyrus, V: 493n, 541-42

Aldrich, Mark, I: 76

Aledo (Ill.) *Record*, IV: 125n

Alexander, Andrew Jonathan, VII: 307n, 312n

Alexander, Barton Stone, VI: 411; VII: 468

Alexander, Charles A., VII: 80

Alexander, Charles M., VII: 525

Alexander, Jediah Franklin, II: 446-47, 532

Alexander, John, IV: 528n; VII: 65

Alexander, John C., I: 14

Alexander, Junius B., VI: 422

Alexander, Mary C., VII: 80n

Alexander, Milton K., II: 218-20

Alexander, Mrs. Paul F., II: 447n

Alexander, Urbin, I: 12

Alexander, William, VI: 356; VII: 260

Alexander, William M., VIII: 68

Alexander II of Russia, V: 74-75, 97, 137, 440; VII: 39, 296

Alexandra, Princess of Denmark (later Queen of Great Britain), VI: 182, 222; VII: 231

Alexandra Josefovna [Joseephowna], Grand Duchess of Russia, V: 440

Alexandra Petrovna, Grand Duchess of Russia, VII: 296

Alexandria (Egypt), IV: 552; V: 229; VI: 105n

Alexandria (La.), VI: 244; VIII: 15n

Alexandria (Va.): Ellsworth killed at, IV: 273n, 386n, 479; recommended occupation of (May '61), 385; mention of military units located near, 446, VII: 137; location of Peirpoint government, VI: 130n, VII: 83, 204; L. plans to visit (June '63) VI: 271n; location of army hospital, 313n; blockade lifted, 479, VIII: 396; recruitment (Mass.) of colored troops, VII: 204; mention of a "Convention" (March '64), 232n; mention of 1864 judge in U. S. district court, 251n; Soldiers Rest, 291n; pass for travel to, VIII: 169n

Mentioned re military operations and: McClellan, V: 34, 396, 399; McDowell, 240, 284n; Burnside, 385n; Haupt, 397-98, 400-402; Hooker, VI: 258n, 271n; McCallum, 481-82; Meade, 534n; Slough, VII: 544, VIII: 9

Alexandria & Orange Railroad, VI: 250n, 270n, 274n, 534

Alger, Russell Alexander, VII: 176-77, 439

Alice Maud Mary, Princess of Great Britain, V: 363

[4]

Aliens, *see* Foreign-born
Alies & Morrison, II: 411
Allard, Luther S., II: 226
Allbright, *see* Albright, Charles Jefferson
Allee, Abraham, VIII: 51n, 52n
Allegheny Arsenal (Pittsburgh), V: 110n
Allegheny County (Md.), VIII: 48n
Allegheny County (Pa.), IV: 208; VI: 512n
Allen, Abner Jones, V: 277n
Allen, Beverly, VII: 235-36, 458-59
Allen, Charles, II: 280
Allen, Cyrus McCracken, IV: 46-47, 410; V: 291; VIII: 117, 119n
Allen, Cyrus McCracken, Jr., IV: 417
Allen, Elisha Hunt, VII: 383
Allen, George Townsend, II: 296, 305
Allen, Helen L., VIII: 422n
Allen, Horace, VI: 112n
Allen, James Cameron, II: 287, 292-93
Allen, James D., I: 139, 153n
Allen, James M., I: 297; II: 424; III: 372, 377; VI: 197
Allen, John, I: 60-61, 287-88
Allen, [Dr.] John, I: 21-22, 359
Allen, Joseph W., V: 136; VII: 231-32
Allen, Julian, IV: 374
Allen, Madison, I: 46
Allen, Nathan, III: 126
Allen, Robert (Ill.), I: 48-49, 122, 289-90, 303, 324, 328-29; II: 39
Allen, Robert, Jr. (Ill.), I: 49n; IV: 560n; V: 192n; VI: 228n, 450, 465n, 473; VII: 229-30; VIII: 363n
Allen, Robert (Tenn.), VIII: 68
Allen, Samuel, I: 32
Allen, William Francis (N.J.), VII: 231-32
Allen, William Francis (N.Y.), VII: 211n; VIII: 212n

Allen, William H., IV: 516
Allen, William Joshua, II: 296; V: 413, 427
Allen, Young W., VIII: 69
Allen & Stone (Athens, Ill.), I: 153, 335
Allen County (Ky.), VIII: 77-78
Allenton (Christian Co., Ill.), I: 130-31, 140, 142n
Allenton (head of Lake Peoria, Ill.), I: 32
Allentown (N. J.), VI: 191; VII: 264n
Alley, J. W., VIII: 69
Alley, Nelson, I: 13, 20-22
Alliance (Ohio), IV: 215
Alliance (ship), VII: 337n
Allibone, Samuel Austin, IV: 178; VIII: 79-80
Allin, James, II: 159
Allin, Thomas, VII: 369n
Allis, Horace B., VII: 335n
Allison, John Stadler, I: 502-503; II: 2
Allison Prairie (Ill.), I: 86
"Alnwick Castle" (poem), IV: 48
Alschuler, Samuel G., IV: 145
Alsop, Thomas, II: 188
Alton (Ill.), I: 111n, 188-90, 192, 398-403, 405; II: 212n, 470n; III: 283-325, 329; V: 170n, 183; VI: 324; VII: 97n, 204, 250; VIII: 122
Alton & Mount Carmel Railroad, I: 250
Alton & Sangamon Railroad, II: 98-103, 105-107, 110-111; IV: 189
Alton & Shelbyville Railroad, I: 250-51
Alton Courier, II: 303, 341n, 432n, 447n; III: 91n
Alton Freie Presse, II: 524n
Alton Telegraph, I: 125n, 143n, 349-53, 363; II: 227n
Altoona (Pa.), V: 441n
Alvey, James W., IV: 122
Alvey, William, I: 298
Alvord, Edward J., VII: 133n

Alvord, H. J., VIII: 220
Alvord, J. W., VI: 44
Alvord, James H., VIII: 412n
Ambler, Charles Henry, VIII: 392n
Ambos, Charles, III: 386-87, 393-94
Am-da-cha (Indian), V: 542
Amelia Court House (Va.), VIII: 390
Amelia Island, V: 167
America (periodical), VII: 419n
America before Europe (Comte de Gasparin), V: 352
American Annual Cyclopaedia, 1863, VI: 235n
American Art Association, catalogs cited, IV: 368n, 475n, 494n; V: 13n; VII: 222n, 305n; VIII: 73n, 160n, 191n, 303n, 321n, 426n
American Art Association Anderson Galleries, catalogs cited in footnotes on the ff. pages: IV: 279, 414, 495, 511, 521, 539; V: 12, 17, 82, 94, 221, 327, 398, 517; VI: 84, 421, 512, 519; VII: 149, 238, 267, 319, 343; VIII: 42, 97, 165, 169, 216, 314, 316, 351
American Autograph Shop, catalogs cited, VI: 553n; VIII: 160n, 161n, 179n
American Bank Note Company, IV: 326n
American Baptist Home Missionary Society, V: 446n; VII: 365n
American Book Prices Current, VI: 437n; VII: 479n
American Chapel (Paris, France), IV: 552n
American Colonization Society, II: 131-32, 544; III: 233; see also Colonization of Negroes
American Firearms (Van Rensselaer), IV: 399n
American House (Springfield), I: 207
American Jewry and the Civil War (Korn), V: 436n

American Knights, Order of, VII: 386n, 436n, 534-35; see also Copperheads
American News Company (N. Y.), IV: 191n
American Notes and Queries, V: 300n
American Party, see Know-Nothing Party
American State Papers, VIII: 206n
American Statesman: A Political History, The (Young), II: 388
American Temperance Union, IV: 419n
American Tract Society, III: 84, 87, 310; IV: 381-82
American Union, The [Steubenville, Ohio], IV: 207n
Ames, Adelbert, VIII: 351n
Ames, Edward Raymond, V: 64; VII: 179, 183n, 351n
Ames, Edward Raymond, Jr., V: 64
Ames, Horatio, VI: 484-85; VII: 510; VIII: 3
Ames, John Worthington, VIII: 351n
Amisville (Va.), V: 488n
Ammen, Daniel, VI: 174n
Ammen, Jacob, VIII: 111n
Amnesty proclamations (Dec. 8, '63, Mar. 26, '64), VI: 498n; VII: 50-52, 53-56 (text of), 60, 63-64, 67-68, 83n, 101-103, 108-109, 124, 126, 130-33, 141-42, 144, 149-50, 153-54, 161-63, 176-77, 180n, 184-85, 209, 239, 269-70 (text of), 351n; VIII: 152, 225, 372, 399n, 401-402; see also Loyalty oath
Amoor, see Amur River
Amory, James S., see Emory, James S.
Amory, Jonathan, VI: 71-72
Amory, Thomas Jonathan Coffin, VI: 71-72, 94
Amos, Joshua F., II: 80n, 343-44, 381, 395
Ampudia, Pedro de, II: 85

Amur River, V: 114; VII: 39n
Ancona, Sydenham Elnathan, V: 202-203
Anderson, Charles E., IV: 411
Anderson, Ephraim F., VIII: 411n
Anderson, Fred P., VIII: 234n
Anderson, George Washington, V: 67
Anderson, George Washington, Jr., VII: 511-12, 519n
Anderson, Hamilton, VI: 551n
Anderson, Isaac, I: 12, 152
Anderson, James H., IV: 278; VI: 507n
Anderson, Joseph, I: 89-93, 97-99, 103-104
Anderson, Mrs. Joseph, see Anderson, Mary
Anderson, Joseph Reid, V: 232, 248, 254
Anderson, Larz, IV: 398n
Anderson, Lucian, IV: 294; VII: 187n, 256n, 274, 291, 400
Anderson, Mary, I: 90n, 92
Anderson, Moses K., I: 152n
Anderson, Richard, I: 90n, 92-93
Anderson, Robert, IV: 279, 299, 321-22, 350, 359, 368-69, 409, 418, 423, 463, 489, 491, 524, 527n, 532, 541, 545; V: 23; VI: 386-87; VIII: 169n, 375n
Anderson, S. H., VIII: 4-5
Anderson, Tavner B., I: 11
Anderson, William G., I: 211; VI: 538n
Anderson, Mrs. Yeatman, III: 395n
Anderson Auction Company, catalogs cited, I: 15n; V: 332n; VII: 225n; VIII: 337n
Anderson Auction Company–Metropolitan Art Association, VIII: 285n
Anderson Cavalry (15th Pa.), VII: 353-54; VIII: 169n
Anderson County (Tenn.), VIII: 68
Anderson Galleries, catalogs cited in footnotes on the ff. pages:

IV: 445; V: 75, 395; VI: 438, 483, 521; VII: 226, 450; VIII: 4, 156, 168, 173, 177, 215, 244, 307, 321, 325, 426, 428
Anderson Zouaves (62d N.Y. Inf.), IV: 406n; VII: 436n
Andersonville (Ga.), VII: 538n
André, John, II: 275
Andrew, John Albion, III: 543n; IV: 148n, 186, 370n, 381-82, 404-405, 408, 550n, 557n; V: 96, 297n, 366-67, 384, 441n; VI: 221-22; VII: 190-92, 204n, 280n, 447; VIII: 108-10, 274n, 425n
Andrews, Edward W., VI: 135n
Andrews, George H., VIII: 231n, 257n
Andrews, George Leonard, VII: 155, 172
Andrews, Henry, VII: 111-12
Andrews, Israel D., VI: 284-85
Andrews, James, VIII: 339-40
Andrews, Rufus F., IV: 325n, 474; V: 410n; VII: 268n
Andrews, Samuel, VI: 425n
Andrews, Timothy Patrick, VI: 63, 109-10, 138-39, 193, 430; VII: 120, 358, 406n, 408, 430; VIII: 97
Andros, Milton, VI: 294n
Angle, Paul McClelland, I: vii, viii, xiv, xvii; see also Mary Lincoln, Wife and Widow; and New Letters and Papers of Lincoln
Angle, Paula, II: 285n
Anglo-African Institute for the Encouragement of Industry and Art, V: 371n
Angola, V: 141n
Anna (Ill.), VII: 74n
Anna Ella Carroll and Abraham Lincoln (Greenbie), V: 382n
Annals of Kansas (Wilder), VI: 335n
Annals of Salem (Felts), IV: 123n
Annals of the City of Trenton (Haven), VII: 458n
Annals of the United States Chris-

tian Commission (Moss), V: 67n; VIII: 246n

Annapolis (Md.), IV: 341n, 344, 346n, 347, 557; V: 132, 432; VI: 136, 491, 520; VIII: 94n, 251n, 423; *see also* Naval Academy, Annapolis

Annapolis Junction (Md.), IV: 347; VIII: 223n

Anthony, Daniel Read, VI: 188n

Anthony, Edward, VII: 123

Anthony, Henry Bowen, IV: 248, 293; VI: 552; VII: 219n; VIII: 288

Anthony, Henry T., VII: 123

Anti-Nebraska Editors Convention (1856), II: 333

Antietam (Md.), V: 426n, 427-28, 442, 448, 474-75, 511; VI: 75-76, 88, 130, 409; VII: 548-50; VIII: 238n

Antietam Creek, VI: 341n

Antietam Ford, V: 249n

Antonia, Infanta of Portugal, V: 105; VII: 478

Antonie, *see* Antonia

Antrim (Ohio), VI: 346n

Antwerp (Belgium), IV: 312

Apache Indians, IV: 307; VI: 153n; VII: 68

Apalachicola (Fla.), VIII: 396

Apia (Samoa), IV: 310

"Appeals to Lincoln's Clemency" (art.), V: 185n; VI: 1n, 35n, 437n; VII: 66n, 194n, 373n, 406n, 421n, 524n

"Apple of Gold" speech, IV: 168-69

Appleby, ———, IV: 218

Appleby, George F., VII: 407

Applegate, Daniel, VI: 433

Applegate, Jesse, VI: 433n

Appleton's Cyclopaedia, IV: 539n, 551n

Appointments: *see* Army appointments: Cabinet; Diplomatic appointments; Indian agencies; Judicial system; Marine Corps; Naval Academy, Annapolis;

Navy; Post Office Department; Territories; West Point

Others, IV: 298-311, 319-20, 323, 325-29, 333-36, 338, 356-57, 359-64, 367, 371, 374, 384, 390-92, 404, 441, 448, 452, 454, 456, 474, 485-86, 493, 495-96, 500-501, 508-509, 537, 542, 547, 551-52, 554, 556

V: 18, 21-22, 28, 33, 68, 71, 75, 81, 89, 93, 95, 104, 110-11, 114-15, 132, 142, 147-49, 157, 159, 163-64, 177, 188-89, 192, 205, 221, 291, 323, 332, 339, 348, 351, 353, 360-62, 375-76, 379, 383, 385-86, 394, 396-97, 403, 437, 464-65, 472-74, 490-91, 516

VI: 16, 67, 69, 83, 94, 118, 122-23, 128-29, 144-45, 150, 165, 167, 172, 174, 178-80, 202, 209-10, 213-14, 224, 232-33, 284, 312, 319, 361, 507, 521, 528, 545

VII: 3, 30, 75-76, 81-83, 91, 97, 101, 120, 133, 156-57, 166, 177, 181-82, 219-20, 238, 304, 332-33, 338, 369, 392, 412-14, 418-20, 442, 451-52, 454, 464-65, 471, 473, 497-98, 548

VIII: 7, 23, 25-26, 38-39, 50, 121-22, 157, 159, 161-62, 168, 197, 288-89, 291, 348, 350-54, 373-76, 408, 411, 420

Appomattox River, VIII: 382-83, 391

Apportionment of representation (Ill.), I: 34, 227-28, 287-88; II: 432-33, 505; III: 337, 351, 356, 364-65

Aquia & Richmond Railroad, VI: 175n

Aquia Creek, V: 121n, 218n, 239-40, 246n, 254n, 385n, 461, 511, 514; VI: 161, 169n, 200n, 274n

Arago (steamship), VIII: 238n

Arapaho Indians, IV: 464n; VI: 153n

Arcade Creek (Calif.), VII: 122

Archer, William B., I: 14, 146n

232, 249; II: 287, 292-93; VI: 198
Archuletta, Diego, IV: 349
Arctic, expedition (1853) to, V: 140
Arenz, Francis A., II: 73, 103
Argentina, IV: 310; VI: 94-95; VIII: 138
Argosy Book Shop, catalog cited, V: 33n
Argüelles, José Augustín, VII: 370n, 399-400
Argument of [Robert J.] Walker & [Frederick P.] Stanton . . . Submitted in the Case of J. & R. H. Porter (pamphlet), V: 451n
Argyll, Duchess of, VIII: 371-72
Arista, Mariano, II: 85
Arizona Territory, III: 137; VI: 113, 141, 167n, 231, 324-25; VII: 40, 521n; VIII: 214n
Arkansas: admission to Union under Missouri Compromise, II: 230, 232, 235, 241, 250-51, 258, 261, 319n; a "border" state, IV: 427, V: 123n, 298; fear of invasion and Indians, IV: 476n, V: 347; and troop movements, V: 1, 178n, VIII: 94; proposed establishment of a court, V: 82; recruitment of troops, 267n; military commands in, 343n, VI: 70-73, VII: 144, 159n, 208-209, 239, 300n, VIII: 229n; reorganization of state government, V: 462-63, 500, 544, VI: 358-59, VII: 83n, 108-109, 141-42, 144-46, 154-55, 160, 161, 173-74, 180, 185-86, 189-91, 199, 204-205, 208-209, 221-22, 226, 239-40, 250-51, 253, 318, 334-35, 388, 398-99, 418, 433-34, 519, VIII: 148-49, 399n; mention of Battle of Prairie Grove, VI: 2n; and the extension of the Pacific R.R., 66, VII: 237n; mention of persons from, VI: 171, VII: 83-84, 213; trading within military lines, VI: 340n, VII: 342n,

VIII: 35n; and the Emancipation Proclamation, VI: 358, VII: 124n; and admission of a Senator from, VI: 358-59, VII: 418; "substantially cleared of insurgent control [Dec. '63]," VII: 49; and free Negro plantation labor, 145-47; plans to send Sickles to confer with Steele (Feb. '64), 160, 176, 204-205; nomination of a U. S. attorney, VIII: 242n
Arkansas Post (Ark.), VI: 70, 82, VII: 56
Arlington Heights (Va.), IV: 385, 450n, 457, 499n
Armes, George Augustus, VII: 443-44
Armesy, Thomas D., VII: 502
Armour, Alexander W., VI: 511n; VIII: 306n
Armour, Charles Lee, IV: 294
Armour, George, II: 182-83, 186
Armour, John, II: 186
Armsby, James H., IV: 446
Armstrong, A. N., III: 339-40
Armstrong, Hannah (Jones), VI: 462
Armstrong, Hosea J., I: 2, 206
Armstrong, Hugh, I: 11, 13-14, 18-20, 24, 206
Armstrong, J. B., VIII: 69
Armstrong, Jesse B., VII: 160-61
Armstrong, John ("Jack"), I: 11, 70, 206-207; VI: 462n
Armstrong, Mrs. John, see Armstrong, Hannah (Jones)
Armstrong, John, Jr., III: 372; IV: 303n; VI: 238n
Armstrong, Pleasant, I: 12; II: 13-14
Armstrong, William ("Duff"), VI: 462
Armstrong, William E., II: 180, 183-84
Army, deserters from, see Deserters
Army absenteeism, V: 322n; VI: 12

Army appointments:
  Generals, IV: 355, 367-72, 384, 394-95, 404-405, 407, 409, 411, 413-14, 418-19, 451, 463, 466-67, 472-74, 479-80, 483, 489, 491-92, 494, 503-505, 511, 517, 524-25, 530, 539, 551-52
    V: 9-10, 15, 28-29, 31, 66, 71-72, 76-78, 90, 93, 100-101, 111, 114, 126, 131, 135-36, 142-43, 167, 170-71, 174, 182-83, 186-87, 191-92, 194-96, 202, 205-207, 221, 253, 261-62, 283, 299, 312-13, 320, 335, 348, 360, 361, 364, 384, 390-91, 405, 407-408, 411, 446, 447, 457, 480, 494-95, 501
    VI: 5-6, 19, 35, 55, 67, 71-73, 81, 82, 94, 101, 106, 117, 125-26, 129-30, 133-34, 136-40, 147-49, 184, 235-36, 291-92, 334, 340, 351-52, 393, 396, 419-20, 528
    VII: 74, 117, 119, 121, 137-38, 142-43, 159, 230, 234-36, 279, 311, 346-47, 379, 416, 439, 450, 452, 463-64, 466, 484, 491-92, 537
    VIII: 175, 255, 307, 314, 362-63, 420, 593-94
  Others, IV: 287, 333-37, 349, 366, 392-93, 398-99, 403, 405, 409, 411-12, 442, 445, 448, 451, 453, 455, 457, 461-63, 467, 470, 472-74, 476-77, 479-80, 484, 486, 488-96, 498-503, 505-508, 513-17, 520-22, 524-26, 529-30, 534-35, 538, 540, 543-44, 548, 553, 555, 557-58
    V: 4, 7-9, 11-12, 14, 17, 19, 22-23, 25, 28, 33, 55-56, 58, 61, 64, 71, 78-80, 83, 89-91, 102-103, 107-108, 130-31, 138, 148, 156, 159, 168-69, 172-73, 175, 179-81, 183, 193, 201-202, 206-207, 211, 216-17, 224, 239, 253, 262-63, 266, 277, 304, 320, 326-27, 332, 334, 340, 342, 348, 351, 361-62, 365-67, 381, 391, 394-96, 398, 410-11, 426, 430, 441, 446, 454-

58, 466, 470-72, 475, 512, 539-40, 543, 552
    VI: 7, 10, 18, 19, 40-41, 44, 50, 63, 76, 86, 94, 96, 98, 107-108, 114, 119, 126, 131-33, 137, 149-50, 158-59, 161, 163-64, 171, 174, 179, 181-82, 191, 194, 197-98, 208, 221, 228, 232, 237-38, 249, 254-55, 259, 290, 351, 364, 386, 403, 426, 430, 452-53, 477, 490, 509, 516
    VII: 3, 11, 15, 73, 88, 92, 97, 114, 137-38, 141, 170-71, 203, 249, 260-61, 289, 317, 357-58, 418, 430, 443-44, 495-96, 502, 511-13, 537-38
    VIII: 12, 35, 44, 72, 79, 118-19, 127, 181, 189, 191, 223-24, 234, 316, 416-18, 420, 422, 424, 594
    See also Army promotions and transfers; Chaplains; Medical Officers; West Point
Army assignments to duty, IV: 320, 344-45, 414, 499, 517, 558-59; V: 103, 177-78, 192, 360, 425, 506; VI: 14-15, 100, 216-17, 234, 253, 312, 386-87, 482-83, 533, 554-55; VII: 78-79, 80, 113-14, 198, 221, 239-40, 272, 312, 400, 464; VIII: 91
Army chaplains, *see* Chaplains
Army Corps (U. S.):
  First, V: 209n, VII: 97n; advance (Apr. '63), VI: 190n; after Chancellorsville, 200n; at Fairfax Station, 280n; Newton commands, 330n; at Gettysburg, 342n; 4th Md. in, 472; 13th Mass. in, 478; reorganization, VIII: 307n
  Second, V: 209n; after Chancellorsville, VI: 200n; near Fairfax Station, 280n; at Petersburg, VIII: 376n, 381-83, 390-91
  Third, V: 209n; change in command, 407n; advance (Apr. '63), VI: 190n; after Chancel-

lorsville, 200n; Sickles and, 322-23; 99th Pa. in, VII: 31

Fourth, V: 209n; VIII: 290n

Fifth, organized, V: 209n; Hooker takes command of, 485n; advance (Apr. '63), VI: 190n; after Chancellorsville, 200n; N. Y. Battery in, 296n; 22nd Mass. in, VIII: 86-87; at Petersburg, 377n, 379-83, 390-91

Sixth, VI: 75n, 439n; organized, V: 209n; advance (Apr. '63), VI: 190n; near Fairfax Station, 280n; 1st N. J. in, 478; Ricketts commands division in, VII: 437n; Sheridan commands, 476n, VIII: 50n; attacked, VII: 511n; Getty commands, VIII: 273; at Petersburg, 382-83; at Burkesville, 389-92

Eighth, V: 455

Ninth, VI: 75n, 130n, 350; change in command, V: 485n; Getty's division in, VI: 238n; 11th N. H. in, VIII: 170; Willcox commands, 276; at Petersburg, 382

Tenth, VI: 490n

Eleventh, Schurz commands division in, V: 493n, VI: 43n; Stahel commands, VI: 6n; changes in command, 80n, 168n; Sigel commands, 93n; advance (Apr. '63), 190n; after Chancellorsville, 200n; at Fairfax Station, 280n; Slocum with, 486n; reinforces Rosecrans, 494n; at Wauhatchie, 554; and Hooker, VII: 263n

Twelfth, VI: 6n, 242n; advance (Apr. '63), 190n; after Chancellorsville, 200n; 3rd Md. in, 400; Slocum with, 486n; reinforces Rosecrans, 494n; at Wauhatchie, 554

Thirteenth, VI: 375n, 380n; VII: 277n

Fourteenth, V: 501n; VII: 61n

Fifteenth, VI: 380n; VII: 248n; VIII: 136n

Seventeenth, at Vicksburg, VI: 380n; Blair commands, 555n, VII: 248n, 307n, 312n

Eighteenth, VI: 255n; Butler commands, VI: 77n; Ord commands, VII: 484n

Nineteenth, VII: 438n, 445n, 472n; VIII: 50n

Twenty-first, VII: 61n

Twenty-third, VI: 516n; VIII: 349n

Twenty-fourth, VIII: 189, 383-84

Army discharges, dismissals and removals, IV: 480, 486, 529; V: 11, 67, 164, 176, 183, 193, 218, 361, 380, 400, 408, 429, 442-43, 458, 471, 476, 508-509

VI: 35, 54, 60, 63, 67, 77-78, 82, 86, 109-10, 114, 126, 127, 153, 161-62, 165, 169, 179, 182, 191-93, 196, 211, 222-23, 224-25, 229, 232, 237-38, 242, 253, 270, 285, 293-94, 308-309, 335-37, 380, 383-85, 419, 421, 426, 429, 442, 460-62, 465, 477, 496, 516, 520, 524, 545

VII: 2, 4-5, 65, 125, 134, 176, 203, 216-17, 230-31, 238, 255, 265, 276, 288, 294, 315, 318, 322, 329-30, 332, 335, 353, 358, 372-73, 375, 427, 447, 455, 465, 486, 491, 495, 497, 511-12, 517, 519, 521, 523-26, 538, 541-42, 545

VIII: 10, 19, 23, 30, 36, 42, 47-48, 76, 80-81, 90, 105, 122, 155-56, 160, 169-70, 198, 215-16, 218-19, 229, 234, 236-38, 246, 289, 307, 313, 363-65, 411, 427, 594

See also Courts-martial; *and* Army resignations, retirements, and reliefs from duty

Army equipment, *see* Troops, equipment and supplies

Army leaves of absence, V: 69-70,

103, 342, 367, 484, 488, 541; VI: 113, 118, 125, 129-30, 372, 382-83, 388, 437, 439, 540-41; VII: 8, 106, 148, 215, 358, 408, 430, 473; VIII: 53, 95, 105, 106; "absenteeism," V: 322n, VI: 12

Army medical officers, see Medical officers

Army mobilization, see Troops, mobilization and recruitment

Army of the Cumberland, VI: 97n, 104n, 105n, 179n, 194n, 395n, 476n, 529; VII: 342n

Army of the James, IV: 553n; VIII: 127, 243, 247, 276, 289

Army of the Ohio, V: 283n, 552n; VI: 97n

Army of the Potomac: McClellan in command of, IV: 394n, V: 155, 164, 287, 289-91; memo to McClellan on Potomac campaign, V: 34-35; McClellan disagreement with orders to advance (Feb. 22, '62) toward Manassas, 111-12, 115, 118-25; ordered reorganized into corps, 149-51; memo of L.'s interviews with officers, 309-12; L.'s visits to 309n, 322, 448-50, VI: 161, 201; numerical strength, V: 322-23 (July '62), 469 (Oct. '62); memo of troops at Antietam 448; McClellan removed from command, 485-86, 509-10; official congratulations (Dec. 22, '62), VI: 13-14; suggested plan (Dec. '62) of operations, 15-16; reported demoralization, 22n; proposed reserve cavalry, 43, 79-80, 93n; Burnside's criticism of Halleck's command, 46-48; Hooker assigned to command, 77-79; Congressional investigation, 128n; report of June '63 position, 280n; pressure to restore McClellan command, 311n; effect of Gettysburg battle, 314, 321, 329n; "Lee's army, not Richmond" the objective

point, 466-68, 534-35; Slocum criticism of Hooker command, 486; mention of Nov. '63 successes, VII: 6n, 32; and Grant's appointment to supreme command, 234n; soldier vote (1864), VIII: 100; plan for Crook command of cavalry, 370-71

Army of the Tennessee, VI: 226n; VII: 240

Army of Virginia, V: 287, 307, 357

Army of Western Virginia, V: 111-12

Army Orders (general):
 AGO 1861, IV: 359, 402; cited in footnotes on the ff. pages, IV: 420, 513, 516, 525, 527, 562; V: 2, 7, 10, 22
 AGO 1862, V: 334-35, 482; cited in the footnotes on the ff. pages, V: 191, 209, 264, 273, 313, 337, 341, 380, 408, 471, 475, 476, 483, 485, 495, 498, 539; VI: 224
 AGO 1863, VI: 132; cited in footnotes on the ff. pages, IV: 516; VI: 67, 77, 82, 110, 133, 148, 189, 285, 313, 357, 432, 460, 478, 539; VII: 14, 92, 502; VIII: 119
 AGO 1864, VII: 208, 239-40, 327; cited in footnotes on the ff. pages, VI: 486; VII: 85, 100, 129, 186, 245, 248, 259, 300, 312, 350; VIII: 119, 166
 AGO 1865, VIII: 293n, 375n. Banks', VIII: 317; Breckinridge's, VIII: 315n; Burnside's, VI: 22n, 74n, 237n; Butler's, VII: 98n, 136n, VIII: 28n; Department of N. C., VI: 127n; Department of the Northwest, VIII: 305n; Department of the Ohio, VIII: 322n; Department of the Susquehanna, VII: 157n; Frémont's, IV: 563n; Grant's, VII: 53n, VIII: 295n; Halleck's, V: 168n; Hooker's, VI: 184n; Hovey's, VIII: 74n; Hunter's,

V: 116n, 222-23, VI: 192n; Mc-
Clellan's, V: 150n; McCler-
nand's, VI: 380n; Meade's, VI:
318, 400n, 472n, 482n, 492n,
506n; Pope's, V: 344n;
Schenck's, VI: 253n, 555-58,
VII: 9n, 26; Schofield's, VI:
343, 396n, 495n; Sedgwick's,
VII: 152; Sherman's, 330n;
Thomas', 211n
Army Orders (special):
  AGO 1861, IV: 373n
  AGO 1862, cited in footnotes
  on the ff. pages, V: 367, 407,
  425, 485, 538; VI: 23
  AGO 1863, cited in footnotes
  on the ff. pages, VI: 55, 131,
  155, 223, 253, 297, 384, VII: 113
  AGO 1864, cited in footnotes
  on the ff. pages, VI: 548, 561;
  VII: 80, 82, 104, 106, 112, 133,
  136-39, 142, 150, 157-59, 170,
  176, 198, 217, 231, 233, 241, 252,
  293, 307, 309, 323, 325, 332, 335,
  386, 427, 439, 460-61, 465, 482,
  512-13, 520-21, 525, 538, 545;
  VIII: 6, 14, 32, 48-49, 52, 81, 90,
  106, 116, 119, 121, 177, 188-
  89
  AGO 1865, cited in footnotes
  on the ff. pages, VIII: 89, 196,
  198, 229, 233, 249, 273, 290, 306-
  307, 315, 364, 366-67
  Army of the Potomac, VI:
  431n; Department of Kansas,
  VIII: 6n; Department of the
  Missouri, VI: 20n, VIII: 102n;
  Department of Washington,
  VIII: 43n; Department of West
  Virginia, VII: 446n; Grant's,
  VIII: 344n; Hunter's, VII: 477n;
  McClellan's, V: 407n; Rose-
  crans', VII: 283-84; Schenck's,
  VI: 253n
Army pay, IV: 509-10; V: 194, 268-
  69, 368-69, 380, 385; VI: 180,
  193, 384, 433, 561; VII: 217, 368-
  69; VIII: 94-95, 97, 106
Army promotions and transfers,

IV: 354, 392, 395, 409-13, 418,
  446, 552-53; V: 21-22, 93-94, 142,
  149, 206-207, 262-63, 316-17,
  405, 446, 486-87, 540; VI: 44,
  72-73, 81, 97, 101, 104, 117, 125-
  26, 135-36, 153, 334, 432, 476;
  VII: 11, 102, 120, 144, 174, 214-
  15, 276, 277, 364-65, 443-44, 463-
  64, 484, 491-92; VIII: 32, 158-
  59, 175, 214, 310, 349, 362-63
Army resignations, retirements,
  and reliefs from duty, IV: 346,
  554; V: 10-12, 178, 249, 296, 358,
  361, 465; VI: 109-10, 257-58,
  359-60, 363, 432; VII: 11-12, 60-
  61, 368-69; VIII: 81; *see also*
  Army discharges, dismissals,
  and removals
Army Square Hospital, VII: 203
Arnett, John T., VIII: 220
Arnold, Charles, II: 223
Arnold, Isaac Newton, II: 284n,
  387, 481; IV: 275n; V: 196n,
  201n, 277n; VI: 110, 230-31,
  279n, 540n; VII: 48n, 66n; 361,
  363-64, 423-24, 453n, 484; VIII:
  102, 422n, 594n
Arnold, John D., II: 289, 296; IV:
  310
Arnold, Lewis Golding, V: 428n
Arnold, S. E., IV: 494n
Arny, William F. M., V: 107,
  354n; VII: 238; VIII: 157
Arterburris, John, VIII: 91n
Articles of Association (1774), IV:
  253, 265
Articles of Confederation, II: 249;
  III: 386; IV: 253, 265, 433
Asboth, Alexander, VI: 147n
Asbury, Henry, II: 380n, 530-31;
  III: 339; IV: 140; VI: 1
Ascension Parish (La.), VI: 29
Ash, Franklin P., VI: 242n
Ashby's Gap, V: 234-35, 461
Ashhurst, John, VIII: 312n
Ashland (Va.), V: 248n, 249; VI:
  199
Ashley, Chester, I: 467
Ashley, James Mitchell, V: 4n,

366-67; VII: 371; VIII: 183, 248, 356

Ashmun, George, I: 446, 448n; III: 183, 319-20; IV: 51n, 52-53, 59, 66, 68-69, 311, 334, 336, 405; V: 165n, 178n; VII: 116n, 451-52; VIII: 38-39, 171, 413

Ashtabula (Ohio), IV: 218

Ashtabula Telegraph, IV: 218n

Ashton, J. Hubley, IV: 510n; VII: 408n

Aspinall, Thomas, II: 331-32

Aspinwall, William Henry, V: 366n; VI: 112n

Aspinwall [Panama], VII: 164n, 415

Assassination of L., threats of, (1860-1861) IV: 132n, 241n; (Apr. 14, '65) VIII: 413

Associated Institute for Soldiers' and Sailors' Orphans (Philadelphia), VI: 376n

Associated Press, VI: 298n, 430n; VII: 19n, 233n

Association of the Surviving Soldiers of the War of 1812, V: 306n

Assumption Parish (La.), VI: 29

Astor, John Jacob, Jr., VII: 5

Astor, William B., VII: 4

Astor House (N. Y.), IV: 133, 229-31; V: 292; VII: 268n, 294, 443, 524; VIII: 170n

Astor Society Library, III: 524n

Astoria Indian Agency, IV: 308

Atacama, Desert of, VII: 339n

Atalanta (ship), V: 64n

Atchison, David Rice, II: 351, 365n

Atchison (Kans.), II: 322n; III: 425n; VI: 334n, 397n; VII: 343n

Athens (Ala.), V: 406n

Athens (Ga.), I: 442

Athens (Ill.), I: 25-26, 37n, 88, 139

Athens (Tenn.), VI: 471n

Atherton's Ferry (Ky.), IV: 61

Athey, Presley G., IV: 309

Atkins, Henry I., III: 352

Atkinson, Andrew J., IV: 309

Atkinson, Robert J., V:21, 204-205; VII: 392; VIII: 419

Atkinson, S. C., IV: 333

Atlanta (Ga.), VI: 517n; VII: 444n, 463, 495, 532-33; VIII: 4, 9, 27, 181, 244n, 331

Atlanta (Ill.), II: 504

Atlanta (Confederate steamer), see *Fingal*

Atlantic & Mississippi Railroad, II: 212-16

Atlantic cable, VIII: 139

Atlantic City (N. J.), VII: 536n

Atlantic Monthly, V: 158n

Atlas and Bee (Boston), IV: 68n

Auburn (N. Y.), VI: 554, 562; VIII: 52, 91, 94, 97, 104

Aud, William T., VII: 290-91

Auditors, Board of, I: 232-33

Augur, Christopher Columbus, VII: 60n, 271n, 423n; VIII: 53, 169n, 232

Augusta (Ga.), V: 552n

Augusta (Ill.), III: 37-38, 134

Augusta (Ky.), IV: 369n

Augusta (slave ship), V: 47n

"Aunt Mary," see Dines, Mary

Aurora (Ill.), III: 258

Aurora Beacon, VII: 15n

Aurt, B. F., VIII: 69

Austin, Benjamin, I: 310

Austria, IV: 292-93, 397; V: 95-96, 197n, 221n, 521; VII: 8

Auth, John, I: 206

Autobiographical sketches, *see* LINCOLN, ABRAHAM, autobiographical references

Autobiography, An (Wallace), VII: 275n

Autograph Album, The (Madigan), V: 502n; VI: 252n

Autograph albums, L.'s inscriptions in, II: 435; III: 347, 504; IV: 339

Autograph Leaves of Our Country's Authors (Bancroft), VII: 22n

Autographs, L. replies to requests

for, IV: 68-69, 145; V: 220-21, 225; VII: 128, 220, 295, 343, 369, 491n; VIII: 77, 92-93, 309
Aux-Cayes (Haiti), IV: 514n
Avary, Myrta Lockett, see *Recollections of Alexander H. Stephens*
Avent, Benjamin F., VI: 233n

Averell, William Woods, VI: 200n; VII: 5-6, 456n, 537n; VIII: 10n
Avery, Edwards, VII: 277-78
Avery, Reeside &, I: 443
Aves Island (West Indies), VIII: 137
Ayres, Eugene, V: 376n

B

Babbitt, Elijah, IV: 483; VI: 119
Babcock, Amos C., II: 289, 297; VI: 307n; VIII: 334-35
Babcock, James Francis, IV: 30, 43-44, 102n, 112, 114-15
Babcock, William, VIII: 334-35
Babcock, Willoughby, VIII: 284
Baber, Richard P. L., IV: 480
Bache, Hartman, IV: 527n
Backus, Abner L., VI: 300-306
Bacon, "Mrs. Dr.," VII: 491
Bacon, D. P., VI: 372n
Bacon, Henry D., II: 341-42, 460n; IV: 526n
Bacon, Reuben, V: 205
Bacon, Wilbur R., VIII: 6
Bacon Church (Va.), V: 121n
Bacon Creek (Ky.), V: 89n
Badger, Alpheus C., IV: 549
Badger, William, VII: 516n
Bagby, Francis C., III: 90n
Bagby, John Courts, II: 531; III: 90, 330, 332
Baggott, Lucy Ann, VI: 432n
Bahama Islands, V: 27n; VIII: 140n
Bahía (Brazil), VIII: 140n
Bail, John D., II: 424-25
Bailey, ———, II: 191
Bailey, Daniel M., II: 194

Bailey, Hiram S., V: 542-43
Bailey, J. F., VII: 181, 195n, 204
Bailey, J. W., V: 516n
Bailey, John S., II: 445n
Bailey, Joseph, VII: 230-31
Bailey, Ozias, II: 426
Bailey, Theodorus, V: 215
Bailey, William W., I: 249
Bailey's Dictionary, I: 2n
Bailhache, Ada, VI: 516n
Bailhache, William Henry, II: 424-25; VI: 238n, 275-76, 516
Bailhache, Mrs. William Henry, see Bailhache, Ada
Baily, ———, VIII: 14-15
Baily, William, VI: 386
Bainbridge, William, VII: 26
Baird, Mrs., VI: 384, VII: 217
Baird, Absalom, IV: 535n
Baird, Chambers, VII: 314n
Baird, E. Z., VII: 4
Baird, Isaac P., VI: 384; VII: 217n
Baird, Virginia W., II: 454n
Baird, William B., II: 310
Baker, A. C., V: 367
Baker, Almon, IV: 529n
Baker, Asa D., V: 441
Baker, Christiana, I: 18-19
Baker, David Jewett, I: 337
Baker, Edward Dickinson: in Ill.

legislature, I: 76n, 123, 183n, 208; and "Sampson's Ghost" letters, 89n; recommends Campbell for prosecuting attorney, 122; L. acts as mediator in controversy with Butler, 138-42; member of Whig committees, 151, 203, 205, 237, 262, 288; loses (1840) election to Senate, 221; supports Servant land office appointment, 253; defense lawyer in Trailor murder case, 256; candidate (1844) for Congress, 319-25, 329, 334, 337, IV: 67; and 1846 Congressional race, I: 349-50, 352, 356, 358n, 360-65, 431; L.'s son named for, 391n; in Mexican War, 395, 419, 446-48, 515, II: 473; L. attests to signature of, I: 430; and support (1848) of Taylor, 467, 491, II: 17-18; promoted for Taylor cabinet post, II: 25, 28-30; and Taylor appointments of Illinoisans, 31-32, 37-41, 58-59, 77; candidate (1860) for Senate, IV: 81-82, 90; supports Cameron (1861) for cabinet post, 248; recommends (1861) territorial and army appointments, 295, 301, 405n, 406, V: 181; raises "California regiment," IV: 419n, V: 60; death, IV: 560n, V: 510-11, VI: 86, VII: 286; L. recommends appointments for relatives and friends of, V: 138n, 147, 239, VI: 86, 94, 119; replies to Breckinridge, V: 382; appointed Brigadier General of Volunteers, VIII: 593-94

Baker, Edward Dickinson, Jr., V: 239; VI: 86, 94, 119

Baker, Edward Lewis, II: 425n; IV: 50n; V: 71n, 175; VI: 275-76, 516n, 561-62

Baker, Edward W., V: 152

Baker, Ezra, I: 67; VIII: 395

Baker, Henry Southard, II: 297, 305

Baker, Isaac, VII: 336n

Baker, James (Ill.), I: 298

Baker, James (Mich.), IV: 529

Baker, James Heaton, IV: 278

Baker, Jehu, III: 106, 175, 215, 220

Baker, Jesse, I: 18-19

Baker, Mrs. Jesse, see Baker, Christiana

Baker, John (Ill.), II: 331

Baker, John (Tenn.), VIII: 68

Baker, John A., II: 419

Baker, John Pope, V: 175

Baker, Joseph F., V: 175

Baker, N. B., VIII: 299n

Baker, Philip R., V: 175n

Baker, Ratcliffe, VI: 544

Baker, S., VII: 213

Baker, Samuel L., II: 444n; III: 505-506, 516n, 521n

Baker, Stephen, V: 188-89

Baker & Van Bergen, I: 290

Baker place (S. C.), VI: 456

Baker's Creek, battle of, VI: 226n

Bakewell, ———, II: 413

Bakewell, Edwin W., II: 91

Balch, George Thatcher, V: 11n

Balcombe, Saint A. D., VIII: 370n

Balderson, J. L., V: 183n

Baldwin, Abraham, III: 527-30; IV: 113, 118-19

Baldwin, Caleb, VIII: 355

Baldwin, Charles Cotesworth Pinckney, IV: 299

Baldwin, Charles H., V: 215

Baldwin, Daniel, I: 243

Baldwin, Mary (McCook), VII: 516, 541n; VIII: 300

Bale, Abram, II: 76

Bale, Jacob, I: 18, 121

Ball, Asahel, I: 76

Ball, Flementine, VII: 27n

Ball, George A., II: 200n; VII: 329n

Ball, Japhet A., I: 208

Ballance, Charles, II: 315, 326n

Ballard, Bland, IV: 499n, 501n, 555-56; V: 464; VI: 118n; VII: 121-22

Ballard, Frank W., VIII: 19

Ballard, John, I: 2
Ballard, Phillip, I: 2
Ballier, John F., VI: 86
Balloch, ———, IV: 404
Balloons, military observation by, IV: 460
Ballot, L. on the, I: 213; II: 271, 454; III: 496; IV: 439; VI: 410
Ballou, DeWitt Clinton, VII: 286n
Ball's Bluff, battle of, IV: 560n; V: 60, 239, 511n; VI: 86; VII: 285-87
Baltic (ship), V: 154n
Baltimore (Md.): rumor of plot to assassinate L. (1861), IV: 241n; appointments, 304, 328, 356-57, 363, 404, V: 159n, VII: 97, VIII: 348n; riots, IV: 340-41, 381n, 386n, V: 343-44, VIII: 84; replies to delegations from, IV: 341-42, V: 24; troops offered from, IV: 368, 388; "Let Baltimore be held . . . with a gentle, but firm, and certain hand [July '61]," 457; arrest of police commissioners, 462n, 522-23; troop and supply movements (1862), V: 237-38, 409n, VI: 218n, 281n, 318; Wool assigned to command at, V: 273n; complaints against care of wounded, 467; complaints against treatment of Negroes by White soldiers, VI: 90; mention of persons from, 309n, VII: 73n; prisoners-of-war in, VI: 323-24, VIII: 296, 304; and imprisonment of Gen. Trimble, VI: 325; Jaquess pursues peace mission from, 329n; Schenck military commander in, 346n, 541; L.'s remarks to Presbyterian Synod (Oct. '63), 535-36; and plans for L.'s trip to Gettysburg, VII: 16n; sale of copy of L.'s Gettysburg speech at Sanitary Fair, 22n, 212n; Wallace assigned to command at, 258-59; Republican national convention (1864), 280n,

289n, 335n, 376n, 380-83; deserters attempt to escape to, 297n; L.'s address at Sanitary Fair (1864), 301-303; disloyalty of Dr. Hawkes, 335-36; Hurlbut authorized (May '64) to visit, 370; arsenal ordered to fire victory salute (Sept. '64), 532; L. presented with Bible by loyal colored people, 542-43; First National Bank and financing of Union Pacific R.R., VIII: 192-93; mentioned, VII: 395; *see also* Maryland
Baltimore (steamer), V: 514
Baltimore American, I: 507; IV: 523n; V: 292; VIII: 399
Baltimore & Ohio Railroad, IV: 328n; V: 24, 184, 413n; VI: 189n, 238-39, 309n, 354; VII: 16n, 424n, 477n; VIII: 208n, 316-17
Baltimore County (Md.), VII: 76
Baltimore Exchange, IV: 342n
Baltimore Patriot, IV: 357n
Baltimore Pike, VI: 310n
Baltimore Sun, V: 371n; VI: 530n; VII: 512n, 529n, 542n
Baltimore Young Men's Christian Association, IV: 342n
Bamberger, Emanuel, V: 258n
Bamberger, Louis, V: 94n
Bamberger, Simon, V: 258n
Bancroft, Frederic, IV: 157n
Bancroft, George, V: 25-26; VII: 22, 212
Bangor (Me.), III: 295, 324; IV: 554; VII: 520n
Bank, Ill. State [Springfield], incorporation of subscribers, I: 43; investigation of, 61-69; payments into state treasury, 74; note for completion of state capitol, 116-17; fee bill for circuit clerks, 140, 142; forfeits charter, 159; report on condition, 179, 185-95; legislative support of, 184, 237-38, 240-42; remuneration for notes destroyed by fire, 224-25; charter of, 240-

41, 333; Stuart & L. account in, 267; value of bank paper of, 285-86, 290, 292-95, 305, II: 174-78; L.'s purchase of certificates, I: 420; a lawsuit against, II: 104n

Bank of Ill. [Shawneetown], payments into state treasury, I: 74; fee bills of circuit clerks, 142; value of bank paper, 285-86; failure of, 290; charter of, 333; lawsuits against, 342

Bank, national, I: 159-79, 184, 189, 210, 307, 312, 317, 333, 454, 502; II: 172-73, 517, 519; III: 28, 102, 232, 243, 278; VI: 61-62; VII: 71; VIII: 143-44; *see also* Sub-treasury system, L. on

Bank of Missouri, I: 134n, 190, 194

Banks, Gordon, I: xiv

Banks, Maude, VIII: 386n

Banks, Nathaniel Prentiss: mentioned as a possible presidential candidate (1856), II: 342-43; accused by Douglas of Black Republicanism, III: 138, 175; and appointments, 378n, V: 167n, 426n, 453, VI: 476n, VII: 156, VIII: 157; mentioned for cabinet post (1861), IV: 147-48, 161; and command of forces near Harpers Ferry (July '61), 457-58; appointed Major General of Volunteers, 463, VIII: 420, 593; commands 5th Army Corps, V: 150; spring (1862) campaign, 184, 230-39, 243n, 246, 247n, 249, 254, 256n, 264, 267-71, 274, 280, 284n, 301; order constituting the Army of Virginia, 287; suggests publication of L. letter, 346n; fall (1862) campaign, 398n, 400, 402n; and memo on Confederate Army, 470n; commands Department of the Gulf, 495, VI: 22n, VIII: 181n; Mississippi R. expedition (1863), V: 505-506, VI: 71n, 73-74, 76-77, 100n; super-

seded by Butler in Department of Gulf command, VI: 73-74, 76-77, 100n; commands new Department in Tex., 100n, 356, 465-66, VII: 148n, 170-71; military arrests, VI: 103n; recruitment of Negro troops in La. and Tex., 154-55, VII: 170-71; and Halleck promotion to General-in-chief, VI: 230-31; and Grant at Vicksburg, 244, 247, 254, 292, 293, 326, 374n; and reestablishment of state government in La., 364-66, 368, VII: 1-2, 89-91, 95-96, 123-25, 161-63, 486-87, VIII: 121, 131, 165n, 206-207, 400n, 402; mentioned in discussion of use of enrolled militia, VI: 503; and trade with insurrectionary states, VII: 63n, 114n; cases of property confiscation in La., 186-87, 492n; and government control of churches, 247-48; and arrest of Gen. Stone, 285-86; wounded in action, 308; Red River expedition (Apr. '64), 308, 334n, VIII: 14-15; leave of absence (Nov. '64), VIII: 106, 121, 366, 386; offers to resign, 121; and compensated plantation labor, 317; mentioned, VII: 196n

Banks, T., VIII: 383

Banks' Ford (Va.), VI: 190n, 200n

Bannack Indians, VII: 113

Bannon, Charles, II: 183

Baptist (Baptiste), R. H., VIII: 302

Baptists, V: 446n; VI: 401n; VII: 365, 368

Barbary States, VIII: 139

Barbee, Isaiah, VIII: 69

Barber, A. D., VII: 498n

Barber, Charles E., VIII: 313n

Barber, Mrs. Clayton, II: 435n

Barber, Herman [alias Edmund W. von Heinecke], VI: 491-92

Barbour County (W. Va.), V: 298

Barboursville (Ky.), IV: 544

Bardstown (Ky.), IV: 61; VIII: 219
Bargdorf, Louis, VI: 175n, 436
Barger, John S., II: 294
Bargie, L. A., IV: 500n
Baringer, William Eldon, I: vii
Barker, A. J., IV: 309
Barker, Adolphus, VII: 511n
Barker, Le Baron R., VII: 331n
Barker, Mary, see Johnston, Mary (Barker)
Barker, Rebecca, VII: 511n
Barker, Richard F., V: 400n
Barlly, see Bedell, Grace
Barnard, Augustus P., VII: 235
Barnard, John L., VIII: 132n
Barnard, William, V: 279
Barnburners, I: 477
Barnes, Emily W., V: 433n
Barnes, James, VI: 483n
Barnes, John, VIII: 70
Barnes, Joseph K., VII: 94n, 203, 222, 496, 526; VIII: 47n, 50, 55n, 170, 388n
Barnes, William B., VII: 214-15
Barnesville (Md.), V: 410n, 412n
Barnett, ———, II: 179-80
Barnett, Clardy, I. 12; II: 311-12
Barnett, Robert, VIII: 370n
Barnett, William, I: 9
Barnett's Ford (Va.), V: 397n, 398n
Barney, H. M., I: 456
Barney, Hiram, IV: 300, 307, 325, 334, 367, 384, 526n; V: 93, 157, 377-78; VI: 206, 361; VII: 9, 120, 181, 268n, 332-33, 413, 543n
Barnhart, William H., IV: 407n
Barnum, Philo F., VII: 82-83
Barnum, Phineas Taylor, II: 371
Barnum's Museum, VII: 249n
Barr, M. W., IV: 534n
Barreda, Federico, V: 142-43
Barren County (Ky.), VIII: 77-78
Barret, James A., II: 99n, 102-103; III: 386-87, 393-94; IV: 551; V: 177-78
Barret, John Richard, II: 537n
Barrett, Charles B., VII: 452

Barrett, George [alias James alias Thomas], VII: 465
Barrett, J., III: 395n
Barrett, James A., VII: 436
Barrett, James W., I: 209; II: 40-41, 47, 188
Barrett, Joseph Hartwell, II: 54n; IV: 325, 356, 361; VII: 279-80, 498; VIII: 214n
Barrett, Oliver D., IV: 361
Barrett, Oliver Rogers, I: xxii, facsimiles preceding page 1; cited (ORB) in footnotes on the ff. pages: I: 1, 17, 38, 120, 121, 253, 254, 266, 268, 270, 281, 282, 285, 288, 299, 303, 304, 306, 323, 329, 389, 407, 417, 445, 448, 449, 466, 499
II: 17, 18, 42, 51, 95, 96, 97, 106, 112, 134, 222, 223, 225, 228, 291, 296, 310, 380, 393, 435, 460, 461, 484, 504, 522, 528, 531, 533
III: 1, 38, 102, 145, 207, 245, 283, 334, 339, 342, 356, 372, 377, 379, 383, 396, 494, 504, 507, 512
IV: 40, 89, 125, 141, 150, 169, 321, 323, 384, 389, 391, 399, 455, 479, 481, 556, 559
V: 57, 81, 91, 99, 128, 168, 177, 192, 194, 238, 263, 354, 406, 436, 485
VI: 13, 111, 154, 214, 400, 497, 509, 518
VII: 30, 196, 229, 249, 296, 308, 419, 420, 423, 442, 496, 498, 527, 531, 538, 546
VIII: 113, 116, 148, 151, 152, 168, 179, 200, 234, 245, 268, 304, 315, 322, 323, 354, 376, 383, 395, 405
Barrett, Richard F., I: 203, 205, 209
Barrett, Roger W., I: 376n; VII: 243n
Barrette, see Barnett, Robert
Barron, Samuel, IV: 318
Barrows, Arad, V: 218n
Barrows, Henry D., IV: 305
Barry, John, VII: 26
Barry, William D., VI: 198n

Barry, William Farquhar, IV: 494
Barry, William Taylor, I: 175-76, 443-44
Barstow, William A., V: 23n
Barten, William, VIII: 69
Bartlett, ———, V: 360n
Bartlett, Mrs. Abner, VII: 331
Bartlett, Asa, VII: 355n, 371-72
Bartlett, Jesse, I: 38
Bartlett, John Russell, IV: 293
Bartlett, Washington A., IV: 386; VII: 363
Bartlett, William O., VIII: 232, 239-40, 308n, 346
Bartley, T. W., VI: 300-306
Barton, Able, VIII: 102n
Barton, Allen A., see Burton, Allen A.
Barton, Clarissa Harlowe (Clara), VIII: 423
Barton, Robert, II: 105n
Barton, Seth M., VIII: 389-90
Barton, William Eleazar, see *The Lineage of Lincoln; Lincoln at Gettysburg;* and *The Paternity of Abraham Lincoln*
Bartram, see Bertram, Charles J.
Bascom, Gustavus Murray, VII: 409
Bascom, William T., III: 400
Bashford, Levi, VI: 231-32
Basle (Switzerland), IV: 298
Basler, Roy Prentice, I: vii-xv, xvii
Bass, Eugenia P. (Bate), VII: 131-32, 149
Bass, Perkins, VIII: 222
"Bass-Ackwards," VIII: 420
Bassett, Richard, III: 527
Basye, Marshall M., II: 196
Bat (steamboat), VIII: 372n
Batavia (Java), IV: 481n
Batavia (N. Y.), IV: 221
Bate, Clarence, VI: 551n
Bate, Henry C., VII: 131n
Bateman, Ephraim, I: 317n
Bateman, Newton, III: 341, 389-90
Bates, ———, VIII: 77n
Bates, Mrs. Arthur L., VI: 199n
Bates, Charles Woodson, V: 152

Bates, David Homer, V: 291n
Bates, Edward: declines place in Fillmore cabinet, II: 92; candidate for 1860 Republican presidential nomination, III: 517, IV: 36, 45-47, 53, 54n; L. receives photograph of, IV: 132; appointed Attorney General, 154-55, 168n, 180; relief for Fort Sumter, 285n, 302n; executive power to establish a militia bureau, 291n; suspension of habeas corpus, 390, 431; recommends appointments, 295n, 411-12, 448n, 471, 473n, 538n, V: 18, VI: 58n; Philadelphian appeal for action to curb Union marauding, IV: 502; troubled situation in Mo., 530n, V: 61n, 347n, 515-16, VI: 33-34, 211n, VII: 86n, 284n; proposed court in Arkansas, V: 82; reprieves of death sentences, 128n; summoned to cabinet meetings, 144n (Mar. '62), VI: 111n (Feb. '63); son fails West Point examinations, V: 152n; supports L.'s relief-from-command orders for McClellan, 155n, 486n; practice of granting judiciary leaves of absence, 195, 267, 268n; simultaneous holding of civilian and military appointments, 275; urges completion of Pacific R.R., 315n, 459n, VII: 224n, 237n; supports preliminary Emancipation Proclamation, V: 337n, 439n; mollifying note to Anna Carroll, 382n; notes L.'s "bitterest anguish" following Second Battle of Bull Run, 404n; comments on "new cure" for wounded soldiers, 444n; military use of paroled prisoners-of-war, 449n; responsibility of the Sec. of the Treasury in payment of war expenditures, 451; executive power to fill Supreme Court vacancy dur-

ing Senate recess, 465n; charged with prosecution of Confiscation Act, 496, VI: 45-46; opposes act to admit W. Va. to Union, VI: 17; suggested revisions for final Emancipation Proclamation, 24n; executive powers to remit fines and forfeitures in prize court cases, 74, 207; opposes proposed "Marque and Reprisal" bill, 126n; accompanies L. on visit to Hooker (Apr. '63), 161; Ninian Edwards replies to charges of using political office for personal gain, 276n; controversy over writ of possession of New Almaden mine, 333n, 394; supports Sec. of War on release of prisoners-of-war, 398-99; on executive power to enforce the draft, 444n; requests wartime transportation for niece, VII: 27; wins freedom for political prisoner son of friend, 250n; controversy over pardon of William Yocum, 256n, 362; dubbed by Weed "a fogy," 268n; Senate confirmation of D. C. appointments, 270n, 408n; rights of Negroes in military service, 280, 332, 404-406, 440, VIII: 400n; Pennsylvanian's protest against Butler's confiscation order, VII: 292n; retaliation for Fort Pillow massacre, 328-29; revises Reconstruction Proclamation, 434n; supported by L. against Butler's charges of meddling in Va. affairs, 487-88; Swayne letter on Harris pardon, 534-35; letter of resignation, VIII: 126n; recommends cotton trader, 177n

Letters from L. on: appointments, IV: 278-79, 290, 295, 299, 323, 329, 336, 345, 366, 383, 391-92, 408, 447-48, 471, 475, 522, 543, 548, 554-56, V: 18, 163, 256, 265, 411n, 464-66, 492, VI: 113,

117, 150, 202, 223-24, 245, 247, 284, 395, 433, 495, VII: 15, 81-82, 128, 145, 153, 215, 219-20, 225, 264, 280, 304, 355, 428, 468, 480, 490, 497, VIII: 23, 82, 121-22; requests for legal opinions, IV: 290-92, 299, 389-90, 510, 538n, V: 82, 128n, 129n, 194, 207, 238-39, 275, 465n, 538n, VI: 74, VII: 270-71, 280, VIII: 80, 106; pardons and remission of fines, IV: 495, 554-55, V: 57, 146-47, 170, 202-203, 205, 211, 258, 266, 270, 285, 300, 333, 336n, 347-48, 352, 366, 390, 500-501, VI: 2, 55, 65, 89, 98, 103, 106-107, 118, 133, 180, 194-95, 211, 240, 278-79, 294, 353, 414, 425-26, 428, 477, 485, 526, 551, VII: 62, 67, 74, 77, 79-80, 91-92, 97-98, 105, 110, 148, 152, 156, 177, 189, 195, 218, 225-26, 276, 280, 286, 292, 304, 336, 391, 456, 463, 511, VIII: 5, 23, 32, 34, 45, 80, 85, 112; others, IV: 281, V: 267, VII: 12, VIII: 98

Bates, George C., V: 465n; VII: 371

Bates, Kinzie, V: 465n

Bates, Moses, V: 472n

Bates, Richard, IV: 448n

Bates, Therena (fiancée of Nicolay), V: 552n

Bates House (Indianapolis), speeches at, IV: 194-96

Bath (Ill.), II: 543-44

Batterton, David, I: 39

Battery, The [Washington], I: 498

Battle Creek (Mich.) Glee Club, II: 361n

Baty, David, VIII: 68

Baughman, John W., VIII: 82n

Baughman, Mrs. John W., VIII: 82n

Baum, John C., IV: 310

Baxter, Algernon Sidney, IV: 529n

Baxter, DeWitt Clinton, VI: 384

Baxter, Elisha, VII: 335n, 399n

Baxter, Henry, VI: 125-26
Baxter, John, VII: 321n
Baxter, Portus, VII: 171-72; VIII: 255n
"Baxter's Fire Zouaves," VI: 364, 384; VII: 320; VIII: 37n
Bayard, George Dashiell, V: 251n
Bayard, Thomas Francis, V: 163n
Bayles, David, IV: 295
Bayles, Jesse, IV: 464
Bayless, Albert S., V: 152
Bayless, John, VIII: 68
Baylor, I. N., VIII: 357n
Baylor, Thomas Gregory, V: 192n
Bayne, Julia (Taft), VIII: 421n, 425n
Bayou Macon (Miss.), VI: 142n
Beach, Moses Sperry, VII: 349n
Beach, Richard H., II: 109, 422
Beal, George Lafayette, V: 234n
Beale, Edward Fitzgerald, IV: 311
Beale, Robert M., VIII: 32n
Beale, Thomas, II: 183
Bealeton (Va.), VI: 257n
Beall, James H., I: 249
Beaman, Fernando Cortez, VII: 315
"Bear Hunt, The" (poem), I: 367n, 386-89, 392n
Beard, Joseph S. [L.], IV: 502
Beardsley, Elliott, V: 138
Beardsley, Henry C., VI: 548
Beardstown (Ill.), I: 4n, 7, 10n, 17, 40, 82-83, 147; II: 24n, 538-41; IV: 63
Beardstown Gazette, I: 350, 354-55, 479n, 492n
Bearsons, Allen, VIII: 69
Beattie, Miss, VII: 257-58
Beattie, Charles J., III: 374
Beattie, Kate [Mrs. Tuck.], VIII: 223
Beattie, Tuck., VIII: 223n
Beatty, John, VII: 311n
Beaufort (N. C.), V: 27, 210; VI: 160; VIII: 20, 396
Beaufort (S. C.), VI: 458-59; VII: 385-86; VIII: 273n, 396
Beaumont (Tex.), VI: 366n

Beauregard, Pierre Gustave Toutant, IV: 324n; V: 286n; VI: 167; VII: 427n
Beaver (Pa.) Argus, IV: 208n
Beaver Dam Depot (Va.), VIII: 37n
Bebb, William, IV: 514
Beck, John B., IV: 165
Beck, Sarah [Mrs. James], I: 325
Beck, William, II: 523n
Becker, George S., VII: 92, 105n, 148n
Beckwith, Amos, V: 317n; VII: 11
Beckwith, Colvin [Calvin], V: 300
Beckwith, Corydon, II: 415n; IV: 389
Beckwith, E. W., IV: 309
Beckwith, Edward Griffin, V: 426
Beckwith, Hiram, IV: 309
Beckwith, Hiram Williams, II: 218; III: 84-85
Beckwith, N. M., V: 157n
Beckwith, William W., VII: 361n
Bedell, Grace, IV: 129-30, 219n
Bedford, Gunning, III: 531n
Bedford (Pa.), VI: 436
Bedford County (Tenn.), VIII: 69
Beebe, Isaac M., VIII: 234n
Beecher, Henry Ward, IV: 38; VII: 512-13; VIII: 318-19, 321n, 375n, 376n
Beekman, Harry E., I: 23n
Beekman, J. Colby, I: 25n, 359n
Beers, Lavania, VII: 291n
Beers, Lewis, VII: 65
Beers, William A., IV: 30
Beers & Mansfield (New Haven, Conn.), IV: 30n
Behring, see Bering Strait
Beidler, Franklin P., VII: 315
Beidler, Mrs. Franklin P., VII: 315n
Beilor, see Bestor, George C.
Beiser, John, VI: 280n
Belger, James W., VII: 202
Belgium, VII: 87, 352, 386n; VIII: 203-204, 244n
Bell, David, VI: 392, 395, 402
Bell, Digby V., IV: 71

Bell, Henry H., V: 215
Bell, Isaac, VI: 112n
Bell, J. Warren, VII: 371
Bell, James, I: 43, 284-85, 306, 389-90
Bell, James A., VIII: 231n, 257n
Bell, John, II: 29-30; IV: 54n, 79n, 83n, 89n, 97-98, 124, 137n, 198, 200, 313; VIII: 128-29
Bell, Joseph McClellan, V: 340; VIII: 298n
Bell, R. B., III: 377
Bell, Samuel, IV: 301n, 335, 363, 500-501
Bell, Samuel B., V: 391n
Bell, Sanford, III: 399
Bell, Theodore S., VI: 394n
Bell, Victor B., IV: 495-96, 521-22
Bell, William, VIII: 70
Bell, William M., VII: 273
Bell & Boice (Springfield), I: 306
Bell, James, & Company, I: 121n, 283n, 285n, 290, 306n, 389
Bell place (S. C.), VI: 455, 457
Bellair (Ohio), VI: 347n
Belle Plain (Va.), V: 218n
Belleville (Canada), VI: 285
Belleville (Ill.), I: 209, 220; II: 379-80
Belleville Advocate, I: 472; II: 380n
Bellows, Henry Whitney, V: 201; VII: 135n
Belmont, August, V: 350-51, 416
Belmont (Mo.), IV: 480n; V: 20-21
Beloit (Wis.), II: 336-39; III: 482-84
Beloit College, II: 314n
Beloit Journal, III: 482n
Bendix, John E., VI: 184
Benedict Landing (Md.), VI: 530n
Benét, Stephen Vincent, VI: 107n
Benham, Henry Washington, IV: 483; V: 69-70, 106; VI: 35; VII: 174
Benicia Barracks (Calif.), VII: 214
Benjamin, Henry R., IV: 141n,

416n, 538n; V: 139n; VII: 288n; VIII: 22n
Benjamin, James H., VI: 516
Benjamin, M., II: 182
Benjamin, O. A., III: 506
Benjamin, Park, IV: 140-41; V: 139
Benke, McManus, *see* Burke, Edward
Bennet, Hiram Pitt, V: 178-79, 309
Bennett, ——, II: 454
Bennett, DeRobigne Mortimer, VIII: 102n
Bennett, Ebenezer J., VIII: 44
Bennett, Isaac R., II: 297
Bennett, James Gordon, IV: 102n, 357n, 539; V: 5, 225-26; VII: 461n; VIII: 240n, 307-308, 346n
Bennett, James Gordon, Jr., IV: 357
Bennett, John, I: 86, 93-94, 154n, 157, 249, 308n, 314n, 318-19, 353, 355; II: 23, 358
Bennett, John C., I: 291
Bennett, Sarah (Short), I: 51
Bennett, William H., V: 163
Bennett, William W., III: 520-21
Bennett, W[illiam] W., & Company, III: 521n
Bennett's Addition to Petersburg (Ill.), I: 157, 179-80
Benning, Henry Lewis, VI: 480
Benson, Rasmus, VI: 2n
Bent, Joseph [alias], *see* Dias, José Bente
Bentley, L. M., VII: 105n
Bentley, Richard, I: 76, 222
Benton, ——, VIII: 369
Benton, C. T., VII: 171-72
Benton, James Gilchrist, VII: 216, 229, 236n
Benton, Josiah Henry, VIII: 321n
Benton, Stephen, IV: 242n
Benton, Thomas Hart, I: 308n, 337; II: 158-59; III: 77, 378; IV: 132
Benton Barracks (Mo.), V: 178n, 432n; VII: 322n
Benton County (Tenn.), VIII: 69

Berdan, Hiram, V: 431; VI: 97n
Berdan, James, I: 380-81; II: 23, 59-60, 75, 347-48
Berdine, William, VI: 126n, 165
Berea, Abigail C., VI: 516
Bergen, George I., VI: 551
Bergen (Norway), VIII: 296
Bergstresser, S. A., IV: 167
Bering Sea, VII: 39n
Bering [Behring's] Strait, VIII: 138
Berington, Thomas, VIII: 80-81
Berington, Mrs. Thomas, VIII: 80n
Berkeley (Va.), V: 303n
Berkeley County (Va.), VI: 29
Berks County (Pa.), III: 511; IV: 37, 60
Berlin (Germany), IV: 276n; V: 131-32; VII: 27-28
Berlin (Ill.), I: 182, 250
Berlin (Md.), V: 481n
Bermuda Hundred (Va.), VII: 346, 367n, 508; VIII: 3, 25, 30
Berney, Alfred, VI: 107, 255n
Bernhisel, John Milton, VI: 62n
Berret, James G., IV: 246-47; V: 195-96
Berrien, John Macpherson, II: 9
Berro, Bernardo Prudencio, VII: 494
Berry, ———, VII: 332n
Berry, Baxter B., I: 13
Berry, Hiram George, V: 142
Berry, J. A., IV: 309
Berry, James, VIII: 159
Berry, John W., VIII: 159-60
Berry, L. G., V: 360n
Berry, Samuel, I: 71
Berry, William Franklin, I: 11, 16n, 20, 23, 25, 96n, 151n; IV: 65n
Berry [Perry] County (Tenn.), VIII: 69
Berryville (Va.), VI: 274; VII: 456n; VIII: 13n
Bertinatti, Joseph, IV: 300; V: 141; VII: 473-74
Bertram [Bartram], Charles J., V: 296n

Bestor [Beilor], George C., V: 82, 162, 180
Bethel (Tenn.), V: 486n
Bethlehem (Pa.), VIII: 8
Betters, Thomas F., VIII: 69
Bettleheim, B. J., V: 158
Betts, Charles R., VII: 143
Beveridge, Albert Jeremiah, I: 2n, 244n, 299n, 466n; II: 17n
Beverly (Va.), VI: 115
Bibles, L.'s, I: 304; IV: 546, VII: 542-43; see also Religion, L. and
Biddle, Nicholas, I: 189
Bielaski, Alexander, IV: 480, 527n
Big Black River (Miss.), VI: 226, 233n, 326
Big Blue River (Ind.), II: 217
Big Eagle (Indian), VIII: 76, 116
Big Sandy River, VI: 177n
Bigelow, Horace, IV: 125n
Bigler, William, III: 148-49, 154-55, 160, 184-85, 189-92, 194
Biglow, John, I: 2
Bilbao (Spain), V: 56n
Bilbo, William N., VIII: 226
Bilisoly, ———, see Boush, Mrs. George Richard
Bilisoly, Joseph A., VII: 232
Bill, Earl, IV: 329
Billinghurst, Charles, III: 519
Billings, Frederick, VI: 333n
Billings, Grace (Bedell), see Bedell, Grace
Billings, H. D., IV: 129n
Billings, Henry W., II: 503
Billingsley, ———, VIII: 165n
Billy Jimmy (Indian), IV: 299n
"Billy the Barber," see Fleurville, William
Bimini Roadstead (Bahama Islands), VIII: 140n
Bingham, James B., VII: 210n; VIII: 70
Bingham, John Armour, V: 19; VI: 245, 363, 405; VII: 468, 472, 496n; VIII: 104, 242n, 346n
Bingham, Kinsley Scott, IV: 248, 512
Binghamton (N. Y.), IV: 311

Bingley, John M., I: 121
Binkley, Marsh, VIII: 69
Binney, Horace, Jr., VI: 279
Birch, J. N., VI: 475n
Birchall, Caleb, I: 158, 206-207, 297; II: 188
Birchall & Johnson (Springfield), I: 237
Birchall & Owen (Springfield), II: 211n
Birchard, Matthew, VI: 300-306
Bird, Robert, I: 32
Bird's Point (Mo.), IV: 545
Birdsall, Ausburn, I: 507
Birdsall [Birdsill], Brice E., VII: 33
Birdsye, J. C., IV: 301
Birely, John, VII: 337
Birney, David Bell, V: 111; VII: 230; VIII: 215
Birney, Frank C., VIII: 215
Birney, William, VI: 494-95, 530n; VII: 28n
Birvies, M. G., IV: 309
Bishop, Horace S., VIII: 50n
Bishop, James E., II: 181
Bishop, John, VII: 213
Bishop, Richard M., IV: 200n
Bishop, Thomas J., VI: 221
Bishop, William W., I: 447-48, 457-58
Bissell, William Henry, I: 226n, 227-28, 243-44, 252; II: 75, 343, 345, 358, 381, 384, 394-95, 426, 432n, 436, 442-43, 445n, 536; III: 109, 335, 364-65, 374, 381-83, 388n, 389, 392; IV: 73n
Bixby, Arthur Edward, VIII: 117n
Bixby, Charles N., VIII: 117n
Bixby, George W. [A.] [alias Way], VIII: 117n
Bixby, Henry C., VIII: 117n
Bixby, Lydia, I: xi-xii; VIII: 116-17
Bixby, Oliver C., VIII: 117n
Black, ———, VII: 448
Black, John Charles, VI: 2n
Black, John S., II: 396n
Black, Robert T., II: 396n

Black, William J., II: 135, 291-92, 310
Black, William M., II: 23-24
Black, William P., VI: 2n
Black Hawk (steamboat), VIII: 336n
Black Hawk War: L. in, I: 5n, 509-10, II: 223, 319, 459, III: 512, IV: 64; receipt for arms, I: 9-10; muster roll of L.'s company, 10-13; cases of identification or claims of veterans, 19, 22n, 100, 152, II: 48, 108, 219n, 311-12, 543, IV: 322n, VI: 134n, VIII: 226n
Black Hole of Calcutta, VII: 170n
Black River (Mich.), VII: 215; VIII: 220
Black River (W. Va.), IV: 420n
Black Sea, V: 28n
Blackburn, William, VIII: 69
Blackburn (England), VI: 121-22
Blackburne, Francis, IV: 166
Blackfeet Indian Agency, IV: 306
Blackledge, Jesse D., II: 161n, 308-309
Blackman, O. M., VIII: 69
Blackstone's Commentaries on the Laws of England, III: 344; IV: 121
Blackwater River (Va.), V: 499n; VIII: 343-44
Blackwell, Robert S., I: 328; II: 115
Blackwood, William G., IV: 471
Bladensburg (Md.), VI: 507
Blaine, James Gillespie, VI: 449; VIII: 2-3
Blair, Austin, VI: 549; VII: 326; VIII: 109, 124
Blair, Elizabeth, VIII: 19n
Blair, Francis Preston, Jr.: mentioned as possible presidential candidate (1856), II: 342; editor of the Missouri Democrat and elected to Congress (1856), 537; defeated in Mo. Congressional election on emancipation issue (1858), III: 256, 265, 314,

500, 553, IV: 6, 11, 21; mention of his photograph, IV: 132; writes article on L.'s political views (Jan. '61), 153n; and Gen. Harney's relief from command in the West, 372-73; recommends Mo. recruiting (Aug. '61), 475-76; opposition to Frémont, 485n, 513n, 520n, 533n; requests commissioning of officers in Mo., 495; and the Chiriqui project, V: 3n; and payment of Sigel's staff, 117n; introduces (Jan. '62) House resolution about appointment of army officers, 140n; requests removal of Colo. governor (Mar. '62), 174n; and cases of military arrests, 348n, VII: 204n; recommends an appointment, V: 369n; and 1862 election in Mo., 496-97; joins McClernand at Helena (Nov. '62), 498-99, 517; a commander under Grant at Vicksburg, VI: 230; support for command in Tex., 356n; leave of absence (Aug. '63), 388; resigns commission to take seat in Congress, 554-55, VII: 319-20, 326-27; represented by Morrison from St. Louis (1864), VII: 189n; assigned to command 17th Corps (Mar. '64), 248, 307n; leaves Congress for active military duty (Apr. '64), 312, 327; and 1864 election of L., VIII: 18n

Blair, Francis Preston, Sr.: publishes (1835) *Congressional Globe*, I: 38n; L. writes on defense of Charleston forts (1860), IV: 157-58; informed of Confederate purchase of ships abroad, 397n; and appointments, 514n, VIII: 181n; opposition to Frémont, IV: 519-20; and the Chiriqui project, V: 3n; L. pardons kinsman, VI: 296n; attacks Banks command in Tex., 356;

asks for leave of absence for Wheaton, 439; and 1864 election of L., VIII: 18n; and preliminaries to Hampton Roads Peace Conference, 188-89, 220-21, 243, 248n, 250-51, 274-85

Blair, Mrs. Francis Preston, Sr., VI: 296n

Blair, Jacob Beeson, V: 319n; VI: 132

Blair, John, III: 531n

Blair, Mary Elizabeth, VI: 185; VII: 531n

Blair, Montgomery: given L.'s reasons for no pre-inaugural policy statements, IV: 155; appointment to L.'s cabinet, 162; and postmaster appointments, 282, 297n, 326-27, 342, 543-44, V: 197, VI: 128, 137, 194, 346; on expediency of provisioning Fort Sumter, IV: 285n; and proposed naval expeditions (Mar. '61), 302n; disagrees with War Department mobilization policies, 369-71, 396n, V: 378-79; recommends army appointment, IV: 473; and commissioning officers of Mo. volunteers, 495n; troubles in St. Louis and Frémont's removal (Sept. '61), 513n, 519-20, 533n, 550n; and the Chiriqui project, V: 3n; annual reports, 44 (*1861*), 524-25 (*1862*), VII: 45-46 (*1863*); Postal Convention (1862) with Mexico, V: 113; and the *Monitor* and the *Merrimac*, 154n; supports Brigadier General appointment for Allen, 191-92; and the Emancipation Proclamation, 337n, VI: 24n; cases of arrests, pardons, etc., V: 348n, VI: 62-63, 194n, 240, 296n, 385, 442n, VII: 11n, 291n, 293n, 463; declines to support censure of McClellan, V: 486n; and admission of W. Va, VI: 17; and West Point cadet appointments,

144n, 443; and requests for passes, 148n, VII: 74n; and Stephens peace mission (July '63), VI: 315n; opinion on the draft, 444n; and captured rebel correspondence, 526; and Gen. Blair's election to Congress, 554-55, VII: 326; and 1863 elections in Md., VII: 9-10, 26n; denounced by radicals, 24n, 268n, VIII: 18n; matters referred by L. to the attention of, VII: 200, 257-58; mention of friends of, 239n; and Fort Pillow massacre, 328; charged with interference in Philadelphia politics, 400n; and judiciary appointments, 404n, 428, 496n; burning of Md. home of, 439; called back to Washington (Sept. '64), 529, 531; resignation, VIII: 18-20; requests (Feb. 2, '65) interview with L., 255-56; mentioned, V: 498, VI: 308-309
Blair, Mrs. Montgomery, *see* Blair, Mary Elizabeth
Blair, Samuel Steel, IV: 300; V: 62
Blair & Rives (Washington), I: 38, 422, 431
Blake, Edward Sanford, VII: 249n
Blake, George S., VII: 194
Blake, Harry E., VII: 249n
Blake, James, VI: 153
Blake, John W., VI: 153
Blake, Marshall B., V: 396
Blake, William H., VI: 153; VII: 82
Blakeley, William, VII: 486n
Blakeman, Curtiss, III: 493n
Blakey, G. T., VII: 156n
Blakey, George D., IV: 481; VII: 496n
Blanca (Spanish ship), IV: 318n
Blanchard, M. A., VII: 3
Blanchard, Valentine, VII: 318
Blanchard, William, IV: 312n
Blanchard, William W., II: 63, 74
Blanchard & Company, II: 180, 184

Blanchard's Fork (Kans.), V: 288
Bland, Harry MacNeill, VII: 164n
Bland, P. E., VIII: 295n
Blane, Frank E., II: 219n
Blankenship, Eli C., I: 19
Blanton, Harrison, VI: 296n
Blatchford, Richard M., IV: 334; V: 241-42; VII: 413
Ble, John [alias Cohoe], VIII: 299
Bledsoe, Albert Taylor, I: 297, 308, 318; VIII: 218n
Bledsoe, Harriet (Coxe) [Mrs. Albert Taylor], VIII: 218
Bledsoe County (Tenn.), VIII: 68
Blenker, Louis, IV: 524n; V: 175-76, 184, 250-52, 273, 360n, 385n
Bleyer, Henry W., III: 471n
Blinn, ———, III: 518-19
Blish, ———, VIII: 393n
Bliss, ———, IV: 294
Bliss, Alexander, VII: 22n
Bliss, George, IV: 99; VI: 300-306
Bliss, John, VIII: 176-77
Bliss, Philemon, IV: 294
Bliss, William S., VI: 279
Bliss, William Wallace Smith, II: 2n
Blittersdorf, August, VI: 506
Blittersdorf, Gustave [alias William Fox], VI: 515-16
Bliven, Miles T., V: 103n
Blizzard, A., VIII: 58-72
Block, Gordon A., I: 279n; IV: 514n; VII: 21n, 126n, 259n; VII: 113n, 393n; VIII: 251n, 329n
Block, Joseph L., VII: 293n; VIII: 268n, 291n, 379n
Blockade: IV: 381n, 389, VIII: 244; and offshore collection of duties, IV: 290, 292, 293; proclamations of, 338-39, 346-47, 428-29; European attitude toward, 376, 378-80, VII: 36, 49; legality of, IV: 444; effectiveness of, 457, V: 345, VII: 43; threat of rebel naval action against, IV: 478; annual message (1861) report of, V: 38, 41, 49; Congress asks for report on, 55; prize

court cases, 109-10, 162, 520, VI: 74, VII: 113; commendation for flag officer, V: 127-28, 134; blockade runners, 167n, VI: 72, 79n, 102, 207, VII: 87-88, VIII: 111, 162-63, 218n, 224n, 251; proclamations lifting blockade of certain ports, V: 210-11, VI: 479, VII: 192-93, VIII: 115, 140, 396-98; order for clearance of vessels in Norfolk, Va., V: 495-96; "blockade errors," 519-20; directive on opening mail of captured vessels, VI: 183-84; Stephens refused passage, 314-16; use of Rio Grande R. in evasion of, 355n; order for clearance of vessels bound for New Orleans, 405; and cotton transport, VIII: 93-94, 103-104, 163-64

Blodget, Lorin, VI: 145n

Blood, Henry Boyden, VII: 23

Bloomfield, Ben, V: 188n

Bloomfield (Ill.), II: 191

Bloomington (Ill.), I: 70, 380, III: 258; L.'s speeches delivered at, (*1854*) II: 230-40, (*1856*) 340-41, 375, (*1858*) 504, III: 85-90, (*1860*) 356n, IV: 41-43, 143-44

Bloomington Pantagraph, II: 205n, 230n, 233n, 375n, 437n, 504n; III: 81n, 85n, 378n

Bloomington Statesman, see *Illinois Statesman*

Bloomington Young Men's Association, II: 437n; III: 356n

Bloor, Alfred J., VI: 248n

Blount, William, III: 524

Blount County (Tenn.), VIII: 68

Blountsville (Tenn.), VI: 470n

Blow, Henry Taylor, IV: 397n; V: 3n; VI: 218, 325; VII: 84n, 105-106, 343; VIII: 187n, 351

Blue Ridge Mountains, V: 235n, 246, 460-61; VII: 466n

Blue River, IV: 61

Blum, Herman, IV: 501n; V: 446n, 543n; VII: 238n, 271n; VIII: 79n

Blumenberg, Leopold, VIII: 238, 348

Blumhaven Library (Philadelphia), see Blum, Herman

Blunt, James Gilpatrick, V: 544n; VI: 188, 334-35, 339-40, 395-97, 495; VII: 119, 300n

Blunt, Orison, IV: 399; VIII: 258n

Boal, Christiana Walker (Sinclair), II: 375

Boal, James St. C. [Sinclair], IV: 311

Boal, Robert, I: 351-53, 355n, 384n; II: 296-98, 375, 387; IV: 311

Boal, Mrs. Robert, see Boal, Christiana Walker (Sinclair)

Boggs, Charles Stewart, V: 215; VI: 52

Boggs, W. F., II: 311-12

Bogotá (Colombia), V: 23

Bogue, Vincent A., I: 13

Bohannon, Thomas, I: 153, 254n

Bohlen, Henry, V: 510-11

Boice, Nicholas, I: 306

Boileau, James P., VIII: 174

Boisdoré, François, VIII: 179

Boisseau, J., VIII: 379n, 380

Boker, George H., VI: 533-34

Boker, Martin Van Buren, VIII: 418

Boker, Herman, & Company (N. Y.), IV: 509n

Bolívar, Simón, II: 123; VIII: 181n

Bolivar (Miss.), VII: 146n

Bolivar Heights (W. Va.), VI: 283n; VII: 548

Bolivia, V: 72-73; VI: 45; VII: 338; VIII: 138

Bollard, see Ballard, Frank W.

Bolles, James G., VI: 123n

Bolles [Bowles], William M., IV: 559n

Bollinger, James W., I: 9n

Bolsom, Jane C., VI: 443

Bonbager, J. C., IV: 165

Bond, Adolphus Freeman, V: 362

Bond, Benjamin, II: 36-38, 45, 64, 73n
Bond, Frank Stuart, VII: 379n, 386n
Bond, Hugh Lennox, IV: 340; V: 402n; VII: 482n
Bond, Lewis Montgomery, IV: 128
Bond, W. P., VIII: 305-306
Bondurant & Primm, I: 254
Bone, Elihu, I: 85
Bonifant, Washington, IV: 304
Bonman, Simon, VIII: 70
Bonner, Miles, VIII: 69
Boone, Daniel, IV: 56
Boone, Levi Day, V: 403
Boone County (Mo.), VI: 37
Boone County (W. Va.), V: 298
Booneville (Miss.), V: 301n
Boonville (Mo.), I: 325; IV: 538
Boorman, James, II: 198
Booth, ———, V: 498n
Booth, Mrs. Charles M., II: 315n
Booth, Jefferson M., VII: 291
Booth, Lionel F., VII: 329n
Booth, Mary Louise, V: 352
Border, District of the, VI: 335n, 423n
"Border Guards" (CSA guerrillas), VI: 415n
Boreman, Arthur Inghram, VIII: 109, 124
Boris, J. P., II: 289
Borrowe, William, VIII: 32n
Boston (Mass.), II: 5, 6n; III: 374-75; IV: 328, 334, 336n; V: 148, 154n, 241, 384n, 492; VI: 93n, 115n, 193; VII: 76, 164n, 394, 406, 523n, 532; VIII: 81n, 92n, 95-97, 194n
Boston Advertiser, II: 1n; VII: 20n; VIII: 80n
Boston & Worcester Railroad, V: 407n
Boston Atlas, I: 516n; II: 5n
Boston Atlas and Bee, IV: 68n
Boston Chronotype, II: 5n
Boston Courier, IV: 146; VI: 559n
Boston Mountain, battle of, VI: 147n

Boston Navy Yard, V: 148n, 241
Boston Transcript, VI: 184n; VII: 429n; VIII: 117n
Boswell, Daniel K., V: 456-57
Boswell, Frederick A., VIII: 5n
Botsford, Alban B., VI: 41
Botts, John F., VII: 287
Botts, John Minor, I: 423-24, 426-27, 429, 499; IV: 95; V: 4
Botts, Randolph, V: 4n, 304
Bouch, Isaac, VIII: 69
Boucher, J. W., VII: 547n
Boucher, Mrs. J. W., VII: 547n
Bouck, William C., I: 316
Bougan, F. S., VIII: 420
Bouligny, John Edward, V: 323, 462, 487-88, 504-505; VI: 172-73
Bounty lands, see Public lands
Bourry, Gotthilf [de], V: 360n, 385n
Boush, George Richard, VII: 232n
Boush, Mrs. George Richard, VII: 232n
Boutwell, Edward B., IV: 366
Boutwell, George Sewel, V: 359n, 433n, 507-508; VI: 364, 366n; VII: 90n, 159, 196
Bovey, John, II: 133-34, 207-208; VIII: 593n
Bowden, Sister Emerentiana, VII: 309n
Bowden, Lemuel Jackson, VI: 130, 132, 137, 419, 438
Bowen, Abram O., I: 418
Bowen, George W., VIII: 79
Bowen, Mrs. George W., VIII: 79
Bowen, James, V: 405; VII: 186n, 248n
Bowen, James W., VIII: 213n
Bowen, John J., V: 216
Bowen, John S., VI: 226n
Bowen, John W., VIII: 69
Bowen, Sherman W., III: 125-26
Bowers, Jacob, VII: 98
Bowers, Theodore S., VIII: 279n, 378n, 379, 383n, 384n
Bowie, ———, VIII: 322n
Bowie, Walter W., VIII: 322-23
Bowles, Samuel, IV: 311, 508n

Bowles, William M., *see* Bolles, William M.
Bowlin, James Butler, V: 161
Bowling, Absalom, I: 52
Bowling, Constantine, VIII: 50
Bowling Green (Ky.), IV: 369n; V: 69n, 84, 87n, 94n, 98-99, 135, 402n, 417n; VI: 424
Bowling Green (Va.), VI: 190n
Bowman, Alexander Hamilton, VI: 443n
Bowman, George W. (Ill.), I: 60
Bowman, George W. (Tenn.), VIII: 68
Bowman, John A., VI: 313n
Bowman, Joseph G., VIII: 117
Bowman, Samuel M., VII: 482
Bowman (Tenn.), V: 264n
Box Elder (Utah Terr.), VII: 112
Boyaya (Indian), VII: 325-26
Boyce, Samuel, V: 165
Boyd, ——— (W. Va.), VI: 130
Boyd, Crosby Noyes, IV: 249n, 518n
Boyd, Linn, I: 442n
Boyd, Marcus, VII: 266n, 372
Boyd, Samuel K., VII: 73
Boyd, Sempronius Hamilton, V: 517
Boyd, William, I: 254
Boyden, August H., VIII: 594n
Boyden, Ezekiel, IV: 563n
Boydtown Plank Road (Va.), VIII: 377n, 378, 379n, 382-83
"Boydville" (Faulkner home), VII: 446n
Boyer, A. Z., VII: 136
Boyle, Francis E., V: 54
Boyle, Francis Xavier, IV: 560n
Boyle, Jeremiah Tilford, IV: 475n, 559n; V: 313n, 321, 334, 367n, 370n, 386, 401-402, 408-409, 416-17, 419n, 427n, 457-59; VI: 87, 298-99, 529, 532n, 537; VII: 98, 106, 109, 121n, 163, 227n, 311n
Boyle, John, VIII: 91n
Boyle County (Ky.), IV: 410n
Boynton, Charles B., VII: 12n

Brabant, Marie Henriette, Duchess of, VII: 477
Bracken, ———, II: 176, 180
Bracken, Matthew, I: 354-55
Brackett, Joseph W., II: 395-96, 427
Braddock, Edward, V: 455n
Bradford, Allen Alexander, V: 256
Bradford, Augustus Williamson, VI: 491, 529, 555-58; VII: 10n, 255, 277, 363n, 445; VIII: 48n, 109
Bradford, James M., II: 297; VIII: 592
Bradford, James M. (Springfield), I: 208, 249, II: 301-303
Bradford, Joshua Thayer, V: 80, 384n
Bradford, Slaughter S., VI: 536-37; VIII: 51, 175
Bradford & Brother, II: 357
Bradford & Smith (Springfield), II: 301-303
Bradford & Son, II: 357
Bradley, Amy M., V: 259
Bradley, Mrs. E. M., VIII: 104n
Bradley, James H., V: 350
Bradley County (Tenn.), VIII: 68
Bradshaw, ———, II: 72, 190, 207-208, 285; VIII: 415
Bradshaw, C. G., VI: 140n
Bradwell, James Bolesworth, II: 532n
Bradwell, Mrs. James Bolesworth, *see* Bradwell, Myra
Bradwell, Myra, II: 532n
Brady, Miss, VIII: 99
Brady, Charles, VIII: 219n
Brady, Jasper Ewing, IV: 76; VIII: 99n
Brady, Mrs. Joseph, IV: 367n
Brady, Mathew Brown, IV: 40n
Bragg, Braxton, V: 301n, 408-10, 416n, 452, 457n, 458n; VI: 233n, 236, 377-78, 425n, 471n, 475n, 476, 478, 535n; VIII: 426n
Bragg, Edward Stuyvesant, V: 447
Bragonier, George H., VIII: 22-23
Brainard, Newton C., VII: 83n

Brainerd, Cephas, III: 522n; V: 339, 367n

Bralton, Joseph, VIII: 167n, 172-73, 198

Bramlette, Thomas E., V: 142n; VI: 202n, 401-402; VII: 34n, 109, 134-35, 163, 272, 281, 283n; VIII: 98-99, 109, 120, 260

Branam, see Branham, David C.

Branch, Lawrence O'Bryan, V: 245, 248

Brand, Alexander, II: 174, 179

Brandt, Peter H., I: preceding page 1

Brandy Station (Va.), VI: 257n, 535n

Branham, David C., IV: 181

Brannen, John, I: 11

Brannon, Mrs., VI: 405

Branson, Annie M., VIII: 85n

Branson, John, I: 284-85, 289

Brashear, Levi, VIII: 193n

Brasher, F. M., VIII: 69

Braxton Co. (W. Va.), V: 298

Bray & Merwin (N. Y.), IV: 386n

Brayman, Mason, I: 393, 407; II: 194, 205, 233-34, 326, 397-98; VII: 308, 322

Brayton, Benjamin B., II: 418

Brazil, II: 274; IV: 293, 359n, 397; VII: 39n; VIII: 97, 140

Brazos de Santiago (Tex.), VIII: 396

Brazos River, VII: 90n

Brearly, David, III: 531n

Breck, Daniel, VII: 219-20; VIII: 165n

Breck, Samuel, V: 228n; VII: 546n

Breckinridge, Charles Henry, IV: 417

Breckinridge, John Cabell, II: 380; III: 452; IV: 82, 90, 98, 123-24, 198, 200; V: 194n, 457n; VI: 39n, 265; VIII: 111n, 128-30, 310n, 315, 374n

Breckinridge, Joseph Cabell, V: 79n, 156n

Breckinridge, Robert Jefferson, V: 79; VIII: 183n, 315

Breckinridge, Samuel M., VIII: 123n

Breckinridge, Mrs. Samuel M., see Breckinridge, Virginia

Breckinridge, Virginia, VIII: 123n

Breckinridge County (Ky.), IV: 61

Breese, Kidder Randolph, V: 215

Breese, Sidney, I: 225, 478-79; II: 23, 529n; III: 105, 138, 172, 175

Brennon, J., & Company, II: 183

Brentsville (Va.), V: 34, 121n, 398n

Brereton, Samuel, VI: 89n

Bressler, B. H., see Brewster, Benjamin H.

Bressler, Ferdinand, see Brewster, Ferdinand

Brewer, ———, VI: 335n

Brewer, Anson L., II: 161, 308-309, 315-16, 327

Brewer, David, VIII: 69

Brewer, E. H., VIII: 171n

Brewster, Benjamin H. [E.], V: 193; VII: 58, 524; VIII: 334n

Brewster, Ferdinand, VII: 58; VIII: 334n

Brewster, Kingman, II: 98n, 101n, 106n

Brice, Benjamin William, VIII: 173

Bridge, Hudson E., VI: 340n

Bridge, Samuel J., IV: 305

Bridge, H[udson] E., & Company, VI: 340n

Bridgeport (Ala.), VI: 494n

Bridgeport (Conn.), IV: 13n; VII: 510

Bridger's Pass (Utah Terr.), VI: 518n

Bridges, Edwin T., III: 505-506

Bridges, George Washington, VII: 540n

Bridges, Hiram, II: 330n

Bridges, Robert Thomas, VII: 540; VIII: 26, 29, 180

Bridges, Thomas R., see Bridges, Robert Thomas

Bridges, William R., see Bridges, Robert Thomas

Bridges (Ill.), construction of, I: 28-30, 72-73
Brien, John S., VII: 130-31; VIII: 211n, 259n
Brierer, Eviend, VII: 371
Briggs, Benjamin, I: 46
Briggs, Charles, II: 73
Briggs, George E., IV: 407n
Briggs, Henry, VIII: 592
Briggs, Henry W., IV: 305
Briggs, Huldah, see Stout, Huldah (Briggs)
Briggs, James A., III: 494, 554; V: 366-67, 403
Briggs, John R., Jr., VIII: 366n
Briggs, Richard, II: 73; VIII: 592
Briggs, Mrs. Richard, II: 73
Briggs, Samuel, II: 423
Briggs, William D., II: 192; VIII: 366-67
Briggs, William S., VI: 241n
Brigham, John C., II: 198
Bright, Jesse David, II: 351, 354; V: 205n
Bright, John, VI: 176n; VII: 71-72
Bright, Marshall H., V: 23n
Brighton (Ill.), I: 401
Brighton (Mass.), V: 406
Brimfield (Ill.), I: 456
Brimstone Hill (Va.), V: 121n
Brink, Peter Cornelius, VII: 523
Brinkerhoff, Fred W., III: 497n
Brinkerhoff, George M., IV: 309
Brinkerhoff, Samuel B., IV: 304
Brintnall, Sewall, VIII: 100
Brinton, William P., IV: 516n
Brisbane, William Henry, VI: 98, 453-59
Briscoe, James C., VIII: 307
Briscoe, Thomas S., VII: 371
Bristoe Station (Va.), V: 280n, 398n, 401n; VI: 528
Bristol (England), IV: 494n, 504n
Bristol (Tenn.), VI: 470n
Bristol County Democrat [Taunton, Mass.], II: 6n
Bristol Station, see Bristoe Station
Bristow, ———, VII: 335
Bristow, Benjamin F., II: 75

Bristow, James H., VI: 532n
Bristow, Samuel B., VI: 532
Bristow Station, see Bristoe Station (Va.)
British Museum, VI: 9-10
British West Indies, II: 298
Britt, W. O., VIII: 69
Britton, Isaac S., I: 335
Britton, James, VIII: 370n
Broad Run (Va.), V: 34, 121n, 240n, 401n
Broaddus, William, I: 340n
Broadhead, James Overton, VI: 34, 329, 501-502, VII: 311n
Broadhead, John M., see Brodhead, John M.
Broadway, Jesse A. [T.], VII: 541n; VIII: 28-29
Broadwell, Charles, I: 39
Broadwell, Dennis P., II: 424-25
Broadwell, John B., I: 182; II: 424-25
Broadwell, M. M., VIII: 16
Broadwell, Norman M., II: 304n, 310
Brocchus, Perry E., VII: 480n, 490; VIII: 243n
Brockman, John M., IV: 121
Broderick, C. S., IV: 309
Broderick, David Colbreth, VII: 13
Brodhead, James Overton, see Broadhead, James Overton
Brodhead, John M., VI: 233
Brodhead, Richard, I: 497
Brodie, John, I: 264, 341
Brodie, Mrs. John, I: 341
Brodie, William, IV: 512
Brogden, H. H., VII: 325
Bromwell, Henry Pelham Holmes, II: 431; VIII: 366
Brooke County (W. Va.), V: 298
Brookline (Mass.), V: 406
Brooklyn (N. Y.), III: 494n, 519; IV: 38, 232; VI: 125n, 361n; VII: 220, 278n, 394
Brooklyn (steamboat), IV: 424
Brooklyn Eagle, III: 81n; VII: 295n

Brooklyn Navy Yard, IV: 313-14
Brooks, Albert I., IV: 356
Brooks, Alfred O., VII: 447
Brooks, Charles Stewart, VIII: 417
Brooks, Edward P., VII: 244-45, 252
Brooks, Erastus, VII: 349n
Brooks, Harold C., VII: 202n
Brooks, James, IV: 98n
Brooks, Noah, VI: 161n; VIII: 98n, 154-55
Brooks, Preston Smith, II: 377-78, 514-15; III: 87, 117, 276, 316, 322; IV: 11
Brooks, William Thomas Harbaugh, V: 67; VI: 75n, 285n, 286, 347n
Broom, Jacob, III: 531n
Broome, Mrs., I: 465
Brosius, Milton L., VI: 106n
Bross, William, III: 52, 54, 58-59, 67
Brough, John, II: 211-12; VI: 287; VII: 130, 175, 196, 308, 312-13, 359, 402, 547; VIII: 109, 124
Brougham, Henry Peter, IV: 101
Broughton, N., Jr., IV: 381-82
Brower, Andrew, VI: 296n
Browker, Benjamin, IV: 295
Brown, Albert [alias], see Brown, Mathias
Brown, Albert Gallatin, III: 549n; VI: 353
Brown, Mrs. Albert Gallatin, see Brown, Roberta E.
Brown, Benjamin Gratz, III: 256, 265, 314; V: 544; VI: 42-43; VII: 13, 78-79, 84-85, 101n
Brown, Bunbry B., II: 188
Brown, Charles D., VI: 421-22
Brown, Charles T., VIII: 363n
Brown, Clara, VII: 258
Brown, David A., II: 310
Brown, Douglas S., III: 352n
Brown, E. Warfield, I: 389; II: 28n
Brown, Egbert B., VII: 407; VIII: 220
Brown, Emily, VIII: 363n
Brown, Fountain J., VII: 357n

Brown, G. L., VIII: 192n
Brown, George E., VI: 436
Brown, George F., VII: 195n
Brown, George [alias George Rock], VIII: 88-89
Brown, George T., II: 303, 432; V: 167n
Brown, George W. (D. C.), VIII: 24n
Brown, George W. (Md.), IV: 340-41, 523n
Brown, George W. (N. Y.), VIII: 301
Brown, H. C., VII: 258n
Brown, Harvey, IV: 315, 320n; V: 187
Brown, Henry A., V: 157
Brown, Henry M., II: 188
Brown, Horace A., II: 297
Brown, J. Henry, IV: 102
Brown, J. Mabbett, VII: 289n
Brown, Jacob, VII: 441n
Brown, James, III: 182; VIII: 298
Brown, James Nicholas, I: 208, 249, 284, 398, 405; III: 327-28; IV: 540; V: 406; VII: 66n
Brown, John: L. on, III: 496-97, 502-503, 538-39, 541-42, 553; IV: 1, 7, 12-13, 23, 33, 42, 132n, 161n; V: 278
Brown, John C., VI: 480
Brown, John C., see Craven, William A.
Brown, John J., I: 230n, 237-39, 242-43, 249, 405-406
Brown, John O., VI: 158, 337
Brown, Jonathan B., I: 2, 3
Brown[e], Joseph (boatbuilder), VI: 163
Brown, Joseph (Cincinnati), V: 174
Brown, Joseph Emerson, VIII: 9n, 27
Brown, Joshua, I: 46
Brown, Julia, VII: 258
Brown, Lloyd Warfield, VII: 65-66
Brown, Mrs. Lloyd Warfield, see Brown, Rebecca P.

Brown, Mathias [alias Albert Brown], VI: 515, 548
Brown, Perc S., I: 474n; III: 342n; V: 144n, 446n, 481n
Brown, Rebecca P., VII: 66n
Brown, Reuben, I: 2
Brown, Robert Young, VI: 353n
Brown, Roberta E., VI: 353
Brown, Samuel E., V: 4
Brown, Samuel W., II: 297
Brown, Stuart, I: 159n, 181n, 208n, 230n; II: 344n; IV: 303n
Brown, Theophilus, VI: 436
Brown, Mrs. Theophilus, VI: 436
Brown, Thomas, IV: 540n
Brown, W. H., VII: 543n
Brown, William (Conn.), VI: 524
Brown, William (Ill.), I: 46n
Brown, William C., I: 335, 389; II: 27-28, 75, 425
Brown, William Gay, V: 319n; VI: 132
Brown, William Hubbard, III: 507-509, 513n, 516
Brown, William L., IV: 295n, 402
Brown, William Murray, VII: 91n
Brown, William Young, V: 54
Brown, Wilson, I: 69
Brown University, I: viii, xiv; IV: 123n
Browne, Junius, VI: 241
Browne, Thomas C., I: 121, 203n, 239, 306; II: 17
Brownell, Francis Edwin, IV: 409-10
Browning, Eliza (Caldwell), I: 95n, 117-19, 156-57, 395
Browning, Orville Hickman: marriage, I: 117n; Ill. state senator (1836), 117n, 119, 156n; appointed (1839) to "Committee of nine," 146n; letter from L. reporting political affairs (June '47), 394-95; legal cases of, 394, II: 103-105, 117-18, 315, 386, 410, 470; "a great admirer" of Clay, I: 468; mentioned for General Land Office, II: 29; and appointments, 62n, 72, IV: 412n, 456, V: 61n, 62n, 143n, 159, 283, 457n, VI: 51n, VII: 373n; signs call for Whig convention (1851), II: 113; letter from L. on 1854 election returns, 286-87; supports Logan for Ill. Supreme Court, 309-10; invited to make political visit to Iowa (1856), 348; asked to draft a Republican party address (Dec. '56), 386; entertained at L.'s home (1857), 388; belief in the ultimate extinction of slavery, 492; Douglas discounts his role in Republican politics (1858), III: 7, 109, 174; recommends a licensing to practice law, 515; suggested revisions to L.'s First Inaugural address, IV: 249n, 254n, 271n; asked by L. to introduce Indian treaty amendment in Senate, 455; and the Frémont proclamation (1861), 531-33; and Emily Helm's White House visit (1863), VII: 63n; requests releases of prisoners-of-war, 66n, 97, VIII: 185n; requests issuance of passes, VII: 84, VIII: 354n; describes Kentuckians discussion with L. on border state problems, VII: 282n; defense lawyer in court-martial of Rear Admiral Wilkes, 342-43; describes L.'s visit to Grant (June '64), 406n; and a permission to trade with insurrectionary states, VIII: 200n, 267n, 353n
His *Diary* cited, II: 285n, 388; IV: 456n; VII: 63n, 66n, 282n, 373n, 406n; VIII: 185n, 267n, 353n, 354n
Browning, Mrs. Orville Hickman, *see* Browning, Eliza
Brownlow, William Gannaway ("Parson"), V: 60; VII: 321n
Brownsville (Miss.), VI: 226

Brownsville (Tex.), VI: 466n; VII: 192-93; VIII: 396

Bruce, ——, V: 402n, 417n

Bruce, E. M., VI: 517n

Bruce, Mrs. E. M., VI: 517n

Bruinsburg (Miss.), VI: 226n

Brumfield, Nancy (Lincoln), IV: 61

Brumfield, William, IV: 61

Brumfield, Mrs. William, see Brumfield, Nancy (Lincoln)

Brummell, George Bryan ("Beau"), IV: 276n

Brune, John C., IV: 340-41

Brunshausen or Stade Dues, V: 58, 131-32, 519

Brunswick (Ga.), V: 167; VIII: 396

Brunswick (Germany), V: 85n

Brush, Daniel Harmon, VIII: 156n

Brush, Daniel Harmon, Jr., VIII: 156

Brush, Henry L., II: 167, 171

Brush Creek (Sangamon Co.), I: 116

Brussels (Belgium), VII: 87; VIII: 204

Bruzual, Blas, VII: 536-37

Bryan, Charles, VI: 30n

Bryan, Silas Lillard, II: 296

Bryan, Thomas Barbour, IV: 144; VI: 30n; VII: 135

Bryan, William F., I: 340n; II: 289n

Bryan Hall (Chicago), IV: 144n; V: 419n

Bryant, John Howard, VII: 366-67

Bryant, Nicholas A., I: 43-44

Bryant, William Cullen, IV: 81, 149n, 163-64, 171, 374n, 550n; V: 361n; VI: 108n, 216-17, 239n; VII: 409-10

Bryantown (Md.), VII: 28n

Bryantsville (Ky.), IV: 542n

Buchanan, Downey, II: 165

Buchanan, Franklin, VI: 265

Buchanan, James: meets L. when Sec. of State (1848), I: 452;

compared with Taylor as 1848 presidential candidate, 463; Republican opposition in elections of 1856 and 1858 and dispute with Douglas on Lecompton Constitution, II: 342-43, 350-85 *passim*, 427n, 447, 448n, 452, 455, 458, 463, 465-66, 471-72, 476-81, 485-86, 503, 508-509, 530, 533, 539, III: 21, 26-27, 34-35, 68-70, 73, 76-77, 83, 116, 156, 166-67, 180, 191-93, 205, 226-27, 259-60, 265, 270, 272-74, 282, 283n, 292-96, 298, 324, 349, 390n, IV: 217, VI: 251n; made honorary member of Washington Agricultural Literary Society, IV: 70n; secession question and reinforcement of Charleston forts, 150n, 157n, 160, 162, 163n, 172-73; and L.'s inaugural (1861), 247n, 339n; views on foreign affairs supported by L., 287-88, V: 38, 144; persons identified as having served in his administration; IV: 384n, 418n, 441n, 544n, V: 25n, 28n, VII: 446n; signature on temperance declaration, IV: 420

Buchanan, Robert Christie, V: 12, 64n

Buchanan County (Mo.), VI: 544; VII: 337

Buchignani, Antonio, IV: 483

Buck, Cornelius F., VII: 355n, 371-72

Buck, Francis N., IV: 512

Buck, H., Jr., IV: 68

Buck, Ira A. W., IV: 43

Buckeye mower, II: 427n

Buckeye State, The [New Lisbon, Ohio], IV: 208n

Buckhart Grove (Ill.), I: 130

Buckheart, Wilbur, VI: 133

Buckingham, Catharinus Putnam, V: 362n, 365n

Buckingham, Eliza (Ripley), IV: 69

Buckingham, William Alfred, IV:

69, 451n; V: 375n; VI: 54, 75n, 113n, 232; VII: 83, 114; VIII: 109

Buckingham, Mrs. William Alfred, see Buckingham, Eliza

Buckland, Ralph Pomeroy, V: 299; VII: 428n

Buckley, Mary (Donovan), IV: 551n, 556n

Buckmaster, Mrs. B. E., V: 542n

Buckmaster, Nathaniel, I: 10n

Buckmaster, Samuel A., II: 524n

Buckner, ———, VI: 286-87

Buckner, Aydelotte H., I: 67

Buckner, Aylette, I: 497

Buckner, Simon Bolivar, IV: 444, 489, 542, 545; V: 14-15, 31n, 381n, 402n, 417n; VI: 265

Buell, Don Carlos: recommends appointments, IV: 503n; commands Department of the Ohio, V: 21; recommends increased officer-training, 31; and defense of East Tenn. and Ky., 54n, 59-60, 84-87, 90-92, 94, 98-99, 130n, 135, 153, 155, 276n, 303n, 313n, 321-23, 409, 416n, 452, 457-59, VI: 475n, VIII: 426; Hunter complains of favoritism toward, V: 84-85; want of cooperation between Halleck and, 84n, 86, VIII: 40n; "delay is ruining us," V: 91; and McClellan's plan (Feb. '62) for Army of the Potomac advance, 122n, 124n; appointed Major General of Volunteers, 142; command of 14th Corps given to Rosecrans, 501n; "dissatisfied with the slowness of Buell and McClellan," 509-10; resigns following investigation, VII: 287-88

Buena Vista (Mexico), battle of, I: 393, 448n, 472, 515; II: 12, 86, 473

Buffalo (N. Y.), II: 4; IV: 31, 220-21, 326n, 501n; VII: 258n, 546; VIII: 1-2

Buffalo Commercial Advertiser, IV: 111n

Buffalo Hart Grove (Ill.), I: 139

Buffalo Morning Express, IV: 221n

Buffington, Joseph, IV: 167

Buffum, John W., I: 251

Buford, John, VI: 200n, 250n; VII: 74

Buford, Thomas Jefferson, VI: 386n

Bulkley, Mrs., VII: 205-206

Bull Run, battles of: mention of various casualties, IV: 336n, 469n, 504n, V: 149, 296, VIII: 85n; memo of military policy suggested by defeat, IV: 457-58; mention of various prisoners, 492n, V: 86n, 268, 381n, VII: 446n; mention of commendable action, V: 79n, VI: 180; comment on first battle, V: 98, 356n, 421, VII: 250n; charges of officer misconduct, V: 70n, 167n, 407n; mention of second battle, 402n, 404n; rumor of third battle (Oct. '63), VI: 528; see also Manassas (Va.)

Bullard, Frederic Lauriston, VIII: 117n

Bulletin of the California State Society Sons of the Revolution, The, III: 492n

Bullitt, Cuthbert, V: 344-46, 504n; VI: 16; VII: 420; VIII: 242n

Bulloch, John M., VIII: 296n

Bulloch, Waller R., VIII: 296

Bullock, Helen Duprey, I: xv

Bullock, Maria L., II: 313, 317, 323-25, 381; III: 348

Bunker, Benjamin B., VI: 255

Bunker Hill (W. Va.), V: 246-47

Bunn, ———, VI: 480

Bunn, Alice Edwards, I: xvii

Bunn, George Wallace, Jr., I: xiv, xvii

Bunn, Mrs. George Wallace, Jr., see Bunn, Melinda (Jones)

Bunn, Jacob, I: 398, 405; II: 120, 396-97; III: 383, 399; VI: 237-38

Bunn, John W., VI: 237-38
Bunn, Melinda (Jones), I: xiv
Buntin, Toussaint Campbell, IV: 309
Burbridge, Stephen Gano, V: 205; VII: 391, 484-85, 509-10, 534-35; VIII: 23, 78, 86n, 88, 89, 99, 120n, 182n, 197-98, 212n, 256, 289, 309-10
Burden, Amos, VI: 353n
Burdick, Raymond E., II: 397n, 433n; III: 336n; IV: 114n, 451n, 484n, 491n, 493n, 502n, 527n; V: 173n, 285n, 446n; VI: 271n, 294n, 420n, 459n, 498n, 506n; VII: 139n, 251n, 261n, 277n, 432n, 523n; VIII: 72n, 156n, 165n, 206n, 235n, 257n
Bureau County (Ill.), III: 352-55
Burge, P., VI: 544
Burgoyne, W. H. S., VIII: 303
Burk, James, II: 183
Burke, Edmund, II: 32n
Burke [Benke, McManus], Edward, V: 143-44, 263; VI: 345-46, 353n, 472n
Burke, John A., VII: 357
Burkesville (Ky.), V: 409n, 417n
Burkesville (Va.), VIII: 385, 389-91
Burket, I. N., IV: 309
Burkhardt, John M., II: 74, 100n, 102; III: 383
Burleigh, Walter Atwood, IV: 298n; VIII: 358n
Burling, George Childs, V: 483n
Burlingame, Anson, III: 518; IV: 292-93, 397; VI: 96n; VII: 147-48; VIII: 139n
Burlington (Iowa) Hawk-Eye, I: 330n; VI: 106n
Burmond, C. F., VIII: 86n
Burnam, John, VII: 80
Burnet, David G., I: 435n
Burnet House (Cincinnati), IV: 72, 76, 197, 200n; VI: 538n
Burnett, Theodore J., VII: 371
Burnett, Ward Benjamin, V: 170
Burnham, Alfred Avery, V: 375n

Burnham, Hiram, VII: 311n
Burnley, J. Hume, VIII: 271
Burns, George Whitfield, V: 381
Burns, Michael (N. Y.), VII: 496
Burns, Michael (Tenn.), VII: 478
Burns, Robert, I: 106, IV: 48; VIII: 237
Burns, William Wallace, VI: 105n
Burnside, Ambrose Everett: and McClellan's proposed plan (Feb. '62) for Army of the Potomac movement, V: 122n; expedition (Jan. '62) to Hatteras, 132, 136n, VII: 232n; and capture of Roanoke Island (Feb. '62), V: 134; appointed major general of volunteers, 142; under McClellan (May-July '62), 216, 288, 293n, 302-306, 311, 323; assigned to Army of Virginia, 334; passes, 354n; and the Eastern front (Aug.-Sept. '62), 366, 385, 395, 397-99, 410n, 412n, 445, 448, VI: 442; and relief of McDowell command (Sept. '62), V: 407; given command of Army of the Potomac, 485; L. visits at Aquia Creek, 511; Nicolay visits at Fredericksburg, 552; supports assignment of Stahl to command of the Eleventh Corps, VI: 5-6, 43n; assignments of officers to, 7, 516n; visits L. in Washington, 10 (Dec. '62), 74-75, 77 (Jan. '63); removed from command of Army of the Potomac, 15n, 22-23, 77-78; controversy over lack of confidence in Halleck and Stanton, 31-32, 46-48; resignation of, 32n, 46-48, 439; supports promotion of Humphreys, 81; Schurz asks for assignment of his Division to, 168n; commands in Department of the Ohio, 196, 200, 350; and Vallandigham case, 215n, 235n, 237, 248n, 266-68; and military arrest cases, 219-

20, 225, 229n, 231, 295-96, 313, 529, VII: 29-30, 93, 96, 106; in East Tenn. and at Knoxville, VI: 238, 285n, 373-74, 434, 436, 439, 516n, 521, VII: 5-6, 14, 30; and enrollment of free Negroes, VI: 298-300; reports on Morgan's raid, 346-47; ordered to join Rosecrans at Chattanooga, (Sept. '63), 469-75, 480-81, 483-86, 498, 510-11; aide-de-camp Cutts reprimand, 538n; succeeded by Foster in command of Department of the Ohio, VII: 109n; proposed transfer of Boyle to command of, 121n; order suspending Chicago *Times* revoked by L., 361, 363-64; recommends West Point cadet appointment, 367n; mentioned at Antietam, 549

Burnside, Mrs. Ambrose Everett, *see* Burnside, Mary Richmond

Burnside, Mary Richmond (Bishop), VII: 6n

Burr, Aaron, IV: 89

Burr, George, VIII: 364-65

Burr, Silas W., VII: 371

Burrage, Henry S., VIII: 229

Burrell, Isaac S., VIII: 81

Burris, John T., IV: 346

Burrowes, Thomas H., VII: 271

Burrows, Daniel, VII: 93, 96, 106

Burt, Armistead, I: 469n

Burt, William C., VIII: 69

Burtle, James, I: 344

Burtnet, D. Henry, V: 193n; VII: 177n

Burton, Allen A., IV: 294, 408, 517n, 521; VI: 56-58; VII: 37n

Burton, Henry Stanton, IV: 392

Burton, Mrs. Henry Stanton, IV: 392

Burton, William, V: 378-79

Burtwell, ———, V: 81

Bush, John M., III: 206-207

Bush, Sarah, *see* Lincoln, Sarah (Bush-Johnston)

Bush, Tompkins, II: 135n

Bushfield, Joseph M., VI: 419n; VII: 175n, 276n

Bushnell, ———, VI: 53

Bushnell, Douglas R., VIII: 261n

Bushnell, Mrs. Douglas R., *see* Bushnell, Emily J. C.

Bushnell, Emily J. C., VIII: 261-62

Bushnell, Nehemiah, II: 72, 103-105

Busteed, Richard, V: 361; VI: 14-15; VII: 15

Buswell, Brigham, VI: 419n

Butler, Andrew J., IV: 301

Butler, Benjamin Franklin (1795-1858), I: 508; II: 338

Butler, Benjamin Franklin (1818-1893): promotion to Major General (1861), IV: 370, 372n, 463, VII: 346-47, VIII: 594; appointment and employment recommendations, IV: 413, 451n, VI: 99, 184, VII: 128, VIII: 25; command of Fort Monroe (1861), IV: 457, 478n; recruitment of troops, 468-69, 515, 518-19, 557n, V: 96; military arrests, V: 8n, VII: 232; command at New Orleans, V: 343n, 420-21, 423, 428n, VI: 16n, 22, 59n, 73-77, 81-82, 100; and reestablishment of state governments, V: 462-63, 504-505, VII: 6, VIII: 174, 186; and compensated plantation labor, V: 487-88; sends Confederate swords to L., 552-53; pardon recommendation, VI: 55n; L. urged to give assignment to, 230-31, 383, 500, 503, VIII: 195; recommended to direct the draft in N. Y., VI: 331n; and court-martial cases at Fort Monroe, VII: 59, 82, 98, 125, 138, 142, 151, 206, 297-98, 341n, 416n, VIII: 30, 47-48, 189-90, 193; and discharge of prisoners at Point Lookout, VII: 103; complaints against his military government in Va., 135-36, 292, 481, 487-88, 508,

VIII: 27-28, 225, 285n; and distribution of copies of amnesty proclamation behind enemy lines, VII: 177n; Cameron visits to Fort Monroe, 203n, 290n; spy cases, 205-206, 356n, VIII: 162n; L. requests interview with Pitts, VII: 203; requests statement of confidence from L., VII: 207; reports death of Col. Dahlgren, 222, 226, 251; and refusal of Maryland visitors to take oath of allegiance, 239; prisoner-of-war exchanges, 244-45, 252, 257, 258n, 260, 265, 289n, 297, 310, VIII; 36-37; L.'s intended visit to Fort Monroe (Apr. '64), VII: 289, 293-94; Fox and Hay visit Fort Monroe, 310; suggested for Sec. of War on false rumor of Stanton resignation, 454n; and procurement of new guns, VIII: 3; N. Y. protests his pressure to maintain order during 1864 election, 91n; abandonment of expedition to take Wilmington, N. C., 187n, 207-208; summoned to appear before Committee on the Conduct of the War (Jan. '65), 215
Butler, Charles, VIII: 97-98
Butler, Charles T., VII: 521n
Butler, Chester, I: 417

Butler, Evan T., I: 206-207
Butler, James P., VI: 163-64
Butler, John George, V: 53
Butler, John M., IV: 167
Butler, Pierce, III: 527; V: 193-94
Butler, Roderick Randum, VIII: 68
Butler, Salome, I: 140
Butler, Speed, IV: 461, 553
Butler, Thomas Harvey, VIII: 311n
Butler, William, I: viii, 92, 97, 99, 106-107, 121, 138-43, 145-46, 149-50, 156n, 229-30, 258n, 286, 288, 300n, 302-303, 322-25, 328-29; II: 39-40, 45n, 47n, 74, 206-207, 209, 291; IV: 168, 303n, 411n, 461n; V: 154n, 186-87, 495n; VI: 97, 228, 340; VII: 213-14
Butler, Mrs. William, I: 140
Butler, William Orlando, I: 441n
Butler's Book, V: 553n
Butterfield, A. D., II: 183
Butterfield, Daniel, VI: 118n, 169, 184, 196, 199-200, 209, 247
Butterfield, Justin, I: 406; II: 43-44, 48-52, 54-55, 57-60, 68, 77, 134-35
Butts, Charles W., VII: 292, 297n
Butz, Caspar, IV: 144
Buzby, George L., VI: 145n
Byrne, Mrs. Edward, VIII: 292
Byrnes, Daniel P., VII: 152
Byrnes, M. C., VI: 309n

C

C. E. Hillman (steamboat), IV: 351-52
Cabaniss, see Cabiness, John M.
Cabell, Edward Carrington, I: 476n

Cabell County (W. Va.), V: 298
Cabiness, John M., I: 297
Cabinet (1861-1865), L.'s: the formation of, IV: 136-37, 141n, 145, 147-50, 154-55, 161-71, 173-

77, 179-81, 248, 273, 278, 279n; "teased to insanity" to make changes in, 173; and relief for Fort Sumter, 284-85, 290n, 301n; legal opinions and arguments requested of Attorney General, 290-91, 390, V: 82, 238-39, 270, 275, 333, 336, VIII: 80, 190-91, 245; and off-shore collection of duties and illegal importations, IV: 292-93; Seward complains of lack of administration policy, 316-18; L. asks resolution of Cameron-Blair differences on mobilization policies, 369; calls for meetings or conferences, 416, 419-20, 454, 551, V: 144, VI: 110-11, VII: 330, VIII: 412; L. approves photographs of, V: 68; and a "proclamation of Jan. 30 1862," 114; N. Y. *Tribune's* prediction (May '62) of changes in, 225-26; Congressional censure of Cameron, 240-43; Chase requested not to leave Washington (Dec. '62), VI: 11; duties of in emergencies, 34-35; and marque and reprisal bill, 126n; complaint of cabinet influence in La. election, 172-73; and Chase's status as candidate for presidential nomination, VII: 212-13; and Fort Pillow massacre, 328-29; interrelationship and relationship to President, 423, 439-40; L.'s war compensation proposal (Feb. '65), VIII: 260-61

Appointments and resignations: Sec. of State, IV: 137, 148-49, 173, 273, VI: 9n, 11-13; Sec. of War, IV: 141n, 165-70, 279n, V: 96; Sec. of the Treasury, IV: 165-68, 171, VI: 9n, 11n, 12-13, VII: 419-20, 422-23; Sec. of the Navy, IV: 170-71; Sec. of the Interior, VI: 35n, VIII: 347; Attorney General, VIII: 126-27;

Postmaster General, VIII: 18-20, 25; *see also names of cabinet members*

Cabinet (Taylor's): L. and appointments in, II: 25, 30
Cabot, Eliza S., *see* Torrey, Eliza S. (Cabot)
Cabot, Stephen, VII: 180, 305-306
Caddo Indians, VI: 153n
Cadiz (Ohio), IV: 206; VI: 347n
Cadiz (Spain), V: 549n
Cadiz Junction (Ohio), IV: 206, VI: 346n
Cadiz Republican, IV: 206n
Cadiz Sentinel, IV: 206n
Cadmus Book Shop (N. Y.), VIII: 595n
Cadwalader, George, IV: 525; VI: 279; VII: 394n; VIII: 249, 273
Caesar, Caius Julius, I: 178
Cahawba (steamer), VI: 254n
Cairo (Ill.), IV: 351-52, 374, 381, 395, 458-59, 510, 517n, 527, 545; V: 20n, 86n, 87n, 110-11, 116n, 177, 187n, 413n, 469n, 488n, 540n; VI: 155, 374n, 494n; VII: 63, 167n, 185, 208-209, 250, 308, 322, 327n; VIII: 178n, 322, 336n
Calcutta (India), V: 32n
Caldwell, Albert Gallatin, II: 100
Caldwell, Charles Henry Bromedge, V: 215
Caldwell, Henry C., VII: 117, 129
Caldwell, John (Ind.), VII: 280n, 304
Caldwell, Mrs. John (Ind.), VII: 280n
Caldwell, John (Tenn.), VIII: 295n
Caldwell, William, I: 264, 284
Caledonia (Ill.), I: 220
Calhoun, John, I: 21, 23, 36-37, 49-50, 149, 170, 211, 284n, 298, 334-35, 336, 393, 398, 405; II: 71n, 229-30, 290, 488; IV: 65, 107, 125n
Calhoun, John Caldwell, I: 181, 310, 419; II: 7, 130, 346, 350-51, 354; III: 77, 301; VI: 507

Calhoun County (W. Va.), V: 298

California: acquisition and admission to the Union as a free state, I: 440, II: 3, 232, 237, 243, 252-54, 259, 279, III: 224, 271, 297, 483, 485; threat to divide state on slavery basis, II: 300-301; delegation pays its respects to L. (Mar. '61), IV: 276n; appointments, 301-302, 304-306, 311, 335, 471, VI: 113n, 249, 290, VII: 215n, 404, 497, VIII: 242n, 408, 420; recruitment of Mexican citizens in, IV: 519; circuit courts, V: 41-42, 267-68, VI: 290; regulations concerning exports, V: 241, VI: 432, VII: 503-504; Senate request for report on trade, VI: 119; land claim, 242n; Republican nominee for governor (July '63), 321n; Campbell a member of the state legislature, 541n; court-martial of person from, VII: 299n; estimated electoral vote (1864), VIII: 46; comparison of election returns (1860, 1864), 128-30, 150-51, 153; telegraph and railroad connection with the East, 146; mentioned, VII: 326

Callam, C. C., VIII: 162n

Callan, Christopher C., VII: 251

Callan, John F., V: 466

Callwell, Mary L., IV: 534n

Calvert, —— (White House employee), V: 491

Calvert, Charles Benedict, V: 187

Cambridge (Mass.), II: 6n

Camden (Ark.), VIII: 324n

Camden (N. J.), VI: 425n

Camden (N. C.), VIII: 396

Cameron, Anderson, VI: 544

Cameron, James, VI: 469n, 504n

Cameron, John, VI: 185

Cameron, Robert Alexander, IV: 181

Cameron, Roderick W., IV: 362n

Cameron, Simon: and 1860 election, III: 491, 521, IV: 55, 71, 84n, 90-91, 103n, 110-11, 113n; appointed Secretary of War, IV: 145, 165-71, 174-77, 179-81, 248, 279n; and appointments, 273, 283, 294, 297, 326, 335, 342n, 358-59, 387, 393-96, 398-99, 403-407, 409, 414, 442-559 passim, V: 4, 6-8, 12, 14n, 17, 19, 22-23, 25, 28, 33, 55, 61, 64-65, 67, 69n, 71, 76, 78-80, 83, 89, 93, 111n, 114n, 332, 437, VI: 185-86, VII: 58, 375, VIII: 157n, 334n, 416-17, 593-94

And Fort Sumter, IV: 280, 285n, 321-22, VIII: 376n; and Fort Pickens expedition, 301-302; and a bodyguard for L., 327; army assignments, 344-45, 517, 551; testimonial to C. Clay, 352; mobilization of troops, 352n, 359, 367-71, 374-75, 376n, 380-81, 384-86, 388, 394, 402-406, 408, 409-11, 414-16, 443, 454n, 455, 456n, 458-59, 464, 468-69, 473, 475-76, 500, 504, 508, 511, 518-19, 556-59, V: 23, 80; and Blair's opposition to War Department policies, IV: 369-71; army promotions, 392, 483, 548, V: 21, 22; procurement of supplies and equipment, IV: 395-96, 410, 464, 499-500, 509, 535-36, V: 197n, VI: 298n

And Frémont's western command, IV: 419-20, 519-20, 524, 549-50, V: 84-85; meeting with L., IV: 420, 551n, VI: 2, VII: 157n, VIII: 421; annual report (1861), IV: 431, V: 37, 40; regularization of Brigadier and Major General appointments, IV: 463; death of brother at Bull Run, 469n; supports Mo. amnesty proclamation (Aug. '61), 470-71; army dismissals, discharges, and paroles, 480,

486, V: 11-12, 67, VI: 324, 522, VII: 521; and men and arms for St. Louis, IV: 485, 529-30; and loyalty of Franklin Pierce, 505; and army pay, 509-10, V: 23n; and civilian communication in military areas, IV: 525
And Port Royal Expedition, 527-28; and work of clergy among N. C. loyalists, V: 3; management of the military telegraph, 6; and Me. coastal defenses, 13-14, 74; and namesake of, 55; adjustment of claims, 57-58; arrest of secessionists, V: 59; and Jewish chaplains, 69; release of suspected kidnapper, 94; Halleck report (Jan. '62) of military situation in the West, 95; minister to Russia, 96-97, 240n, 368, 425n, VI: 103-104; false-arrest lawsuit against, V: 193-94; Congressional censure of, 240-43; reports (July '63, Oct. '64) on Army of the Potomac movements, VI: 329-30, VIII: 40-41; disloyalty of Trimble, VI: 325n; and L.'s reelection, VII: 118, 289-90, 517n, VIII: 43-44; visit (Feb. '64) to Fort Monroe, VII: 203, 289n; and arming Negroes, 282; mentioned also, I: 416n, IV: 125n, VI: 105n, 385n, VIII: 421
Camp, Amos, II: 188
Camp, Benjamin F., IV: 186n
Camp, Irwin, III: 385
Camp, John N., VII: 403n
Camp Beauregard (Ky.), V: 87n
Camp Butler (Ill.), VII: 253n; VIII: 316n
Camp Calvert (Ky.), V: 54n
Camp Carroll (Md.), IV: 396n
Camp Casey (Va.?), VII: 369
Camp Chase (Ohio), V: 278n, 369n, 376, 432n, 539n; VI: 50, 219-20, 394; VII: 136n, 242n; VIII: 79, 86, 428
Camp Defiance (Ill.), IV: 457n

Camp Dennison (Ohio), IV: 535n; V: 183n
Camp Dick Robinson (Ky.), IV: 542, 544
Camp Douglas (Ill.), V: 377, 403n, 432n; VI: 20n, 110, 532; VII: 34n, 66n, 100, 129, 257, 430; VIII: 30, 86
Camp Ella Bishop (Ky.), VI: 12n
Camp Hamilton (Va.), VIII: 34n
Camp Jefferson (Ky.), V: 89n
Camp Lincoln (D. C.), VI: 76n
Camp McClellan (Iowa), VII: 325-26; VIII: 299n
Camp Morton (Ind.), V: 275-76; Confederate prisoners at, VI: 398; VII: 195n, 274, 421n; VIII: 123n, 348n
Camp Nelson (Ky.), VII: 106, 109
Camp Parole (Md.), VIII: 94n
Camp Perry (Mass.?), VII: 155n
Camp Piatt (W. Va.), VII: 486n
Camp Stanton (Md.), VII: 28n
Camp Sumter [Sumpter] (Ga.), VII: 538
Camp Wildcat (Ky.), V: 21-22
Campbell, ——, II: 91
Campbell, Alexander, II: 473
Campbell, Ann (Todd), I: 266, 325; V: 288n
Campbell, Antrim, I: 122, 393, 490; II: 63, 310
Campbell, Baptiste (half-breed), V: 542
Campbell, C. B., IV: 309
Campbell, Charles C., IV: 457
Campbell, Charles Harrod, VI: 185-86
Campbell, David B., II: 62n, 310-11
Campbell, Edward Wallar, I: 154n
Campbell, Elbert, VIII: 68
Campbell, Hugh, V: 22n
Campbell, Isaac, VIII: 68
Campbell, James, I: 416-17; IV: 137n; VI: 237-38, 290n
Campbell, James Hepburn, V: 202n; VIII: 296

Campbell, James L. [M.], VII: 371

Campbell, James M. (Ill.), II: 296

Campbell, James M. (Tenn.), VIII: 370

Campbell, John Archibald, III: 543n; IV: 137n; V: 41; VIII: 246-48, 250, 258, 269, 276-87, 302, 386-89, 406n, 406-408

Campbell, John H., VIII: 69

Campbell, Josephine (Goodwin), VI: 477n

Campbell, Lewis Davis, V: 314n

Campbell, Quintin, V: 288

Campbell, Shadrick J., I: 298

Campbell, Stephen C., VII: 362

Campbell, Thomas, I: 336; II: 183

Campbell, Thomas (Sangamon Co., Ill.), I: 336

Campbell, Thomas H., II: 75, 220; V: 153-54; VI: 85, 90

Campbell, Thomas M., VI: 225, 231

Campbell, Thomas M. (Mo.), I: 325

Campbell, Mrs. Thomas M., see Campbell, Ann Todd

Campbell, Thomas P., IV: 300; V: 62n

Campbell, Thompson, I: 336; III: 123-24, 139, 144; VI: 540-41; VII: 404

Campbell, Turner, I: 490n

Campbell, William Bowen, VI: 393n; VIII: 58-72

Campbell, William P., V: 458n

Campbell, William P. (Tenn.), VIII: 69

Campbell, William S., VIII: 69

Campbell & Hundley, II: 435

Campbell County (Tenn.), VIII: 68

Campbell place (S. C.), VI: 455, 457

Campbell's Station (Tenn.), VII: 14n

"Campbellites," see Disciples of Christ

Canada, I: 509; II: 272; III: 500; IV: 284; V: 503; VI: 70n, 285-86; VII: 160n, 187, 416n, 504; VIII: 141, 209

Canady, John, I: 249

Canajoharie and Catskill Railroad, II: 171

Canal Bank (Evansville, Ind.), IV: 44n

Canals (Ill.), construction and development of, I: 40, 43, 48, 147, 149, 181, 184, 195-98, 232, 243-44, 344, 483-84; II: 26-27, 162-87, 189; III: 390; IV: 37n, 128-29; V: 526; VII: 48

Canals (Md.), IV: 455n; V: 130n, 191n

Canals (N. Y.), development of, V: 270, 526; VI: 508; VII: 48, 274

Canby, Edward Richard Sprigg, VI: 220n, 286n, 325n, 390n; VII: 457, 488-89, 492n, 532; VIII: 14-15, 91, 93-94, 104n, 107-108, 131, 162n, 163-65, 202n, 363

"Candide Secure" [pseud.], VI: 125n

Canedy, Peleg C., I: 92, 207-208

Canfield, J. B., VIII: 69

Canfield, Robert W., I: 336

Canisius, Theodor, II: 524; III: 380-81, 383, 391n; IV: 44, 418; V: 476

Cannan & Harlan, I: 323

Cannelton (Ind.), V: 509n

Cannon, John R., VIII: 28

Cannon, Robert T., VIII: 69

Cannon, William, VI: 180; VIII: 109

Cannon County (Tenn.), VIII: 69

Canseco, Pedro Diez, VI: 212-13

Canton (China), V: 38n

Canton (Miss.), VIII: 336

Cantrall, Elizabeth, II: 162

Cantrall, Levi, I: 26

Cantrall, Thomas, II: 162

Cantrall, Mrs. Thomas, see Cantrall, Elizabeth

Cape Girardeau (Mo.), III: 456

Cape Lookout (Va.), V: 123n
Cape of Good Hope, V: 265n
Cape Town (Africa), V: 76
Capell, Charles G., VII: 155
Capen, Francis L., VI: 190-91
Capers place (S. C.), VI: 456-57
Capital and labor: L. on, I: 163-64, 408-15, II: 364, 379, III: 459, 462-63, 468-69, 477-80, IV: 7-9, 12, 24-25, 202-203, 212, 214, V: 51-53, VII: 40, 259-60, 466-67; receives book on, III: 518-19; on establishment of free-labor systems on Southern plantations, V: 487n, VI: 108, VII: 145-47, 185, 212, 217-18, 378-79, 385-86, 466-67, 492, VIII: 30-31, 317, 325; replies to expressions of support from English working-men, VI: 63-65, 88-89
Capitol Hospital (Washington), V: 444n
Caple, see Capell, Charles G.
Capps, Jabez, III: 391
Capps, John, see Capps, Jabez
Caraher, Andrew Patrick, VIII: 40
Carberry, Catherine, VIII: 43n
Cardale, ———, VII: 311n
Cardiff (Wales), IV: 504
Carey, Thomas [alias], see Lamplaugh, Thomas
Carillo, Joaquin, VI: 242n
Carlile, John Snyder, IV: 443n, 451n, 464n, 491n
Carlin, Thomas I: 149, 212, 283-84, 294; II: 185; III: 278
Carlin, William H., II: 296, 481; III: 277-78
Carlin, William Passmore, VI: 117
Carlinville (Ill.), I: 209, 221, 399, 401; III: 77-81; VIII: 593n
Carlinville Democrat, III: 77n
Carlisle, James Mandeville, IV: 444n
Carlisle, John S., VII: 393, 493n
Carlisle (Pa.), VI: 310n, 322, 328, 330n
Carlos Fernando, Prince of Portugal, VII: 110

Carlson, Oliver, VIII: 240n
Carlton, Caleb Henry, VIII: 91, 169
Carlton, James H., VIII: 69
Carlyle (Ill.), I: 147
Carlyle (Pa.), see Carlisle (Pa.)
Carman, Merritt M., I: 12
Carmichael, Richard B., V: 285-86
Carnahan, Robert B., IV: 329; VIII: 80n, 418n
Carnegie, Dale, IV: 478n; V: 73n, 193n, 201n, 398n, 493n, 499n; VI: 22n, 385n; VII: 80n, 293n, 416n; VIII: 50, 194n, 210n, 293n, 310n
Carnegie Book Shop, catalogs cited, VIII: 35n, 351n, 426n
Carnes, Adolphus, IV: 310
Carney, Thomas, VI: 179n, 188, 334-35, 339-40, 395-96; VII: 338n, 340-41; VIII: 109, 124
Caroline (steamboat), II: 146
Carothers, Andrew G., V: 27, 76n
Carpenter, ———, IV: 326
Carpenter, Charles, VII: 305-306
Carpenter, Francis Bicknell, V: 337n; VII: 34n
Carpenter, Franklin [alias Harry J. Carpenter], VIII: 232n
Carpenter, George F., VII: 419-20
Carpenter, John Orcutt, VI: 211
Carpenter, Milton, I: 226, 294
Carpenter, W. H., IV: 310
Carpenter, William, I: 44n, 298; II: 62n
Carper, John, VIII: 69
"Carpet-Bag Papers, The," I: 416n
Carr, Charles D., III: 348
Carr, Overton, V: 70
Carrington, Mrs., VII: 419
Carrington, Edward C., IV: 372n, 494n, 522n; VII: 281n, 419
Carrington, Henry Beebe, VI: 158n; VIII: 136n
Carroll, Anna Ella, V: 381-82
Carroll, Daniel, III: 527
Carroll, Patrick, VIII: 85, 87-88

Carroll, Thomas King, Jr., VII: 363n; VIII: 411n
Carroll, William C., VI: 198, 232
Carroll County (Mo.), VII: 337
Carroll County (Tenn.), VIII: 69
Carroll Prison (Md.), VI: 431; VII: 290
Carrollton (Ill.), II: 227
Carrollton (La.), VII: 322n
Carryl, William H., & Brother, IV: 407
Carson, John M., IV: 39-40
Carson (steamboat), see *S. B. Carson*
Carson City Land Office, V: 316n; VIII: 358n
Cartagena (Spain), VI: 258n
Carter, James T. P., VIII: 58-72
Carter, John P. [B.], VIII: 125n
Carter, Joshua B., VII: 468n
Carter, Nick, I: 387
Carter, R. C., VIII: 68
Carter, Samuel Powhatan, V: 54n; VI: 470n; VIII: 7n
Carter, Timothy J., VI: 497, 504-505, 545; VIII: 38-39
Carter, Tunstall G., V: 170n
Carter, William B., I: 105; V: 501n
Carter County (Tenn.), II: 218; VIII: 68
Carter's Station (Tenn.), VI: 470n, 481
Carthage (Ill.), I: viii; III: 330-31
Carthage (Tenn.), VI: 393n
Cartmell, John, I: 206
Cartter, David Kellogg, IV: 136; VI: 167; VII: 80n; VIII: 160n
Cartwright, Peter, I: 39-40, 85, 298, 383-84; III: 492n; IV: 109
Carusi's Saloon (Washington), I: 495-96
Carver, Cyrus H., VIII: 125n
Carver, Thomas G., VI: 313n
Cary, C. C., IV: 165n
Caryl, James B., VI: 256-57
Case, A. P., VIII: 301n
Case, Charles, IV: 520-21; VII: 358; VIII: 233n
Case, Francis M., IV: 294-95

Case, Zophar, III: 513
Casey, George F., VIII: 595n
Casey, Joseph, IV: 83-84, 166, 383; VI: 526n; VII: 428-29, 468
Casey, Peter, VII: 213
Casey, Samuel Lewis, V: 319n, 367n, 503; VI: 212; VII: 62-63, 187n, 213-14, 256n; VIII: 595
Casey, Silas, V: 256n, 361, 413, 446; VI: 82n
Casey, William, VI: 528
Casey, Zadoc, III: 135
Cason, W. W., VIII: 223n
Cass, Lewis, I: 463, 480-81, 503-17; II: 3-4, 7, 14, 156, 159, 236, 343n, 351n, 353, 451; III: 2, 35, 47, 52, 61, 85, 91, 94-95, 102, 105, 169-71, 270, 273, 293
Cass, Thomas, IV: 486
Cass County (Ill.), I: 333, 354, 358n
Cassville (Mo.), V: 267n
Castalian Springs (Tenn.), V: 546n
Castillero, Andres, VI: 205
Castle, Edward H., VI: 100
Castleman, John Breckinridge, VIII: 123
Castleman, Virginia, see Breckinridge, Virginia (Castleman)
Catalogue of Lincolniana, A, (Madigan), I: 367n; IV: 344n; V: 18n, 249n, 299n, 415n, 464n; VI: 175n, 323n; VII: 159n, 166n, 305n; VIII: 110n, 364n, 411n
Cataract House (Niagara Falls), VII: 436n
"Cathleen" [pseud.], I: 292n
Catholics, I: 337-38; II: 316, 323; IV: 559-60; VI: 51n
Catlettsburg (Ky.), VIII: 99, 120n
Caton, John Dean, II: 336; IV: 448n
Catron, John, III: 543n; V: 481; VII: 188, 273, 288
Caudine Forks, V: 122n
Cavarly, Alfred W., I: 220n, 231, 334-35; IV: 125n
Cawfield & Moffett, III: 521

Cayuse Indian Agency, IV: 308
"Cecil" [pseud.], see Fisher, Sidney George
Cedar County (Mo.), V: 2n
Cedar Creek (Va.), battle of, VIII: 74n
Cedar Grove (S. C.), VI: 456
Census Bureau, V: 68; see also Population
Centenarian Deacon John Phillips, The (pamphlet), VIII: 118n
Center-Street Hospital (Newark?, N. J.), VI: 429
Centerville (Va.), V: 34, 120n, 234, 399-401, 443n
Central America, IV: 561-62; VII: 265-66; see also names of individual countries
Central Pacific Railroad, VII: 122; VIII: 146
Central Park (N. Y.), VII: 123n
Central Transcript [Clinton, Ill.], II: 398n, 525n; III: 389-90, 488n
Centre College (Danville, Ky.), I: 304n
Century Magazine, cited, V: 185n; VI: 1n, 18n, 35n, 437n; VII: 17n, 66n, 194n, 373n, 406n, 421n, 485n, 524n; VIII: 98n, 296n
Ceres (Confederate ship), VII: 87
Cerro Gordo (Mexico), battle of, I: 418, 447, 464, 519
Cessna, John, VIII: 29
Chadbourn, Moses, VII: 96
Chadsey, Henry C., & Company, III: 517
Chadwick, H. A., VII: 318
Chaffee, Calvin Clifford, III: 167, 260
Chaffee, Mrs. Calvin Clifford, III: 167, 260
Chalker, James S., IV: 337
Chalmers, James Ronald, VI: 39n; VIII: 169n
Chamberlain [Chamberlin], Jacob Payson, V: 383
Chamberlain Creek, VIII: 379n
Chamberlin, Culver P., VIII: 242n

Chambers, A. B., II: 58-59
Chambers, Alexander, VII: 279
Chambers, David, IV: 136
Chambers, James S. [M.], IV: 444; V: 129n
Chambersburg (Pa.), IV: 395n; VI: 293n
Chamblin & Wilson (Springfield), II: 96n
Chambrun, Charles Adolphe Pineton, Marquis de, VII: 102n
Champaign County (Ill.), III: 37; V: 398n
Champlin, John D., VIII: 230-31
Champlin, Stephen Gardner, VII: 311n
Chancellorsville (Va.), VI: 190n, 196n, 198-201, 211n, 216n, 273, 450n; VII: 230
Chandler, L. H., VI: 419n, 438, 522n
Chandler, Louis W., I: 445
Chandler, William, V: 59n
Chandler, Zachariah, II: 361n; IV: 102-103, 248, 274n, 512; V: 12n, 88n, 205, 207n; VI: 125, 549; VII: 23-24
Chan-ka-hda (Indian), V: 543
Channing, William Henry, V: 464-65
Chantilly, battle of, V: 511n
Chapin, Aaron L., II: 314
Chapin, S. R., VIII: 70
Chapin's Farm, battle of, VIII: 189
Chaplains: appointments, IV: 413, 559-60, V: 69, 171, 464-65, VI: 44, 58, 137, 193, 420-21, 512, VIII: 50, 225; and organization of N. C. loyalists, V: 3n; and compensation for, 8-9, 40, 53-54, 297, VII: 280; assignments, V: 340, 473, VI: 194; on proposed reduction of hospital assignments, VI: 313-14; dismissal, VII: 293; on appointment of women, VIII: 102-103
Chaplin, Ben, VI: 455
Chaplin, J. Bond, IV: 328
Chaplin, J. C., II: 171

Chaplin, James, VI: 456-57
Chaplin, John F., VI: 457
Chaplin, Saxby, VI: 456
Chaplin, Thomas B., VI: 456
Chapman, Augustus H., II: 97n, 112; V: 80n
Chapman, Mrs. Augustus H., *see* Chapman, Harriet
Chapman, Ervin S., IV: 37n
Chapman, Harriet (Hanks), II: 96-97, 112n
Chapman, Mrs. J. L., Jr., VIII: 416n
Chapman, John Lee, VII: 438n; VIII: 348
Chapultepec (Mexico), battle of, IV: 413n
Character of Napoleon . . ., The (Phillips), II: 281n
Charles V, King of Spain, II: 298-99
Charles XV, King of Sweden and Norway, IV: 287; V: 18; VII: 475; VIII: 228
Charles, John F., I: 249
Charles William Lewis, Prince of Hesse, V: 363
Charles Town (W. Va.), III: 539n; V: 245-46, 249, 462n; VI: 283n; VII: 134, 511n
Charleston (Ill.), I: 261, 263n; III: 145-201, 213-14, 221, 237-39, 247-50, 252-53, 262-64, 280-81, 319, 327; IV: 182, 326; VII: 421-22
Charleston (S. C.), IV: 248; V: 122n, 284n, 520; VI: 72, 250n, 389n, 474n; VII: 81, 185, 348n; VIII: 131, 321n, 358n, 396; *see also* Fort Sumter; *and* Fort Moultrie
Charleston (W. Va.), VI: 137; VIII: 417
Charleston (Ill.) *Courier*, I: 447
"Charleston Riot, March 28, 1864, The" (art.), VII: 422n
Charlestown (Mass.), VII: 100n
Charlottesville (Va.), V: 278n, 287; VI: 354n, 534; VII: 477n

Charrney, Theodore S., VI: 334n
Chase, Charles D., VIII: 186-87
Chase, Helen, VIII: 195n
Chase, John A., VI: 189
Chase, S. W., VII: 543n
Chase, Salmon Portland: mentioned as possible 1856 presidential candidate, II: 342-43; and the Kansas-Nebraska bill, 466, III: 23, 35, 46-48, 52-53, 251, 299; accused by Douglas of "Black Republicanism," III: 3, 6, 60-61, 105, 138, 175; accused by Douglas of sectionalism, 321; L.'s appreciation of 1858 campaign support, 378, 395, 400-401, IV: 34; letters from L. on 1859 Ohio state elections, III: 384, 386, 470-71; attacked by Democrats in Congress (1860), 542n; mentioned as possible 1860 presidential candidate, IV: 34, 36, 94n; support of L. (1860), 53; appointment to L.'s cabinet (1860), 136n, 168, 171, 248; presented with a pitcher by free Negroes, 156; and relief for Fort Sumter, 285n; and collection of duties, 292, 293n, 487-88, V: 139, VI: 157, 479, VII: 192; and Fort Pickens expedition, IV: 302n; and contracts for engraving Treasury notes, 326; government acquisition of privately owned boats, 357; and purchases for White House, 407, 557-58, V: 394
Annual reports, (*1861*) IV: 431, V: 39-40, (*1862*) V: 508, 524, (*1863*) VII: 41, 42; and war expenditures, IV: 499, V: 451n, VI: 60; appointments of Department acting heads, IV: 537, V: 22, 75, 221, VI: 179-80; and the Chiriqui project, V: 3n; drafts letter for L. on retirement of Gen. Scott, 10n; letter from L. on McClellan's health, 88; and

Port Royal contrabands, 132, 210-11; and adjustment of Ill. state claims, 153-54; complaints against Third Auditor, 204-205; and revocation of Hunter emancipation order, 219, 225n; reports military situation (May '62) from Va., 233-35; and censure of Cameron, 243; and compensated emancipation, 324-25, 487-88; pardon cases, 336, VII: 314n; and Emancipation Proclamation, V: 337n, 433n, 434n, 439n, VI: 24n, 428-29; and the draft, V: 338n, VI: 444n, 445n; requests audience for Md. legislators, V: 402; and McDowell's relief from command (Sept. '62), 407n; supports army medical experimentation with new "Balm," 444n; supports removal of McClellan (1862), 486n; and report on New Orleans newspapers (Nov. '62), 489; and sale of public lands, 511-12; and commercial intercourse with insurrectionary states, 540, VI: 150, 157, 159-60, 294, 307, 340, 479, VII: 148-49, 151-52, 156, 166

Resignation from cabinet, VI: 11-13, VII: 414n, 418-20; and admission of W. Va., VI: 17; and confiscation of property, 98, 455; and L.'s invitation to preside at a religious meeting, 111n; favors Senate extra session, 111n; and marque and reprisal bill, 126n; attends L.'s audience to Indian chiefs, 152n; and requests for interviews, 175, 195, 252, 397, 420, 460, 531n, 537-38, VII: 15, 60, 178; and blockade runners, VI: 207n; and Union raid in Ala. (1863), 213-14; and Vallandigham case, 215, 300n, 445n; use of revenue cutters by navy, 272-73; and seizure of Almaden mine, 322n;

and a claim against government purchase of cotton, 481; plans to attend Gettysburg ceremony, VII: 15; querried by law partner on deserter case, 112n; arranges for bas relief heads of L. and cabinet, 187n; support for 1864 presidential nomination, 200-201, 212-13, 222-23, 268n, 285n; and exports, 279n, 331; and the Fort Pillow massacre, 328-29; advice from L. on a "five per cent loan," 347; purported L. draft of a proclamation, 347; L. plans to visit office of (June '64), 376; and investment of L.'s securities, 384-85; attitude toward "the Blairs," VIII: 18n; appointed Chief Justice of the Supreme Court, 154; L. expresses confidence in, 195; supports release of a prisoner-of-war, 322n; views on reconstruction, 399n; mentioned, IV: 491n, V: 450, VII: 28-29, 187n, VIII: 421

Appointments, III: 378, 491n; IV: 294, 310, 325-27; 329n, 334n, 356-57, 359-64, 371, 373-74, 390, 452, 499, 502, 537, 556; V: 33, 228, 256, 323, 332-33, 348, 353, 360-62, 375-76, 379, 472, 490-91; VI: 16, 122-23, 144-46, 172n, 185, 202, 209-10, 213-15, 224, 232-33, 362n, 517-18; VII: 120, 156-57, 181-82, 184, 195, 204, 338n, 392, 412-14

See also *Account of the Private Life and Public Services of Salmon Portland Chase*; *Diary and Correspondence of Salmon P. Chase*; and *Life and Public Services of Salmon Portland Chase*

Chase, William Henry, IV: 414

Chaskay-don [alias Chaskay-etay alias Robert Hopkins] (Indian), V: 542; VI: 7n

Chatham (Canada), III: 538n

Chattahoochee River, VII: 449

Chattanooga (Tenn.), V: 261, 263, 264, 284n, 292, 295, 300, 305n, 308, 322n, 410n; VI: 378n, 470-75, 478, 481, 483-85, 498, 505n, 510, 517n, 562; VII: 53, 85n, 120n, 122, 319, 540n; VIII: 27n, 91, 169

Chattanooga Times, II: 218n

Chauncey, John S., VI: 107n

Chay-ton-hoon-da (Indian), V: 543

Cheatham County (Tenn.), VIII: 69

Cheeseborough, Ellsworth, VII: 338n

Cheeseman, David W., IV: 305

Cheever, Daniel A., II: 522-23; VIII: 415

Cheever, George B., VI: 239n

Cheever, Washington Irving, II: 523n

Chenery, William Dodd, II: 387

Chenery House (Springfield), II: 387

Cheney, T. Apolion, IV: 93, 309

Chenoweth, George D., V: 215-16

Cherokee Indians, II: 158-59; V: 415-16, 439-40, 456; VII: 196n; VIII: 34n

Cherrystone (Va.), VIII: 396

Chesapeake & Ohio Canal, *see* Canals (Md.)

Chesapeake Bay, V: 50, 118, 122n, 151, 185; VI: 36, 56n, 69n

Chesley, R. V., VI: 319

Chesney, James, IV: 526

Chesnut, John Alexander, II: 188

Chester, A., IV: 30, 112n

Chester, Anson G., IV: 111-12, 125n

Chester, Augustin, IV: 30n; VI: 233, 279

Chester, Eliphalet Nott, VI: 88

Chester (Pa.), VI: 421n

Chester (Va.), V: 247n

Chester County Times [West Chester, Pa.], III: 512n

Chester Gap, V: 461

Chester (Pa.), Military Institute, VI: 7n

Chesterfield, Philip Dormer Stanhope, 4th Earl of, IV: 276n

Chestertown (Md.), VI: 494n

Chestnut, John, VI: 544

Chevanne, Henry, VIII: 179

Chevarre, *see* Chevanne, Henry

Chew, Henry, III: 202-203; IV: 35n

Chew, John J., VII: 358

Chew, Robert S., IV: 323-24

Cheyenne (Wyo.), VI: 518n

Cheyenne Indians, IV: 464n; V: 397n; VI: 153n

Chicago (Ill.): report on branch of state bank located at (1840), I: 191-92, 194; incident of Whig convention baggage mix-up (1840), 210; river and harbor convention (1847), 395; construction of railroad connections to Alton and Springfield (1854), 395n; Cass expenditures in (1821-1822), 513; questions posed by L. as defense attorney in the "Sandbar Case," II: 430-31; L. arranges to meet Hamlin and Speed at (Nov. '60), IV: 136, 141; mention of Chicago Union Defense and War Committee, V: 406n; emancipation memorial presented to L. by Chicago Christians, 419; Sanitary Fairs at, 512n, VI: 30n, 539-40, VII: 75n, 394, 442; sale of copy of Emancipation Proclamation for the benefit of the Soldiers Home, VI: 30n, 539-40; protests against effecting the draft in, 417n, 435n; press release of L.'s letter to Conkling (1863), 430n; extension of communication with the northeastern seaboard, VII: 48; L. presented with a watch from the Sanitary Commission, 75; mention of Board of Trade, VIII: 359n; mention

of persons from, II: 91n, 431n, V: 361n, 512n, VII: 167.

L.'s speeches at: (*Oct. '48*) II: 11; (*July '50, eulogy on Zachary Taylor*) 83-90; (*Oct. '54*) 283-84; (*July '56*) 348-49; (*Dec. '56*) 383-85; (*Feb. '57, notes for speech*) 390-91; (*July '58*) 484-502, III: 213-14, 216, 221, 237, 238, 247, 253, 262-64, 280-81, 300, 326, 373; (*Mar. '59*) 365-70, 429n, 432n

Mention of Douglas speeches at: (*1850*) III: 139, 170; (*Nov. '57*) II: 449-50; (*July '58*) 373. Mention of Seward speech at, (*1860*) IV: 126-27

Chicago, University of, IV: 71n

Chicago American, I: 151-52, 229

Chicago and Alton Railroad, II: 330n; III: 342, 359

Chicago and Rock Island Railroad, II: 189-91; VIII: 192-93

Chicago Book & Art Auctions, catalogs cited, VI: 259n; VIII: 303n

Chicago, Burlington & Quincy Railroad, II: 329n

Chicago Commercial Advertiser, II: 11n, 186

Chicago Democrat, II: 429n, 484n; IV: 140n

Chicago Democratic Press, cited, II: 349n, 378n, 383n, 415n, 450n, 471n; see also *Chicago Press & Tribune*

Chicago Historical Society, III: 377n, 509n; VI: 540n

Chicago Journal, II: 68, 83n, 91n, 186, 284n, 444n; III: 355-56, 506n

Chicago Post, VI: 252n

Chicago Press & Tribune, II: 475n, 484-85, 488n, 491n, 494n, 496n-501n, 543n, 544n; III: 1, 14n, 30n-32n, 38, 52n, 77n, 91n, 102n, 145, 148, 207, 245, 283, 329, 331n, 332n, 343, 365n, 372-73, 385, 471n-81n, 519n; IV: 60n,

86n; see also *Chicago Democratic Press*; and *Chicago Tribune*

Chicago Record, IV: 48n

Chicago Times, II: 448, 472-74, 528; III: 1, 14n, 31n, 38-39, 102n, 145, 163, 183, 207, 245, 283, 302, 373, 515n; V: 517n; VI: 248, 251-52; VII: 361, 363-64

Chicago Times & Herald, IV: 112n

Chicago Tribune, II: 304n, 410, 444n, 455, 456n, 461n, 468n, 469n, 471n, 474n; III: 81n, 385n; IV: 111n, 139n, 140n, 176n, 184n, 456n; V: 419n; VI: 184n, 430n; VII: 20n, 75n, 364n; VIII: 289n, 304n; see also *Chicago Press & Tribune*

Chicago Voice, IV: 75n

Chickahominy River, V: 232, 236n, 240n, 257-58, 289-92, 295, 499n; VI: 207n; VIII: 204

Chickamauga (Ga.), IV: 335n; VI: 472-76, 478, 480, 517n; VII: 14n, 108n, 333n

Chickamauga Creek, VII: 30n

Chickasaw Bayou, VI: 43n

Chickasaw Indians, IV: 283n, 299n

Chicopee (Mass.) Works, IV: 343-44

Childress, D. B., VIII: 317n

Childress, Sam L., VIII: 68

Chile, IV: 293, 396-97, 521; V: 19, 451n, 521; VI: 271; VII: 37, 143, 338; VIII: 138

Chillicothe (gunboat), V: 174n

Chillicothe band of Shawnee Indians, VII: 261n

China, IV: 293, 310, 397; V: 38, 79n, 430, 521; VI: 96; VII: 40, 147-48; VIII: 139, 145n

Chincha Islands, VIII: 138n

Chipley, C., VI: 394n

Chipley, William S., VI: 394

Chipman, Norton Parker, VII: 511; VIII: 120n

Chippewa Indians, V: 397n, 455n; VI: 135; VII: 116, 215, 299, 345; VIII: 219-20

Chiriqui project, IV: 561-62; V:

2-3, 48n, 370-75, 414, 418-19, 434
Chittenden, Lucius Eugene, IV: 448; V: 359n; VII: 197-98
Chitty's Pleadings, III: 344; IV: 121
Chitwood, Pleasant, VIII: 69
Choate, Joseph Hodges, VIII: 170
Choctaw Indian Agency, IV: 283n, 456; VIII: 194n
Chowan County (N. C.), VII: 258n
Chowan River, VIII: 368n
Chrisman, Elizabeth (Lincoln), IV: 117n
Chrisman, John, IV: 117
Chrisman, Joseph, Sr., IV: 117n
Chrisman, Mrs. Joseph, Sr., see Chrisman, Elizabeth
Chrisman, Joseph, Jr., IV: 117n
Chrisman, St. Clair, I: 148n
Christian IX, King of Denmark, VI: 222; VII: 111, 231, 336-37
Christian Advocate, The, IV: 451n
Christian Commission, V: 67, 349n; VI: 114-15; VII: 187, 394; VIII: 241-42, 245n
Christian [formerly Dane] County (Ill.), I: 127-32, 140n, 144-46
Christian Indians of Kansas, see Munsee Indians
Christliche Apologete, Der [Cincinnati], VIII: 83n
Christopher, Jackson, VI: 544
Christy, ———, VI: 128
Christy, Samuel C., I: 67
"Chronicles of Reuben," purportedly by L., I: 1n
Chrysler, Morgan Henry, V: 103n
Chrysopolis Mills (San Francisco), IV: 296n
Chrystal Springs (Miss.), see Crystal Springs
Chumasero, William, VI: 137
Church, Lawrence S., VI: 460
Churches: divided on the slavery question, II: 452, III: 77, 84, 87, 204-205, 256, 310-11, 445; "should minister . . . without interference by others differing from them," V: 445; disloyalty charges against St. Louis minister, VI: 20, 33-34; "government must not undertake to run the churches," VII: 85-86, 178-80, 182-83, 223, 247, 283-84, 339, 427-28; disloyalty charges against a Baltimore church, 335-36, 339-40; restoration of a confiscated Tenn. church, VIII: 264; directives concerning the holding of Episcopalian services in Richmond (Apr. '65), 405n
Churchill, George, I: 146n
Churchill, Richard Cuyler, V: 75, 152
Churchill, Samuel B., V: 127; VI: 219, 223; VIII: 342
Churchill, Mrs. Samuel B., VI: 219n
Churchill, W. C., VIII: 187n
Churchill, William Hunter, V: 75n
Churchill's Military School, VI: 221
Cicero (Sangamon Co., Ill.), I: 220
Cienfuegos (Cuba), V: 73n
Cincinnati (Ohio), I: 428, 518; II: 315n, 325-26; III: 365n, 400, 425, 429n, 432n, 435n, 437n, 438-63, 467; IV: 156, 182, 197-203, 310, 368, 398n, 458, 478n, 542, 544-45; V: 402n, 416, 419, 452, 501, 511n; VI: 50, 196, 225, 298; VII: 14n, 29, 53n, 76, 150, 321, 394, 422n; VIII: 83n, 192n, 193, 291, 323n
Cincinnati Commercial, IV: 153n, 194n, 196n, 197n, 199n, 201, 203n, 276n; VIII: 183n
Cincinnati Gazette, III: 438n, 456n, 461n; IV: 73n, 92n, 194n, 199n, 202-203, 216n; V: 327n, 516n; VI: 366; VII: 13n, 131n
Cincinnati Hochwächter, IV: 283n
Cincinnati Inquirer, VIII: 315n
Cincinnati, Past and Present, Or, Its Industrial History (M. Joblin & Co.), VIII: 222n

Cinkpa Tawa (Indian), VII: 325-26

Cintas, Oscar, VII: 22n

Circassian (steamboat), VIII: 43n

Circuit Court Order Book No. 9 (Jefferson Co., Ky.), VI: 140n

Cisco, John J., IV: 514n; VI: 525n; VII: 413-14

Cist, L. J., VII: 343

City Book Auctions, catalogs cited, VII: 102n

City Point (Va.), VI: 203, 220n, 258n, 517n, 553; VII: 74, 120, 240, 252n, 325, 416, 492, 531, 538n; VIII: 4, 86n, 87, 116n, 203, 248n, 276, 314, 367, 369, 371-92, 409n

Civil rights, *see* Liberty, equality, and civil rights, L. on

Civil War in Song and Story, 1860-1865, The (Moore), VII: 249n

Claghorn, Mrs. James L., VI: 376n

Claghorn, Mrs. John W., VI: 376n

Claiborne County (Tenn.), VIII: 68

Clapp, Daniel, V: 541

"Clara Barton, Humanitarian" (art.), VIII: 423n

Clark, A. H., IV: 536-37

Clark, Ambrose Williams, V: 316n; VI: 97n

Clark, Barney, VI: 544

Clark, Daniel, IV: 248; V: 44n

Clark, Daniel P., VII: 323

Clark, Edward, II: 319n

Clark, Ezekiel, VI: 241n

Clark, Henry, I: 18

Clark, Henry A., III: 385

Clark, Isaac, IV: 328

Clark, Jesse R., V: 114-15

Clark, John, VII: 137

Clark, John H., VI: 296n

Clark, John S., V: 470n; VII: 287n

Clark, John Wesley, VII: 261n

Clark, Jonas J., IV: 392n

Clark, Josephus M., V: 266n

Clark, Levi, IV: 309

Clark, William M., VII: 156n

Clark, *see* Clarke, William Penniman

Clark & Morrison, II: 332n

Clarke, Beverly Leonidas, I: 502

Clarke, D. W. C., VIII: 154n

Clarke, Daniel, VIII: 198n

Clarke, Henry J., I: 354-55

Clarke, James M., VII: 371

Clarke, Robert M., I: 354-55

Clarke, Sidney, VIII: 338-39, 355n

Clarke [Clark], William Penniman, V: 470n

Clarke's Exchange Bank (Springfield), II: 324

Clarksburg (Md.), V: 412n, 418

Clarksburg (W. Va.), IV: 481n; VI: 195n; VII: 502n

Clarksville (Tenn.), V: 135, 408; VII: 105n

Clary, John, I: 13, 26, 35-36

Clary, Robert E., IV: 560n

Clary, Royal, I: 12, 18

Clary, William, I: 12

Clary's Grove (Ill.), I: 25n, 36n, 255, 257, 371-72

Clay, Brutus Junius, VI: 366n, 372; VII: 34, 129, 136n, 146-47, 187n, 256n, 274, 291

Clay, Cassius Marcellus, I: 447; IV: 5, 11, 53-54, 85, 88, 92-93, 281, 294, 352; V: 96-97, 368, 390n, 425, 428n, 439n; VI: 103-104, 372

Clay, Christopher Field, VII: 146-47

Clay, Clement Comer, VII: 441n, 443n, 459-60

Clay, Ezekiel F., VIII: 218

Clay, Green, V: 458n

Clay, Henry: presidential candidacy (1832), I: 14, 419n, III: 78, IV: 64; and sale of public lands, I: 50n, 307, 312-14; invitation to speak in Springfield (1842), 297; mention of Clay Clubs, 297, 326, 332-33, 341, III: 203n; and annexation of Texas, I: 337, 431; presidential candidacy (1844), 338-40, 347, 378, III: 78,

85, IV: 65, 125; not supported by L. for 1848 presidential nomination, I: 447, 463, 467-68, 507, II: 7, 43, 49, III: 213; son killed in Mexican War, I: 515; L.'s eulogy on, II: 121-32, IV: 557; L.'s support of his position on the tariff, III: 487, IV: 49, 125; L. receives bronze medal of Clay (1861), IV: 183-84; son Thomas appointed minister to Nicaragua, 555, 559, V: 452n; his snuff box presented to L., V: 363-64; mention of his "half-brother," VI: 6

His position on slavery question: L. on, II: 137-38, 251, 282, 318, 341, 370, 373, 378, 380, 518-19, 543-45, III: 29, 38, 42, 77-80, 89, 93-94, 224, 233-34, 244, 250, 280, 300, 302-305, 314, 327-29, 333, 424, 484, IV: 104, 108, 230-31, 262n; Douglas on, III: 2, 61, 102-103, 163, 168-70, 217, 270-73, 288, 293-94, 320-21, 323

Clay, Mrs. Henry, *see* Clay, Lucretia

Clay, Henry, Jr., II: 86

Clay, John M., V: 363-64

Clay, Lucretia (Hart), V: 364

Clay, Thomas H., IV: 555, 557n, 559; V: 452-53

Clay County (Mo.), VIII: 234

Clay County (W. Va.), V: 298

Claybrook, Edwin C., VII: 91-92, 97-98

Claybrook, R. A., VII: 91n

Clayton, J. Paul, I: xvii

Clayton, James W., VIII: 411n

Clayton, John Middleton, II: 31, 36-38, 48, 56, 60-65, 68-69, 144-46

Cleburne, Patrick R., VI: 480

Clemens, Orion, IV: 295

Clemens, Sherrard, V: 180

Clements, Andrew Jackson, V: 319n, 333n; VI: 373

Clements, George W., VIII: 69

Clements, L. S., VIII: 69

Clements, Thomas, I: 344

Clemment, James, I: 12, 18, 20

Clemson, Anna Maria (Calhoun), VI: 507-508

Clemson, Mrs. Thomas G., *see* Clemson, Anna Maria

Clemson, Calhoun, VI: 507-508

Cleveland (Ohio), III: 506n, 517n; IV: 188, 215-16, 282; V: 300; VIII: 347n

Cleveland (Tenn.), V: 295; VI: 471

Cleveland Commercial, IV: 216n

Cleveland Leader, IV: 282n

Cleveland Plain Dealer, IV: 218n

Clevenger, John C., VII: 298n

Clever, Charles P., VIII: 157

Clifford, Nathan, V: 481; VII: 92; VIII: 298n

Clift, ———, II: 308

Clifton, Joseph W., VII: 133, 152

Clinch, Charles P., VI: 123n; VII: 9n

Cline, William, IV: 189

Cline, William M. [N.], II: 297

Clingam, K., VIII: 68

Clinton, DeWitt, V: 455-56

Clinton (Ill.), II: 525-27; III: 81-84, 487-89

Clinton (Tenn.), VI: 522n

Clinton County (Ill.), I: 142, 147, 150n; II: 457

Clinton County (Mo.), VI: 489

Clinton County (Pa.), VIII: 41n

Clothing, importance to man, II: 437-38

Cloud, Newton, I: 183n

Clover, Seth, V: 147

Cloyd, John C., I: 344n

Clyde (N. Y.), IV: 222

Clymer, George, III: 527, 546n

Clymer, Meredith, V: 206n; VI: 41

Coakley, Gabriel, VII: 419n

Coalter, John D., VII: 85-86

Coan, William H., VII: 92n

Coan River, VII: 27n

Coates, H. Crawford, V: 76n

Cobb, H. W., IV: 309

Cobb, Howell, I: 501; VIII: 204
Coburn, Abner, VI: 547
Coburn, John, VIII: 224
Cochran, Mrs. Olin J., VIII: 81n
Cochran & Hall, III: 385
Cochrane, John, VI: 22n, 75n
Cocke, John Pope, see Pope, John
Cocke County (Tenn.), VIII: 68
Cockran, Francis S., see Corkran, Francis S.
Codding, Ichabod, II: 288; III: 30-31, 57, 284
Cody, H. H., III: 126
Cody, Richard, II: 183
Coety, James, VIII: 69
Coffee County (Tenn.), VIII: 69
"Coffee Mill" guns, V: 75-76, 365
Coffeeville (Miss.), VI: 17n
Coffenberry, Charles C., VIII: 338
Coffey, George A., IV: 167
Coffey, Titian J., VI: 290
Coffin, Nathaniel, II: 198-99
Coffin, William G., VII: 68-69; VIII: 34n
Coffing, Churchill C., II: 113-14, 535n
Coffman, Aaron, I: 206
Coffman [alias Philips], Maria, VII: 79-80
Coffman, Moses, I: 206
Coffroth, Alexander Hamilton, VIII: 235n
Coflin, Robert F., I: 158
Cogdall, Joseph, I: 18
Cohe, Henry [alias], see Cole, Henry
Cohen, John, VII: 291
Cohoe, John [alias], see Ble, John
Colburn, D. G., I: 467n
Colburn, Richard T., VI: 241
Colby, Abraham U., VIII: 290
Colby, Mrs. Abraham U., VIII: 290
Colby, Harvey M., VII: 520
Colby, L. B., IV: 555n
Colchester (Va.), V: 119
Cold Harbor (Va.), V: 227n; VII: 393n, 506n
Cole, ———, II: 91
Cole, Ashley T., IV: 336n

Cole [alias Cohe], Henry, VIII: 309
Cole, Thomas, I: 2
Cole & Wall, III: 350
Coleman, Charles H., VII: 422n
Coleman, Isaac, IV: 456
Coleman, Littleton, I: 310
Coleman, Thomas E., VI: 424
Coler, William N. [J. N.], IV: 477
Coles, Henry A., VII: 134
Coles County (Ill.), I: 380-81, 389; II: 217; IV: 181; VII: 421-22, 455; VIII: 90
Colfax, Schuyler, III: 390-91; IV: 54, 57-58, 110-11, 114, 278, 362; V: 14n, 169, 475; VI: 433n; VII: 123, 128; VIII: 204, 253-54, 274n, 286n, 328, 334
Colgrove, Silas, IV: 309; VII: 144n
Collamer, Jacob, I: 469, 471n; II: 39; III: 538n; IV: 248, 282, 284; V: 67, 283, 394n; VI: 9, 53-54, 549-50; VIII: 255n, 303, 419n
Collamer, William, V: 394n
Collector, The, cited, IV: 474n; V: 29n, 82n; VI: 147n, 405n, 528n; VII: 133n, 358n, 520n; VIII: 44n, 249n, 327n
College of New Jersey, see Princeton University
Collier, David L., IV: 336n
Collier, William B. [C.], VII: 458-59
Collingsworth, James, I: 436n
Collins, Daniel, VI: 371n
Collins, James L., VIII: 157
Collins, John L., VII: 430
Collins, Mary, VIII: 95n
Collins, Mary Emmons, VIII: 95n
Collins, Perry M., VII: 39n
Collins, Thomas, I: 422; V: 161
Collins, William, VII: 293, 301
Collins, William A., VIII: 95n
Colombia [New Granada], IV: 393, 408n, 517n, 521; V: 23, 140-41, 521; VI: 56-58; VII: 37, 389; VIII: 6-7, 137
Colonization of Negroes, L. on: II: 131-32, 298-99, 409-10; III: 15,

192, 233-34; IV: 561-62; V: 2-3, 48, 318, 370-75, 414, 418-19, 434, 520-21, 530, 534-37; VI: 41-42, 178-79; VII: 164-65, 241, 417-18; *see also* Chiriqui project

Colorado River Indian Agency, IV: 308

Colorado Territory: appointments, IV: 184n, 294-95, 475, 543, V: 173-74, 178-79, 182, 256n, 265, 309n, 485n, VII: 100n, VIII: 356; recruitment in, IV: 500n; need of military equipment and supplies, 536; organization of, V: 47; request for a pass, VI: 86n; request for troops from, 141; suspension of a death sentence, 335n; lack of labor to develop mineral resources, VII: 40; Indian attacks on mail routes, 530n

Colt, James B., VI: 398

Colton, G. A., VIII: 325n

Colton, John B., V: 396

Coltrin, Isaac Newton, III: 389-90

Columbia (Ill.), *see* Lacon (Ill.)

Columbia (Ky.), V: 402n, 417n

Columbia (Pa.), VI: 324n

Columbia (S. C.), VIII: 192n, 238

Columbia College (now University), IV: 362n; VII: 149; VII: 462n; VIII: 85n, 184n

Columbus, Christopher, II: 10; III: 90, 94

Columbus (Ky.), V: 84, 86-87, 94n, 95n, 98-99, 135, 540n; VI: 58n

Columbus (Miss.), I: 166n

Columbus (Ohio), III: 399n, 400-25, 437n; IV: 185, 203-205; V: 369n; VI: 20; VII: 274, 517n; VIII: 25, 79n

Columbus Machine Manufacturing Company, III: 387n, 393

Colville, Sam L., VIII: 69

Colwell, Stephen, VII: 77n

Colyer, Mary (Hancock), IV: 319

Colyer, Walter, IV: 39n; VIII: 310n

Comanche Indians, VI: 153n; VII: 68

Comayagua (Honduras), VIII: 167

Combs, T. M., VII: 177n, 291

Combs, Thomas, I: 11

Comegys, Cornelius Lee, VII: 465

Comingo, Abraham, VI: 423n

Commercial Law Journal, II: 316n

Commodore Perry's Expedition to Japan, IV: 88n

Compañia, Church of the (Santiago, Chile), VII: 143

Compilation of the Messages and Papers of the Presidents, 1789-1897, A (Richardson), IV: 414n; V: 481n; VI: 290n; VIII: 227n

Complete Works of Abraham Lincoln, The (Nicolay & Hay), I: viii; cited in footnotes on the ff. pages: I: 5, 108, 150, 207, 221, 266, 297, 377, 392, 407, 417, 431, 445, 477, 494, 498; II: 11, 17, 65, 82, 110, 218, 221, 222-23, 346, 445, 448, 459, 460, 484, 547, 552

III: 81, 97, 205, 326, 328, 332, 394, 425, 434, 463, 518; IV: 33, 63, 69, 85, 88, 91, 93, 110, 122, 125, 145, 147, 161, 164, 168, 280, 299, 301, 314, 347, 357, 361, 363, 364, 371, 373, 387, 414, 428, 439, 452, 454, 467, 485, 554

V: 30, 64, 88, 110, 176, 212, 213, 216, 226, 312, 323, 332, 351, 360, 362, 375, 376, 404, 409, 444, 473, 478, 489, 511, 544; VI: 10, 16, 26, 59, 123, 142, 150, 157, 165, 182, 214, 233, 245, 281, 292, 293, 317, 320, 371, 384, 405, 406, 435, 443-44, 450, 463, 534, 538, 548

VII: 16, 83, 103, 112, 149, 156, 173, 196, 223, 324n, 351, 365, 379, 383, 427, 439, 474, 506, 520; VIII: 96, 119, 155, 175, 180, 220, 229, 248, 255, 266, 267, 289, 326, 378, 382, 384, 387, 392, 413

Compromise of 1820, *see* Kansas-Nebraska Act and repeal of the Missouri Compromise

Compromise of 1850, *see* Kansas-Nebraska Act and repeal of the Missouri Compromise

Compton, J., IV: 305

Compton, William B., VI: 227, 233-34

Comstock, John, IV: 137

Comyges, *see* Comegys, Cornelius Lee

Conant, Phineas H., III: 399

Concord (Mass.), VII: 287n

Concord (N. H.), III: 552n, 554; VI: 355n, 368; VII: 298n

Concord Daily Monitor & New Hampshire Patriot, VIII: 415n

Concord Gazette Press, II: 148n

Concord Statesman, IV: 505n

Concord Tribune, II: 148n

Condell, Thomas, I: 407n

Condict, Alden S., VI: 414n

Cone, David D., IV: 54n

Cone, Sylvester Wells, IV: 54

Cone River, *see* Coan River

Conejos (Colo. Terr.), VII: 70

Confidential Correspondence of Gustavus Vasa Fox (Thompson & Wainwright), IV: 507n

Confiscation Act, IV: 506, 518, 531-32; V: 48-49, 337n, 389n, 435, 548n; VI: 45-46

Conger, Patrick H., VIII: 358n

Congregationalists, VII: 388

Congress, acts cited: swamp lands, III: 352-54; a fast day, IV: 482; suppression of insurrection (Confiscation Act), IV: 506, 518, 531-32, V: 48-49, 337n, 389n, 435, 496, 548, VI: 45-46, 493; VII: 54; commendations for military action, IV: 527n, V: 352, VIII: 285, 339; discharge of minors, IV: 529n; supplementary piracy acts, V: 5-6; efficiency of the Navy, 127, 134, 166, 214, VI: 116, VIII: 134-35; collection of duties, V: 139, 210, VI: 157, 479, VII: 192, VIII: 115, 396; release of persons held to labor in the District of Colum-

bia, V: 195, 370n, 418; awards resulting from Indian uprising, 205n; settlement of individual claims, 238-39, VII: 202n; medical officers, V: 275, 302; prohibition of bank notes of less than five dollars in the District of Columbia, 282-83; collection of direct taxes in insurrectionary districts, 298, VI: 454; increased revenue, V: 299, VI: 453, VII: 41n, 47n; government possession of railroad lines, V: 314; treason and rebellion, 336-37, 341-42; draft law, 384n, VI: 132-33, 203-204, 369, 390n, 435, 446-49, VII: 39n, 45n, 448-49, 534n, VIII: 171-72, 349-50; appointments to Annapolis, V: 387-88; supplemental appropriations, 419; additional Article of War, 434-35; amending the judicial system, 480, VI: 290; Treasury agents in rebel states, VI: 16n, 98-99; admission of West Virginia, 17, 181; continuation of a railroad to the Pacific, 68, 491, 504-505, VII: 16, 122, 228, 451, 464, VIII: 38-39, 192; commissary department, VI: 94n; Navy and Marine Corps promotions, 112, VII: 56-57; Navy line officers, VI: 116; organization of the military establishment, 116, 386-87; Michigan judicial districts, 119n; donation of public lands for colleges (Morrill Act), 123-24; letters of marque and reprisal, 126; Committee on Conduct of War, 128n; Peruvian convention, 134n; foreign recognition of the Confederacy, 177n; settlement on lands ceded to the United States, 205; reorganization of District of Columbia courts, 284; circuit courts for California and Oregon, 290; treason cases, 361; Illinois enabling act, 403-404; the organi-

zation of the House, 406n, 546-50, 552-53; revenue frauds, VII: 39n; telegraphic communication between the Eastern and Western continents, 39n; national banking law, 41-42; amending the Homestead Law, 47n; diplomatic and consular systems, 59, VIII: 332; tonnage and impost duties, VII: 72; reinvestigation of a dismissal case, 94n; troops in Kentucky, 109n, 272; maximum compensation of special agents, 156; oath for all civil and military government employees, 170n; 13th amendment, 172n, VIII: 253-54, 287n; revival of the grade of Lieutenant General, VII: 236; assignment of officers of same grade, 240n; enlistment bounties, 245; a jail warden for District of Columbia, 270n; Negro pay, 280n; returning Indians to homes, 342n; support of the Military Academy, 375n; the support of the Army, 404-406; consular clerks, 407n; District of Columbia marshal's compensation, 415n; habeas corpus suspension, 425; a day of prayer, 431-32; guarantee to certain states of a republican form of government, 433-34; Negro recruiting, 449-50; immigration, 489, VIII: 141n; cotton trading, VII: 495n; collection districts, 503-504, VIII: 208-209; exports to Canada, VII: 504; government purchases of Southern products, VIII: 20; admission of Nevada, 83-84; advance of Naval officers within grades, 133-34; regulation of steamship passengers, 141n; mail service to China, 145n; the grade of Vice Admiral, 145n; Navy reserve officers, 345; postwar Regular Army, 409n

Congress, annual messages to: (*1861*) V: 35-54 (text of), 145-46, VII: 259; (*1862*) V: 499n, 508n, 518-37 (text of); (*1863*) VII: 23-24, 36-53 (text of), 66, 124n, 162, VIII: 107; (*1864*) VIII: 90n, 108, 136-53 (text of), 328n, 329

Congress, appropriations for: Negro colonization, V: 370n, 419, VII: 241; White House books, V: 394; payment of a judgment, 514n; salary for a Department of Agriculture chemist, VI: 343n; habeas corpus act, 368-71; salary of a federal engineer, 508; payment of Pa. militia, VII: 178; relief of loyal Indians, VII: 196n

Congress, contested seats in, I: 317n; IV: 504n; VI: 365, 410-11, 555n; VII: 418

Congress, investigating committees: IV: 531, 533n, 556n, 560; V: 20n, 23n, 25n, 88, 94, 167n; VI: 118n, 128; VII: 285-86; VIII: 215; see also *Report of the Joint Committee on the Conduct of the War*

Congress, L. in, his speeches, bills, reports, resolutions, and letters on: the Mexican War, I: 420-22, 431-42, 446-48, II: 23; post-office affairs, I: 423-31, 442-43, 456-57, 500; public lands, 442, 460-61, 464, II: 26-27; House rules, I: 462-63, 501; payment of Tex. volunteers, 468-69; admission of Wis., 469-71; internal improvements, 480-90, VIII: 419n; judge's salary, I: 494-95; absentee Congressmen, 499; Taylor and Cass as presidential candidates, 501-16; public printing, 517; record of his vote on a bill, II: 19; abolition of slavery in D. C., 20-22

Later references to his term in Congress, III: 6, 16, 56, 319-

21, 512, IV: 62, 65-67, 84, 104, 106, 391

Congress, messages to: on presidential electoral count, IV: 246, VIII: 326-27; special message of July 1861, IV: 332, 420-41; international exhibitions, 450-51, V: 77, 88, VI: 51, VII: 140, VIII: 296-97; northeastern coastal fisheries, IV: 453-54; fortification of seacoast and lakes, V: 74; the *Trent* affair, 82-83, 95-96, 102, 115, 137, 141; foreign damage claims, 109-10, 140-41, 162, 539, VII: 113, 188; abolition of Stade Dues; V: 131-32; commendations for gallantry, 134, 166-67, 214-15, 299, 315-16, 547, 549-50, VI: 82, VII: 57, VIII: 134-35; acceptance of gifts to government or military personnel, V: 137, 331-32, 552-53, VI: 9-10, VII: 198-99, 311; VIII: 271; cooperation of federal government with states initiating emancipation, V: 144-46, 324-25; salaries of territorial officials, 171; abolishment of slavery in D.C., 192; a charge of false arrest, 193-94; Congressional censure of Cameron, 240-43; Erie and Oswego canals, 270, VII: 274; on 1862 bill to suppress insurrection and confiscate property, V: 328-331; consular pupils, VI: 19; cabinet members' power to appoint their own acting heads, 34-35; payment of military forces, 60-62; VII: 107-108; construction of railroads, VI: 68-69, VII: 321; regulation of diplomatic and consular systems, VI: 76, VII: 59, VIII: 331-32; relief for "distressed operatives of Blackburn," England, VI: 121-22; land grants for colleges, 123-24; proposed Bureau of Emancipation, VII: 76-77; relief for East

Tenn., 321; repeal of \$300 clause in enrollment act, 380; compensated emancipation recommended (1865), VIII: 260-61; validation (1865) of electoral votes, 270-71; *see also* Congress, annual messages to; Senate, messages to; House of Representatives, messages to; Treaties and agreements with foreign powers; *and* Treaties, Indian

Congress, petitions to and from members of, I: 287; V: 227

Congress, powers of: to establish a national bank, I: 170-72; to declare war, 451-52, II: 153; to appropriate money for internal improvements, I: 485-86; to suspend writ of habeas corpus, IV: 390n, VI: 300n, 302, 368-71, 451-52, VII: 425-26; in property confiscation, IV: 531-32, VII: 264n; to regulate currency, VI: 61; to raise and support armies, 446; in organization of government departments, VII: 266-67; in reestablishing state governments, VIII: 107n; *see also* Congress, the slavery question and

Congress, the slavery question and, I: 75; II: 7, 370, 400-402, 451, 462, 464, 514; III: 4, 27, 35-36, 41-42, 46, 53, 97, 99-101, 116, 123-24, 127-33, 288, 299, 307, 317, 324, 334-35, 369, 386, 403-404, 411-12, 415, 419, 422, 427-28, 464-65, 523n, 526n, 528, 537-38, 552; IV: 27, 41, 105-106, 108, 156-57, 172, 176, 256-57, 532; V: 195-96, 422-23, 465n; VI: 387, 411; VII: 81, 102n, 172n; VIII: 253-54, 280

Congress (ship), V: 154n

Congress of the Confederation, III: 414-15, 523-25

Congressional Globe, I: 38n, 419-20, 422-23, 430n, 434n, 448n,

461n, 463n, 469n, 471n, 480n, 491, 498-501, 517n; II: 19n, 20n, 27n; III: 47, 129, 154-56, 164, 184, 190-92, 200, 228-29; IV: 66, 106-108, 299n, 428n, 439n; V: 66n, 326n, 405; VIII: 249n, 254n, 326n

Congressional Medal of Honor, V: 58n; VIII: 175n

Conkey, A., I: 52

Conkling, Cyrus, II: 395-96

Conkling, Frederick Augustus, V: 396; VII: 374

Conkling, James Cook, I: 308; II: 113, 144n, 290n, 310, 360; III: 399; IV: 473n; VI: 85, 90, 399, 406-10, 414, 420n, 423, 430, 443n, 444n; VII: 471, 500

Conkling, Mrs. James Cook, see Conkling, Mercy Ann

Conkling, Mercy Ann Riggs (Levering), I: 308n

Conkling, Roscoe, IV: 307; VII: 194, 498

Conkling, William J., II: 310

Conley, Edward, VII: 544-45; VIII: 9

Conn, John S., VIII: 30

Conneaut (Ohio), IV: 218-19

Conneaut Reporter, IV: 219n

Connecticut, I: 75n; V: 361-62, 375-76, 386n; VI: 54, 113n; VII: 82-83, 133; VIII: 128-29, 150, 153

Connelley, John, Sr., II: 206, 323

Connelly, Henry, VI: 124n; VII: 40n; VIII: 157n

Conness, John, VII: 13, 323, 404; VIII: 227n

Connor, John (Indian), IV: 401; VII: 309

Connor, Thomas, VII: 460-61

Connors, see Conness, John

Conover, Robert, I: 16n, 18, following 48, 53

Conrad, V. L., V: 158n

Conscientious objectors, VII: 535-36; VIII: 290n

Conspiracy in the U.S. Navy Department . . . ., The (Smith), VIII: 364n

Constable, Charles Henry, I: 345-46; II: 48, 97, 342-43

Constant, Archibald, I: 220

Constant, John, VIII: 421

Constantin Nikolaievich, Grand Duke of Russia, V: 440

Constantinople (Turkey), IV: 358-59, 397; V: 176

Constellation (frigate), VIII: 271

"Constitution" (locomotive), IV: 228

Constitution (U. S.), L. on: establishment of a national bank, I: 170-72, II: 402; presidential electors, I: 450-51, VIII: 270; war-making power, I: 451-52, VI: 261-69; internal improvements, I: 480, 485-88; the Missouri Compromise, II: 7-8, 229, 244-45; naturalization, 142-43; the institution of slavery, 230-31, 274-75, 363, 366, 466-67, 492, 494, 501, 513, 515, 520-21, III: 78, 87, 96-101, 128-33, 230-33, 279, 307, 334-35, 386, 398, 408, 420-21, 439-40, 466, 522-35, 543-45, IV: 11-12, 22-23, 29, 251, 262-63, 270; Negro-White (5-3) basis of representation, II: 246; supersedes Articles of Confederation, 249; and amendments to, IV: 162-63, 260, 268-69; and the Union, 168-69, 260-63; right of a state to secede, 195-96, 264-69, 432-38, 440; who shall interpret, 206-207, 252-58; writ of habeas corpus, 430-31, 451-52; attainder, V: 331; and treason, VI: 261-63; and the draft law, 370, 446-48; and Emancipation Proclamation, 408, 428-29; reinstatement of state governments, VII: 50-51, VIII: 59-72; see also Thirteenth Amendment; Dred Scott case; Kansas Nebraska Act and repeal of the Missouri Com-

promise; Congress, powers of; *and* Supreme Court
Constitutional Union [Washington], VII: 200n
Constitutional Union party, IV: 54n, 83n
Consular system, *see* Diplomatic appointments
Contidoka Duta (Indian), VII: 325-26
Continental Congress, III: 411
Continental Hotel (Philadelphia), IV: 239n; VI: 520; VII: 106, 398; VIII: 174, 346
Contner, Albert, VIII: 5n
Contner, Ellen, VIII: 5n
Converse, George Leroy, VI: 300-306
Converse & Priest (Springfield), I: 405, 420n
Conway, Martin Franklin, III: 371-72, 379
Conway, Thomas W., V: 3n, 26n; VIII: 325
Conwell, George, IV: 166
Cony, Samuel A., VII: 519-20; VIII: 3n, 108-10
Cook, Burton Chauncey, II: 296, 305, 347n, 480, 532-33, 537; III: 355-56; IV: 168n, 477, 553; VII: 376n
Cook, Daniel Pope, II: 70-71
Cook, Isaac, III: 125, 390n
Cook, John, II: 291-92, 324; IV: 189; V: 142, 179-80, 348
Cook, Josiah, I: 51
Cooke, Edwin Francis, VII: 222n
Cool Harbor (Va.), *see* Cold Harbor (Va.)
Cooley, Albert B., IV: 525n
Cooley, Francis Morgan, IV: 309
Coolidge, E. Channing, VI: 513n
Coolie trade, V: 79
Coombs, J. J., IV: 319
Coon, Amos B., VI: 197
Coon, Reuben, II: 188
Coons, John, VII: 372
Cooper, ———, II: 337, 339
Cooper, Edward, VII: 195n

Cooper, F. F., VII: 195n
Cooper, Henry, VII: 195; VIII: 58-72
Cooper, J. R., I: 340n
Cooper, James, IV: 396, 472, 507; V: 28, 90, 148-49
Cooper, Jonathan K., II: 396, 445
Cooper, Leopold, *see* Cowper, Leopold C. P.
Cooper, Lewis L., I: 53
Cooper, Samuel, VI: 476n
Cooper, Wickliffe, VII: 119
Cooper, William M., VI: 344
Cooper Institute (N. Y.), L.'s address (1860) at: III: 399n, 494n, 519n, 522-50 (text of), IV: 38-39, 58-59, 113n; mentioned, V: 26n, VI: 108n, VII: 32
Cooper Shop Volunteer Refreshment Saloon (Philadelphia), V: 217-18; VI: 344n; VII: 394
Coosaw Island (S. C.), VI: 455-57
Copes, J. S., II: 442
Copperheads, VI: 191n; VII: 216-17, 288n, 334-35, 422n, 436n, 549n; VIII: 46; *see also* American Knights, Order of; *and* Knights of the Golden Circle
Corby, William, VII: 314-15
Corcoran, Michael, IV: 418-19, 492; V: 381, 466; VI: 84, 295n, 361
Corcoran & Riggs (Washington), I: 419n
Corder, Abraham C., VI: 7
Corder, Anderson P., II: 296
Corey, John H., V: 103n
Corinth (Miss.), V: 231, 250, 252, 254, 259, 264, 276, 291, 293, 295, 300, 304-305, 308, 313, 321-23, 358n, 451, 453n, 465n, 478, 546n; VI: 71n, 147n, 472; VII: 104n; VIII: 74
Cork (Ireland), VIII: 337n
Corkran, Francis S., IV: 304, 357; VI: 488; VIII: 82
Corliss, Carlton J., V: 407n
Corn Island (S. C.), VI: 457

Corneau, Mrs. Charles S., *see* Corneau, Elizabeth
Corneau, Elizabeth (Ridgeway), IV: 362
Corneau, Stephen A., II: 311-12; VI: 63n
Cornelius, Ida (Brockman), IV: 121n
Cornell, Paul, II: 396-97
Corner, John B., VII: 152n
Corning, Erastus, VI: 235, 260-69, 271, 372n
Corning, Jasper, II: 198
Cornwallis, Charles, 1st Marquess, VII: 458n
Corps d'Afrique, VIII: 313n
Corpus Christi (Tex.), II: 84
Correll, William F., III: 519-20
Corse, John Murry, VII: 308
Corse, Montgomery D., VIII: 389-90
Corsey, Abraham C., *see* Corder, Abraham C.
Corton, Joseph, VI: 544
Corwin, Thomas, II: 8, 93; III: 319-20, 401; IV: 153, 281, 312; V: 73, 109, 113, 281; VI: 39; VII: 524n; VIII: 15n, 106
Corwine, Richard M., IV: 36, 47-48, 77n, 151; VII: 29n, 168n, 275, 409n; VIII: 323
Cory, Thomas H., III: 395
Corydon (Ind.), I: 462
Costa Rica, IV: 286n, 397; V: 312, 371n, 521; VI: 259-60; VIII: 137-38
Cottman, Thomas E. H., V: 487n; VI: 287-89; VII: 66-67, 71
Cotton and other products, trade in, IV: 313; V: 36, 139, 141, 472, 507, 540; VI: 72, 157, 159-60, 207n, 212n, 294, 307, 340, 397n, 481; VII: 62-64, 78, 114-16, 126, 145-46, 148-49, 151-52, 156, 166, 178n, 213-14, 258, 342n, 354, 457, 488-89, 495-96, 519, 527-28
    VIII: 7-8, 20-22, 28n, 35, 73, 93-94, 103-104, 119-20, 163-64,
175-76, 177n, 182n, 185-86, 187n, 196-97, 199-201, 202n, 209-10, 221, 230-31, 243-44, 267-68, 288-89, 306n, 330, 334-37, 339-42, 368, 395, 419, 595
Couch, Darius Nash, V: 402n; VI: 184, 293, 299, 310, 327-30; VII: 394n
Coulter, ———, VII: 309n
Coulter, Guy, IV: 34n
Coulter, John, IV: 109
Council Bluffs (Iowa), III: 355, 396-97
Council Bluffs Bugle, III: 397n
"Council of War, The" (statuary group), VII: 389n
Counterfeiters, VIII: 80n, 290n, 309n
Courts-martial, IV: 286-87, 366, 503, 516; V: 198-99, 201, 204, 228, 349, 362, 369-70, 406, 538-39; VI: 54, 75, 142-43, 158, 208, 211, 257, 285, 426, 431-32, 538-39, 562; VII: 26-27, 93-94, 175, 197, 342-43, 505-506, 516-17; VIII: 34, 300; *see also* Death sentences
Courtney, James, II: 297
Covell, Merrit L., I: 381
Covington (Ky.), IV: 326-27; VII: 29, 59, 112; VIII: 120n
Covode, John, IV: 298, 327, 445; V: 88n, 116n; VI: 5
Cowan, Edgar, IV: 298; VI: 50n
Cowan, Temple, VIII: 70
Cowan, Thomas, I: 2
Cowardin, Peter G., I: 139-40
Cowden, John H., V: 158n
Cowgill, W. B., II: 188
Cowgill, W. M., II: 188
Cowles, Edwin, IV: 282
Cowles, Leslie, V: 104n
Cowley, Patrick, VII: 318
Cownover, Robert, *see* Conover, Robert
Cowper, Leopold C. P., VI: 132
Cowperthwait, George W., V: 376n
Cox, A., VIII: 68

Cox, Christopher C., VII: 537-38
Cox, Henry, I: 12
Cox, Jacob, VI: 544
Cox, Jacob Dolson, IV: 463; V: 230n, 270n, 497n; VIII: 417n
Cox, Jeremiah, I: 249
Cox, John T., VIII: 114-15
Cox, Lewis H. [alias John M. Dillon], VI: 463-64
Cox, Samuel Sullivan ("Sunset"), III: 210; V: 408n; VI: 19; VIII: 249, 328
Cox, William, I: 12, 18
Coxe, Richard S., VI: 284
Coxe, Robert Edward, VIII: 199-200, 354
Coyle, Daniel, VIII: 595
Craddock, Mrs., VI: 452
Craddock, J. M., IV: 309
Craft, William Henry, VII: 89
Crafton, Greek, III: 492n
Crafts, F. D., II: 25n
Crafts, William A., II: 25
Craig, Allen Andrew, IV: 483n
Craig, C. W., II: 113-14
Craig, Charles, VI: 73n; VII: 83-84
Craig, Mrs. Charles, see Craig, Susan
Craig, Daniel H., VII: 233n
Craig, James (Ill.), I: 71n, 76
Craig, James (Mo.), V: 142; VIII: 176n
Craig, Samuel G., II: 195n, 197; IV: 95n
Craig, Susan, VI: 73n; VII: 83-84
Crain, James M., I: 119-20
Crain, John, I: 147n
Crain, Lewis F., I: 120
Cramer, James Lawrence, V: 7-8
Crampton, E. C., II: 121n
Crampton's Gap (Md.), V: 426n
Crane, ———, II: 336-37, 339
Crane, Charles Henry, VIII: 50n, 225n
Crane, James H., VIII: 299n
Crane, R. E., VII: 60n
Crater, George E., V: 178n
Craven, Thomas Tingey, V: 215

Craven, William A. [alias John C. Brown], VIII: 298-99, 305
Cravens, John R., V: 291
Crawford, Andrew, IV: 62
Crawford, George Washington, II: 43, 74-76
Crawford, Josiah, I: 18
Crawford, Mrs. Josiah, I: 1n
Crawford, Medorem, VI: 161n
Crawford, Robert, VIII: 237n
Crawford, Robert Parks, V: 471
Crawford, S. A., I: 1n
Crawford, Samuel Johnson, VIII: 115n, 338n, 339n, 355n
Crawford, Samuel Wylie, VI: 418
Crayon (periodical), VII: 392n
"Crayon" (pseud.), see Strother, David H.
Creager, J. P., IV: 396n
Creek Indians, VII: 69
Creswell, John Andrew Jackson, VII: 9n, 226-27, 251, 331; VIII: 369, 411, 412n
Crete, Valentine, I: 11
Crimean War, V: 79n
Crisfield, Arthur, VII: 10n, 26
Crisfield, John Woodland, V: 64n, 285-86; VI: 8; VII: 9-10, 26-27
Crisis, The [Columbus, Ohio], IV: 206n
Crispin, Silas, V: 189, 197n
Crist, Nelson L., VI: 421
Crittenden, Henry, VII: 456n
Crittenden, John Jordan, I: 419, 457-58; II: 2n, 28-29, 50, 93, 483-84; III: 305, 335-36, 367, 452; V: 23n, 80, 103-104, 170n, 451; VI: 8, 65n, 97n, 106n, 372; see also Crittenden-Montgomery bill
Crittenden, Thomas Leonidas, IV: 368, 544-45; V: 320; VII: 14n, 108n, 127
Crittenden-Montgomery bill, III: 60, 368, 434
Crock, Michael, V: 177
Crockett, John A. L., II: 161-62
Crofoot, H. K., IV: 121n; V: 304n

Cromwell, H. B., VI: 112n
Cronan, James, & Company, II: 183
Crone, Dave, VIII: 214n
Crook, George, V: 270n; VII: 445, 456n, 537n; VIII: 22n, 297n, 370-71
Crook, William H., VIII: 328, 372n
Crook, Mrs. William H., VIII: 328n
Crooked Creek, I: 42
Crooks, William, IV: 446n; V: 542-43
Crosby, Hiram B., VII: 114n
Crosby, J. W., I: 352
Crosby, Pierce, V: 215
Crosby, William, VII: 132-33
Crosman, George Hampton, V: 207n; VI: 5
Cross, ———, V: 73n
Cross, Edward E., VI: 133
Cross, Osborn, IV: 503
Cross, Thomas, VII: 417n
Cross, Thomas H., VII: 417n
Cross Keys (Va.), battle of, V: 272n, 275n; VI: 232n
Crossman, George Hampton, see Crosman, George Hampton
Crosster, Joseph Henry, VII: 291
Crothers, Hugh W., VI: 136-37
Crotty, Jeremiah & Company, II: 183
Crouse, William, VIII: 25
Crow, William, I: 39-40, 85-86
Crowder, Matthew, Jr., I: 206
Crowder, Victoria, VIII: 423
Crowell, John, Jr., VI: 194n
Crowell, John, Sr., IV: 511; VI: 194n
Crowell, Robert L., VII: 98, 106, 109
Crowen, T. J., V: 394
Crozier, John Hervey, II: 218
Crumb, Samuel D., VI: 287n
Crumblin, Charles, see Crumpton, Charles
Crume, Mary (Lincoln), IV: 61; V: 57

Crume, Ralph, IV: 61; V: 57
Crume, Mrs. Ralph, see Crume, Mary
Crume, Susannah, see Weathers, Susannah (Crume)
Crumpton, Charles, VII: 297-98
Cruttenden, Joel D., V: 55
Crystal Springs (Miss.), VI: 226
Cuba, II: 153, 258; III: 115, 356, IV: 172; VI: 110n; VII: 37, 331, 370n
Cudjo's Cave (Trowbridge), IV: 75n
Cullom, Richard Northcraft, I: 76, 82n
Cullom, Shelby Moore, II: 310, 387, 424; V: 71n, 491; VI: 237-38; VII: 180
Cullum, George Washington, VI: 193
Culpeper County (Va.), VIII: 51, 175
Culpeper Court House (Va.), V: 366n, 397n, 460, 488; VI: 169n, 250n, 258n, 276n, 280n, 354n, 450n, 535n, 537; VII: 313n, 473n; VIII: 16n, 51n
Culver, William E., V: 67n
Cumback, William, VII: 371
Cumberland (Md.), IV: 472n; VI: 189n, 473-74, 515; VII: 175, 437n; VIII: 22-23, 371n
Cumberland (ship), V: 154n
Cumberland (sloop of war), V: 550
Cumberland, Department of the, V: 21-22, 501n; VII: 14n, 240; VIII: 371n
Cumberland County (Me.), VIII: 3n
Cumberland County (Tenn.), VIII: 68
Cumberland Gap, IV: 524n, 541-42, 544-45; V: 37, 91, 264, 276n, 392, 425, 452-53, 484n; VI: 439, 471n; VII: 29-30, 169n, 331n
Cumberland Island, V: 167
Cumberland Mountains, V: 409n; VI: 425n

Cumberland River, V: 135, 409n, 417n, 545; VI: 522n
Cumberland Sound, V: 167
Cumberland Valley, VI: 310n, 318, 322
Cumins, Solon, II: 72n, 190, 436
Cummings, Alexander, V: 242-43; VII: 371
Cummings, Joseph, VII: 351n
Cummings, William H. [H. H.], VII: 344
Cummins, William, I: 12
Cunningham, George, VI: 544
Cunningham, James T., I: 124n, 157n, 249
Cunningham, Joseph Oscar, III: 37
Cunningham, Mary, IV: 92n
Cunningham, Patrick, IV: 92
Cunningham, Samuel W., V: 390
Cunningham, William A., VI: 185
Curl, Jennie G., VII: 100n
Curly, Thomas, V: 517
Curran, Isaac B., V: 61n
Curry, Jabez Lamar Monroe, III: 542n
Curry, Thomas C., VIII: 86-87
Curtin, Andrew Gregg: Pa. gubernatorial candidate (1860), IV: 84n, 111, 117; quarrel between Cameron and Curtin factions of Pa. Republicans, 103n, 113n; L.'s advice on his inaugural speech as governor of Pa., 158; appointment recommendations, 184, 552n, V: 29n, 111, 207n, 239, 380, 400n, 495, VI: 228, 422n, VII: 97n, 444, VIII: 44; speaks on the occasion of L.'s stop at Harrisburg en route to inaugural, 243; and preparation for armed conflict (spring '61), 324, 326, VII: 249n; and arrest of Cameron, V: 194n; and 1862 call for troops, 294n, 339, 363n, 368; and the defense of Pa. (Sept. '62), 414-15, 417-18, 427-28; protests McClellan recruiting order (Oct. '62), 482; L. suggests (April '63)

a future diplomatic post for, VI: 170; and fear of enemy invasion of Pa. (spring '63), 189, 193, 195, 238; requests U. S. supplies for state troops, 298n; and the draft, 300n, 435, 477-78, VIII: 84-85; court-martial cases and discharges, VI: 464n, VII: 2n, 455; and 1864 election in Pa., VI: 513, VIII: 41, 109, 124; and recruitment of troops in Pa., VII: 57-58; disloyalists attack soldiers cheering for, 216; call for 100-day troops, 424n; on the presentation of a cane to L., 457-58, 460; and complaints of women government workers, 467n; fear of enemy raids into Pa. (1864), VIII: 50; asks verification of rumor that three states have offered to come back into the Union, 121; protests violations of Enrollment Act (Jan. '65), 245n
Curtin, Mrs. Andrew G., see Curtin, Catherine
Curtin, Catherine Irvine (Wilson), VII: 97n
Curtis, Benjamin Robbins, II: 400, 403, 466; III: 251, 543n; V: 544
Curtis, George William, VII: 381n, 411n
Curtis, James, IV: 413
Curtis, Samuel Ryan, III: 400; IV: 43, 463, 527n, 549-50, 560n, 562-63; V: 2n, 7, 14, 65-66, 101n, 142, 178n, 203n, 323n, 456, 459-60, 517, 548; VI: 2, 6, 8, 10-11, 20-21, 33-34, 36-38, 52-53, 65-66, 131n, 210-11, 219, 223n, 234, 253-54, 326n, 345n, 383, 501-502; VII: 78, 85-86, 100, 157-58, 178-79, 300n, 340n, 343, 530; VIII: 6n, 57, 94, 293n, 300n
Cushing, Caleb, III: 543n; V: 451
Cushing, William Barker, VIII: 134-35
Cushing's Block (Cleveland), III: 506n, 517n

Cushman, ———, II: 314
Cushman, C. Seth, IV: 453n
Cushman, Joseph, IV: 308
Cushman, W. H. W., II: 167, 170
Cuthbert, John, I: 162n
Cuthbert, Mary Ann, V: 492; VI: 371, 474
Cutler, Lysander, IV: 295n
Cutler, R. King, VIII: 207n
Cutting, William, VI: 538n

Cutts, James Madison, Jr., I: viii; IV: 409; VI: 538-39
Cutts, James Madison, Sr., VI: 232-33
Cutts, Richard Dominicus, VI: 518n
Cutts, Richard Malcolm, V: 388
Cuyler, John Meck, V: 206n
Cuyler, Theodore L., IV: 240-41
Cynthiana (Ky.), VII: 391
Czapkay, L. J., VIII: 227

D

Dabblee, C. B., VII: 158n
Dabney, W., VIII: 378-79
Dabney's Mills (Va.), VI: 548n; VIII: 379n
Dade County (Mo.), V: 1
Dahlgren, John Adolphus, IV: 383-84, 399, 551; V: 21, 112-13, 156, 196, 203, 251n, 262-63, 316, 365n, 463, 476, 545; VI: 3-4, 111-12, 367; VII: 84, 118, 222
Dahlgren, Ulric, V: 262, 446n; VI: 281-82; VII: 222, 226, 251
D'Ahna, Henry C., see De Ahna, Henry C.
Daily, Enos, VI: 248
Daily, Samuel Gordon, VI: 21
Daines, Adam K., VI: 475n, 488
Daines, Thomas, VI: 475
Dainese, Francis [?], VIII, 139n
Dake, O. E., V: 68
Dakota (ship), V: 154n
Dakota City land office, IV: 306
Dakota Territory, appointments for, IV: 294, 408, 550n; V: 47, 148n; VI: 494-95; VII: 141n, 206-207, 215, 372; VIII: 358n, 359n

Dale, Michael G., I: 147-48; III: 493-94
Dallas, Alexander James, IV: 484, 491
Dallas, George Mifflin, IV: 101, 376-77
Dallas, S. J., V: 474n
Dalrymple, Mrs. [nee Duvall], V: 183n
Dalton (Ga.), V: 261n, 263; VI: 471n, 510
Damascus (Md.), V: 412n
Dana, Charles Anderson, VI: 358-59, 374, 475n, 521, 554n; VII: 166, 170n, 277n, 479; VIII: 10n, 15-16, 28, 50, 125, 303, 322-23, 387n, 405n
Dana, Napoleon Jackson Tecumseh, V: 78; VIII: 35n, 201-203, 288n, 299n, 305-306
Dana, Richard Henry, VI: 294n
Dane, Nathan, III: 525n
Dane County (Ill.), see Christian County (Ill.)
Danenhower, William Weaver, IV: 327; VI: 118
Danforth, J. B., Jr., VI: 162n, 182

Daniel, Peter Vivian, III: 543n; V: 41

Daniels, Samuel, VII: 400n

"Danites," III: 283, 345; IV: 47; see also "National Democrats"

Danville (Ill.), I: 46; IV: 191-92; V: 541; VI: 319; VIII: 290n

Danville (Ky.), V: 321n

Danville (Va.), VIII: 384n

Darien (Ga.), VIII: 396

Darlin, John, II: 183

Darling, A. B., VIII: 409

Darling, Clarence, IV: 486

Darling, Nathan, VI: 106-107

Darling, William Augustus, IV: 486; V: 25, 296

Darlington District (S. C.), IV: 526

Darneille, John, I: 208, 249

Dart, Anson, IV: 403-404

Dartmouth College, I: 22n

DaSilva, Ritta Angelica, II: 224-25

Dauber & Pine Bookshops, V: 358n

Davenport, J. E., II: 430n

Davenport, Simeon J., V: 207n

Davenport, William, I: 354, 360; II: 455n

Davenport, William H., II: 429-30, 454-55

Davenport (Iowa), VII: 325-26; VIII: 76, 116, 269, 298, 305, 309

Davenport Democrat & Leader, VI: 40n

David, George W., VII: 422n

Davidson, ———, II: 191

Davidson, Hunter, VI: 315n

Davidson, James M., I: 391

Davidson, John, I: 405n

Davidson, John Wynn, V: 93; VII: 208-209

Davidson, William H., I: 61, 67, 146n, 253, 264, 391; see also Davidson, James M.

Davidson, Mrs. William H., I: 253

Davidson County (Tenn.), VIII: 69

Davies, John P., II: 223-24

Davies, Thomas Alfred, V: 180

Davis, Allen, VIII: 69

Davis, Charles Henry, V: 316; VI: 111-12

Davis, David, I: 416n; II: 62n, 94n, 97n, 104-105, 290-92, 306, 310, 314, 325n, 329, 394-95, 426n, 436n; III: 335, 347n, 490n; IV: 35n, 43, 46, 48, 79n, 84, 91, 93, 168n, 185-86, 189n, 287n; V: 22, 465-66, 481, 501-502; VI: 18n, 113n, 235, 276n; VII: 120n, 268n, 421-23; VIII: 343n

Davis, David (IV), II: 218n; III: 513n; IV: 55n, 57n, 84n; VII: 385n

Davis, Edmund Jackson, V: 357n

Davis, Edward, VI: 428n

Davis, Edwin A., VIII: 74

Davis, Elias, VIII: 313

Davis, Eliza, I: 261, 281

Davis, Mrs. Frank, I: 148n

Davis, Garrett, IV: 369n; V: 104n, 156n; VI: 97n; VIII: 293-94

Davis, George, I: 211

Davis, George Perrin, III: 347

Davis, George Turnbull Moore, I: 447-48; II: 65; IV: 132-33, 139n; V: 93n; VI: 526n

Davis, H. Gail, VIII: 221n

Davis, Hasbrouck, VI: 198, 207

Davis, Henry Winter, IV: 79, 173, 328; VI: 140-41, 562n; VII: 277

Davis, Isaac, VIII: 124n

Davis, Jacob Cunningham, II: 296; III: 277, 332

Davis, James, VIII: 69

Davis, James M., II: 342, 377

Davis, Jefferson, III: 295, 324, 423, 429, 538n; IV: 5, 10, 21; V: 484n, 517-18; VI: 31, 203, 314-16, 526n, 535n; VII: 429n, 435-36, 460-61, 501, 517-18; VIII: 10n, 27, 151, 188n, 216n, 220-21, 243, 275-76, 281n, 283, 406n, 407n

Davis, Jefferson Columbus, VI: 148-49

Davis, Jeremiah, I: 23

Davis, John [alias John Lewis], VIII: 269

Davis, John, Jr., VI: 271n
Davis, John Givan, III: 367, 435
Davis, John Moore Kelso, VI: 162
Davis, John W., IV: 522-23
Davis, Jonah M., VIII: 290n
Davis, Levi, I: 38, 47-48, 60-61, 77-78, 116; II: 58, 113, 330; IV: 448
Davis, Levi, Jr., IV: 448n
Davis, M. P., VII: 100
Davis, Maria, I: 464-65; VIII: 213n
Davis, Martin, VI: 241
Davis, N. W., VII: 371
Davis, Oliver L., II: 220, 426n, 443; VIII: 290n
Davis, Philip R., VII: 292n
Davis, Ray W., VIII: 355n
Davis, Richard E., IV: 529n
Davis, Robert B., VII: 94n
Davis, Samuel Boyer, VIII: 291-92
Davis, Samuel H., I: 340n
Davis, Susan Fry (Speed), I: 261n
Davis, Thomas, I: 464-65, 493n; II: 18
Davis, Thomas E., VIII: 124n
Davis, Thomas Treadwell, VIII: 82, 368
Davis, W. R., VIII: 68
Davis, Walter, I: 158, 446n, 464, 493; II: 18-19, 40, 42, 44-47, 64, 135n
Davis, William D., II: 187-88
Davis' Creek, VIII: 57n
Davis' Ford, V: 120n
Davis, Samuel C., & Company (St. Louis), II: 434-35; III: 338, 342-43, 346
Dawes, Henry Laurens, V: 20n; VII: 320n, 398-99
Dawson, John, I: 35n, 156-57, 221, 264, 298
Dawson, John Littleton, VIII: 327n
Dawson, L., VII: 314-15
Dawsonville (Md.), V: 410n
Day, Charles H. B., V: 376n
Day, Frederick S., II: 297, 304
Day, G. E. H., IV: 309

Dayton, Jonathan, III: 529
Dayton, William Lewis, I: 498; II: 346, 349-50, 364; IV: 234n, 248, 281-82, 292-93; V: 130; VII: 359n
Dayton (Ohio), III: 425n, 436-37, 463n; IV: 187
Dayton Empire, III: 437n
Dayton Journal, III: 437n
Dayton News, IV: 347n; VIII: 300n
Dazey, Mitchell, VII: 97n
Dazey, William T., VII: 97
De Ahna [D'Ahna], Henry C., V: 369
Dean [Deaw], ———, VI: 137
Dean, Ezra, V: 375
Dearborn, Frederick M., I: 475n; IV: 492n; VI: 5n; VII: 98n, 180n, 418n
Dearborn, Jonathan, II: 297
Dearborn Park (Chicago), II: 348-49
Death sentences, V: 475-76; VI: 148, 158, 167-68, 189, 225, 227, 229, 231-34, 244, 248, 253, 287, 292, 295-97, 313, 335, 337, 340, 347, 356, 362, 392, 395, 400, 402, 414-15, 419, 424, 428, 437-38, 441-43, 459, 466, 472, 474-75, 478, 481-82, 488, 491-92, 498, 504-506, 508-10, 514-15, 519, 522, 529, 531, 537, 548, 561-62
VII: 2, 12, 25-26, 29, 31-34, 58-61, 64-65, 75, 82, 93-94, 96, 99, 104, 106, 109, 111-12, 122, 129, 133, 136-38, 140, 143, 150-52, 155, 157-59, 163, 171-76, 180, 182, 205-206, 211, 219-20, 227, 252, 261, 270-71, 278, 293, 297-99, 305-307, 313-17, 320, 341, 344, 356-360, 375, 416, 436, 502-503, 509, 516, 522, 536, 540-41, 544-45
VIII: 4-5, 9, 12-13, 19, 22-23, 26, 28-30, 37-38, 49, 75, 85-89, 91, 102, 120-21, 133, 135-36, 159-60, 167-68, 174, 176-77, 180-81, 188-90, 194, 203, 205-

206, 210-13, 223, 226-27, 229, 232, 235, 237-41, 243, 245, 249, 255-56, 259, 263, 269, 273-74, 291-92, 297-302, 305, 309-10, 313, 325, 357

Deatonville (Va.), VIII: 391

Deaw [Dean?], ——, VI: 137

DeCamp, John, V: 215

Decatur (Ga.), I: 442

Decatur (Ill.), I: 2, 3; II: 333; III: 356n; IV: 48-49

Decatur County (Tenn.), VIII: 70

Decatur Gazette, II: 112n

Decatur Magnet, IV: 100n

Decatur State Chronicle, see *Illinois State Chronicle*

Declaration of Independence, L. on the, I: 112; II: 121,130-31, 245, 249, 255, 266, 275-76, 283-84, 346, 368, 380, 403-407, 499-501, 519-21, 527, 544-47

III: 9-10, 14, 16, 29, 31, 57, 79-81, 88-91, 94, 112-13, 177, 205, 213-14, 216, 220, 222, 234, 237-38, 248-50, 262-63, 280, 284-85, 296, 300-304, 327-28, 402, 423-25, 430, 444, 469-70, 486, 500

IV: 4, 10, 16-17, 19, 169, 239-41, 253, 258, 265, 433, 438; V: 498; VI: 319-20

Defoe, Mrs., VIII: 24

Defrees, John D., IV: 155, 539; V: 499; VII: 12, 128, 172-73, 513n; VIII: 136n, 148n, 149n, 152n, 287n

Defrees, Morris W., VIII: 148n

DeGroot, William H., V: 238-39

Deitrich, John E., see Detrich, John E.

DeJanon, Patrice, VII: 496

DeJanon, Mrs. Patrice, VII: 496n

DeKalb County (Tenn.), VIII: 69

DeKalb County Sentinel [Sycamore, Ill.], III: 126-27

DeKalb Regiment (N. Y.), IV: 368n

Delafield, Richard, VII: 345n, 468; VIII: 264-65

Delahay, Mark William, I: 350; II: 341, 447; III: 355, 365n, 371-72, 378-79, 425n, 489-90, 497n, 504n; IV: 31-32, 40, 44, 49, 283, 364; V: 164n, 416n; VI: 507

Delahay, Mary, III: 504

DeLand, Hooker A., VIII: 246n

Delany, ——, II: 7

DeLany, Hayden, VIII: 346

Delany, Martin Robison, VIII: 272-73

Delany, Michael, VI: 335n

Delavan, Edward C., IV: 420n

Delavan (Ill.), I: 354-55; II: 423

Delavan House (Albany, N. Y.), IV: 227n

Delaware, I: 476; IV: 426; V: 29-31, 49, 153, 160, 376, 378n, 535; VI: 324n, 429; VIII: 46, 128-30, 150, 153

Delaware Indian Agency, IV: 306

Delaware Indians, IV: 400-402, 453, 455, 476-77, 540n; VII: 403

Delaware River, VII: 337n

Delaware State Journal [Wilmington], I: 476n

Delgado, Felipe, VIII: 157

Delker, Christian [Christoper], VII: 94

DeLong, James, IV: 514; V: 549n

Dement, John, I: 77

Demerara (British Guiana), IV: 475, 527; VIII: 196n

Demming, Hercules, I: 21

Demmon, Archelaus, I: 79-80

"Democrat, A" [pseud.], I: 327n

"Democratic Battle Hymn" (poem), II: 152

Democratic Hall (Chicago), II: 450n

Democratic Party: policy on public lands, I: 50n; debate on subtreasury issue, 140-41, 159n; Ill. state convention (1839), 155; essential "difference" (1839) between Whigs and Democrats, 177; and apportionment bill, 287; and officering army in the Mexican War, 381;

national convention, (*1848*) 480, II: 236, (*1844*) 232; government advertising (1849) in Democratic newspapers, II: 42-43; national convention (1852) and election of Pierce, 235, 254; the essential "difference" (1858) between Democrats and Republicans, III: 91-93; complaints of army control by (1862), V: 494-95, 510n, VI: 117n; success (1862) in Ill. election, VI: 100n; and Vallandigham arrest, 237n, 267-68, 300n; and the draft, 331n; and the Thirteenth Amendment, VII: 172n, 501n; national convention (1864), 459-61, 506, VIII: 123n; estimated electoral vote (1864), VIII: 46; *see also* Douglas, Stephen Arnold; Van Buren, Martin; Cass, Lewis; *and* Pierce, Franklin

Dempster, John, V: 419n

Denio, Cyrenius B., III: 58; VII: 401

Denio, Walter S., IV: 301, 305

Denison, Andrew Woods, VIII: 411n

Denison, George, IV: 296, 307, 334, 371, 373-74

Denison, George S., V: 487-88; VII: 114n, 124, 420, 486n

Denman & Company (Phila.), I: 188

Denmark, IV: 447; V: 162, 521; VI: 69n; VII: 37

Dennett, Tyler, see *Lincoln and the Civil War in the Diaries and Letters of John Hay*

Dennis, Edgar Whetten, VII: 496n

Dennis, George R., V: 409n

Dennis, James Shepard, I: 332n

Dennison, Charles Wheeler, IV: 413

Dennison, Erasmus, VI: 144

Dennison, George, *see* Denison, George

Dennison, William, IV: 186-87, 333, 410, 451n, 550; V: 155n, 183n, 495; VI: 144n; VII: 381n, 411-12, 517n, 524n; VIII: 20, 25, 99, 145, 261-62, 323, 330

Dennison, Mrs. William, VIII: 20n

Denny, ———, II: 72, 190, 207-208

Denny, Arthur Armstrong, IV: 308-309

Denny, Christopher C., IV: 535

Denny, John E., I: 249; II: 188, 424-25

Denny, Thomas, II: 198

Denver, James William, IV: 418, 502n; V: 71, 168, 180

Denver (Colo. Terr.), IV: 294-95; V: 526; VII: 322n

Denver Mint, V: 256, 516n

Depew, Chauncey Mitchell, VI: 224n

D'Epineuil, Lionel J., V: 132n

DePuy, Henry W., IV: 348; VI: 21, 246, 355-56; VII: 371

Derby & Miller, II: 388n

Derickson, David V., V: 484-85

Derringer, ———, V: 129

Derringer, Mrs., see Dessinger, Mrs.

Derrom, Andrew, VI: 295

Description of Ancient Marbles, VI: 10n

Deserters, V: 322n, 491; VI: 97n, 132-33, 232, 244, 248n, 249n, 264, 266-67, 280n, 293n, 295-96, 304-305, 313, 335n, 336n, 360n, 384, 400, 414n, 441, 451, 466n, 471n, 472, 475, 478n, 491-92, 504, 506-507, 510, 519, 548, 550, 561

VII: 14, 25, 28-29, 32-34, 89, 96, 98-99, 104, 106, 129n, 133n, 137, 140, 143, 153n, 158, 172-73, 175-76, 182, 185, 196, 206n, 208, 211n, 251, 261, 271, 277-78, 280n, 297n, 301, 305-307, 309, 320-23, 325, 328, 344, 378, 385n, 416, 425, 438n, 453n, 460, 465,

470n, 479n, 520, 525n, 540n, 543n, 545-46
VIII: 36-37, 88-89, 106, 112, 117n, 120-21, 135-36, 159n, 176, 189-90, 192n, 203, 212-14, 219n, 224, 229n, 232n, 233, 235n, 238, 243, 249n, 252-53, 255, 263n, 273n, 297n, 306, 315, 349-50, 366-68, 377n, 405n
Deshler, James, VI: 480
Des Moines (Iowa) Capital, VIII: 99n
Dessinger, Mrs., VII: 390
Detrich, John E., II: 296; VI: 198
Detroit (Mich.), V: 369
Detroit Daily Advertiser, II: 361n
Develin, Bernard, VII: 157
Devens, Charles, V: 15, 174; VII: 294
Devin, Michael L., II: 119
Devin, Thomas Casimer, V: 397n, 398; VII: 158; VIII: 380-81
DeVoss, Lewis, VI: 544
Dew, Francis, VI: 335n
Dewees, Samuel B., I: 2
Dewey, ———, IV: 499
Dewey, William F., VIII: 35
Dewing, Thomas S., VIII: 225n
DeWitt, David Porter, IV: 507n
DeWitt, Samson, III: 374
DeWitt, William C., VII: 538n
DeWitt County Republican [Clinton, Ill.], II: 381n
Dexter, George T., VII: 133n
Dezeyk, Albert J., IV: 510n
Diary and Correspondence of Salmon P. Chase, V: 337n, 338-39, 407n
Dias, José Bente [alias Joseph Bent], VIII: 298n
Dick, Franklin A., VI: 8n, 20n, 66n, 327n, 501-502; VII: 85-86, 178
Dick, Henry, I: 52
Dicke, L. E., IV: 460n; V: 257n, 376n; VII: 119n, 196n
Dickerman, Mrs. H. S., IV: 87n
Dickey, Charles, VI: 119-20

Dickey, Hugh Thompson, II: 162, 535n; III: 384-85
Dickey, John, I: 2; VI: 172
Dickey, Oliver J., VI: 172
Dickey, Theophilus Lyle, V: 457
Dickey, William, I: 2
Dickinson, B. F., see Dickinson, David
Dickinson, Daniel Stevens, II: 535; IV: 555; V: 7, 411; VI: 150, 152n, 239n; VII: 413n
Dickinson, David, I: 20, 24, 360
Dickinson, J. Nevin, IV: 309
Dickinson, John, III: 531n, 546n
Dickinson, Joseph, VI: 93n
Dickson, ———, VIII: 319
Dickson, A. C., VII: 216n, 236n
Dickson, Annie M. (Parker), III: 491n; IV: 72-73, 77
Dickson, Archimedes C., II: 341-42
Dickson, Cyrus, VII: 454n
Dickson, John, VII: 202
Dickson, John, see Dixon, John
Dickson, Jonathan Bates, VIII: 23n, 182-83, 212
Dickson, William, II: 107
Dickson, William M., III: 490-91; IV: 72-73, 76-77; VIII: 342
Dickson, Mrs. William M., see Dickson, Annie M.
Dickson & Zane (Philadelphia), VII: 236n
Dickson County (Tenn.), VIII: 69
Dictionary of American Biography, II: 30n; IV: 273n, 281n; VI: 108n; VIII: 374n
Dictionary of the United States Congress (Lanman), II: 459n; IV: 74n
Dieffendorf, Oliver, II: 18
Diego Paredes, Victoriano de, VI: 57
Diehl, Israel S., IV: 481n
Dienkhard, Charles B., IV: 309
Diggins, Wesley, II: 297, 303
Diggs, ———, VI: 216
Dignowity [Dignowitz], Anthony M., IV: 503

Dill, John S., IV: 309
Diller, Isaac Roland, V: 354, 385; VI: 3-5, 59, 163, 342-43, 367, 521, 530, 559-61; VII: 3-4
Diller, Jonathan Roland, I: 343, 444-45; II: 39
Diller, William H., II: 391n
Dillingham, ———, II: 336-37
Dillon, James, VI: 385n, 485n, 488-89
Dillon, John M. [alias], see Cox, Lewis H.
Dimick, Justin, VII: 544n
Dimick, Mrs. Justin, VII: 544
Dimitry, Alexander, V: 190
Dimmick, Kimball H., IV: 305
Dimmick, Milo Melankthon, VII: 393-94
Dines, Mary ("Aunt Mary"), V: 492
Dingee, S[olomon], & Company (N. Y.), V: 189n, 196-97
Dingman, A., VI: 285
Dinsmore, Richard, VIII: 131
Dinwiddie Court House (Va.), VIII: 377n, 379n
Diplomatic appointments:
    Consuls, IV: 278, 284, 298, 300, 302-303, 310, 312-13, 348, 362, 396-97, 418, 445-47, 460, 466, 471, 475, 478, 481, 483, 490-91, 493-94, 498, 504, 509, 514-15, 527-28, 536-38, 540, 553; V: 6-8, 12-13, 27, 32, 56, 62, 76, 85, 102-103, 114, 158; VI: 70, 167, 195, 507; VII: 370-72, 375, 403; VIII: 195-96, 247, 337, 360
    Ministers, IV: 280-83, 292-93, 310, 358-59, 521, 555; V: 96, 100n, 368, 383, 425n; VI: 104n, 269n; VIII: 232, 239-40, 307-308, 346
    Consular pupils, VI: 19n, VII: 407, VIII: 132; others, IV: 310, 311, 521, V: 73, 138, 187, 451, VI: 51, 77, 134, 170, VIII: 343
    Operation of consular system, VI: 76, VII: 39-40, VIII: 331-32;

arrest of U.S. consul to Montreal, VII: 187-88
Disciples of Christ ("Campbellites"), I: 320
Discourse on the Bottle—Its Evils, and the Remedy ..., A (pamphlet), II: 188n
Discoveries and inventions, L.'s lectures on, II: 437-42; III: 356-63
Disney, Mrs., V: 449
District of Columbia: abolition of slavery, (L. on) I: 74-76, II: 20-22, 243, 259-60, III: 40-42, 96, 123, 127, 255, IV: 104-108, 152, 172n, 183, V: 169, 192, 195-96, 370n, 418-19, VI: 62, (Douglas on) III: 4-5, 33, 105, 258; abolition of slave trade, II: 253-54, III: 225; mention of cases brought before District courts, II: 382n, V: 352n, VI: 106-107, 195n, 361, VII: 80n; appointments, IV: 319, 323, 334-35, 522, V: 72, 150, 205, 348, VI: 22n, 167n, 284, VII: 270-71, 408; complaints against arbitrary arrests, IV: 372n; mention of penitentiary in, 555n; suggested raising of regiments in, V: 15, VI: 212n; L. recommends restoring original boundaries, V: 45; L. asks Congress to consider claims of citizens of, 47; economic value of slaves in, 153, 160; L.'s objections to repeal of bill prohibiting circulation of bank notes under five dollars, 282-83; ratio of free colored persons to whites in, 535; reorganization of courts in, VI: 284; report on appropriation for colonization of District Negroes, VII: 417n; L. serenaded by Maryland residents of, VIII: 52-53; mention of District's Supreme Court justices, 126n, 160n; L. asks for Congressional support of "the benevolent in-

stitutions" of, 147; *see also* Washington (D.C.)

Ditlow, Reuben A., VII: 491

Dittenhoefer, Abraham Jesse, VIII: 212n

Divine, Joseph, VIII: 68

Dix, Dorothea Lynde, V: 206, 259n; VI: 41n

Dix, John Adams: and appointments, IV: 384n; appointed Major General of Volunteers (1861), 384n, 407, 463, VIII: 593n; recommends organization of an East Md. military force, IV: 508; assignment of officers to, 527n, VI: 490n; and spy cases, V: 8n, VIII: 226; courts-martial and military arrests, V: 163n, 285n, VI: 295n, VII: 163, 182, 213, 298, 306, 328n, 375, 513n, VIII: 13n, 85, 87-88, 216n, 251n, 253n; and report of a Baltimore secessionist plan (May '62) to attack Washington, V: 221; and the advancement to him of public money for defense of the government (Apr. '61), 242-43; assigned to command at Fort Monroe, 255, 272-73; and action on the Eastern front (June '62), 289, 294-96; and McClellan's request for reinforcements (July '62), 301-302, 304-305; pass issued by, 354; difficulties in maintaining Williamsburg insane asylum on evacuation of Union troops (Aug. '62), 387n; assignment of brigades to (Sept. '62), 405n; and election of a Congressman from loyal Va. district, 476-77, VI: 26; reports on enemy troop locations (Nov. '62), V: 499; asks recognition of loyalty of Accomac and Northampton counties in Eastern Va., 502, VI: 401; assignment of Busteed to a command at Yorktown, VI: 14-15; defines parts of Va. to be exempted

by Emancipation Proclamation, 30n, 187; relays reports in Richmond papers to L. (Jan., May, June '63), 43, 83-84, 198-99, 210, 252, 254; and expediency of using colored troops to garrison Fort Monroe and Yorktown (Jan. '63), 56; reports on movements of ironclads at Hampton Roads (Jan. '63), 84; and threat of enemy invasion of Md. (May-June '63), 207, 250n, 258n, 270n, 277n, 293; and mission of Confederate peace emissary Stephens, 316n; assigned to N. Y. to control opposition to draft, 389-91; and amnesty in Eastern Va. (fall '63), 427n; president of the Union Pacific R.R., 525n, VIII: 39; and the holding of elections in Md., VI: 557; offered N. Y. mayoralty nomination (1863), VII: 5; mentioned as possible presidential candidate (1864), 290n; criticizes L.'s actions in cases of military crime, 328n; ordered to arrest editors and take possession of N. Y. papers publishing purported L. proclamation, 347-50, 513n; position on use of U. S. troops to maintain order in N. Y. elections, VIII: 92n; informed of capture of Ewell and others (Apr. 6 '65), 389n; mentioned also, VIII: 155

"Dixie" (song), VIII: 393

Dixon, Archibald, VII: 281, 283n

Dixon, Elizabeth (Cogswell), VII: 272

Dixon, George C., I: 416-17

Dixon, James, I: 492; IV: 248; V: 339-40, 375n, 376, 385-86; VI: 122-23, 221; VII: 82-83, 272n; VIII: 310n

Dixon, Mrs. James, *see* Dixon, Elizabeth

Dixon, John (Ill.), I: 90, 92, 121

Dixon, John (Private), VII: 546n

Dixon, Noah M., I: 453n
Dixon, William, V: 205
Dixon, William M., *see* Dickson, William M.
Dixon [Dixon's Ferry] (Ill.), I: 10n, 19, 152, 200
Dixon Land Office, V: 541-42
Dixon Telegraph & Herald, I: 474n
Dobbin, George W., IV: 340-41
Dobson, Joseph, I: 11
Doctors, taxation of (Ill.), I: 252
Dodd, H. S., IV: 309
Dodd, William, II: 201
Doddridge County (W. Va.), V: 298
Dodge, Abram R., I: 243-44
Dodge, Grenville Mellen, VII: 117, 129; VIII: 166, 210n, 217-18, 223, 234, 298n, 320n, 343n, 372
Dodge, William Earle, Jr., VIII: 327-28
Dodge, William Sumner, see *Robert Henry Hendershot . . .*
Dodson, B. E., IV: 89
Dodson, Nathan B., III: 396
Dodsworth, ———, VII: 311n
Doheny, Morgan, V: 466
Dole, George Washington, I: 191; II: 83; III: 507-509, 513n, 516-17
Dole, William P., IV: 349, 389, 391, 401, 403-404, 442, 456n, 476-77, 540; V: 46, 89, 102, 104, 107, 189, 307, 315, 346, 397n, 455, 485, 526, 540, 550
   VI: 152-53, 164, 212, 382n; VII: 27, 68-69, 113, 116, 196, 215, 261, 284, 300n, 326n, 341n, 344-45, 407, 501n, 507; VIII: 34n, 220, 322, 339, 347n, 410
Dollins, Achilles D., I: 252
Dollner, Horace, V: 162n
Dominican Republic, *see* Santo Domingo
Don Carlos, William C., II: 429-30
Donahue, Edward J., Jr., VIII: 321

Donaldson, Edward, V: 215; VI: 102
Donavan, Michael, *see* Donovan, Michael
Donaven, John, I: facing 49
Dondero, George, IV: 129n
Donerty, Thomas, *see* Dorerty, Thomas
Doney, Thomas, IV: 89
Doniphan, Alexander W., I: 447-48
Doniphan (Kans.), III: 425n, 497n
Donley, Nellie W., VIII: 76n
Donn, Alfonso, VIII: 381n
Donnell, Richard Spaight, V: 26
Donnelley, Peter, VII: 59n
Donnelly, Charles, VIII: 177n
Donnelly, Dudley, V: 237n
Donnelly, Ignatius, VIII: 358n
Donnelly, Maria A., VI: 128n
Donnelly, Neil, III: 125
Donnohue, D. C., IV: 539
Donovan, Michael, IV: 551
Doolittle, James Rood, III: 538n, 549n; IV: 248, 283, 449, 453, 462n; V: 149, 152n, 224n, 332; VI: 70, 88, 137n, 437n; VII: 84n, 174, 225n, 249n, 265, 317n, 368
Dorchester (Mass.), II: 5n
Dorchester County (Md.), VIII: 48n
Doremus, John Erskine Caldwell, I: 308
Dorerty, Thomas, VII: 341
Dormady, William, I: 224-25, 240
Dorman, William M., I: 305, 352, 370, 445; II: 193
Dorman, Mrs. William M., I: 305n, 370
Dorr, Carl E., V: 72n
Dorrence, Charles B., IV: 309
Dorset, Folsom, I: 286
Dorsett [Dorset], ———, VIII: 363-64
Dorsett, Charles T., VIII: 363-64
Dorsey, Azel Waters, IV: 62
Dorsheimer, Philip, IV: 307, 501n
Doty, Ezra S., VI: 360

Doty, James Doane, IV: 462n; VII: 113
Doty, Peter, II: 205
Doubleday, Abner, IV: 409, 418; VI: 431
Dougherty, Daniel, VII: 397n
Dougherty, James, VIII: 69
Dougherty, John, I: 343; III: 106, 122, 172, 175, 337; VII: 74n
Dougherty, Lewis B., VIII: 311
Doughty, William, I: 154
Douglas, Adele (Cutts) [Mrs. Stephen A.], V: 32; VI: 538n
Douglas, Martha Denny (Martin) [Mrs. Stephen A.], V: 32n
Douglas, Robert Martin, V: 32n
Douglas, Stephen Arnold: his bill for division of Sangamon Co. amended by L., I: 56n, 57n; in Ill. Congressional race with Stuart, 107, 120, 151-52, 154, 184; and the 1840 political campaign, 158n, 159-60, 172-75, 177, 206; L. sees in Washington (Dec. '47), 416, 419; resigns as Representative-elect (1847), 432n; serves on Congressional committee with L., 449n; and the 1852 political campaign, II: 135-57; and the Ill. senatorial election (1855), 306-307; withdraws as candidate for presidential nominee (1856), 343n; L. on comparative ambitions of himself and, 382-83
  Political opponent of L. and his stand on slavery question: (*1854-1855*) II: 232-86, 288, 293-94, 322; (*1856*) 341, 347, 352-53, 362-63, 373, 376n, 380; (*1857*) 388n, 398-410, 427-28, 430; (*1858*) 444-554 *passim*, III: 1-325 (L.-Douglas debates), 326, 329, 330-34, 337n, 339-45, VII: 508; (*1859-1860*) III: 349, 351, 366-69, 373, 378-79, 390n, 394-554 *passim*, IV: 4, 7-8, 10, 12, 19, 23, 28, 32, 41-43, 45-47, 58, 67, 82, 84n, 85, 88n, 90, 97-98, 107,

123-24, 134, 150, 152, 154, 155n, 156, 198-200, 205, 208, 216-17, 278n, 327, 493n, VII: 508, VIII: 128-29
  Mention of brother-in-law, IV: 409, VI: 538n; L. advises his widow on children's property in the South, V: 32; his connection with the Chicago *Times*, VI: 251-52; mention of his position on suspension of writ of habeas corpus, VI: 268-69; a tribute to, VII: 484n
Douglas, Stephen Arnold, Jr., V: 32n
Douglas Hospital (Washington?), V: 429
Douglass, Frederick Augustus Washington Bailey, II: 344-45; III: 3, 6, 10, 55-56, 60-61, 105, 138, 171, 175, 263; VII: 508
Douglass, John M., II: 398n, 429
Dover (N. H.), III: 552-54
Dover (Pa.), VIII: 214
Dover Inquirer, III: 554n
Dow, George S. C., VIII: 116n
Do-wan-sa (Indian), V: 542
Dowdy, Rufus, VIII: 68
Down in Tennessee (Gilmore), VII: 429n
Downey, George M., IV: 486n
Downey, James M., VI: 62-63, 65n
Downey, John, VI: 313
Doyle, Joseph, VII: 534n
Doyle, Thomas [alias], see Lennan, John Doyle
Doyle, Thomas A., IV: 365
Doyle, Mrs. Thomas A. [nee Sprague], IV: 365n
Draft (1862-65): proposed, V: 338-39; L. commends order for, 359n; habeas corpus suspended for opponents of, 436-37, VI: 451, VII: 425-26; exemption of aliens, V: 470, VI: 203-204; effect on recruiting, VI: 44, 523-24; form draft order, 239-40; enrollment of Negroes, 298-300; effect of lack of military success

on, 311n; substitutes for, 414-15, VIII: 206, 234-35, 415-16; L.'s opinion on, 444-49; reimbursement of state expenses, 477; draft *vs.* volunteer system, 553-54, VII: 107-108; crediting naval service to, VII: 44-45, 519-20, 534, VIII: 48, 86-87; orders for (Feb.-Dec. '64), VII: 164, 245, 344, 347, 349n, 448-49, VIII: 172; recommended repeal of $300-clause in enrollment act, VII: 380; Grant on importance of (Aug. '64), 499n; exemptions for rejected volunteers, VIII: 168; a complaint against exemption refusal, 194; L.'s memo (Jan. '65) on, 231; order to review and correct quotas, 264-65; cases of exemptions requested by L., 328-29; Stanton stops draft, 409n; mentioned also, V: 355, 366n, 479, VII: 435n, 490n

Troubles in interpretation and enforcement: in N. Y., V: 349, VI: 331n, 361-62, 369-70, 381-82, 388-92, 412-13, 416-17, 419-20, 551-52, VII: 194n, 210-11, VIII: 231-32, 257-58, 262-63, 271-72, 290; in Mass., V: 361n, 384n; in Philadelphia and Pa., V: 362n, VII: 58n, 299-300, 393n, VIII: 29n, 80n, 84-85, 245n, 311-13, 418n; in Del., V: 378-79; in Ky., V: 387n, VI: 298-300, VII: 272; in Minn., V: 396-97; in Ind. and Iowa, V: 469n; in Chicago and Ill., V: 469n, VI: 417-18, 435-36, VIII: 8; in Ohio, VI: 304-305; in N. J., VI: 337-38, 347-48, VII: 523n; in N. H., VI: 352, 355; in Mich., VII: 469n; in Ind., 11-12; in Tenn., VIII: 295n

Drake, Alexander Edwin, V: 22
Drake, Mrs. Alexander Edwin, V: 22
Drake, Charles Daniel, VI: 218, 493n, 499-504, 545n

Drake, John V., II: 430
Drake, Nathan, I: 12
Draper, Simeon, IV: 376; VII: 120n, 126, 298n, 543
Dred Scott case:
  L. on, II: 387-88, 400-409, 449, 452n, 453, 454, 462-67, 475, 494-502, 516-19, 526, 539-41, 548-53; III: 11, 19, 21-24, 27-30, 47-48, 78, 80, 89-90, 92, 95, 97-98, 100-101, 130, 179, 230-33, 250-51, 255, 277-79, 282-83, 298-300, 302, 315-18, 349, 369, 398, 404-405, 413, 417-21, 423-26, 430-31, 434, 449-50, 488, 533, 543-46, 548n; IV: 4, 67n
  Douglas on: II: 398, 400-401, 405, 495-98, 502, 516-19, 526, 539-41, 548-53; III: 9, 69, 112, 114, 143, 166-67, 177, 217, 242-43, 259, 266-70, 284-85, 500
  Mentioned also, II: 343n
Dreer, F. J., VII: 369n
Dresser, Charles, I: 331; II: 121n
Dresser, Nathan, I: 150, 355; III: 521n
"Drifting About"; or, What "Jeems Pipes, of Pipesville," Saw-and-Did (Massett), VII: 34
Driggs, John Fletcher, VIII: 257
Driggs, Leroy C., VII: 202
Driscoll, Emily, VII: 126n, 262n
Drum Beat, The [Brooklyn & Long Island Sanitary Fair], VII: 220n
Drummond, Thomas, I: 214-15, 239; II: 117n, 199
Drury's Creek (Ill.), I: 146
Dry Tortugas Fort (Fla.), *see* Fort Jefferson (Fla.)
Dry Tortugas Islands, IV: 365; VI: 253n, 548n, 561n; VII: 25n, 33n, 104n, 133n, 208, 265, 307n, 317n, 378, 546; VIII: 13n, 37n, 219n, 246n, 263n
Dryden, David, I: 263
Dryden, John D. L., VI: 18n

Dryer, Thomas J., V: 147n, 162; VI: 51n

Dublin (Ireland), Royal College of Surgeons, V: 79n

Dubois, Alexander McKim, II: 198-99; VIII: 593

Dubois, Jesse Kilgore, I: 206-207, 286; II: 345, 360, 393, 410, 414, 429; III: 341, 381-83, 389, 392, 486, 509, 516, 521; IV: 44, 46, 48-50, 132, 136, 168, 288, 302, 303n, 411n, 413n; V: 178n, 425-26, 491n, 548-49; VI: 100n, 117, 237-38, 290n, 319, 323, 382n, 383, 450, 473; VII: 201n; VIII: 110, 422

Dubois, William Archer, IV: 413

DuBose, Dudley McIver, VIII: 389-90

Dubuque (Iowa), II: 224; IV: 126-27

Dubuque & Pacific Railroad, II: 417n

Dubuque County (Iowa), II: 224

Dudley, H. A., IV: 445n

Dudley, Nathan Augustus Monroe, VII: 186n

Dudley, S. D., IV: 445n

Dudley, Thomas H., IV: 466; VI: 121-22; VII: 238

Duell, Robert Holland, V: 187; VI: 426n

Duer, G. Rush, VI: 145n

Duffie, Alfred Nattie, VI: 291-92; VII: 5-6

Duffie, E. [alias], see Lae, Emile

Duffield, Milton H. [P.], VIII: 214n

Duffy, B., & Company, II: 183

Dugan, Mrs. Edward C., II: 395n

Dugan, John, VIII: 233-34

Duggan, Henry, VIII: 68

Dugger, Jefferson L., III: 379, 497n

Dugger, Susan, VII: 257-58

Duke, ———, VI: 154n

Duke, Emily, VI: 154n

Duke, William, VI: 414

Duke's Landing (Md.), VI: 530n

Dulce y Garay, Domingo, VII: 331

Dulin, William Y., VIII: 169

Dumfries (Va.), V: 121n

Dummer, Henry Enoch, I: 20n, 287-88, 330, 350, 392; II: 24, 73, 192, 196, 203, 204, 206-207, 209, 307-308, 309, 327, 432-33, 521, 536; III: 517

Dumont, August P., VIII: 180n

Dumont, Ebenezer, IV: 505; V: 546n; VII: 304

Dunawin, James E., VI: 180

Dunawin, Mrs. James E., VI: 180

Dunbar, Alexander P., I: 73n, 457-58

Dunbar, Fred H., II: 288n, 294n

Duncan, ———, VIII: 213

Duncan, Craven, VIII: 68

Duncan, Henry Timberlake, V: 161

Duncan, James, I: 76-77

Duncan, Jason, I: 18

Duncan, John R., II: 146n

Duncan, Joseph, I: 38, 54-55, 61n, 76-78, 107, 121-22, 149, 166n, 264, 361

Duncan, Mary, VI: 481n

Duncan, Thomas, V: 93-94

Duncan, Mrs. Thomas, V: 93

Duncan, William Garnett, II: 29

Dundee (Scotland), VI: 51n, 58

Dungan, Lemuel, VIII: 68

Dungy, William, III: 492, 494

Dunkirk (N. Y.), IV: 219-20

Dunlap, Adam, I: 14; II: 75, 531

Dunlap, Alva, II: 75

Dunlap, George A., II: 104

Dunlap, George Washington, IV: 464n; V: 458n

Dunlap, James, VI: 44n

Dunlap, James M., II: 104n

Dunlap, James T., I: 342

Dunlap, Lloyd Allen, I: xv

Dunlap, Matthias Lane, II: 297

Dunlap, Robert, II: 111

Dunn, David M., IV: 309

Dunn, William McKee, IV: 539; V: 8, 66; VII: 372

Dunnell, Mark Hill, IV: 284

DuPont, Samuel Francis, V: 127-28, 166-67, 241, 389n; VI: 166n, 170, 173-74, 256n
Durant, Thomas Clark, VI: 518, 525-26; VIII: 89n
Durant, Thomas J., V: 344-45; VI: 365, 368n; VII: 1-2, 90n; VIII: 179
Durbin, John, I: 130
Durell, Edward H., VI: 224n; VII: 420
Durkee, Charles, IV: 248
Durley, John, I: 298
Durley, Madison G., I: 347
Durley, Williamson, I: 347-48
Durrett, Reuben T., IV: 534n

Dusseldorf (Germany), VII: 538
Dutch, Alfred, II: 186
Dutch Gap, VIII: 235n
Dutch Gap Canal, VIII: 3n
Dutton, Arthur Henry, VII: 367
Dutton, M. R., VIII: 338
Dutton, Samuel, I: 11
Duval, Isaac Hardin, VI: 136-37
Duvall, see Dalrymple, Mrs.
Duvall, Amos, IV: 319
Duvall, Charles T. M., V: 183n
Dwight, George, IV: 311
Dyer, E. C., VII: 318
Dyer County (Tenn.), VIII: 69
Dyson, Howard F., I: 210n; III: 352n, 515n; VIII: 427n

E

Eads, James Buchanan, IV: 412n; V: 108n
Eads, Wesley, I: 254
Eagan, William P., VI: 293
Eager, Henry J., VIII: 209-10
Eagle Artillery (Baltimore), IV: 388n
Eagle Brigade (N. Y.), IV: 471n; V: 506n; VI: 41
Earle, Edward S., IV: 499n
Earlham Lodge (N. J.), VII: 535n
Early, Frank L. [S.?], I: 464
Early, Jacob M., I: 10n, 206-207, 298
Early, Jubal Anderson, VI: 273n; VII: 103n, 216, 424n, 434-35, 437-40, 456n, 466n, 548; VIII: 13n, 29, 74n, 188n
Early Engagements: and Florence, (a Sequel) (Hayden), II: 211n
Earnest, Peter L., II: 424-25
East, Edward H., VII: 209-10; VIII: 68

East Burke (Vt.), VIII: 409n
East St. Louis [formerly Illinois-town] (Ill.), II: 212n
Eastep, Abigail (Teter), I: 4n
Eastep, E., I: 15
Eastep, James, I: 3-4, 15, 18-19
Eastep, Mrs. James, see Eastep, Abigail
Eastern Virginia, District of, VII: 416n
Eastham, John, V: 193
Eastham, Marvellous, I: 281
Eastman, Arthur M., VI: 122
Eastman, Harvey G., IV: 39-40
Eastman, Seth, VII: 29-30
Eastman, Zebina, IV: 494, 504
Easton, Charles, VI: 92
Easton, Langdon Cheves, VI: 179
Eastport (gunboat), V: 156n
Eastville (Va.), VII: 356n; VIII: 186n
Eastwood, Joel H., VIII: 120-21
Eathers, A. H., VIII: 69

Eaton, Abel, VII: 93, 96, 106
Eaton, John, Jr., VII: 212n, 492;
VIII: 218, 274
Eaton, Lucien, VIII: 35n
Eaty, S. B., I: 264
Eberhardt, Conrad, VII: 175n
Eberstadt, Charles, V: 433n; VI:
30n
Eberstadt, Edward, & Sons
(N. Y.), VI: 242n
Eccles, Joseph T., II: 113-14, 523,
533
Eckert, George Nicholas, IV: 165n
Eckert, Thomas Thompson, VI:
155n, 225n, 284, 293n, 297n,
491; VII: 101, 104, 137, 150, 152,
155, 157, 163, 171-72, 174, 205-
206, 211, 220, 227, 252, 298, 316,
332n, 346n, 360, 509; VIII: 4-5,
136, 159, 190, 206, 212, 239, 246-
49, 252, 256, 259, 265, 269, 273-
74, 277-84, 297-99, 301-302, 305,
313
Eckley, Ephraim Ralph, VIII: 173
Ecton, John, VIII: 293
Ecuador, IV: 283n; VI: 35-36; VII:
247; VIII: 10
Eddings Point (S. C.), VI: 455-56
Edds, Thomas, VI: 441-43
Eddy, Adelbert S., VI: 211n, 220n,
441
Eddy, Asher Robbins, IV: 538n;
V: 178
Eddy, Henry, I: 203n, 342, 345
Eddy, John, IV: 69
Eddy, John M., IV: 305
Edenton (N. C.), VIII: 396
Edgar County (Ill.), I: 380-81; II:
191
Edgerton, Sidney, VII: 357n, 371-
72, 403
Edinburg (Va.), VI: 203n
Edinburgh (Scotland), VII: 471n
Edmonds, Alexander, II: 219
Edmonds, Charles L., VII: 265
Edmonds, John W., VII: 133
Edmondson, Young C., VIII: 38n,
75

Edmunds, George, Jr., II: 115; III:
332
Edmunds, James M., IV: 325,
442; V: 474n; VI: 96-97; VII:
207n, 217
Edmunds, Newton, VI: 494-95
Edson, Tracy R., IV: 326n
Education: L. on, I: 8, 320, II: 124,
III: 126, 362-63, 479-81, 511, IV:
62, 65, 87; state (Ill.) funds, I:
71; state (Ill.) examinations for
teachers, 213-14; school lands
(Ill.), 461, 478-79; for Negroes,
II: 21, V: 259-60, VI: 365, VII:
55; land grant colleges, VI: 123-
24
Edward VII of Great Britain, see
Albert Edward, Prince of
Wales
Edwards, Abraham, V: 262-63
Edwards, Benjamin Franklin, I:
221
Edwards, Benjamin Stephenson, I:
258-59; II: 113, 160, 188, 212-16,
226, 291-92, 301-303, 309-10,
314; III: 350, 352
Edwards, Cyrus, I: 10n, 221, 233,
242n, 249, 251, 466n; II: 29, 41,
50, 57-59
Edwards, Elizabeth P. (Todd), I:
331; II: 195n
Edwards, George R., V: 81
Edwards, James L., I: 422
Edwards, John W., II: 469
Edwards, Matilda, see Strong,
Matilda (Edwards)
Edwards, Ninian, I: 49n, 259n
Edwards, Ninian Wirt, I: 43, 49,
93n, 121-22, 148, 208, 259n, 285,
288, 298, 308, 331; II: 77, 144,
163-64, 166n, 170-71, 173, 181,
184-85, 188, 194-95, 203-205,
219; III: 350n; IV: 107, 188-89,
412, 492, 562n; V: 175, 488; VI:
238n, 275-76; VIII: 422, 426
Edwards, Mrs. Ninian Wirt, see
Edwards, Elizabeth P.
Edwards, N[inian] W[irt], &

Company (Springfield), I: 491n; II: 188
Edwards, Richard M., VII: 169n
Edwards, Theodore D., IV: 294, 475, 527, 547n; VI: 255n
Edwards, Thomas, I: 93n
Edwards, William, I: 52
Edwards' Ferry (Md.), IV: 560n
Edwards' Station (Miss.), VI: 226
Edwardsville (Ill.), II: 31, 447-48, 523; III: 91-96; VIII: 416n
Effie Afton (steamboat), II: 415n, 417-21
Egbert, Edward B., IV: 131n
Egbert, Milton C., VIII: 204n
Egbert, Mrs. Milton C., VIII: 204-205
Eggleston, Benjamin, IV: 77n, 182
Egypt, IV: 552; VI: 105n; VII: 40; VIII: 139
"Egypt" [southern Ill.], III: 5, 33, 53, 106, 133-36, 140, 176, 214-15, 249, 270, 280, 287
Ehler, John, VII: 294; VIII: 4
Einstein, Max, IV: 386
Eisendrath, Joseph L., Jr., V: 221n
Eisenschiml, Otto, VII: 524n
Ekblaw, Mrs. K. J. T., V: 454n
Elbe River, V: 132n
Elbert, John L., V: 104n
Elbert, Samuel H., V: 182
Elder, Alfred R., VI: 208-209
Eldredge, ———, VI: 93
Eldridge, Joseph, IV: 309
Elections in Illinois (1830-1858): place of holding in Decatur (1830), I: 2; bill on holding in Schuyler Co. (1836), 41-42; illegal voters and election frauds, 151, 212-13; contested Pike Co. election, 157; Springfield election notice, 207-208; opinion on election laws, II: 160, III: 325-26; right of foreigners to vote, II: 355-56
    Forecasts and returns: (*1832-1836*) I: 13-14, 23-26, 48n, 297-99, IV: 64; (*1854*) II: 286-87,

292, 304; (*1856*) 356, 358-60, 374, 381-82, 503; (*1858*) 503-504, 523-24, III: 336-37; (*1860, 1864*) VIII: 46, 128-30, 150, 153
Electors, the purpose of, I: 450-51; IV: 170
Elementary Treatise on Strategy, VI: 81n
Elgin (Ill.), IV: 89n; VI: 194
Eliot, Miss, VIII: 123n
Eliot, Thomas Dawes, VII: 77n; VIII: 323-24
Elizabeth City (N. C.), VIII: 396
Elizabeth City County (Va.), VI: 29
Elizabethtown (Ky.), IV: 56-57, 62, 139n
Elkhorn (Mo.), V: 544n
Elkin, Aaron, VII: 436n
Elkin, Garrett, I: 24, 106-107, 121, 446
Elkin, William F., I: 208, 284-85, 298, 305-306, 446; II: 223-24; VI: 237-38
Ellet, Alfred Washington, V: 490
Ellet, Charles, V: 490n
Elliot, John, VIII: 68
Elliott, Charles, VII: 351n
Elliott, J. W. [S. W.], VIII: 211, 237-38
Elliott, W. P., VII: 502n
Elliott, William, IV: 167
Elliott places (S. C.), VI: 457
Ellis, Abner Yates, II: 39, 64
Ellis, Abraham, IV: 309
Ellis, Edward F. W., VIII: 330n
Ellis, Mrs. Edward F. W., VIII: 330
Ellis place (S. C.), VI: 457
Ellsworth, E. M., VIII: 422n
Ellsworth, Edward Augustus, IV: 479; VIII: 422n
Ellsworth, Elmer Ephraim, IV: 273, 291, 333, 372n, 385-86, 409, 479, 534-35; V: 54n, 192n; VIII: 422
Ellsworth, Ephraim D., IV: 273n, 385-86; V: 192

Ellsworth, Mrs. Ephraim D. *see*
Ellsworth, Phoebe
Ellsworth, Frederick, VII: 133n
Ellsworth, Lewis, V: 394
Ellsworth, Phoebe, IV: 273n, 385-86
Ellwood Township (Vermilion Co., Ill.), VIII: 290n
Elmira (N. Y.), VI: 533n; VII: 227n, 313-14, 406n; VIII: 225n, 368
Elmore, Benjamin, I: 17-18, 47
Elmore, Cyrus, I: 11
Elmore, Frances C., VIII: 6n
Elmore, Julius, I: 18
Elmore, Travice, I: 12, 47
Elmore, William, VIII: 5-6
Elmore, Mrs. William, *see* Elmore, Frances C.
El Salvador [San Salvador], V: 198, 253; VIII: 138
Elwood (Kans.), III: 425n, 495-97, 506
Elwood Free Press, III: 497n
Ely, Alfred, IV: 469n; V: 216n; VII: 446n
Ely, Alfred Brewster, V: 69n
Ely's Ford, V: 366n; VI: 190n
Emack, ———, V: 221n
Emancipation: L. on a gradual system of, II: 131, 255-56, 260, 278, 318, 404, III: 256, IV: 11, 21 (*see also* Colonization of Negroes); Frémont proclamation (Aug. '61), IV: 506-507, 517-18, 520, 531-32, VII: 281-82; L.'s recommendations to Congress, V: 144-46, 324-25, 527-37; opposition to L.'s policies on, 152-53, 160-61, 388-89, 545n; revocation of Hunter order, 219, 222-26; Quaker support of, 278-79, VI: 40n
  Texts of 1862 proclamations, V: 336-38, 341-42, 433-36, VI: 23-26, 28-31; comments on and references to 1862 proclamations, V: 356n, 357, 404n, 419-25, 428n, 431n, 438-39, 441,

444, 471, 476-77, 503-504, VI: 48-49, 54n, 56, 73, 89n, 120n, 186-87, 192, 372n, 374, 407-409, 411, 423, 428-29, 440-41, 539-40, 546, VII: 49-52, 66, 75n, 76-77, 81, 135, 381n, 411n, 507, VIII: 152, 254, 286n, 318n; establishment of Freedmen's Bureau, VII: 76-77, VIII: 274; emancipation in Russia suggested as lecture topic, VII: 93; a review of L.'s views on, 281-82, 499-500
  In Ark., V: 500, VI: 358; in border states in general, V: 317-19, 545n; in Del., V: 29-31; in D. C., *see under* District of Columbia; in Ky., V: 503-504, 512n, VI: 42n; in Md., VII: 49, 226-27, 251, 277, 543n, VIII: 41-42, 52-53, 84, 113-14; in Mo., V: 497n, VI: 52n, 54n, 210n, 289n, 291, 345n, 358, 499n, VII: 141, 145; in La., V: 343n, 462-63, VI: 365, VII: 1, 124n, VIII: 106-107, 179, 402-406; in Tenn., VI: 440-41, VIII: 216-17; in W. Va., VI: 181n; in the U. S., *see* Thirteenth Amendment to the Constitution
"Emancipation March," VI: 78
Embarrass River (Ill.), I: 86
Emberet, John R. H., VII: 522n
Emboy, ———, VII: 309n
Embree, Elisha, II: 51, 63
Emerick, Christian, VIII: 326n
Emerson, Charles, I: 129; III: 350; IV: 73
Emery, Harvard B., VII: 128n
Emery, Woodward, VIII: 326n
Emmons, F. W., VIII: 118n
Emmons, Sylvester, I: 355n; II: 72-73
Emory, James S., VII: 220
Emory, William Helmsley, II: 23; IV: 409; VIII: 301n
Emory, William Helmsley, Jr., V: 388

Enfield rifles, IV: 399n; V: 197n
Engelmann, ———, V: 476n
England, see Great Britain
Engle, John Beard, VII: 235
Englewood Soldiers' Memorial Association, IV: 126n
English, Duval, VIII: 310n
English, James Edward, VII: 138-39
English, John B., VII: 227-28; VIII: 310-11
English, Revel W., I: 301n
English, S. S., VII: 227-28
English, William Hayden, II: 445; III: 210, 290-91
English Bill, II: 445, 447, 510; III: 43, 87, 97, 101, 128, 208-11, 290-92
Enloe, Benjamin S., I: 76-77
Ennis, John F., VII: 318
Enos, Albert Gallatin, IV: 336
Enos, Pascal Paoli, Jr., I: 398, 405; II: 424-25; VI: 238n
Enos, Zimri Allen, I: 491; III: 372
"Enquirer" [pseud.], V: 353n
"Enquiry, The" (poem), VIII: 423n
Episcopalians, I: 320; VIII: 405n
Epperson, Thomas, I: 100-101
Eppes, William D., VIII: 68
Equality (Ill.), II: 106n
Equality of men, see Liberty, equality, and civil rights, L. on
Erie (Pa.), IV: 219; V: 81n; VIII: 41
Erie (slave ship), V: 47n
Erie Canal, V: 270
Erie Gazette, IV: 219n
Ernenwine, Charles, IV: 553
Erskine, ———, VI: 420
Erwin, John, I: 11
Escambia Bay, VIII: 94
"Escape of Lee's Army, The" (art.), VI: 341n
Esher, Linden B., VIII: 37n
Eshrick, Joseph, II: 396n
Essett, Russell, IV: 166

Essex Institute (Salem, Mass.), VII: 63n
Este, William Miller, IV: 462n
Estill, Clifton F., VII: 34
Estrays, I: 3, 8, 27-28
E-tay-hoo-tay (Indian), V: 542
Etheridge, Emerson, IV: 111n, 295, 395-96; V: 489-90; VIII: 58-72
Ethiopian Serenaders, I: 495
Eubank, John L., IV: 330
Eugénie, Empress of the French, V: 130n
Eulogies delivered by L. on: Benjamin Ferguson, I: 268-69; Zachary Taylor, II: 82-91; Henry Clay, 121-32; Van Buren, V: 340-41
Eureka [formerly Walnut Grove] (Ill.), I: 355n
Eustace, John V., VI: 197
Eustis, George, Jr., V: 64n
Eutaw House (Baltimore), VII: 376n
Evans, Alexander, I: 497; IV: 354n
Evans, Andrew Wallace, IV: 354
Evans, Charles, IV: 509n
Evans, Daniel, V: 56n
Evans, Mrs. E. M., VII: 354
Evans, E. P., VII: 28-29
Evans, Elwood, IV: 509n; V: 467; VII: 188
Evans, French S., IV: 328, 356-57
Evans, George, II: 46
Evans, Isaac W., II: 206n
Evans, James, I: 14
Evans, John, IV: 550n; V: 173-74; VII: 70, 530n; VIII; 356
Evans, Rachel S., VI: 375
Evans, Samuel M., VIII: 411n
Evans, Thomas, III: 340n
Evans, Wash, VIII: 68
Evans, William J. [alias], see Evers, William T.
Evans, Willis F., VII: 446n
Evansport (Va.), V: 120n
Evansville (Ind.), IV: 131n, 533, 541, 545; VI: 531
Evarts, William Maxwell, V: 241

Evening Mirror (Willis'), I: 377n
Everett, ———, I: 283
Everett, Edward, IV: 54n, 137n; V: 26, 437-38; VII: 18n, 21, 24-25, 167-68, 396n; VIII: 79-80, 236
Everly, William, I: 84
Evers, William T. [alias William J. Evans], VI: 496; VII: 307n
Everson, Alfred, VIII: 111
Ewell, Leczinska Campbell (Brown), VIII: 372
Ewell, Richard Stoddert, V: 230n, 232-33, 235, 237, 245-47, 250n, 252, 254, 280n, 287; VI: 273-74, 280n, 282n, 293n, 450n, 468n, 510, 518, 534-35; VII: 438n; VIII: 389-92
Ewell, Mrs. Richard Stoddert, *see* Ewell, Leczinska Campbell
Ewing, Henry, I: 2

Ewing, Hugh, VII: 511-12, 519n, 535n
Ewing, Robert M., II: 381
Ewing, Thomas, II: 31, 39-42, 44-47, 50-52, 55-58, 61, 65-68; 78; IV: 137n; VI: 67; VII: 342-43
Ewing, Thomas, Jr., VI: 67n, 334-35, 415n, 423n
Ewing, William Lee Davidson, I: 84n, 127, 143, 211, 235-36, 314, 336
Ewing, William Pinckney, IV: 304
"Excelsior Regiments," VI: 561n
Executive Letter Book (1854-1866) [Md.], IV: 341n
Executive Power (Curtis), V: 544n
Exeter (N. H.), III: 554-55; IV: 31
Extradition, VII: 370n; VIII: 166-67

F

Fabronius, D. C., VIII: 192n
Fagan, George, I: 206-207
Fagan, John, I: 206-207
Fagan, William, I: 206-207
Fair Oaks, battle of, V: 255n, 429, 446n, 471n; VI: 82n, 236n
Fairbairn, Frank, VIII: 159
Fairbanks, Erastus, V: 67
Fairchild, Lucius, VI: 528
Fairchild, T. S., I: 343
Fairfax County (Va.), VIII: 169
Fairfax Station (Va.), V: 121n, 401n, 402n; VI: 129, 280n
Fairfield, William B., V: 95n
Fairfield (Md.), VI: 318
Fairleigh, Thomas B., VIII: 159, 190

Falcón, Juan Crisóstomo [José], VIII: 137n
Faline, John [alias Geacinto Lerchize], VI: 414-15
Falls Church (Va.), IV: 450n
Falls Village (Conn.), VI: 484-85
Falmouth (Mass.), VIII: 77n
Falmouth (Va.), V: 235n, 240, 366, 395, 397-98, 511; VI: 5n, 165; VII: 249n
Falmouth (slave ship), V: 47n
Falstaff, Sir John, I: 118; VI: 392-93, 559n
Faneuil Hall (Boston), IV: 319n
Faris-el-Hakim, IV: 552; V: 229
Farleigh, Thomas B., *see* Fairleigh, Thomas B.

Farleigh, William, IV: 56
Farley, Frederick A., VII: 278
Farmer, Lewis W., I: 11
"Farmington" (Speed plantation), I: 259
Farmville (Va.), VIII: 390
Farnham, H. N., IV: 309
Farni, Christian, III: 381n
Farni, Peter, III: 381n
Farnsworth, Addison, V: 321
Farnsworth, Hiram W., V: 218; VII: 407
Farnsworth, John Franklin, III: 10, 55, 61, 133, 140, 174, 176, 241; V: 321, 410n, 539-40; VII: 327; VIII: 102
Farragut, David Glasgow, V: 214-15, 495; VII: 489n, 532-33; VIII: 93-94, 103-104, 164
Farrar, Lysander, V: 216n
Farrell, Charles H., IV: 408
Farrington, James, V: 351
Farwell, Charles Benjamin, VI: 460
Farwell, Nathan Allen, VIII: 306n
Farwell, Willard B., IV: 301n
Fauchet, Joseph, V: 547-48
Faulkner, Charles James, Sr., VII: 445-46; VIII: 205n
Faulkner, Mrs. Charles James, Sr., see Faulkner, Mary
Faulkner, Elisha Boyd, VIII: 205
Faulkner, Mary (Boyd), VII: 446n; VIII: 205
Fauquier County (Va.), VI: 442n
Fawcett, George E., VI: 78
Faxon, William, VII: 87n
Fay, Herbert W., see Fay, Horace W.
Fay, Herbert Wells, I: 453n, 464n; II: 73, 206n; IV: 555n; V: 176n; VI: 193n; VII: 491n; VIII: 313n
Fay, Horace W., II: 292
Fayette County (Ill.), I: 142, 149-50
Fayette County (Ky.), II: 195, 203-205
Fayette County (Tenn.), VIII: 70
Fayette County (W. Va.), V: 298

Fayetteville (Ark.), VIII: 94
Feaman, George, IV: 319
Fechhemmer, Marcus, III: 521
Federalist, The, III: 524n
Feeley, Stephen V., IV: 248n
Felipe, Ramón María, V: 392; VIII: 54
"Felix, Dr.," see Regnier, Felix
Fell, Jesse Wilson, I: 120, 454-55; III: 376, 511-12, 514; IV: 126; V: 78-79, 175; VI: 113
Fellows, Hart, II: 62
Fellows, John Quincy Adams, VII: 186n, 243n
Fellows, Mrs. John Quincy Adams, VII: 186-87
Felsinger, George, VI: 296n
Felts, Joseph B., IV: 123n
Fendall, Mary L., VI: 353
Fendall, P. R., VI: 353
Fendall, Mrs. P. R., see Fendall, Mary L.
Fendon place (S. C.), VI: 456
Fenn, Benjamin, IV: 309
Fenn, Ira I., I: 52
Fenno, Isaac, IV: 179
Fenton, Alonzo, VI: 127n
Fenton, Charles Davis [David], VII: 470n, 474
Fenton, Ellen, VII: 470n
Fenton, James W., VI: 127n
Fenton, Reuben Eaton, VIII: 231-32, 257n
Fenton, Sallie A., VI: 39-40
Fentress County (Tenn.), VIII: 68
Feran, Thomas, V: 89
Ferguson, ———, V: 180
Ferguson, B. W., IV: 542
Ferguson, Benjamin, I: 268-69
Ferguson, Colin Bannatyne, VI: 197n, 271
Ferguson, John, I: 4
Ferguson, Richard L., VIII: 203
Ferguson, Robert, II: 110
Ferguson, William I., II: 115-16
Fernandina (Fla.), V: 167; VIII: 115, 140, 185, 396
Fernando (Infante of Portugal), V: 104-105

Ferree, James J., II: 470
Ferrero, Edward, VI: 75n
Ferrill, William, VI: 544
Ferriss gun, V: 99n
Ferry, Orris Sanford, V: 142
Ferry, Thomas White, VII: 469; VIII: 367n
Ferry, William, see Firey, William
Ferry, William H., IV: 272n
Ferry, William M., VIII: 367n
Ferry, William M., II, VIII: 367n
Fessenden, Cortes, II: 424-25
Fessenden, Francis, VII: 422n, 423n
Fessenden, Samuel Clement, IV: 110
Fessenden, William Pitt: his brother a candidate for Congress (1860), IV: 110n; and Congressional legislation on fugitive slaves, 157n; and appointments, 248, 284, VI: 102n, VII: 454, 496n, 497, VIII: 7-8, 117, 168, 184, 269; and northeastern coastal defenses, VI: 320n; and the accrediting of duly elected members of the House, 547-48; pardon requests, 548n, VII: 67, 276, VIII: 45n; appointment to L.'s cabinet (1864), VII: 420n, 422-23; absence from Washington, 471, VIII: 50; L.'s approval of Treasury regulations, VII: 471-72, VIII: 175-76; authorization for crediting funds to State Department, VII: 489; recommends export privileges for Newport, Vt., 504; and proposal to send peace commission to Richmond (Aug. '64), 518n; cotton permits and trade with insurrectionary states, 527, VIII: 20-22, 31, 35, 93n, 115, 185-86, 199, 209-10, 221, 243-44, 305-306, 330, 335-36, 339-42; persons referred by L. for an audience with, VIII: 38, 88, 110, 113, 310; withholds clearance for Amer-ican-built Japanese gunboats, 45n; annual report (1864), 142-43; nomination of his successor as Sec. of the Treasury, 408n; mentioned also, VIII: 194
Few, William, III: 524, 527, 530
Few Letters and Speeches of the Late Civil War, A (Belmont), V: 351n
Fick, Henry W., VII: 267
Ficklin, Orlando Bell, I: 179, 185n, 195, 327, 389; II: 389n; III: 182-83, 319; VII: 455
Field, Mrs. [nee Peters], VII: 369
Field, Alexander Pope, I: 149-50
Field, Ben, V: 472-73; VI: 420
Field, Charles William, VIII: 292n
Field, Christopher F., VII: 146-47
Field, David Dudley, IV: 325; VI: 84n
Field, George, & Company (Peoria, Ill.), IV: 137
Field, George W., VII: 450n
Field, Maunsell B., VII: 412-14
Field, R. H., I: 447
Field, Stephen Johnson, VI: 113n, 290; VII: 404
Fields, Henry, VI: 533n
Fiery, Lewis P., IV: 494n
Fifield, Benjamin F., V: 401n
Fifth Avenue Hotel (N. Y.), VI: 323, 327, 471, 474, 478; VII: 401; VIII: 409n
"Fifty-Four Forty or Fight," IV: 66
Fifty Years Observation of Men and Events (Keyes), IV: 320n
Figaniere é Moraô, J. C. de, IV: 277; VIII: 296-97
Fighting Politician Major General N. P. Banks (Harrington), VIII: 595n
Figyelmesy, Philip, VIII: 195-96
Filbert, John A., IV: 309
Filisola, Vicente, I: 435n
Filley, Giles F., VI: 34, 37n
Filley, Oliver Dwight, VII: 85-86, 179

Fillmore, George Millard, V: 33n; VI: 222-23

Fillmore, Millard: candidacy for vice president (1848), I: 498, II: 5; and appointments, II: 93n, 103, V: 33, VI: 508n; mention of persons connected with his administration, IV: 57n, 83n, 537n; signature on temperance declaration, 420; and nephew's dismissal from army, VI: 222-23

His presidency and his politics: L. on, (*1852*) II: 136, 145, 151-53; (*1856*) 347-49, 354, 356, 358, 360, 362-63, 365, 368, 372-75, 385; (*1858*) 443, 476-81, 503, III: 38, 85, 227; (*1860*) IV: 71, 93n, 98n. Douglas on, (*1858*) III: 61, 103, 162-63, 169-70

"Finality" [pseud.], II: 227n

Financial affairs of L.: promissory notes, (*given*) I: 13, 16n, 20, 143, 145-46, 420, (*received*) II: 109, 162, 188, 201, 224-25, 307, 313, 323-25, 343-44, 422-23, III: 348, 490n, IV: 188-89, 232; bonds, I: 16-17, 263, II: 76; deposit on road application, I: 25; collections for clients, 153, II: 194-97, 201-205; receipts, I: 210-211, II: 395; purchase·and sale of Coles Co. land, I: 262-63, II: 108-13; pays taxes for client, I: 330; contract to purchase home, 331; underwrites, 405, 420, II: 96, III: 399, IV: 131, 146; contract to lease home, I: 406-407; drafts to wife, 473-74, 495-96; pays wife's bills in Washington, 475; warranty deed for Menard Co. land, II: 13-14; sends money to parents, 15-17; forgets money entrusted to his care, 29-30; patent application fee, 32; buys brick for fence, 79-80; purchase of carpet from St. Louis firm, 120; pays court fees, 192; fee collection, 193, 233-34, 521, IV: 35, V: 118; land for Black Hawk War service, II: 223-24, 319; newspaper subscription payments, 312, III: 385, 391; railroad pass, II: 330; cost of politics, 382, 395, 413, 446, III: 347, 388, 396-97, 400, IV: 32-33, 44, 72-73, 77n, 131; purchase of German newspaper, III: 383; lecture fee, IV: 38; wages as flatboatman, 63-65; sale of furniture (1861), 189; checks by, V: 154, VI: 380, VII: 320; son Robert's college expenses, V: 309; deposits salary warrants; VI: 371, refuses offer of bank stock, VII: 316; personal finances handled by U. S. Treasury, 384-85; requests cost of horse feed, VIII: 123

Financial panic, threats of (1860), IV: 138-39

Finck, William Edward, VI: 300-306

Findley, Joseph R., VIII: 47-48

Fingal (Confederate steamer), VII: 57

Fingle, Peter, VII: 104

Finley, Clement Alexander, V: 129n

Finney, Darwin Abel, IV: 188

Firearms of the Confederacy (Fuller and Stewart), IV: 399n

Firey, William, VII: 134

Fischel, Arnold, V: 69

Fish, Hamilton, IV: 376n

Fish, Mrs. Hamilton, *see* Fish, Julia

Fish, Julia (Kean), VII: 168n

Fishback, William M., III: 338, 342-43, 346; VII: 173n, 189-90, 239, 335n, 399n; VIII: 187n

Fishback, Mrs. William M. [nee Welton], VIII: 187n

Fisher, Alexander, II: 475

Fisher, Archibald, I: 254-57, 371-77

Fisher, Charles H., IV: 98, 101

Fisher, George, V: 194n
Fisher, George Purnell, V: 30n, 319n, 378-79; VI: 167n; VIII: 293
Fisher, Joseph W., VI: 129
Fisher, Sidney George ("Cecil"), see *Kanzas and the Constitution;* and *Law of the Territories*
Fisher, Theodorus, I: 46
Fisher, W. H., VII: 26n
Fisher & Bennett, III: 521
Fishkill (N. Y.), IV: 229
Fisk, Clinton Bowen, V: 411n; VI: 511, 545; VII: 337n; VIII: 300
Fisk, George P., VII: 511n
Fisk University, VII: 542n
Fitch, Graham Newell, III: 538n; V: 14n
Fitch, Harriet V., VII: 225n
Fitch, Thomas, IV: 301
Fithian, William, II: 63, 74, 210, 307; III: 84-85, 202; IV: 95; VI: 2, 197
Fitzgerald, John, II: 294-95
Fitzgerald, Roy G., IV: 411n; VII: 288n
Fitzgerald, Thomas, V: 203
Fitzgibbon, James, VIII: 305
Fitzhugh, Harrison G., III: 372; V: 71
Fitzpatrick, David, VI: 544
Fitzpatrick, John Bernard, IV: 404n
Fitzsimmons, Thomas, III: 527
Five Forks (Va.), VIII: 36n, 380
Flack, Abner, I: 14
Flag, American, IV: 192, 220, 241-42, 244-45, 382-83; VI: 375-76, 382-83
Flagg, George A., IV: 490
Flagg, Willard Cutting, VII: 177
Flagg & Savage, II: 332
Flanders, Alvan, V: 262n, 500n
Flanders, Benjamin Franklin, V: 488n, 505n; VI: 213-14, 223n, 365-66, 368; VII: 1-2, 6-7, 114n, 186n, 243n, 420, 457n; VIII: 157

Flanders, John L., I: 286
Flathead Indian Agency, IV: 308
Fleetwood Academy (Va.), I: 518n
Fleming, Charles E., V: 198-99
Fleming, John, I: xiv
Fleming, John M., VI: 373-74; VII: 321n
Fletcher, Calvin, IV: 539
Fletcher, Job, IV: 109
Fletcher, Samuel F., IV: 309
Fletcher, Thomas Clement, VIII: 308, 319-20, 365n
Fleurville, William ("Billy the Barber"), II: 159; III: 518
Flinn, John, VII: 59n
Flint, Abel, IV: 65
Flint, Charles L., V: 211-12
Flood, William G., I: 138n
Florence, Rowena, V: 552n
Florence (Italy), IV: 310
Florey, David, I: 2
Florida, II: 251; IV: 364-65, 435, 465n; V: 41, 166-67, 222, 298; VI: 108, 245, 363, 474n, 518n; VII: 126, 185; VIII: 242n
Florida (Confederate steamer), VIII: 97, 140n
Florida War, *see* Seminole War
Florville, William, *see* Fleurville, William
Flournoy, Thomas Stanhope, I: 452
Floyd, George P., II: 332-33
Floyd, John Buchanan, IV: 279n; V: 70n, 238n
Floyd, S. C., VII: 213
Fly, Thomas, VI: 544
Flying Quill, The, IV: 524n; VI: 469n; VIII: 422n, 428n
Foegelmeisy, *see* Figyelmesy, Philip
Fogg, ———, VIII: 421
Fogg, Francis B., VII: 541n
Fogg, Mrs. Francis B., *see* Fogg, Mary Middleton
Fogg, George Gilman, IV: 94, 96-97, 99n, 102, 110-11, 135-36
Fogg, Mary Middleton (Rut-

ledge) [Mary McBaldwin], VII: 541n
Folaney, John, see Faline, John
Foley, James, IV: 389
Folger, Frank, IV: 301
Follett, Oran, IV: 78
Follett, Foster & Company, II: 461n; III: 510n, 515; IV: 79-80, 556
Fonda (N. Y.), IV: 223-24
Fondey, William B., II: 77; III: 337
Fonerden, John, VII: 541n
Foochow (China), IV: 310; V: 38n
Food, importance to man, II: 440
Foot, Mary Ann (Hodges), VI: 89
Foot, Samuel A., VI: 247
Foot, Solomon, IV: 248, 299; V: 283, 325, 326; VI: 28, 89, 185, 207n, 549-50; VII: 84n, 187n, 267n; VIII: 426
Foot, Mrs. Solomon, see Foot, Mary Ann
Foote, Andrew Hull, IV: 313-14, 533n; V: 108, 112, 135n, 156, 187n, 299, 352; VII: 199-200
Foote, Henry Stuart, VIII: 216
Foote, Mrs. Henry Stuart, VIII: 216
Foote, John A., VI: 245n
Foote, L. H., IV: 304
Foote, Mary Ann (Hodges), see Foot, Mary Ann
Foote, Solomon, see Foot, Solomon
Forbes, Mary Bowditch, IV: 40n
Forbes, Paul S., VI: 42n, 112n
Forbes, R. B., V: 6
Forbes & Hill case, I: 305
Force, Peter, VII: 318
Force Bill of 1795, V: 338n
Ford, Allen Nicholas, I: 383-84
Ford, George S., IV: 448
Ford, John A., IV: 472
Ford, Peter, IV: 166, 181n
Ford, Robert, VII: 336n
Ford, Samuel, VI: 431-32
Ford, Thomas, I: 294, 336, 346-47, 349; III: 28, 182; IV: 448n
Ford, Thomas H., III: 3

Ford County (Ill.), III: 364
Ford's Theatre (Washington, D. C.), VIII: 413n
Foreign affairs: support of Hungarian freedom (1849, 1852), II: 62, 115-16; pre-inaugural expression of Mexican friendship, IV: 177-78; urgency (Mar. '61) of appointing ministers to England, France, Spain, and Mexico, 281-82; replies to foreign diplomats presenting credentials, 286, 300, 393, V: 17-18, 141-42, 198, VI: 56-58, 548-49, VII: 37, 383, 473, 536-37, VIII: 6-7, 228, 355; Vancouver boundary dispute, IV: 287-88; Seward's complaint of lack of administration foreign policy, 316-18

Spanish interference in Santo Domingo, IV: 316, 318n, 446; European interference in Mexico, 318-19, V: 61, 73-74, 105, 108-109, 230, 234, 257n, 356n, VI: 38-39, 66-67, 90, 105, 355n, VII: 265-66, 359, 365, 394, 411, VIII: 137, 259-60; L. accepts San Marino honorary citizenship, IV: 360

European attitude toward the Civil War, 376-80, 459-60, 462, V: 55, 92, 355, 416, 422, VI: 18n, 64-65, 88-89, 99, 101-102, 126n, 176-77, VII: 36, 49, 473, VIII: 97n, 140, 157-58; U. S. participation in London Industrial Fair, IV: 450-51, V: 47, 77, 88, 97-98; American-British development of northeastern coastal fisheries, IV: 453-54

Opening of Japanese ports to U. S. trade, 468; maltreatment of American missionaries in Egypt, 552, V: 229; the Trent affair, V: 26, 62-64, 82-83, 92, 95-96, 102, 115, 137, 141, 166n; annual reports on, (1861) 35-39, (1862) 319n, 518-21, (1863)

VII: 36-41, 46, 49-50, (*1864*) VIII: 136-41; increasing and extending foreign trade, V: 55-56; foreign damage claims in seizures of vessels, 109-10, VI: 92-93, VII: 37, 188, VIII: 137-38

Difficulties in presenting American citizens to French Court, V: 130; U. S.-New Granada claims commission, 140-41, VIII: 137; Portuguese plan for African cotton culture, V: 141; "the general principles which govern . . . " U. S. foreign relations, 142-43; U. S. claims against Paraguay and Chile, 144, 161, 260, VI: 271-72, VIII: 138; analysis of French railroad system, V: 156-57; foreign systems of revenue and finance, 181

Rebel privateers in foreign ports, 199; order on allegiance of aliens, 334-35; shipment of gunpowder to China prohibited, 430; unofficial European ambassadors, 437-38, VI: 160-61; proposed extension of telegraph to Europe, V: 521, VII: 39, VIII: 138-39, 146; British gift to Library of Congress, VI: 9-10; investigation of Butler seizure of foreign consul's property, 16; U. S. participation in German Agricultural Exhibitions, 51, 206, VII: 140, VIII: 227; construction and delivery of gunboats to Japan, VI: 95-96, VIII: 45, 131-32, 139; the Chinese rebellion, VI: 96, VIII: 139

Conduct and privileges of U.S. navy in foreign ports, VI: 342-43, 348-50, 378-80, VIII: 397-98; exemption of foreigners from military service, VI: 351n; Spanish jurisdiction in Cuban waters, VII: 37; destruction of U. S. embassy in Japan, 39; tax-

ation of incomes of foreign consuls, 41; reciprocity of tonnage and import duties, 72-73; pursuit of hostile Indians across Canadian border, 160; British gratitude for acts of U. S. sea men, 198-99, 311, VIII: 271

Suggested negotiations (Apr. '64) of a foreign loan, VII: 285; Chile-Bolivia boundary dispute, 338-39; revocation of recognition of Belgian consul at St. Louis, 352; extradition without treaty, 370, 399-400; rumors of U. S. recruiting abroad, 415-16; regulation of exports to Canada, 503-504; settlement of U. S., Peru, and Venezuela claims, VIII: 137; survey of San Juan R., 137; rights of transit from Canada through the U. S., 141; commerce with British North American provinces, 208-209; U. S. participation in International Exhibitions in Norway and Portugal, 296-97

See also Diplomatic appointments; *and* Treaties and agreements with foreign powers

Foreign-born: L. on the rights of, I: 151, 181, 337; II: 234, 284-85, 316, 323, 341, 347, 355-56, 406-407, 475, 502-503, 523-24, 536-37; III: 80-81, 202, 328-30, 333, 376-77, 380, 390-91; IV: 78-79, 164; V: 99-101, 106, 334-35, 470; VI: 203-204, 216-17; VII: 38; *see also* Immigration; *and* Naturalization

Foreign intervention and domestic division, L. on, V: 36-37

Foreign sovereigns: formal letters of congratulations or condolence to, IV: 417, 490, 546-47; V: 19, 74-75, 104-105, 117-18, 125-26, 133-34, 199, 363, 393, 440, 448-49, 482-83; VI: 18-19, 45, 91-92, 94-95, 124, 136, 162, 170-71, 182-

83, 212-13, 222, 259-60, 357-58;
VII: 110-11, 165, 231, 283, 296-
97, 336-37, 373, 475-76, 477-79,
493-94, 550-51; VIII: 53, 54, 56-
57
Foren, William, I: 2
Forest Grove Landing (Md.), VI:
530n
Forman, Jacob G., VI: 72n
Forney, John Wein, III: 495; IV:
311, 456; V: 454n; VI: 59n, 62,
118n, 214, 430n; VII: 157, 360n,
468-69, 481n, 525; VIII: 35n,
87n, 204-205, 312n, 314n
Forrest, Dennis, I: 326-27
Forrest, Nathan Bedford, V: 402n;
VI: 214n, 233; VII: 327n, 329n
Forrest Hall Prison, VII: 479n
Forrester, William, IV: 521
Forsha, S. W., V: 444n
Forsyth, Jacob, I: 159n
Forsyth, James William, V: 77n
Forsyth, Robert, II: 315n
Forsythe, John, VI: 51n
Fort Adams (R. I.), VI: 386-87
Fort Albany (Va.), IV: 499n
Fort Beauregard (S. C.), V: 127
Fort Bridger (Utah Terr.), VII:
112
Fort Brown (Tex.), I: 439, 473; II:
84-85
Fort Buchanan (N. M. Terr.), IV:
354n
Fort Clark (Ill.), I: 79
Fort Clark (N. C.), V: 316
Fort Corcoran (Va.), IV: 450n,
458
Fort Darling (Va.), V: 224, 226n
Fort Delaware (Del.), VI: 189,
324n, 422, 452; VII: 89, 309n,
325, 422n, 474, 502n, 527n; VIII:
6n, 103, 160, 292n, 293n, 314n
Fort Donelson (Tenn.), V: 135,
142, 299, 342n, 352, 471n, 486n,
491n; VI: 67n; VII: 322n
Fort Fisher (N. C.), VIII: 187n,
236n, 285
Fort Gaines (Ala.), VII: 532-33

Fort Gibson (Indian Terr.), II: 84
Fort Harrison (Ind.), II: 83-84
Fort Hatteras (N. C.), IV: 525; V:
50, 316
Fort Henry (Tenn.), V: 299, 352,
489; VI: 71n; VII: 322n
Fort Holt (Ky.), IV: 545; V: 87n
Fort Hoskins (Oreg.), I: 466n
Fort Independence (Mass.), VII:
143
Fort Jackson (La.), V: 214, 316
Fort Jefferson (Fla.), IV: 422; VI:
461n; VII: 31n, 307n
Fort Kearney [Kearny] (Nebr.
Terr.), IV: 132
Fort Klamath (Oreg.), VIII: 322
Fort Lafayette (N. Y.), IV: 522n,
534; V: 167n, 193n, 196n; VII:
213, 350n; VIII: 13n, 314n
Fort Laramie (Colo. Terr.), IV:
480n
Fort Leavenworth (Kans.), IV:
132n, 159n; V: 71n, 84-85, 116n,
164n, 180n; VI: 179, 495n; VII:
120n; VIII: 6n
Fort Lincoln (D. C.), IV: 559n
Fort McHenry (Md.), IV: 462;
V: 255; VI: 135, 227, 234n, 323n;
VII: 120, 531
Fort Magruder (Va.), VII: 82
Fort Mifflin (Pa.), VII: 157, 394n;
VIII: 249
Fort Monroe (Va.), see Fortress
Monroe
Fort Morgan (Ala.), VII: 521-22,
532-33; VIII: 422n
Fort Moultrie (S. C.), IV: 158n,
159n
Fort Pickens (Fla.), IV: 285n, 313-
20, 350-51, 366-67, 422, 424,
465n; V: 187
Fort Pillow (Tenn.), V: 263, 316;
VI: 111; VII: 302-303, 328-29,
345-46
Fort Powell (Ala.), VII: 532-33
Fort Preble (Me.), VII: 155
Fort Randall (Dakota Terr.), V:
148n; VI: 134n

Fort St. Philip (La.), V: 214, 316
Fort Scott (Kans.), V: 168n, 456
Fort Scott Land Office, IV: 307
Fort Smith (Ark.), VI: 396n, 495n; VII: 100, 185n, 239, 300n; VIII: 159n, 399n
Fort Snelling (Minn.), III: 544n; VIII: 120, 121n
Fort Stedman (Va.), VIII: 374n, 378n
Fort Stevens (D. C.), VIII: 42-43
Fort Sumter: threats of rebel seizure, IV: 137, 151n, 157-59, 162, 172-73, 175n, 178, 195; chances of holding, 277, 279; possibility of provisioning, 284-85, 289; considerations in favor of withdrawing troops, 288-90; "inexpedient" to release Anderson dispatches to Senate, 299; relief expedition to provision, 301-302, 314n, 316-18, 321-22; conference with Gov. Pickens, 323-24; probable government action in the event of an assault, 330-31; Anderson and Fox commended, 350-51; review in 1861 message, 422-27; references to significance of, V: 49, 241, VIII: 1; failure of naval attack (Apr. '63), VI: 165-67, 170, 173-74, 256n; report of Union reoccupation, 421; plans for 1865 flag-raising, VIII: 375-76; mentioned also, IV: 341, VII: 518n
"Fort Sumter" (art.), IV: 319n
Fort Taylor (Fla.), IV: 422
Fort Townsend (Wash. Terr.), IV: 308
Fort Trumbull (Conn.), VII: 338
Fort Vancouver (Wash. Terr.), VII: 290n
Fort Wagner (S. C.), VI: 339n, 421
Fort Walker (S. C.), V: 127
Fort Warren (Mass.), V: 549n; VII: 180n, 305, 306, 421n, 502n; VIII: 15-16, 185, 292n

Fort Wayne (Ind.), I: 513
Fort Wood (Tenn.), VII: 30n
Fort Wool (Va.), V: 209n
Fortress Monroe (Va.), IV: 343, 367, 371-72, 375-76, 383-84, 386, 388, 413, 457, 478, 525n; V: 59n, 111, 122n, 123n, 124n, 132n, 154n, 157, 164, 174, 192n, 207-10, 255, 259n, 273n, 293n, 294, 298, 302, 304, 309, 322n, 354, 476, 495-96
VI: 56, 84n, 252, 256n, 315n, 329n, 353, 362, 437-38; VII: 7, 59, 64n, 203, 232, 244, 250, 252, 257, 260, 265, 289, 290n, 297, 298, 310, 341, 344, 357, 359, 363, 367, 416, 438, 469-70; VIII: 28n, 34, 161n, 162-63, 167n, 182, 187n, 247, 250, 256, 278-84, 318n, 373n, 380
Fosha, see Forsha, S. W.
Foss, Robert H., II: 297
Fosselman, John B., II: 188
Foster, ———, V: 498n
Foster, A. Lawrence, VI: 513
Foster, Charles H., IV: 504n; V: 377
Foster, Charles Warren, VIII: 264-65
Foster, Corra (Bacon), VIII: 423n
Foster, Dwight, V: 15
Foster, Frances H., III: 340n
Foster, Frank E., IV: 556
Foster, Frederick, VII: 33
Foster, George F., II: 297
Foster, George W., I: 11
Foster, Horace, VIII: 68
Foster, John, VIII: 155-56
Foster, John Gray, VI: 72, 147n, 173n, 184, 362, 371, 389, 419, 483, 505n, 514, 522; VII: 30, 35n, 109, 134, 153-54; VIII: 186-87
Foster, John W., VI: 85n, 87n, 470n
Foster, Lafayette Sabine, IV: 248; V: 375n; VI: 114; VII: 82-83, 114; VIII: 354n
Foster, Lemuel, I: 70
Foster, Robert Sandford, VIII: 384

Foster, Sanford, IV: 418
Foster, Solomon, VI: 184n
Foster, Thomas, IV: 553
Foster, William, I: 12
Fouke, Philip Bond, IV: 477
Foulke, William Dudley, VIII: 11n
Fourth of July, L. on, VI: 319-20
Fowler, Cecil, IV: 124n
Fowler, Edward B., VII: 473
Fowler, Emanuel, IV: 73
Fowler, Moses, IV: 124
Fox, Benjamin Franklin, III: 385
Fox, Gustavus Vasa, IV: 285n,
    314n, 321-22, 350-51, 363, 507;
    V: 154n; VI: 145n, 155, 199n,
    433n; VII: 246, 310, 355, 456;
    VIII: 17, 423
Fox, Philip L., IV: 512-13
Fox, William [alias], see Blit-
    tersdorf, Gustave
Fox Indians, I: 152; V: 189, 307;
    VII: 69-70
Fox River, I: 10
Foy, Peter L., VI: 178
France, I: 175, 177; III: 457, 540n;
    IV: 281, 292, 311, 376-78, 453;
    V: 61, 64n, 82, 96n, 109, 130,
    157n, 257n, 519n, 520, 521; VI:
    38, 51n, 66-67, 355n; VII: 8, 229,
    359n, 411, 446n, 461n; VIII: 45n,
    240n, 307-308
Francis II, King of the Two Sici-
    lies, VI: 18
Francis, Allen, II: 61, 188; IV: 90
Francis, Calvin, I: 139
Francis, Eliza (Rumsey), IV: 90
Francis, J. Newton, I: 297
Francis, Jacob, II: 182
Francis, Joseph, VII: 221n
Francis, Josiah, I: 139, 153, 208,
    240n, 249, 254, 335; II: 61n,
    319n; IV: 90
Francis, Simeon, I: 89n, 108n, 121,
    139n, 153n, 154, 158, 206-208,
    210n, 264n, 292n, 299, 300, 351;
    II: 61, 62n, 64-65, 67, 93, 188,
    319n; IV: 89-90; V: 163n
Francis, Mrs. Simeon, see Francis,
    Eliza

Francis, William H., VII: 543n
Francis, Allen & Stone, I: 335
Francis, Simeon, & Company, I:
    202n
Francis H. Pierpont (Ambler),
    VIII: 392n
Francisco María Isabel Gabriel
    Pedro, Infante of Spain, V: 133
Frank, Paul, VII: 304
Frankfort (Ill.), I: 146
Frankfort (Ky.), IV: 369n; V:
    262n, 296, 370n; VII: 497n;
    VIII: 256
Frankfort (Pa.) Arsenal, VI: 343n,
    531n, 560n
Frankfort (Ky.) Commonwealth,
    VII: 282n, 497n
Franking privilege, I: 449, 465-
    66
Franklin, Benjamin, III: 8, 178,
    531-32
Franklin, Homer, VIII: 350-51
Franklin, John, Sr., III: 347-48
Franklin, Mrs. John, Sr., III: 347
Franklin, Martha W., I: 468n
Franklin, Nelson N., III: 347
Franklin, Wesley P., III: 347
Franklin, William Buel, IV: 382n,
    411n, 484n, 491; V: 175n, 208-
    209, 226, 312, 407n, 448, 481n,
    499n; VI: 15-16, 63, 75n, 77n,
    312n, 366n; VII: 470n, 549
Franklin (La.), VIII: 396
Franklin (Tenn.), VIII: 169n
Franklin (Va.), V: 230-32, 236,
    264, 274, 275n
Franklin County (Ill.), I: 142,
    146, 150n
Franklin County (Ohio), IV: 205
Franklin County (Tenn.), VIII:
    69
Franklin Square (Washington),
    VI: 397-98
Franklin Tavern (Tremont, Ill.),
    I: 154n
Franklin's Crossing (Va.), VI:
    190n
Franks, Herman, V: 258
Franz Josef I [Emperor of Austria-

Hungary], V: 95; VI: 18-19; VII: 475-76
Fraser, Philip, VI: 150n
Frazer, ———, VI: 93n
Frazer, William E., III: 491
Frazier, Mrs. C. W., VIII: 241n
Frazier, Samuel, VI: 198n, 319n
Frederic, Grand Duke of Baden, V: 482-83; VI: 170-71
Frederick VII, King of Denmark, VI: 182-83, 357-58; VII: 111
Frederick, Prince Royal of Prussia, VIII: 56
Frederick (Md.), V: 409n, 412n, 418n, 426, 450; VII: 434n, 472n, 477n, 549; VIII: 82n, 112n, 371n
Frederick Ferdinand, Prince of Denmark, VI: 357
Frederick William, Prince of Hesse, V: 363
Fredericksburg (Va.), V: 195, 226-27, 232-33, 234, 236-37, 240, 245, 254, 276, 284n, 308, 334n, 401n, 461, 514-15, 552n; VI: 13-14, 15, 47n, 81n, 88, 126n, 130, 190n, 196, 197, 207, 249-50, 258n, 273, 291, 354n, 399-400, 535n; VII: 96n, 249n, 357n, 358; VIII: 353n
Fredericksburg & Richmond Railroad, see Richmond & Fredericksburg Railroad
"Free Democracy," III: 106, 175, 215, 220-21
Free Soil Party, I: 347-48; II: 3-14 passim, 156-57
Freedmen's Aid Societies, VII: 76-77; VIII: 321n
Freedmen's Bureau, VIII: 274n, 374n
Freeland, James, VII: 181-82
Freeland, Paul B., VIII: 417n
Freeland's Grove (Sullivan, Ill.), III: 201-202
Freelinghoysen, see Frelinghuysen, Frederick Theodore
Freeman, ———, V: 548-49
Freeman's Ford, battle of, V: 511n
Freeport (Ill.), III: 38-76, 97, 123, 125, 127, 132-34, 142, 171, 179, 227, 230, 234, 260-61, 267, 270, 272, 281, 287, 294-95, 349, 417-18, 449, 514; IV: 107-108
Freer, Joseph W., II: 24n
Freese, Jacob R., VII: 11, 203; VIII: 12, 25-26
Frelinghuysen, Frederick Theodore, VI: 460-61
Frelinghuysen, Theodore, I: 317n, 339
Frémont, Jessie (Benton), IV: 515, 518n, 519-20
Frémont, John Charles: presidential candidate (1856), II: 342-85 passim, IV: 159n; mentioned in 1858 L.-Douglas senatorial race, II: 450, 476-81, 503, III: 227, 265; mentioned in 1860 election, IV: 90, 111; Seward recommends for Sec. of War, 164; L. recommends for minister to France, 281-82; reports Confederate foreign purchase of war steamers, 397n; his command of the Western Department, 420, 457, 465-66, 469, 477, 484-85, 499, 506-507, 510n, 513, 515n, 517-20, 524, 531-34, 545, VI: 501, VII: 281-82; appointed Major General, IV: 463; relinquishment of his command in the West to Hunter, 533, 549-50, 562-63, V: 7, 14n, 65n, 85n; and appointments, V: 107-108, 168, 179n, 193, 262n, VI: 180; given command of the Mountain Department, V: 155, 175-76; Greeley asks for resolution of differences between Stanton and, 169n; in valley campaign (May-June '62), 230-33, 236, 243, 246-52, 254, 258n, 264, 267-75, 280n, 284n, 301; his command reorganized as 1st Army Corps of the Army of Virginia, 287; the question of a new command for (1863), VI: 127, 230-31, 239, 243, 282-83, 383; and

the election of 1864, VII: 268n, VIII: 3; opposition to Montgomery Blair, VIII: 18n
Frémont, Mrs. John Charles, *see* Frémont, Jessie
Frémont, Pathmarker of the West (Nevins), IV: 397n, 515n
French, Augustus Chaplin, I: 393-94, 405-406; II: 75, 77, 94n, 161-87
French, Benjamin Brown, IV: 522n, 542; V: 71, 394, 463; VI: 107, 187, 312-13, 397-98; VII: 197-98, 266-67, 419n; VIII: 98
French, Ezra Bartlett, IV: 452n
French, Matilda C., *see* Gray, Matilda C. (French)
French, Richard, I: 461n
French, Stephen, I: 69
French, Thomas, II: 24
French, William Henry, V: 360; VI: 184, 317-18, 342n; VII: 7
French and Indian War, V: 455n
French Revolution of 1789, II: 123
French Revolutions (1830, 1848), V: 28n
Fretwell, ———, VII: 309n
Fribley, Charles W., IV: 309
Frick, Jacob G., IV: 167
Friend, Henry C., II: 316n
"Friend in the Swamp" (statuette group), VII: 389
Friends, Society of, *see* Quakers
Friends of Union and Liberty, VII: 333
Frink, William Stanton, I: 140-42
Frisby, Miner, Jr., IV: 306
Frogmore (S. C.), VI: 456
Froman, Isaac, I: 249
Front Royal (Va.), V: 232, 235-36, 246-48, 251, 254-55, 258, 264, 268-69, 271, 280, 324n; VI: 309n; VII: 456n; VIII: 94n
Frontier Guard, IV: 345
Frontier State, 1818-1848, The (Pease), I: 344n
Froskett, Joseph, IV: 309
Frost, Emily S., VI: 443
Frost, Norman B., III: 399n

Fry, Benjamin S., VII: 539n
Fry, Cary Harrison, V: 360, 368-69, 380, 385
Fry, James Barnet, IV: 450n; VI: 153n, 197-98, 232n, 298n, 337, 347, 361n, 382, 390n, 413n, 416-17, 417n, 523-24, 551-52, 554n; VII: 16n, 57-58, 77, 107, 194, 207n, 211n, 230, 245, 299-300, 330n, 369, 380n, 457n, 469, 523, 530-31; VIII: 8, 14, 25-26, 40, 48, 72, 123n, 155-56, 172, 238n, 245n, 258, 262-63, 265, 272n, 311n, 328, 416n
Fry, James R., VII: 323-24
Fry, John, IV: 410
Fry, John B., IV: 95
Fry, Nelson, I: 389-90
Fry [Frye], Speed Smith, VI: 97
Fry, William H., V: 333
Fry, William M., VI: 198
Fryers Point (Miss.), VI: 307n
Fugitive slaves, I: 126, 272; II: 21, 157, 227n, 232, 233n, 237-38, 243, 253, 256, 260, 273; III: 4-5, 15-16, 32, 40-41, 56, 59, 79, 105, 107, 123, 131-32, 225, 258, 307-308, 317-18, 334, 384, 386, 390-91, 394, 395n, 435, 460, 496, 498, 514, 553; IV: 93, 150-57 *passim*, 172n, 176n, 183, 216, 251-67 *passim*, 269; V: 224n, 502-503, 512-14, 524n; VI: 72-73, 492; VII: 133n
Fulgham, J. H., VIII: 69
Fuller, Allen C., V: 365n
Fuller, Charles E., VIII: 330
Fuller, Claud E., IV: 399n
Fuller, Clinton, VII: 196
Fuller, Frank, IV: 558
Fuller, George, VII: 92n
Fuller, Henry C., VII: 138
Fuller, Samuel W., II: 481; III: 381
Fuller, William, I: 442-44
Fuller, William Greenleif, VI: 228-29
Fuller, Mrs. William G., VI: 229n
Fuller place (S. C.), VI: 456-57

Fullinwider, Jacob N., III: 519-20
Fulton, Charles C., V: 292-93
Fulton, Edington, VIII: 411n
Fulton (steamboat), VII: 293n
Fulton County (Ill.), I: 90, 92
Fulton County Ledger [Canton, Ill.], IV: 101n
Fulton County Republican [Lewistown, Ill.], II: 289n

Funayma Solace (steamer), VIII: 45n, 131-32
Funk, Isaac, I: 249
Funkhouser, Presley, II: 297
Furlong, Franklin B., VII: 276n; VIII: 45n
Furr, Argyle W., I: 430
Fusigama (steamer), VIII: 45
Fyffe, Edward P., VIII: 173
Fyffe, James, I: 85

G

Gabon (Africa), IV: 310
Gage, George, II: 292-93, 296, 303, 480
Gage, Rodney, VI: 313n
Gaines, Edmund Pendleton, I: 381
Gaines, Erasmus D., V: 152
Gaines, John Pollard, I: 447-48, 458, 460, 515
Gaines' Cross Roads (Va.), VI: 273n
Gaines' Mill, battle of, V: 362n, 454
Gainesville (Va.), V: 399n
Galatza (Moldavia), VI: 507
Galaxy, The (periodical), IV: 319n
Galena (Ill.), I: 192; II: 349n, 353-55; IV: 67
Galena (gunboat), V: 207
Galena Advertiser, II: 356n
Galena and North-Western Gazette, II: 355n, 356n; IV: 67n
Galena Courier, II: 356n
Galena Jeffersonian, II: 303
Gales, Mrs., *see* Galez, Mrs.
Gales, Joseph, II: 24
Gales & Seaton (Washington, D. C.), VIII: 206n
Galesburg (Ill.), III: 207-44, 247,

250-51, 253-54, 262, 277, 281, 301-302, 374
Galez, Mrs., VI: 507
Galishen, Isaac, *see* Gulihur, Isaac
Gallaer, William W., VI: 84-85
Gallagher, Hughey, VI: 466
Gallagher, John [alias Jacob Watson], VI: 466
Gallaher, Benjamin F., V: 101
Gallaher, John S., IV: 359-60
Gallatin (Tenn.), V: 545
Gallatin County (Ill.), II: 106
Galleher, H. L., & Company, II: 183
Galleher, Thomas, & Company, II: 182
Galloway, Andrew Jackson, I: 257
Galloway, Samuel, III: 387n, 393-95; IV: 33-34, 43, 79-80, 94; V: 509; VII: 517n
Gallup, William, V: 197n
Galveston (Tex.), VI: 102n, 366n; VII: 489; VIII: 103, 230-31, 396
Gamage, Samuel, IV: 488, 501-502, 507
Gamble, Hamilton Rowan, IV: 470-71, 495n, 530; V: 12, 15-17, 61n, 347, 411n, 497, 500-501, 515-16, 538, 548n; VI: 9, 10, 21,

23, 36-38, 211n, 234, 291n, 344-45, 489, 499n, 526-28, 546n; VII: 230n
Gamble, James, VIII: 68
Gambrel, James, I: 279
Gammon, William A., VII: 33-34
Gannell, see Grinnell, Henry D.
Gansler, W. H., VIII: 48
Gantt, ———, II: 331
Gantt, Daniel, VII: 264n
Gantt, Edward W., VII: 154-55
Gantt, Thomas Tasker, IV: 498n
Garber, Hezekiah H., I: 466
Garber, Jacob ("Uncle Jakey"), I: 466n; VI: 462n
Garcia, Belle, VI: 479-80
Garcia y Tassara, Gabriel, V: 109
Garcy, Jacob, VI: 335n
Gardiner, Emanuel A., V: 90n, 111n, 148n; VI: 158n, 235n; VII: 357n
Gardiner, George F., V: 211
Gardiner, Michael [alias], see Sullivan, George M.
Gardner, ———, VIII: 36n
Gardner, Awful, IV: 123n
Gardner, Daniel Pierce, IV: 122-23
Gardner, Frank A., IV: 123n
Gardner, Symmes, V: 217, 317n
Gardner, Thomas, IV: 123n
Gardner Memorial; A Biographical and Genealogical Record . . . (Gardner), IV: 123n
Garfield, James Abram, V: 382n; VI: 213, 225n; VII: 333n, 379n
Garland, James Maurice, II: 424-25
Garrard, Israel, VII: 6n
Garrard, Jeptha, V: 390n
Garrard, Mrs. Jeptha, see McLean, Sarah Bella
Garrard, Kenner, V: 390
Garrard, Sarah Bella, see McLean, Sarah Bella
Garretson, Charles, VII: 216-17, 230-31
Garretson, John H., VI: 270
Garretson, William, VII: 216

Garrett, George W., V: 205, 266n
Garrett, John W., VII: 424, 429, 434-35; VIII: 208, 303n
Garrett, Thomas, V: 279n
Garrett, W. W., VIII: 69
Garrison, ———, VI: 236-37
Garrison, Amos F., IV: 473n
Garrison, Andrew Jackson, VIII: 69
Garrison, William Lloyd, II: 344-45; III: 213, 263; VIII: 265-66, 289n
Gartell, see Gartrell, Lucius Jeremiah
Garton, ———, VIII: 417
Gartrell, Lucius Jeremiah, III: 542n
Garvin, Cornelius, VII: 304
Gasparin, Agenor-Etienne, Comte de, V: 83, 352, 355-56
Gaston, Miss, VII: 239
Gates, James C., VII: 89
Gates, William, IV: 509-10; VIII: 106
Gatewood, William Jefferson, I: 61
Gaulden, ———, III: 549n
Gausler, W. H., see Gansler, W. H.
Gay, Sydney H., V: 353, 364; VI: 241n; VII: 349n
Gayle, John, I: 497
Gazzam, Edward D., V: 187n
Gear, see Giers, Jean Joseph
Geary, John White, V: 234, 235, 236, 240, 246, 251n; VI: 441-42, 554; VII: 65
Geary, Thomas, VIII: 411
Geiger, Joseph H., VI: 376n
General Accounting Office, IV: 407n, 528n; V: 394n
"General Grant" (ox), VIII: 96n
General land office, see Public lands
General Regulations for the Purchase of Products of the Insurrectionary States . . ., VIII: 22n
General war orders, see Army Orders; and President's Orders
Geneva (N. Y.), IV: 297n; VI: 508

Genoa (Italy), IV: 445n
Genoa (Nebr. Terr.), VI: 21n
Gentry, Allen, IV: 62n
Gentry, James, IV: 62n
Gentry, Josiah, VIII: 86
Gentry, Matthew, I: 384-85
Gentry, Meredith Poindexter, IV: 173; VII: 242-43
Genuine Autograph Letters from the Most Distinguished Men of Our Country . . ., IV: 123n
George, Samuel (Indian), VII: 27
George III, King of Great Britain, II: 371; III: 324
George V, King of Hanover, V: 58, 131
Georgetown (D. C.), II: 21-22; IV: 364n, 450n; V: 32; VII: 434n
Georgetown (S. C.), VIII: 396
Georgia, I: 48n, 126n; IV: 146; V: 122n, 166-67, 222, 298, 552n; VI: 250n, 256n, 425n, 471n; VII: 58, 425-26, 532-33; VIII: 9n, 10n, 27n, 33, 344n
Georgia Pen (Washington, D. C., slave trade center), II: 237-38, 253
Georgiana (ship), VI: 92
Gerard, George, V: 85
Gere, John A., V: 215-16
Gere, John W., II: 120-21
Gerhard, William, VII: 545
Germania Hills, VI: 190n
Germans: II: 345, 380, 475, 523n, 524; III: 328-29, 377n, 380; IV: 166, 201-203, 367-68, 388, 418n, 476n, 479, 563n; V: 100-101, 106, 419n; VI: 168n, 217n; VIII: 83
Gerolt, Baron von, V: 102
Gerrish, George M., IV: 305
Gerry, Elbridge, III: 523n
Getty, George Washington, VI: 238; VIII: 273
Gettys, James, VIII: 68
Gettysburg (Pa.), V: 409n; VI: 76n, 133n, 293n, 299n, 314, 321, 323n, 324n, 325n, 327-30, 341-42, 353n, 409, 429, 513n, 516,

520, 533n, 544, 557; VII: 34n, 88, 89n, 97n, 158, 273n, 317, 472n; VIII: 236, 311n; *see also* Gettysburg address
Gettysburg address, VII: 7, 15-17, 17-23 (drafts of address), 24-25, 167-68, 212; VIII: 372
Ghent, Treaty of, VI: 268
Ghislin, J. D., Jr., VI: 443
Gibbon, John, VII: 506n
Gibbs, Addison Crandall, VIII: 124
Gibbs, Benjamin, I: 121
Gibbs, Oliver C., VI: 221-22; VII: 190, 204n
Gibbs, Theodore H., VIII: 69
Gibney, William H., VII: 298
Gibson, Augustus Abel, VII: 444n
Gibson, Charles, VII: 224n, 237n, 462-63, 468, 472n; VIII: 243n
Gibson, Ella E., *see* Hobart, Ella E. (Gibson)
Gibson, H. C., I: 359
Gibson, Isaac, II: 101
Gibson, Moses Sidney, V: 224n
Gibson, Robert, IV: 65
Gibson, Samuel C., V: 61n, 62n
Gibson, William, VII: 64
Gibson, William Harvey, VI: 104n
Gibson County (Tenn.), VIII: 70
Giddings, Ammi, VII: 355n, 371-72
Giddings, Grotius Reed, VII: 137-38
Giddings, Joshua Reed, II: 249; III: 3, 6, 10, 60-61, 105, 138, 174-75, 213, 263, 321; IV: 51-52, 80-81; VII: 137, 187-88, 371n, 375n
Gideon, J. & G. S. (printers), I: 449n
Giers, Jean Joseph, VIII: 112
Giesborough Point (D. C.), VII: 495n
Gifford, Edmund, V: 539-40
Gifts presented to L., I: 261; IV: 71, 74, 75, 89, 98, 120-21, 127, 132, 137, 179, 183-84, 296, 319, 546; V: 57, 125-26, 137, 158, 177, 193, 200, 211-12, 352, 363-64,

466, 544; VI: 78, 375-76, 392-93;
VII: 13, 34, 75, 123, 133, 258,
278, 331, 337, 389, 396-97, 442,
457-58, 471, 485-86, 529; VIII:
51, 96-97, 166, 179, 183, 222,
236, 265-66
Gilbert, Miss, VII: 355
Gilbert, Charles Champion, V:
416-17, 552n
Gilbert, George W., VII: 238n
Gilbert, Joseph L., VII: 19n, 20n,
21n
Gilbert, Samuel Augustus, VI: 19
Gilbert, William, VIII: 68
Gilbreath, ———, I: 200
Giles, Moses, VII: 31
Giles County (Tenn.), VIII: 69
Gilfillan, Charles D., II: 395
Gill, Richard T., V: 65n
Gill, Robert, VII: 150, 152, 158
Gillam, B. C., IV: 309
Gillem, Alvan Cullom, V: 501n;
VI: 393; VII: 466, 520n; VIII:
111-12
Gillem, John, VIII: 69
Gillespie, Charles S., II: 57n, 59n,
212n, 432n, 433n, 503n
Gillespie, Joseph, I: 232-33, 237,
249, 343, 416; II: 31n, 50, 57-59,
99, 113, 211-12, 228, 290, 296,
357, 432, 433, 447, 476n, 480,
503, 523-24, 533; III: 493; VI:
463n; VIII: 416, 592
Gillespie, Joseph J., VI: 463
Gillespie, Matthew, II: 31
Gillespie, W. H., IV: 187
Gillett, J. T., VI: 211
Gillette, A. D., V: 410n
Gillette, James, V: 410n
Gillham, James, I: 288n
Gillis, John P., V: 241
Gillmore, Quincy Adams, VI: 421;
VII: 81, 84, 126, 510; VIII: 375n,
376n
Gilman, Nicholas, III: 527
Gilman, Samuel, Jr., VII: 92
Gilman, Winthrop Sargent, I: 67
Gilmer, John Adams, IV: 151-53,
155, 164, 170-71, 173

Gilmer, Joseph, VI: 337
Gilmer County (W. Va.), V: 298
Gilmore, Ephraim, IV: 529n
Gilmore, James Ross, VI: 225n,
330-31; VII: 429, 461
Gilmore, Joseph Albree, VI: 355,
368; VII: 517n; VIII: 109
Gilmore, Quincy Adams, see Gill-
more, Quincy Adams
Gilmore, Robert, I: 257, 374-76
Gilner, Peter, VII: 317; VIII: 12-
13, 49
Gilpatrick, Rufus, IV: 476
Gilpin, Edward W., V: 378-79
Gilpin, William, IV: 294, 536; V:
174n
Gimber, Mrs., VIII: 110
Gingerich, Joseph, II: 206n
Girard Hotel (Philadelphia), III:
521
Give, Laurent de, VIII: 244n
Give, Mme Laurent de, VIII: 244n
Given, John S., VII: 76
Glasgow (Ky.), V: 321n, 402n
Glasgow (Scotland), II: 61; IV:
300, 310, 483n, 490
Glasgow (steamboat), IV: 557
Glen (British schooner), VII: 113
Glendy, William Marshall, VI: 1
Glenn, John, VIII: 266
Glidden, John S. M., VII: 315n;
VIII: 411n
Globe Tavern (Springfield), I:
324-25; II: 96n
Gloucester County (N. J.), VII:
523n
Gloucester Point (Va.), VI: 86n
Glover, Henry R., II: 330n
Glover, Joseph Otis, II: 167, 537;
III: 30
Glover, Samuel Taylor, IV: 392n,
533, 538; V: 3; VI: 66, 210n;
VIII: 177n
Glynn, Michael, I: 206-207
Gobin, E. C., VII: 371
Gobright, Lewis A., VI: 430n
Godbey, Russell, I: 20-21
Goddard, Addison S., I: 294
Goddard, C. P., VII: 106, 109

Goddard, Conrad G., IV: 81n; VI: 217n; VII: 410n
Goddard, John H., VII: 408-409
Godey's Lady's Book (Hale), VI: 497n; VIII: 56n
Godfrey (Negro), V: 551n
Godfrey, Benjamin, I: 67
Godfrey, John S., IV: 516
Godfrey, Gilman & Company (Alton, Ill.), I: 189
Godwin, Parke, IV: 373n; VII: 410n
Godwin, William Thomas, VI: 477n
Goff, Nathan, Jr., VII: 502
Goggin, L. B., VI: 553
Goggin, William Leftwich, I: 429-30; III: 387-88; VI: 553; VIII: 427
Gold, Thomas, VII: 419
Golden, Harry G., V: 114n
Goldie, William, V: 202n
Goldman, M., VIII: 68
Goldsboro (N. C.), V: 288n, 303; VI: 147
Goldsborough, Arnold, V: 79n
Goldsborough, Henry H., V: 286n, 402n
Goldsborough, Louis Malesherbes, V: 134, 207, 209, 226n, 289, 293n, 294n
Goldsby, James, I: 39, 121
Golliher, *see* Gulihur, Isaac
Gonyeag, Mother Mary, VII; 67
Gooch, Daniel Wheelwright, V: 88n; VII: 329n
Goodell, Roswell Eaton, II: 172, 186-87
Goodenow, Ira, *see* Goodnow, Ira
Gooding, David S., VIII: 168
Gooding, Edward L., VI: 403
Gooding, William, II: 185; IV: 36-37
Goodloe, Daniel R., V: 464-65
Goodloe, Green Clay, VII: 375
Goodloe, William Cassius, VII: 127-28
Goodman, Caswell, VI: 544
Goodman, Christian, II: 330-31

Goodman, Edward, VI: 122
Goodnow [Goodenow], Ira, VIII: 166
Goodrich, Aaron, IV: 86n
Goodrich, Frank Chester, V: 370n
Goodrich, George Samuel, Jr., VII: 171
Goodrich, Grant, II: 329; VI: 361n
Goodrich, John Zacheus, IV: 166; V: 114-15; VIII: 351-53
Goodrich, Mrs. John Zacheus, VIII: 352n
Goodspeed's Book Shop (Boston), I: xiv
Goodwin, Daniel, Jr., VIII: 221
Goodwin, M. B., IV: 505n
Goodwin, Richard D., IV: 416, 443; V: 101
Goodwin, Stephen A., VIII: 221
Goodwin, Thomas F., V: 148-49
Goodwin, William F., V: 198n; VII: 61
Goodwin, William Thomas, *see* Godwin, William Thomas
Goodyear, A. Conger, I: preceding page 1; IV: 285n
Goose Creek Salt Works (Ky.), VI: 83
Gorchakov, Alexander (Russian Prince), V: 137
Gorden, John, IV: 116
Gorden, R. J., VIII: 69
Gordon, George Henry, V: 237n; VII: 464; VIII: 395
Gordon, Isaac G., IV: 166
Gordon, John Brown, VIII: 374n
Gordon, Jonathan Wesley, IV: 43-44
Gordon, Nathaniel, V: 47n, 128-29
Gordon, W. J., VI: 300-306
Gordon, Mrs. W. R., VIII: 150n
Gordon, William F., VII: 26
Gordonsville (Va.), V: 276-77; VI: 169n, 249n, 258n, 354n, 468; VII: 477n
Gorham, Nathaniel, III: 531n, 545n
Gorin, Jerome Rinaldo, II: 387

Gorman, Willis Arnold, IV: 511
Gortchacow, see Gorchakov, Alexander (Russian Prince)
Goslin, John, VI: 544
Gosport (Ind.), II: 105n
Gosport (Va.), IV: 427; VII: 232n
Goss, George Gideons, V: 53
Gotlieb, Henry E., V: 483n
Gott, Daniel, II: 20n
Gould, ———, VI: 343
Gould, Miss, V: 147n
Gould, John, VIII: 122n, 242n
Gould, Jonathan K., VII: 420n
Gould, Norman Judd, III: 337n, 516n
Government: L. on, I: 111, 113, 246, II: 220-22, 245, 266, 355, 379, 385, III: 435; L. on "self-government," II: 235, 239, 250, 265-66, 269, 275, 278-81, 370-71, 398-99, 451-52, 462, 493 (see also Popular sovereignty)
Governor's Island (N. Y.), IV: 301; VIII: 304n
Governors' Letter-Books, 1840-1853 (Greene & Thompson), I: 406n
Grafton (W. Va.), V: 497n; VI: 189n, 195n
Graham, Benjamin, II: 296
Graham, James (Ill.), I: 317
Graham, James (La.), VI: 224n; VIII: 242n
Graham, Jeremiah, I: 18
Graham, John A., IV: 448
Graham, Lawrence Pike, IV: 503n, 505n
Graham, Mentor, see Graham, William Mentor
Graham, Michael, VI: 534-35
Graham, Samuel, VI: 75
Graham, Thomas, Jr., I: 417-18, 422
Graham, William Alexander, II: 140
Graham, William Mentor, I: 24-25
Granada [New Granada], see Colombia
Grand Ecore (La.), VII, 308n

Grand Gulf (Miss.), VI: 202, 210, 326
Grand Junction (Miss.), V: 259n; VI: 7
Grand Rapids (Mich.) Press, IV: 539n
Grand Ronde Indian Agency, IV: 308
Grandin, William Gain, V: 437
Granger, Bradley Francis, V: 332; VII: 310
Granger, Gordon, VI: 474n; VII: 14n, 532-33
Granger County (Tenn.), VIII: 68
Granier, E. D., VI: 443
Grannis, John C., VIII: 337, 346-47
Grant, Agnes Mary, VIII: 98n
Grant, Hiram P., V: 542-43
Grant, J. C., VII: 225n
Grant, Jesse Root, VII: 350; VIII: 189
Grant, Julia (Dent), VII: 272
Grant, Lewis Addison, VII: 261n, 311n
Grant, Ulysses Simpson: appointed Brigadier General, VIII: 593-94; McClernand under his command in Mo. (Nov. '61), V: 21n; commands movement up the Tennessee River (Feb. '62), 108n; and courts-martial and arrests, 116n, VI: 142-43, VII: 75n, 122, 242-43, 436n, VIII: 87, 167, 203, 212-13, 216, 235, 237, 239-40, 263, 274, 301, 302, 313; surrender of Fort Donelson, V: 135; appointments and discharges, 148n, VI: 465, VII: 80, 235, 272, 443-44, 452, 463-65, VIII: 122, 189, 226-27, 274, 375; assumes command at Corinth, Miss., V: 313n, 323n, 453; and reorganization of state government in La., 462-63, 470-71; Mississippi R. expedition and surrender of Vicksburg, 469n, VI: 71n, 155n, 226, 230-31, 233,

[99]

236, 244, 247, 293, 319, 321, 326, 350, 374-75, 377-78, 499n, 503; order expelling Jews revoked, VI: 71n

Supports promotion of Gen. Steele, VI: 73n; appointed Major General, 139-40; proposed shift of a part of Ky. to Burnside command, 200; commended by L., 230, 326, 350, VII: 53, 79, 109, 234, 324, 332, 334, VIII: 58, 339, 374; relieves McClernand from his command, VI: 293, 380n, 383-84; born in Ohio, 304; assigns Hurlbut to command, 358; on emancipation and arming of Negroes, 374n; and prisoners-of-war, 514, VIII: 10n, 14n, 17-18, 36-37, 314-15, 347-48, 370-71; Fisk transferred from command of, VI: 545n

Given command of the Military Division of the Mississippi, VII: 14n, 109n; in Tenn. and at Chattanooga, 5-6, 14n, 30-31, 35n, 53, 85n, 113-14, 134-35, 149; presented with a medal and Congressional resolution of thanks, 79, VIII: 339; receives copies of Foster-Longstreet correspondence on circulation of amnesty handbills to Confederate soldiers, VII: 153n; and free-labor operation of Miss. plantations, 212n, 492; promotion to Lieutenant General, 234-36, 239-40, 319; invited to dinner at the White House, 235; criticism of Hooker, 244n; assignment and subsequent resignation of Blair, 248, 312n, 319n, 327

Directs final campaign of the war from Va., VII: 272, 312n, 324-25, 332, 334, 346, 348n, 350, 359, 360n, 374, 384, 393, 395-96, 406, 416, 437, 438, 444-45, 452-53, 476, 477n, 493, 499, 513, 521-24, 548; VIII: 29, 50n, 58, 97,

148, 182n, 201n, 316-17, 320-21, 329, 372-92, 394n, 400, 407

And protest against rumor of Buell assignment at Knoxville, VII: 287; requests extension of Department of Ark. and transfer of Blunt, 300n; and the recruiting of 100-day troops, 312n; Hurlbut protests replacement by Sherman, 327-28; and permission for unofficial peace mission to go south (July '64), 429; L. visits at Fort Monroe (July, '64), 469-70; confers with L. in Washington (Aug. '64), 482n; and the draft, 499n; asked to review protest against 3-year service regulations for officers, 539; Sherman mentions (Sept. 15 '64) awaiting a courier from, VIII: 9n; informed by Sheridan of victory at Opequan Creek (Sept. '64), 13n; and requests for passes, 26n, 72-73, 75, 198, 200n, 218, 321n; and the 1864 election, 45, 100; failure of expedition to Wilmington, N. C., 187, 207-208; adds L.'s son, Robert, to his staff, 223-24

And the Hampton Roads peace conference, 249-50, 252, 256, 258, 265, 269-70, 274-85; and trade with insurrectionary states, 267-68, 288-89, 343-45, 353, 354; and amnesty in Tenn., 295n; and report to Sec. of War (Mar. '65), 328, 329; forbidden by L. to confer with Lee on any political aspects of peace terms, 330-31; L. visits City Point, 367, 372-95; and Lee's refusal to receive the Russell letter, 373-74; attends cabinet meeting (Apr. 14, '65), 411, 412

Grant, Mrs. Ulysses Simpson, see Grant, Julia

Grant, Ulysses Simpson III, VII: 234n

Grant County (Ind.), VIII: 125n

Grant, Lincoln and the Freedmen (Eaton), VII: 492n; VIII: 218n, 274n

Gratiot Street Prison (St. Louis), VIII: 316

Gratton, James C., VII: 142, 151

Gratz, Benjamin, VI: 148

Gravelly Run, VIII: 376n, 378n

Graves, William Preston, V: 71n, 159

Gray, ———, VI: 229

Gray, A. H., VII: 171

Gray, Franklin C., II: 427

Gray, Mrs. Franklin C., *see* Gray, Matilda C., and Gray, Mary A.

Gray, George W., II: 297

Gray, H. Jouette, VIII: 268n

Gray, John P., VI: 429, 437-38, 443; VII: 227n, 313-14

Gray, Mary A., II: 427n

Gray, Matilda C. (French), II: 427-28

Gray, R. A., VIII: 268

Gray, W. H., II: 457-58

Gray, William H., VI: 426-27

Gray Hill (S. C.), VI: 456-57

Grayson, James, VIII: 68

Grayson, P. W., I: 436n

Great Britain: controversies over Canadian boundaries, I: 177, IV: 287-88, VII: 160, VIII: 140-41; responsibility for introduction of institution of slavery in the American colonies, II: 361, 370, 518; suppression of slave trade, 482 (*see also under* Treaties and agreements with foreign powers); appointment of ministers to, IV: 281, 292-93; and the blockade, 376-80, VI: 79n, VII: 36-37, 49, 87n, 113; building of Confederate vessels, IV: 397n, VI: 126n; intervention in Mexican affairs, V: 61n, 109; attitude toward Civil War, 519-21, VI: 63-65, 88-89, 121, 176n, 348-50, 378-80, VIII: 140; gifts to Library of Congress and American seamen, VI: 9-10, VII:

198-99; letter of introduction for American visitor to, VI: 160-61; mention of a reciprocal trade treaty with the U.S., 284n; dismissal of English officer from Union army, 351-52; settlement of claims of Hudson's Bay and Puget Sound Agricultural Societies, VII: 76, 246-47, VIII: 140; and Japanese anti-foreign sentiment, VIII: 45n; and Canadian-U. S. commerce, 208-209, *see also* Telegraph

Great Lakes, VII: 274; VIII: 141, 206

Great Western Railroad, IV: 131n, 182n; VI: 497n

Great Whig Demonstration in Favor of the Nomination of Gen. Taylor to the Presidency . . ., I: 449n

Greece, II: 123, 129

Greeg, *see* Gregg, John

Greeley, Horace: L.'s objections to his position on Texas boundary question, I: 493-94; called a leader of Black Republicanism (1856), II: 345; L. on his support of Douglas (1858), 456-57, III: 365n, 506-507; L. recommends Nicolay for *Tribune* correspondent, III: 336; relays Buffalo speaking invitation to L. (Mar. '60), IV: 31; and the Republican convention in Chicago (1860), 89; L. gives *Tribune* as source of questioned statement in Cooper Union speech, 118-19; use of L.'s name in promoting his senatorial candidacy protested by L. (Feb. '61), 185-86; and appointments, 325, 361-62, 367; and removal of Frémont, 550n; correspondence with L. on administration policies (Mar., Aug. '62), V: 169, 364n, 388-89, 421, VII: 499-502; release of text of Emancipation Proclamation to newspapers, VI: 30n; Weed

charges with presidential ambitions, 83n, 514n; urges Frémont command of colored troops, 239n; correspondence with L. on conference with peace emissaries reported to be at Niagara Falls, VII: 435-36, 440-43, 451n, 459-60, 482-83, 485, 489-90, 494; recommends a prisoner-of-war exchange, VIII: 314n

Greelish, *see* Gulish, Michael J.

Green, Bowling, I: 13-14, 17-19, 21-22, 24, 26, 86, 93

Green, Duff, I: 419; II: 49-50, 52n, 53; IV: 162-63; VI: 33

Green, E. H., V: 403n

Green, Henry, II: 167, 170

Green, Henry R., VII: 150-51

Green, James M., VI: 339n

Green, James Stephen, V: 173

Green, John, VI: 76

Green, Mrs. John, VI: 76

Green, John A., Jr., VIII: 92n

Green, Mrs. M. J., IV: 118

Green, Peter, I: 241n

Green, Robert, VI: 339n

Green, Robert P., VII: 274

Green, Robert R., I: 67

Green, William H., III: 364n

Green Bay (Wis.) *Advocate,* VII: 501n

Green County (Ky.), I: 203n, VIII: 211n

Green River (Ky.), IV: 533; V: 14

Greenbie, Marjorie Barstow, V: 382n

Greenbie, Sydney, V: 382n

Greenbush (Ill.), I: 255n

Greencastle (Pa.), V: 415n; VI: 293n, 330n

Greene, Evarts Boutell, I: 406n

Greene, Gilbert J., II: 96n

Greene, Henry R., *see* Green, Henry R.

Greene, Henry S., III: 515

Greene, James Stephen, *see* Green, James Stephen

Greene, John Wesley, V: 517-18

Greene, Oliver Duff, V: 313n

Greene, R. G., VI: 488n

Greene, William Graham ("Slicky Bill"), I: 10n, 15-17, 20, 53n, 96n; VI: 383-84

Greene, William Griggs, I: 13-14

Greene County (Tenn.), VIII: 68

Greeneville (Tenn.), VI: 470n, 481

Greenleaf, M., II: 188

Greenleaf's Evidence, III: 344; IV: 121

Greenly, A. H., II: 429n; IV: 127n; V: 230n

Greensburg (Ill.), I: 70

Greenup (Ill.), II: 96

Greenupsburg (Ky.?), V: 453n

Greenville (Ill.), III: 96, 592

Greenville Advocate, II: 447n; III: 96n

Greenwich (Conn.) Institute, VII: 138n

Greenwood (Miss.), VI: 142n

Greenwood Academy (Muscatine, Iowa), VI: 78n

Greer, Edmund, I: 13

Gregg, ————, VIII: 70

Gregg, A., VIII: 70

Gregg, David L., II: 75, 79n; VI: 51n; VIII: 358n

Gregg, David McMurtrie, VI: 207n; VII: 438n

Gregg, Hugh, II: 297

Gregg, John, VI: 480

Gregg, Lafayette, VII: 173n

Gregg & Weld (Boston), I: 188

Gregory, Charles, I: 60-61

Gregory, Daniel S., VI: 520

Gregory, Dudley Sanford, VII: 413

Gregory, Francis Hoyt, IV: 303

Gregory, George, I: 184, 206

Gregory, John Shaw, IV: 303n; V: 107

Gregory's Gap, V: 461

Greiner, John, VIII: 157

Grenada (Miss.), VIII: 336

Greyhound (British ship), VII: 311n

Grider, Henry, IV: 464n; V: 79n;

VLı: 105, 156n, 309n; VIII: 77-78
Gridley, Asahel, I: 227n; II: 159, 190n, 538; IV: 336
Grier, Robert Cooper, III: 543n; V: 481
Grierson, Benjamin Henry, VI: 502; VIII: 295n, 418; see also *Record of Services Rendered the Government by B. H. Grierson in 1865*
Griffin, Anne Mary, IV: 509n
Griffin, Asberry, VIII: 69
Griffin, Charles, V: 202, 407n; VIII: 203n, 376-77, 391
Griffin, Elihu, V: 475
Griffin, William, V: 285
Griffith, ———, I: 518; VIII: 421
Griffith, Ezra, II: 113-14
Griffith, Thomas, I: 46
Griffiths, John W., IV: 311, 340
Grigg, John, II: 30n
Grigsby, Aaron, II: 95
Grigsby, Mrs. Aaron, see Grigsby, Sarah
Grigsby, Charles, IV: 116
Grigsby, Joseph Warren, VI: 148n
Grigsby, Mrs. Joseph Warren, see Grigsby, Susan
Grigsby, Nathaniel, IV: 116
Grigsby, Sarah (Lincoln), II: 94-95; IV: 56-57, 61
Grigsby, Susan (Shelby), VI: 148
Grigsby, William, IV: 116n
Grigsby, William H., II: 535-36
Grimes, James Wilson, II: 348, 413-14; III: 400; IV: 43, 248, 298, 445n, 460n; V: 68n, 70n, 198n, 261n; VI: 128n, 515, 546-47; VII: 117, 121, 142-43, 415n; VIII: 358n
Grimshaw, Arthur H., V: 163n, 378-79; VI: 351
Grimshaw, Joseph Jackson, II: 432n, 482-83; III: 509-10; V: 116n; VI: 351; VII: 377n
Grimshaw, William A., VII: 377n
Grimsley, Elizabeth J. (Todd), I: 491n; II: 437n; III: 356n; IV: 303; VI: 252, 376n, 385-86, 403
Grimsley, Harrison J., I: 491; II: 437n; VI: 252n
Grimsley, Mrs. Harrison J., see Grimsley, Elizabeth J.
Grimsley, John, I: 2
Grimsley, John Todd, VI: 252, 376, 386, 403
Grinnell, Henry D., V: 205
Grinnell, Moses Hicks, V: 241
Griswold, William D., IV: 47
Groesbeck, John, IV: 485
Groesbeck, William Slocum, III: 210
Grose, William, VII: 144n
Gross, Samuel E., V: 139
Grove, Henry A., II: 297
Grover, Alonzo J., III: 514
Grow, Galusha Aaron, IV: 452, 548n; V: 326; VI: 12, 52n, 104, 185-86
Grubb, George G., II: 206-207, 209
Grubb, Samuel, Sr., II: 188
Grundy, ———, VII: 427n
Grundy County (Ill.), III: 396n
Grundy County (Tenn.), VIII: 69
Gruver [Gruvier], William, VI: 295
Guadalupe Hidalgo, Treaty of, II: 50n
Guayaquil (Ecuador), IV: 310; VI: 36; VII: 247
Gubby, James, VI: 157
Guest, John, V: 215
Guinea, II: 298
Guinnip, Lyman, VI: 140
Guion, Elijah, VII: 247n
Guitar, Odon, VI: 133-34
Gulf, Department of the, V: 428n, 495n; VI: 7, 73, 100n, 294n, 312n, 476n; VII: 179n, 286n; VIII: 121n, 131, 325, 366n
Gulf and the Mississippi, Department of the, VI: 100n
Gulf of Mexico, see Mexico, Gulf of
Gulihur, Isaac, I: 12, 19

Gulish, Michael J., V: 164n
Gum, Jesse, I: 22-23
Gum, Thomas, I: 23
Gummere, Barker, IV: 500n
Gumpert, Gustave, VI: 531n; VIII: 168
Gunn, Lewis C., VI: 210n, 213
Guns and ammunition, see Troops, equipment and supplies
Gunter, Edmund, I: 391
Gunther, Charles, II: 437n
Gurley, John Addison, IV: 310, 410-11, 485, 550; V: 182-83, 202n; VI: 141, 167n, 325n
Gurley, Phineas Densmore, VI: 378n, 536n; VIII: 291n
Gurley, William H. F., VIII: 355n

Gurney, Eliza P. (Kirkbride), V: 478; VII: 535-36
Gurney, Joseph John, V: 478n
Gurney, Mrs. Joseph John, see Gurney, Eliza P.
Gurney, Seth, II: 416
Gussett, Abraham, VIII: 69
Gussett, Ellison, VIII: 68
Gute, William, VII: 458n
Guthrie, James, IV: 141n, 368, 549; V: 14-15, 31, 386; VI: 147n, 219, 223
Guthrie, William A., VIII: 193n
Guy, B. F., VII: 318n
Gwin, John, III: 202n
Gwinn, Charles J. M., VII: 318n, 522n

H

Habeas corpus: and Lovejoy's resolution on principles of the Republican Party, III: 64; and the fugitive slave law, 395n; see also Habeas corpus, suspension of Habeas corpus, suspension of: L. on, IV: 344, 347, 364-65, 390, 414, 419, 429-31, 554, VI: 302-303; Halleck empowered (1861) to suspend in Mo., V: 35; proclamations, (1862) 436-37, (1863) VI: 451-52, 460, (1864) VII: 425-27; in Vallandigham case, VI: 215-16, 263-69, 300-306; appropriations for Congressional act put under control of Seward and Staunton, 368-71; and the draft, 444n, 493n, 503; in case of imprisoned N. Y. detectives, VIII: 233-34
Hackelman, see Hackleman, Pleasant A.

Hackelton, Samuel, I: 58
Hacker, William P., IV: 216
Hackett, James Henry, VI: 392-93, 558-59
Hackett, John Keteltas, VI: 559n
Hackleman, Pleasant A., V: 453
Hackney, Benjamin, II: 297
Haddock, Lorenzo K., VII: 371
Hadley, Henry, I: 11
Hagan, Charles Thomas, VII: 136
Hagen, Erhard, VII: 391n
Hagen, Mrs. Erhard, see Hagen, Louisa
Hagen, Louisa, VII: 391n
Hagenbuch, Benjamin T., VII: 369n
Hagenbuch, Jacob C., VII: 297
Hagerstown (Md.): loyal Virginians congregated at (1861), IV: 395n, 536; and military movements, (1862) V: 415, 418, 426, (1863) VI: 318, 323, 328; and

construction of railroad from Washington to, VI: 69n
Haggard, Mrs., VII: 129
Haggard, David R., VI: 224-25, 229
Haggard, Edward, VII: 129
Haggard, Linnie, III: 203-204
Haggard, Rosa, III: 203-204
Hagner, Alexander B., VI: 378n
Hagner, Mrs. Alexander B., VI: 378n
Hagner, Peter, I: 79-80, 100-101
Hagner, Peter Valentine, V: 189, 197n
Hague, The, I: 162n
Hahn, Michael, V: 505n; VI: 30n, 224n, 288n, 365, 368n; VII: 2n, 162n, 243, 248, 307-308, 454, 486n, 492n; VIII: 110
Haight, Augustus, IV: 481
Haight, Edward, V: 136n
Haight, Fletcher M., IV: 471
Haight, John Mason, IV: 75
"Hail to the Chief" (song), IV: 248n; VIII: 334n
Haines, Alfred, III: 371n; IV: 189
Haines, Jonathan, II: 382, 426-27, 436-37; III: 206-207, 370-71, 380, 384-85; IV: 189; VI: 124n
Haiti, III: 540; V: 39, 520-21; VI: 41n, 178; VII: 417n; VIII: 138, 166-67
Haldeman, Jacob S., IV: 166, 283
Hale, Albert, IV: 139
Hale, Artemas, I: 455-56; II: 356
Hale, Calvin H., V: 78; VII: 284
Hale, Charles, VII: 20n, 21n; VIII: 139n
Hale, Edward L., VII: 14
Hale, J. D., VIII: 68
Hale, James Tracy, IV: 172
Hale, John Parker, III: 53, 138, 175; IV: 248, 295, 470n, 516; V: 103n, 112-13, 127n, 316n, 320; VI: 133, 255, 479
Hale, Mary Jane, see Welles, Mary Jane (Hale)
Hale, Sarah Josepha, VI: 497n; VIII: 56n

Haley, James, VI: 548
Halfway House (S. C.), VI: 456-57
Haliburton, Samuel P., VIII: 242n
Hall, ———, I: 139; VI: 469
Hall, "Ab," V: 159n
Hall, Alfred, I: 2
Hall, Alfred L., II: 96
Hall, Amanda H. (Ferry), VIII: 367
Hall, Benjamin F., III: 125; IV: 294
Hall, Charles W., VIII: 322
Hall, Curtis H., V: 157
Hall, Mrs. Curtis H. [nee Ruckel], V: 157n
Hall, Dominick A., VI: 268
Hall, Edward, V: 358
Hall, Edward H., V: 353
Hall, Elizabeth Jane, II: 96
Hall, F., VIII: 69
Hall, Fleming, I: facing page 48
Hall, Henry C., VIII: 367n
Hall, John J., I: 263n
Hall, L. W., VI: 58
Hall, Leonard G., VII: 371
Hall, Matilda (Johnston), II: 96n
Hall, Myron V., VII: 15
Hall, Oliver Perry, III: 519-20
Hall, Samuel, VI: 93n
Hall, Sarah Louisa, II: 96
Hall, Squire, I: 2; II: 96n; IV: 116
Hall, Mrs. Squire, see Hall, Matilda
Hall, Willard Preble, I: 468-69; VII: 206n, 230; VIII: 109, 124, 156
Hall, William (Macon Co., Ill.), I: 2
Hall, William (Tazewell Co., Ill.), I: 290, 323-24
Hall, William A., II: 315
Hall, William Augustus, VI: 8, 10-11; VIII: 217n
Halleck, Fitz-Greene, IV: 48
Halleck, Henry Wager: appointed Major General, IV: 489; given command at St. Louis, V: 21-22;

Halleck, Henry Wager (*continued*):
authorized to proclaim martial law and suspend writ of habeas corpus in Mo., 27-28, 35; opposition to Schofield, 61n, 203, VI: 501; opposition to Lane, V: 80; and lack of cooperation with Buell (1862), 84, 86-87, 91, 94, 95, 98-99, 130n, 135, 153, VIII: 40n; and the resolution of difficulties with Mo. Germans, V: 99-101; and McClellan's plans for the Army of the Potomac (Feb. '62), 122n, 124n; given command of the Department of the Miss., 155; L. suspends order sending Denver to Kans., 168, 180; transfers of military units, 177-78, 200, 349; arrests and courts-martial, 183-84, VI: 75, 106, 229n; receives news of destruction of the *Merrimac*, V: 210; his request for reinforcements (May '62), 231; occupation of Corinth, 254, 259, 260-61

Plan to move against Chattanooga and McClellan's need of reinforcements at Richmond (June-July '62), V: 261n, 263-64, 276, 289-91, 295, 300-301, 303, 305, 307n, 308, 322

Appointed General-in-Chief, V: 312-13, 323, 325n; and Buell's request for help against Morgan raids (July '62), 313, 321, 322; his advice on facilitating recruiting in N. Y. (July '62), 349n; L. suggests Stanton conference on sending arms to Tex., 357, VI: 354; dines at White House (Aug. '62, Mar. '64), V: 380-81, VII: 235n; mention of dispatches received from Pope, Burnside, McClellan, and Banks (Aug. 27-31, '62), V: 395n, 396n, 398n, 400, 402n; L. asserts no wish to interfere with control of military movements, 399, 407, 416-17;

criticism of his military ability, 403; and the defense of Washington (fall '62), 404, 452n; Keyes complains of reductions in his command, 405; and Pa. fears of invasion (Sept. '62, May '63), 409n, 411, 417-18, VI: 195; McClellan asks for reinforcements (Sept. 11, '62), V: 415n; and support to succeed Stanton as Sec. of War, 416

Receipt of dispatches to and from McClellan (Sept.-Oct. '62), V: 418n, 426n, 428n, 460, 462n, 474n, 477, 482; and Confederate parole of prisoners forbidding Indian fighting, 432, 449; receipt of dispatches from Boyle (Oct. 11, '62), 457n; and proposed McClernand Miss. expedition, 469n, 498-99; and defense of East Tenn., 483-84, 497, VI: 373-74, 377-78, 424-25, 436n, 450n, 470-71, 474-75, 480-81, 483-84, 511, 522n, 534-35, VII: 29n, VIII: 111n, 169

And removal of McClellan from command of the Army of the Potomac, V: 485-86; receives report of absence of enemy at Culpeper Court House (Nov. 6, '62), 488; and transfer of Miss. war vessels to the navy, 490n; L. accused of being unsympathetic toward, 510n; rejects L.'s plan for driving the enemy from Fredericksburg (Nov. 27, '62), 514-15; L. asks explanation for presence of an isolated brigade at Hartsville, 545-46; controversies with Burnside, McClernand, and Humphreys (Jan. '63), VI: 31-33, 46-48, 70-71, 77-78, 81n, 293n, 380n; receives Rosecrans' dispatch on victory at Murfreesboro, 39n; and Ky. opposition to the Emancipation Proclamation, 42n; and a proposal to form a reserve

Halleck, Henry Wager (*continued*):
cavalry unit for the Army of the Potomac, 43; receives dispatch from Dix on naval vessels at Hampton Roads, 84n; agrees to necessity of river patrols, 101; proposed organization of a mounted infantry command to oppose enemy cavalry raiders, 105, 352-53; and W. Va. fear of a spring (1863) invasion, 115-16, 238-39; opposes new command for Frémont (Mar. '63), 127; and protection of Ariz., 141; and Hunter's cooperation with Navy on operations against Charleston (Apr. '63), 170n; visits Hooker with L. (May '63), 200n

Pressure for his removal from top command, VI: 214n, 230-31; rejects proposal to organize military units of Negroes to construct a railroad from Washington to Pittsburgh, 246; and Hooker's military operations against Lee (June '63), 249-51, 257-58, 270, 274n, 280-84; Hooker complains of lack of cooperation, 281-82; urges Banks action in Tex., 292, 364, 366n; and Milroy's defeat at Winchester, 308-309, 541-42; and Meade's failure to attack Lee, 317n, 318-19, 327-28, 330n, 354, 450-51, 466-68, 518-19, 534-35; and the New Almaden mine case, 333n, 393-94; support of Hurlbut, 358, VII: 328n; views on Rock Island bridge, VI: 386n; receives news of bombing of Fort Sumter (Aug. '63), 421n; and control of outrages following sack of Lawrence, Kans., 423-24, VII: 123, 157-58; receives dispatches from Grant and Meade (Oct.-Dec. '63), VI: 509n, VII: 6n, 7n, 30n, 35n; recommends acceptance of Palmer's resignation, VII: 61n; orders court of inquiry on Crittenden dismissal, 108, 127n; receives copies of Foster-Longstreet correspondence on circulation of amnesty handbills, 153n; relief of West and Davidson from their commands, 159, 208-209

Grant succeeds him as General-in-Chief, VII: 234n, 239-40; on transfer of title or private use of government property, 264n; and the enlargement of the Department of Ark., 300; attends meeting of L. and western governors, 308; mention of dispatches from Grant (May-July '64), 327, 359n, 393n, 438n; dispatch received from Burbridge on action at Cynthiana, 391n; orders Wallace rally of forces after defeat at Monocacy, 435n; exchange of telegrams with Grant on pursuit of Early (July 10, '64), 437; and Blair's criticism of army generals, 439-40; and Hunter's complaint of being a "scape-goat," 445n; Grant extends command of (July 28, '64), 470; Hunter asks for military advice of (July 30, '64), 472n; informed by Grant of Sheridan assignment (Aug. 3, '64), 476n; and removal of Frederick, Md., secessionists, 477n; telegram from Grant on enforcement of the draft, 499n; and Sigel's relief from duty, 521n; messages from Sherman in Ga., 450n, VIII: 9n, 27n, 201n; and exchange of naval prisoners, VIII: 37n; telegram from Curtis on engagement with Price in Mo. (Oct. '64), 57n; receives news of threatened raid in W. Ky., 74n; and assessments of Mo. disloyalists for care of refugees, 298n; and

the release of prisoners-of-war,
320-21, 371n
Appointments, assignments,
leaves and dismissals, V: 56, 72,
80, 100-101, 148n, 229-30, 262,
353-54, 360, 361, 364, 384, 390,
405-408, 425, 428, 447, 453,
457, 458n, 480, 495, 506, 508,
547; VI: 35n, 70, 77, 81n, 101,
147, 193, 210, 279, 312, 386-87,
419-20, 465n, 541n; VII: 79, 137-
38, 212, 276n, 307, 371n
Haller, James, *see* Halter, James
Haller, Samuel, II: 113-14
Hallion, James, VIII: 30, 34
Halloway, Thomas S., VII: 213
Hallowell, Morris L., VIII: 35
Halltown (Va.), VII: 472n
Halpine, Charles G. ("Miles O'-
Reilly"), VI: 490
Halsey, George A., V: 376n
Halsey, William A., V: 383n
Halstead, William M., II: 198
Halsted, John B., V: 383n
Halsted, Oliver S., Jr., V: 498; VI:
255n
Halter, James, VII: 58
Hambleton, Alice Eliza, V: 279n
Hamburg (Germany), I: 162n;
IV: 278; VI: 51, 206, 507; VII:
140
Hamby, James, VIII: 68
Hamby, James H., VIII: 68
Hamilton, Alexander, I: 334, 502;
III: 8, 178, 523n, 524n, 531-32
Hamilton, Andrew Jackson, IV:
286; V: 357n, 492; VI: 399, 465-
66; VII: 488-89; VIII: 93n, 103
Hamilton, Charles Smith, V: 208-
209, 227, 243n, 246
Hamilton, Eliza Ann (Wright),
IV: 134
Hamilton, J. G., VI: 361n
Hamilton, John A., IV: 134n
Hamilton, Mrs. John A., *see*
Hamilton, Eliza Ann
Hamilton, John W., V: 65n
Hamilton, Mrs. Lindsey, VIII:
425n

Hamilton, Perry, VI: 544
Hamilton, Richard Jones, I: 67; II:
91
Hamilton, Mrs. Samuel P., VII:
184
Hamilton (Ohio), III: 437n
Hamilton County (Ohio), III: 490-
91
Hamilton County (Tenn.), VIII:
68
Hamilton Crossing (Va.), VI: 249n
Hamlet (play), VI: 392
Hamlin, Augustus Choate, V:
171n
Hamlin, Charles Eugene, VIII:
353n
Hamlin, Cyrus, VI: 439-40; VII:
416
Hamlin, Hannibal: called a Black
Republican (1860), III: 542n;
receives vice-presidential nomination (1860), IV: 53n; L. sends
respects to, 55; and L.'s nomination (1860) speech, 59, 69n; L.
suggests conference with (July
'60), 84-85; and 1860 election,
110, 113-14, 130n, 234; and
formation (1860) of L.'s cabinet,
136, 145, 147-49, 161; and resolutions drawn up for Committee of Thirteen, IV: 158-59;
recommends appointments, 284,
V: 171, 327n, VII: 216; recommends increased production of
cannon, IV: 343; requested to
give daily reports on N. Y. mobilization, 357-58; requested to
procure recommended preacher,
445-46; receives communications from L. to transmit to
Senate, 464, V: 201, 204n, VI:
116, VIII: 250, 324, 329; on the
Emancipation Proclamation, V:
444; requests investigation of
arsenal employee's accounts,
458n; and coastal defenses, VI:
320n; and son's command of colored troops, 439-40; advice from
L. on certification of House

members (1863), 547-48; urges commissioning of an army sergeant, VII: 92; supports pardon for constituent, 276; on a permit for cotton trading, VIII: 197n; endorses Thirteenth Amendment, 253-54; appointment as Boston collector of customs, 352-53

"Hammet letter" of Van Buren, I: 336n

Hammill, Joseph R., VII: 223n

Hammond, George T., VIII: 288-89, 291

Hammond, Helen (Nisbet), VII: 474-75

Hammond, Henry, V: 375, 385-86; VII: 81-83; VIII: 122n, 242n

Hammond, James Henry, IV: 11

Hammond, John Henry, VII: 452

Hammond, William A.: use of new medical treatments, V: 228-29, 444-45; personnel grievances in Hospital Transport Service, 259; appointments and assignments of hospital chaplains, 340, 473, VI: 44, 157, 194, 313-14; endorses work of Christian Commission, V: 349n; appointments, assignments, and discharges of medical personnel, 380n, 382-83, VI: 294n, 420-21; and reports on cases of medical fitness, V: 429, VI: 97; hospital use of Capitol building and Washington school, V: 443n, VI: 397; on complaints of care of wounded, V: 467, VI: 344n; and Sanitary Commission appointment, VI: 53; N. Y. *Times* erroneously reports removal of, 450n; court-martial and dismissal of, VII: 93-94, 475n, 503; mentioned also, V: 449

Hammond, Mrs. William, *see* Hammond, Helen

Hampshire County (W. Va.), IV: 536

Hampton, George, VIII: 69

Hampton, Moses, IV: 119-20

Hampton, Wade, V: 481n

Hampton Roads (Va.), IV: 528n, V: 154n, 305n, 550, VI: 84, VIII: 285; conference at, VIII: 188-89, 220-21, 243, 246-52, 256, 258, 259, 265, 269-70, 274-85, 286n, 288n, 318-19

Hanchett, Luther, V: 224n

Hancock, Charles, IV: 521n

Hancock, John, III: 533n; IV: 319n

Hancock, Winfield Scott, VII: 97n; 395, 443-44; VIII: 26n, 307, 370-71

Hancock County (Ill.), I: 462; II: 217; IV: 61

Hancock County (Ind.), IV: 61

Hancock County (Tenn.), VIII: 68

Hancock County (W. Va.), V: 298

Hancock Station (Va.), VIII: 383n

Hand, Moses, I: 2

Handy, Mrs., VIII: 426

Hanks, Amanda, *see* Poorman, Amanda (Hanks)

Hanks, Charles, IV: 100

Hanks, Dennis Friend, II: 97n; IV: 120; VII: 342n

Hanks, Mrs. Dennis Friend, *see* Hanks, Sarah Elizabeth

Hanks, Harriet, *see* Chapman, Harriet (Hanks)

Hanks, John, I: 2-3; IV: 48n, 63-64, 100-101, 181

Hanks, John Talbot, IV: 120

Hanks, Mary L., *see* Shriver, Mary L. (Hanks)

Hanks, Nancy, *see* Lincoln, Nancy (Hanks)

Hanks, Sarah Elizabeth (Johnston), II: 97n; IV: 120

Hanks, Thomas, IV: 49n, *see also* Hanks, John

Hanks, William, Jr., IV: 100

Hanks, William, Sr., I: 2; IV: 100

Hanna, Joshua, VII: 242n

Hanna, Valentine C., IV: 463

Hanna, William H., II: 502; III: 374; IV: 37

Hannegan, Edward Allen, II: 145-46
Hannibal (Mo.), VIII: 156
Hanover, treaty with, V: 58, 131-32, 519
Hanover County (Va.), II: 124
Hanover Court House (Va.), V: 240n, 245, 515; VI: 169n, 199
Hanover Junction (Va.), V: 244-45
Hanscom, Albert, VII: 195
Hanscom, Simon P., IV: 408; VI: 120, 221, 552n
Hanscom, William L., V: 148
Hanseatic Republics, VI: 51
Hansen, Arthur, VIII: 33n, 155n
Hanson, Daniel, VI: 498, 504, 515
Hanson, George M., I: 157; IV: 306, 326
Hanson, Joseph R., VIII: 358n
Hanson, Roger W., VI: 39n
Ha-pan (Indian), V: 542
Ha-pink-pa (Indian), V: 542
Happy, William W., I: 179
Harbaugh, Springer, VI: 491; VIII: 39
Hardee, A. J., VI: 362n
Hardee, William Joseph, V: 69n, 458n
Hardeman, Franklin, VIII: 69
Hardeman County (Tenn.), VIII: 70
Hardie, James Allen, VI: 351n, 477n, 521; VII: 155, 183n, 327, 361n, 363n, 436n, 463n, 513n; VIII: 197, 405-406
Hardiman, B., I: 436n
Hardin, John J.: in the Black Hawk War, I: 10n; in Ill. legislature (1838-1841), 122-23, 133, 201n, 217n, 219n, 231, 237, 244n, 249; and lack of ladies in Springfield social life (1839), 156-57; and L.'s illness (1841), 228n; intervenes in proposed Lincoln-Shields duel, 301n; candidacy (1843) for Congress, 319-22, 325; letters from L. on political affairs (1844), 336, 342-43; candidacy (1845) for

Congress, 349-66, 380, IV: 66-67, 95n; letter from L. on appointment of officers in Mexican War, I: 381; L. on the death of, 392-93, 515, II: 86, 473; L. recommends (1861) appointment of brother-in-law, IV: 302; L. endorses request (1861) from widow of, VIII: 426n
Hardin, Mrs. John J., see Hardin, Sarah Ellen
Hardin, Martin Davis, VI: 373n, 388
Hardin, Sarah Ellen (Smith), I: 156n; VIII: 426
Hardin County (Ky.), I: 456; II: 459; III: 511; IV: 56-57, 60, 75, 96
Hardin County (Tenn.), VIII: 70
Harding, Aaron, V: 457n; VI: 97n; VII: 136, 309n, 430
Harding, Abner Clark, V: 447
Harding, George, II: 315n; IV: 295
Harding, Jacob, II: 286, 312, 313n, 483n
Harding, Stephen Selwyn, V: 432n
Hardy, Charles M., IV: 178
Hardy, Isaac, II: 113-14
Hardy, John, IV: 98n
Harell, Landy [Orlando], I: 2
Harford County (Md.), VII: 427
Harker, Charles Garrison, V: 77n
Harkness, James, II: 23
Harlan, James (Iowa), IV: 248, 294, 298, 445n, 493, 537n; V: 56n, 68n, 148, 261n, 283, 335, 470n; VI: 39-40, 128n, 134n, 157n, 546; VII: 279, 524; VIII: 358n, 363n, 366n, 409n, 410
Harlan, James (Ky.), IV: 369n
Harlan, John, V: 546n
Harlan, Josiah, V: 335n
Harlan, Justin, I: 264; II: 426; VIII: 34n
Harlan, Mary, see Lincoln, Mary (Harlan)
Harmon, Mary C., V: 406n
Harmon, Oscar F., III: 84-85
"Harmon's Sandal Sock," VII: 416

Harney, James F., V: 174-75
Harney, William Selby, I: 464-65; IV: 372-73, 387
Harper, B. C., I: 206
Harper, Benjamin, VI: 386
Harper, Charles, I: 206
Harper, J. P., VIII: 202n
Harper, Samuel, I: 206
Harper, Walter, & Company (Washington), I: 495
Harper's Ferry (W. Va.): seizure of U. S. armory, IV: 427; and L.'s military policy (July '61), 457-58; and plan to construct bridge of canal boats near, V: 130n; Hamilton under command of Saxton, 227n; disposition of paroled soldiers captured at, 432, 453n; construction of fortifications, VI: 15n, 246n; request of troops to vote in state elections (1863), 554; mentioned also, IV: 472, VII: 419, 486n, VIII: 298, 301, 305, 325
   And military movements: (*spring '62*) V: 232, 234, 236-38, 244-56 *passim*; (*fall '62*) 409, 418, 460-61, VII: 548-49; (*spring '63*) VI: 250n, 253n, 273-74, 276, 278, 280-83, 308; (*fall '63*) 399n; (*Jan. '64*) VII: 102-103; (*July '64*) 424n, 437, 445, 456, 465-66, 472; (*Aug. '64*) 511; (*Feb. '65*) VIII: 317n
   See also Brown, John
Harper's New Monthly Magazine, III: 399n, 405-406, 408, 411-12, 418, 426-28, 436; VII: 392n; VIII: 155n
Harper's Weekly, IV: 191n
Harrell, Abram Davis, V: 215
Harriet Lane (revenue cutter), IV: 301
Harriman, Walter, VI: 352n
Harrington, ———, I: 177
Harrington, Carlos, VI: 248
Harrington, Fred H., VIII: 595n
Harrington, George, IV: 537n; V:

22, 75, 159n, 221; VI: 179-80, 209n; VII: 418-19, 471; VIII: 50, 345, 422n
Harrington, Henry F., VIII: 122
Harriott, Edgar, VI: 107-108
Harriott, James, II: 455
Harris, A., VII: 534-35
Harris, Arnold, IV: 469n
Harris, Charles C., VIII: 198n
Harris, Clara, IV: 443n
Harris, G. W., V: 473
Harris, George H. [alias], *see* Root, Newell W.
Harris, George T., V: 473; VI: 362
Harris, Ira, IV: 387, 443, 446, 501, 506n; V: 10n, 263n, 379n, 383n; VI: 55n, 136; VII: 84n, 391, 413
Harris, Isham Green, IV: 351-52; VI: 440; VIII: 60n
Harris, J. T. [S. T.], VIII: 238
Harris, John, VII: 353n
Harris, John H., I: 329
Harris, Mary, V: 174n
Harris, Nathan, V: 175n
Harris, Thomas Langrell, I: 355, 519; II: 115, 227, 228, 287, 330-31, 483-84; III: 57, 108, 173, 227-29, 239-40, 258-59, 281-82, 345n; VII: 508
Harris, Thomas W., V: 495n
Harris, Townsend, IV: 468
Harris, W. P., I: 166
Harris, William, VIII: 68
Harris, William Hamilton, IV: 506n
Harris Light Cavalry, VII: 203
Harrisburg (Pa.), I: 201n; IV: 188, 239, 243-46, 404n; V: 417, 501; VI: 2, 87-88, 103-104, 285n, 293, 299, 321, 322, 324n
Harrisburg National Bank, IV: 283n
Harrisburg Telegraph, IV: 244n, 246n
Harrison, James, VIII: 177-78
Harrison, Napoleon Bonaparte, V: 215
Harrison, Peachy Quinn, III: 492-93

Harrison, Peyton (Ill.), III: 492n
Harrison, Peyton (Md.), VI: 378
Harrison, Reuben, I: 35-36, 85
Harrison, Samuel, VII: 280n
Harrison, William Henry, I: 184, 200, 201-206, 208, 210, 295, 317, 458-509; II: 83, 125, 136, 148, 351, 354; III: 78, 85, 162; IV: 36, 65, 420n; VIII: 181n, 374n
Harrison County (Ind.), I: 462; II: 217; IV: 61
Harrison County (Ohio), IV: 206
Harrison County (W. Va.), V: 298
Harrison Literary Institute (Philadelphia), IV: 39-40
Harrison Township (Gloucester Co., N. J.), VII: 523n
Harrisonburg (Va.), V: 230, 232, 236, 243, 246, 264, 267-68, 271, 275n; VI: 534; VIII: 268n
Harrison's Island, IV: 560n
Harrison's Landing [Bar] (Va.), V: 303n, 307n, 309n, 347n, 405n; VI: 15
Harrodsburg (Ky.), V: 321n, 459n
Harrow, William, VII: 11-12, 106, 113
Hart, Abraham, V: 212
Hart, Benjamin Kirtland, I: 251
Hart, David, I: 18, 44
Hart, Ellis, I: 258
Hart, Harvey B., I: 83-84
Hart, James (Ill.), II: 184
Hart, James (Tenn.), VIII: 70
Hart, Joseph D., VIII: 304
Hart, Margaret, VIII: 304n
Hart, Martha, see Wilson, Martha (Hart)
Hart, Moses, I: 83-84
Hart, Mrs. Moses, see Hart, Rhoda
Hart, Moses P., I: 83-84
Hart, Nancy, I: 83-84
Hart, Rhoda, I: 80, 83-84
Hart, Rhoda, Jr., I: 83-84
Hartford (Conn.), III: 554; IV: 1-13; VI: 122-23

Hartford Courant, IV: 2n.
Hartford Press, IV: 2n, 8
Hartsuff, George Lucas, V: 450n; VII: 549
Hartsville (Tenn.), V: 545-46; VI: 20
Hartt, Edward, V: 174
Hartt, Jedediah W., IV: 307
Hartwick Seminary, V: 213n
Hartz, Edward L., VII: 164n
Harvard University, IV: 82, 87, 249n; V: 480n; VI: 443n; VIII: 223
Harvel, P. S., I: 18
Harvey, ———, II: 180
Harvey, Alexander W., IV: 31
Harvey, Cordelia A. P., VI: 437
Harvey, James E., IV: 73, 94-95, 122, 125; V: 141
Harvey, Jonathan S., IV: 454-55
Harvey, Lewis P., VI: 437n
Harvey, Mrs. Lewis P., see Harvey, Cordelia A. P.
Harvey, William, I: 284-85, 323
Harvey Hospital (Madison, Wis.), VI: 437n
Harwood, Andrew Allen, V: 266n; VII: 27n
Harwood, Mrs. Andrew Allen [nee Luce], V: 266
Harwood, Sprigg, VIII: 198n
Harwood, Wilson F., IV: 399n; V: 266n; VII: 27n
Haskell, James R., V: 365n
Haskell, William T., I: 447-48, 458, 476n, 497, 515
Haskin, John Bussing, III: 367, 435
Haskins, Abraham Lincoln, V: 55n
Haskins, Gideon Welles, V: 55n
Haskins, Leonard, V: 55n
Haskins, Simon Cameron, V: 55n
Hassaurek, Frederick, IV: 283; VIII: 10n, 263-64
Ha-tan-in-koo (Indian), V: 543
Hatch, Edward, VII: 117, 129, 279, 311n

INDEX

Hatch, Ellen (Smith), I: xiv
Hatch, John Porter, V: 237n
Hatch, Ozias Mather, II: 345, 368, 410, 432-33; III: 90, 333n, 341, 342, 374n, 389, 392, 397n; IV: 73n, 136, 411n, 461n; V: 365n, 495n; VI: 100n, 237-38, 383, 450, 473; VII: 201-202
Hatch, Pascal Enos, I: xiv
Hatch, Mrs. Pascal Enos, see Hatch, Ellen
Hatch, Reuben B., IV: 461; V: 116n, 177n
Hatcher's Run, VIII: 380n, 382
Hatfield, James T., V: 136
Hathaway, William, VIII: 69
Hatteras (N. C.), V: 3n, 26n
Hatteras Inlet (N. C.), IV: 525n; V: 132n, 136n; VII: 231
Hatterscheidt, John P., IV: 312
Hatton, John, VII: 204
Hauberg, John Henry, VI: 182n
Hauley & Healy, II: 183
Haupt, Herman, V: 395, 397-402; VIII: 424
Hauser, Samuel T., VII: 371
Havana (Cuba), IV: 310, 318n; V: 110, 162; VI: 195; VII: 370n, 399-400; VIII: 230
Havana (Ill.), II: 541-43
Havelock, Charles Frederick, VI: 351
Haven, C. C., VII: 458n
Haven & Haven, II: 185
Havens, G. C., IV: 305
Hawaiian [Sandwich] Islands, V: 147; VI: 51, 69n, 77; VII: 165, 169, 383
Hawes, J. H., V: 474
Hawkes, Charles K., VII: 114-16, 156
Hawkins, John, II: 298
Hawkins, L., I: 166
Hawkins, Lucian, VIII: 69
Hawkins, Pierce B., VIII: 256n, 289
Hawkins, Rush Christopher, V: 59, 304-305

Hawkins County (Tenn.), VIII: 68
Hawks, Francis L., VII: 335-36, 339-40
Hawley, Chauncey G., VII: 59, 112
Hawley, Eliphalet B., II: 204-205, 424; III: 372, 399; VI: 237-38
Hawley [Eliphalet B.] & Edwards (Springfield), II: 205
Hawley, G. W., I: 285
Hawley, Isaac A., II: 424; III: 372, 377, 399
Hawley, Joseph Roswell, VII: 450
Hawley, Thomas G., I: 251
Hawley, William A., IV: 508
Hawley, E[liphalet] B., & Company (Springfield), II: 425n
Hawthorn, L. K., VIII: 262n
Hawthorne, Nathaniel, V: 158n
Hawxhurst, John, VI: 130
Hay, John (grandfather of John Milton Hay), II: 80n, 114, 313, 381n
Hay, John Milton: II: 80n, III: 337n, 506n, 517n; V: 34n, 164n, 202n, 370n; VI: 30n, 174n, 461n, 477n, 497n, 552n, 561n; VII: 25n, 33, 58n, 67n, 103, 126, 218n, 289n, 310n, 360, 376n, 386-87, 411n, 440-43, 451n, 479n, 481n, 482, 513n; VIII: 19n, 85n, 96n, 101n, 103n, 117n, 126n, 173n, 212n, 240, 333, 349n, 370n
Penned for L., IV: 296n, 394n; V: 9, 20n, 83n, 99n, 101n, 108n, 139n, 157n, 177n, 180n, 184n, 194n, 203n, 207n, 212n, 309n, 333n, 343n, 346n, 352n, 354n, 356n, 380n, 391n, 400n, 406n, 454n, 466n; VI: 15n, 38n, 40n, 54n, 78n, 309n, 360n, 368n, 373n, 375n, 382n, 485n, 490n, 534n, 537n, 556n; VII: 32, 65n, 95n, 324n, 358n, 386n, 462, 486n, 514n; VIII: 42n, 97n, 122n, 126n, 159n, 174n, 179n,

[113]

182n, 186n, 219n, 227n, 240n, 243n, 255n, 263n, 266n, 273n, 297n, 300, 301n, 313n, 325, 327n, 343n, 411n, 417n
His *Diary* cited or quoted: V: 433n; VI: 328n, 390n, 488n, 499n, 539n; VII: 79n, 83n, 84n, 103n, 118n, 386n, 514n; VIII: 42n, 101n
See also *Complete Works of Abraham Lincoln*; and *Abraham Lincoln: A History*
Hay, Logan, I: vii, xiv
Hay, Mrs. Logan, *see* Hay, Lucy Langdon
Hay, Lucy Langdon (Bowen), I: xiv, xvii, 228n, 254n; II: 80n, 307n, 313n, 395n; VII: 7n; VIII: 341n
Hay, Milton, I: 151; III: 352, 372
Hay, Nathaniel, II: 79-80, 307, 313, 323, 343-44, 381, 395
Hay, W. H., VII: 495n
Hay, order prohibiting (1865) export of, VIII: 227
Haycock, Judson, VIII: 417
Haycraft, Julius E., VII: 139n
Haycraft, Samuel, IV: 56-57, 69-70, 97, 99, 139
Hayday, Horace A., VII: 88n
Hayden, ———, V: 66
Hayden, Julius, IV: 442
Hayden, Sarah (Marshall), II: 211n
Hayes, Mrs. [nee Bainbridge], VII: 26
Hayes, Isaac Israel, V: 140
Hayes, Richard Somers, VII: 26
Hayes, Samuel Snowden, VI: 417-18, 435-36
Haymarket (Va.), V: 461
Hayner, Henry Z., VI: 427n, 434-35, 461-62, 482
Haynes, John, *see* Haines, Jonathan
Haynes, John L. [P.], V: 357n
Haynes' Bluff (Miss.), VI: 142n
Haynie, Isham Nicholas, VIII: 314n

Haynor, *see* Hayner, Henry Z.
Hay-pee-don (Indian), V: 542
Hays, Alexander, VI: 342n
Hays, David S., V: 380
Hays, J. W., VIII: 70
Hays, Lewis M., II: 105, 160, 201-202, 206
Hayti, *see* Haiti
Hayward, John T. K., VIII: 156
Haywood, ———, *see* Hayward, John T. K.
Haywood, Abel, VI: 65n
Haywood County (Tenn.), VIII: 70
Hazard, E. W., VII: 28n
Hazard, John, I: 354-55
Hazel, Caleb, IV: 61
Hazel Farm (S. C.), VI: 457
Hazen, William Babcock, VI: 194n
Hazlehurst, ———, IV: 166
Hazlett, William J., VII: 65
Hazzard, George Washington, V: 66, 126
Hda-hin-hday (Indian), V: 543
Head, Lafayette, VII: 70
Headley, S. F., VIII: 125
Heap, Gwinn H., IV: 320
Heard, John Theodore, VIII: 290
Hearn, Samuel B., VII: 522n
Heartman, Charles F., VI: 144n; VIII: 419n
Heath, Henry, II: 94
Heath, Herman H., VIII: 6
Heath, Randolph, II: 297
Heathsville (Va.), V: 123n
Heaton, O. B., III: 78
Heaverer, Jacob, I: 12
Hecker, Friedrich Karl Franz, II: 376, 380, 502-503, 524; IV: 390
Hecox, William T., VI: 340n
Hedden, Josiah, V: 163, 165
Hegon, ———, V: 85
Heineman, D. N., VII: 84n
Heintzelman, Charles Stewart, VI: 60, 185-86
Heintzelman, Samuel Peter, V: 150, 208-209, 226n, 256n, 310-12, 325n, 399n, 415; VI: 60n,

82n, 135, 185, 211n, 250n, 280, 337, 363n; VII: 391, 402, 499n

Heise, John, catalogs cited, VII: 95n, 120n, 143n; VIII: 48n, 218n

Heiskell, Daniel, VIII: 68

Heiskell, Joseph B., VII: 520

Heiskell, William, VII: 321n

Helena [St. Helena] (Ark.), I: 166n; V: 476n, 498-99; VI: 72n, 307n; VII: 83, 109, 185

Hellman, Alfred M., V: 259n

Helm, Benjamin Hardin, IV: 56, 70, 335; VI: 478, 480, 517n; VII: 63-64, 484-85

Helm, Mrs. Benjamin Hardin, see Helm, Emily (Todd)

Helm, Emily Todd, IV: 70; VI: 517; VII: 63-64, 484-85

Helm, John, VI: 480

Helm, John L., VI: 517n

Helm, Katherine, see Mary, Wife of Lincoln

Helm, Meredith, IV: 298

Helmick, William, IV: 325n; VII: 498

Helms, Richard, II: 65n; V: 116n

Helper, Hinton Rowan, III: 541

Hemingway, Thomas, II: 194-97, 200, 204, 216

Hemingway, William, VII: 371

Hempstead, Charles S., VIII: 423

Hempstead & Washburne (Galena, Ill.), VIII: 423n

Hempston, C. T., IV: 282

Hempstow, see Hempston, C. T.

Hendershot, Robert Henry, VII: 249; VIII: 194-95

Hendershott, Henry Bascom, VI: 162n

Henderson, Isaac, IV: 334; VII: 409-10

Henderson, James M., VIII: 68

Henderson, John Brooks, V: 253, 543; VI: 18, 53n, 100, 211n; VII: 13, 78-79, 84, 173n; VIII: 76, 156

Henderson, Ray, VIII: 214n

Henderson, Samuel, VIII: 69

Henderson, Thomas Jefferson, II:

288, 293-94, 297, 307n, 480; VI: 12

Henderson, William H., I: 238, 242-43, 249; II: 306-307

Henderson (Ky.), VII: 390; VIII: 266

Henderson County (Ky.), VI: 85-86

Henderson County (Tenn.), VIII: 70

Hendersonville (Ill.), I: 69-70

Hendricks, Thomas Andrews, VIII: 322

Hendricksburg (Ohio), VI: 346n

Hendrickson, George R., IV: 167

Hening, Henry, VI: 340n

Henkels, Stan. V., catalogs cited in footnotes on the ff. pages: IV: 114, 320, 324, 355, 363, 397, 444, 476, 517; V: 13, 33, 85, 129, 138, 201, 277, 340, 354, 473, 498; VI: 52, 127, 222, 395, 422, 430, 551; VII: 92, 127, 144, 171, 200, 442, 514, 522; VIII: 43, 106, 112, 132, 191, 227, 381, 420, 428

Hennepin (Ill.) Herald, I: 492n

Hennessy, James [alias], see Lynch, James

Hennessy, Thomas W., II: 183

Henning, Fanny, see Speed, Fanny (Henning)

Henrietta (yacht), IV: 357n

Henry, Alexander, IV: 238-39; V: 417-18; VI: 435; VII: 470n; VIII: 312n

Henry, Anson G., I: 77-78, 80, 90n, 93-94, 121, 158, 203, 205, 221, 228, 262, 288, 297, 308, 327, 337, 353-54, 356, 500; II: 14n, 31, 46, 68-69, 74, 78, 116n; III: 339-40; IV: 81-82, 118; VI: 111, 128-29, 144, 161n, 202n, 215; VII: 200n; VIII: 98, 414

Henry, Mrs. Anson G., see Henry, Eliza

Henry, Anson M., VI: 119n

Henry, Bushrod W., III: 202n

Henry, David W., IV: 84n

Henry, Edwin, V: 334, 430n

Henry, Eli_a (Dunlap), III: 340; IV: 82, 118
Henry, James, Jr., VIII: 68
Henry, James Dougherty, I: 13, 22, 101
Henry, John, I: 58, 129, 334; II: 473-74; III: 183
Henry, Joseph, VI: 151-52; VII: 378n, 385
Henry, Miles S., II: 297
Henry, Patrick, II: 127; III: 526n; V: 502-503
Henry (Ill.), III: 134
Henry IV (play), VI: 393n
Henry V (play), VI: 559n
Henry VIII (play), VI: 392
Henry County (Ky.), VI: 50
Henry County (Tenn.), VIII: 70
Henry E. Huntington Memorial Library and Art Gallery (San Marino, Calif.), I: xiv; IV: 249n, 348n
Henshaw, John C., III: 518-19; IV: 287, 321n
Herara, *see* Herrera, José Joaquín
Herbruger, F. C., IV: 39-40
Herkimer (N. Y.) *Democrat*, IV: 223n
Hermann, *see* Herrmann, Prince of Hohenlohe-Langenburg
Hermitage, The (Port Royal Is., S. C.), VI: 455
Herndon, Archer Gray, I: 82n, 121, 149, 233, 239n, 298; II: 40, 533; VIII: 429n
Herndon, Elliott Bohannon, II: 310, 386
Herndon, John Rowan, I: 13, 18, 150-51
Herndon, William, I: 268
Herndon, William D., I: 158, 284-85
Herndon, William Henry: mention of his relatives, I: 233n, 268n; administrator of Bell estate, 389n; cases in his law partnership with L., 416-17, 420, 445, II: 17, 70, 74, 101, 203, 410-12, 434-35, 535-36, III: 338, 343, 513, IV: 74; letters from L. on political affairs (1847-1849), I: 416-17, 419-20, 430-31, 446-48, 451-52, 476-77, 490-92, 497-98, 519n, II: 18-19; supports Hungarian freedom, II: 115; supports Davis for circuit court judge (1855), 310; signs calls for Republican local conventions (1856, 1857, 1859), 340n, 424, III: 372; and Palmer's 1856 candidacy for Congress, II: 357; and the 1858 Ill. senatorial race, 444, 455, III: 335; and the 1860 political campaign, III: 516, IV: 126, 140n; letter from L. on "money matters" (Feb. '62), V: 118; L. proposes brief assignment in St. Louis [Feb. '63], VI: 111
  References to his biographical material on L., I: 1n, 53n, 55n, 266n, 271n; II: 44n, 47n, 390n, 460n, 476n, 544n; III: 332n, 371n, 374n,-377n; IV: 50n, 57n, 104n, 126n, 141n, 191n; VII: 258n; VIII: 166n, 248n, 423n, 424n
Herpert, Wilton M., *see* Hupert, Milton L.
Herrán, Pedro Alcántara, V: 140-41; VI: 57-58
Herrera, José Joaquín, I: 472
Herrick, E. W., II: 176
Herrick, Edward, Jr., IV: 68n
Herrick, Hugh M., VIII: 350-51
Herrick, Josiah B., II: 23-24, 52, 378n
Herrick, William B., II: 24n
Herrington, A. M., III: 125
Herrmann, Prince of Hohenlohe-Langenburg, V: 482
Herron, Francis Jay, VI: 171n, 218n, 503; VII: 114n
Hertford, Joseph, IV: 495; VI: 94
Hertz, Emanuel, see *Abraham Lincoln: A New Portrait*; and *The Hidden Lincoln*
Herzog, William, VI: 242n

Hesing, Anton Caspar, II: 475
Hesler, Alexander, IV: 115n
Hesse, Grand Duke of, V: 363
Heth, Henry, VI: 199; VIII: 383
Heusken, Henry C. J., IV: 468n
Hewett, Josephus, I: 122, 450-51
Hewitt, Christopher C., IV: 308, 447-48; VIII: 368
Hewitt, Mary Elizabeth, I: 495-96
Hewlings, Mark, VII: 457n
Heymann, Roy A., V: 168n; VI: 346n
Heyn, J. G., VIII: 50n
Hiatt, Abraham, see Hyatt, Abraham
Hiatt, J. M., VIII: 409
Hibbard, Hiram, VIII: 315
Hibbitt, John B., VIII: 191n
Hibbs, John, II: 394-95
Hibernia (fire engine), VIII: 319
Hicklin, Hicklin & Spratt, VIII: 203
Hickman, John, III: 367, 408, 435, 451; IV: 311; V: 56, 342
Hickman, William, I: 284
Hickman (Ky.), IV: 510n
Hickman County (Tenn.), VIII: 69
Hickox, Addison, I: 255-56, 258; II: 76n
Hickox, Horace, I: 255-56, 258; II: 76n
Hickox, Virgil, I: 405, 444-45; II: 76n, 110, 331
Hicks, B. Chapin, VII: 367n
Hicks, George Montagu, V: 206, 229
Hicks, Mrs. Gordon, I: 10n
Hicks, James L., VIII: 273
Hicks, Jane (Wilson), VII: 367n
Hicks, Stephen G., I: 221n
Hicks, Thomas, IV: 76n
Hicks, Thomas Holliday, IV: 328, 340-41, 364, 508; V: 4; VI: 136, 420n, 491; VII: 350, 367, 432n, 482n; VIII: 82, 158, 369n, 409n, 423
Hicks, Mrs. Thomas Holliday, *see* Hicks, Jane

Hidden Lincoln, The (Hertz), VIII: 420n
Hiestand, John Andrew, IV: 167
Higbee, Chauncey L., II: 297
Higby, Lemuel, II: 74
Higgins, James M., II: 197-98
Higgins, William H., VII: 114n
Higginson, Henry C., VII: 538
Higginson, Thomas Wentworth Storrow, VI: 158n
High, George, II: 426
Highland (Ill.), II: 524n
Highland County (Ohio) Union Central Committee, V: 453n
"Highland Guard," V: 296n
Highlander (ship), VII: 198-99
Highley, Silas H., VII: 250
Highsmith, Henry W., VI: 544; VIII: 176, 205-206, 210
Highsmith, Richard, VI: 544
Higswith, *see* Highsmith, Henry W.
Hildegarde, Archduchess of Austria, VII: 476
Hill, Alexander S., VIII: 313n
Hill, Ambrose Powell, V: 310, 409n, 481n; VI: 199, 276n, 280n, 282n, 293n, 450n, 468n, 510n, 518, 535n; VII: 438n
Hill, Charles W., V: 4; VIII: 259
Hill, Cornelia H., V: 23n
Hill, Daniel Harvey, V: 310; VI: 184n, 354n
Hill, George Dana, IV: 294-95
Hill, J. S., IV: 455n
Hill, James, III: 494n
Hill, John, I: viii; IV: 104-108
Hill, John L., VII: 227-28
Hill, John Z. [?], III: 202n
Hill, Joshua, VIII: 27n
Hill, Luther, II: 374n
Hill, Michael, I: 283-84
Hill, Samuel, I: 14, 21-22; IV: 104n
Hillhouse, Thomas, VII: 413
Hilliard, Henry Washington, I: 425, 499n
Hillman, Jesse, IV: 167
Hillman (steamboat), see *C. E. Hillman*

Hills, E. O., II: 297
Hillsboro (Ill.), I: 327
Hillsborough (Ohio), V: 453n
Hilton (Fla.), see Milton (Fla.)
Hilton Head (S. C.), V: 110n, 222,
304n; VI: 157, 174, 235n, 256;
VII: 126n, 532, 544; VIII: 93n,
187n
Hinch, Benjamin P., II: 297
Hines, Reuben, VIII: 68
Hingham (Mass.), I: 456n; IV:
60n
Hin-han-shoon-ko-yag (Indian),
V: 542
Hinkell, Bailey, VIII: 70
Hinkle, William F., VIII: 232-33
Hinton, E., V: 403n
Hise, John, III: 125
"Historicus" [pseud.], VII: 273n
History of Abraham Lincoln, and
the Overthrow of Slavery, The
(Arnold), VII: 424n
History of America in Documents,
The, IV: 147n
History of Berkeley County, West
Virginia (Evans), VII: 446n
History of Edward W. Kinsley
Post No. 113, Department of
Massachusetts, Grand Army of
the Republic (Parker), VIII:
425n
History of Illinois (Ford), III: 28,
182
History of Massachusetts in the
Civil War, A (Schouler), IV:
370n
History of the Brooklyn and Long
Island Fair, VII: 278n
History of the City of New York
(Booth), V: 352n
History of the Early Settlers of
Sangamon County, Illinois
(Power), I: 116n
History of the Great Western
Sanitary Fair (Boynton), VII:
12n
History of the One Hundreth
Regiment of New York Volun-
teers (Stowits), VII: 171n

Hitchcock, ———, V: 85
Hitchcock, Ethan Allen, V: 151n,
164n, 179n, 180n, 196; VI: 59n,
394n, 398n; VII: 42, 119-20, 139,
143n, 195n, 208n, 309n, 458, 502,
538, 540; VIII: 10, 16, 37n, 51-
52, 95, 110, 123n, 131, 192, 224,
310-11, 324
Hitchcock, Phineas Warren, IV:
336n, 366; VIII: 349n
Hitchcock, Roswell D., IV: 445-
46
Hitt, Robert Roberts, II: 415n; III:
351n, 365n
Hitt, Samuel Merritt, III: 350-51
Hitt, Wright, III: 351n
Hittle, William, II: 396n
Hoadley, George, VII: 112n
Hobart, Ella E. (Gibson), VIII:
102n
Hobbs, Albert, VIII: 86
Hobbs, William C., IV: 37
Hobby, James M., VII: 360
Hoblitzell, William T., VI: 229n
Hobson, Atwood G., VI: 424
Hobson, Edward Henry, VII: 391
Hodge, Andrew, I: 446
Hodge, W. H., I: 446
Hodge, William L., IV., 537
Hodgenville (Ky.), IV: 56, 70, 75;
VIII: 166n
Hodges, Albert Gallatin, VII: 281-
83, 308-309, 497; VIII: 79, 120
Hodges, John M., IV: 295
Hodges, William H., VI: 89-90,
185-86
Hoed, J. K., VII: 371
Hoelke, H. E., IV: 132
Hoes, Calvin, VIII: 68
Hoes, James H., VII: 75
Hoey, John, V: 163, 165
Hoffman, Benjamin F., VII: 94
Hoffman, Henry William, IV:
304, 333, 404; VII: 75-76; VIII:
23, 41-42, 48-49, 100
Hoffman, Jacob, I: 393
Hoffman, John, VIII: 120-21
Hoffman, Josiah Ogden, VII: 67-
68

Hoffman, William, V: 369, 403n; VI: 220n, 398n; VII: 80n, 123; VIII: 10n, 16n, 30, 37, 205, 314n

Hoffmann, Francis Arnold, II: 345; VII: 315

Hoffmann, Francis Arnold, Jr., VII: 315

Hoffmann, Julius T. C., VII: 315

Hofner, William, VIII: 68

Hogan, Christopher V., VIII: 233-34

Hogan, John, I: 61, 210-11, 499-500; VII: 179n, 182-83; VIII: 316n

Hoge, Abraham H., V: 512n

Hoge, Mrs. Abraham H., see Hoge, Jane Currie

Hoge, George Blaikie, V: 512n; VI: 126n

Hoge, Holmes, V: 512n; VI: 40-41, 96n

Hoge, Jane Currie (Blaikie), V: 512; VI: 40-41, 96n; VII: 75n

Hogeboom, John T., V: 93n; VII: 182n, 269n, 413

Hogg, George, IV: 447

Hoheimer, Joseph, I: 12

Hoheimer, William, I: 12

Hohenlohe-Langenburg, Herrmann, Prince of, V: 482

Hohenzollern-Sigmaringen, Leopold, Hereditary Prince of, V: 105; VII: 478

Holbrook, Amory, IV: 101

Holbrook, James C., II: 297; VII: 358

Holcomb, A. Barton, VII: 367

Holcomb, Florence, VII: 28n

Holcombe, James B., VII: 443n

Holcombe, John M., Jr., VII: 136n

Hole-in-the-day (Indian), VII: 345

Holiday, Benjamin, VII: 343n

Holland, James P., VIII: 176, 205-206, 210

Hollander, ———, VI: 268

Hollaway, Henry, VIII: 68

Holliday, George H., II: 297

Holliday, J. B., VIII: 244

Holliday, Mrs. J. B., see Holliday, Lallie

Holliday, Lallie, VIII: 244

Hollister, David F., V: 375

Holloway, David Pierson, IV: 294-95; V: 198, 385; VI: 50n, 124

Holloway, Henry Clay, VIII: 81n

Holman, ———, VI: 459

Holman, William Steele, V: 20n

Holmes, James H., IV: 312; V: 107; VIII: 594

Holmes, Theophilus Hunter, VI: 31n

Holmes, William J., VI: 443

Holston River, IV: 61; VI: 470n, 471n, 481, 483n

Holt, Frank B., VIII: 90n

Holt, Joseph: and relief of Fort Sumter, IV: 172-73, 277n, 279; L. requests interview with (Mar. 13, '61), 282; and appointments, 327n; V: 129, VIII: 416n; protests Frémont proclamation (Sept. '61), IV: 518n, 520; recommends commands in the West for Sherman and Halleck, V: 21-22; and the parole of Union prisoners-of-war (Oct. '62), 449n; support of emancipation in Ky., 503-504; and the execution of Minn. Indians, 537-38; appointed Judge Advocate General, (Sept. '62) 538n; VIII: 424, (June '64) VII: 372; recommends cancellation of revocation of Benham's brigadier general appointment, VI: 35; and the loss of Milroy's division, 541-42; on the transfer or private use of government property, VII: 264n; mentioned for Vice President (June '64), 376-78; declines to accept attorney general appointment and recommends Speed, VIII: 126n; mentioned also, IV: 343n, VI: 105n

Cases of pardons, courts-martial, dismissals, etc.; VI: 54.

169n, 211, 220, 222-23, 227, 229,
241, 246, 253, 258n, 270-71, 279-
80, 285-87, 292-93, 296-97,
335-37, 340, 347, 385, 392n, 397,
400, 402n, 419, 421, 426, 442,
477, 505, 508-509, 519n, 532n,
548n; VII: 2, 25n, 58n, 82n, 93-
94, 103, 104n, 129n, 160-61,
163n, 167-68, 173-76, 197,
208n, 209n, 219, 223, 227,
232-33, 265, 271, 276, 292-
94, 298-99, 314, 322, 332,
353, 357, 421, 436, 447-48, 465,
470, 479-80, 491, 493, 497, 516-
17, 519, 531, 536, 543, 545-47;
VIII: 8, 10, 16-18, 22, 24, 32-33,
37, 39, 76, 87, 89n, 90, 100, 104,
122, 133, 180, 187-88, 193, 210,
213, 219, 224, 229, 233, 240n,
246, 269n, 270, 273n, 291, 303-
304, 309, 313, 321-22, 326, 329,
353-54, 357, 368, 405, 594
Holt, W. D., IV: 327n
Homestead Law, IV: 202-203; V:
525; VII: 46-47; VIII: 146
Honduras, IV: 397; V: 371n, 521;
VII: 373; VIII: 167
Honolulu (Hawaii), V: 147, 162;
VIII: 132n, 360n
Hood, Archibald, I: 264
Hood, John Bell, VI: 249n, 480;
VII: 499n; VIII: 9n, 27, 33,
182
Hood, Michell, VIII: 70
Hood, P. H., & Company (Washington), I: 495
Hoodley, David, V: 498n
Hook, John, V: 503n
Hooker, Joseph: his appointment
(May '61) as Brigadier General
of Volunteers, IV: 412-13, VIII:
593-94; and appointments, IV:
516, VI: 180, 184, 249, VII:
355n; invites L. to Fort Lincoln
flag-raising (Oct. '61), IV: 559;
and the Army of the Potomac
(Feb.-Aug. '62), V: 123n, 130n,
184, 281n, 399n, 400n, 407n,
448; given command of Fifth

Corps, 485; L. blocks his dismissal by Burnside, VI: 74-75,
77; given command of Army of
the Potomac, 77n, 78-79; his
promotion to Major General,
82n; and assignment of Sigel
to command of the Eleventh
Corps, 93; and expediency of
transferring regiments to W.
Va. (Feb. '63), 115-16; dismissals, leaves of absence, and
courts-martial, 118, 125, 126,
244, 248, VIII: 210-11, 291-92
Visit to Washington (Feb.
'63), VI: 118n; transfers Stahel
to Heintzelman's command,
135; L.'s visits to (Apr., June
'63), 161, 270; and the Army of
the Potomac (Apr.-June '63),
164-65, 168-69, 173, 175-76, 188-
90, 193, 196-203, 207, 215, 217-
18, 233, 249-51, 255, 257-58,
270-71, 273-74, 276-78, 280-84,
289-90, 293n, 297-98, 309n;
Schurz's complaints against,
VI: 168, VII: 244n, 263n; criticized by the Philadelphia Press
(May '63), VI: 214n; and pressure to remove Halleck as General-in-Chief, 230; complains of
Halleck's lack of confidence in
him, 281-82; suggested for command of a corps under Meade,
350, 381, 383; Slocum protests
serving under his command,
486; at Chattanooga (fall '63),
486, 494n, 510-11, 554, VII: 30n
Hooper, Samuel, VII: 548; VIII:
352n
Hope, Thomas M., III: 283-84, 295
Hope of Israel Congregation
(Philadelphia), V: 212
Hope place (S. C.), VI: 456
Hopkins, ———, VII: 309n
Hopkins, C. C., II: 297
Hopkins, Henry, V: 54; VI: 313n
Hopkins, Moses B., VII: 371
Hopkins, Robert [alias], see
Chaskay-don (Indian)

Hopkins, Robert G., VIII: 419n
Hopkins, Samuel Taylor, II: 84
Hopkins, William R., V: 335-36
Hopkins County (Ky.), VI: 85, 87n
Hopper, John, VII: 265
Horatio Seymour of New York (Mitchell), VIII: 321n
Hord, John K., IV: 295
Hornbuckle, Tilman, I: 60
Horner, Robert E., I: 417-18, 497
Horner, William H. W., VI: 177
Hornsecker, Tilman, *see* Hornbuckle, Tilman
Horses and mules, export of, VI: 432; VII: 331
Horsford, Eben N., VII: 378n, 385n
Horsman, J., III: 126
Horton, Valentine Baxter, V: 218
Hosea, Robert, IV: 197
Hoskins, Charles, VI: 413n; VII: 139n
Hoskins, John Deane Charles, VII: 139, 235
"Hoskinsville Rebellion," VII: 131n
Hosmer, Addison Augustus, VIII: 90n
Hosmer, Charles Hawes, IV: 467
Hosmer, Hezekiah Lord, VII: 355n, 371-72
Hosmer, James Ray, VI: 171n
Hosmer, P. E., II: 297
Hostick, King V., I: xiv
Hotchkiss, Benjamin Berkeley, VII: 236
Hotchkiss, Giles Waldo, VIII: 364-65
Houck, Soloman J., V: 408
Hough, Charlotte [Lotty], VIII: 35, 340
Hough, Daniel, I: 38
Hough, Henry A., I: 331
Hough, John A. (Jack), I: 493n; III: 399
Hough, Rosell M., VIII: 359
Houghan, Thomas, I: 43
Houghton, Elijah, I: 44n

Houghton, Horace Hooking, II: 356n
Houghton, Joel, IV: 349
Houghton, John H., I: 11
Houk, David A., VI: 300-306
House Divided doctrine: in 1843 Whig campaign circular, I: 315; preliminary draft of L.'s 1858 speech, II: 448n; text of 1858 speech, 461-69; comments on 1858 speech, 471, 490-94, 512-14, III: 67, 140, 178, 218-19, 241, 265-66, 286, 519-20, 550-51; defends doctrine in debate with Douglas, III: 7-8, 17-18, 72-73, 78, 82-83, 86-88, 120-21, 305-306, 308-10, 407-408, 438, 464; certified transcript (1860) of passage from 1858 speech, IV: 147; printing of 1858 speech, VIII: 415
House Journal, V: 66n, 181n; VIII: 414n
House of Representatives, messages reporting or transmitting reports on: Spanish incorporation of the Dominican Republic, IV: 446; relations with foreign powers, 459-60, V: 55, 319; arrest of Baltimore police commissioners, IV: 461-62; Confederate imprisonment of loyalists, 469; extension of foreign trade, V: 55-56; European intervention in Mexico, 61, 188, 230, VI: 38-39, 90, VII: 359; Chinese coolie trade, V: 79; employment of U. S. army officers in recruiting, 140; Dutch taxation methods, 181; insurgent privateers in foreign ports, 199; maltreatment of American missionaries in Egypt, 229; N. C. education of Negro children, 259-60; judiciary leaves of absence, 267n, 268; reorganization of the army medical department, 275; adjournment postponement (1862), 326; U. S. arrest

of Confederate seamen in Tangier, 549; diplomatic representation in New Granada, VI: 56-58; Indian uprising, 104; arrest of U. S. consul to Montreal, VII: 187-88; re-enlistment of veteran volunteers, 214; a questioned officer assignment, 290; questioned holding of Blair's military commission upon election to Congress, 319-20, 326-27; correction of clerical errors in 1864 internal revenue act, VIII: 199; exchange of prisoners-of-war, 204; Hampton Roads conference, 269, 274-85; see also Congress, messages to

House of Representatives Executive Documents, cited in footnotes on the ff. pages: IV: 459, 460, 462; V: 14, 74, 77, 79, 110, 115, 188, 199, 270, 319, 518, 549, 552; VI: 39, 90, 104; VII: 36, 43, 45-47, 88, 140, 187, 307, 312, 327, 359; VIII: 22, 136, 139, 140, 142, 144, 145, 147, 153, 204

House Reports, V: 20n; VIII: 43n

Houston, D. W., VIII: 194n

Houston, George S., I: 463

Houston, John B., VIII: 98-99

Houston, John Wallace, I: 476n, 497; VI: 180

Houston (Tex.), VI: 366n; VIII: 108, 230-31

Hovey, Alvin Peterson, VI: 230; VII: 463-64; VIII: 74n, 123, 211

Hovey, Charles Edward, VI: 231n, 340

Howard, Frank, VII: 491n

Howard, Jacob Merritt, VII: 84n, 469n

Howard, James Quay, II: 22n; IV: 80

Howard, John C., IV: 286n

Howard, Joseph, Jr., VII: 348n, 350n, 512-13; VIII: 13n

Howard, Mrs. Joseph, Jr., VII: 513n

Howard, Justin H., IV: 447

Howard, Mark, IV: 310; VI: 122-23

Howard, Oliver Otis, IV: 504-505; VI: 168n, 330n, 341-42, 486, 494n, 554n; VII: 244n; VIII: 136n

Howard, Robert, VI: 422

Howard, Sam, VIII: 68

Howard, William Alanson, VI: 549

Howard County (Mo.), VII: 189n

Howe, Albion Parris, VII: 437

Howe, Frank W., VIII: 157

Howe, George, IV: 299

Howe, S. D., VII: 284

Howe, Thomas M., VI: 189n

Howe, Timothy Otis, IV: 462n; V: 224

Howell, Eunice E., III: 520

Howell, Joseph C., I: 221

Howell, Samuel H., IV: 493n

Howell, William T., VIII: 410

Howells, William Dean, see *Lives and Speeches of Abraham Lincoln and Hannibal Hamlin*

Howland, Allen H., II: 167

Howland, George, VII: 77n

Howland, John D., VIII: 158n

Hoyne, Thomas, III: 125

Hoyt, Charles, II: 286, 314, 328-29

Hoyt, Charles J., VI: 364

Hoyt, John W., IV: 551

Hubbard, Asahel Wheeler, VII: 207n

Hubbard, E. K., I: 191

Hubbard, Gurdon Saltonstall, II: 431; III: 507-509, 513n, 516

Hubbard, John Henry, VIII: 122n

Hubbard, W. B., V: 98n

Hubbell, Augustus, VII: 368

Hubbell, Henry Wilson, VI: 112n

Hubbell, Sydney A., VII: 480, 490; VIII: 243n

Huckleberry, John W., I: 422

Hudgin, Moses, VI: 443

Hudgins, Prince L., VIII: 324n

Hudson, Charles, I: 475, 499

Hudson, Frederick, VII: 349n

Hudson, Jonathan T., I: 251
Hudson, Peter Todd, VIII: 382n
Hudson (N. Y.), IV: 227-28
Hudson (Ohio), IV: 217-18
Hudson (steamboat), VI: 389
Hudson Bay Territories (Canada), VII: 160
Hudson's Bay Company, VII: 76, 246-47; VIII: 140
Huey, William, V: 342
Huff's Ferry (Tenn.), VII: 14n
Huger, Benjamin, V: 310
Hughes, James, V: 407-408; VI: 526n; VII: 11n, 214-15; VIII: 54, 73, 74, 200n, 287n, 343-44, 353
Hughes, John D., I: 31n, 44n, 45n
Hughes, John Joseph, IV: 418-19, 559; VI: 154n, 185, 309n
Hughes, Thomas W., VII: 321
Hughlett, James W. W., VIII: 94-95
Huidekoper, Henry Shippen, VI: 533; VII: 530-31; VIII: 14n, 17n; book cited, VI: 533n, VII: 317n
Huidekoper, Herman, VII: 317
Hull, Alden, I: 249, 306-307
Hull, Andrew, VIII: 68
Hull, Morton Denison, II: 303n
Hull, Peter K., II: 475n
Hull, Thomas, II: 374n
Hull, William, I: 509-10
Hulsemann (Chevalier), V: 95
Humboldt Land Office, IV: 305; V: 262n, 500n; VIII: 356n
Humphrey, Mary E., I: xvii
Humphreys, Andrew, VIII: 74n, 210-11
Humphreys, Andrew Atkinson, VI: 81, 342n; VIII: 382-83, 390-91
Humphreys County (Tenn.), VIII: 69
Hungary, II: 62, 115-16; IV: 293n, 510n
Hungary Neck (Md.), VII: 9n
Hunnycutt (S. C.), VIII: 68
Hunt, A. Cameron, V: 265
Hunt, Charles, VII: 352, 386n
Hunt, Daniel, VII: 296n

Hunt, Mrs. Daniel, *see* Hunt Sallie (Ward)
Hunt, Henry Jackson, VI: 164n
Hunt, Leavitt, VI: 497n
Hunt, Lewis Cass, VIII: 253n
Hunt, Randall, IV: 164, 173
Hunt, Sallie (Ward), VII: 295-96
Hunt, Timothy Atwater: VI: 107n
Hunt, Ward, VII: 498
Hunt, Washington, I: 497; IV: 89, 98
Hunter, D. C., VIII: 379n
Hunter, David: reports rumors of plans to prevent L.'s inauguration (1860), IV: 132, 159; appointments and dismissals, 335, 395, 413, 553, V: 369n VI: 191-92, 490n, VII: 364-65, 392n; promoted to colonel, IV: 418; and Union defeat at Vienna, Va., (1861), 450n; appointed Major General, 483; relieves Frémont in Mo., 513, 560n, 562-63, V: 1-2, 7, VI: 501; in command of Department of Kans., V: 22n, 71, 84-85, 115-16, 131, 155; Benham assigned to command of, 69n; L.'s revocation of his emancipation order, 219n, 222-26, 318, VII: 282; sends reinforcements to McClellan (July '62), V: 303-306; L.'s order to take over command of Burnside's Corps (Nov. '62), 485; authorization for confiscation of S. C. land, VI: 98-99; and the use of Negro troops in Fla., 158; cooperation with naval forces in operations against Charleston (spring '63), 170, 173-74, 256; and pressure to dismiss Halleck (May '63), 230; his relief from command of the Department of the South, 310, 383; assigned to command of the District of Western Va., VII: 364n; at Harper's Ferry (July '64), 437, 438, 456, 465-66, 472, 476n; attempts to

resign (July 17, '64), 445; complaints against his military arrests in Frederick, Md. (Aug. '64), 477-78, VIII: 82n
Hunter, Robert Finley, V: 78, 218
Hunter, Mrs. Robert Finley, V: 78
Hunter, Robert Mercer Taliaferro, IV: 443n; VIII: 246-48, 250, 258, 269, 276-87, 388
Hunter, Thomas, I: 206
Hunter, William, IV: 397
Hunting Island (S. C.), VI: 455
Hunting Run (Va.), VI: 200n
Huntington, Elisha M., V: 492n
Huntington, George L., I: 393
Huntington, J. W. Perit, VIII: 322
Huntington Memorial Library, see Henry E. Huntington Memorial Library and Art Gallery
Huntsville (Tenn.), see Hartsville (Tenn.)
Hupert, Milton L., VI: 292
Hurd, Jacob S., II: 415n
Hurd, Washington, VIII: 68
Hurdle, Henry M., V: 266n
Hurlbut, Sophronia (Stevens), IV: 134
Hurlbut, Stephen Augustus, I: 498; II: 456; IV: 124, 134, 349, 407, 463, 533; VI: 70, 142, 179n, 226, 324, 358-59, 387-88; VII: 75, 104, 276n, 327-28, 370, 428n; VIII: 106-108, 164n, 325
Hurlbut, Mrs. Stephen Augustus, see Hurlbut, Sophronia
Huron (Ill.), I: 130, II: 14n; facsimile of survey, following page I: 48

Hurst, Charles R., I: 284-85, 305-306, 323, 325, 328-29, 389; II: 39-40
Hurtado, Marcelino, IV: 393
Hurtt, Francis W., VII: 375
Husband, Henry Morris, VII: 31
Huson, Calvin, IV: 469n
Huson, Calvin, Jr., IV: 469n
Hussey, Nathan, I: 79
Hutches, M. L., I: 52
Hutches, Moris, I: 52
Hutchins, Charles, IV: 407n; VII: 284
Hutchins, Horace Andrews, VIII: 173n
Hutchins, John, VII: 114n
Hutchins, Waldo, VI: 312n
Hutchins, Wells Andrews, VI: 300-306
Hutchinson, Mrs., VI: 517n
Hutchinson, George E., VIII: 78-79
Hutchinson, John (Ill.), III: 399
Hutchinson, John (Kans.), IV: 294
Hutchinson's Cemetery (Springfield), III: 399
Hutter, E. W., VIII: 90n
Hutter, Mrs. E. W., see Hutter, Elizabeth
Hutter, Elizabeth E., VI: 375-76, 519, 523; VIII: 90
Huttinger, Paul, VI: 59n
Hutton, Charles Gordon, VI: 538n
Hutton, Hamilton, V: 17n
Hutton, John C., VIII: 159
Hyatt, Abrahm, VI: 224
Hycks, see Hicks, James L.
Hyde, Alfred, II: 535
Hypolite Ange (Indian), V: 543

I

Iankiewicz, Stephen J., I: 327
Icawtuze (Indian), VII: 325
"Ichabod" [sobriquet], *see* Smith, Israel S.
Idaho Territory, VI: 195n; VII: 163-64, 166, 188, 372; VIII: 145, 412n
Ide, Clara J., IV: 73n
Ide, George B., VII: 368
Ide, Mrs. Roy W., *see* Ide, Clara J.
Ihrie, George Percy, VI: 465
Iles, Elijah, I: 10n, 14, 43; II: 70-71, 324; VII: 167n
Iles, Washington, I: 79
Illinoian [Jacksonville, Ill.], I: 134n; II: 44n
Illinois: apportionment of representation, I: 34, 225, 287-88, II: 432, 505, III: 336-37, 351, 356, 364-65; capital moved to Springfield, *see* Illinois, capital of; establishment of new counties, I: 41-42, 54-60, 72, 127-32, 138-42, 144-46, 198-99, 240; agricultural wealth, 135, 397, 402-404; state constitutions, (*1818*) 138n, 235-36, 247, 249, (*1848*) II: 191, 209, III: 9-10, 242, 457-58; tribute to Mexican War soldiers, I: 392-93; Constitutional convention (1847), 394-95, 449, III: 320; disputed removal of superintendent of state insane hospital, II: 197-98, 286-87, 434; slavery in, 263, 277, 282, III: 456-58, 467, 485; L.'s speech to Colonization Society, II: 298-99; banking laws of, 414; mention of Ill. State University, III: 395n, IV: 189; L.'s remarks (1861) to a state delegation, IV: 275; mobilization, recruitment, and the draft,

349n, 374n, 381, 388, 390, V: 365n, 391-93, 406n, 430-31, 469n, VI: 300n, 417-18, 435-36, VII: 312n, VIII: 8, 33-34; mention of agricultural society, V: 406; advocacy of division of state, 413n; fear of insurrection (Feb. '63), VI: 100n; list of provost marshals and enrolling board appointments (1863), 197-98; erection of a Soldiers Home, VII: 167, 316n; ratification of the Thirteenth Amendment, VIII: 254-55
See also Bank, Ill. state; Elections in Illinois; Illinois, capital of; Illinois Legislature, L. in; Internal improvements; Judicial system (Ill.); Public lands, sale of; Revenue and expenditures (Ill.); and *Laws of Illinois*
Illinois, capital of: removal from Vandalia to Springfield, I: 54, 73, 87n; erection of a state house at Springfield, 77-78, 80, 84-85, 116-17, 126-27, 184, 230-31, 327; purchase of house for the governor, 197
Illinois, Military District of, VII: 492n
Illinois Advocate and State Register [Vandalia], see *Illinois State Register*
Illinois and Michigan Canal, *see* Canals (Ill.)
Illinois and Mississippi Telegraph Company, II: 432n
Illinois Central Railroad, I: viii, 146-47, 250, 407n; II: 134, 189, 194n, 202, 205, 207, 209, 210n, 233-34, 325-26, 333-35, 336n, 389, 392, 397-98, 429, 460n,

538n; III: 206, 244, 330-31, 393n, 486; IV: 456n; V: 350n; VI: 227-28

Illinois College (Jacksonville), II: 199n, 379n; III: 356n; VI: 160; VIII: 593

Illinois Gazette [Lacon], I: 322n, 360n, 366, 382n, 383n, 384n, 492n; II: 11n, 14n

Illinois Historical Survey (Urbana), I: 120n

Illinois Journal [Springfield], see *Illinois State Journal*

Illinois legislature, L. in, his bills, speeches, committee reports and resolutions on: jurisdiction of justices of the peace, I: 26, 28, 124; estrays, 27-28; House regulations and organization, 29, 55, 125, 211, 219, 231; construction of bridges, 28-30, 72-73; relief for purchasers of Vandalia lots, 30-31; contingent fund, 31; surveyor of Schuyler Co., 31; sale of public lands, 32, 132-38, 147-48; road construction, 32-36, 39-40, 42, 45-47, 69-72, 82, 85-87, 93, 181-83

Marks and brands, 33; apportionment of representation, 34, 225-28; insolvent debtors, 39, 41; canal companies, commissioners, and scrip, 40, 43, 147, 195-98, 232, 243-44; establishment of new counties, 41-42, 54-60, 72, 127-32, 138-42, 144-46, 198-99, 240; state bank, 43, 61-69, 179, 184-95, 237-38, 240-42; fire insurance company, 43; public printing, 44, 212, 221-24, 241; state budgets (1836, 1837), 45, 74; school funds, 71; moving capital to Springfield, 73; protest on slavery, 74-75; new state house, 80, 84-85, 126-27, 184, 230-31; sale of real estate, 80, 83-84; incorporation of Springfield, 81-82, 238-39; railroad and fund commissioners, 122-23

Judgments and executions, 123; election of House members to state or federal office, 124-25, 138; fugitive slaves, 126; depositories for tax monies, 134; relief for county clerk, 142, 149-50; sub-treasury system, 143, 159-79; internal improvements, 144, 184, 200-201, 232; judiciary reorganization, 145, 239, 244-49; location of railroad, 146-47; tax collection, 155; contested elections and election frauds, 157, 212-15; Springfield Mechanics Union, 158; surveying or vacating town plats, 179-80, 183, 220; tax exemptions for veterans, 181-82; relief of incorporated towns, 183-84

Purchase of house for governor, 197; divorces, 198; interest on promissory notes, 200; teachers' examinations, 213-14; state debt, 215-18, 219-21, 238, 243; burning of bank notes, 224-25, 240; commemoration of the battle of New Orleans, 226; a burlesque petition, 226-27; creation of a board of auditors, 232; incorporation of a railroad, 233; election of a public binder, 237; appropriations, 239; incorporation of turnpike company, 250-51; taxing doctors and lawyers, 252; incorporation of mining company, II: 189-91

House Journal, cited in footnotes on the ff. pages: I: 32, 40, 43, 75, 125, 135, 145, 211, 222, 244; VIII: 429

Illinois Patriot [Jacksonville], I: 5n

Illinois Reports, VI: 97n, 404n, 405n

Illinois Republican [Shawneetown], I: 291n

Illinois Republican [Springfield], I: 80, 95, 99, 101, 105-106

Illinois River, I: 34
Illinois Sentinel [Jacksonville],
II: 368n, 449n, 450n; III: 329n
Illinois Staats-Anzeiger [Spring-
field], II: 524n; III: 381n, 383,
391n
Illinois State Bank, *see* Bank, Ill.
State
Illinois State Chronicle [Deca-
tur], II: 333n, 398n
Illinois State Democrat [Spring-
field], II: 533
Illinois State Historical Library
(Springfield), I: xii, xiv; II:
211n; V: 463n; VII: 339n
Illinois State Hospital for the Insane (Jacksonville), II: 198n,
286, 434
Illinois State Journal [Spring-
field]: L. and, II: 25, 61, 68
(letter to editors), 79, 93, 211,
226, 412, 522, 523, 531, 537; III:
84; IV: 32, 39, 131, 150 (editorial by L.); VII: 399 ("always
my friend")
Cited in footnotes on the ff.
pages, I: 10, 49, 60, 431; II: 62,
96, 113, 115-16, 118, 120-21, 133,
135, 160, 218, 227, 230, 240,
247, 290, 299, 310, 311, 317, 340,
355, 383, 386, 398, 425, 461, 468,
469, 483, 504-11, 513, 515-16,
518-19, 538; III: 202, 203, 334,
350, 356, 365, 372, 377, 381, 400,
438, 459, 463, 489, 493, 497, 510,
551; IV: 50-51, 71, 87, 91, 94,
108, 112, 123, 129, 143, 144, 150,
161, 191, 232, 249, 303; VII:
117, 144
See also *Sangamo Journal*
Illinois State Library (Springfield), I: 332
Illinois State Penitentiary (Alton), I: 45
Illinois State Register [Vandalia-
Springfield], I: 95n, 154n,
292-93, 306n, 492; II: 160, 211,
447-48, 531, 537; III: 57, 183,
227-28, 258, 281; VI: 252n

Cited in footnotes on the ff.
pages, I: 34, 56, 132, 134, 197,
201, 215, 217, 219-22, 226-27,
231-33, 237-40, 242-44, 252, 327,
333-35, 338, 398; II: 5, 13, 68,
79, 115, 149, 227, 229, 341, 345,
359, 368; IV: 42
Illinois State University (Springfield), III: 395n; IV: 189
Illinois Statesman [Blooming-
ton], IV: 42n
Illinois Wesleyan University, II:
294n
"Illinoisian" [pseud.], VI: 252n
Illinoistown [now East St. Louis]
(Ill.), II: 212n
Imboden, John Daniel, VI: 534-35
Immigration, L. on, II: 263; IV:
202-203; VII: 40, 489; VIII: 141
*Impending Crisis in the South and
How to Meet It, The* (Helper),
III: 541
Inauguration (1861), L.'s: plans
for trip to Washington, IV: 92,
170-71, 181-82, 184-88, 217, 239,
281n; preparation of address,
92-93, 169n, 184, 201n, 249-62;
rumors of plans to prevent inauguration, 159n, 170-71, 175n,
177, 241n; text of address, 262-
71; comments on and references
to address, 110, 274-75, 316, 330-
31, 423, 425, 439; V: 49, 527-28,
554n; VII: 132; VIII: 332
Inauguration (1865), L.'s: text of
address, VIII: 332-33; invitation to inauguration ball, 334,
337; references to address, 356,
367
Independence (Mo.), VIII: 57n
Independence Hall (Philadelphia), II: 275, 284; IV: 240-42,
244; VI: 118n
Indian agencies: appointments,
IV: 283, 288, 296-98, 302-307,
326, 348-49, 389, 391, 403-404,
406n, 442, 456, 462, 498; V: 78,
104, 346, 354, 485; VI: 21, 134,
142, 164, 208-209, 246, 355-56;

VIII: 114-15, 194, 225-26, 325, 338-39, 355, 358-59, 370, 410
  Federal disbursements for, (*1863*) VII: 42, (*1864*) VIII: 142; recommended reorganization of system of, VIII: 146-47
Indian Hill (S. C.), VI: 456
Indian Territory, IV: 476n; V: 180n, 456n; VII: 100n, 119n, 300n, 341n
Indiana, I: 132-33, 222, 342n, 378; IV: 179, 181, 192-97, 276n, 362, 384-85, 388, 402, 410, 415, 454, 537n; V: 283, 356-57, 392-93, 469n, 492; VI: 88n, 237n, 300n, 515; VII: 80n, 128, 312n, 356n; VIII: 11, 27n, 33-34, 38n, 45-47, 128-29, 150, 153, 224n
Indiana, District of, VIII: 74n
Indiana Legion, V: 408n
Indiana Territory, III: 415, 455-56, 465-66, 484-85
Indianapolis (Ind.), I: 297; III: 463-70; IV: 179, 181-82, 193-96; VI: 158, 488, 514n; VIII: 46-47, 74n, 177
Indianapolis Atlas, III: 463n
Indianapolis Journal, IV: 194n, 196n
Indianapolis Sentinel, IV: 193n, 194n, 196n
Indianola (Tex.), VI: 366n
Indians: costs of Seminole War, I: 174-75; costs of removal to west of the Mississippi R., 175, II: 158-59; L.'s grandfather killed by, I: 456, III: 511, IV: 37, 61; Zachary Taylor in wars with, II: 83-84; and white supremacy, III: 9, 113, 296; executions of, IV: 299, V: 493, 537-38, 542-43; VI: 6-7; order for bond issue for use of, IV: 400-402; establishment of reservations, 548, VII: 300; uprisings and hostile attacks on mail and telegraph, V: 46, 200, 204n, 396-97, 432, 449, 455, 525-26, 550-51, VI: 104, VII: 40, 47-48, 160, 530, VIII: 359-60;
  complaints of injustice and neglect, V: 173; payment of property claims from hostilities (1813), V: 194; relief and protection, V: 415-16, 439, 456, VII: 196, 341-42, VIII: 34; chiefs call on L., VI: 151-53; unlawful enlistment of, VII: 27; on removal of Kans. Indians to Indian territory, VII: 119; sale of lands, 246, 515-16; religious work with, 275n; order for pardon of Sioux, 325-26; release of "Big Eagle" from Iowa prison, VIII: 76, 116
  See also Indian agencies; Black Hawk War; *and* Treaties with Indian tribes
Infantry, *see* Troops, specific infantry regiments
Ingalls, Rufus, V: 293; VI: 197, 200, 322
Ingersoll, Ebon Clark, VII: 366, 403n; VIII: 102
Ingersoll, Jared, III: 531n
Ingersoll, Joseph Reed, I: 497
Ingerton, William Henry, VII: 520n
Ingham, Samuel, IV: 364
Ingraham, Timothy, VIII: 19n, 100
Inman, M. M., III: 341
Insects Injurious to Vegetation, V: 211
Insley, Merritt Hitt, IV: 474n
Inslow, John, VII: 400n
Interior Department, U. S., III: 352-53; IV: 561; V: 137n; VII: 417-18
Internal improvements, L. on, I: 5-7, 48, 76, 87, 122-23, 135-36, 144, 184, 200-201, 232, 246, 480-90, 503-507, II: 158; *see also* Bridges (Ill.); Canals (Ill.); Canals (N.Y.); Roads (Ill.); *and* Railroads
Internal Revenue, Bureau of, IV: 495n; V: 353n; VI: 94n; VII: 187n

Invalid Corps, VI: 512; VII: 42, 165n, 265

Inventions, L. and: a method for buoying vessels, II: 32-36; lectures on, 437-42, III: 356-63; a steam ram for harbor defense, VI: 163; *see also under* Troops, equipment and supplies

Iowa, II: 231, 236, 241, 250, 256, 261; III: 120; V: 41, 189, 469n; VI: 40n, 515; VII: 67, 312n; VIII: 33-34, 46, 55n, 128-30, 150, 153

Iowa, District of, VIII: 116n, 269n

Ireland, VII: 415n

Ireland, Thomas, VI: 136

Ireland, Thomas A., VII: 227-28

Irish, III: 328, 330; IV: 404n; VI: 283

Irish Brigade, V: 25, 79n; VI: 101; VII: 293

Iron, importance to man, II: 438-39

Ironclads, VI: 84, 155, 166, 174n, 256n; VII: 43; VIII: 3n, 134

Irons, William, VII: 60

Ironton (Mo.), IV: 518n

"Irrepressible conflict," L. on, IV: 1, 3, 6, 9, 12, 17, 23, 50

Irvin, ———, IV: 391

Irving, *see* Irwin, John W.

Irwin, David M., II: 69-70

Irwin, James S., I: 304

Irwin, John, I: 290, 328; II: 188

Irwin, John W., VI: 337n

Irwin, Richard B., IV: 496n

Irwin, Robert, I: 92, 290n, 297; II: 423n; IV: 188-89, 232, 296, 373n; VII: 178n

Irwin, W. W., VII: 353n

Irwin, John, & Company (Springfield), I: 407

Irwin, Robert, & Company (Springfield), I: 208, 290n, 324

Isabel II (Queen of Spain), IV: 490, 547; V: 133-34, 392, 393; VI: 136, 162; VII: 283; VIII: 53, 54

Isabella Indian Reservation (Mich.), VIII: 219

Isherwood, Benjamin Franklin, IV: 297n; V: 174

Island Grove (Ill.), I: 208

Island Number Ten, V: 177n, 187n, 299, 352

Isle à Vache, VI: 41n, 178-79; VII: 164-65

Israelites, *see* Jews

Italy, IV: 292-93, 300; V: 141, 521; VII: 473-74

Iuka (Miss.), V: 453n

Iverson, Alfred, I: 507; III: 351n, 542n

Iyasamani (Indian), VII: 325

Iyemoshi (Shogun of Japan), IV: 468; VII: 39

J

Jack, Thomas J., VII: 329n

Jackman, Porter, VII: 189n

Jackson, ———, VIII: 305

Jackson, Albert, VI: 6n

Jackson, Andrew, I: 7n, 14n, 170, 172, 175-76, 226, 310, 419n, 506, 508; II: 60, 125, 137, 150, 159, 346, 350-51, 354, 384, 402, 496, 517, 526, 552; III: 28, 141, 147, 162, 195, 232, 243, 278, 293, 321; IV: 64, 93n, 158n, 262n, 341, 420; VI: 268-69; VII: 459

Jackson, Mrs. Andrew (N. Y.), VI: 509n
Jackson, Claiborne Fox, IV: 471n
Jackson, Fred R., IV: 145
Jackson, James H., VII: 470-71, 511
Jackson, James Streshly, IV: 464n, 477; V: 11n, 458n
Jackson, Nathaniel James, VII: 471n
Jackson, Thomas Jonathan ("Stonewall"), V: 230, 232-37, 240n, 244-48, 250n, 252, 254, 258, 264, 267-69, 271, 274-77, 280n, 286n, 287, 289n, 310, 395n, 401n, 409n, 412n, 415n, 417-18, 481n; VI: 199, 214; VII: 446n
Jackson, William M., II: 182; III: 125-26
Jackson (Miss.), VI: 226, 247n, 350; VII: 63-64
Jackson (Mo.), VI: 6
Jackson (Tenn.), V: 405n, 453, 457n
Jackson County (Ill.), I: 146
Jackson County (Tenn.), VIII: 69
Jackson County (W. Va.), V: 298
Jacksonville (Fla.), V: 167; VI: 158; VIII: 396
Jacksonville (Ill.), I: 5, 21, 24, 34-35, 70, 282, 323n, 329-30; II: 11-13, 368-73, 449-50, 483n; IV: 131n
Jacksonville Journal, II: 522n
Jacksonville Sentinel, see Illinois Sentinel
Jacob (Indian), VI: 153n
Jacob, Richard Taylor, VIII: 120, 182-83, 198, 222, 250
Jacobs, H. H., VII: 216-17
Jacobs, Richard T., see Jacob, Richard Taylor
Jacoby, George L., VII: 216
James, Benjamin Franklin, I: 337, 349-56, 359-60, 363n, 365-66, 379; IV: 103, 121; V: 353n
James, Mrs. Benjamin Franklin, IV: 103, 121
James, Calvin, VI: 544

James, Charles Tillinghast, IV: 69, 382
James, John, V: 170n
James, Josiah L., I: 330n
James, Louis, IV: 103, 121
James, Tandy, I: 35
James, William, VI: 197
James, William Levis, VIII: 373
James Island (S. C.), VI: 35n
James rifled guns, V: 151n
James River, IV: 525n; V: 123n, 207, 210, 216, 289-90, 293n, 294n, 301n, 303n, 305n, 306, 334n, 499n; VI: 15, 76n, 164, 258n, 315n; VII: 222n, 393n, 499n, 547; VIII: 3n, 57
Jameson, Charles Davis, IV: 504-505; V: 471
Jameson, David, VIII: 15-16
Jameson, E. H. Emery, II: 424-25; VII: 13
Jameson, George W., VIII: 15-16
Jameson, James B., VII: 423n
Jameson, John A., II: 396-97
Jameson, Thorndike C., VIII: 289-90
Jamestown (Va.), V: 207
Jamison, David Flavel, IV: 322n
Janes, Edmund Storer, V: 12-13
Janes, William L., VII: 517n
Janesville (Wis.), III: 484-86
Janesville Morning Gazette, III: 484n
Janney, John, IV: 330
Janney, John J., VII: 517
January, Derrick A., VI: 65n
Japan, IV: 397, 468; V: 521; VI: 95n; VII: 39, 40; VIII: 45, 131-32, 139
Jaquess, James Frazier, VI: 225, 236, 329; VII: 429, 461
Jarrot, Nicholas, VIII: 226n
Jarrot, Vital, I: 138n; VIII: 225-26
Jarvis, ———, II: 516
Jarvis, Lewis, VIII: 68
Jay, John (1745-1829), III: 8, 178; IV: 23
Jay, John (1817-1894), V: 10n

Jayne, Gershom, I: 121; II: 13-14, 188, 357n; VI: 238n
Jayne, Mrs. Gershom, *see* Jayne, Sibyl
Jayne, Julia Maria, *see* Trumbull, Julia Maria (Jayne)
Jayne, Perry, VII: 207n
Jayne, Sibyl (Slater), II: 13-14
Jayne, William, II: 357, 424; III: 489n, 516; IV: 294-95, 303, 550; V: 148n; VI: 495n; VII: 141n, 206-207, 215n
Jeffers, William Nicholson, VI: 521n, 530-31
Jefferson, Samuel [alias], *see* Shaffer, Simon J.
Jefferson, Thomas, I: 172, 310, 485, 487, 502-503; II: 83-84, 128-29, 130, 231-32, 235, 249-50, 340, 378, 516-17, 552; III: 2, 8, 18-19, 28, 80, 124, 162, 178, 195, 216, 220, 232, 374-76, 410, 414, 453, 469, 484, 525n, 541; IV: 6, 23, 89, 112n, 124-25, 199, 303, 438; V: 48; VI: 319-20
Jefferson (Va.), VI: 535n
Jefferson City (Mo.), IV: 538; VI: 66n, 499n; VII: 8n
Jefferson County (Ill.), I: 146
Jefferson County (Ky.), I: 259n
Jefferson County (Tenn.), VIII: 68
Jefferson County (Va.), IV: 516n
Jefferson Parish (La.), VI: 29
Jeffersonville (Ind.), V: 14
Jeffries, John R., II: 45
Jeffries, William, VII: 122
Jeffs, William H., VIII: 239, 245
Jenckes, Thomas Allen, V: 431n
Jenifer, Daniel, III: 531n
Jenkins, Alexander M., I: 67
Jenkins, G. Taylor, VIII: 409
Jenkins, George Sumner, VI: 185
Jenkins, Thornton A., Jr., VI: 433; VII: 246
Jennings, Henry L., VII: 371
Jennings, William A., II: 389
Jérez, Maximo, VIII: 137n

Jericho (S. C.), VI: 457
Jermon, J. Wagner, IV: 490-91
Jernigan, Gabriel R., II: 296
Jerome, Edward Baker, V: 138n
Jerome, John Adams, V: 171
Jerome, Leonard W., VI: 42n
Jersey City (N. J.), IV: 233-34; V: 284; VI: 520n
Jersey City Journal, VIII: 218n
Jerusalem (Palestine), V: 8
Jessup, Edgar, IV: 507n
Jesup, Thomas Sidney, II: 84
Jesus, Society of, I: 344
Jeter, William G., I: following page 48
Jetersville (Va.), VIII: 391
Jewell, J. Grey, IV: 493
Jewett, ———, I: 323
Jewett, Daniel T., III: 393, 515
Jewett, William Cornell ("Colorado"), VII: 435n
Jews, V: 69n; VI: 71n; VII: 323; VIII: 238
Jímenez, Jesús, VI: 259-60
Jimmy, Billy (Indian), IV: 299n
João (Infante of Portugal), V: 199
Job, Zephaniah B., II: 503
Joblin, M., & Company (Cincinnati), VIII: 222n
John D. Perry (steamboat), IV: 352n
John Gilpin (ship), VI: 207
John Trucks (ship), V: 132n
Johns, ———, IV: 165
Johns, Charles, VI: 424
Johns, Edmund George, I: 405; II: 188
Johns, Harvey C., II: 297; V: 110-11
Johnson, ———, V: 70, 71
Johnson, A., VIII: 119n
Johnson, Mrs. A. D., VIII: 424n
Johnson, Andrew: L. mentions meeting in Washington, II: 218; and appointments, IV: 295, 313, 478n; V: 333n, 501n, VI: 393, VII: 466, VIII: 410n, 412n; and defense of East Tenn., V: 59-60,

91, 260, 302-303, 313-14, 323n,
483-84, 497, 501n, VI: 48, 53,
238, 373-74, 462-63, 471n, 505,
VII: 287n, 520; member of
Committee on the Conduct of
the War, V: 88n; his proposal
to exchange prisoners held under military arrest, 260, 264-65,
344n; and the holding of state
elections in Tenn., 462-63, 470-
71, 489-90, VII: 196, 209-10;
and recruiting in Tenn., V:
546, VI: 149-50, 393n, VII:
169n; and re-establishment of
state government in Tenn., VI:
187, 440-41, 462-63, 465, 468-69,
VII: 130-31, 149-50, 183-84, 205,
351-52, VIII: 235; and emancipation in Tenn., VI: 440-41,
VIII: 216-17; L. requests Washington consultation with (Oct.
'63), VI: 543, VII: 59; arrests
and clemency cases, VII: 184,
225, 273, 502-503, 509n, 540-41,
VIII: 26, 33, 38n, 125-26, 133,
180-81, 211n, 259n, 347, 370;
elected Vice President (1864),
VIII: 4n, 216-17, 235; and the
1864 election, 58-72, 108-10;
and the restoration of confiscated property of a Nashville
church, 264; erroneously signs
Senate resolution, 346n; and a
post for retiring Vice President
Hamlin, 352n; mentioned also,
VII: 149n, 200n, 478n, VIII:
108n, 112n

Johnson, Andrew J., VIII: 14n, 40
Johnson, Benjamin, I: 125n
Johnson, Beverley, VIII: 309n
Johnson, Bradish, VI: 287-89
Johnson, Bradley Tyler, V: 409n
Johnson, C. K., VIII: 309-10
Johnson, Cave, I: 423-29
Johnson, Charles F., V: 300
Johnson, Charles Philip, VII: 101n
Johnson, David Dick, VII: 110, 235
Johnson, Edward, V: 235, 247n,
    254

Johnson, Henry C., VII: 110n,
    157n
Johnson, Horace B., VII: 12n
Johnson, J. H., I: 206-207
Johnson, James (Ill.), I: 2
Johnson, James (Negro), VII: 369
Johnson, John (S. C.), VI: 456-57
Johnson, John M., I: 417n; II: 38
Johnson, John O., II: 424, 429;
    VIII: 415
Johnson, Joseph, VIII: 5
Johnson, Lewis, IV: 188-89; VII:
    318
Johnson, Louis E., IV: 461
Johnson, Oliver, V: 278-79
Johnson, R., II: 183
Johnson, Reverdy, IV: 342-43, 390,
    461; V: 342-44; VI: 16, 463n,
    481n, 491, 529, 556n; VII: 203n,
    522n
Johnson, Richard Mentor, III: 146,
    403
Johnson, Richard W., IV: 477; V:
    12n; VI: 104
Johnson, Robert (Ohio), VII: 175
Johnson, Robert (Tenn.), VIII:
    38n
Johnson, Robert C., VI: 191n; VII:
    318
Johnson, Robert W., I: 460-61
Johnson, Sarah, II: 186
Johnson, Solomon James, VII:
    156-57; VIII: 354n
Johnson, Thomas, VI: 85n
Johnson, Thomas W., VIII: 224n,
    303n
Johnson, W. H., VIII: 70
Johnson, William (Ill.), II: 186
Johnson, William (N. Y.), IV:
    297n
Johnson, William (Ohio), VIII:
    35, 54
Johnson, Mrs. William, see John-
    son, Sarah
Johnson, William H., IV: 277, 288;
    V: 33, 446-47, 474; VI: 8-9, 69,
    125n; VII: 156-57
Johnson, William S., III: 525n,
    527

Johnson, Willis H., II: 332n
Johnson County (Kans.), III: 516n
Johnson County (Tenn.), VIII: 68
Johnson, Saunders & Company (Cincinnati), IV: 72
Johnson's Island (Ohio), VI: 225n, 231n, 325n, 507; VII: 131n, 171n, 205, 274, 310, 362, 373; VIII: 155, 165, 223n, 244, 259, 296n, 302, 310n
Johnsonville (Tenn.), VIII: 94
Johnston, Abraham L. B., II: 94, 112
Johnston, Adam, III: 372
Johnston, Albert Sidney, V: 31n
Johnston, Andrew, I: 366-67, 371n, 377-79, 384-86, 392n; VIII: 185n
Johnston, Daniel, II: 94
Johnston, Mrs. Daniel, see Johnston, Sarah
Johnston, Daniel W., II: 95
Johnston, Dennis F., II: 95
Johnston, John D., I: 2-3, 263; II: 15-17, 76-77, 94-97, 108-113; IV: 63-64, 116
Johnston, Mrs. John D., see Johnston, Nancy Jane
Johnston, John D., Jr., II: 95n
Johnston, John M., V: 453n
Johnston, Joseph Eggleston, IV: 458n; VI: 226, 233n, 236, 250n, 265, 293, 377-78, 503; VII: 330n; VIII: 27n, 33, 394
Johnston, Maria Jane (Wright), IV: 134
Johnston, Marietta Sarah Jane, II: 95
Johnston, Mary (Barker), II: 94-95
Johnston, Matilda, see Hall, Matilda (Johnston)
Johnston, Nancy Jane (Williams), II: 95
Johnston, Noah, II: 162-87
Johnston, Richard M., II: 95
Johnston, Robert P., IV: 134n

Johnston, Mrs. Robert P., see Johnston, Maria Jane
Johnston, Sarah (Bush), see Lincoln, Sarah
Johnston, Squire H., II: 95
Johnston, Thomas L. D., II: 94
Johnston, William Preston, VI: 517n
Johnston, William S., II: 430-31
Johnston, William S., Jr., V: 202n
Joint Committee on the Conduct of the War, reports of, VI: 196n, 209n, 244n, 280n; VIII: 324n
Joliet (Ill.), III: 124-25, 133, 135
Joliet Signal, II: 186
Jolly, Ellen Ryan, VIII: 428n
Jonas, Abraham, II: 380, 533-34; III: 516; IV: 85-86; VI: 1; VII: 373
Jonas, Mrs. Abraham, VII: 373n
Jonas, Charles H., VII: 373
Jones, ———, I: 463
Jones, A. E., V: 183n, 202
Jones, Albert, VI: 459-61
Jones, Albert G., II: 297
Jones, Alfred H., V: 28
Jones, Andrew, V: 390
Jones, Aquilla, IV: 539
Jones, Burrel T., VI: 198n
Jones, C. A., VII: 517n
Jones, Caleb, VIII: 69
Jones, Charles, VIII: 43
Jones, Charles T., IV: 166
Jones, Clinton, VI: 197
Jones, Daniel, VIII: 167n, 172-73, 198
Jones, Edgar DeWitt, I: xvii
Jones, Edward, I: 418; VIII: 414
Jones, Fernando, III: 514
Jones, Ferney, VIII: 68
Jones, Francis F., V: 152
Jones, George [?] C., VIII: 106n
Jones, Haidie M., VIII: 183
Jones, Horatio, IV: 295
Jones, James, II: 436
Jones, Jehu Glancy, III: 210
Jones, John, Jr., I: 12
Jones, John, Sr., I: 42, 71-72
Jones, John Albert, IV: 73

Jones, John Paul, VII: 545n; VIII: 39n
Jones, John William, I: 497
Jones, Jonathan D., VIII: 86
Jones, Levant L., III: 504-505
Jones, Martha M., VIII: 292
Jones, Newton F., VII: 74n
Jones, Orin B., III: 335
Jones, Owen, III: 210
Jones, Patrick, VII: 509
Jones, Richard, I: 12
Jones, Samuel (C. S. A. general), VII: 6n
Jones, Samuel (Ill.), II: 436
Jones, Samuel H., VIII: 341
Jones, Thomas, IV: 298
Jones, Thomas D., VIII: 337
Jones, Thomas L., VI: 50
Jones, W. W., VIII: 69
Jones, William [alias], see Smith, Samuel J.
Jones, William (Chicago), II: 430-31
Jones, William (New Salem), I: 25
Jones, William (St. Joseph), VI: 544
Jones, William A., VII: 545n; VIII: 39n
Jones, William Hemphill, VI: 312
Jones, William J., VIII: 411n
Jones, William O., IV: 473n
Jones, William P., Jr., IV: 392
Jones, William P., Sr., IV: 392n
Jones, William W., IV: 498
Jones, Willis F., VIII: 292n
Jones, Mrs. Willis F., see Jones, Martha M.
Jones House (Harrisburg, Pa.), IV: 244n
Jonesboro (Ill.), III: 5, 97n, 101, 102-44, 176, 179, 221, 237, 247, 269; VIII: 416
Jonesboro (Tenn.), V: 484n; VI: 470
Jordan, Charles E., VIII: 242n
Jordan, Edward, V: 359n

Jordan, Edward (Tenn.),.VIII: 69
Jordan, Warren, VII: 196, 209, VIII: 69
Jorgen Lorentzen (Danish ship), V: 162
Jouett, George P., V: 458n
Journal of the American Temperance Union and the New-York-Prohibitionist, IV: 420n
Journal of the Illinois State Historical Society, IV: 39n; VI: 462n; VII: 422n; VIII: 310n, 422n
Joy, James Frederick, II: 207, 209-10, 325-26, 329, 397-98
Juárez, Benito Pablo, IV: 178n; VIII: 137n
Judah, Henry Moses, V: 111, 135, 392n
Judd, Adeline (Rossiter), III: 337n; VII: 28n
Judd, Frank Rossiter [alias Frank Judson alias William Stanley], VII: 27-28; VIII: 189-90, 224
Judd, Norman Buel, II: 296, 305, 348, 412, 414n, 415n, 480, 522, 528n, 537; III: 174, 202, 329-30, 332, 336-37, 341, 355-56, 376, 397n, 506-509, 512, 516, 517, 521n; IV: 99-100, 102n, 116, 171, 187, 189, 276; VII: 27; VIII: 189
Judd, Mrs. Norman Buel, see Judd, Adeline (Rossiter)
Judge, James, VIII: 104n
Judicial decisions, L. on, II: 400-401
Judicial system (Ill.): judiciary districts, I: 145; opposition to reorganization of, 234-37, 239, 244-49, 394-95; judges' salaries, 494; see also Supreme Court (Ill.)
Judicial system (U. S.): importance of judicial decisions, II: 400-401; recommended revisions (1861), V: 41-44; proposal of one district court for Ark., 82; on interruption of Calif. circuit

court business, 267-68; establishment of a provisional court in La., 467-68; transmits report on consular courts, VI: 76; division of Mich. into two judicial districts, 119-20; *see also* Supreme Court (U. S.)

Appointments (1861-1865), IV: 305, 322, 334, 336, 345-46, 383, 391-92, 408, 447-49, 471, 475, 522, 543, 548, 555-56; V: 28, 41, 68, 332-33, 451, 465-66, 492; VI: 52, 113, 117, 129, 167n, 202, 223-24, 245, 247, 255, 290, 363, 395, 495, 518; VII: 15, 94, 128, 153, 264, 280, 371-72, 404, 408-409, 428-29, 468, 472, 480, 483-84, 490, 497; VIII: 47, 82, 121-22, 158, 160, 168, 212, 221-22, 242n, 287, 324-25, 346-47, 355, 368-70, 410, 412

Resignations, dismissals, and leaves, V: 195, 256, 309, 408n; VI: 526n; VII: 462-63

Judson, Frank [alias], *see* Judd, Frank Rossiter

Judson, Philo Purdy, VII: 15

Jules et Marie (brig), V: 539

Julian, George Washington, V: 88n

Justice, Alfred B., VII: 529; VIII: 51

Justice, Mrs. Alfred R., VII: 529n; VIII: 51n

Justices of the peace (Ill.), jurisdiction of, I: 26, 28, 124

K

Kagi, J. H., III: 539n

Kalamazoo (Mich.), II: 358-59, 361-66; IV: 102

Kalb, Absalom, III: 399

Kalpantpan Ku (Indian), VII: 325

Kam Hill, battle of, VI: 147n

Kamehameha IV (King of Hawaii), VI: 51n; VII: 165

Kamehameha V (King of Hawaii), VII: 165

Kanawha, District of, VIII: 417n

Kanawha County (W. Va.), V: 298

Kanawha River, V: 416n, 497n

Kane, Elisha Kent, V: 140

Kane County (Ill.), III: 44

Kankakee (Ill.) *Gazette*, IV: 30n

Kanner, William D., VIII: 68

Kansas: L.'s speeches in (Nov.-Dec. '59), III: 495-504; election of first Senator from, III: 490n, IV: 31-32; Seward speaks in (1860), 87n; the thirty-fourth state to enter the Union, 242n; appointments, 283, 290, 306-307, 309, 346n, 419n, 455n, 474, 476, 543, VI: 507, VII: 220, 304n, 338, VIII: 338n, 339, 356n; recruitment in, IV: 414, VI: 334-35, 339-40, VII: 340-41; Confederate encouragement of Indian hostilities, IV: 551, V: 46, 415n; retreat of Price's army, V: 1-2; need of circuit courts, 41; assignment of Denver to command in, 168, 180; treaties with Indians in, 218-19, VII: 68, 407; controversy between Blunt and Gov. Carney (1863), VI: 339-40, 395-

97; the sack of Lawrence, 415-16, 423-24, VI: 502-503; support of a command for Curtis in, VII: 78, 84n; relief for refugee Indians, 119n, 341-42, VIII: 34n; Lane charges of rebel discrimination against captured Kans. troops, VII: 123; the "Russell Fraud," 246n; election returns in (1860, 1864), VIII: 46, 129-30, 150, 153

Kansas, Department of, V: 22n, 71n; VI: 334, 339-40; VII: 100n, 158n; VIII: 6n, 55n

Kansas City (Mo.), VI: 335n, 424n; VII: 157-58

Kansas City Star, VI: 360n

Kansas City Times, III: 505n

Kansas Historical Quarterly, III: 497n

Kansas Indian Agency, IV: 306; VIII: 338n

Kansas Nebraska Act and repeal of the Missouri Compromise:
L.'s opposition to, II: 7-8, 125, 127-29, 137-38, 226-86, 296, 299-301, 318, 320-23, 333n, 340-49, 352-53, 361-71, 375, 378, 398-400, 404-405, 462-67, 514-16, 539-40, 550-51; III: 14, 19, 23-24, 71, 77-78, 82-83, 86-87, 90-91, 93-94, 98, 119-21, 144-45, 179-81, 205, 224-26, 251, 288, 298-99, 305-306, 310, 334, 388, 391, 403, 410-11, 414, 449, 468, 483, 485, 487, 498-99, 507-508, 512, 524n, 529, 544n; IV: 14-15, 19, 67, 164n, VI: 251

Douglas on: III: 2-3, 5, 35-36, 45-48, 51-53, 55, 61, 64, 68-69, 102-106, 133, 139, 166-73, 207-208, 217-18, 259-61, 269-73, 293-96, 323, 326

"Kansas Tour of Lincoln the Candidate, The" (art.), III: 497n

Kanzas and the Constitution (Fisher), IV: 101n

Kapp, Friedrich, V: 106n; VI: 282

Karl Ludwig [Charles Louis], Archduke of Austria, VI: 18

Karr, ———, I: 340

Kaskaskia (Ill.), II: 277; III: 456

Kaskaskia Indians, V: 147

Kaskaskia Land Office, I: 253n; II: 42

Kasson, John Adam, VII: 456n

Kaufmann, Sigismund, VI: 283n; VII: 199n

Kavanaugh, Archibald W., VIII: 86

Kearny, Philip, IV: 463; V: 159n, 209n, 227n, 256n, 510-11

Kearsarge (steamer), VIII: 134-35

Keasbey, A. Q., VIII: 177n

Keatly, John L., VII: 58, 152

Keats, Emma, *see* Speed, Emma (Keats)

Keats, George, I: 261n

Keats, John, I: 261n

Keeling, Hayden, III: 371

Keenan, Mrs., VII: 295

Keicherd, T. A., VIII: 28n

Keiley, Patrick, II: 324-25

Keim, William High, V: 28-29

Keinle, Edward, V: 347-48

Keith, Charles B., V: 315

Keithly, Levi J., V: 354n; VI: 142

Keitt, Laurence Massillon, III: 78

Kell, Theodore, IV: 166

Keller, A., Jr., V: 296n

Keller, Abram H., I: 264

Keller, Oliver J., VI: 172n

Kelley, Alexander, VIII: 68

Kelley, Benjamin Franklin, IV: 451n, 492; VI: 274; VII: 103n; VIII: 593-94

Kelley, Benjamin Franklin, Jr., IV: 451

Kelley, Dennis, II: 183

Kelley, Milton, VIII: 412n

Kelley, Thomas F., V: 258n

Kelley, Timothy, II: 183-84

Kelley, William Darrah, IV: 122, 127, 509n; VI: 292; VII: 393, 400n, 402, 452, 481, 529; VIII: 36n, 51, 168n, 312n, 424

Kelley, Zeno, VIII: 323-24

Kellinger, Thomas J., VII: 139
Kellog, Orton, VII: 322
Kellogg, Benjamin, Jr., I: 466-67
Kellogg, Edward, III: 518n
Kellogg, Ensign H., II: 1
Kellogg, Francis William, VI: 528; VII: 326, 521n
Kellogg, Palmer V., VII: 498n
Kellogg, Mrs. R. T., IV: 290n, 299n
Kellogg, William, I: 340n; II: 289, 447, 534, 544; III: 506-507; IV: 150, 176n, 183, 321, 448; V: 261, 277n, 317n; VI: 12, 167, 294, 307; VIII: 410
Kellogg, William, Jr., IV: 448n; V: 261
Kellogg, William Pitt, IV: 295; VII: 420n; VIII: 410
Kelly, ———, III: 126
Kelly, George Fox, VI: 242n
Kelly, James, II: 161, 308-309; VII: 318
Kelly, John (Ill.), II: 183
Kelly, John (Oreg.), IV: 406n
Kelly, Moses, IV: 554, 556n
Kelly, Patrick (Ill.), II: 183
Kelly, Patrick (Minn.?), VIII: 120-21
Kelly, Patrick (N. Y.?), VI: 101
Kelly, William, VIII: 212n
Kelly's Ford (Va.), VI: 190n, 400, 441-42; VII: 6, 7n
Kelsey, D. M., IV: 294-95
Kelso, John A., I: 24n
Kelton, John Cunningham, V: 458n; VI: 76n
Kemper, ———, II: 190, 199, 206; VIII: 415, 593
Kendall, Amos, I: 426, 443-44
Kendall, Bion F., IV: 389n, 404n
Kendall, William, I: 298
Kendall's Hall (Quincy, Ill.), II: 285; IV: 86n
Kendrick, Benjamin, I: 34-35
Kendrick, Henry Lane, VII: 139n
Kendrick, Silas F., IV: 349
Kenesaw Mountain (Ga.), V: 77n
Kenly, George T., V: 324n

Kenly, John Reese, V: 324; VI: 195n
Kennedy, Mrs., VII: 101
Kennedy, Hugh, V: 504-505
Kennedy, John Pendleton, VII: 22n
Kennedy, Joseph C. G., V: 161n
Kennedy, Michael, II: 183
Kennedy, William K., V: 253n
Kennerly, Henry A., IV: 325
Kenney, Patrick, & Company, II: 183
Kenrick, Francis Patrick, IV: 560n
Kent, J. H., III: 399
Kent, James, I: 485-86
Kent, Victoria Maria Louisa, Duchess of, IV: 417
Kent, William H., VIII: 26n
Kent County (Md.), VI: 494
Kentucky: L. on results of legislative interference with the courts (1841), I: 248; Clay's career in, II: 124, III: 93-94; admission as a slave state, II: 231, III: 466; emancipation in, III: 93-94, V: 152-53, 160, 329, 503-504, 512n, VI: 42, 428-29; mobilization, recruitment, and the draft, IV: 359, 398n, 464, 492n, 497, V: 50, 142n, 283, 387n, VI: 42, 141n, 147n, 298-300, VII: 272; military defense of, IV: 368-69, 497, 510n, 524, 529, 533-34, 541-42, 544-45, V: 292, 313, 384n, 406, 409n, 416-17, 452-53, VI: 141n, 147n, 200, VII: 109, 134-35, 387n, VIII: 74; appointments, IV: 411, 555-58, V: 80n, 142n, 384n, VI: 202n, 285n, VII: 145
    Magoffin and his claims of neutrality, IV: 444, 497n, V: 113n, 384; and the Frémont proclamation (1861), IV: 506-507, 532; Anderson assigned to command in, 524; "to lose Kentucky is nearly the same as to lose the whole game [Sept. 22 '61]," 532; arrests, 534, 549,

V: 227, 426n, 512-14, VII: 108n, VIII: 120, 182-83, 198, 222, 250; mention of persons from, IV: 549, VIII: 79n; proposed construction of a railroad to loyal regions in Tenn. and N. C. (1861), V: 37; and the use of Negro troops, 357, VI: 299n, VII: 272, 390; suggested Morton replacement of Boyle as military governor, V: 367n; protest against confiscation of property, 502-503

L. on the use of Confederate scrip in, 507; assessment of secessionists, VI: 85-86, VII: 400, VIII: 77-78; assignment of Fry to command in Eastern District of, VI: 97n; election (1863) in, 366, 372; Emily Helm returns to (1863), VII: 64; reorganization of state government, 227-28, 281-83, 308, VIII: 120, 148-49, 182-83, 198, 222, 250; election (1864) in, VII: 308-309, 510n, VIII: 46, 98, 120, 128-29, 150, 153; suspension of writ of habeas corpus, VII: 426; discharge of Meade (Sept. '64), VIII: 23; support for Butler command in (Jan. '65), 195; and trade with Ohio, 197; certified copy of Thirteenth Amendment submitted to, 260; orders concerning prisoners-of-war in, 315n; mentioned also, VII: 182

Kentucky, Department of, IV: 369n; V: 264n; VII: 511n
"Kentucky Brigade," IV: 398n; V: 80n
Kentucky River, V: 402n
Keokuk (Iowa), III: 400; VII: 67
Kercheval, Gholson, II: 182
Kercheval, Lewis C., II: 82-83, 91
Kernan, Francis, VIII: 301n
Kerns, Wilson B., VII: 125
Kerr, A. & G. W., & Company, I: 153
Kerr, Henry C., VIII: 424

Kerr, John Bozman, V: 451
Kerr, Richard, I: 157n
Kerr, William H., IV: 167
Kershaw, Joseph B., VIII: 389-90
Kessman, Charles, VI: 283n
Ketcham, Daniel, IV: 310
Ketchum, Morris, V: 350n
Ketchum, William Scott, V: 72n, 430-31; VI: 141n
Ketchum, William W., VIII: 157
Ketchum, Winthrop Welles, IV: 274n
Kettle Run (Va.), V: 401n
Kevas, Wilson B., see Kerns, Wilson B.
Key, James [Joseph] Rudd, V: 509n
Key, John James, V: 442-43, 508-509; VI: 20
Key, Thomas Marshall, IV: 489; VIII: 204
Key West (Fla.), IV: 285n, 317n, 365, 479n; V: 167n; VI: 160, 363, 517-18; VII: 185; VIII: 396-97
Keyes, Edward, II: 186
Keyes, Elias, II: 186
Keyes, Erasmus Darwin, IV: 304, 320; V: 150, 208-209, 226n, 256n, 311-12, 405n; VI: 15n, 82
Keyes, James W., I: 97, 100-101, 104, 255, 257; II: 14n
Keyes, John, VI: 544
Keys, Isaac, VI: 197
Keystone Club, III: 272
Kickapoo Indian Agency, IV: 306; V: 315; VIII: 338n
Kickapoo Indians, V: 315
Kickapoo Land Office, IV: 306
Kidder, Edward, VI: 330n
Kidder, Frederic, VI: 330n
Kidwell, ———, V: 228-29
Kilborne, B., I: 52
Kilburn, Cyrus G., VII: 479n
Kilburn, Mrs. Cyrus G., VII: 479n
Kilduff, Patrick M., II: 183
Kilgore, ———, I: 340
Kilgore, David, V: 12n
Killela, Michael, II: 183

Killinger, John Weinland, IV: 167
Killingworth, ———, VII: 4-5
Killion, Michael, I: 24
Killpatrick, Thomas M., I: 332-33
Kilpatrick, Judson, VI: 207; VII: 178, 222n, 226
Kimball, Legh R., I: 491
Kimball, Nathan, VII: 108-109, 174n, 325
Kimmel, Anthony Z., IV: 511
Kimyan Hiotan (Indian), VII: 325
Kimyan Hiyaya (Indian), VII: 325
Kincaid, Archibald, I: 37
Kincaid, J. Kennedy, I: 37n
Kincaid, John K., I: 37
Kinderhook (N. Y.), V: 340
Kindrick, Benjamin, see Kendrick, Benjamin
King, Allen, I: 11
King, Anna S., VII: 25
King, Austin Augustus, VI: 211n, 423n; VII: 152n, 153n, 218n, 368n; VIII: 193n, 218n, 290n, 293n, 311, 324
King, Benedict A., VII: 271
King, Charles, VI: 149
King, Edward, VII: 25
King, Francis T., V: 92; VIII: 76
King, Franklin T. [L.], I: 286-87; II: 331
King, H. P., VI: 98n
King, James, VI: 351n
King, John C., VII: 97
King, John L., IV: 490n
King, Norman L., VIII: 291
King, Peter, VIII: 18n
King, Preston, IV: 248, 319-20, 326n, 452, 480; V: 8, 156n, 365; VI: 208n; VII: 181n
King, R. P., IV: 167
King, Rufus (1755-1827), III: 524n, 525n, 527, 529-30, 534n; VI: 149
King, Rufus (1814-1876), IV: 295n, 463n; V: 244-45, 276, 284n, 308-309, 320, 366; VI: 149; VIII: 593-94

King, T. Butler, I: 517
King, Turner R., I: 286-87; II: 40-42, 44-47, 64, 135n
King, William, VIII: 10n
King, William Rufus deVane, II: 141, 158, 351, 354-55, 364
King and Queen Court House (Va.), VII: 226
King Lear (play), VI: 392
Kings County (N. Y.), VI: 370n
Kingsbury, Charles Peoble, IV: 534-35; V: 76n
Kingsbury, Henry Walter, VI: 75-76
Kingsbury, Mrs. Henry Walter, VI: 75
Kingsbury, John J. D., VI: 75-76, 185-86
Kingston (Jamaica), VII: 403n
Kingston (Tenn.), VI: 436, 481, 510-11
Kinkead, George B., II: 194-95, 197, 200, 203-205, 216-17, 219-20
Kinney, ———, VII: 272
Kinney, Alexander B., VIII: 125
Kinney, Ernest L., VI: 221
Kinney, Louis, VII: 524
Kinney, Thomas J., II: 435
Kinney, William C., II: 297, 304
Kinsley, Andrew, II: 183, 186
Kinsley, Edward W., VIII: 425
Kinsley, James, II: 183
Kinsloe, Thadeus A., VII: 325
Kinzie, Arthur Magill, VI: 256
Kinzie, John, I: 159n; II: 83n
Kinzie, John Harris, II: 83
Kinzie, Robert Allen, I: 158-59, 208; II: 430-31; IV: 35n, 335
Kiowa Indians, VI: 153n; VII: 68
Kip, Lawrence, VI: 236
Kirby, Byron, VI: 139n
Kirby, Spencer, VII: 32
Kirchner, Hermann, V: 270n
Kirk, Robert C., IV: 205n
"Kirke, Edmund" [pseud.], see Gilmore, James R.
Kirkham, Robert, VI: 97
Kirkham, Samuel, I: 38n

Kirkham's Grammar, I: 38n
Kirkland, Charles P., V: 544
Kirkpatrick, James T., VIII: 69
Kirkpatrick, John, II: 375n
Kirkpatrick, William, I: 11, 298
Kirkwood, Samuel Jordan, V: 297n; VI: 546
Kitchell, Wickliffe, I: 232, 237-38, 242-44, 252
Kitchen, Joseph, VI: 184
"Kitchen Cabinet" (Jackson's), I: 419n
Kizer, Robert, VIII: 70
Klamath Indian Agency, IV: 306
Klamath Indians, VIII: 322
Klasprath, Dorcas, VI: 429n
Klasprath, William J., VI: 429
Klein, Joseph, I: 43, 99, 207-208; II: 99n, 102
Kline, Levi, IV: 166
Klippart, John H., V: 98n
Knapp, Charles, VI: 112n
Knapp, John Sullivan, IV: 548n; V: 464
Knapp, Joseph G., IV: 449, 471; VII: 490
Knapp, Moses L., I: 154
Knapp, Nathan Morse, II: 75, 373; IV: 548n; V: 138n, 464
Knapp, William H., VII: 77n
Knaur, Don, VIII: 55n
Knight, Cain, III: 202n
Knight, Edward B., VII: 523n
Knight, Hattie, V: 348; VII: 291n
Knight, N. B., V: 379n
Knight, Robert T., V: 348; VII: 291n
Knight, Mrs. Robert T., *see* Knight, Hattie
Knight, Sylvester R., V: 86
Knight, Mrs. Sylvester R., V: 86
Knights of the Golden Circle, VI: 158n; *see also* American Knights, Order of; *and* Copperheads
Knob Creek, IV: 61, 70
Knobelsdorf, Charles, IV: 456n
Knob-view (Ky.?), I: 328
Knorr [?], ———, V: 99

Knott, Andrew L., VIII: 68
Knowles, Elizabeth, VI: 278n
Knowles, John, VI: 278-79
Knowlton, Lincoln B., I: 340n
Know-Nothing (American) Party, I: 477; II: 229, 234, 284, 287, 316, 323, 333n, 345, 349n, 373, 387, 447, 523, 524; III: 108, 173, 329, 333, 488; IV: 70, 79n, 85-86, 122n, 124, 184n, 327, 334n; VIII: 416
Knox, James, II: 287
Knox, James B., VII: 60-61
Knox, Joseph, II: 347n, 415n
Knox, Samuel, VI: 555n
Knox, Thomas W., VI: 142-43
Knox, William, I: 367n, 378n
Knox College (Galesburg, Ill.), III: 374n; VIII: 184n
Knox County (Ill.), I: 72
Knox County (Tenn.), VIII: 68
Knoxville (Ill.), I: 32
Knoxville (Tenn.), V: 37, 135, 155, 273-74; VI: 373, 434, 436, 444, 469-70, 481, 486; VII: 14, 29n, 30, 53, 109n, 134, 184n, 219, 220n, 287n, 319, 321, 431n
Kock, Bernard, VI: 41n, 178-79
Koehnle, Frederick C. W., III: 391
Koepfli, Salomon, III: 515n
Koerner, Gustave Philip, II: 332, 410-11, 425, 433, 502-503, 524, 536-37; III: 376-77, 514-15; IV: 78, 418n, 476, 479; V: 99-101, 106n, 383; VII: 177n; VIII: 138n
Koerner, William K., II: 433n
Kolb Sale Catalog, VIII: 100n
Koontz, George S., V: 413n
Koppel, Herman, VI: 72
Korn, Bertram Wallace, *see American Jewry and the Civil War*
Koscialowski, Napoleon, II: 74-76
Kossuth, Lajos [Louis], II: 115-16, 118
Krager, George, V: 366
Kreismann, Herman, III: 109; IV: 276

Kretschmar, Julius C., VIII: 105
Kretz, Herman, VI: 473-74, 515
Kronovet, Milton, VII: 502n; VIII: 214n
Krzyzanowski, Wladimir, IV: 319

Kuhne, George [alias G. Weik], VI: 414-15
Kurtz, G. F., VII: 432n
Kuykendall, Andrew Jackson, II: 296, 481; VI: 198

L

Labor, see Capital and labor
Labor and Other Capital: The Rights of Each Secured and the Wrongs of Both Eradicated (Kellogg), III: 518-19
Lacey, R. A., II: 24n
Lackey, Robert J., IV: 392n; VIII: 242n
Lacon [formerly Columbia] (Ill.), I: 52n, 354, 381-82, 384n; II: 14
Lacon Gazette, see *Illinois Gazette*
Lacy, Albert A., VII: 138
Ladies Island (S. C.), VI: 455-57
La Due, Mrs. R. M., IV: 70n
Lae, Emile [alias E. Duffie], VI: 414-15
Lafayette, Marquis de, III: 524n, 537; IV: 27
Lafayette (Ind.), I: 400; II: 211; IV: 192, 288n
Lafayette County (Mo.), VI: 343
Lafayette (Ind.) *Courier*, IV: 192n
Lafayette (Ind.) *Journal*, IV: 228n
Lafferty, John, II: 182
Lafferty & Larkin, II: 183
Lafourche Parish (La.), VI: 29
Lager, the Misses, VI: 375-76
La Guayra (Venezuela), IV: 485n; V: 7n
La Harpe (Ill.), I: 462

Laidley, Theodore T. S., VI: 521n, 530-31, 560n; VII: 127
Lake, Delos, VII: 404, 497; VIII: 242n
Lake, Peter, VIII: 368
Lake Borgne, VIII: 196
Lake Huron, VIII: 257n
Lake Ontario, II: 10
Lake Pontchartrain, VIII: 196
Lake Providence (La.), VI: 142
Lake Superior, V: 455n
Lake Winnibigoshish, VI: 135; VII: 345
Laland, Joseph, VII: 526
Lalumiere, Stanislaus P., I: 343-44
La Manche (French ship), VII: 188
Lamar, Charles A. L., VII: 87n
Lamb, Adam, II: 182-83
Lamb, Andrew, II: 186
Lamb, Daniel, IV: 464n
Lamb, Evan T., I: 12
Lamb, James G., I: 190
Lamb, James Lea, II: 106-107; IV: 515-16; VI: 340n
Lambert, Isaac, IV: 555n; V: 266
Lamborn, Josiah, I: 172, 177-78, 256, 343
Lamon, Judson A., II: 219n
Lamon, Robert S., II: 313n
Lamon, Sally (Logan), VII: 7
Lamon, Ward Hill: and his associations with L. in the prac-

tice of law, II: 210, 218n, 347, 426n, 436n, III: 335n, IV: 34-35, VIII: 427; letter from L. on 1858 Republican nomination for congressman, II: 458-59; serves as D. C. marshal, IV: 319, 323, 327n, V: 72, 247, VI: 128, VII: 270-71, 278, 414-15, VIII: 23n; and mobilization and recruitment, IV: 395, 416-17, 461, 504n, VI: 184n; and appointments, IV: 495n, V: 472n; asked to act as marshal at Gettysburg ceremony, VII: 7; and refutation of Copperhead story of his visit with L. to Antietam battlefield, 548-50; L. consults on costs of feeding two horses and two ponies, VIII: 123; and discharge of W. A. McCullough, 307n; obtains pass to Richmond, 395
  See also *Life of Abraham Lincoln from His Birth to His Inauguration as President;* and *Recollections of Abraham Lincoln*
Lamon, Mrs. Ward Hill, *see* Lamon, Sally
Lamplaugh, Thomas [alias Thomas Carey], VIII: 226-27
Lancaster (Ky.), IV: 303n, 369n
Lancaster (Pa.), IV: 242-43; V: 368n
Lancaster County (Pa.), IV: 242
Lancaster County (Va.), VII: 27n
Lancaster (Pa.) *Express*, IV: 242n
Lander, Frederick West, IV: 355; V: 150; VIII: 593-94
Land-grant colleges, VI: 123-24
Land's End (S. C.), VI: 455
Lane, George W. (Ind.?), V: 256, 516n; VII: 15
Lane, George W. (N. C.?), VII: 258; VIII: 368, 395
Lane, Henry Smith, V: 103, 174n, 256n, 516; VII: 119, 128, 235, 350; VIII: 165, 287n
Lane, James, VII: 140, 152

Lane, James Henry, III: 489-90; IV: 31-32, 312n, 345n, 346n, 414, 466-67, 473-74, 476, 533n, 538n; V: 1, 9n, 12, 71, 80, 115-16, 131, 164, 180n, 256n; VI: 188, 334-35, 415n, 418; VII: 85n, 100, 119n, 123n, 246n, 267, 338, 340-41; VIII: 115n, 338n, 339n, 355, 424
Lane, John, I: 305n, 345, 352, 370; II: 193n
Lane, John Y., I: 12
Lane, Levin, I: 77
Lane, Nathaniel, V: 376n
Lane, Richard, I: 12
Lane, Scanon, *see* Lane, Levin
Lane, William, I: 60-61, 76
Lane, William Bartlett, V: 11n
Lanferseick, F. W., VII: 211
Langdon, John, III: 527-28, 530
Langford, James R., I: 258
Langford, Nathaniel P., VII: 372
Langley, James, Jr., VIII: 68
Langley, James, Sr., VIII: 68
Lanman, Charles, II: 459n; IV: 74
Lanphier, Charles Henry, III: 57, 227-30, 239-40, 258-59, 281
Lansden, David Smith, I: 343n; II: 198n
Lansing, Charles B., VI: 96n; VIII: 45n
Lansing, John, III: 523n
Lanterman, James, I: 85
Lapsley, Arthur Brooks, see *Writings of Abraham Lincoln, The*
Lardner, James L., V: 315-16
La Reintrie, Henry R., VI: 134n
Larimer, William, IV: 294-95
Larkin, Thomas, II: 184
Larned, Benjamin Franklin, IV: 451n; V: 64n, 268-69, 297; VI: 139n
Larned, Charles Trowbridge, V: 64; VI: 138-39
Larned, Edwin C., VIII: 221-22
Larner, Thomas D., VIII: 34n
Larrabee, ———, V: 4
Larrance, Isaac, III: 336

Larrance's Post Office Key, III: 336

Larrimore, John N., III: 518

Larue County (Ky.), IV: 60, 75; VIII: 166n

La Salle (Tex.), VIII: 396

La Salle (Ill.) *Democrat*, III: 124

La Seine (French ship), VI: 105n

Latest Light on Abraham Lincoln and War-Time Memories (Chapman), IV: 37n

Latham, ——, V: 383

Latham, George C., IV: 87

Latham, John, I: 220

Latham, Milton Slocum, IV: 418-19, 484n, 519, 537n; V: 195n, 200n, 268n; VIII: 417

Latham, Philip C., I: 106-107, 207-208, 286; IV: 87n

Latham, Richard, II: 424

Latham, Robert B., II: 74

Lathrop, Charles C., V: 188

Latimer, Alexander, I: facing p. 20

Latimer Brothers & Seymour (N. Y.), V: 544n

Latshaw, William D., I: 458

Latta, Emmett, VIII: 218n

Latta, Samuel N., VIII: 218n, 358n

Lauck, James F., VI: 424

Lauderdale County (Tenn.), VIII: 70

Lauman, Jacob Gartner, V: 142

Laurel Bay (S. C.), VI: 455-57

Laurence, Mrs. G. J., VIII: 192n

Lavely, William, I: 256, 420; II: 424

Lavely & Stout (Springfield), I: 420

Lavender, ——, VII: 118

Law, Thomas, I: 2

Law of the Territories (Fisher), IV: 101n

Lawe, George, VIII: 136n

Lawrence [alias Wright], Alfred G., VIII: 19

Lawrence, Amos Abbott, V: 361

Lawrence, Charles B., II: 193

Lawrence, Ed., II: 374n

Lawrence, Ellis, III: 336n

Lawrence, George W., II: 218; IV: 370

Lawrence, James, V: 15

Lawrence, L. W., II: 297, 303; III: 65

Lawrence, Rheuna D., VII: 141

Lawrence, Samuel Betts, VIII: 167n

Lawrence, T. Bigelow, IV: 310

Lawrence, William W., VI: 363n, 517-18

Lawrence (Kans.), III: 504; VI: 415n, 423-24, 502

Lawrence (Mass.), IV: 543-44

Lawrence County (Ill.), I: 85-86

Lawrence County (Tenn.), VIII: 69

Lawrenceburg (Ind.), IV: 197, 541

Lawrenceburg (Tenn.), VII: 105n

Lawrenceville (Ill.), I: 85-86, 211

Laws: L. on, I: 109-15, VI: 438, 448-49; recommends classification of statute laws, V: 42

Laws, A. M., VIII: 267-68

Laws of Illinois, cited in footnotes on the ff. pages, I: 28, 30, 33, 35, 36, 40, 42, 44, 70, 72, 73, 82, 83, 86, 127, 142, 145, 147, 150, 158, 183, 214, 218, 220, 232, 239, 241, 250

Lawson, William C., IV: 167

Lawson Hospital (St. Louis), VIII: 298n

Lawyer, the Statesman, and the Soldier, The (Boutwell), V: 433n

Lawyers, taxation of (Ill.), I: 252

Lay, James, VIII: 68

Lay, Joseph Carbery, VI: 426

Lay, Richard, VIII: 43n

Lazelle, Henry Martyn, V: 369n, 376n, 377n

Leach, A. H., VI: 544

Leach, Charles, VII: 59n

Leach, DeWitt Clinton, VII: 300n; VIII: 220, 410n

Leach, W., VIII: 51

League Island (Pa.), VIII: 144n

Leaman Place (Pa.), IV: 242

Lean Bear (Indian), VI: 153n
Leathe, Charles B., VI: 336n
Leatherman, D. M., VI: 179, 324, 431
Leatherman, George P., VI: 179n
Leatherman, J. A., VI: 324
Leatherman, Paul, VI: 431n
Leavell, William S., VI: 526n
Leavenworth, Edward, IV: 362n
Leavenworth, Jesse Henry, VII: 371
Leavenworth (Kans.), II: 341n; III: 371, 425n, 497-504; IV: 402n, 477n, 540n; VI: 188, 416n, 423n, 489; VII: 322n; VIII: 34n; see also Fort Leavenworth
Leavenworth County (Kans.), IV: 401
Leavenworth, Pawnee & Western Railroad Company, IV: 400-401, 455; VI: 68
Leavenworth Register, III: 497n
Leavenworth Times, III: 497n, 502n
Leavitt, Humphrey Howe, VI: 215-16
Lebanon (Ind.), IV: 192-93
Lebanon (Ky.), V: 37, 402n
Lebanon (Mo.), V: 314-15, 459n; VII: 224n
Lebanon (Tenn.), V: 546n
Lebanon (steamboat), I: 260
Lebanon (Pa.) Reporter, VIII: 90n, 91n
Leberman, L. J., VII: 442
Le Blond, Francis Celeste, VI: 300-306
Lebo, William B., IV: 165; V: 172
Lebold, Foreman M., I: facsimiles preceding page 1; II: 533n; IV: 347n, 537n; V: 334n, 396n, 399n, 412n, 511n, 552n; VI: 240n; VII: 73n, 393n; VIII: 127n, 223n
Lecker, Norm, IV: 306
Lecompton Constitution: L. on, II: 427-28, 445-46, 448-52, 462-67, 489-90, 497, 508-12; III: 25-26, 49, 74-76, 83, 86-87, 148-56, 180, 185-201, 226-27, 306, 345, 349n,

364, 368, 398, 408, 435n, 495n, 506-507; IV: 2, 9, 14-15; 107n
    Douglas on, II: 507; III: 115, 208-11, 289-92
Lecompton Land Office, IV: 306
Ledlie, James Hewitt, VI: 147
Ledlie, Joseph, II: 70-71
Lee, Arthur Tracy, V: 152
Lee, Blair, IV: 157n
Lee, Fitzhugh, VIII: 377n
Lee, George Washington Custis, VIII: 389-92
Lee, Henry, V: 205
Lee, James H., II: 329-30
Lee, John C., IV: 131-32
Lee, John Fitzgerald, V: 69-70, 78, 103, 116, 170-71, 349, 362, 369-70; VII: 74n
Lee, Richard Henry, VIII: 103
Lee, Robert Edward: warns McClellan of retaliatory measures in the event of guerrilla executions, V: 278n; L. explains why he was not arrested in early stages of the rebellion, VI: 265; L. requests mutual prohibition against destruction of private property, VII: 493; and peace terms, VIII: 330-31, 373-74
    And military operations: (fall '62) V: 395n, 426n, 481n, 514; (spring-summer '63) VI: 47n, 196n, 199, 203n, 218n, 249n, 257, 273, 276-77, 281, 285n, 293n, 308n, 318n, 319, 321-23, 327-30, 341-42, 354, 399n, VII: 178n; (fall '63) VI: 407, 450, 466-68, 471n, 509n, 510n, 512n, 518-19, 525n, 534-35; (spring '64) VII: 406n; (fall '64) VIII: 29; (spring '65) 384-85, 389, 392, 409n
Lee, Samuel Phillips, V: 215; VI: 314-16, 317; VIII: 336n
Lee, Samuel Yorke At, see Yorke At Lee, Samuel
Lee, Mrs. Stephen P., VI: 353n
Lee, William H., VIII: 184
Lee, William L., VIII: 184

Lee, William M., II: 297
Lee County National Bank (Dixon, Ill.), I: 474
Leesburg (Va.), V: 235, 481n; VI: 289-90, 295
Leet, George Keller, VIII: 208n
Leffingwell, Christopher William, IV: 499n
Legal cases mentioned by L.: I: 116-464 *passim*, II: 14-482 *passim*, III: 335-521 *passim*, IV: 74
  Specific cases mentioned (listed alphabetically): Alton and Sangamon Railroad Co. suits, II: 98-103, 105-107, 110, 111; Ambos *vs.* Barrett *et al.*, III: 386-87, 393-94; Anderson *vs.* Miller, I: 91, 99; Aspinall *vs.* Lewis *et al.*, II. 331-32; Atwood *vs.* Caldwell, II: 100n; Bakewell *vs.* Allin, II: 413; Bell, James, & Company *vs.* Lockridge, I: 283n; Bell & Co., *vs.* Hall, I: 290n, 324n; Bell & Speed *vs.* Nesbitt, I: 306n; Bunce [Bruen] *vs.* Schuyler, I: 344; Cabot *vs.* Regnier, I: 348; Castillero *vs.* United States, VI: 205; Chicago, Burlington & Quincy Railroad *vs.* Wilson, II: 329n; Clark & Morrison *vs.* Page & Bacon, II: 332n; Cochran & Hall *vs.* Camp *et al.*, III: 385; Cochran & Hall *vs.* Morrison, III: 385; Constant *vs.* White, VIII: 421n; Crain *vs.* Crain *et al.*, I: 119-20
  Davenport *vs.* Sconce *et al.*, II: 430n; Davidson *vs.* Bailey, II: 191n; Dickhut *vs.* Dunell, I: 344; Dorman *vs.* Lane, I: 305, 342, 345, 352, 370-71, 445, II: 193n; Eshrick, Black & Company *vs.* Tobias, Hittle & Company, II: 396; Farni *vs.* Tesson, III: 381n; Fitzpatrick *vs.* Brady *et al.*, I: 344; Forsyth *vs.* Peoria, II: 315n, 386n; Gardner *vs.* Brown, II:

339; Gatewood *vs.* Wood & Wood, I: 342, 345; Gilman *et al vs.* Hamilton *et al.*, II: 198n, 199n, VIII: 593n; Gingerich *vs.* Evans *et al.*, II: 206n; Grable *vs.* Margrave, I: 290-91; Graves *vs.* Bruen, I: 344; Gray *vs.* French *et al.*, II: 427n; Haines & Haines *vs.* Talcott *et al.*, II: 427n, III: 370-71; Hall *vs.* Wilson, II: 205; Harris Lime Rock Company *vs.* Harris, II: 192n; Hays *vs.* Turley, II: 105, 160, 201-202, 206; Heirs of Payne *vs.* Hall, II: 69-70; Hinman *vs.* Pope, I: 344; Houghton *vs.* Heirs of Hart, I: 44n; Illinois Central, *see* Illinois Central Railroad
  Johnston *vs.* Jones & Marsh, II: 431n, IV: 35n; Kelly *vs.* Blackledge, II: 161n, 308-309, 316n, 327; Kemper *vs.* Adams, II: 133-34, 190, 199-201, 206-208, 285, VIII: 592-93; Kinzie & Forsythe *vs.* Musick, I: 158-59, 208; Lehmann *vs.* Schroeder, II: 444n; Lincoln *vs.* Illinois Central Railroad, II: 392, 397-98; McCormick *vs.* Manny & Company, II: 314-15, 325, 326n; McIver *vs.* Walker, II: 336; McNutt *et al. vs.* Bean & Thompson, I: 344; Manning *et al. vs.* Warren *et al.*, II: 330n; Miller *vs.* Anderson, I: 99; Miller *vs.* Miller, II: 319-20; Moore *vs.* Brown, I: 394; Moore *vs.* Latourette, I: 394; Morgan *vs.* Curtenius *et al.*, II: 339; Morrison *vs.* Briggs, II: 224; Morrison *vs.* Illinois Central Railroad, II: 389n; Nicholas *vs.* Herbert, I: 391; Northrup *vs.* Reynolds *et al.*, II: 193n; Oldham *et al. vs.* Lincoln *et al.*, II: 194-97, 200, 203-205, 216-17
  Page & Bacon *vs.* Ohio & Mississippi Railroad, II: 411;

Papin *vs.* Hall, II: 315n, 326n; Parker *vs.* Hoyt, II: 83n, 103-105, 286n, 314; People of the State of Illinois *ex. rel.* Koerner *et al. vs.* Ridgely *et al.*, II: 411n, 425n; People of the State of Illinois *ex rel.* Lanphier & Walker *vs.* Hatch, II: 432n; Phares *vs.* Jennings & Oatman, II: 389n; Phelps *vs.* Blakeman, III: 493n; Powell *vs.* Ament *et al.*, II: 482n, III: 510n; Rawlings *vs.* Field, I: 345; Reinhardt *vs.* Schuyler, I: 344; Rock Island, *see* Rock Island Bridge case; Rockwell *et al. vs.* Bradford, II: 357n; Rowland, Smith & Co. *vs.* Francis, Allen & Stone, I: 335; Rugg *vs.* Haines, II: 382n; School Trustees *vs.* Prather, II: 118-19; Shaw, Buel & Barber *vs.* Hill & Hill, III: 494; Smith & Dunlap, assignees, *vs.* Dunlap, II: 104-105; Smith *vs.* Gardner, II: 117-18; Smith *vs.* Smith, II: 425n, 427, 436, III: 384-85; Sniffin *vs.* Harris, II: 397; Speed *vs.* Branson & Branson, I: 289n; Sprague *vs.* Illinois River Railroad Company, II: 433n, 521n; Stickney *vs.* Cassell, I: 342; Sullivan *vs.* Andrews, I: 344; Summers, administrator, *vs.* Sears, I: 150n

Thayer *vs.* Farrell, I: 363; Thompson, White & Pryor *vs.* Wilson & Park, II: 469, 474; Todd *vs.* Wickliffe, II: 66n; Tonica & Petersburg Railroad *vs.* McNeely, III: 343n; United States *vs.* Randall & Scott, VIII: 80n; United States *vs.* Rifferd, V: 211n; Untied States *vs.* Williams, VIII: 369n; Valk *vs.* Crandall *et al.*, II: 213; Van Bergen *vs.* Berry *et al.*, I: 20n; Van Bergen *vs.* Walters, I: 290n, 306n; Vance *vs.* Kilgore *et al.*, I: 340; Webb *vs.* Parrin, I: 271n;

Whiting *vs.* Mudge, III: 393n; Wilson *vs.* Wilson, I: 336; Wright, administrator, *et al. vs.* Adams, I: 92n

Legal Titles to Mining Claims and Water Rights, in California (Yale), VI: 206n

Leggett, J. M., VII: 338n

Leggott, George, III: 399

Le Havre (France), IV: 312, 313

Lehmann, Julius, II: 444

Leib, Charles N., IV: 492

Leigh, Charles C., VIII: 321

Leinart, John, VIII: 68

Leland, Edwin S., II: 163

Leland, Warren, VII: 320n

Leland, William W., V: 25, 148n

Lellyett, John, VIII: 58-72

Lemaster, Hugh, II: 289

Lemmon, John C., VI: 258n, 532-33

Lemon, John J., I: 183n

Lemon case, III: 548n, 549n

Leningrad (U.S.S.R.), IV: 347n

Lenk, Baron von, V: 476n

Lennan, Felix, VIII: 177n

Lennan, John Doyle [alias Thomas Doyle], VIII: 177, 192, 194

Lennon, John, VIII: 120-21

Lenon, Walter, VII: 531

Lenthall, John, V: 174

Leonidas (ship), V: 79n

Leopold I, King of the Belgians, VI: 92, 271-72; VII: 37, 477; VIII: 138n

Leopold, Hereditary Prince of Hohenzollern-Sigmaringen, V: 105; VII: 478

Leopoldine, Princess of Baden, V: 482

Lerchize, Geacinto [alias], *see* Faline, John

Le Roy, Robert, VI: 254-55

Le Roy, William Edgar, VIII: 104n

Le Roy (Kans.), VII: 68

Le Roy (N. Y.), VI: 372n; VII: 193

Lesley, James, Jr., IV: 91, 125n, 310
Leslie, Charles P., VII: 371, 402-403
Lester, ———, VII: 75
Lester, George S., IV: 112
Lester, John H., VIII: 27-28, 354n, 357
Lester, Mrs. John H., VIII: 357
Lester, Sigler H., I: 394
Lester, W. W., II: 37n, 55n
Letcher, John, III: 542n
Letcher, Robert Perkins, I: 317
Letter from President Lincoln to Mr. Hackett, A (Hackett), VI: 393n
Letter to the Hon. Benjamin R. Curtis, A (Kirkland), V: 544n
Levering, Mercy Ann Riggs, *see* Conkling,´ Mercy Ann Riggs (Levering)
Levy, Cheme M., VII: 4-5
Levy, David, VIII: 213-14
Lewis, ———, IV: 384, 561
Lewis, Alpheus, VII: 145-46, 212, 217-18
Lewis, Charles, I: 2
Lewis, Charles S., II: 347n
Lewis, James Taylor, VII: 312n, 356; VIII: 33, 109, 124
Lewis, Jesse, VII: 60
Lewis, John [alias], *see* Davis, John
Lewis, John C., VIII: 105
Lewis, Joseph J., III: 512n; VI: 531n; VII: 333, 517
Lewis, Joseph K., IV: 188-89
Lewis, Sely, V: 475
Lewis, Thomas (D. C.), IV: 319
Lewis, Thomas (Ill.), I: 158; II: 62n, 188, 331-32; IV: 188-89
Lewis, Thomas (Tenn.), VI: 241n
Lewis County (Tenn.), VIII: 69
Lewis County (W. Va.), V: 298
Lewisburg (Va.), VII: 5
Lewiston (Me.) *Journal*, II: 289n
Lewistown (Ill.), I: 35, 42, 71-72, 86-87, 257; II: 544-47
Lexington (Ill.), IV: 144

Lexington (Ky.), I: 266, 495; II: 124; IV: 544; V: 37, 402n; VII: 431n, 510n; VIII: 88, 108n, 182n, 212, 309
Lexington (Miss.), VI: 226
Lexington (Mo.), IV: 538; V: 58; VI: 343; VII: 12; VIII: 57n
Lexington (Ill.) *Globe*, IV: 144n
Libby Prison (Richmond, Va.), VI: 522n; VII: 235, 260, 297, 502n; VIII: 10n
Liberia, II: 255, 409, 515; III: 15, 499; V: 39, 373, 520-21, 550; VII: 417n; VIII: 138
Liberty (Mo.), VI: 489
Liberty (Tex.), VI: 366n
Liberty, equality, and civil rights, L. on: I: 108-15, 279, 338; II: 126, 129-31, 222-23, 249-50, 262-63, 270, 318, 341, 366, 385, 405-406; III: 16, 29, 47, 83, 92-95, 126-27, 145-46, 205, 220-22, 247-49, 257, 276, 280, 299, 301-304, 315, 327-28, 339, 366, 368-69, 375, 380, 401-405, 423, 435-37, 440, 444-46, 453-57, 462-63, 465-69, 478-80, 488, 489, 495-97, 503-504, 522-35, 541; IV: 193-94, 198, 240, 252, 264, 426; V: 18; VI: 39-40; VII: 301-302; *see also* Declaration of Independence
Liberty Party, I: 347-48; *see also* Free Soil Party
Library of Congress: appointment of an assistant librarian, IV: 537; copy of Vanderbilt medal deposited in, V: 331n; British Museum presents volumes to, VI: 9-10
Lick Creek (Tenn.), VII: 520n
Licksville (Md.?), V: 412n
Liebenau, Henry F., VIII: 329n
Liebman, Henry, V: 81
Life and Public Services of Abraham Lincoln, The (Raymond), VIII: 40n
Life and Public Services of Martin R. Delany (Rollin), VIII: 273n

Life and Public Services of Salmon Portland Chase (Schuckers), VII: 201n

Life and Public Services of William Pitt Fessenden (Fessenden), VII: 422n, 423n

Life and Services of Gen. Pierce, Respectfully Dedicated to Gen'l Lewis Cass, II: 148n

Life and Times of Hannibal Hamlin, The (Hamlin), VIII: 353n

Life of Abraham Lincoln [Scripps], IV: 60n

Life of Abraham Lincoln (Tarbell), I: viii; cited in footnotes on the following pages: I: 19, 49, 291, 322, 336, 344, 359; II: 360, 536; III: 332, 346; IV: 69, 382, 386; V: 472, 473, 544; VI: 2, 7-8, 74, 247, 249, 313, 356, 437, 441, 442, 450, 461, 478, 492, 496, 509, 516, 518, 519, 529; VII: 2, 31, 33, 58, 61, 64, 65, 104, 125, 129, 133, 137, 140, 150, 152, 155, 157, 163, 171, 172, 174, 205, 206, 211, 220, 233, 265, 301, 315, 317, 318, 320, 362; VIII: 175

Life of Abraham Lincoln from His Birth to His Inauguration as President (Lamon), I: 371n

Life of Cassius Marcellus Clay: Memoirs, Writings, and Speeches . . . , The (Clay), IV: 352n; V: 425n

Life of Chief Justice Parsons, III: 533n

Life of Edward H. Rollins (Lyford), VIII: 413n

Life of John Bright, The (Trevelyan), VII: 71n

Life of Oliver P. Morton, (Foulke), VIII: 11n

Life of Patrick Henry (Wirt), V: 503n

Life of Thurlow Weed, Including His Autobiography and a Memoir (Weed), VI: 112n

Life of Washington (Weems), IV: 235

Life of William H. Seward (Bancroft), IV: 157n

Life on the Circuit with Lincoln (Whitney), II: 313n; IV: 33n; V: 433n

Lightburn, Joseph Andrew Jackson, VI: 137

Light-House Inlet (S. C.), VI: 256n

Lightner, A. S., V: 188n

Lightner, Alice, V: 188

Lights and Shadows of a Long Episcopate (Whipple), V: 173n

Lilla (British ship), VI: 79n

Lilley, William, V: 365; VI: 149n, 158-59, 181-82, 208; VIII: 310n

Lima (Peru), VI: 92, 134n; VII: 37; VIII: 137n

LINCOLN, ABRAHAM, autobiographical references: His humble beginnings and financial problems, I: 8-9, 289, 320; II: 204, 315, 413, 446; III: 16, 337, 348, 396-97, 400; IV: 24, 32-33, 48

His health, I: 54-55, 78-79, 228-30, 260-61, 268, 282, 289; II: 14, 389; III: 336; IV: 82, 134, 216, 218-19, 221, 225, 234, 242, 296; V: 436; VI: 277, 345; VII: 32, 34n, 57, 182; VIII: 179, 373n

Characteristics of his personality: "being a politician myself," I: 66, VII: 298; desire for social life, I: 78-79, 156; mentions being superstitious, 280-90, II: 348; no experience with farming, I: 282, III: 473; "not a very petulant man," I: 283; ability to keep resolves the "chief gem of my character," 289; hope to "distinguish myself" in Congress, 420; dislikes (1848) use of "Honorable" on his letters, 465-66; not a military hero, 509-10; "not very sentimental," II: 19; "nothing about me which would author-

ize me to think of a first-class office," 28-29; "not an accomplished lawyer," 81; sight of slaves "a continual torment," 320; "never professed an indifference to the honors of official station," 482; "hurts me very much to suppose that I have wronged anybody on earth," III: 254; no less selfish than the "average of men," 310; do not think myself fit for the Presidency," 377, 395, *see also under* LINCOLN, ABRAHAM, Presidential nominee, *and* LINCOLN, ABRAHAM, President-elect; "not a professional lecturer," IV: 39, 40; claims "no greater exemption from selfishness than is common," 43; "not since [election as Captain in Black Hawk War] had any success . . . [brought] so much satisfaction," 64; "rather inclined to silence," 209; "no pleasure to me to triumph over anyone," VIII: 96, 101, *see also* LINCOLN, ABRAHAM, his comments on

Mention of books, music, and art, I: 184, 367n, 377n, 378n; II: 211, 317-19, 384, 388; III: 350, 480-81, 513; IV: 48, 74-75, 89, 98, 101, 120-21, 127, 141, 235; V: 502, 544; VI: 392-93, 558-59; VII: 389; VIII: 166

Family records and biographical sketches, I: 304, 320, 455-56, 459-62; II: 94-96, 217-18, 459; III: 16, 463, 511-12; IV: 37, 48, 56-57, 60-68, 70, 75-77, 79-80, 85, 100, 116-17, 120, 130-31, 410; V: 57

Physical characteristics: I: 450, II: 1, III: 512; his beard, IV: 129-30, 144n, 145n, 219; *see also* Photographs and portraits of L.

See also: Autograph albums; Gifts presented to L.; Financial affairs of L.; *and names of members of his family*

LINCOLN, ABRAHAM, Commander in Chief (Civil War): on the threat of armed conflict, IV: 132, 141-42, 145-46, 170-73, 177, 240-41, 243-45, 254-55, 266, 271, 280, 324, 341-44, *see also* Fort Sumter; on "first war casualty" Ellsworth, 273, 333, 385-86; on off-shore collection of duties, 290, 292-93; on establishing a militia bureau, 291-92; on *Powhatan* expedition to Fort Pickens, 313-20, 350-51, 366-67, 424-25, 465n; requests daily reports from Scott and Hamlin, 316, 338, 357-58; on intended policy toward seceded states, 329-31, 341-43, 358, 385; on appointment of a militia commander for D. C., 334-35; proclaims a blockade, *see* Blockade

On Md. protest of passage of troops through state, 340-42, V: 343-44; on the defense of Washington, IV: 341-43, 346, 348-49, 352, 541, V: 151, 157, 184, 219-20, 236, 287, 289-90, 294-95, VI: 285, 525, VIII: 189; production and procurement of war materiel, *see* Troops, equipment and supplies for; on course of action in the event of a Md. legislature assembly, IV: 344; on suspension of habeas corpus, *see* Habeas corpus; requests interview with Gen. Totten, 350; on Tenn. protest of seizure of munitions boat, 351-52; on Md.'s probable rejection of secession, 355-56; on defense of Ohio R., 362, 533-34; on seizure of Md. customs house and canal boats, 364

Presidential responsibility for appointment of generals, IV: 367, 370-71; on Schurz and command of Fort Monroe, 367-68,

LINCOLN, ABRAHAM, Commander in Chief (*continued*): 371-72, 388, 406n; on distribution of arms to loyal Kentuckians, 368-69; mobilization, *see* Troops, mobilization and recruitment; on arbitrary military arrests, 372; on relieving Gen. Harney from command, 372-73; on uncertain position of Mo., 372-73, 387, 466n, 470-71, 475-76, 495, 499, 506-507; on defense of Cairo, Ill., 374-75, 381, 395-96, 510, 527; approves plan for religious work among soldiers, 381-82, V: 67; orders military units to Fort Monroe, IV: 386, 388, 457, VII: 363; on Cameron's objection to Meigs' appointment, IV: 394-95; on Hooker's promotion, 412-13; Lane assigned to Kans., 414; requests detailed reports from War and Navy Departments, 415

On Frémont's command in the West, IV: 419, 465-66, 469, 477, 484-85, 499, 506-507, 510n, 513, 515, 517-20, 524, 529-34, 549-50, 562-63, V: 7, 14n, 65-66, 169n; requests Congressional legislation to increase war appropriations and military forces, IV: 420-21, 431-32; reviews war situation in July '61 message to Congress, 426-28; on Ky. armed neutrality policy, 444; on defeat of Schenck near Vienna, Va., 449-50; "let Baltimore be held . . . with a gentle, but firm, and certain hand," 457; memo on military policy (July '61), 457-58; on arrest of Md. officials, 461-62, 522-23, V: 285-86; on treatment of political prisoners, IV: 466; on Wool assignment to command at Fort Monroe, 478; lack of trained officers, 481, 500; on newspaper

reporter's offer of information from the South, 484

Proclamation forbidding intercourse with rebel states, IV: 487-88; on Ky. protest of military use of state, 497; opinion on army pay, 509-10; Anderson assigned to command in Ky., 524; commends military action at Wilson's Creek, 526-27; on expedition to Port Royal, 527-28, 557, V: 26-27, 50, 127-28; "lose Ky. . . . lose the whole game," IV: 532, 541, V: 113, 357; on Md.'s request for salt, IV: 536; on action at Muldraugh's Hill, Ky., 537-38; on conditions and military action around St. Louis, 538, 560, V: 27; on Zollicoffer's movements near Cumberland Gap, IV: 541-42

Memo (Oct. '61) on a plan of campaign, IV: 544; order on rank of flag officers, 548; on release of governor and other political prisoners in Ky., 549, V: 81; decides against visit (Oct. '61) to Sherman, IV: 557; on military action near Poolesville, Md., 560; on military policy in the West, V: 1-2; authorization for seizure of enemy ships, 5-6, 38; endorses plan for military telegraph, 6; on retirement of Scott and appointment of McClellan as General in Chief, 9-11, 13, 50-51, 494-95; memo (Nov. 2 '61) of current pressing problems, 12; re fortification of northern seacoast and lakes, 13-14, 74; on Buckner threat to Louisville, 14-15, 31; on military action at Belmont, Mo., 20-21

Assignment of western commands, V: 21; commends action at Camp Wildcat, Ky., 21-22; on Baltimore complaints of unemployment, 24; on N. Y. meeting

LINCOLN, ABRAHAM, Commander in Chief (*continued*): for relief of N. C. loyalists, 25-26; on the *Trent* affair, 26, 62-64, 82-83, 95-96, 102, 115, 137, 141, 166n; pressure for action in defense of East Tenn. and Ky., 31, 54, 59-60; suggests Buell promotion, 31; on erection of Potomac R. bridges, 31, 130n; on Mrs. Stephen A. Douglas's fear of property confiscation, 32; memo to McClellan on Potomac campaign, 34-35; urges railroad construction in Ky.-Tenn. area, 37; gives "a general review" of events, 48-51; "one bad general is better than two good ones," 51; requests that Schofield remain in Mo., 61-62

On command troubles with Hunter and Lane at Fort Leavenworth V: 71, 80, 84-85, 115, 131; McClellan's illness (Dec. '61), 84, 86-88, 94; urges Halleck-Buell concerted action in Ky., 84, 86-87, 90-92, 94-95, 98-99; on McClellan's appearance before investigating committee, 88, 94; "delay is ruining us," 92; "my general idea of this war" is . . ., 98; urges military appointment of Koerner, 99-101; presses for gunboats on Tennessee R. to support Grant, 108, 110, 112; endorses reorganization of ordnance departments, 110, 112-13; General War Order No. 1, 111-12

On McClellan disagreement with proposed movement (Feb. '62) toward Manassas, V: 111-12, 115, 118-25, 130; regulation re active duty for retired naval personnel, 127-28; on Burnside expedition to Hatteras Inlet, 132; on importance of holding Fort Donelson, 135; list of pro-motions to rank of general, 142; on organization of Army Corps, 149-51, 207-209; warns Buell (Mar. 10, '62) of threat of enemy attack, 153; on the *Merrimac* and the *Monitor*, 154, 210; limits McClellan command, 155, 164; directs McClellan (Mar. 13, '62) to move toward Fort Monroe, 157-58; on proposed change in division organization, 159; suspends order to send Denver to Kans., 168, 180

Pressed to strengthen Frémont command in W. Va., V: 175-76, 193n; on settlement of Cairo, Ill. claims, 177; on McClellan complaint against McDowell, 195; on Tenn. governor's complaint against transfer of troops, 200; on arrest of Stone, 201, 204, VII: 285-86; on pressure for Mo. command for Schofield, V: 203; on McClellan request for James R. gunboats, 207, 210; mention (May 7, '62) of intended visit to Wool, 207; accepts responsibility for naval action at Sewell Point, 209; on McClellan complaint of lack of War Department support, 216; correspondence (May 16-July 14, '62) with McClellan, McDowell, Frémont and others on Peninsular Campaign, 218-323

On revocation of Hunter emancipation order, V: 219, 222-26, 318; correspondance (May 24-July 14, '62) with Halleck and others on action in the West, 231, 254, 259-61, 263-64, 276, 295, 300-301, 305, 308, 313-14, 321-23; confers at West Point (June 24, '62) with Scott, 284n; order for Army of Virginia under Pope, 287; "my view of the present [June 28, '62] condition of the War is

LINCOLN, ABRAHAM, Commander in Chief (*continued*):

about as follows . . .," 291-92; proclamation naming insurrectionary areas, 298-99; "*time* is everything [July 3, '62]," 304; memo of interviews with Army of the Potomac officers, 309-12; appoints Halleck General in Chief, 312-13, 325n; on assignment of Burnside's troops (July '62), 334; on the draft, *see* Draft (1862-1865); on La. complaints against army control, 342-46, 350-51

Comments on course of the war, V: 355-56; use of colored troops, *see* Negro troops; record of dismissal of Major Key, 442-43, 508-509, VI: 20; removes army bakeries from Washington, V: 443, 463; memo on troops at Antietam, 448; on western request for Morgan's forces, 452-53, 483-84; on McClellan's wish to see his wife, 452; Grant's report of action at Corinth, Miss., 453n; on Buell's movements (Oct. '62) in Ky., 457-58; correspondence with McClellan (Oct.-Nov. '62) on lack of Army of the Potomac action, 460-62, 474-75, 477, 481; on lack of hospital facilities, 467; memos (Oct. '62) on Army of the Potomac and Confederate Army, 469-70; annoyed that Rosecrans still (Oct. '62) at Corinth, 478; order removing McClellan from command of Army of the Potomac, 485-86

On reported rebel movement near Culpeper Court House, V: 488; on a plan for naval action, 489, 490n; assigns Banks to command Department of the Gulf, 495; on a proposed (Oct. '62) Mississippi R. expedition, 498-99, 517, VI: 71n; on enemy

strength at Richmond and Petersburg, 499; on complaints of neglecting Mississippi R. area, 501-502; warns Banks against delay, 505-506; confers (Nov. '63) with Burnside near Aquia Creek, 511, 514-15; on unofficial peace missions, 517-18, VI: 225, 236, 329, VII: 429; on presence of an isolated brigade at Hartsville, Tenn. (Dec. '62), V: 545-46

On Tangier arrest of rebels by U. S. consul, V: 549; refers to Nicolay visit to Fredericksburg (Dec. '62), 552, VI: 2; on removing all but militia forces from parts of Mo., VI: 9-11, 23, 36-38, 66; on arrangements (Dec. '62) for Washington meeting with Burnside, 10; on absenteeism, 12; congratulates Army of the Potomac, 13-14; on a plan of operations for the Army of the Potomac, 15-16; on treatment of paroled regiments captured at Hartsville, Tenn., 20; on a "peculiar and important service" for Butler, 22; asks Burnside to make no major move "without letting me know," 22-23; on Halleck opposition (Jan. '63) to Burnside's plans, 31-33

On justifications for guerrilla executions, VI: 31; suggests cancellation of revocation of Benham's appointment, 35, VII: 174; on Murfreesboro victory, VI: 39, 43n, 48, 53; on Ky. loyalty, 42; on Grant at Vicksburg, 43, 83, 142, 155, 226, 228-29, 233, 236, 244, 247, 252, 254, 293, 319, 321, 326, 350; on commands for Sigel, Schurz, and Stahel, 43, 55, 79-80, 93; approves dismissal of Porter, 67; discourages Hurlbut complaints, 70; on McClernand charges of Halleck incompe-

LINCOLN, ABRAHAM, Commander in Chief (*continued*):

tency, 70-71; on opposition to Steele promotion, 72-73; on Butler and Banks commands in Departments of the Gulf and Texas, 73-74, 76-77, 81-82, 100; assigns Hooker to command of Army of the Potomac, 77-79

Burnside, Sumner, and Franklin relieved of their commands, VI: 77n; on promotion for Humphreys, 81; asks for news (Jan. '63) from Dix at Fort Monroe, 84; on Union sentiment in Memphis, 84-85; memo on fines collected from Ky. secessionists, 85-87; on Baltimore assault (Feb. '63) on Negroes by white soldiers, 90; on conditions of unrest (Feb. '63) in Ill., 97, 99-100; on patrol of rivers, 101; on plan to counteract rebel cavalry raids, 105, 108-109; on charges of fraud against Warren, 106; on W. Va. fear of invasion, 115-16; report of number of quartermasters, paymasters and commissaries in volunteer force, 116; on new command for Frémont, 127; memo on rebel capture of Joseph Fisher, 129; on need to relieve Curtis of Mo. command, 131n, 210-11

On Rosecrans' complaints against the Sec. of War, VI: 138-40; on Wiegand request for a command, 146-47; on visit (Apr. '63) to Hooker near Aquia Creek, 161; on harbor defenses, 163, 193; memo (Apr. '63) on army strength, 164; memo on plan of Hooker campaign against Richmond, 164-65; unsuccessful Fort Sumter naval action (Apr. '63), 165-67, 170, 173-74, 256n; Schurz request to remove division from Army of the Potomac, 168; correspond-ence with Hooker and others on spring (Apr.-July '63) campaign, 169, 173, 175-76, 188-90, 193, 195-97, 202-203, 207, 209-10, 215, 217-18, 233, 249-51, 257-58, 270-355 *passim*, 389, 399-400, 541-42

Rosecrans' protest of complaints against him, VI: 186; on attaching part of Ky. to Burnside command, 200; on Milroy arrest after defeat at Winchester, 203, 253n, 273-75, 308-309, 355n, 522n, 541-42, VII: 80; on failure of Streight raid in Alabama, VI: 213-14; on arrest and deportation of Vallandigham, 215n, 235, 237, 248n, 266-69, 300-306, VII: 208n, 386n, 402; on William C. Bryant's request for reassignment of Sigel, VI: 216-17; on factional disputes in Mo. and appointment of Schofield, 218, 234, 253-54, 344-45, VII: 78; on Arnold's advice to dismiss Halleck, VI: 230-31; rejects Burnside's offer to be relieved of command in Ohio, 237; on Burnside plan for an East Tenn. expedition, 238

Schenck appeal for cavalry units, VI: 238-39; on a command of colored troops for Frémont, 239, 242-43; on use of troops and Negroes to build privately owned railroads, 246; relieves Hunter from command in the South, 256, 310-11; authorizes use of revenue cutters to protect commerce, 272-73; on Hooker's complaint of Halleck's lack of confidence in him, 280-82, 284; on request for martial law in Pittsburgh, 286; on removal of McClernand, 293n, 383-84; on rumors of Hooker visit to Washington (June '63), 297-98; on pressure to call McClellan to

LINCOLN, ABRAHAM, Commander in Chief (*continued*):
command Army of the Potomac, 311-12; consents to suggested assignment for Franklin, 312; on battle at Gettysburg, 314, 321, 353n, VII: 273n, VIII: 236

On question of receiving a peace emissary from Davis (July '63) VI: 314-17; on naval protection for New England fishermen, 320-21; on military protection for Ariz., 324-25; on imprisonment of captured rebel General Trimble, 324-25; on Meade request (July '63) to be relieved of his command, 327-29, 341; on willingness to receive peace overtures from Southern governors, 330-31; on quarrels between Kans. governor and Blunt, 334-35, 339-40, 343, 395-97; on reported arrest of slaves in Mo., 343-44; on army-civilian dispute in Philadelphia, 344; on Morgan's raids (July '63), 346-47

On Meade's agreement to a command for Hooker under him, VI: 350, 381, 383; Halleck disapproval of a special cavalry force to combat guerrillas, 352-53, 394-95; on importance (July-Aug. '63) of a military movement into Tex., 354-56, 364, 368, 374-75; order of retaliation for violations of "the laws of war," 357; on Hurlbut resignation, 358-59; on conditions of contraband Negroes, 362-63, 387-88; directs Stanton control of appropriations for habeas corpus act, 370-71; on East Tenn. complaints (Aug. '63) of insufficient military protection, 373-74, 377-78

On Grant, Rosecrans, and action at Chattanooga, Chickamauga, and Knoxville, VI: 377, 424-25, 434, 436, 439-41, 470-498 *passim*, 505, 510-11, 521-22, 562, VII: 5-6, 14, 29-31, 35, 53, 108; on Anderson assignment to Fort Adams, VI: 386-87; on relieving Blunt from command in Ark., 396n, 495; on amnesty difficulties in Eastern Va., 401, 427, 434-35, 461-62, 472; endorses colored ministers' work among soldiers, 401; Mississippi R. "again goes unvexed to the sea [Aug. '63]", 409; "peace does not appear so distant . . . [Aug. 26, '63]," 410-11

On Lawrence massacre and other Kans. disturbances, VI: 415, 418, 423-24, 489, 502-503; compliments Meade, 418; on army drunkenness, 438, 486-90; rejects (Sept. '63) Burnside's resignation, 439; on making Lee's army, not Richmond the "objective point," 450-51, 466-68, 509-10, 512, 518-19, 528, 534-35; on false report of Meigs removal, 450n, 473; on Hooker-Slocum relations, 486; on removal of Schofield from command of the Department of the Mo., 492-93, 498-504, 511, 526-28, 543-46, VII: 61-62, 78-79, 84-85; on death penalty for youthful deserters, VI: 506, 510, 515-16

A reprimand to Capt. Cutts, VI: 538; report on the war in 1863 annual message, VII: 42-43; on a medal for Grant, 79; on dim prospects (Dec. '63) for army-navy joint movement against Charleston, 81, 84; on dismissal of Hammond, 93-94, 474-75, 503; visits rebel prisoners at Pt. Lookout (Dec. '63), 95; on arsenal employees' grievances, 100; Curtis assigned command of the Department of Kans., 100; reports (Jan. '64) on

LINCOLN, ABRAHAM, Commander in Chief (*continued*):
military situation from Sullivan at Harper's Ferry, 102-103; supports continuation of bounty payments to veteran volunteers, 107-108; on Ky. complaints of troop shift to Tenn., 109, 134-35; on resignation of Boyle, 121-22, 163

Assignment of Sigel to command of Department of W. Va., VII: 129, 199; on military confiscation of private property, 131, 149, 186-87, 229-30, VIII: 27-28, 42-43, 119-20, 228-29; on the distribution of amnesty proclamation handbills, VII: 153-54, 176-77; on "renewed troubles" in Mo. (Jan.-April '64), 157-58, 283-84, 287, 310-11, 337, VIII: 156; removal of West from command of the Department of N. Mex., VII: 159; summons Kilpatrick to Washington, 178; memo on confidence in Butler, 207; order commuting deserter death sentences, 208; on Blunt replacement of Davidson in Ark. command, 208-209, 300; report of a James R. diversionary action (Mar. '64), 222; on Grant's appointment to supreme command, 234-36, 239-40

On validity of Schenck and Blair military commissions after election to Congress, VII: 248, 307, 312, 319, 326-27; views (Mar. '64) on prisoners-of-war, officer dismissals, rebel sympathizers, and military passes, 254-57, VIII: 77-78, 99n, 347-48; Lockwood removed from command at Baltimore, VII: 258-59; on resignation of Buell, 287-88; on contemplated visit (Apr. '64) to Butler at Fort Monroe, 289, 293-94, 310; on protest against Butler confiscation order, 292;

on Fort Pillow massacre, 302-303, 328-29, 345-46; on proposed reorganization of the militia, 305; news of action in Red River area (Apr.-May '64), 308n, 334n

Confidence in and praise for Grant, VII: 324, 333, 350, 354, 374, VIII: 57-58; Hurlbut's demand for a court of inquiry hearing on replacement by Sherman, VII: 327-28, 370; Tenn. protest of Sherman order re military provisions for civilians, 330-31; cheered (May 9, '64) by military news "within the last five days," 333-34; on Butler request to be made a major general, 346-47; on reinforcing Sherman with 100-day troops, 355-56; on military news from Grant (May-June '64), 359, 393; on American Knights' conspiracy to overthrow the government, 379, 386-88, 402, 436; on defeat near Cynthiana, Ky., 391-92

Predicts Grant will take Richmond, VII: 395; a false report of the capture of Petersburg, Va., 399; visits Grant (June, July '64), 406, 469-70; on Coles County, Ill., riots (Mar. '64), 421-23, 455, VIII: 90; on Early's advance toward Baltimore and Washington, VII: 424, 429, 434-35, 437-38, 444-46, 456, 465-66, 472; on negotiations with enemy peace emissaries at Niagara Falls, 435-36, 440-42, 451, 459-61, 482-83, 485, 489-90, 494-95; on Halleck's protest of Blair's criticism of military officers, 439-40; on Hunter complaint of order to join Wright, 445, 447n; on Sherman complaint of army promotions, 463-64; approves Sheridan command of field troops, 476;

suspends Hunter order banishing Md. secessionists, 477-78; on military possession of North Western R.R., 478

Grant visits Washington, VII: 482; suggests Grant-Lee agreement suppressing destruction of private property, 493; urges Grant to "hold on with a bulldog gripe" (Aug. 17, '64), 499; a report (Aug. 21, '64) of fighting near Harper's Ferry, 511; authorizes Raymond conference with Davis on peace terms, 517-18; on Sherman's march to the sea, 532-34, VIII: 9-10, 27, 148, 154, 181-82, 201, 329, 331; revision of regulations for 3-yrs. men, 539n; on newspaper complaints of handling war news, 546, VIII: 26; orders of thanks to 100-day troops, VII: 547, VIII: 33-34

On Sheridan action in Shenandoah Valley, VII: 548, VIII: 13, 29, 40-41, 57-58, 73-74, 316-17, 320-21, 329; memo on Lamon and Antietam episode, VII: 548-50; views on terms of peace, VIII: 1-2, 151-52, 386-88; authorizes Sigel visit (Sept. '64) to Washington, 8-9; on relief for destitute people in La., 14-15; difficulties between War and Navy Departments over exchange of naval prisoners, 36-37; testifies to shelling of houses near Fort Stevens, 42-43; discourages Pa. fear (Oct. '64) of enemy raids, 50; on Rosecrans and Curtis actions in Mo. (Oct. '64), 57; "satisfactory but not important" news from the front (Nov. '64), 97

On military vs. civil authority in La., VIII: 106; report of military action in Tenn. (Nov. '64), 111; Alabama loyalists ask for ammunition, 112; on Banks assignment to New Orleans, 121, 131, 386; on investigation of military division west of the Mississippi R., 161-62; on report (Dec. '64) of fighting near Nashville, 169; on capture of Wilmington, N. C., 187, 207-208, 235-36; on peace moves and Hampton Roads conference, 188-89, 220-21, 243, 246-52, 255-56, 265, 269-70, 274-87, 318-19; on complaints against Butler, 195, 215, 225; on a military appointment for son Robert, 223-24; directs Grant not to let peace moves influence military plans, 252, 258, 280

Proposes war compensation plan for insurrectionary states, VIII: 260; congratulates Porter on capture of Fort Fisher, 285; report of Petersburg mine explosion, 324; on employment for disabled and discharged soldiers, 327-28; directs Grant not to confer with Lee except for capitulation of Lee's army, 330-31; on Banks resumption of command of Department of the Gulf, 366; reports military action from City Point and visits Richmond, 367, 369, 372-92; on capture and exchange of Crook, 370-71; on amnesty for Mrs. Ewell, 372; on Lee's refusal to accept Russell letter, 373-74; requests serenade band to play "Dixie," 393-94; memo on reduction of army, 408-409

See also Army; Navy; Marines; and LINCOLN, ABRAHAM, President (1861-65)

LINCOLN, ABRAHAM, his comments on (listed alphabetically): accusations, III: 13-14; ambition, I: 8, 114, 420, II: 378-79, 382-83, 548, III: 334, V: 36, VII: 13; America, I: 108-15, III: 356-58, 363, IV: 192, V: 36-37; "Amer-

INDEX

icanism," II: 447; anarchy, IV: 256, 268; anger, I: 356; arbitrary actions, IV: 394; arguments, II: 283; bargains, I: 280; bitterness, I: 314; borrowing, I: 311; character (defense of), I: 100; coercion, IV: 195, 343; communication, III: 359-63; compromise, VI: 407; conservatism, III: 501, 537, IV: 1, 27; consistency, II: 56; corruption, I: 178; death, I: 165-66, 267-68, II: 90, 97, IV: 385-86, VI: 16-17, VIII: 116-17; deliberation, IV: 261, 270-71; democracy, II: 532; denunciation, I: 272-73; despotism, III: 95, 375-76, V: 51; dictators, I: 113-14, II: 264; disappointment, I: 9; dishonesty, I: 167, II: 82; divine right of kings, II: 278, III: 315; dreams and forebodings, I: 280-81, 289, VI: 256; duty, II: 3-4, 89, IV: 8, 13, 29-30

Editorial correction, III: 510, 515, IV: 58-59, 77, 89, 113, 118-19; eloquence, II: 81, 125-26, 129; embarrassment, III: 438; enemy and stranger, III: 471-72; events (control of), VII: 282; evil, *see* good and evil *infra*; experience, I: 165-66; failure, I: 178, III: 344, IV: 81, 87; fair play, I: 352, 361, IV: 480; falsehoods, I: 384, II: 17, III: 21-23; fashion, I: 277; favoritism, V: 102; favors, I: 49; forgiveness, V: 343, VIII: 169; freedom, I: 109, II: 126, 276, III: 376; friendship, I: 49, 87, 273, 281-83, 320, 357, II: 58, 211, 484, IV: 184, V: 295-96, 343, VI: 167; gamblers, I: 110; good and evil, I: 347-48, 484-85, II: 270, 278; greatness, II: 125-26

Habit, III: 358; handwriting, I: 280; happiness, I: 260; honesty, I: 167, 269, II: 82; honor, V: 85; hope, III: 462-63,

IV: 191; human nature, I: 273, VIII: 101; humility, II: 90; idleness, I: 269-70, 411-12, 415, II: 16, 111, III: 479; inconsistency, IV: 41; indifference, IV: 1, 4, 10; inequality, I: 484-85; injunction (meaning of), I: 104; injustice, II: 221; intelligence, IV: 36; invasion (of territory), I: 451-52, IV: 195, 343; judgment, II: 3-4, 125; justice, II: 271; laziness, II: 16; loquaciousness, IV: 242; malice, III: 388, VIII: 333; misrepresentation, III: 13; modesty, I: 8-9; motivation, I: 66, II: 26; observation, III: 358; patience, III: 334, V: 343; persuasion, I: 272-73; poverty, *see* wealth *infra*; prosperity, II: 273, 406, IV: 168-69

Reading, III: 360, 480-81; reason, I: 115, 279; "rebellion" and "secession," IV: 432-36; rectitude, II: 56; reflection, III: 358-59; repentance, V: 343; resolutions, I: 289; revenge, VII: 345-46; right and wrong, I: 8, 94, 113, II: 58, 273, 353, III: 315, 484, IV: 3-4, 8, 17, 29, 120, VII: 542; right makes might, III: 550, IV: 8, 13, 30; slander, II: 234, III: 389-90, IV: 12, 23, 24; statesmanship, II: 451; success, III: 482, IV: 513; superiority, I: 62, 278; traitors, I: 49; tyrants, *see* dictators *supra;* wealth, I: 69, 147-48, 311-12, V: 52-53; will (strength of), II: 125; wisdom, IV: 482; work, I: 5, II: 16, 437, IV: 556, V: 75, 109, VII: 495

See also subject entries, especially: Abolitionism; Agriculture; Ballot; Bibles; Capital and labor; Civil rights; Clothing, importance to man; Congress, powers of; Conscientious objectors; Constitution (U. S.); Declaration of Independence;

Education; Electors, the purpose of; Emancipation; Equality of men; Eulogies delivered by L.; Extradition; Flag, American; Food, importance to man; Foreign-born; Foreign intervention and domestic division; Fourth of July; Government; Habeas corpus, suspension of; Immigration; Internal improvements; Inventions; Iron, importance to man; Irrepressible conflict; Judicial decisions; Laws; Liberty; Loyalty oath; Minorities; Naturalization; Patent laws, importance of; Patronage; Political acclaim; Political institutions; Political parties; Politicians; Polygamy; Power, the utilization of; President, office of; President, powers of; Press, L. and the; Printing; Prisons; Public office; Public opinion; Rail-splitting; Religion; Revolution, American; Revolution, the right of; Sectionalism; Secession; Shakespeare's plays; Shoe strike (Mass.); Slave trade; Slavery; Slaveholders; Soldier vote; Speech, the "first invention"; Speechmaking, L. and; States rights; Steampower; Tariff; Taxation; Temperance; Toasts by L.; Transportation, importance of; Treason; Usury; Verses composed by L.; Veto power; Weather; Women and marriage; Writing, the "great invention"; Young men, advice to

LINCOLN, ABRAHAM, lawyer: documents drafted before being licensed to practice, I: 3, 4, 15-17, 18-19, 51 (for other documents and specific cases, *see* Legal cases mentioned by L.); his fees and bills, 120, 122, 159n, 209, 264, 270, 279, 285-86, 290-91, 416-17, 420, II: 186-87, 193n,

202, 233-34, 315, 425, 521, III: 338, 342, IV: 35; memo of L.-Stuart bank account, I: 267; notes for a law lecture and for argument of a case, II: 81-82, 459-60; answers charges of failure to deliver funds collected on a claim, 194-97, 200, 203-205, 216-17, 219-20; certifies applicants to practice law, 218, III: 352; advice to law students, II: 327, 535, III: 344, IV: 33, 121

L. & Herndon: subscribers to *American Statesman*, II: 388n; letters signed by, III: 338, 343, 513; student in office of, IV: 146n, VI: 464n

Opinions on: election laws, II: 160, III: 325-26; Ill. two-mill tax, II: 209; railroad act, 212-16; aliens as public charges, 294-95; public lands, 333-39, III: 348-49, 352-55; bank law, II: 393; interpretation of a will, III: 347-48; pardon of convicts, I: 283-84, 393-94, II: 94n, 161-62, 187-88, 329-30, 394, 414, 426, 436, 442-43, III: 335, IV: 73, 92, 93

LINCOLN, ABRAHAM, political career of:

Campaigns of 1832-1838: platform in 1832 candidacy for legislature, I: 5-9; support (1834) of Henry for governor, 21-22; platform in 1836 candidacy for legislature, 48; reply to charges of unfitness for office, 48-49; speech at 1836 Springfield rally, 49-50; attack on 1837 candidacy of Adams for probate judge, 89-93, 95-106; on candidacies of Stuart and Douglas (1838) for Congress, 107, 120, 151-52, 154

Campaign of 1840: resolutions adopted at 1839 Springfield Whig meetings, I: 146, 155; speeches at Springfield,

157-79; a plan of campaign, 180-81; letters to Stuart and others relevant to campaign, 181, 184, 195, 206-208, 209, 211, 221; Whig circular, 201-203; communication to readers of *The Old Soldier*, 203-205

For L.'s activity in the General Assembly, *see* Illinois legislature, L. in

On Springfield appointments (1841) and Stuart's probable re-election to Congress, 228-30, 233; letter to Davidson on party affairs, 253; call for 1841 Whig state convention, 261-62; results of Whig county conventions (1842), 284-85; confidential Whig circular (1842) on Senate candidates, 287-88; duel with Shields, 291-97, 299-303; invitation to Clay to speak in Springfield, 297

Campaign of 1844: willingness to run for Congress, I: 306-307, 309; Whig campaign circular, 308, 309-18; failure to win nomination, 319-22; Whig recommendation of Baker's nomination, 322; support of Hardin, 322-25; Whigs invite opposition debate, 325-26; campaign speeches in Ill., 327, 329-30, 332-34, and in Ind., 341-42; debate with Calhoun and Cavarly on election issues, 334-35; on lack of Springfield support of Van Buren, 336; on annexation of Tex., 337, 347-48; on Philadelphia riots, 337-38; Peoria convention endorses Clay ticket, 338-40

Campaign of 1846: on contest with Hardin over nomination for Congress, I: 349-66, 379-80; promise to speak at Jacksonville, 380-81; speech at Lacon, 381-82; replies to campaign charges of infidelity, 382-84;

comments on his election to Congress, 391

For L.'s activity in U. S. House of Representatives, *see* Congress, L. in

On probable results of 1847 Ill. constitutional convention, I: 394-95; Whig organization (1847) in Congress, 416-17; appointment recommendations addressed to Polk, 417-19; attitude toward possible re-election to Congress, 430-31, 463-64, II: 79, IV: 66-67

Campaign of 1848: support of Taylor, I: 419, 422, 449-50, 452-54, 463-64, 467-68, 476-77, 479, 490-93, 498-99, 501-16, 517-19, II: 1-9, 11-14, IV: 67; mentioned attendance at Whig convention, 476-78, 495, II: 1

Candidacy for land office commissioner, II: 28-29, 41, 43-44, 48-55, 57, 67, 68, 91-93; on indifference of Taylor administration to his appointment recommendations, 30-32, 36-48, 56, 59, 78, 93-94, 97, 103; declines appointments (1849) as Secretary and Governor of Oreg. Territory, 61, 65; call for Whig state convention (1851) and Springfield meeting, 113, 120; eulogy on Henry Clay, 121-32

Campaign of 1852: support of Whig presidential candidate Scott, II: 135-59, IV: 67

Campaign of 1854: support of Yates' reelection to Congress, II: 226, 284-85; campaign speeches, 226-27, 229-86, IV: 77; on election results, 286-87, 292, IV: 67

Campaign of 1855: solicits support for 1855 election to Senate, II: 286, 288-90, 292-95, 303-304; declines election to Ill. legislature, 287-88, 289; protests an official connection with Republican party, 288; list of

Ill. legislators (1855) prepared for use in campaign, 296-98; on his defeat, 303-307

Campaign of 1856: speech at Decatur, II: 333; call for Republican county convention, 340; speeches at Bloomington, 340-41; on Buchanan nomination, 342-43; campaign speeches, 344-49, 353-55, 359-60, 361-73, 375-80; fragment on sectionalism, 349-53; editorial on right of foreigners to vote, 355-56; party election strength, 356, 358-60, 374; invitations to speak, 356, 358-60, 373, 376, 380; form letter to Fillmore men, 374; post-campaign comments, 381-82; speech at post-election banquet in Chicago, 383-85, IV: 67

Letters (1857-May '58) on party affairs, II: 387, 395, 412-14, 424, 427-30, 435-36, 443-47, 455; fragment on Dred Scott case, 387-88; notes (1857) for a Chicago speech, 390-91; fragment on formation of Republican party, 391; speech (1857) in Springfield, 398-410, 412; promotes circulation of Republican newspaper, 410; call for 1857 county convention, 424-25; speech at Edwardsville, 447

Campaign of 1858: candidacy for nomination to Senate, II: 456-59; House Divided speech, 448-54, 461-69, 471; letters concerning campaign, 469-75, 483-84, 502-503, 522-24, 530-38, III: 37, 84-85, 90, 144-45, 329-30, 332-33; message to Chicago German Republicans, II: 475; outline of campaign strategy, 476-82; fragment on struggle against slavery, 482; campaign speeches, 484-502, 504-21, 525-27, 538-47, III: 37-38, 76-96, 328-29, 330-31, 333-35; debates with Douglas, *see* Lincoln-

Douglas debates; response to a Springfield serenade, III: 203; fragment on pro-slavery theology, 204-205; notes (Oct. '58) for speeches, 205; extracts (L.'s) from his speeches on slavery, 326-28; comments on his defeat, 335-37, 339-43, 346, 349, 355, 365-67, 378, 385

Letters on party affairs (Nov. '58-May '60), III: 335-37, 339-46, 349, 351, 355-56, 371-80, 384-90, 394-97, 399-400, IV: 30-34, 36-40, 43-47, 49; drafts Ill. governor's veto message on apportionment bill, III: 364-65; speech (1859) at Chicago, 365-70; calls (1859) for Springfield Republican meetings, 372, 377; contract to publish German Republican paper, 383; speech in Iowa, 396-97; notes (1859) for speeches, 397-99; speeches in Ohio, 400-62; fragment on free labor, 462-63; speeches in Indianapolis, 463-70, in Wis., 471-86, in Ill., 487-89, 493, in Kans., 495-504, at Cooper Institute, 522-50, IV: 38-39, in R. I., III: 550-51, in N. H., 551-54; notes for and speeches (1860) in Conn., IV: 1-30; speech in Bloomington, Ill., 41-43; remarks to convention in Decatur, 48

See further LINCOLN, ABRAHAM, Presidential nominee

LINCOLN, ABRAHAM, postmaster, I: 25, 38, 459; IV: 65

LINCOLN, ABRAHAM, President (1861-1865): inauguration, *see* Inauguration (1861), L.'s; Nicolay appointed his secretary, IV: 271; formation of cabinet, *see* Cabinet; remarks to state delegations paying calls of respect, 272-76, 280-81; attitude toward insurrectionary states (Mar.-July '61), 272-73,

288-90, 341-44, 439; reply to greeting from diplomatic corps, 277; foreign affairs, *see* Foreign affairs; emancipation decrees, *see* Emancipation; the "Russell fraud," 281, VII: 246; patronage, *see* Appointments; *and* Patronage; engraving of treasury notes, IV: 326; personal bodyguards, 327, 353, V: 108, 484-85, VII: 423; national financial affairs, *see* Revenue and expenditures, national; official newspapers for government advertising, IV: 328, VI: 188, 313, VII: 399, VIII: 343; delays Md. appointments, IV: 328

Proclamation (Apr. '61) convening Congress and calling out militia, IV: 331-33; removal of secessionists from government employ, 333; suspension of writ of habeas corpus, *see* Habeas corpus; wartime protection of White House, 348-49 (for all other references to White House, *see* White House); remarks at band concerts and serenades, 352, 390, V: 438-39, VI: 319-20, VII: 332, 334, VIII: 4, 57-58, 96, 100-102, 393-95; approves distribution of religious books to soldiers, IV: 381-82; remarks at flag raisings, 382-83; condolence letter to Ellsworth's parents, 385-86; on unfitness for office of recommended appointee, 403-404; on Ninian Edwards' request for appointment, 412; relations with Congress, *see* Congress; signs temperance declaration, 420

Remarks to regiments passing through Washington, IV: 441-42, 458, V: 213, VII: 388-89, 504-505, 512, 528-29, VIII: 75, 81, 84, 360-62; arranges to hear church sermon, IV: 445-46; on refunding monies to states for equipping volunteers, 454-55; support of Sanitary Commission and Sanitary fairs, *see* Sanitary Commission; proclamation of a fast day (Aug. '61), 482-83; on suspected loyalty of Ex-President Pierce, 505; receipt of Oxford Bible, 546; completion of telegraph to Salt Lake City, 558; Chiriqui project, *see* Chiriqui project

On expressions of administration support (Oct. '61-Nov. '64): from church groups, V: 7n, 165-66, 215-16, 327, 478, VI: 39-40, 244-45, 531-32, 535-36, VII: 350-51, 365, 368, 388, VIII: 83; from state groups, V: 325, VI: 54, 499n; from newspapers, V: 391, VII: 360, 361; from Britons, VI: 63, 64, 65, 88-89, 121, 122, VIII: 97-98; from schoolteachers, VII: 271

Order for day of Thanksgiving (Nov. '61), V: 32; advice to Mrs. Stephen A. Douglas on her Southern property, 32; namesakes, 55, VI: 511

Movements to reorganize state governments, L. on, V: 553-54, VI: 8, 31-32, VII: 24, 48, 52, 55-56, 101-102, VIII: 121, 412n; *see also under names of individual states*

On holding slaves in D. C. jails, V: 72; composition of National Union March, 125; grants stay of execution for convicted slave trader, 128-29; proclamation for celebration of Washington's birthday, 136-37; on engravings of McClellan, 157; gift of an "elegant whip," 158; admission of West Virginia, 166, VI: 17, 26-28, 181; proclamation (Apr. '62) of Thanksgiving for military victories, V: 185-86; and volunteer

LINCOLN, ABRAHAM, President
(*continued*):
work re refreshment and care
of troops, 217-18, 406-407, 444-
45, VII: 117, VIII: 204-205 (*see
also* Christian Commission)

Complaints of nonenforce-
ment of fugitive slave law in
Md., V: 224; education of Negro
children, 259, VI: 365; interruption of Calif. circuit court
business, V: 267-68; construction and improvement of N. Y.
canals, 270, VI: 508, VII: 274;
remarks in N. J. on return from
West Point conference with
Scott, V: 284; taxes in insurrectionary states, 298-99, 502,
507-508, VI: 98-99, 453-59, VII:
98-99; remarks to veterans of
War of 1812, V: 306; extension
of the Union Pacific R.R., *see*
Union Pacific R.R.; on "An act
to suppress treason . . .," 328-
31, 341-42, 435, 496, VI: 45-46;
an error to suppose "any important portion of my correspondence escapes my notice,"
V: 333

Order for official mourning
for Van Buren, 340-41; support
of Terre Haute Republican Congressional candidate, 351-52;
complaints of lack of administration policy, 353, 364; address
at Washington Union meeting,
358-59; remarks on colonization to Negro delegation, 370-
75 (*see also* Colonization of
Negroes); address and writings
of Anna Carroll, 381-82; correspondence with Greeley on administration policy, 388-89,
421; "My paramount object in
this struggle [Aug. '62] . . .,"
388; meditation on the divine
will, 403-404; conversion of
D. C. penitentiary to an arsenal,

429-30; reply to delegation of
loyal governors, 441; endorses
conduct of N. C. military governor, 445; on "some collision"
between church groups ministering to Negroes, 445-46

Speeches (Oct. '62) at Frederick, Md., V: 450; Treasury
payments for war expenditures,
451; trade with insurrectionary
states, *see* Cotton and other
products, trade in; and 1862
state elections, 472-73, 487, 493-
95, 496-97, 509-11; allotment of
supreme court judges to circuits,
480-81 (*see also* Judicial system (U. S.)); order for military forces observance of the
Sabbath, 497-98; fugitive slave
question in Ky., 502-503, 512-
14; orders re exports, 503, VI:
432, VII: 8, 229, 279, 331, VIII:
25, 227; construction of an international telegraph, V: 521, VII:
39, VIII: 138-39, 146; suspension
of Schofield order to assess Mo.
secessionists, V: 548; on government policy toward churches,
see Churches; on inadvisability
of appointing a military governor for D. C., VI: 21-22; requests navy aid for removal of
Va. refugees, 36

On Weed's complaint against
Greeley's dangerous "fanati-
cism," VI: 83; on Democrats plan
to end war, 88n; and Ill. claims
to 2% fund, 96-97, 403-405, 411-
12, 463; on acceptance of captured Confederate flags, 106-
107; convenes special sessions of
Congress, (*1863*) 111n, 120-21,
(*1865*) VIII: 304; approves division of Mich. judicial district,
VI: 119-20; on a voluntary return of money stolen from government, 125; on an indictment
for aiding a slave escape, 140;

LINCOLN, ABRAHAM, President (*continued*):
1863 state elections, 140-41, 170, 287, 366, 401 402, 449, 477n, 512n, 513, 515, 542-43, 546-58, VII: 4-5, 8-10, 13, 26-27; Ariz. request for military protection, VI: 141; reimbursement of state expenditures for militias, 141, VII: 178; military expulsion of a newspaper reporter, VI: 142-43; on cooperation of N. Y. governor in matters of national policy, 145-46

Proclamation (Mar. '63) of a National fast day, VI: 155-57; Senate rejection of nominations, 158-59; resolution against international recognition of a slave nation, 176-77; memo on patronage in St. Louis, 178; on definition of Tenn. military governor's authority, 187, 468-69; government repossession of New Almaden mine, 205-206, 322, 333-34, 393-94, 422; employment of disabled war veterans, 212; death of Stonewall Jackson, 214; remarks to wounded veterans, 226-27; settlement of U. S. accounts with Ill. Central R.R., 227-28; Confederate arrests of newspaper correspondents, 241-42; letter to editor of *Washington Chronicle* on inaccuracies of a published article, 251-52; harassed by "my life-long friends" in Springfield about appointments, 275-76; replies to government agent's complaint of personal discrimination, 284-85; disapproves arrest of *Missouri Democrat* editor for unauthorized publication of a letter, 325-27, 329, 338, 344-45

Proclamation (July '63) of Thanksgiving, VI: 332; salary for a chief chemist in Department of Agriculture, 343, 367-68; misses White House appointment with Schenck, 345-46; declines invitation for N. H. vacation, 368; relief for Va. civilians, 371; letters to Hackett on Shakespeare performance, 392-93, 558-59; military use of Washington school buildings, 397-98; letter to Springfield (Ill.) meeting (Aug. '63) of Union sympathizers, 399, 406-410 (text of letter to Conkling), 411n, 414, 420, 423, 430, 443; to "those who are dissatisfied with me . . . I would say . . .," 406-410; "what is decided by the ballot cannot be reversed by the sword," 410-11; on temperance in the army, 486-88; proclamation of Thanksgiving (Oct. '63), 496-97; misunderstanding with Weed, 513-14; receives medal from Philadelphia Union League, 533-34

"a second term would be a great honor and a great labor, which together, perhaps I would not decline, if tendered [Oct. '63]," 540-41; military service *vs.* a seat in Congress for Gen. Blair, 554-55; Gettysburg address, *see* Gettysburg address; "I do not often decline seeing people who call upon me," VII: 10; accepts gift of a cane, 13; "I hope to stand firm enough to not go backward, and yet not go forward fast enough to wreck the country's cause [Nov. 20, '63]," 24; reply (Dec. '63) to invitation to attend Cooper Union meeting, 32; encouragement of immigration, VII: 40, 489, VIII: 141; proclamations of amnesty and reconstruction, VII: 50-53, 53-56 (proc. of Dec.

8, '63), 66-68, 83, 269-70 (proc. of Mar. 26, '64); amnesty for Emily Helm, 63-64, 484-85 "I wish to avoid both the substance and the appearance of dictation," VII: 67; proclamation on reciprocal tonnage and impost duties, 72; establishment of a Freedmen's Bureau, 77, VIII: 274; death of Caleb B. Smith, VII: 118-19; administration of oath of allegiance in Tenn., 130-31, 149-50; comments on Lowell's article on his policies, 132-33; friction between civil and military authority in Va., 135-36; mention (Jan. '64) of Washington small-pox epidemic, 137; establishment of free-labor systems on Southern plantations, *see under* Capital and labor; rumored N. C. loyalty movement, 158; Sickles sent on Southern observation tour, 160, 176, 180, 185, 204-205, 250; establishment of Springfield (Ill.) Soldiers Home, 167, 316; opinion on loyalty oaths, 169-70; Thirteenth Amendment abolishing slavery, 172-73, VIII: 253-55, 260; investigation of N. Y. Customs House, VII: 181-82, 184, 195, 204; remarks at patent office fair, 197-98; "dislike to make changes in office so long as they can be avoided," 206

Reelection (*1864*): support of L., VII: 118, 243-44, 262-63, 468n, 474, 497n, 509-10, 529n, 535n, VIII: 18-19, 96, 105n, 118, 318n, 371-72; opposition to L., VII: 120n, 197, 200-201, 212-13, 222-23, 268n, 285n, 289-90, 447n, 459-63, 548-50, VIII: 52, 98-99, 155-56; state elections, VII: 201-202, 361n, 498, VIII: 2-4, 41, 43-45, 58-72, 81, 102; "Nor could I be justified to detail any officer to the political campaign during its continuance and then return him to the Army," VII: 244-45, 262-63; nomination, VII: 376-78, 380-84, 402, 409, 411-12, 424, VIII: 4; "not best to swap horses when crossing streams," VII: 384; "seems exceedingly probable that this Administration will not be reelected," 514-15, 517n, 524n, 539n, VIII: 12; declines to make public statements as presidential nominee, VIII: 2; memo of a pre-election poll, 3; N. Y. protests use of U. S. troops to maintain order during elections, 91-92; returns, 46, 98, 102, 108-10, 124, (*1860-1864 comparison*) 128-30, 153, 270-71, (*see also* Soldier vote); election victory, 96, 98, 100-102, 154, 326-27; necessity of holding elections in wartime, 100-101; reported in annual message, 150-51; inauguration, *see* Inauguration (1865), L.'s

Seeks appointment for a "gallant drummer-boy," VII: 249; permission for N. J. railroad use of government land, 264; political intrigue in Capitol construction work, 266-67; petition of Concord (Mass.) children to free slave children, 287-88; call (May 9, '64) for prayers and thanksgiving, 333; on charges of disloyalty against Baltimore minister, 335-36, 339-40; political frictions "the means of tormenting my life out of me," 338, 340-41; N. Y. newspaper publication of a false Presidential proclamation, 347-51, 512-13, VIII: 13-14; Burnside's suppression of the Chicago *Times*, VII: 361, 363-64; erection of a monument to Owen Lovejoy, 366-67; appointment lists and memos, 371-72, 420,

VIII: 348, 369, 411; significance
of Hawaiian Islands to U. S.,
VII: 383; speeches in Philadelphia (June 16, '64), 394-98;
opposes use of patronage power
to defeat nomination of Congressional candidates, 400, 402,
423-24, 452-53, 469n, 480-81
Correspondence with Bryant
on a navy dismissal, VII: 409-10;
declines to veto bill reducing
fees of D. C. marshal, 414;
proclamation (July '64) for a
day of prayer, 431-32; wages of
women workers in arsenals,
466-67; approves (July '64) new
treasury regulations, 471-72;
conflict between civil and military authority in Norfolk, Va.,
481, 487-88, 508; reply to letter
on white supremacy, 483; position on slavery in respect to
acceptable terms of peace, 499-
502; reported conversation on
policy and reminiscences, 506-
508; proclamation (Sept. 3,
'64) of thanksgiving and prayer,
533-34; presented with Bible by
Baltimore Negroes, 542-43; accused of joking on Antietam
battlefield, 548-50
"my present [Sept. '64] position in reference to the rebellion
is . . .," VIII: 1-2; consents to
publication of memo of Jan. '62
meeting with McDowell, 39-40;
proclamation (Oct. '64) for
Thanksgiving Day, 55-56; admission of Nevada, 83-84; on
care of war orphans, 90; message to Boston Sailors' Fair, 95;
suggested purchase of Confederate newspapers, 114; on war
pensions, 147; nominates Chase
for Chief Justice of the Supreme
Court, 154; "The President's
Last, Shortest, and Best Speech,"
154-55; commemoration of the
landing of the Pilgrims, 170;

declines invitation to attend
Springfield (Mass.) Soldiers'
Fair, 171; suspension of Butler's
order for Eastern Va. election,
174, 186; accepts Doctor of Laws
degree from Princeton Univ.,
183-84; authority of Mo. provost
marshals, 203, 292-93, 297-98,
300, 342-43; lack of coal for
Washington lighting system,
208; arrest of Confederate Congressman, 216; Johnson leaves
Tenn. post to take office of Vice-
President, 216-17, 235; on requested new trial for Baltimore
and Washington merchants,
224, 303-304; memo on Robert
Burns, 237; comment (Jan. '65)
on a House speech, 249; 1865
Ill. senatorial election, 288n;
Seward's driving accident, 388;
last public address, 399-405;
Grant invited to cabinet meeting, 411-12; warned (Apr. 14,
'65) of assassination dangers,
413; appointment card (last
autographed document), 413
See also LINCOLN, ABRAHAM,
Commander-in-Chief (Civil
War)
LINCOLN, ABRAHAM, President-
elect (1860-61): plans for trip
to Washington, IV: 92, 170-71,
181-82, 184-86, 188, 217, 239,
281n; on preparation of inaugural address, 92-93, 169n, 184,
249-62; on reaction of slave
states to his election, 137, 139-
146, 150-65, 170, 172-73, 175-78,
195, 198-99, 208, 211, 215-16,
238-41, 243-48, 250-51, 255-59,
262-63, 266, 271; declines to
make public policy statements
or compromise on slavery extension, 138-40, 143, 145-46, 149-
55, 160-64, 172, 182, 183, 200-
204, 210-11, 230-31, 236-39, 259;
on commercial and financial
uneasiness, 138, 139; formation

of cabinet and patronage, *see* Cabinet (1861-1865), L.'s, *and* Appointments

Replies to election congratulations, IV: 140-41, 145; drafts passage for Trumbull's Springfield speech, 141; remarks at Springfield celebration and en route to Chicago, 142-44; requests copy of Stephens' Georgia speech, 146; resolutions for Committee of Thirteen, 156-57; advice on inaugural address of Pa. governor-elect, 158; on threats to prevent inauguration, 159n, 170-71, 175n, 177, 241n; comments on himself as pres.-elect, 160, 194, 197, 204-207, 220-21, 223, 226, 228, 235-36, 239, 243, 264, 274

On states rights and amendment to Constitution, IV: 162; fragment on the Constitution and the Union, 168-69; on official count of electoral vote, 170, 246; reply to good will call of Mexican diplomat, 177-78; addresses letter of introduction for friend to all U. S. diplomats, 178; remarks at Charleston, Ill., 182; protests use of his name in Greeley candidacy for Senate, 185-86; receipts for sale of furniture and notes left for collection in Springfield, 188-89, 232; farewell address at Springfield, 190-91

Speeches and remarks en route to Washington: in Ill. and Ind., IV: 191-97, in Ohio, 197-208, 215-19, in Pa., 208-15, 219, 238-46, in N. Y., 219-33, in N. J., 231, 233-38, in Del., 239; fragment of speech intended for Kentuckians, 200-201; responses to Washington's civic welcome, 246, 247

See further, LINCOLN, ABRAHAM, President (1861-65)

LINCOLN, ABRAHAM, Presidential nominee (1860): pre-nomination comments on availability and fitness for office, III: 377, 395-96, 491, 505, IV: 32-34, 36, 43, 45-49, 80-81, 91-92, 127; on Seward's position on slavery question, IV: 50; response to Springfield serenade, 50-51; accepts nomination, 51-53, 59, 68; replies to nomination congratulations, 51-59, 68-71, 73; form letter replies to requests for biographical data and policy statements, 60; autobiography written for campaign use, 60-67; declines to make further public statements on policy, 60, 71, 75, 81, 93-94, 102-103, 134-35; acknowledges receipt of gifts, 71, 74, 75, 98, 120, 127, 137, 179, 183; letters on unpaid campaign (hotel) bill, 72-73, 76-77; letters on party affairs, 76-79, 81-91, 94-103, 109-22, 124-28, 130-36; comments on patronage, IV: 83, 88, 94; remarks at Springfield rally, 91-92; reply to advice on preparation of inaugural address, 92-93; criticism of Hill's pamphlet on "Opposing Principles of Henry Clay and Abraham Lincoln," 104-108; imaginary dialogue between Douglas and Breckinridge, 123-24; invites potential cabinet members to tea, 136

See further LINCOLN, ABRAHAM, President-elect

LINCOLN, ABRAHAM, storekeeper, mentioned, I: 4n, III: 512, IV: 64; receipts and statements, I: 9, 15; L.-Berry store, 15-16, 20, 96n, 151n, IV: 65

LINCOLN, ABRAHAM, surveyor: fees and bill rendered, I: 15, 24; certificates and reports of surveys, 20-24, 36-37, 44, 52-53; facsimiles of surveys, facing pages 20,

24, 25, 48-49; legislative authorization of surveys, 146-47, 183; a contract request, 252-53; an opinion on land surveys, III: 348-49; mentioned, IV: 65
Lincoln, Abraham (an "ancestor" of L.), IV: 319
Lincoln, Abraham (cousin of L.), I: 459, 462
Lincoln, Abraham (grandfather of L.), I: 456, 459, 461-62; II: 217; III: 511; IV: 37, 60-61, 117
Lincoln, Abraham (grandson "Jack" of L.), I: 304n
Lincoln, Abraham Lucius, I: 459n, 462n
Lincoln, Austin, IV: 37
Lincoln, David, I: 459, 461-62; II: 218; IV: 37
Lincoln, Davis, IV: 37
Lincoln, Edward Baker (L.'s son "Eddie"), I: 304, 391, 395, 465-66, 478, 496; II: 77; IV: 65, 190
Lincoln, Elizabeth, see Chrisman, Elizabeth (Lincoln)
Lincoln, George, II: 86
Lincoln, George B., IV: 122
Lincoln, George Gould, IV: 526n
Lincoln, Hananiah, IV: 37
Lincoln, Isaac, I: 459, 462; II: 217; IV: 61, 117
Lincoln, Jacob, I: 459, 462; IV: 61, 117
Lincoln, James, I: 459
Lincoln, Jeanie Gould, IV: 526n
Lincoln, Jesse, II: 217-18
Lincoln, Jessie Harlan, I: 304
Lincoln, John, I: 459, 462; IV: 61, 117
Lincoln, Josiah, I: 459, 462; II: 217; IV: 61
Lincoln, Mary, see Crume, Mary (Lincoln)
Lincoln, Mary (granddaughter of L.), I: 304n
Lincoln, Mary Harlan (daughter-in-law of L.), I: 304n
Lincoln, Mary Todd: her engagement to L. broken, I: 228n, 230n, 282; mentioned in L.'s letters to Speed, Browning, Henry, and others, I: 258, 306, 325, 328, 391, 395, II: 323, III: 340, IV: 52, 81, 82, 103n, 122-23, 129, 141, 217-18, VI: 295, 488; persons identified as her relatives, I: 266, 320, 325, 491n, II: 66n, 195n, 196, 203, 313n, III: 491n, IV: 70, 73n, 303, 323, 335n, V: 22-23, 288n, VI: 48, 517, 537, VII: 7-8, 484-85; and the "Rebecca" letters, I: 292n, 299n; marriage to L., I: 303n, 304, 331n, II: 95, 196, IV: 65; births of her children, I: 304, 391, II: 97, IV: 65; mention of her death, I: 304; mention of her friends, I: 308n, 325; church affiliations, 320, VI: 536n; mention of her health, I: 466, II: 97, V: 168, 327n, 386, VI: 314, VII: 285, 293; transfers of property, II: 13-14, 108-109, 193; makes copies of a L. political form letter, 52n; mention of a book read, 211; born in Ky., 217; entertains at Springfield, 388; criticizes Springfield *Republican*, 389-90; mention of her confinement in a mental institution, 532n; receives photograph of L., IV: 122n
Accompanies L. to Chicago (Nov. '60), 143n, 144n; with L. en route to Washington, 218, 242; holds levee at Willard's Hotel, 248; mention of staying at Washington boarding house, 391n; sends revolvers and sabre to a company commander, 410; and appointments and employment recommendations, 498, V: 71, 447n, VI: 108n, VII: 65n; sends photographs of her family to Cassius Clay, V: 368n; and Sanitary Fairs and hospital relief, 377-78, VI: 540n, VII: 390n; requests for passes and return of confiscated property, V: 386,

VI: 517n, VII: 245n, 296n, VIII: 218n; mention of her servants, V: 492; and White House functions, VI: 28, VII: 235, 262, VIII: 334n; L. invites Sumner to accompany her to the opera, VI: 185; proposed military trips with L., VI: 161n, VII: 95, 289, 293, VIII: 367, 372n, 373n, 384, 388n; mention of theatre attendance (Apr. 14, '65), VIII: 413n

Letters and telegrams from L.: (*1848*) I: 465-66, 473-74, 477-78, 495-96; (*1860*) III: 555; (*1862*) V: 492; (*1863*) VI: 256, 260, 277, 283, 353, 371-72, 421, 431, 434, 469, 471-72, 474, 478, VII: 34-35; (*1864*) VII: 34-35, 106, 112, 320, 401, 406, 417, 526, 544, 547, VIII: 174; (*1865*) 381-82, 384

Lincoln, Mordecai (uncle of L.), I: 2n, 459, 462; II: 217; IV: 61
Lincoln, Mordecai (cousin of L.'s), I: 459, 462
Lincoln, Nancy (aunt of L.), IV: 61
Lincoln, Nancy Hanks, II: 94-95; III: 511; IV: 56-57, 61-62, 64
Lincoln, Nathan S., IV: 526
Lincoln, Richard V. B., IV: 37
Lincoln, Robert Todd: birth, I: 304, 325n, IV: 65; marriage, I: 304n; mentioned in L.'s letters to Speed, Browning, Henry, and others, I: 391, 395, II: 217, IV: 82, 87, 103, 129, VIII: 373; mentioned in L.'s letters to Mary Todd Lincoln, I: 466, 478, 496, VI: 353, VII: 526, 544, VIII: 381-82; mention of L. documents disposed of or endorsed by him, II: 482n, III: 399n, IV: 165n, VII: 373n, 411n, 444n, VIII: 287n, 328n; notes return of a claim against Ill. Fund Commissioners addressed to L., III: 363; L. visits (1860) at Phillips Exeter

Academy, 555n; instance of his editing of Nicolay and Hay manuscript, IV: 63n; mention of his friends, 87n, V: 480; L. asks Nicolay to forward funds to (1862), V: 309; his unexplained search for John Reed, 347; letters and telegrams to and from L., VI: 314, 323, 327, VII: 121, 137, 392, VIII: 44, 326n, 369, 372n, 383n; reports L.'s grief over escape of Lee (1863), VI: 328n; L. suggests army commission for, VIII: 223-24, 314n; L. assumes cost of a telegram sent by him, 234n
Lincoln, Mrs. Robert Todd, see Lincoln, Mary Harlan
Lincoln, Sarah, see Grigsby, Sarah (Lincoln)
Lincoln, Sarah (Bush-Johnston), I: 1n, 262-63; II: 15, 94-96, 109-13; IV: 56-57, 62-64, 181n
Lincoln, Solomon, I: 455-56, 459-60
Lincoln, Thomas (L.'s brother), IV: 61
Lincoln, Thomas (L.'s cousin), I: 459, 462
Lincoln, Thomas (L.'s father), I: 262-63, 280, 304n, 456, 459, 462; II: 15-17, 94-97, 109, 217; III: 511; IV: 37n, 49n, 56-57, 60-64, 96, 100, 116-17; V: 57n
Lincoln, Thomas (L.'s great-uncle), I: 459, 462; II: 218; IV: 61, 117
Lincoln, Thomas (L.'s son "Tad"), mention of: his birth, I: 304, IV: 65; in his parents' correspondence, II: 217, IV: 122n, 129, 441, V: 28n, VI: 256, 260, 371-72, 471-72, 474n, VII: 35n, 320, 401, 406, 526, 544, VIII: 384; his illness, V: 154, 327n, VII: 24-25; his pets, V: 177, VI: 371-72, VII: 320, 544; his cannon, V: 463; his pistol, VI: 256, 520-21; his trips with L. to military headquar-

ters, V: 161n, VII: 95, 406, VIII: 372n; delivers letter for father, VI: 214n; his attendance at serenades, VIII: 58n, 393n; his tutor, 237n; a gift of a hymnal, 246n; navy sword and flags for, 395; *see also* VIII: 319, 424

Lincoln, Thomas (L.'s uncle), I: 459, 462

Lincoln, Mrs. Thomas, *see* Lincoln, Sarah (Bush-Johnston); *and* Lincoln, Nancy Hanks

Lincoln, Thomas B., VIII: 354-55

Lincoln, Timothy D., II: 415n

Lincoln, William Wallace (L.'s son "Willie"), I: 304; II: 217; IV: 65, 82, 122n, 129, 441; V: 28n, 154n, 168n; VI: 144, 422n; VIII: 237n

Lincoln (Ill.), IV: 143; VIII: 51n

"Lincoln" (printed Congressional speech of Richard Yates, Feb. 12, 1921), I: 419n; II: 226n, 285n

Lincoln and His Wife's Home Town (Townsend), I: 466n

Lincoln and Ohio (Ryan), III: 437n

"Lincoln and Retaliation" (art.), VIII: 116n

Lincoln and the Civil War in the Diaries and Letters of John Hay (Dennett), VI: 174n; VII: 84n, 378n, 386n

Lincoln at Gettysburg (Barton), VII: 17n, 19n

Lincoln at New Salem (Reep), I: 10n

Lincoln Autographic Album, The (Whitney), IV: 35n, 79n

Lincoln Bibliography 1839-1939 (Monaghan), I: 159n; II: 504n, 537n

Lincoln Centennial Association, I: vii; *see also* Abraham Lincoln Association

Lincoln County (Tenn.), VII: 541n; VIII: 69

Lincoln-Douglas debates: arrangements for, II: 522, 524, 528-34; III: 201; at Ottawa, II: 547-53, III: 1-37 (text of); at Freeport, III: 38-76 (text of), IV: 107-108; at Jonesboro, III: 97-101, 102-44 (text of); at Charleston, 145-201; at Galesburg, 207-44 (text of), 245; at Quincy, 245-83; at Alton, 283-325 (text of), 329
Comments on debates and the publication of, III: 37, 285, 339, 341, 343, 349, 365-70, 372-74, 401-403, 510, 514-16; IV: 152

Lincoln Fellowship of Wisconsin, III: 471n

Lincoln Guards (N. Y.), V: 257n

Lincoln Herald [periodical], VIII: 116n

"Lincoln in Rushville" (art.), I: 210n; III: 352n, 515n; VIII: 427n

Lincoln in the Telegraph Office (Bates), V: 291n

"Lincoln in Wisconsin" (art.), III: 477n

Lincoln Kinsman, The, IV: 57n

Lincoln Memorial: Album-Immortelles, The (Oldroyd), VI: 511n

Lincoln National Life Foundation (Fort Wayne, Ind.), IV: 84n

Lincoln on Agriculture (pamphlet), III: 471n

Lincoln on the Eve of '61, a Journalist's Story (Villard), IV: 191n

Lincoln (Nebr.) *Star*, IV: 347n

"Lincoln, the Constitutional Lawyer" (art.), II: 431n

Lincoln the President: Springfield to Gettysburg (Randall), V: 64n

Lincoln's Crisis in the Far West (Wiel), VI: 206n

"Lincoln's Emancipation Proclamation" (art.), V: 433n; VI: 30n

Lincoln's Parentage and Childhood (Warren), IV: 57n

"Lincoln's Re-election" (art.), VIII: 98n
"Lincoln Riflemen" (Chicago), IV: 184n
Lincoln's Secretary (Nicolay), V: 552n
Linder, Daniel W., VII: 87, 91, 94-95
Linder, Usher Ferguson, I: 56-57, 61-62, 66-67, 453, 457-58; II: 45, 68, 191, 431; VII: 87, 92n, 94, 95
Lindley, Philo, II: 167
Lindsay, David G., VIII: 32n
Lindsay, Isaac, III: 399; IV: 188
Lindsay, James, V: 249n
Lindsay, John M., IV: 303n
Lindstrom, Ralph G., I: xvii
Lineage of Lincoln, The (Barton), IV: 57n
Link, William H., V: 213n
Linn, William, I: 67, 166
Linton, John L., IV: 508
Lippy, John D., Jr., VIII: 48n
Lisbon (Portugal), V: 141
Little, David, VIII: 69
Little, S., *see* Littler, S.
Little, Sidney H., I: 237
Little, Wallace A., II: 297, 303; III: 65
Little Baynard (S. C.), VI: 456-57
Little Blue River, VIII: 57n
Little, Brown & Company (Boston), V: 544n
Little Falls (N. Y.), IV: 223
Little Heart (Indian), VI: 153n
Little Piney Creek (Mo.), V: 314-15, 459n
Little River Turnpike (Va.), V: 234
Little Rock (Ark.), VII: 109, 142, 208n, 325, 464n
Little Traverse Indian Reservation, VII: 300n
Little Vermilion River (Ill.), II: 189
Littlefield, H., VI: 464
Littlefield, John H., IV: 146; VI: 464
Littler, S., III: 203n

Livermore, Mrs. Daniel Parker, *see* Livermore, Mary Ashton (Rice)
Livermore, Mary Ashton (Rice), VI: 539n; VII: 75n
Liverpool (England), IV: 466n; VI: 121-22; VII: 238n
Liverpool Point (Va.), V: 130n
Liverpool (England) *Post*, VI: 559n
Lives and Speeches of Abraham Lincoln and Hannibal Hamlin (Howells), II: 383n; IV: 80n
Livingston, H. P., VIII: 75, 114, 227
Livingston, William, III: 531n
Livingston (Ill.), I: 220
Lizzie Thompson (ship), VI: 92
Lloyd, Richard H., II: 482-83
Lloyd, Mrs. W. Ross, III: 341n
Loan, Benjamin Franklin, VI: 545n; VII: 78, 197, 428n
Locke, Eric, IV: 181-82
Locke, Joseph Morris, VIII: 122
Locke, Walter L., IV: 347n
Lockhart, Jacob T., IV: 471n
Lockridge, John, I: 283-84, 290, 319
Lockwood, Henry Hall, V: 163n, 379n; VI: 399; VII: 10n, 60, 258-59; VIII: 167n
Lockwood, John, VI: 137-38
Lockwood, Samuel Drake, I: 52, 392; II: 71-72, 75, 120-21; VIII: 179-80
Lockwood, William F., IV: 336n, 345
Locofocos, *see* Democratic Party
Loe, Moses, II: 414
Loes, F. T., IV: 166
Logan, Christopher, I: 491
Logan, David, IV: 81-82, 90, 101, 120
Logan, Elsie, II: 391n; III: 205n
Logan, John, I: 242-43
Logan, John Alexander, IV: 477, 555n; V: 142, 413n; VI: 107, 230, 382-83; VII: 248n, 327; VIII: 105, 182n, 197

Logan, Samuel M., VII: 161n
Logan, Stephen Trigg: and the "Sampson's Ghost" letters, I: 89n; his law cases and law partnership with L., 92n, 97, 99, 106n, 256, 267, 270-71, 279n, 283n, 285, 291, 304-305, 324n, 329, 331, 335, 342, 344, 352, 370-71, 394, 406, 444-45, II: 17, 69, 104-105, 114, 118, 197-201, 203, 206-208, 224n, 291-92, 397-98, 482-83, III: 392, IV: 131, V: 541, VIII: 421n; and appointments, I: 122; defeats Prickett (1839) for judge of eighth judicial circuit, 153n; and L.'s melancholia (1841), 230; nominated (1842) for state (Ill.) representative, 284-85, 288; on committee to draft Whig campaign circular (1843), 308, 318; Brown succeeds as judge of first judicial district, 389n; L. mentions similarity of speaking voice of Stephens to, 448; mention of his sons, 491n, IV: 81-82, 120; defeated in Congressional election (1848), I: 518-19; L. urges his appointment (1850) as district court judge, II: 71-72; on committee to draft resolutions on death of Judge Pope, 79n; opinion on election laws, 160; listed as member of Ill. legislature (1855), 297; unsuccessful candidacy (1855) for supreme court judge, 309-10, 312-13; signs call for county convention (1857), 424-25; opinion on state debt, III: 381-83; recommended as delegate to Washington peace conference (1861), IV: 168n; member of commission investigating Cairo, Ill., claims (1862), V: 177; mentioned as father-in-law of Lamon, VII: 7
Logan, Thomas J., VII: 371
Logan, William, IV: 407n

Logan & Baker (Springfield), I: 92n
Logan County (Ill.), I: 127-32, 139n, 144-45, 198-99, 351, 354, 357-58
Logan County (W. Va.), V: 298
Logan County Democrat [Lincoln, Ill.], II: 375n
Logansport (Ind.), I: 32
Logue, Felix, VI: 443
Lombard, Robert P. (half-breed), VIII: 398n
London (England): IV: 284, 397n, 417n, V: 92, 550, VI: 88-89; World's Fair (1862), IV: 450-51, 551n, V: 47, 77, 88, 98n
London (Ky.), V: 54n
London (Ohio), IV: 203-204
London (England) *Daily News*, VI: 89n
London (Ohio) *National Democrat*, IV: 204n
London (England) *Post*, VI: 177n
London Printing & Publishing Company, Ltd., V: 157n
Lone Wolf (Indian), VI: 153n
Long, Mrs., VIII: 268
Long, Alexander, VI: 300-306
Long, John F., IV: 167
Long, Lee W., VI: 529, 531, 537
Long, Stephen Harriman, VI: 247-48
Long, Thomas, I: 10n
Long Branch & Sea-Shore Railroad Company, VII: 264
"Long Nine," I: 73n, 227
Longnecker, Henry C., VIII: 48
Longstreet, James, V: 250n, 252, 276n, 310; VI: 199, 203, 218n, 273n, 274, 280n, 282n, 293n, 450n, 475n, 476, 518; VII: 14n, 35n, 153-54, 438n; VIII: 331n
Longworth, Abel, VI: 137n, 197
Lookout Mountain (Tenn.), VII: 30n, 539n
Loomis, Dwight, VI: 122
Loomis, Francis Butler, VII: 338
Loose, Jacob G., III: 399

López, Carlos Antonio, V: 161;
VI: 91
López, Francisco Solano, VI: 91-92
Lord [?], James H., IV: 369n
Loring, William Wing, VI: 226
Los Angeles Land Office, IV: 305
Los Angeles Times, IV: 81n; VII:
534n
Lossing, Benson John, VI: 30n
"Lost Speech," delivered by L.
at 1856 Bloomington conven-
tion, II: 341n
"Lost Townships" letters, I: 291-
97, 300-301
Louaillier, Louis, VI: 268
Louderman, J. C., & Company,
(St. Louis), II: 120
Loudon (Tenn.), VI: 436, 471n,
481; VII: 14n
Loudon & Hampshire Railroad,
IV: 450n
Loudon Heights (Va.), VI: 283n;
VII: 549
Loughborough, James M., II: 328
Loughborough, John, II: 326, 328n
Loughborough, P. S., II: 328
Louis Napoleon, *see* Napoleon III,
Emperor of the French
Louis-Philippe d'Orléans, Comte
de Paris, VIII: 53
Louise Charlotte (of Hesse), VII:
336
Louisiana: admission as a slave
state, II: 231, 235, 250; and Mc-
Clellan's plan of military opera-
tions (Feb. '62), V: 123n; pro-
claimed an area of insurrection
(July '62), 298-99; re-establishment of state government, 342-
46, 350-51, 467-68, 487-89, 504-
505, VI: 287-89, 364-66, VII: 1-2,
6-7, 66-67, 71, 89-91, 95, 123-25,
161-63, 185, 243, 248, 420, 433,
486-87, VIII: 106-108, 121, 131,
148-49, 163-65, 179, 206-207,
399-405
The holding of state elections
(1862), V: 462-63, 504-505, VI:
172; and cotton trading, V:

472n, VI: 160, VII: 488-89, VIII:
20, 103-104, 178, 196-97; employment of free Negroes on
plantations, V: 487n, VIII: 317;
and Banks Red R. expedition,
V: 506n, VIII: 14-15; claims
against military seizure of
property, VI: 16n, VII: 186-
87, 247-48, 296n, 492n; and
the Emancipation Proclamation, VI: 29, 30-31, 73, 428-29;
recruitment of Negro troops, 41,
154n; appointments, 223n, VII:
420, VIII: 181, 242n; reported
destitute condition of loyalists,
VIII: 14-15; election returns,
(1860, 1864), 128-29; *see also*
New Orleans (La.)
Louisiana (Mo.), I: 302-303
Louisiana Purchase, I: 137, 434;
II: 128, 231, 235, 237-38, 250;
III: 54, 528; V: 48
Louisville (Ky.), I: 153, 254n, 258,
259n, 260n, 428; IV: 369n, 499,
505n, 529, 534n, 535n, 541-42,
544-45; V: 14, 21-22, 92n, 321,
401, 408, 416-17, 419, 501; VI:
140, 219, 223n, 425n, 426n, 462;
VII: 98, 100n, 120n, 122n, 128,
513n, 535n; VIII: 119-20, 190,
292, 315, 323n
Louisville & Nashville Railroad,
V: 313n, 552n
Louisville City Railroad, VII:
163n
Louisville Journal, IV: 135; V:
61n; VIII: 183n, 337n
Louisville Post, VIII: 123n
Louisville Times, VII: 184n
Lounsberry, John S., VII: 176n
Louttit, W. Easton, Jr., V: 101n,
391n; VII: 411n; VIII: 302n
Love, Charles, VIII: 243, 302
Love, John, V: 407-408; VI: 177n;
VII: 211n
Love, Oscar, I: 157n
Love, S. Palace, IV: 533
Loveaire, J. G., VIII: 252n
Loveaire, John S., VIII: 252

Lovejoy, Elijah Parish, I: 111n
Lovejoy, Owen, II: 297, 316-17, 340, 347, 435-36, 458-59, 534, 537; III: 3, 6, 10, 13, 55, 60-64, 105, 107, 109-10, 113, 133, 136, 138, 140, 172, 174-76, 213, 241, 250, 262-63, 280, 284; V: 297n, 396; VII: 366-67; VIII: 102
Lovettsville (Va.), V: 481n
Low, Alexander, VIII: 338
Low, Frederick Ferdinand, V: 267n; VI: 321, 322, 393-94, 395n, 550; VII: 214-15; VIII: 109
Low, S., & Son (London), V: 352n
Lowe, John G., IV: 187
Lowe, O. F., IV: 129
Lowe, Samuel, VIII: 68
Lowe, Thaddeus S. C., IV: 460
Lowe, William H., VIII: 68
Lowe, William W., V: 489-90
Lowell, James Russell, VII: 132n
Lowell (Mass.), II: 6, 8; VI: 81
Lowell Daily Journal, II: 6n
Lower, Abraham, VI: 364
Lower Sioux Indian Agency, V: 493n
Lower Yellow Banks, see Oquawka (Ill.)
Lowery, Thomas, see Lowrey, Thomas
Lowery, William, VIII: 68
Lowndsbury, Jonathan, I: 52
Lowrey, Thomas, VII: 335
Lowrie, Walter H., VI: 445n
Lowry, George W., II: 396
Lowry, Horace, II: 93n
Lowry, Samuel R., II: 92-93
Loyalty oath: and aliens, V: 334-35; and prisoners-of-war, 344n; L. on the principle of, VII: 169-70, 283-84; see also Amnesty proclamations
Loyed [Lloyd?], Robert, I: 18, 24n
Lucas, J. C., VII: 369
Lucas, Josiah M., II: 43-44, 59, 67, 445; III: 517-18; IV: 492
Luce, William, V: 266
Luckett, Henry F., VII: 75, 275
Luckey, S. J. W., VII: 225n

Luckey, Theron Baldwin, VI: 294
Ludlow, William H., VI: 241, 315n
Ludlum, Cornelius, I: 406-407
Lufkin, Richard F., IV: 319n, 473n, 505n; V: 443n; VI: 111n, 436n; VII: 258n; VIII: 54n, 112n, 227n
Luis Jesús (Infante of Spain), VI: 162
Luiz I, King of Portugal, V: 104-105, 199; VII: 110, 478; VIII: 297
Lukens, C. L., II: 183
Luna, Ramon, IV: 349
Lundy, Benjamin, II: 357n
Lundy, Benjamin Clarke, II: 356-57, 412-13; III: 342
Luray (Va.), V: 258n, 280n
Lusby, James H., V: 205; VII: 75
Luse, James P., IV: 288n, 302
Luse, Mrs. James P. [nee Dubois], IV: 302n
Lushbaugh, Benjamin F., VI: 21n, 246n
Lusk, Edward, III: 333
Lusk, Samuel, IV: 369n
Luster, Harvey, I: 34
Luther, Diller, IV: 337
Lutherans, V: 212-13
Lutz, ———, VIII: 191-92
Lyford, James Otis, VIII: 413n
Lyle, John R., VI: 229, 231
Lyman, Azel S., VI: 272
Lyman, Roswell D., II: 163-68
Lyman, William, II: 297, 303; III: 65
Lyman, William T., V: 148n
Lynch, Henry W., I: 464n
Lynch [alias Hennessy], James, VIII: 297
Lynch, Jesse, I: 463-64
Lynchburg (Ill.), I: 130
Lynchburg (Va.), V: 122n, 278n; VI: 534-35
Lynn, George, Jr., III: 202n
Lyon, ———, II: 102
Lyon, Caleb, VI: 195; VII: 163-64, 166, 194

Lyon, James G., VI: 292n
Lyon, Nathaniel, IV: 412n, 463, 526-27; V: 14n, 491n, 510-11
Lyons (France), IV: 310
Lyons, Alonzo, III: 363
Lyons, Branton, VII: 522n

Lyons, Lord Richard Bickerton Pemell, IV: 287, 341n, 450, 453; V: 38, 62, 115, 186, 225, 265; VI: 110, 349n, 378-79; VII: 160n, 198, 311
Lypert, Jasper, VIII: 69

M

McAber, ———, IV: 165
McAdam, James George, VII: 385-86
Macallister, Charles, III: 392n; V: 548
McAllister, Mathew H., V: 195n, 267n, 268n
McAlpin, A., IV: 182
McArthur, John, V: 142
McAtee, Smith, II: 330-31
McBernie, ———, VIII: 110
Macbeth (play), VI: 392
McBlair, John Hollins, Jr., IV: 417
McBride, James, V: 147n; VI: 51n, 69n, 77; VIII: 132n
MacBride, Van Dyk, VIII: 427n
McCaleb, C. C., VIII: 68
McCall, Charles Archibald, VII: 526n
McCall, George Archibald, IV: 463; V: 195n, 254, 272, 380-81, 454
McCalla, J. M., I: 446, 493
McCallen, Andrew, I: 448-49; II: 106, 469
McCallen, James, VII: 156n
McCallum, Daniel Craig, VI: 472n, 474n, 481-82; VII: 89n
McCammon, Joseph, II: 418
McCammon, Samuel, VIII: 68
McCandless, J. B., II: 188
McCarthy, James, VII: 378, 385
McCarthy, William H., Jr., I: xiv

McCarty, Dennis, VI: 473-74, 515; VII: 175-76
McCauley, Mark, VIII: 324n
McCaulley, William S., IV: 240n
McCaullie, A. J., VIII: 68
McChesney, Joseph H., V: 62
McClain, Dudley, II: 297
McClary, Charles, VIII: 68
McClellan, Ellen Mary (Marcy), V: 452
McClellan, George Brinton: appointed Major General, IV: 370, 463; and mobilization and recruitment, 388n, 394, 402, V: 15n; and war contracts, IV: 400, V: 20, 75-76; and suspension of the writ of habeas corpus, IV: 414n; and L.'s memo on military policy (July '61), 457; and use of balloons for military observation, 460n; and need of trained military officers, 481; and appointments, 489, 494, 496n, 498n, 503-505, 516n, 525n, 530, V: 12n, 56, 72, 90, 93n, 167n, 202, 457-58

Report of conditions in Western Va. referred to him by L., IV: 491; persons referred to him for conference by L., 543, V: 173; his attitude toward the Port Royal expedition (1861), IV: 545, 557; requested by L.

to inspect a battery of repeating guns, V: 4-5; appointed General in chief, 9-11, 13, 51, 494-95; courts-martial and arrests, 15n, 59n, 69n, 106, 129, 369-70; his plans for commands in the Departments of the West and of the Cumberland (Nov. '61), 21-22, 31; authorized to declare martial law in St. Louis, 27; erection of Potomac foot bridge suggested to him, 31 L.'s memo to him on Potomac campaign, V: 34-35; and the defense of East Tenn. (Dec. '61), 54, 59-60, 90n, 91-92, 94, 98-99; duty assignments and promotions, 60, 75-78, 159, 175-76, 360n, 451, 464, VI: 76n; quells rumor of plan to transfer Schofield from Mo. command, V: 61-62; and Halleck complaints against Lane (1861), 80n; his illness (1862) and investigation by the Committee on the Conduct of the War, 84, 86-88, 94, VIII: 40n; and L.'s General (No. 1) and Special (No. 1) War Orders, V: 111-12, 115; and proposed Lane expedition from Fort Leavenworth, 115-16; conflicting plans for Army of the Potomac movement (Feb. 3, '62), 118-25, 130; and disposition of troops on vessel forced back from Burnside expedition to Roanoke Island, 132

His reaction to organization of Army Corps, V: 150n, 207-209, and military operations, (*spring '62*) 130, 151, 153, 155, 157-59, 164, 175-85 *passim*, 195, 202-310 *passim*, 322-23, 334, (*Aug.-Nov. '62*) 387n, 396, 398n, 399-400, 405n, 407, 410, 412, 415, 418, 425-28, 448n, 452, 460-62, 474-75, 477, 479, 481, VI: 281, 467; his command limited to the Army of the Potomac, V: 155,

164; L. receives engravings of, 157

His removal from command of the Army of the Potomac, V: 325n, 404n, 416n, 485-86, 509-11; his relations with Stanton (Aug. '62), 358-59; L. visits his headquarters (Oct. '62), 448n; and his order No. 154 on recruitment of volunteers, 482; mention of publication of letter from L., VI: 59n; mention of his comparative army rank, 230; pressure to give him a command (1863), 311-12, 383, VII: 470n; dismissal of his former aide-de-camp, VI: 351n; and elections in Pa. (1863), 512n; mention of his report on 1862 arrest of Stone, VII: 285-86; L.'s portrait painter identified as former member of his staff, 392n; Democratic party candidate for President (1864), 506, 514-15, VIII: 3, 46, 58n, 98, 128-30, 156n; refutation of Copperhead press story of his visit with L. to Antietam battlefield, VII: 548-50

McClellan, Mrs. George Brinton, *see* McClellan, Ellen Mary
McClellan's Own Story, V: 176n
McClelland, John, VIII: 180-81
McClenahan, Henry, I: 69
McClennan, Donald, IV: 296
McClernand, John, *see* McClelland, John
McClernand, John Alexander: in Ill. legislature, I: 213n, 227n, 238, 242; Congressman from Ill., 461, II: 23, 151, III: 429; argues illegality of apportionment act veto in Ill. Supreme Court, II: 432-33; and his proposal to suppress Utah polygamy, IV: 41; mobilization and recruitment, 374n, 381, 527; and purchase of produce deprived of Southern outlets, 381;

L.'s permission for him to visit Fort Monroe, 383-84; appointed Brigadier General, 477, VIII: 593-94; appointments and assignments to duty, IV: 480, 492, 517, 527, V: 180, 405, 427, 457n, 471n, 498-99, VI: 44n, 96; in command at Cairo, Ill., IV: 527; letter from L. commending military action at Belmont, Mo. (Nov. '61), V: 20-21

Appointed Major General, V: 142; urges discharge of imprisoned secessionist, 413, 427; and organization of an expedition to Vicksburg (Oct. '62), 468-69, 498-99; correspondence with L. on his support of a Confederate peace move (Jan. '63), VI: 48-49; attacks Halleck's competency, 70-71; and court-martial of N. Y. *Herald* war correspondent, 142-43; and La. elections (1863), 173n; mentioned by L. in 1863 reappointments of generals, 230-31; his removal from command, 293n, 380, 383-84; his illness and leave of absence (July '64), VII: 473

McClintock, John, IV: 551-52
McCloud, John B., VI: 26n
McClun, John E., II: 297
McClure, Alexander Kelly, IV: 103, 112-13, 169; VI: 311; VIII: 29, 81
McClure, Charles, VII: 371
McClure, John W., VI: 476
McClure, Thomas B. [R.], II: 297
McClurg, Joseph Washington, VII: 343n
McColet, Joseph Rhea, VIII: 69
McComas, Elisha W., VI: 251n
McComb, Henry S., VII: 457n
McConihe, Isaac, IV: 227n
McConnel, John Ludlum, II: 75
McConnel, Murray, I: 76; II: 12-13, 75
McConnell, John, VI: 490
McConnellsburg (Pa.), VI: 293n

McCook, Alexander McDowell, IV: 449-50, 505; V: 14, 320, 417n, 458n; VII: 14n, 235n
McCook, Charles M., VII: 516n
McCook, Daniel, VII: 516n
McCook, Edward M., VII: 311n; VIII: 229n
McCook, Edwin S., IV: 392
McCook, Mary, *see* Baldwin, Mary (McCook)
McCook, Robert L., VII: 516n
McCormack, Michael, II: 106n, 107
McCormack, Thomas Joseph, IV: 479n
McCormack House (Danville, Ill.), III: 494n
McCormick, Andrew, I: 76-77, 147n, 148-49, 298
McCormick, Cyrus Hall, II: 315n; VI: 251n
McCormick, William J., I: 417
McCoy, Henry C., VII: 374n
McCoy, Joseph, V: 79n
McCracken, Hugh B., VIII: 80n
McCran, William, VIII: 69
McCrea, James A., VII: 385-86
McCreay, James B., VII: 274
McCrellis, Lafayette, II: 297
McCroskey, David, VIII: 68
McCulloch, Edward D., I: 452n
McCulloch, Hugh, VII: 128; VIII: 352-54, 408
McCulloch, Ross, VIII: 408n
McCullough, Fanny, VI: 16-17; VIII: 307n
McCullough, Hugh, *see* McCulloch, Hugh
McCullough, William, VI: 17n
McCullough, William A., VIII: 307n
McCurdy, Robert H., V: 325
McCurdy, Solomon P., VII: 153n
McDaniel, Jonathan, II: 297
McDaniels, ———, VII: 284n
McDierman, Michael, I: 47
McDonald, David, VIII: 47n, 158n
McDonald, Michael, II: 182
McDonald, Walter D., II: 182-83

McDonall, Alexander J., V: 19n
McDonell, Charles, III: 125
MacDonough, Leo, IV: 441n
McDonough County (Ill.), I: 73n;
IV: 124
McDougall, James Alexander, IV:
419, 481, 501n, 537n; V: 32,
160-61, 195n, 268n; VI: 50n, 236
McDowell, Helen (Burden), V:
168
McDowell, Henry C., V: 464n
McDowell, Irvin: his army promotions, IV: 411n, 463n, V: 142;
his cousin given a military commission, IV: 501; an expression
of L.'s confidence in, V: 98;
given command of First Corps,
149, 209n; arranges for his wife
to call on Mrs. L. (Mar. '62),
168; and military operations,
(*spring '62*) 179, 184, 195, 206,
218-80 *passim*, 284n, 301, (*fall
'62*) 399n, 400n; L. visits
(May '62), 231, VI: 291; his
command incorporated into the
Army of Virginia, V: 287; his
request for a court of inquiry on
his action at Second Bull Run,
407n, VI: 59n; presides over
court of inquiry of cotton trade
cases, VI: 397n; L. authorizes
his memo on their meeting
(Jan. '62), VIII: 39-40
McDowell, Mrs. Irvin, *see* Mc-
Dowell, Helen (Burden)
McDowell, James, I: 345-46, 459-
60, 462
McDowell, James L., IV: 290; VII:
304
McDowell, William P., IV: 501n
Macedonian (brig), VI: 272n;
VIII: 138
McElrath, Mrs., VIII: 7
McElrath, Thomas, IV: 334; VII:
181-82, 269n
McElroth, Thomas, *see* McElrath,
Thomas
McElroy, James Newton, VII: 513
McElwee, F. B., VIII: 68

McEwen, James H., VII: 288
McFadden, Richard, II: 182
McFarland, Henry, IV: 505n
McFarland, J. B., II: 373
McFarland, James E., V: 64n
McFerran, James, VII: 12n
McFerson, Theodore R., VIII: 119n
McGaffey, A. A., V: 90n
McGahan, David, VII: 99n
McGaughey, Edward Wilson, II:
29
McGill, John D., I: 518n
McGilvra, John J., IV: 308
McGinnis, H. B., II: 149n
McGirr, John, II: 183
McGlouflin, George, V: 164n
McGrath, Thomas, VIII: 233n
McGuire, George W., VI: 392, 395,
402
McHannon, Charles, V: 15n
McHatton, Samuel, I: 31n
McHenry, Henry, I: 82
McHenry, James, III: 524
M'Henry, John H., Jr., VI: 67
McHose, Samuel, VII: 369n
McIlvaine, Abraham Robinson,
IV: 167
McIlvaine, Charles Pettit, V: 473;
VI: 362; VII: 128; VIII: 218n,
424
McIndoe, Walter Duncan, IV:
462
McIntosh, ———, I: 110
McIntosh, Alexander, V: 394
McIntyre, James B., V: 397n
McIntyre, Joseph S., II: 112
McIntyre, Roswell, VIII: 36
Mack, Alonzo W., IV: 400; V: 541n
Mack, Mrs. George E., VIII: 148n
Mackay, Alfred, VII: 353
Mackay, Charles, VIII: 423n
McKay, Gurdon, VI: 60
McKay, James, V: 167n
McKay, James H., IV: 534
McKay, William, IV: 543
McKean, Thomas Jefferson, V: 261
McKee, Alexander R., IV: 302-303
McKee, Francis M., VIII: 69
McKee, John, VII: 213

McKee, Martin, I: 229n
McKee, William, VI: 325n, 326n, 329, 338
McKee, William Robertson, II: 86
McKenny, Thomas J., IV: 563n
McKenzie, Alexander, VIII: 189, 268n
Mackenzie, Morris R. S. [A.], V: 388
McKenzie, William L., II: 146n
McKilbin, Joseph C., VII: 371n
McKimmons, William, VIII: 69
Mackinac Indian Agency, VII: 300n
Mackinac Island (Mich.), V: 342n
Mackinaw (Ill.), I: 46; V: 342n
Mackinaw River, I: 450
McKinley, James B., II: 475
McKinney, ———, VIII: 317n
McKinney, David, VII: 102n
McKinney, James, VIII: 69
McKinney, John Franklin, VI: 300-306
McKinney, Thomas J., see Mc-Kenny, Thomas J.
McKinstry, Justus, IV: 515-16; VI: 82
Macklin, Charles, VI: 559n
McKnabb, see McNab, John
McKnight, ———, I: 465
McKown, Thomas, II: 182
McLain, Dudley, II: 297
McLane, Ellen V., V: 266n
McLane, L. A., IV: 107n
McLane, Robert Milligan, I: 516; IV: 356n, 358
McLaran, Charles, VIII: 297-98
McLaren, Robert Neill, VIII: 120
McLaughlin, Augustus, IV: 361
McLaughlin, Patrick, VI: 296-97
McLaughlin, Robert K., I: 67
McLean, D. H. A., VII: 455
McLean, E. P., VII: 455
McLean, Frank J., VII: 310
McLean, James M., I: 249; II: 22, 52
McLean, John, I: 467, 474; II: 291, 314, 342-43, 400, 417, 466; III: 251, 543n; IV: 36, 40-41, 45-46; V: 41, 390n
McLean, Mrs. John, see McLean, Sarah Bella
Maclean, John (1800-1886), VIII: 183-84
McLean, Nathaniel Collins, VIII: 182n
McLean, Nathaniel Henry, VII: 290
McLean, Sarah Bella, V: 390
McLean, Washington, VIII: 314n
McLean, William Alexander, VI: 126n
McLean County (Ill.), II: 210n, 311n, 325, 458; III: 331; VI: 17n
McLean County Bank (Blooming-ton, Ill.), II: 233, 325; III: 519n
McLear, John P., V: 376n
McLetchie, Andrew, VII: 332
McMahon, John, VII: 483
McMahon, William D., VIII: 206
McManus, see Burke, Edward
McMichael, Morton, V: 454; VII: 469, 480-81
McMillan, James Winning, IV: 402
Macmillan's [McMillan] Maga-zine, VIII: 371-72
McMinn County (Tenn.), VIII: 68
McMurtrie, Theodore, VII: 531n
McMurtry, William, I: 70n, 73n; II: 75
McMynn, John G., VII: 225n
McNab, John, IV: 480; V: 11n
McNally, William, VIII: 213n
McNamar [alias McNeil], John, I: 13, 60, 330
McNamara, F. G., VII: 166n
Macnamara, Francis S., VII: 166n
McNamara, Michael H., IV: 486
McNary County (Tenn.), VIII: 70
McNeely, William, I: 13, 36-37; III: 343
McNeil, John (Ill.) [alias], see McNamar, John

McNeil, John (Mo.), VI: 31, 493n, 495n
McNeill, Cornelius F., IV: 38
McNeill, Francis A., I: 284-85, 334, 381
McNulty, John [alias Joseph Riley], VIII: 167-68
Macomb, William H., VIII: 133
Macomb (Ill.), III: 38, 134, 333
Macomb Eagle, IV: 112n
Macomber, O. O., V: 99n
Macon (Ga.), VII: 169n; VIII: 27n
Macon County (Ill.), I: 2, 3n; IV: 48, 49, 63, 64, 100
Macon County (Tenn.), VIII: 69
Macoupin County (Ill.), I: 401-405; II: 524n
McPhail, Daniel H., V: 286n
McPheeters, Samuel B., VI: 20, 33-34; VII: 85-86
McPheeters, Mrs. Samuel B., VI: 20n, 33
McPheeters, Thomas, VII: 86n
McPheeters, Mrs. Thomas, VII: 86n
McPherson, Edward, VII: 65n, 183n; see also *A Political History of the United States during the Great Rebellion*
McPherson, James Birdseye, VI: 230, 380n; VII: 240, 248, 307n
McPherson, John, VIII: 68
McPherson, John D., VI: 526n; VII: 428-29, 468; VIII: 243n
Macpherson, Mrs. John Francis, *see* Macpherson, Lydia Edna
Macpherson, Lydia Edna (Orendorff), II: 335n, 336n, 392n, 398n, 476n; VIII: 421n, 429n
McPherson, William M., V: 500
McRae, John Jones, III: 542n
Macready, Mary, II: 470
McReynolds, Andrew Thomas, IV: 406
McRoberts, Samuel A., I: 221
McTurens lands (S. C.), VI: 456
McVay, Perry, VI: 544
McVeagh, Isaac Wayne, VI: 512-13

McVitty, S. H., IV: 456n; V: 452n
McWilliams, Amzi, II: 310
McWilliams, Daniel, VIII: 68
Macy, Daniel, II: 466
Macy, Oscar, IV: 305
Madagascar, VI: 110n
Maddux, J. B., VI: 420
Madigan, Thomas F., see *The Autograph Album* and *A Catalogue of Lincolniana*
Madison, James, I: 172, 312, 333, 502; II: 84; III: 8, 12, 18-19, 78, 162, 178, 195, 453, 484, 527, 532n, 533n, 544n, 545n; IV: 199, 262n, 420
Madison (Ga.), VIII: 27n
Madison (Ind.), IV: 541
Madison & Indianapolis Railroad, II: 212n
Madison County (Tenn.), VIII: 70
Madlener, Otto, VI: 414n
Madlener, William C., VI: 414n
Madrid (Spain), IV: 406n
Magnolia (Ill.), I: 463-64
Magnolia (S. C.), VI: 455, 457
Magoffin, Beriah, IV: 444n, 497; V: 113n, 170n, 384n
Magoffin, Ebenezer, V: 170n, 183
Magrath, F. M., IV: 560n; V: 8-9, 54
Magraw, Henry S., IV: 469n
Magruder, John Bankhead, V: 123n, 310; VI: 265; VII: 335n
Maguire, George A., VII: 307n, 312
Mahan, Dennis Hart, V: 13
Mahan, Frederick Augustus, V: 13n, 152
Maher & Castello, II: 184
Mahoney, John, VIII: 68
Mahpe-o-ke-na-ji (Indian), V: 542
Maidof, Joachim, IV: 408n
Maine, I: 126n, 177; II: 146, 246, 269, 313, 363; III: 11, 19, 114, 217; IV: 276n; V: 14n, 74; VI: 83n, 321n, 449n; VII: 67, 519-20; VIII: 2-4, 100n, 128-29, 150, 153

Majer, Adolph, V: 382-83
Major, William, VI: 402n
Majors, John B., VIII: 176, 205-206
Ma-kat-e-na-jin (Indian), V: 543
Malhiot, E. E., VI: 287-89
Mallery, Garrick, VI: 119
Mallery, John Conrad, VI: 119
Mallett, Edward Jones, V: 377; VI: 430
Mallison, Francis A., VIII: 13-14
Mallory, C. H., VII: 220n
Mallory, Egbert M., I: 257
Mallory, James R., VIII: 180-81, 188, 259
Mallory, Robert, IV: 464n; V: 71n, 159
Mallory, Stephen Russell, VIII: 37n
Malmros, Oscar, VI: 507n
Malone, Benjamin, VIII: 233n
Maltby, Charles, VIII: 408
Maltby, Harrison, II: 374n
Man of the World, The (play), VI: 559n
Man Who Made the News, James Gordon Bennett, The (Carlson), VIII: 240n
Manassas (Va.): military movements near, (Jan.-April '62) V: 115, 118-25, 135, 157, 179, 184-85, (May '62) 233, 235-36, 240, 246, 248, 252n, 280n, 284n, (Aug.-Oct. '62) 395n, 397-403, 443n, 461, VI: 528; mention of L. visit (June '62), V: 280n; see also, Bull Run, battles of
Mancer, ———, IV: 165
Manche, La (French ship), VII: 188n
Manchester (England), VI: 63-65
Manchester (Ky.), VI: 83n
Manchester (N. H.), III: 551-52, 554; VII: 389n, 520n
Manchester (Vt.), VI: 421, 431, 434; VII: 526, 544, 547
Manchester (N. H.) Daily American, III: 552n
Mangum, Berrien, II: 9

Mangum, Willie Person, II: 53, 351, 355n; IV: 310
"Maniac, The" (poem), I: 385-86, 392n
Manierre, Benjamin F., VII: 32
Manikiya (Indian), VII: 325-26
Mankato (Minn.), VI: 6n
Manly, Miss, VII: 239
Manly, Hiram P., VIII: 103n
Manly, Uri, V: 183; VI: 18
Mann, Mary Tyler (Peabody), VII: 287-88
Mann, Uriah, I: 298
Mann, William B., IV: 165
Manning, Charles, II: 330n
Manning, E. A., VIII: 194n
Manning, Joel, II: 181-82
Manny, John H., II: 315, 325, 437; III: 371n
Mansfield, H. Livingston, V: 387-88
Mansfield, John L., IV: 312
Mansfield, Joseph King Fenno, IV: 370, 372n, 385, 412-13, 463n, 467, 517, 524n; V: 510-11
Mansfield, Sereno, IV: 30
Mansion House (Leavenworth, Kans.), III: 497n
Manter, Francis H., V: 517
Manypenny, George W., III: 401n
Maple Valley (Va.), V: 119
March, Jason, see Marsh, Jason
March, Walter, see Marsh, Walter
Marchand, John B., VIII: 104n
Marchant, Edward D., VI: 118n
Marchant, Henry A., VI: 118, 125
"Marco Bozzaris" (poem), IV: 48
Marcy, Randolph Barnes, IV: 479-80; V: 244n, 248, 249, 305-306
Marcy, William Larned, I: 466, 496, 500
Mare Island Navy Yard (Calif.), VII: 401n
Mareil, H. de, VIII: 343
Margraff, Philip, VI: 244, 248
Maria Annunziata, Archduchess of Austria, VI: 18

Maria Cristina, Infanta of Spain, V: 133; VI: 162
Maria de la Concepción, Infanta of Spain, V: 133
Maria de la Paz, Infanta of Spain, V: 393
Maria de Regla, Infanta of Spain, IV: 547
Maria del Pilar, Infanta of Spain, IV: 490
Maria Eulalia, Infanta of Spain, VII: 283
Maria Isabel, Infanta of Spain, VIII: 53
Maria L. Day (ship), VII: 164n
Marie Clotilde Napoleon (French Princess), VII: 550
Marie Henriette (later Queen of the Belgians), VII: 477
Marietta (Ga.), VIII: 10n
Marine & Fire Insurance Company, III: 342
Marine Corps: concerts by band, IV: 248n, VII: 332; appointments, IV: 356, 484n, 494n, 521n, V: 13, 23n, 175n, VI: 154, 214, VII: 353; promotion, IV: 470n; Ill. artillery unit charged with mutinous conduct, VI: 127; draft order for, VII: 245; dismissal, VIII: 170n
Marion, Francis, II: 275
Marion County (Ill.), I: 146
Marion County (Tenn.), VIII: 68
Marion County (W. Va.), V: 298
Mark, David, II: 47
Markbreit, Leopold, VIII: 10n, 263-64
Markens, Isaac, *see Abraham Lincoln and the Jews*
Markland, A. H., IV: 517
Marley, *see* Manly, Hiram P.
Marriage, *see* Women and marriage, L. on
Marrs, John, VII: 205
Marryat, Frederick, II: 157
Marseilles (France), IV: 310
Marsh, Charles (consul to Egypt), VIII: 139n

Marsh, Charles (Mass.), VIII: 171n
Marsh, Elston, V: 376n
Marsh, George Perkins, IV: 292-93
Marsh, Jason, VIII: 161
Marsh, John, II: 198
Marsh, Richard Symmes Thomas, II: 81n
Marsh, Sylvester, II: 431n
Marsh, Walter, I: 206; IV: 181
Marsh, William, VI: 544
Marshall, D. D. T., IV: 307, 334
Marshall, George, VII: 189
Marshall, James F. B., V: 147
Marshall, James M., IV: 398
Marshall, Jessie Ames, V: 487n
Marshall, John, II: 210-11
Marshall, Samuel D., I: 290-91, 304-305, 342, 345, 352, 370-71, 445, 515; II: 193n
Marshall, Samuel Scott, II: 106n, 116n
Marshall, Thomas A., II: 443; IV: 398, 400; VII: 378-79
Marshall, Thornton F., IV: 369n; VIII: 197
Marshall, William, I: 12
Marshall, William L., IV: 304
Marshall, William Rainey, V: 542-43
Marshall County (Ill.), I: 354, 358n, 360, 384n
Marshall (now Menard) County (Ill.), proposed establishment of, I: 57n
Marshall County (Tenn.), VIII: 69
Marshall County (W. Va.), V: 298
Marston, Gilman, IV: 516; VI: 350n; VII: 87, 91-92, 95n, 98n, 103, 139
Marston, Ward, V: 13
Martin, ———, VI: 144, 214
Martin, Anna B., VIII: 122
Martin, Benjamin N., VI: 35
Martin, Henry, IV: 462
Martin, Henry W., VII: 69; VIII: 339n

Martin, James, I: 2
Martin, James Stewart, VIII: 314
Martin, John, III: 543n
Martin, Luther, III: 523n
Martin, Nathaniel B., I: 198
Martin, Mrs. Nathaniel B., *see* Martin, Sarah
Martin, Robert, VII: 371
Martin, Samuel H., II: 297, 470
Martin, Sarah, I: 198
Martin, Wesley, VIII: 293
Martin, William, V: 94
Martin, William (Ill.), II: 98-103, 105-107, 110
Martindale, Franklin G., VII: 445-46
Martindale, John Henry, VI: 145n, 452n; VIII: 16n
Martínez, Tomás, IV: 286; VIII: 137n
Martinique, V: 76n
Martinsburg (W. Va.), IV: 420n; V: 236-37, 247n, 249, 418; VI: 253n, 273-74, 276, 309n, 534; VII: 102-103, 424n, 446n, 511n
Marvin, Asa, VIII: 309n
Marvin, James Madison, VI: 163-64
"Mary, Aunt," *see* Dines, Mary
Mary, Princess of Baden, VI: 171
Mary Lincoln, Wife and Widow (Angle and Sandburg), I: 478n; VII: 8n
Mary, Wife of Lincoln (Helm), VI: 472n, 474n, 517n; VII: 34n, 64n, 320n
Maryland: appointments, IV: 304, 328, 356-57, 363, 404, V: 159n, 453n, VII: 97, VIII: 348, 369, 411; position as a border state, IV: 340-44, 355-56, 358, 381n, 386n, 532, V: 24, 49-50, 221n, 241, 343-44, VI: 56n; mobilization and recruitment, IV: 368, 386n, 388, 455n, 508, VI: 277-78; military arrests, IV: 462n, 522-23, V: 86-87, 114n, 221n, 285n, VI: 378, 463-

64, VII: 60, VIII: 167, 198n, 303-304; and McClellan's plan of campaign, V: 123n; number and value of slaves in (1862), 152-53, 160, 535; complaints of non-enforcement of fugitive slave law, 224n; L. and Anna Carroll on the circularization of her defense of the war policy, 381-82
Military operations in, (*fall '62*) V: 417n, 418, 425-28, (*spring '63*) VI: 193, 249n, 257n, 280n, 282n, 317-18, 323-24, (*July '64*) VII: 424n, 435n, 437-38, 440n, 444n, 445-46; and enlistment of Negroes, VI: 317n, 491n, 495, 529-30, VII: 363n, 482n; and emancipation, VI: 428-29, VII: 49, 226-27, 251, 276-77, 302, 432-33, VIII: 41-42, 84, 254-55; holding of elections in (1863), VI: 542-43, 555-58, VII: 9-10, 26-27; clemency for condemned spies, VII: 26, 522; ratification of new constitution (Oct. '64), 227n, 251n; VIII: 23, 41-42, 52-53, 148-49, 251n; removal of Lockwood from command in, VII: 258-59; secessionist interference with church services for Negroes, 374n; retaliation for Confederate burning of governor's house, 445-46; and the 1864 election, VIII: 46, 48n, 100, 111n, 113-14, 128-29, 150, 153; investigation of loyalty of federal appointees in, 158; *see also* Baltimore (Md.)
Maryland Heights (Md.), VI: 283n; VII: 424n, 438n, 549
Maryman, Horatio R., IV: 522
Maryville (Calif.) Land Office, IV: 305
Mason, Amasa, IV: 312
Mason, Charles, VIII: 59n
Mason, George (1725-1792), III: 523n, 545n

Mason, George (prisoner, 1863), VI: 452

Mason, James Murray, III: 429, 538n, 549n; IV: 11-12, 25; V: 26, 64n, 83n

Mason, Rodney, V: 408

Mason, Roswell B., II: 417

Mason, Vance, VIII: 88, 89n, 229n

Mason and Dixon's Line, IV: 271

Mason County (Ill.), I: 354, 357-58, 360

Mason County (W. Va.), V: 298

Massachusetts, II: 299; III: 377n, 380, 390-91; IV: 186, 274-75, 370-71, 408, 557n; V: 158, 212n, 361n, 384n; VII: 81n, 190-91, 204; VIII: 128-30, 150, 153

Massachusetts (steamer), V: 38

Massachusetts Bay Colony, IV: 319n

Massachusetts Historical Society, I: 519n, VII: 168n

Massett, Stephen C., VII: 34

Massey, George V., VII: 258-59

Massie, Jesse E., I: 87-88

Masson, Mrs., VII: 288

Masten, William, V: 383, 490-91

Mastern, ———, V: 102n

Masters, Squire Davis, II: 297

Matamoros (Mexico), I: 473; II: 84; VI: 355n

Matanzas (Cuba), IV: 480n

Matheny, Charles Reynolds, I: 25, 92, 97, 99, 121, 129, 152n, 154n, 491n; II: 324-25

Matheny, Charles W., I: 491; II: 424; VI: 237-38

Matheny, James Harvey, I: 108n, 151, 308; II: 310, 386, 424; III: 3, 7, 108-109, 119, 138, 173, 181

Matheny, Noah W., I: 154, 267, 299n, 453; II: 14n, 108n, 109n, 225n, 287-88, 304n, 319n, 423n

Mather, Rufus, *see* Matherson, Rufus

Mather, Thomas, I: 67, 179

Mather, Thomas S., II: 424-25; III: 372; VII: 371n

Mathers, John, II: 522

Matherson, Rufus S., V: 375

Matheson, Roderick, IV: 301

Mathews, R. Stockett, VII: 542n; VIII: 224n

Mathewson, Charles, VIII: 370n

Mathewson, J. W., VIII: 70

Mathias Point (Va.), VII: 238

Mathis, F. J., VIII: 68

Mathis, Stephen, VIII: 68

Matlock, A. G., I: 497

Matlock, Robert, V: 402n

Matlock, William T., IV: 406n

Mattapony River, V: 515

Matteson, Joel Aldrich, II: 180, 187-88, 304-306, 329-30; III: 125, 342, 390; IV: 128-29

Matteson, Orsamus Benajah, VII: 498n

Matteson House (Chicago), II: 360

Matthews, Bordry, I: 11

Matthews, James L., VI: 37

Matthews, John, IV: 478

Matthews, Matilda (Young), VIII: 307

Matthews, Robert A., VIII: 307n

Matthews, Mrs. Robert A., *see* Matthews, Matilda

Matthewson, *see* Matheson, Roderick

Mattingly, George, IV: 319

Mattingly, Mrs. R. F., V: 69n

Mattoon, Calvin S., VIII: 360n

Mattoon (Ill.), III: 91n

Maulsby, William P., IV: 494n

Maury County (Tenn.), VIII: 69

Mausinares, José Antonio, IV: 349

Max, Louis H., VIII: 205n

Maxcy, James, I: 255-57

Maximilian, Emperor of Mexico, VIII: 137n

Maxson, Allen G., VII: 129, 152

Maxwell, A., II: 188

Maxwell, Robert A., V: 499; VI: 331-32, 475-76

Maxwell, Thomas, VIII: 70

May, George, V: 68

May, Thomas M., VII: 420

May, Thomas P., VI: 364n; VIII: 107-108, 165n

May, William Lewis, I: 25, 206-207, 208, 256, 262
Mayer, Adolph, *see* Majer, Adolph
Mayer, William, VI: 419-20
Mayers, E. D., VII: 173n
May-hoo-way-wa (Indian), V: 543
Maynadier, John H., VII: 26
Maynard, George A., VIII: 313, 405n
Maynard, Horace, IV: 313; V: 54n, 91, 200n, 319n, 328n; VI: 373; VII: 149-50, 183-84
Mayo, Ezekiel R., VII: 277n
Mayo, Z. B., III: 126
Maysville (Ky.), VI: 295; VIII: 268
Maza Adidi (Indian), VII: 325-26
Mazatlán (Mexico), IV: 445n
Maze, J. H., VII: 521n
Meaddows' Mill, I: 53
Meade, ———, VIII: 23
Meade, Abraham B., V: 93
Meade, George Gordon: and military operations, (*summer '63*) VI: 310n, 318-19, 321, (*fall '63*) 399n, 407, 450-51, 466-68, 509, 510, 512, 518-19, 534n, VII: 6-7, (*summer '64*) 395-96, (*spring '65*) VIII: 374, 390-91; and the escape of Lee's army after Gettysburg, VI: 327-30, 332n, 341-42, 354; acquiesces to proposed Hooker command under him, 350, 381; leaves of absence, 372-73, 437, 439, VII: 106; presented with a sword, VI: 418; mention of his removal of Doubleday (July '63), 431n; Naglee ordered to report to, 483n; resignations, VII: 60-61; Harrow assigned to report to, 113n; relays report of death of Dahlgren, 226; and the soldier vote (1864), 233, VIII: 100; invited to White House dinner (Mar. '64), VII: 235; orders discharge of Pa. reserve corps, 250n; his request for a court of inquiry on his action at Gettysburg, 273-74; requests for and revocation of passes, 360-62, VIII: 26n; Grant proposes new command for (July '64), VII: 469-70; recommends a West Point applicant, 545
Courts-martial and discharges: VI: 347, 356, 400, 414-15, 441-43, 459-61, 472, 478, 481-82, 491-92, 496, 498, 504, 506-507, 515-16, 519, 548, 550, 561; VII: 2, 25, 31-34, 58, 61, 64-65, 94, 96, 99, 104, 129, 133, 150, 160-61, 219-20, 261, 265, 293, 301, 307, 314-15, 317-18, 320, 378, 385n; VIII: 12-13, 19n, 87-89, 167n, 226n, 249n
Meade, Mrs. George Gordon, *see* Meade, Margaretta
Meade, Margaretta (Sergeant), VI: 332n
Meade, Richard Kidder, I: 487, 494n
Meagher, Thomas Francis, II: 106n; IV: 418; V: 25n, 76, 79; VI: 101, 283
Means, Joseph, II: 446
Means place (S. C.), VI: 455-57
Mechanic Fusiliers (Ill. Infantry, 56th Regt.), V: 202n; VI: 97n
Mechanics & Farmers Bank (Springfield), II: 291
Mechanics Union (Springfield, Ill.), I: 158
Mechanicsburg (Ill.), III: 493
Mechanicsville (Va.), V: 410n
Mechem [Machin?], ———, II: 358-59
M[echen?], James E., IV: 295n
Meck, Henry A., VIII: 357
Meconkey, Elbridge, V: 454
Meconkey, Sarah B., VII: 333
Medical officers: appointments, IV: 469, 478, 503, 512, V: 17, 65, 67, 79-80, 129, 140, 171, 179-80, 206n, 228-30, 302, 358, 380, 382-83, 400, VI: 41, 53, 211, 294,

351-52, VIII: 25, 210; assignment, V: 451; dismissals and resignations, VI: 55, 285, 312-13, VII: 537-38
Medicine Creek Indian Agency, VI: 209n
Medill, Joseph Meharry, II: 455, 472n, 473-74; III: 516n; IV: 110-11, 114; VII: 377n
Medina, José María, VII: 373
Meeker, George W., II: 79n, 113
Meeker, Usil, I: 12
Meese, J. D., IV: 71n
Meharry, James, II: 394n
Meharry, Thomas, II: 393-94
Meharry, Vinton, II: 394n
Mehringer, John, VI: 86n
Meier, John J., VII: 538-39
Meigs, Montgomery: naval instructions (Apr. '61) written by him and signed by L., IV: 318-19; secret service fund payment to, 320; and opposition to War Department's mobilization policies, 370n; Cameron's opposition to his appointment as Quartermaster General, 394-95, 398; his promotion to Brigadier General, 394n, 411n; procurement and care of supplies, 499-500, 543n, V: 162, 230n, 390, VI: 59n, 519, 523, VIII: 213; makes inspection tour of St. Louis (Sept. '61), IV: 513n; appointments and assignments of quartermasters, 534, 538, 560, V: 89-91, 104, 217, 304n, 454, VI: 119, 171, 208n, 476, 516, VII: 260, 511-12, VIII: 363n; persons referred to him by L. for conference, IV: 555, V: 75, 257, VI: 85, 150, 432-33, 519, VIII: 213
        Charges of quartermaster frauds and corruption, V: 116n, 178, VI: 161n, 196; and restoration of privately owned boats used in repairing and navigating the Chesapeake and Ohio

Canal, V: 191n; prepares military instructions (May '62) for McClellan and McDowell, 219n; receives Ingalls report of abandonment of White House depot (June 29, '62), 293n; requests for passes, 377; settles U. S. accounts with Ill. Central R.R., VI: 228n; N. Y. *Times* erroneously announces his removal, 450n; procurement of a ship to return Negroes from Isle à Vache colony, VII: 164; and adjustment of wages of women government workers, 467n; mentioned also, V: 180, 252n, VIII: 424
Meigs County (Tenn.), VIII: 68
Melbourne (Australia), IV: 312, 490-91
Mellen, William P., VI: 340n, 531; VII: 212, 218n
Melvin, Bradford M., II: 437n
Melvin, E. P., IV: 189n
Melvin, Samuel Houston, II: 437n; IV: 189; VIII: 8n
Memoir and Letters of Charles Sumner (Pierce), VIII: 364n, 372n
Memoirs of Gustave Koerner (McCormack), IV: 479n
Memoirs of Henry Villard, IV: 191n, 484n
Memphis (Tenn.), IV: 458, 484n; V: 122n, 259, 263, 276n, 305n, 313n, 316, 323n, 469n, 475n, 490n; VI: 85n, 111, 131n, 229n, 324, 431; VII: 75, 104, 146n, 185, 276n, 327n, 339, 427-28, 464; VIII: 8n, 20, 74, 178, 202n, 296n, 299n
Memphis Bulletin, VI: 380n
Menard, Peter, I: 120, 249
Menard, Pierre [Sr.], I: 14
Menard County (Ill.), I: 127-32, 139n, 144-45, 155n, 198-99, 240, 319-20, 353-55, 358n
Menard County Axis [Petersburg, Ill.], IV: 104n

Menard Index [Petersburg, Ill.],
II: 381; III: 333n
Mendenhall, Mrs. Dana, II: 425n
Mendenhall, Dinah, V: 279n
Mendocino Indian Agency, IV:
306
Menzies, G., VIII: 70
Menzies, John William, VI: 366n,
372; VIII: 236n
Menzies, William A., VIII: 235-
36
Mercer, Samuel, IV: 313n, 314,
366-67
Merchants' National Bank (Boston), VIII: 192
Mercier, Henri, V: 130n; VI: 99
Meredith, Joseph F., IV: 304
Meredith, Solomon, IV: 196
Meredith, William M., II: 32
Meredosia (Ill.), I: 34; III: 328-
29, 333
Meriden (Conn.), III: 554; IV: 13n
Merriam, Henry M., I: xvii
Merrick, Richard Thomas, VII:
167
Merrimac (C.S.S. *Virginia*), V:
154n, 177n, 207, 209-10, 547,
550; VII: 457n
Merriman, Amos L., I: 452
Merriman, Halsey O., I: 452; II:
113
Merritt, Nehemiah, V: 179n
Merriwether, William A., VII:
145, 227-28; VIII: 23n
Merry Wives of Windsor, The
(play), VI: 559n
Merryman, Elias H., I: 256, 300-
303; II: 62n; VI: 214n
Merryman, James H., VI: 214;
VII: 292
Mersey (British brigantine), VIII:
271
Mershow [Mershon?], ———, II:
201-202
Mervine, William, IV: 479n
Merwin, James Burtis, IV: 451n;
V: 297, 340
Merwin & Bray (N. Y.), *see* Bray
& Merwin

Meserve, Frederick Hill, I: xv; IV:
115n
Meservey, Charles C., VIII: 103n
Messager Franco-Américain, Le
[N. Y.], VIII: 343
Messages and Papers of the Presidents, see *Compilation of the
Messages* . . .
Messina (Sicily), IV: 310
Meszaros, Emeric, VI: 63n
Metamora (Ill.), I: 355n; II: 191n
Metcalf, Richard L., V: 180n
Methodists, II: 452; III: 84, 87,
310; IV: 542n, 550; V: 215-16;
VI: 225n; VII: 179-80, 182-83,
350-51, 374n; VIII: 83, 194n,
264, 595
Metropolitan Art Association,
catalogs cited, IV: 537n; V: 14n,
347n; VI: 464n; VII: 539n
Metropolitan Hall (Chicago), II:
391n
Metropolitan Hotel (N. Y.), VI:
215; VII: 34-35, 320
Metropolitan Hotel (Washington), V: 206n; VII: 367n
Metropolitan Railroad, VI: 246n
Metz, Christian, IV: 325-26
Mexican Boundary Survey Reports, IV: 88n
Mexican Navy, V: 28n
Mexican War, I: 381-82, 392-93,
420-22 (spot resolutions), 431-
42 (speech in Congress), 446-49,
451-52, 454-55, 457-58, 468-69,
472-76, 492-94, 514-15; II: 4-5,
8-9, 18, 84-88, 148-50, 155, 232,
237, 241, 252, 472-74, 527; III:
6, 16-17, 56, 107, 121, 168, 180,
182, 183, 206, 235-36, 239, 245,
319, 320; IV: 66, 413n, 418n,
472n, 502n, V: 142n; VI: 301n,
302
Mexicans (in California), IV: 519
Mexico, I: 431-33; II: 251; IV: 177-
78, 281, 467; V: 61, 73-74,
109, 113, 138, 188, 189-90, 230,
234, 257n, 281, 356n, 521;
VI: 66-67, 90, 105n, 205, 364,

366, 374, 393, 548-49; VII: 359, 365, 394, 411; VIII: 137, 259
Mexico, Gulf of, V: 111
Mexico City, VI: 39n
Meyer, Henry F., V: 194
Meyers, John C., *see* Myers, John C.
Miami (gunboat), V: 207
Michael, C. W., II: 534
Michigan, IV: 103n, 274n; V: 332, 360; VI: 117n, 119n; VII: 469n; VIII: 46, 100n, 128-29, 150, 153, 410
Michigan, University of, VI: 18n
Michigan Pioneer and Historical Collections (Ferry), VIII: 367n
Middle Department, V: 273n; VI: 253; VII: 259n
Middle Military Division, VII: 513n
Middleburg (Va.), V: 240n; VI: 289, 292
Middleport (Ill.), IV: 38n
Middleport Press, IV: 38
Middleton, Charles H., V: 83n
Middleton, Edward, VIII: 27
Middleton, Elijah C., VIII: 27n, 191-92
Middleton, George, VI: 460-61
Middleton, Johnson Van Dyck, VII: 526n
Middleton, Richard, V: 148-49; VI: 247-48
Middleton, Strabridge & Fabronius (Cincinnati), VIII: 192n
Middletown (Ill.), I: 53
Middletown (Va.), V: 234n, 280
Mifflin, Thomas, III: 524
Mihalotzy, Geza, IV: 184
Mikhail Mikhailovich, Grand Duke of Russia, V: 74
Milburn, Benedict, IV: 319; VII: 148n
Milderborger, John, VII: 10
Miles, Dixon Stansbury, V: 70, 234
Miles, George U., I: 318-19, 321-22; II: 330-31, 332
Miles, James G., II: 220

Miles, Joseph W., IV: 31n
Miles, Nelson Appleton, VIII: 381-83
Miles, Rufus W., IV: 31
Military arrests, IV: 372, 429-31, 462, 466, 469, 522-23, 534, 549; V: 8, 27, 86-87, 127, 188, 193-94, 221, 227, 260, 277, 285-86, 344n, 370n, 403, 413, 426-27, 429
    VI: 18, 20, 128, 144, 208, 219, 223, 260-70, 286, 303-306, 325, 361, 378, 421, 426-27, 437-38, 441, 452, 504, 536-37
    VII: 208, 232, 250, 269-70, 318, 421, 454-55; VIII: 15-16, 74, 104, 132, 166, 167, 172-73, 210-11, 229-30, 234, 322
    See also Pardons; Paroles; *and* Spies
Military Laws of the United States . . ., The, V: 466n
Military Telegraph during the Civil War, The (Plum), V: 6n
Militia Bureau, proposed establishment of, IV: 291
Mill Stone Landing (Md.), VI: 530n
Millard, ———, IV: 535
Millard, E. A., VIII: 68
Millard, Harrison, VII: 332-33
Milledgeville (Ga.), I: 442; VIII: 27n
Miller, Abram O., V: 546n
Miller, Alvera, III: 340n; VI: 480n
Miller, Anson S., III: 340; VII: 483-84; VIII: 330n
Miller, Daniel Bright, VIII: 127
Miller, David, I: 2
Miller, E. Kirby, VI: 18n
Miller, George C., VIII: 222
Miller, George Funston, VIII: 127
Miller, George G., I: 35, 52
Miller, George W., VI: 480
Miller, Horace, II: 113-14
Miller, Isaac, I: 2
Miller, Isaac S., IV: 530-31
Miller, J. F., VIII: 269n
Miller, Jacob W., I: 510

Miller, James, II: 287, 345, 360, 476-81; III: 337, 381-83, 389, 392
Miller, James (Macon Co.), I: 2
Miller, John, I: 2
Miller, John Franklin, VII: 509; VIII: 28-29, 38, 75, 188, 211, 237-38, 241, 259
Miller, John L., II: 319-20
Miller, Mrs. John R., see Miller, Susan F.
Miller, Joseph, I: 90-92, 99, 103-104; II: 70
Miller, Joseph T., VIII: 210n
Miller, Madison, I: 181n
Miller, Morris Smith, VII: 362
Miller, Nehemiah H., VIII: 160
Miller, Samuel Freeman, V: 481; VII: 280n
Miller, Samuel K., I: 85
Miller, Solomon, I: 206
Miller, Stephen, IV: 511n; VII: 311n; VIII: 109, 121n
Miller, Susan F., II: 320n
Miller, Thomas K., VIII: 38
Miller, W. W., VII: 200
Miller, William, IV: 100; VII: 200n
Miller & Jaquith, II: 470
Miller's Ferry (Ill.), I: 35, 52
Millersburg, see Middleburg (Va.)
Milligan, Samuel, IV: 295
Milliken, Richard M., VI: 537-38
Milliken's Bend (La.), VI: 293, 537
Mills, Benjamin, I: 25
Mills, J. C., VIII: 324n
Mills, Joseph T., VII: 501n, 506-508
Mills, William S., V: 360n
Millwood (Va.), VI: 293n
Milord, Henry (half-breed), V: 542
Milroy, Robert Huston, IV: 505; VI: 137, 203, 253n, 273-75, 308-309, 355n, 522n, 541-42; VII: 80
Milton (Fla.), VIII: 94

Milwaukee (Wis.), III: 471-82; VI: 138n; VIII: 300n
Milwaukee Sentinel, III: 471n, 474n, 478n, 480n, 481n
Miner, Edward Griffith, II: 434; grandson with same name, II: 434n, III: 203n, 204n
Miner, Martin B., IV: 93
Miners, Verne, IV: 187n; VIII: 173n, 307n
Minick, John R., VI: 167-68
Mining and Scientific Press (San Francisco), VII: 323n
Minnesota, I: 62n; II: 231, 236, 250, 256, 261; III: 116, 130, 188, 273, 397, 400, 485; IV: 86n, 276, 296-97, 446; V: 41, 396-97, 432n, 455n, 525-26, 537, 542-43, 550-51; VI: 6-7, 240n; VII: 160n, 345, 515-16; VIII: 46, 128-29, 150, 153, 358n
Minnesota (steamer), V: 154n, 333n
Minnesota Territory, II: 31, 46
Minor, Franklin, I: 182-83
Minorities, L. on: I: 244-45; II: 372-73; IV: 256
Minshall, William A., I: 107, 249
Minutes of the Twenty-fifth Annual Session of the Synod of Pennsylvania . . ., VI: 459n
Mis-qua-dace (Indian), VII: 345
Mission Dolores (San Francisco), IV: 296n
Missionary Ridge, VII: 30n
Mississippi, I: 75n, 109-11, 483; V: 298, 456; VI: 41, 250n, 340n, 387; VII: 124n, 131, 147, 217-18, 342n; VIII: 363n
Mississippi, Department of the, V: 155, 180n; VIII: 55n, 203n
Mississippi, Military Division of the, VII: 11n, 14n, 109n, 209n, 240, 248n, 457n, 488, 492n
Mississippi & Atlantic Railroad, III: 493n
Mississippi River, I: 483; IV: 412n; V: 123n, 174, 187n, 214, 259,

292, 316, 469n, 490n, 501; VI: 71n, 73-74, 77, 100, 111, 226n, 340n, 364, 374; VII: 44n, 49, 83, 154, 345; VIII: 196

Mississippi Squadron, VI: 82, 103; VIII: 43n, 336n

Mississippi Territory, III: 528-29

Mississippi Valley Sanitary Fair (St. Louis), VII: 343, 353-54, 395

Missouri: Sangamon Co. citizens petition for release of thief imprisoned in, I: 87-88; federal policy of depositing Ill. tax monies in the Bank of Missouri, 134n, 194; Col. Doniphan "the favorite Whig" of (1848), 447; admission to the Union as a slave state, II: 128-29, 231-32, 235, 250-51, 261, III: 456-57, 529-30 (*see also* Kansas Nebraska Act and the repeal of the Missouri Compromise); effect of the inapplicability of the Ordinance of 1787, II: 277, III: 456-57, 467; appointments, IV: 309, 392n, VI: 131, 486n, VII: 407, VIII: 358n; state defense bonds printed by American Bank Note Co., IV: 326n

Troubled conditions in: (*1861*) IV: 369n, 372-73, 387, 407n, 457, 466n, 484-85, 513n, 527n, 529-30, 532-33, 538, 545, 560, 562-63, V: 1-2, 15-17, 27, 35, 50, 80n, VII: 218n; (*1862*) V: 95n, 100, 203, VI: 8-11, 20, 21, VIII: 424; (*1863*) VI: 31, 33-34, 36-38, 42-43, 52-53, 54n, 66, 218, 234, 344-45, 360n, 415n, 489, 492-93, 499-504, 526-28, 543-45, VII: 78-79, 84-86; (*1864*) 157-58, 230, 283-84, 287, 407, 462n, VIII: 40n, 78; (*1865*) 217-18, 292-93, 308, 319-20, 365-66

Recruitment in, IV: 475-76,

495, 550n, V: 347, 411n, 515-16, VI: 59; Confederate operations in, IV: 485n; authorization for suspension of writ of habeas corpus, V: 35; support of Schofield command, 61-62, 203; Halleck's criticism of Lane, 80n; military operations, (*Jan. '62*) V: 95n, (*spring-summer '62*) 292, 347n, 501-502, (*fall '64*) VIII: 57n, 220; and emancipation, V: 152-53, 160, VI: 53n, 54n, 289, 291, 344n, 358, 428-29, 499n, VII: 49, 91; treaty with Indians, V: 189; election (1862), 496-97; protests against trade restrictions, 540; mention of Mo. R.R., VI: 236-37; repercussions from the Lawrence massacre, 415n, 423-24; election (1863), 556-58, VII: 8, 10; election (1864), 101n, 377n, VIII: 24-25, 46, 128-29, 150, 153; Methodist churches exempted from Stanton's order, VII: 182-83; expediency of completing railroad from Rolla to Springfield, 224, 237-38; reorganization of state government, VIII: 148, 365-66; court martial case, 176; state penitentiary deemed a military prison, 300; mentioned also, I: 62n, V: 500-501; *see also* St. Louis (Mo.)

Missouri, Bank of, *see* Bank of Missouri

Missouri, Department of the, V: 22n, 35; VI: 8n, 20n, 131n, 210n, 218n, 234, 253-54, 500-502; VII: 78-79, 85n, 158n, 179n, 284; VIII: 102n, 166n, 293n

Missouri Compromise, *see* Kansas Nebraska Act and repeal of the Missouri Compromise

Missouri Democrat [St. Louis], II: 410, 537; IV: 50, 153n, 154; V: 544n; VI: 178, 325-27, 344-45; VIII: 187-88

Missouri Railroad, VI: 236
Missouri Republican [St. Louis],
II: 58-59, 376n, 527n; III: 133,
186, 335-36; IV: 104n, 140n;
VIII: 159n, 223n, 351n, 365n
Missouri River, VI: 9-11, 68, 134n,
246n, 526n; VII: 16
Missouri State Guard (C.S.A.), IV:
538n; VI: 6n
Missouri State Militia (U. S. A.),
V: 15-17, 61n, 203n; VI: 9, 10-
11, 21, 23, 31n, 492-93, 500-501,
503; VIII: 366n
Missroon, John Stoney, VI: 107n
Mitchel, John, II: 116
Mitchel, Ormsby McKnight, IV:
545; V: 89
Mitchell, Benjamin, I: 58, 76, 129
Mitchell, Charles B., VII: 335n
Mitchell, Charles F., IV: 54-55
Mitchell, Edward, I: 19, 332; II:
71
Mitchell, George Anson, IV: 472
Mitchell, James (Ill.), II: 182; V:
177
Mitchell, James (Ind.), IV: 547;
V: 370-71
Mitchell, James (N. Y.), VI: 112n
Mitchell, John W., VIII: 86
Mitchell, Robert, IV: 526
Mitchell, Robert B., VI: 148-49,
167-68
Mitchell, Stewart, VIII: 321n
Mitchell, T. E., VIII: 112n
Mitchell, William, IV: 520-21,
539; VI: 272n; VIII: 46
Mitchell's Station (Va.), VI: 450n,
506
Mitre, Bartolomé, VI: 94-95
Mittman, ——, V: 476n
Mix, Charles E., IV: 391; V: 104,
147, 346; VI: 164; VII: 299
Mob Jack Bay (Va.), V: 123n
Mobile (Ala.), V: 38n, 250, 260n,
265n, 268, 284n; VI: 102, 374;
VII: 464n, 522n, 532-33; VIII: 4,
93-94, 396, 409, 421
Mobile & Ohio Railroad, V: 540n
Mobilization of troops, see Troops,
mobilization and recruitment
Mobley, Mordecai, II: 63, 74; IV:
70
Mobley, Mrs. Mordecai, IV: 70
Modoc Indians, VIII: 322
Moelich, Frederick, VI: 438
Moffett, George, II: 425n
Moffett, James W., III: 378n
Moffett, John B., II: 332n
Moffett, Thomas, I: 44n, 254, 286,
323; II: 188, 310; III: 378n, 399
Moffett, Thomas, & Son (Spring-
field), III: 378
Mohammed Saïd Pacha, Viceroy
of Egypt, IV: 552; V: 229n; VI:
105n; VIII: 139
Mohan, Francis, VII: 318
Molina, Cirilo, VI: 258
Molina, Luis, IV: 286; VI: 258;
VII: 72-73
Molony, Richard Sheppard, III:
124-25, 139
Monaghan, Jay, see Lincoln
Bibliography 1839-1939
Monday, see Mundy, Marcellus
Monitor (ironclad), V: 154, 177n,
209-10, 547; VI: 561-62
Monmouth (Ill.), I: 32; III: 244-
45
Monmouth Review, III: 245n
Monocacy River, IV: 455n; V:
412n, 418n; VII: 434-35, 437,
547
Monongahela House (Pitts-
burgh), IV: 208-10
Monongalia County (W. Va.), V:
298; VI: 130
Monroe, ——, IV: 374
Monroe, Byrd, I: 179, 195; VII:
174n
Monroe, Calvin, VIII: 68
Monroe, George, VII: 174
Monroe, James, III: 162, 195,
523n; IV: 23; VIII: 206n
Monroe County (Tenn.), VIII: 68
Monrovia (Liberia), IV: 310
Monrovia (Md.), VII: 434n
Montague, ——, VIII: 157
Montague, Charles P., IV: 304

Montana Territory, VII: 216n, 280n, 355-57, 371-72, 402-403, 428n; VIII: 145

Montano, Stephen G., VI: 92; VII: 88n

"Monteray passes," V: 269n

Monterey (Calif.), IV: 304

Monterrey (Mexico), II: 85-87; V: 552n; VII: 139n

Montevideo (Uruguay), IV: 310

Montgomery, Alexander, VI: 385

Montgomery, James, VI: 158n

Montgomery, John Berrien, VIII: 87n

Montgomery, William (Ill.), I: 70

Montgomery, William (Pa.), III: 368; *see also* Crittenden-Montgomery bill

Montgomery (Ala.), IV: 427; V: 122n, 241; VIII: 336

Montgomery (ship), V: 358n

Montgomery County (Ill.), I: 72, 140-41

Montgomery County (Md.), VI: 148n

Montgomery County (Tenn.), VIII: 69

Month at Goodspeed's, The, VII: 452n

Monticello (Ill.), II: 527

Montpensier, Duchesse de, V: 392; VI: 136

Montpensier, Philippe Raymond Marie, V: 392

Montreal (Canada), VII: 370-72, 375n

Montufar, Lorenzo, V: 198

Monument Square (Baltimore), VIII: 42n

Moody, Granville, VII: 351n

Moody, Seymour B., V: 381

Mooney, ———, VI: 335n

Mooney, Thomas J., IV: 389n

Moore, Absalom B., V: 546n

Moore, Andrew, VII: 274

Moore, Charles C., VII: 9n, 26-27, 197n

Moore, Charles L., IV: 182

Moore, Clifton H., II: 336, 389

Moore, Daniel T., I: 197n

Moore, David, VIII: 299n

Moore, Ebenezer, VII: 371

Moore, Ezekiel C., VII: 523n

Moore, Frank, VII: 249n

Moore, Henry DeWitt, IV: 167

Moore, Henry H., VI: 297n

Moore, Henry Miles, VII: 371

Moore, Henry T., V: 162n

Moore, Henry T. (Mo.), V: 411n

Moore, James B., I: 14

Moore, James J., VII: 274

Moore, James Miles, IV: 167; VII: 534n

Moore, John, I: 179, 347n; II: 75, 287, 476-81; V: 61n

Moore, John D., VIII: 69

Moore, Lazarus Loury, VII: 495n

Moore, Leighton G., I: 420n

Moore, Nicholas, I: 148n

Moore, Thomas P., I: 317

Moore, Tredwell, VI: 249

Moore, William H., VII: 129

Moorefield (Va.), V: 243, 246-47, 250-51, 254

Moorhead, James Kennedy, IV: 166; V: 81n; VI: 286, 325n, 512; VIII: 49, 213n

Moorhead, Matthew, I: facing page 48

Morais, Sabato, V: 212n

Moran, William, IV: 509

More, Alfred, VIII: 32n

More, E. J., VII: 369n

Morean, Alexander B., II: 227-28

Morehead, Charles Slaughter, IV: 534n, 549; V: 81

Morel, Pierre Louis, VI: 268

Morely, *see* Manly, Hiram P.

Morey, George, IV: 59

Morey, Joseph S., IV: 167

Morey, Mrs. Townsend, IV: 160n

Morgan, Charles H., VII: 371

Morgan, Edwin Denison: and the 1860 election, IV: 94, 102n, 116-17; L. speaks in Albany, N. Y. (Feb. '61) at his invitation, 185, 224-25; mobilization and re-

cruitment, 368n, 375-76, 382, 384, 406, 416, V: 294n, 302, 304, 349-50, 361, 431n, 483n, VI: 211n; recommends a sermon to L., IV: 445-46; suggests Wool be sent to Fort Monroe to train troops, 478n; and appointments, V: 28n, 81, 216n, 362, 379n, 408, VI: 163n, 224, 508n, 511n, VII: 85n, 269n, 402-403, 412-14; and Congressional censure of Cameron, V: 241-42; and Weed's complaints of abolitionist opposition to, VI: 84n; courts-martial, dismissals, and pardons, 256-57, VII: 410n, 526-27; his support of L.'s policies (1863), VII: 23-24; recommends invention to remove under-water obstructions, 118n; relays a present to L., 133; summoned by L. to Washington conference (Aug '64), 474; and a cotton permit, VIII: 200n
Morgan, Elijah, VIII: 160
Morgan, George Denison, V: 241; VI: 511n
Morgan, George Washington, V: 264, 452-53, 483-84
Morgan, H. T., II: 296n, 375n, 387n; III: 343n
Morgan, John Hunt, V: 321n, 384n, 402n; VI: 346-47, 394n, 502, 532n; VII: 34n, 136n, 296, 391n, 520n; VIII: 123n
Morgan, John Pierpont, VIII: 287n
Morgan, Lewis Henry, VII: 378n, 385n
Morgan, N. D., VI: 511n
Morgan, Obadiah, I: 11
Morgan, Richard P., II: 330; VI: 519-20
Morgan, Thomas, V: 57n
Morgan, Thomas P., VII: 318
Morgan, William E., VI: 433
Morgan, William G., VI: 511n
Morgan County (Ala.), VIII: 112n

Morgan County (Ill.), I: 322, 323n, 330n, 354, 357-58; II: 449n
Morgan County (Tenn.), VIII: 68
Morgan Journal [Jacksonville, Ill.], I: 360, 364-66, 492n; II: 449n; see also *Jacksonville Journal*
Morgan Rifles (N. Y.?), IV: 374n
Morgantown (W. Va.), VI: 189n
Morgenthau, J. C., & Company, Inc., VIII: 106n
Morison, John B., VII: 247n
Morley, H. P., see Manly, Hiram P.
Morley, William D., Inc., catalogs cited, IV: 385n; V: 65n, 90n, 514n, 516n; VII: 137n, 323n; VIII: 100n
Mormons, I: 207n, 291; II: 399; IV: 41-43
Morning Light (ship), V: 162
Morocco, V: 521; VII: 40
Morrell, see Morrill, Lot Myrick
Morrill, Ashley C., VII: 116-17
Morrill, Justin Smith, IV: 43n; VIII: 255n
Morrill, Lot Myrick, IV: 248; V: 104n, 458n; VI: 105n, 321n, 547
Morrill, Milton M., III: 332
Morris, Achilles, I: 129, 131, 182, 298
Morris, Buckner Smith, I: 405-406; II: 82-83; IV: 92
Morris, Edward Joy, IV: 358-59, 397n; V: 176
Morris, George A., IV: 537n
Morris, George Upham, V: 549-50
Morris, Gouverneur, III: 531-32, 545n
Morris, Henry W., V: 215
Morris, Hiram, VIII: 69
Morris, Isaac Newton, II: 182, 184-86; IV: 86n, 161, 281; VI: 96-97, 404, 411-12, 463
Morris, James Remley, VI: 300-306
Morris, Josiah W., VII: 353-54

Morris, Martin Sims, I: 319-21, 321-22, 355
Morris, Robert, III: 527, 537n
Morris, Samuel, I: 43
Morris, Thomas Armstrong, IV: 539
Morris, Thomas E., VII: 353
Morris, William M., III: 356n, 374
Morris, William Walton, VI: 135
Morris (Ill.), III: 396
Morris Book Shop (Chicago), VIII: 118n
Morris Island (S. C.), VI: 170, 173, 256n
Morrison, D. A., II: 389
Morrison, Ephraim, V: 333n, 336n
Morrison, James ("Don"), I: 515; II: 29, 41-42, 50, 58, 67, 75, 296, 305, 342-43; III: 385; VII: 60
Morrison, Pitcairn, V: 392n
Morrison, William Ralls, II: 297; V: 342, 486-87; VII: 167, 189, 260, 315
Morristown (Tenn.), V: 60n; VI: 481; VIII: 111n
Morrow, Aquilla I., VI: 544
Morrow, M. W., VII: 326n
Morrow, Robert, VI: 373-74
Morrow, William, VI: 544
Morse, Adolphus, VII: 31
Morse, Charles E., see Moss, Charles E.
Morse, Charles F., V: 400
Morse, Daniel, III: 372
Morse, Freeman Harlow, IV: 284
Morss, James, IV: 474
"Mortality" (poem), I: 367n, 378n; II: 90
Morton, Joseph, II: 296
Morton, Mary E., VIII: 228-29
Morton, Oliver P.: welcomes L. to Ind. (Feb. '61), IV: 193-94; mobilization and recruitment, 402n, 410, 415n, 416n, 454n, 485, VII: 308, 312n, 355-56, VIII: 33; and appointments, IV: 404-405, 514-15, V: 14, 17, 64, 66, 126, 275-76, 291, 407, 428, 492n, VI: 177n, VII: 144n, 350, VIII: 72n, 339; and military operations in the West, (Sept. '61) IV: 533-34, 537-38, 541-42, (spring '62) V: 231; L. rejects suggestion to make him military governor of Ky., V: 367; and trouble (1863) with Ind. "peace Democrats," VI: 87-88; and the Vallandigham case, 237n; courts-martial and pardons, 337, VII: 122, VIII: 136n; county election returns in Ind. (1863), VI: 515; and the 1864 election, VII: 518n, VIII: 11n, 46-47, 109; and exchange of prisoners-of-war, VIII: 224n; presented with a captured Confederate flag, 360
Morton, Rosalie S., see A Woman Surgeon
Morton, Stratford Lee, I: 422n
Morton's Ford (Va.), VI: 468n
Mosby, John Singleton, VI: 129n
Moschcowitz, Eli, VI: 351n
Moscow (Russia), IV: 312n
Moseley, Jourdan, VII: 541n
Moseley, Robert, II: 483
Moses, L. on the language of, III: 360
Moses, Isaac, IV: 514
Moses, John, II: 430; III: 332
Mosher, Mrs. Harris P., V: 157n
Mosquera, Tomás C. de, VI: 56
Moss, A. W., VIII: 69
Moss, Charles E., IV: 445
Moss, James H., VI: 489
Moss, Lemuel, V: 67n
Motley, John Lothrop, V: 221n
Motley, Mary, V: 220-21
Mott, Gershom, VI: 334n; VII: 491-92
Mott, Gordon Newell, IV: 295, 302n; VI: 188, 395n
Mott, M., II: 182
Moulton, Samuel Wheeler, II: 297, 359; VI: 198, 359-60

Mounce, John, I: 12
Mound City (Ill.), IV: 545; VII: 229-30
Mount Auburn (Ill.), I: 183
Mount Jackson (Va.), V: 258n, 268-69, 271, 273-74
Mount Pleasant General Hospital (Washington), VII: 526
Mount Pulaski (Ill.), I: 130-31, 206
Mount Sterling (Ill.), I: 34
Mount Vernon (Ill.), I: 146
Mount Vernon (Va.), VII: 225
Mount Vernon Hotel (Washington), VIII: 4n
Mountain Department, V: 155, 176n, 273, 287
Mozambique, V: 141n
Mozart, Mrs. J. M., III: 350
Mudd, Charity, VII: 136n
Muddy River (Ill.), I: 147
Mudge, Benjamin W., IV: 305
Mudge, Solomon H., III: 393n
"Mud-sill" theory, III: 478-80
Mueller, Adolph F. C., II: 388n
Mulattoes, I: 110; II: 407-409; III: 80, 84, 88-89, 504
Muldraugh's Hill (Ky.), IV: 537-38, 541-42, 544
Mulfinger, C. L., V: 172n, 202n
Mulford, John Elmer, VII: 7, 325; VIII: 311n
Mullany, James, II: 182
Mullenax, William, VIII: 68
Muller, James N., IV: 363, 390; V: 159
Mullica Hill (N. J.), VII: 523n
Mulligan, James Adelbert, IV: 538n; V: 25, 58; VII: 484
Mulligan, Mrs. James Adelbert, VII: 484n
Mullins, Michael, VII: 203
Mumma, David, Jr., IV: 167
Mundy, Marcellus, VII: 229-30
Munfordville (Ky.), V: 111; VI: 424
Munroe, Thomas B., IV: 556n
Munroe, Timothy, IV: 346
Munsee Indians, VII: 215

Munsell, Leander, I: 233, 249
Munsey's Magazine, IV: 361n
Murdoch, Alexander, IV: 329
Murdock, Charles A., V: 500n
Murfreesboro (Tenn.), VI: 39, 43n, 48, 53, 86, 138, 203n, 324, 409, VII: 249n; see also Stone's River, battle of
Murillo Toro, Manuel, VI: 56; VIII: 7
Murphy, Edmund, VII: 420
Murphy, Isaac, VII: 155n, 173-74, 205, 209n, 239n, 240, 250-51, 253, 318, 418n, 519n
Murphy, Jesse, I: 141-42
Murphy, John, VI: 506, 510, 516; VIII: 249
Murphy, Patrick, VI: 361; VII: 298-99
Murphy, Richard G., I: 124, 179, 224-25, 242-43
Murphy, William C., I: 211
Murray, Bronson, V: 339-40
Murray, F. G., VI: 163
Murray, F. M., IV: 558
Murray, Mrs. H. L., II: 25n, 77n
Murray, John, II: 24-25, 77
Murray, M., see Mundy, Marcellus
Murray, Thomas J., VIII: 120-21
Murray, Thomas K., VI: 443
Murtaugh, William J., IV: 328n; V: 205
Musick, Samuel, I: 21, 28-30, 39, 53, 85, 158-59
Musick's Bridge, I: 39, 53, 85-86
Musick's Ferry, I: 21, 24, and following page 48
Mustin, Thomas, IV: 298
Muza Kiyemani [alias Wakan Inapedan] (Indian), VII: 325-26
Muzzey, Loring William, VI: 259
Muzzy, Leonard F., VIII: 72
"My Childhood-Home I See Again" (poem), I: 367-70, 378-79, 384-86
Myer, William H., I: 255, 257, 371-72, 375-76

Myers, Amos, VII: 110n
Myers, Catharine, VII: 491n
Myers, Clemens J., VII: 473
Myers, Henry, V: 549n
Myers, John, VIII: 69
Myers, John C., IV: 167, 337

Myers, Jonathan, II: 396n
Myers, Leonard, VIII: 215-16, 311-12
Myers, Samuel B., VI: 203n
Myers, William, VII: 237n
Mygatt, George S., IV: 511n

N

Nabb, James, I: 86
Nagasaki (Japan), V: 158n
Naglee, Henry Morris, VI: 371n, 482-83
Naglee, James, VI: 362n
Nahant (ironclad), VI: 84n
Nance, Catharine, II: 133
Nance, John C., I: 18
Nance, Joshua, I: 121
Nance, Thomas Jefferson, I: 38, 121, 154n; II: 133n
Nance, Mrs. Thomas Jefferson, *see* Nance, Catharine
Nanking (China), VIII: 139n
Na-pay-shue (Indian), V: 543
Naper, Joseph, I: 76, 197n; III: 126
Naperville (Ill.), III: 126
Naples (Ill.), III: 328-30; IV: 85
Naples (Italy), IV: 446n
Napoleon I, Emperor of the French, II: 123, 281; III: 391n; IV: 23; VI: 79
Napoleon III, Emperor of the French, III: 541; V. 130n; VI: 105n, 355n; VII: 36, 331, 550-51
Nash, Michael, VII: 173n
Nashville (Ill.), I: 147
Nashville (Tenn.), IV: 61, 544; V: 87, 91, 122n, 135, 200, 305n, 313-14, 409, 410n, 417n, 457n, 484n
VI: 48, 135n, 167-68, 186, 393, 494n, 505

VII: 11n, 80n, 108n, 150, 184, 209, 234n, 242n, 248, 308n, 328n, 330, 478n, 496n, 509
VIII: 20, 27n, 28, 38, 58n, 60n, 61n, 65-67, 71-72, 74, 75, 120n, 169, 175, 188, 211, 237, 241, 259, 264, 342, 372
Nashville & Chattanooga Railroad, VII: 478n
Nashville Press, VII: 209
Nashville Railroad, V: 31n
Nashville Times, VIII: 60n
Nast, William, VIII: 83
Natchez (Miss.), I: 450-51; VIII: 196, 396
National Archives (Washington), I: xiv; IV: 414n, 421n, 447n, 454n; V: 147n, 342n; VI: 30n
"National Democrats" ["Buchaniers"], III: 122, 221, 226-27, 332, 373
National Hotel (Washington), IV: 217; VI: 41
National Intelligencer [Washington], II: 24n, 154-56; cited, IV: 286n, 300n, 353n, 356n, 393n; V: 213n, 341n, 419n, 430n, 439n, 441n; VI: 227n, 430n, 487n, 530n, 536n; VII: 200n, 474n; VIII: 393n
National Magazine, II: 6n
National Republican [Washington]: as official publication for

Executive Department notices and advertisements, IV: 328, VI: 188-89, 221, 313; Hanscom editor of, IV: 408n, VI: 120n; cited in footnotes on the following pages: IV: 275, 352, 383, 442, VI: 487, 532, 536, VII: 334, 537, VIII: 4, 7, 58, 84, 114, 394

"National Union March," V: 125

Nativists, see Know-Nothing Party

Naturalization, I: 337-38, 452; II: 136, 142-43; III: 376-77, 380; IV: 133; VII: 38-39

Nauman, Ethel M., VII: 166n

Naumkeag River, IV: 123n

Nautical Magazine and Naval Journal (Griffiths), IV: 311n

Navajo Indian Agency, IV: 307

Naval Academy, Annapolis: president's power to make cadet appointments, V: 66, VI: 385-86; dismissal of instructor on disloyalty charges, V: 335-36; report in annual message (1863), VII: 45; cadet appointments, IV: 381, 392n, 526, V: 59, 66, 387-88, VI: 252, 299, 376, 385-86, 403, 511, VII: 194, 315, 513, VIII: 215

Naval History of the Civil War (Porter), IV: 314n

Naval Records, cited, IV: 313n, 314n, 315n, 361n, 367n, 478n; VI: 166n; VII: 258n, 310n; VIII: 103n

Navy, U. S.: importance of internal improvements to, I: 483; call for volunteer enlistments (1861), IV: 354, 429; procurement of boats and ships, 357, 370, 397, 412, V: 33-34, 82, 108, 112, 156, 162, 174, 191, 331-32, 489, 498; Fox appointed Assistant Secretary of, IV: 363; on determination of rank, 470, 548; and the Chiriqui project, 561, V: 414n; and proposed reorgan-

ization in, V: 41, 112-13; navy force in Gulf of Mexico alerted (Feb. 22, '62), 111-12; in McClellan's plan of campaign (Feb. '62), 123n; President's General War Order No. 3 (Mar. '62), 151; list of commanding officers in Apr. '62 action around New Orleans, 215; *Monitor-Merrimac* action, 547, 550; removal of Va. refugees, VI: 36

On retirement pay, VI: 116-17; proposals for harbor defenses, 163, VII: 468; attack (1863) on Fort Sumter, VI: 165-67, 170, 173-74, 256n, VII: 81; new inventions, VI: 209, 272, VII: 118; use of revenue cutters, VI: 272-73; conduct of U. S. personnel in foreign ports in respect to neutral ships and prize courts, 342-43, 348-50, 378-80, VII: 40-41; L. pays tribute to (1863), VI: 409-10, VIII: 394n; reports in annual messages, (*1863*) VII: 43-45, (*1864*) VIII: 144-45; shipyard strikes, VII: 84; and the draft, 245, 519-20, 534, VIII: 48, 86-87; and recruitment (1864), VIII: 14n; prisoner-of-war exchange, 36-37; and 1864 sailor vote, 43n; availability of court-martial files to individuals, 190-91; *see also* Welles, Gideon

Appointments: IV: 296-97, 311, 334, 337, 340, 356-57, 363, 371, 373-74, 411, 444, 447, 507, V: 127-28, 134, 166-67, 214, 395, 447, 480, VII: 267, 491, VIII: 86-87; duty assignments, IV: 314-15, 318-19, 335, 366-67; retirements, resignations, and courts-martial, 343, 361, 484n, V: 59, 101, 198-99, VI: 102-103, 116-17, VII: 342-43, 409-10, VIII: 111, 182; promotions and commendations, IV: 548, V: 127-28, 134, 166-67, 214-15, 299,

315-16, 352, 389, 547, 549-50, VI: 1, 52, 82, 91, 102, VII: 56-57, 199-200, 360, VIII: 133-35, 345

Navy in the Civil War, The (Ammen), VI: 174n

Navy Register, IV: 340

Nay, Robert B., VI: 55n, 103, 151

Nazareth (Ky.) Academy, VIII: 219

Neagle, V. C. K., VII: 199

Neale, Harriet (Blakemore), II: 71

Neale, John M., I: 252-53

Neale, Thomas M., I: facsimiles facing pp. 48 and 49, 53, 93, 298; II: 70-71

Neale, Mrs. Thomas M., *see* Neale, Harriet

Neally, Edward B., VII: 355n, 371-72

Neave, Joseph J., VIII: 72-73, 76n

Neblett, William R., VIII: 191n

Nebraska Territory, II: 231, 236, 241; III: 4, 14-15, 59, 91, 94-95, 137, 151, 288, 294, 447; IV: 295, 298n, 306-307, 322, 336-37, 345, 347, 366, 452n, 548; VII: 100n, 264n; VIII: 349n, 410

Ne-con-he-con (Indian), IV: 401

Needles, John O., VIII: 215n

Neff, Henry K., V: 400

Negley, Henry Morris, *see* Naglee, Henry Morris

Negley, James Scott, VI: 483n; VII: 14n

Negro troops: recruitment, organization, and officering, V: 330, 337n, 338, 506n, VI: 41, 59, 154-55, 212, 239, 242-43, 292, 298-300, 317, 342, 374, 396n, 439n, 440, 462-63, 493-95, 499n, 529-30, 532, VII: 11, 42, 137-38, 170-71, 190-92, 204, 212, 253n, 272, 284, 295, 317n, 363n, 388n, 390, 449-50, 452n, 482n, 506, VIII: 24n, 120n, 151, 266, 268, 273n, 357n; expediency and justification for their use, V: 356-57, 423, VI: 56, 342, 374,

VII: 49-50, 281-83, 302-303, VIII: 2, 360-62; protests against their use, V: 431, VI: 90n, 188, 482-83, 491n, 494, VII: 431n, 446-47, 480, VIII: 120, 151

Effect on enemy, VI: 149-50, 158, 408-409, 423; and the construction of privately owned railroads, 246; murder of officer of a colored company, 362, 437-38, 443; pay and clothing, 362-63, VII: 198, 280, 404-406, 432, 440, 482; Negro chaplains, VI: 401, VII: 280, 332; status as slaveholder property, VI: 408-409, VII: 432-33, 482; Fort Pillow massacre, VII: 302-303, 328-29, 345-46; on Confederate use of, VIII: 360-62

Negroes: social and political equality, I: 48, 210; II: 256, 266, 391, 403-409, 449-50, 453, 464, 498, 515, 519, 526-27, 539, 541; III: 9-11, 16, 20, 31, 37-38, 79-81, 83-84, 88-89, 96, 113-14, 126-27, 145-46, 158, 178-79, 213-14, 220-22, 237-38, 248-49, 280-81, 299-301, 326-28, 398-403, 504; IV: 9, 32, 156; V: 370-72; VII: 101-102, 243, 411-12

Effects of mob law in Miss. and St. Louis, I: 109-10; education of children, II: 21, V: 259n, VI: 365, VII: 55; the "humanity" of the Negro, II: 239, 245-46, 264-66, 281-82, 321, 323, 453, 520, III: 95-96, 181, 220, 296-97, 304, 327, 423-25, 430-32, 444-45, 469-70, 486, IV: 4-5, 9-10, 16-20, V: 158, VI: 407; references to Negroes and crocodiles, III: 445-46, 470, 483-84, 486, 500, IV: 4, 5, 10, 18-20

Population concentration, (*1854*) II: 265, (*1862*) V: 535; L.'s flatboat attacked by (1828), IV: 62; difficulties in the religious ministering of, V: 445-46, VI: 401, VII: 280, 332, 374n;

cases of white persons charged with immoral conduct, VI: 73n, 208n, VIII: 193n; French use of Negro troops in Mexico, VI: 105n; L.'s check to "colored man with one leg," 380; "wish [him] to be appointed ... regardless of whether he can tell the exact shade of Julius Caesar's hair," VII: 11; on sale of Negroes captured in Cuba, 370n, 400n; reply to a letter on white supremacy, 483; *see also* Colonization of Negroes; Mulattoes; Negro troops; Slavery; Capital and labor; *and* Emancipation

Negus, ———, II: 180

Neill, Edward Duffield, VII: 252n, 514n, 529n, 539n; VIII: 5n, 136n, 273, 299n, 302, 306n

Neiswender, Philip D., II: 455n

Nellis, ———, V: 201

Nelson, David, V: 484

Nelson, David P., I: 4

Nelson, Samuel, II: 466; III: 251, 543n; V: 481

Nelson, Thomas, VI: 77n

Nelson, Thomas Amos Rogers, IV: 313; V: 484n; VII: 194; VIII: 27n, 58-72, 226n

Nelson, Thomas H., IV: 397; VII: 143n, 339n

Nelson, William (Ky.), IV: 398; V: 71n, 80, 225n, 320, 401-402

Nelson, William (N. Y.), I: 497; II: 53n

Nemaha Indian Agency, IV: 306; VIII: 338n

Neosho (Mo.), VII: 218n

Nesbitt, George F., & Company (N. Y.), III: 522n

Nesbitt, James, I: 305-306

Nesmith, ———, VII: 235

Nesmith, James Willis, V: 103, 163, 426n; VI: 181-82; VII: 413n

Nesqually (Wash. Terr.), IV: 308

Netherland, John, VIII: 317

Netherlands, IV: 287; V: 181n, 521; VIII: 45n

Nevada, VIII: 46, 83-84, 129-30, 145, 146, 150, 153

Nevada Territory, IV: 293, 295, 298, 471n; V: 47, 171, 316n, 391n; VI: 188, 255, 395n; VII: 40, 322-23

Nevah (Indian), VI: 153n

Nevins, Allan, see *Frémont, Pathmarker of the West*

Nevins, William R., VI: 174n

Nevins, Townsend & Company (N. Y.), I: 187

New Albany (Ind.), IV: 541, 545

New Almaden quicksilver mine (Calif.), VI: 205-206, 322n, 333-34, 393-94, 422

New Baltimore (Va.), V: 493n

New Bedford (Mass.), VII: 77n

New Berlin (Ill.), I: 182, 399-402, 404-405

New Bern (N. C.), V: 288n, 316, 377; VI: 72, 127n, 150, 255n; VII: 532; VIII: 396

New Boston (Mass.), II: 157n

New Bridge (Va.), V: 226n

New Brunswick (Canada), II: 146n

New Brunswick (N. J.), IV: 235

New Brunswick Fredonian, IV: 235n

New Colophon, The, V: 433n; VI: 30n

New England, IV: 515, 518-19, 557n; VIII: 46; *see also names of individual states*

New England Kitchen (Brooklyn and Long Island Sanitary Fair), VII: 220

New England Society in the City of New York, VIII: 170

New Granada, *see* Colombia

New Hampshire, III: 390-91; V: 360; VI: 113n, 352, 355, 368n; VIII: 100n, 128-29, 150, 153, 271-72

New Hampshire in the Great Rebellion (Waite), VI: 355n

New Haven (Conn.), IV: 5, 13-30;
V: 352
New Haven Palladium, IV: 13n,
21n, 30n
New Ironsides (ship), VI: 166n
New Jersey, I: 317n, 500; IV: 186,
233-38, 355, 458-59, 500n; V:
188n, 376; VI: 311-12, 337-38,
347-48, 354-55; VII: 24n, 195n,
VIII: 46, 98, 128-30, 150, 153,
329
New Jersey, College of (now
Princeton University), VIII:
183-84
New Kent Court House (Va.), V:
226n, 294n, 296
New Letters and Papers of Lincoln
(Angle), cited in footnotes on
the ff. pages: I: 392; II: 100, 188,
212; IV: 1, 35, 49, 335, 385, 409;
V: 136; VII: 128, 149, 202, 274,
506, 531, 549; VIII: 353
New Lisbon (Ohio), II: 161n
New London (Conn.), VI: 232n
New Madrid (Mo.), V: 169n
New Market (Va.), V: 258n, 412n
New Mexico, Department of, VII:
159n
New Mexico Territory, II: 3, 232,
237-38, 243, 252-54, 259-60, 279-
81; III: 137, 224-25, 261, 271-72,
288; IV: 183, 307, 312, 349, 449,
471; V: 46, 56n, 93-94, 103,
107n, 177-78, 283, 354n; VI:
123-24, 142; VII: 40, 157-58,
480n, 483-84, 490; VIII: 17n,
157, 168n, 243n, 369-70, 594
New Orleans (La.): L. takes flatboat of produce to (1831), I:
4n, IV: 62-64; mention of Jackson's victory (War of 1812) at,
I: 226, VI: 262, 268; mention of
newspaper correspondent's trip
to (1861), IV: 484n; proposed
Butler expedition to, 519n; and
McClellan's plan of campaign
(Feb. '62), V: 122n; and the
blockade, 162n, 210-11, VIII:
396-97; and military operations

(spring '62), V: 214, 293, 316;
appointment of port surveyor
of, 323; unsettled affairs in,
(*1862*) V: 343n, 389n, 468, VI:
262, (*1864*) VIII: 107-108, 162n;
and peace overtures by a plantation owner (July '62), V: 350-
51; cancellation of Cassius
Clay's assignment to, 425, 428-
29; plans to open Mississippi R.
navigation to, 469n, 501-502,
VI: 73, 100n; mention of mayor
of (1864), V: 540; L. suggests
Bullitt as port collector, VI:
16; complaints against military
seizure of property, VI: 16n,
VII: 186-87, 247-48, 296n
Banks assumes command at,
VI: 22n, VIII: 121, 131n, 366n,
386n; and Emancipation Proclamation, VI: 29; reassignment of Butler to command at,
73, 76-77, 100n, VIII: 195; trade
regulations, VI: 160, VII: 488-
89, VIII: 20, 103-104, 178,
196-97; ironclads sent to, VI:
174n; attack on vessel bound
from, 254n; order of clearance
for vessels bound for, 405;
Hamilton awaits Union control
of Texas at, 466n; L.'s letter of
introduction of Illinoisan in-
tending to establish himself in
business in, VII: 150-51; organization of Negro troops, 170-71;
included in Sickles tour of observation (1864), 185, 250; victory salute of guns (Sept. '64),
532; appointment of commission to investigate conditions in
(Dec. '64), VIII: 161-62; L. rejects Todd's request for a military appointment in, 181;
commissioning of port collector
(Apr. 13, '65), 410n; mentioned
also, I: 22n, V: 487, VI: 55n,
172-73, 288n, VIII: 15, 317
See also Louisiana; *and* Gulf,
Department of the

New Orleans Picayune, V: 489
New Orleans Times, VI: 364n;
VIII: 108n
New Orleans True Delta, V: 489
New Salem (Ill.), I: 4, 5n, 6, 13-14,
15-17, 20, 21-22, 23-26, 36n, 47-
48, 87, 93n, 96n, 151n, III: 5,
512; IV: 64-65, 104, 310n, 322n;
VI: 383n
New York (city): bank suspension
of specie payments (1837), I:193;
operating cost of boat transportation to Troy (1848), 428;
Douglas visits (1858), II: 507,
512; L.'s Cooper Institute address, III: 494n, 522-50 (text of
address), IV: 113n, 118-19; L.
disavows Wall Street pressure
for slavery compromise, IV:
163-64; *Courier and Enquirer*
editor seeks L.'s views on secession, 164-65; L.'s speeches en
route to his inaugural, 229-33;
appointments, 296n, 300, 307,
325, 373-74, 474, V: 93, 265n,
339n, 367n, 405, VI: 123, 430,
VII: 92n, 181, 195n, 333n, 412-
14, 543n, VIII: 232; mobilization and recruitment, *see* New
York (state); and relief for
N. C. loyalists, V: 25-26; German citizens protest reported
treatment of Sigel, 106; mention
of seizure of Spanish vessel en
route to, 109-10; L. invited to attend a mass loyalist meeting
(July '62), 325; clergymen urge
better army observance of the
Sabbath, 497-98
    Citizens committee urges
armed free labor colonization in
Fla., VI: 108n; mention of public meetings of Christian
Commission, 115n; British
workingmen's appeal to N. Y.
Relief Committee, 121-22;
Chase visits to negotiate a loan
(Apr. '63), 180n; support for
Frémont command of colored

troops, 239, 243n; Burnside suspension of N. Y. *World*, 248n;
L. summons son Robert from
(July '63), 323, 327; letters addressed to Mrs. L. at, 353, 469,
471-72, 474, 478, VII: 34-35,
320, 401, 417, 547; committee of
merchants request conference
with L., VII: 4; Dix declines
mayoralty nomination (1863),
VII: 5
    Copy of Gettysburg address
sold at Sanitary Fair, VII: 21n,
168n; Freedmen's Aid Society
urges establishment of a Bureau
of Emancipation, 76-77; publication of captured letters sup-
pressed, 87-88; and the cotton
trade, 114n, 126n; Crittenden
given permission to visit, 127;
proposed investigation of operation of Customs House, 181, 195;
Schurz makes political visit to
(Mar. '64), 244n; Nicolay's report of Astor House meeting
with Weed (Mar. '64), 268-69;
telegram from L. addressed to
Seward at Astor House (Apr.
'64), 294
    Newspaper publication of a
bogus Presidential draft proclamation (May '64), VII: 347-
50; disposition of a claim for
cost of transportation of a naval
brigade from, 363; the case of a
Spanish officer returned to Cuba
for trial, 370n; L.'s reply to invitation to mass meeting honoring Grant (June '64), 374; L.
commends holding of Sanitary
Fairs, 394; L. transmits report
on maltreatment of persons on
ships bound for New Granada,
415; Hay visits on mission for
L. (July '64), 442-43; firing of
victory salute ordered (Sept.
'64), 532; L. receives delegation from Young Men's
Republican Union, VIII: 19n;

request for passes to, 24, 160; Cherokee agent instructed to purchase clothing in, 34n; suspension of clearance for Japanese gunboat built in, 45; permit for cotton trader resident of, 230-31; federal arrest of metropolitan police detectives, 233-34; delegation serenades L. in celebration of Sherman's victories, 331n; L. addresses telegram to Banks at (Apr. '65), 386; L. requests reports on vessels bound for Mobile, 421-22; mentioned also, III: 524n, V: 154n, 293n, VI: 389n, 430n, 497n, VII: 164n, 171n, 357, 416n, VIII: 22n, 257n

New York (state): and interchange of state resolutions on slavery (1837), I: 75n; L.'s interest in records of 1821 state convention, 209-10; strength of Whig party (1840-44), 316, 347; and Congressional act to establish post routes (1848), 500; slavery introduced in 1626, II: 299; Douglas on Negro suffrage and abolitionists in, III: 11, 104, 114, 217; and the Constitutional Convention of 1787, 523n; and the Ordinance of 1787, 525n; and the Missouri Compromise, 529, 531n; and the Fifth and Tenth Amendments to the Constitution, 533n; slavery and the state constitution, 548n; L.'s speeches en route to his inaugural, IV: 185, 219-34; L.'s remarks to state delegation paying call of respect (Mar. '61), 272

Appointments, IV: 334 (see also New York (city); mobilization and recruitment, 371-72, 374-76, 382, 384, 416, 471, V: 291n, 292n, 294n, 349, 350, VI: 279; L.'s remarks at a review of state regiments, IV: 441-42; Congressional censure of Cameron for procurement of supplies by state agencies, V: 240-43; development of canals, 270, 526, VI: 508, VII: 48, 274; state purchase of autograph Emancipation Proclamation, V: 433n; elections, (1862) 472-73, (1863) VII: 24n; appeal for Republican Party funds, VI: 112n; support for McClellan command of the Army of the Potomac (July '63), 311n, 312n

And the draft, VI: 361n, 369-70, 381-82, 388-92, 412-13, 416-17, 419-20, 551-52, VII: 210-11, 424n, 437, VIII: 231, 257n, 258, 262-63, 311-12; election (1864), VII: 24n, 233, 244n, VIII: 43, 46, 91-92, 100n, 128, 130, 150, 153, 239, 321n; L.'s reply to Workingmen's Democratic Republican Assoc. upon being tendered an honorary membership, VII: 259-60; state prison (Clinton), 545n, VIII: 300

New York County (N. Y.), VI: 370n; VIII: 262n

New York Courier & Enquirer, IV: 165n

New York Day-Book, III: 205

New York Evening Bulletin, V: 153n

New York Evening Post, V: 153n, 213n; VII: 410; VIII: 325n

New York Express, VII: 349n

New York Herald, IV: 38, 96-97, 99, 102, 539; V: 5, 225-26; VI: 120, 142-43; VII: 273-74, 349n, 461n; VIII: 240n

Cited in footnotes on the ff. pages: IV: 114, 144, 156, 163, 176, 179, 182, 191-92, 205, 210, 216, 221-22, 224-31, 233, 246-48, 357, 383, 388, 408, 458, 484, 520, 558; V: 70, 143, 153, 225, 436, 515; VI: 90, 143, 145, 320, 559; VII: 19, 223, 273, 384, 512; VIII: 170, 255, 334, 362, 393, 395; see

also *New York Tribune*
New York Hotel (N. Y. C.), VI: 279
New York Journal of Commerce, VII: 347-50
New York Mercury, VI: 155
New York Observer, V: 391n
New York Prohibitionist, IV: 420n
New York Sun, VII: 349n; VIII: 425n
New York Times, III: 522; IV: 140, 146; V: 152-53; VI: 331n; VII: 360, 482n, 494n; VIII: 26n
Cited in the footnotes on the ff. pages: IV: 89, 126-27, 136, 181, 182, 221, 222, 224-26, 243, 244, 246, 272, 469, 556; V: 26, 106, 158, 284, 359; VI: 113, 129, 314, 320, 450, 549; VII: 8, 19, 71, 201, 338, 384, 505; VIII: 75, 92, 96, 233, 255, 326, 395
New York Tribune, II: 96n, 381, 430; III: 365n, 368, 506-507, 522n; IV: 38-39, 73n, 119, 186n; V: 169n, 333n, 353, 364, 388-89; VI: 106n, 241, 332n, 514n; VII: 349n, 494n, 508n; VIII: 26n
Cited in the footnotes on the ff. pages: IV: 48, 51, 138, 140, 143, 144, 176, 191, 196, 210, 211, 222, 224-31, 233, 234, 236-39, 241, 243, 244, 246, 275, 277, 286, 341, 345, 416, 471, 509, 543, 553, 554, 556
V: 11, 18, 24, 27, 33, 59, 60, 106, 126, 132, 153, 176, 198, 224, 279, 306, 319, 349, 357, 365, 370, 439, 441, 450, 457, 465, 470, 478, 498, 504, 517
VI: 4, 13, 55, 127, 129, 239, 245, 260, 262, 266, 268, 269, 306, 320, 341, 346, 499, 537, 552, 554
VII: 11, 17, 19, 95, 102, 153, 187, 198, 235, 260, 306, 365, 381, 383, 384, 388, 399, 400, 471, 505, 506, 512, 529, 542
VIII: 53, 118, 154, 195, 241, 255, 262, 331, 362, 384, 389; see also *New York Herald*

New York Voice, IV: 75n
New York World, IV: 235n, 238n, 239n; V: 153n; VI: 241n, 248n; VII: 347-51, 400n, 550n; VIII: 58n, 59n, 60n, 61n, 226n
Newark (N. J.), III: 554; IV: 231, 234-35; VI: 285n, 477n
Newark (Ohio), IV: 206
Newark (N. J.) Advertiser, IV: 553n
Newark Galleries Catalog, IV: 461n; VIII: 290n
Newark (Ohio) North American, IV: 206n
Newberry, Walter Loomis, II: 83
Newberry Library (Chicago), II: 83n
Newburyport (Mass.) Gaol, V: 57n
Newcastle (England), V: 62n
Newcastle (Ky.), VI: 50
Newcomer, Charles, V: 377
Newell, John W., IV: 502n
Newell, Mason W., V: 386
Newell, William Augustus, I: 497; IV: 405, 502n; V: 136, 179n; VI: 165, 191, 460; VII: 263-64, 353, 543
Newhall House (Milwaukee), III: 482n
Newlands, David, I: 317
Newman, Henry, II: 15n, 18
Newman, Joseph, II: 15, 18
Newman, Ralph G., I: xiv
Newnes, Albert A., *see* Nunes, Albert A.
Newport (Ky.), IV: 369n; VI: 50; VII: 198n, 532
Newport (R. I.), VI: 387
Newport (Vt.), VII: 504
Newport (R. I.) Daily News, VIII: 288n
Newport News (Va.), V: 255, 323; VI: 84n
Newspapers, L. and the: endorses statements in, I: 48, III: 385, VI: 214; attacks political opponents in, I: 89n; subscriptions to, 291n, II: 312; complains of being ignored by, I: 491-92; dis-

agrees with statements in, 349-51, 493-94, II: 68, 79, 381, 389-90, 429-30, 472-74, III: 228-30, 240-41, 251-53, 281-82, 355-56, 368, 389-90, 506-507, 550, IV: 38, 67, 96-97, 99, 102, 104-108, 111-12, 124-25, 139-40, 145-46, VI: 62, 251-52, 325, 430, VII: 347-51, 409-10, 512-13

Government advertising in, II: 42-43, IV: 328, VI: 188, 313, VII: 197, 399n; support in an election a "fair index" of the vote, II: 374; financial support of party papers, 410, III: 383, 391; offers article to, II: 483; printing of debates with Douglas, III: 373; apologizes for failure to keep appointment, 506; guest of Conn. editor (1860), IV: 30; writes biographical sketches for, 60-67; relationships with correspondents, 484, 539, VI: 142-43, 241, VII: 332, 546, VIII: 26n; cooperation of N. Y. papers (1862-1864), V: 353, 391, VI: 120, 155, 331n, VII: 360-61, VIII: 39-40, 343; advice of N. Y. Times editor on Emancipation Proclamation, V: 544-45; asks that publication of a letter include revisions, VI: 59; revokes Burnside's suspension of Chicago Times, 248, VII: 361, 363-64; disapproves arrest of St. Louis editor, VI: 326-27, 329, 338; "care very little for the publication of any letter I have written," 326-27

Newton, Isaac, IV: 512-13; V: 143n, 228, 353n; VI: 163, 343, 367-68; VII: 3n, 48, 536n; VIII: 147, 227n

Newton, John, VI: 22n, 75n, 330n, 342n

Newton, Thomas Willoughby, I: 495-96

Newton (Mass.), V: 406

Nez Percé Indians, VII: 284

Niagara Falls, II: 10-11, 146n; VII: 435n, 440n, 459, 461, 482n, 494, 501n

Niagara River, II: 146n

Nicaragua, IV: 286, 555n; V: 190-91, 371n, 451n, 452n, 521; VI: 258n; VII: 37, 72-73; VIII: 137

Nice (Italy) [now France], IV: 483, 538n

Nicholas I, Emperor of Russia, VIII: 181n

Nicholas I (ship), VIII: 111

Nicholas County (Ky.), VIII: 244n

Nicholas County (W. Va.), V: 298

Nicholasville (Ky.), V: 37, 512n

Nicholl, ———, VI: 429n

Nichols, ———, VII: 82-83

Nichols, Edward T., V: 215

Nichols, Henry P., VII: 132-33

Nichols, John H., Jr., V: 263n

Nichols, William, IV: 166

Nichols, William Augustus, VII: 139n

Nicholson, Alfred Osborn Pope, I: 511; II: 7, 236; III: 91, 94-95

Nicholson, Augustus S., IV: 356

Nickols, D. F., II: 374n

Nickols, Noah, VIII: 124n

Nicolas Auguste, Prince of Sweden and Norway, IV: 475

Nicolay, Helen, see Lincoln's Secretary; and Personal Traits of Abraham Lincoln

Nicolay, John George, II: 44n, 45n, 410; III: 336

IV: 34n, 60, 83-85, 88, 101n, 127n, 136, 165n, 175, 177n, 185n, 186n, 187n, 191n, 212, 246n, 249n, 262n, 271, 285n, 328n, 334n, 385, 393n, 415n, 506n, 513n

V: 26n, 71n, 132n, 152n, 161, 267n, 309, 342n, 346n, 397n, 464, 552

VI: 2, 17-18, 30n, 58, 83n, 111n, 152n, 167n, 174n, 198n, 220n, 223n, 261n, 301n, 303n, 304n, 307n, 344, 412n, 497n

VII: 17n, 18n, 25n, 97n, 104,

132n, 137, 150, 152, 155, 157, 163, 171-72, 174, 176n, 205-206, 207n, 211, 220, 224n, 227, 234n, 246n, 252, 268n, 279n, 298, 316, 324n, 345n, 376n, 408n, 458n, 483n, 505n, 509, 522n, 539n, 540n, 541n

VIII: 4-5, 9n, 28n, 57, 118n, 131n, 136, 173n, 190, 206, 212, 238n, 239, 249, 251n, 256, 259, 263, 269, 273-74, 297-99, 301-302, 305, 313, 327n, 345, 354n, 422n

See also *Complete Works of Abraham Lincoln, The:* and *Abraham Lincoln: A History*

Nicolay, Mrs. John George, *see* Bates, Therena

Nields, Ben., V: 379n

Nightingale (slave ship), V: 47n

Nikolai Nikolaievich, Grand Duke of Russia, VII: 296

Niles, Nathaniel, V: 257

Niles' Register, I: 436, 511; II: 83n

Ningpo (China), IV: 310; VI: 96n

Nininger, Alexander Ramsey, V: 59

Nininger, Mrs. John [nee Ramsey], V: 59

Niobrara (Nebr. Terr.), V: 106-107

Nixon, John Thompson, IV: 391, 442, 466n

Noble, ———, VI: 279n

Noble, Joshua Francis, VII: 2, 545-46

Noble, Mrs. Joshua Francis, VII: 545

Noble, Silas, I: 474

Noble, Warren Perry, V: 197n; VI: 300-306

Noble County (Ohio), VII: 131n

Nodle Book Nook, catalog cited, V: 178n

Noell, John William, V: 319n; VI: 6n

Noell, Thomas Estes, V: 130-31

Noggle, Charles Leavit, IV: 453n; V: 369-70

Nolan, Thomas J., VI: 544

Nolin Creek, IV: 70, 76; VIII: 166n

Noll, Virginia, *see* Williams, Virginia (Noll)

Norfolk (Va.): mention of navy yard near, IV: 427; and McClellan's plan of campaign (Feb. '62), V: 122n; *Monitor* ordered not to proceed to, unattended to, 154; Union capture of (May 10, '62), 164n, 210, 293; L. suggests Sigel command for forces at, 255; and Emancipation Proclamation, 477n, VI: 25n, 29; and the blockade, V: 495-96, VIII: 115, 140, 396; and election (1862), VI: 26n; ironclad *Weehawken* reported at (Jan. '63), VI: 84n; murder of officer of colored troops, 362, 437-38; report of destitute condition of secessionist families (Aug. '63), 371; Peirpont visits (Dec. '63), VII: 103n; Butler investigates condition of financial institutions (Jan. '64), 135-36; court-martial cases, 297, VIII: 245; requests for passes to, VII: 305, VIII: 321n; hospital surgeon presented with gift from British seamen, VII: 311; conflict between military and civilian authority (Aug. '64), 487-88; trade regulations, VIII: 20; mention of Shepley at, 34n; purchase of cotton by U. S. agent at, 185; supplies smuggled to rebel army from, 344n; detention of Lane at, 368

Norfolk County (Va.), VI: 26n, 29

Norman, John, VIII: 69

Norment, Samuel, IV: 319

Norris, Benjamin, IV: 393n

Norris, George H., II: 164-65, 167-70

Norris, P. W., VII: 371
North, Howard, VI: 411
North, John W. [M.], IV: 295;
VI: 395
North, Townsend, V: 360n
*North American & United States
Gazette* [Philadelphia], IV:
73n, 101n, 125n; V: 454; VII:
481n
North American Review, III:
365n; VII: 132-33
North American Telegraph Com-
pany, II: 65n
North Anna River (Va.), VI: 207;
VII: 359
North Atlantic Blockading Squad-
ron, V: 128n, 134; VIII: 285
North Carolina, IV: 346-47, 426-
27, 504, 525; V: 3n, 26, 37, 50,
122n, 259-60, 298, 445; VI: 250n,
471n, 479; VII: 158, 435n, 441n,
479, 490n; VIII: 72, 76, 344n
North Carolina, Department of,
VI: 77n, 127n, 184n
North River (Va.), V: 123n
Northwest, Department of the,
VIII: 305n
*North-Western Gazette & Galena
Advertiser*, I: 238n, 309n
North Western Railroad (Tenn.),
VII: 478n
Northampton County (Pa.), V:
362n
Northampton County (Va.), V: 50,
502n; VI: 29, 186-87, 401, 427,
434n; VII: 203n
Northeastern Virginia, Depart-
ment of, IV: 450n
Northern Central Railroad (Pa.),
V: 24; VI: 299n; VII: 16n
Northern Cross Railroad (Ill.), I:
250-51; V: 386n; VIII: 419n
Northern Home for Friendless
Children and ... Soldiers' and
Sailors' Orphans (Philadel-
phia), VI: 376n
Northumberland County (Va.),
VII: 27n, 91n

Northwest, Department of the,
VIII: 293n
Northwest Ordinance, *see* Ordi-
nance of 1787
Northwest Territory, II: 235, 237,
240, 248-49, 267, 274, 276-77,
299; *see also* Ordinance of 1787
Northwestern Confederacy, pro-
posed, VI: 88n
Northwestern Sanitary Commis-
sion, VI: 30n, 539-40; VII: 75,
167n, 394
Norton, Eugene L., IV: 334n
Norton, Jesse Olds, II: 113-14, 287,
304; III: 57, 228, 282; V: 394;
VI: 137, 403; VII: 418; VIII:
102
Norton, Milton D., VIII: 82
Norton, William, VIII: 72-73, 76n
Norvell, John Mason, IV: 499n
Norway, *see* Sweden and Norway
Norwich (Conn.), IV: 13n
Norwich Courier, IV: 13n
*Notes and Comments upon Certain
Plays and Actors of Shake-
speare, with Criticisms and Cor-
respondence* (Hackett), VI:
393n
"Notes of a Military Reconnais-
sance, from Fort Leavenworth
... to San Diego ...," II: 23n
Nott, Charles Cooper, III: 522n;
IV: 58-59, 113, 118-19; VIII:
287n
Nov, John F., VIII: 68
Novelty Iron Works (N. Y.), VI:
112n
Nowlin, David, I: 57n
Noyes, Mrs. Thomas S., II: 104n
Noyes, William Curtis, IV: 307
Nueces River, I: 433-34, 437-38,
472, 493-94; V: 357
Nugent, Robert, VI: 101, 552n,
554n
Nullification, II: 125, 127, 129,
146, 158, 346; III: 86, 293, 310,
321
Nunes, Albert A., VII: 97

Nunes, Joseph A., IV: 302; VI: 63
Nunn, D. A., VIII: 305-306
Nuns of the Battlefield (Jolly), VIII: 428n

Nutter, C. D. VII: 291
Nye, D. S., VIII: 69
Nye, James Warren, IV: 293n, 295; V: 171n; VII: 323; VIII: 109, 358n

O

Oak Mulligan (S. C.), VI: 456-57
Oakes, James, IV: 492; V: 12n, 21n; VI: 435n; VII: 455
Oakes, Mrs. James, V: 21
Oakes, John, V: 12n
Oakland (S. C.), VI: 456-57
Oakley, Charles, I: 76
Oaks, The (S. C.), VI: 456
Oatman, James R., II: 389
Oberkline, Frederick, IV: 203n
Oberteuffer, John H., VII: 305
Obion County (Tenn.), VIII: 70
O'Brien, James, II: 116
O'Brien, William, VII: 318
O'Brine, Larry, VII: 525n
Ocampo, Francisco, IV: 178n
"Occasional" [pseud.], *see* Forney, John Wein
Occoquan (Va.), V: 119, 121n; VIII: 216n
Occoquan Creek, V: 34, 119-21
O'Connell, John, VII: 219n
O'Conner, Henry, II: 376; V: 95n
O'Connor, Henry, VII: 371
O'Conor, Charles, III: 548n, 549
Ocracoke (N. C.), VIII: 396
Odell, Moses Fowler, V: 88n, 487; VI: 562n; VII: 410n, 473
Odessa (Russia), IV: 310, 348n
Official Records, see *War of the Rebellion ...*
Official Roster of the Soldiers of the State of Ohio, V: 509n
Offutt, Denton, I: 4, 9; IV: 63-64

O'Flagerty, Bernard [Barney Williams], VI: 120
Ogden, Amos, I: 52
Ogden, William Butler, II: 178; IV: 136
Ogden, William H., VII: 12
Ogden Land Office, IV: 307
Ogle County (Ill.), I: 145
Oglesby, John Gillett, II: 536n
Oglesby, Richard James, II: 333; V: 142, 453; VII: 201n; VIII: 247n, 255n, 288n, 299n
O'Hair, John H., VIII: 90
O'Hara, Daniel, V: 411; VI: 153
O'Hara, J., VI: 50
O'Hara, James A., V: 411
Ohio, I: 133, 313; III: 384, 386, 391, 394, 395n, 400-62, 510; IV: 186, 197-208, 215-19, 276n, 333, 410, 511n, 550; VI: 20, 22n, 131, 277, 287n, 300-306, 512n, 515; VII: 24n, 312n, 384, 423n, 547; VIII: 27n, 45, 46, 100n, 128, 130, 150, 153, 197, 300
Ohio, Department of the, V: 22n, 402n; VI: 97n, 200n, 294n; VII: 14n, 109n, 153n, 240, 290n; VIII: 88n, 322n
Ohio & Illinois Railroad, III: 385n
Ohio & Mississippi Railroad, II: 411, 460n; IV: 47n
Ohio County (W. Va.), V: 298
Ohio Farmer [Cleveland], IV: 540n

Ohio River, IV: 362, 381, 398n, 533, 545; V: 452; VIII: 197

Ohio Staats-Zeitung [Cincinnati], IV: 283n

Ohio State Journal [Columbus], III: 400n

Ohio Statesman [Columbus], III: 401

O'Kean, Mortimer, II: 296; VI: 198

Okeechobee, battle of, II: 84

O'Keefe, Francis B., V: 349, 362

Okolona (Miss.), V: 250

Olaf, Crown Prince of Norway, V: 308n

Old Capitol Prison (Washington), V: 413n; VI: 35, 361, 427n, 436, 442n, 452, 504n, 536; VII: 144, 208, 271, 330n; VIII: 123n, 233n, 304n, 323n

Old Hickory [Springfield, Ill.], I: 202n

"Old Line Whig, An" [pseud.], III: 302

Old Point Comfort (Va.), VII: 74n, 367

"Old Settler, An" [pseud.], I: 89n

Old Soldier, The [Springfield, Ill.], I: 202-206

Olden, Charles Smith, IV: 186, 355, 458-59, 500n

Oldham, ———, VII: 309n

Oldham, Edward, II: 195-96, 204, 216

Oldham, Todd & Company (Lexington, Ky.), II: 194-97, 200, 203-204

Oldroyd, Osborn Hamiline, VI: 511n

Olds, Francis A., I: 223-24, 251

Olga Teodorovna, Grand Duchess of Russia, V: 74

Olin, Abram Baldwin, VI: 167n; VII: 177n

Olin, Rollin C., V: 542-43

Oliphant, Ethelbert P., II: 48; IV: 322; VIII: 368

Oliver, John H., VII: 369n

Olmstead, Frederick Law, IV: 543n

Olney, John, II: 469; III: 521

Olney (Ill.), II: 376

Olsen, Charles W., II: 91n, 482n; IV: 282n, 284n, 381n, 398n, 453n, 469n, 509n; V: 25n, 170n, 171n, 207n, 410n, 466n; VI: 54n, 101n, 163n, 223n, 351n, 364n, 426n, 429n, 464n; VII: 158n, 337n, 346n, 456n; VIII: 95n, 213n, 258n

Olson, Julius E., III: 477n

Olustee (Fla.), VII: 507

Olympia (Wash. Terr.), IV: 308; VI: 208

Omaha (Nebr. Terr.), IV: 303n, 307; VII: 16, 233; VIII: 89, 146

Omaha Indian Agency, IV: 306

Omnibus Bill, *see* Compromise of 1850

"One-Legged Brigade," VI: 226-27

O'Neill, Bernard S., VII: 301

O'Neill, Charles, VIII: 48, 312n

O'Neill, Howard D., VII: 208

O'Neill, James, VIII: 111

O'Neill, John, VI: 300-306

Oneille, Edward J., I: 86

Onstot, Henry, I: 15; II: 66n

Onstot, Isaac, II: 66, 94

Onstot, John, II: 66n

Opdycke, Stacy B., I: 251, 398, 405

Opdyke, George, IV: 307, 325, 373, 447; V: 242, 403n, 554n; VI: 154, 239n, 435; VII: 32

Opequan (Va.), IV: 517n; VIII: 13n

Oporto (Portugal), VIII: 296-97

Opposing Principles of Henry Clay and Abraham Lincoln (pamphlet), IV: 104

Oquawka [Yellow Banks] (Ill.), I: 32-33

Orange & Alexandria Railroad, *see* Alexandria & Orange Railroad

Orange County (Va.), II: 83

Orbe (Switzerland), V: 355

Ord, Edward Otho Cresap, V:

246n, 251n, 453n; VII: 277n, 438n, 445n, 484n, 522n; VIII: 207n, 224, 243, 246, 247, 250, 265, 276-78, 285, 289-90, 331n, 357, 368, 378-82
Order of American Knights, *see* American Knights, Order of
Ordinance of 1784, III: 414, 524n, 525
Ordinance of 1787, II: 235, 240-41, 245, 249, 263, 267, 277, 280-81, 299, 346, 354, 515; III: 93, 124, 414-15, 422, 427, 437, 448, 454-57, 465-68, 483-84, 523-25, 527, 530n, 533, 537n; IV: 113n, 118
Ordner, John, VI: 533n
Ordway, Nehemiah G., VI: 352
Oregon, I: 382; II: 237, 280; III: 351; IV: 66, 280-81, 308, 404, 406-407; V: 41-42, 77, 163, 204n; VI: 111n, 119n, 290, 432; VII: 290n; VIII: 46, 129-30, 140, 150, 153, 359; *see also* Oregon Territory
Oregon Farmer [Portland], IV: 90n
Oregon Territory, II: 61-63, 65; III: 50-51, 54, 261; *see also* Oregon
O'Reilly, Miles [Charles G. Halpine], VI: 490
Orendorff, Alfred, II: 476n
Oreto (Confederate steamer), VI: 102
Orin, *see* Olin, Abram B.
Orleans (Va.), V: 236
Orleans Parish (La.), VI: 29
Orme, William, VII: 318
Orme, William Ward, V: 353-54; VI: 352n, 441; VIII: 7-8, 307
Ormsbee, Joseph W., I: 222, 243-44
Orozembo (ship), V: 64n
Orr, James C., V: 465n, 473n
Orr, James Lawrence, III: 218, 269, 295, 543n, 547n
Orsini, Felice, III: 541
Ortan, Allison, VII: 261, 265
Orth, Godlove Stein, VII: 3-4, 128; VIII: 47

Orton, William, V: 396; VIII: 194
Osage Indians, VII: 68
Osage River Indian Agency, IV: 306; VIII: 115n
Osawatomie (Kans.), III: 371, 378
Osborne, Thomas A., VII: 304
Osceola (Mo.), IV: 538n
Osgood, Uri, II: 296, 305
Ospino, Mariano, VI: 57
Osterhaus, Peter Joseph, VII: 463-64; VIII: 136n
O'Sullivan, John P., V: 32n
O'Sullivan, Thomas, II: 183
Oswego Canal, V: 270
O-Ta-kla, V: 551n
Otero, Miguel Antonio, IV: 349n
Otis, George K., VII: 530
Otis, James, II: 127
Otoe and Missouri Indian Agency, IV: 306; VIII: 338n
Ottawa (Ill.), III: 1-37, 39, 43, 45, 48-49, 52, 56-58, 88, 119, 125, 127, 133, 135, 179, 183, 227, 229, 239-41 245, 248-49, 251, 253, 260-61, 280, 285, 287, 326, 401
Ottawa County (Mich.), VIII: 367n
Ottawa (Ill.) *Free Trader*, II: 186; III: 124
Ottawa Indians, V: 287-88
Ottawa Republican, III: 388n
Ottawa Republican-Times, II: 537n
"Ottawa's Old Settlers" (art.), VIII: 367n
Otto, William T., VI: 69, 231-32, 242; VIII: 34, 424
Ottoman Empire, *see* Turkey
Ouachita expedition, VIII: 244n
Ouiatenon [Wea] Indians, V: 147; VII: 246n
Ould, Robert, VI: 207n, 315n
"Out with Mosby's Men" (art.), IV: 526n
Overland Mail Line, V: 200n; VII: 530
Overton County (Tenn.), VIII: 68
Owen, C. Norton, III: 520n; V: 4n,

147n, 192n, 205n; VI: 77n, 187n, 397n; VII: 114n, 245n, 358n, 505n
Owen, David, I: 2
Owen, David R., VIII: 69
Owen, George S., VIII: 190
Owen, Joshua J., VII: 255
Owen, Joshua Thomas, VII: 505-506
Owen, M. P., VII: 430n
Owen, Robert Dale, IV: 415-16, 454n; VI: 88n
Owen, Samuel W., IV: 524n

Owens, F. L., II: 182
Owens, Mary S., I: 54-55, 78-79, 94-95, 117-19
Owens, Parnick, I: 32
Owens, Samuel A., VIII: 125
Owens, Wesley, VII: 241n
Owensboro (Ky.), IV: 533; VIII: 181n
Oxford (Md.), IV: 364n
Oxnam, G. Bromley, VII: 540n
O-ya-tay-a-koo (Indian), V: 543
Oye Muza (Indian), VII: 325-26
Ozark Mountains, V: 459n

P

Pace, H. T., I: 143
Pacific, Department of the, VI: 325n
Pacific Ocean, VI: 68
Pacific Railroad [Mo.], IV: 88n, 121n; V: 314-15, 459-60, 526; VI: 66; VII: 224, 237-38
Pacific Telegraph Company, IV: 558n
Packard, Major W., III: 378, 518
Paddock, Algernon Sidney, IV: 337n, 347
Paddock, Orville, II: 45
Paducah (Ky.), IV: 510n, 529n, 533, 545, 558; V: 86n, 87n; VII: 212n
Page, Charles A., IV: 527n
Page, Daniel D., II: 92, 341-42
Page, Elwin L., II: 148n; IV: 94n
Page, Peter, IV: 177
Page, William T., IV: 43-44
Page & Bacon (St. Louis), II: 332n, 341-42, 411, 460n
Paige, Wilkinson W., VI: 400, 533n

Paine, Adolphus, see Payne, Dolphus
Paine, Eleazar A., III: 339, 340; IV: 448, 505, 529; VII: 400
Paine, Halbert Eleazar, VII: 492n
Paine, N. E., V: 7-8
Paine, Phelps, IV: 529n
Paine, Robert F., IV: 279n; VI: 353n
Painesville (Ohio), IV: 218
Painesville Telegraph, IV: 218n
Palestine (Ill.), I: 406; II: 22; V: 541
Palfrey, John Gorham, IV: 106
Palmer, George Henry, V: 58
Palmer, Innis Newton, VI: 254-55
Palmer, John McAuley, II: 228, 296, 305, 340, 357, 447, 480, 524, 536; III: 109, 174, 355-56, 384, 492-93; IV: 168n, 466n; V: 168-69; VII: 61; VIII: 315, 316
Palmer, Luther T., VIII: 300-301, 325
Palmer, Mrs. Luther T., VIII: 301n
Palmer, Robert M., IV: 167

Palmetto (Ga.), VIII: 27n
Palmyra (Mo.), VI: 31n
Palo Alto, battle of, II: 60
Pamunkey River (Va.), V: 219n, 232, 293n, 515
Panama, IV: 303n, 561n; V: 56n; VII: 37n, 415n; VIII: 137n
Pancoast, Samuel A., IV: 536
Panizzi, Sir Anthony, VI: 9-10
Panoche Grande land grant (Calif.), VI: 402n
Pantaninniye (Indian), VII: 325-26
Pantier, David M., I: 12
Pantier, James, I: 25, 71-72
Paola (Kans.), V: 147
Papin, Joseph L., II: 315n
Paraguay, IV: 397; V: 144, 161, 260; VI: 91-92; VIII: 138
Pardee, Theron, II: 234
Pardons, IV: 389, 495, 554-56; V: 57, 68-69, 94, 146-47, 170-71, 183-85, 202-203, 205, 211, 249, 258, 266, 285, 300, 347-48, 352, 366, 390, 475-76, 491, 500-501, 538-39

VI: 2, 35, 55, 62-63, 75, 89, 98, 103, 106-107, 109-10, 118, 132-33, 135, 148, 158, 180, 189, 191-95, 211, 225, 229, 231, 240, 241, 280, 294, 337, 340, 353, 360, 364, 414, 425-26, 428, 463-64, 477, 485, 488-89, 510, 515-16, 526, 551

VII: 14, 32-33, 62, 67, 71-72, 74, 75, 77, 79-80, 82, 89, 91-92, 98, 105, 110, 130, 131, 136-39, 148, 150, 152, 156, 158, 173, 175, 177, 187, 189, 195-96, 218, 221-22, 225, 226, 232-33, 253, 275-78, 286, 292, 298-99, 301, 304-305, 309, 314-15, 321-23, 325-26, 328, 336, 350, 357, 362, 385, 389-91, 393-94, 446n, 447-48, 456, 460, 465, 474, 511, 525, 536, 543, 547

VIII: 5, 16-18, 23, 32-34, 36, 45, 85, 112, 119, 152, 176-77, 180, 192-93, 196, 203, 205, 213-14, 219, 233, 238, 251-53, 270, 289-90, 306, 309, 313, 315, 317, 323-24, 326, 349-50, 357, 366-67, 369, 370, 398-99, 425
Paredes y Arrillago, Mariano, I: 472
Paris (France), IV: 311, 313, 379, 397, 466, 478, 498n, 552n; VII: 46
Paris (Ill.), II: 211, 359; III: 90-91
Paris (Ky.), IV: 369n, 558n
Parke, John Grubb, V: 385; VIII: 239n, 240n, 276, 374n, 378n, 381-82
Parke-Bernet Galleries, I: xxii; cited in footnotes on the ff. pages: II: 482; III: 554; IV: 88, 323, 336, 339, 349, 384, 444, 455, 503; V: 8, 177, 180, 187, 206, 300, 538; VI: 124, 212, 257, 422; VII: 121, 178, 188, 272; VIII: 7, 166, 218, 249, 253, 422, 424
Parker, ———, VII: 25n
Parker, Albert, II: 538
Parker, Amasa Junius, VIII: 212n
Parker, Bowdoin S., VIII: 425n
Parker, Courtland, IV: 405
Parker, Ely Samuel, VI: 150n
Parker, Frank W., VII: 163
Parker, George S., VI: 367n
Parker, H. A., IV: 126n
Parker, J. M. G., VII: 420
Parker, James, I: 477-78
Parker, James P., VI: 537-38
Parker, Jane L. (Allen), III: 491n
Parker, Joel, VI: 311-12, 334n, 337-38, 347-48, 354-55, 460-61; VIII: 109
Parker, John, VI: 537-38
Parker, John H., IV: 166
Parker, John Todd, I: 465, 495-96; II: 66; III: 491n
Parker, Mrs. John Todd, see Parker, Jane L. (Allen)
Parker, Leopold Oscar, VI: 132
Parker, Nathaniel W., II: 418, 420
Parker, Oliver Hazard Perry, IV: 181n
Parker, Samuel H., IV: 301
Parker, Willard, VIII: 290n
Parker, Z., II: 314

Parkersburg (W. Va.), IV: 559n
Parkinson, James, I: 249
Parkinson, John, V: 465n, 473n
Parks, Bushrod Washington, VII: 406n
Parks, Gavion D. A., II: 298, 304, 480
Parks, Mrs. M. Davis, VII: 406
Parks, Samuel C., II: 296n, 298, 383n; VIII: 412
Paroles, V: 163, 167, 170, 176, 300, 432n, 449, 453n, 461-62; VI: 1-2, 50, 135, 203, 219-20, 241n, 324n, 325, 429, 441, 520; VII: 65-66, 98n, 199, 322n, 373, 391, 430-31, 436n, 446-47, 480n; VIII: 51, 94n, 112, 218, 226, 259, 285, 302-304, 310n
Parrott, Edwin A., IV: 34
Parrott, Lena, I: 95n
Parrott guns, V: 203-204; VI: 255
Parry's Island (S. C.), VI: 455-57
Parsons, ———, IV: 310
Parsons, George J., VII: 371
Parsons, George M., II: 461n; III: 510, 515
Parsons, Lewis Baldwin, II: 341-42; IV: 526; VI: 552; VIII: 349, 362-63
Parsons, Mosby M., VII: 393n
Parsons, Solomon, I: 231
Parsons, Theophilus, III: 533n
Partridge, James R., V: 88
Pascagoula River (Miss.), VIII: 196
Paschall, Nathaniel P., IV: 138n, 139-40
Pasfield, George, I: 43, 79
Passes, military, IV: 383-84, 389, 481, 525, 539; V: 4, 174-75, 300, 354, 377, 386; VI: 80-81, 86, 148, 436, 444, 517, 553, 561
VII: 4, 27, 74, 83-84, 127, 136, 169, 184, 203, 205-206, 219-20, 240, 242, 256-57, 294, 295, 305, 360-62, 367, 369, 419, 429, 492, 525, 531, 544
VIII: 4, 24, 38, 51, 54-55, 57, 72-73, 75, 76, 82, 95, 108, 160,
169, 177, 188-89, 200-201, 218, 227, 238, 244, 290, 292, 302-303, 307, 317, 321, 342, 351, 354, 363, 365, 395, 409-10
Patapsco (ironclad), VI: 84n
Patent laws, importance of, III: 363
Patent Office, U. S., I: 466-67; II: 32-36; IV: 295, 514n; V: 28n, 45, 553n; VI: 50n; VII: 197-98, 236-37; VIII: 334n
Paternity of Abraham Lincoln, The (Barton), IV: 57n
Paterson, William, III: 527
Patrick, Amos F., II: 56
Patrick, J. N. H., VIII: 324n
Patrick, Marsena Rudolph, VIII: 19n, 105-106
Patronage, L. on, I: 339-40; II: 12, 32, 42-43, 60, 144-46, 444-45; IV: 83, 88, 94, 152, 163, 173, 296, 302, 321; V: 147, 278; VI: 178, 275-76; VII: 188, 197, 266-67, 340, 400, 402, 423-24, 452-53, 469n, 480-81
Patten, George, VI: 7
Patten, George Evans, IV: 294
Patten, William, II: 298; IV: 398-99
Patterson, David Trotter, VII: 225n
Patterson, Francis Engle, V: 90
Patterson, George W., VII: 502n
Patterson, Golden, IV: 35n
Patterson, J. G., II: 182
Patterson, Joseph, II: 220
Patterson, Robert, IV: 420n, 457-58; V: 90n, 98
Patterson, Thomas, IV: 93
Patterson, William, IV: 35n
Patterson, William M., VIII: 357n
Patton, Charles L., I: xvii
Patton, William, see Patten, William
Patton, William W., V: 419n
Patuxent River (Md.), VI: 530, 532
Paul, Augustus Choteau, VIII: 311n
Paul, E. A., VII: 360

Paul, Gabriel René, V: 390-91; VIII: 311

Paul, Mrs. Gabriel René, V: 390-91

Paul, John, VII: 393-94

Pawnee (steamboat), IV: 301, 311n, 351n

Pawnee Indian Agency, IV: 306, 348; VI: 21n, 246n

Paxton, Elisha F., VI: 199

Paxton, James W., IV: 464n

Payne, Alexander, VIII: 69

Payne, Daniel R., VII: 251

Payne, Dolphus S., VII: 371; VIII: 412n

Payne, M. J., VIII: 290n

Pa-zee-koo-tay-ma-ne (Indian), V: 543

Pea Ridge (Ark.), V: 196; VI: 147n

Peabody, Charles A., V: 468; VII: 420; VIII: 242n

Peabody & Company (Philadelphia), V: 473

Peacher, Cornelius E., VIII: 211, 241

Peacock, William, VIII: 252-53

Pearce, James Alfred, II: 97, 137-38; V: 285

Pearce, Samuel, VI: 116-17

Pearl (British ship), VII: 198

Pearl River (Miss.), VIII: 196, 396

Pearson, Abe, VIII: 68

Pearson, Eliza, II: 27-28

Pearson, Isaac E., V: 33

Pearson, John, I: 287-88, 332-33

Pease, Edward B., II: 188; IV: 147

Pease, Theodore Calvin, I: 344n

Peay, Austin, I: 261n

Peay, Mrs. Austin, *see* Peay, Peachy Walker (Speed)

Peay, Peachy Walker (Speed), I: 261

Peck, Mrs. [nee Richardson], VII: 454n

Peck, Anning R., VII: 454

Peck, Ebenezer, I: 212, 231, 238, 239n; II: 115-16, 348, 433; III: 174, 337; IV: 395; VI: 167n, 526n; VIII: 38

Peck, George, VII: 351n

Peck, Harry, VII: 138n

Peck, Isaac A., V: 15n

Peck, John James, VI: 84n, 173n, 176n, 218n, 295

Peck, John Mason, I: 472-73

Peck, S., V: 446n

Peck, William Walker, IV: 395n, 413

Peckham, ———, VI: 206n

Pedro V, King of Portugal, V: 104

Pedro de Alcantara, Infante of Spain, VI: 136

Peekskill (N. Y.), IV: 229

Peggy (packet ship), V: 548n

Pegram, Benjamin R., IV: 536

Peirpoint, Francis Harrison, IV: 511; V: 166, 387n, 465, 473, 477n; VI: 17n, 26n, 130, 136, 371, 472; VII: 83, 103, 135-36, 191, 204, 481, 487-88; VIII: 392, 399n

Pekin (Ill.), I: 45-47, 52, 322, 349-51, 354n, 363-66; III: 206-207; IV: 389

Pemberton, John, I: 121

Pemberton, John Clifford, VI: 226, 247

Pembroke (ship), V: 5-6, 38n

Pendergrast, Garrett J., IV: 318-19

Pendleton, E. Boyd, V: 17, 65, 129

Pendleton, George Hunt, III: 210; VI: 300-306; VIII: 65

Penfield, George H., V: 172n

Pengra, B. J., IV: 406n

Peniston, Fergus, VIII: 196-97, 243-44

Pennebaker, Charles D., VIII: 197n, 310n

Pennington, Edward D., VIII: 69

Pennington, William, III: 495n

Pennock, Alexander M., VI: 155

Pennsylvania: L. accepts honorary membership in State College Literary Society, IV: 70; and Cameron's appointment to L.'s cabinet, 165-71, 179-81; L.'s speeches en route to his inaugural, 188, 208-15, 219, 238-46; L.'s reply to state delegation

paying call of respect (Mar. '61), 273-74; appointments, 311, 327, 329, 337-38, 342, 444, V: 206-207, VI: 119, VII: 110, 353n, 357n, 369n, 374n, VIII: 346n

Mobilization and recruitment, IV: 380-81, 402, 419n, 511n, V: 29n, 339, 368n, 391-93, 414-15, VI: 277-78, 279n, 282-83, 292, 298n, VII: 57-58, 178n, 249-50, 299-300, 424n, 437; and the draft, V: 362n, VI: 240n, 444n, 477-78, VII: 58n, 299-300, VIII: 29n, 48, 84-87, 311-13; military operations, (fall '62) V: 409n, 411-12, 415, 417-18, 477n, (spring '63) VI: 189, 193, 195, 249n, 280n, 293, 299, 310-12, 321-24, 553n, (fall '64) VIII: 50

Reserve corps presents sword to Meade, VI: 418; election (1863), 512-13, 515; L.'s address at Gettysburg, VII: 16-23; election (1864), 118n, 452, VIII: 17n, 38, 43-46, 81, 96, 100n, 101n, 129-30, 150, 153; school teachers' support of L., VII: 271; organization of prisoners-of-war as Union troops, 530-31, VIII: 17-18; mentioned also, VI: 119n, 375n, 459n, VII: 120n, 157n

See also Philadelphia (Pa.)

Pennsylvania, Historical Society of, VII: 396n

Pennsylvania, University of, VI: 62n

Pennsylvania Railroad, VI: 493n

Pennsylvania State Agricultural Society, IV: 166

Pennsylvania State College, IV: 70n

Penny, Myram, I: 82-83

Penny, Solomon, I: 82

Penrose, Charles Bingham, VIII: 372n, 381-82

Pensacola (Fla.), IV: 315, 318-19; V: 38n, 428n; VII: 185, 532; VIII: 20, 94n, 115, 140, 396

Pensacola (steam sloop), V: 33-34

Pension Office, U. S., IV: 526n; V: 45-46; VIII: 214

Peoria (Ill.), I: 45-47, 69-70, 338-40; II: 158-59, 247-83, 315n, 326, 375, 379; III: 14-15, 79, 83, 88, 326; IV: 77, 137n

Peoria Democratic Press, II: 159n

Peoria Indians, V: 147

Peoria Register & North-Western Gazetteer, I: 226n, 229

Peoria Republican, II: 159n, 234n, 333n, 349n, 379n

Peoria Transcript, III: 77n, 207n; IV: 92n, 137n

Perczel, see Pretzel, Nicholas

Perea, Francisco, VII: 238; VIII: 157

Pérez, José Joaquín, V: 19

Perkins, A. J., VII: 550n

Perkins, Benjamin W., IV: 472

Perkins, Delavan Duane, V: 462n

Perkins, George F., VI: 548

Perkins, John, Jr., VIII: 77n

Perkins, Pryor, VIII: 68

Perkins, Tarrant Augustus, V: 229-30, 277n; VIII: 417

Perkins, William J., VIII: 319n

Perry, ———, VII: 316-17

Perry, Mrs., VIII: 152n

Perry, Mrs., [nee Adams], VII: 544

Perry, Amos, IV: 313n

Perry, Charles O., VII: 317n

Perry, John A., V: 431

Perry, John J., I: 354-55

Perry, Leslie J., see "Appeals to Lincoln's Clemency"

Perry, Roger, VI: 102-103

Perry County (Ill.), I: 147

Perry County (Ind.), I: 378n; IV: 37n

Perry [Berry] County (Tenn.), VIII: 69

Perryman, John D., VIII: 58-72

Perryville (Ky.), IV: 477n; V: 457n, 509n; VI: 86

Perryville (Md.), IV: 347

Persia, VIII: 319n

Personal Finances of Abraham

Lincoln, The (Pratt), II: 224n,
315n; V: 394n; VII: 385n
*Personal Narrative of the Ac-
quaintance of My Father and
Myself with Each of the Pres-
idents of the United States, A*
(Hagner), VI: 378n
*Personal Notes and Reminiscences
of Lincoln* (Huidekoper), VI:
533n; VII: 317n
"Personal Recollections of Abra-
ham Lincoln" (art.), VIII: 155n
*Personal Recollections of Abra-
ham Lincoln and the Civil War*
(Gilmore), VI: 330n; VII: 429n
*Personal Recollections of John M.
Palmer: The Story of an Earnest
Life* (Palmer), VII: 61n
*Personal Traits of Abraham Lin-
coln* (Nicolay), IV: 35n
Perthshire (British ship), V: 38
Peru, IV: 293, 396n, 397; V: 142-
43, 521; VI: 92-93, 124, 134, 167n,
212-13; VII: 37, 88; VIII: 137-38
Petefish, William, IV: 137
Peter, Zachariah, I: 24, 298
Peterhoff (ship), VI: 183n
Peters, Mrs., VI: 483
Peters, John H., IV: 313, 526; V:
296n
Peters, Onslow, II: 120-21, 285
Peters, Richard, Jr. [?], VII: 369n
Petersburg (Ill.), I: 17, 23n, 58-59,
82-83, 87, 93, 129-31, 157, 179-80,
182-83, 330n, 353-55, 359-60,
379; II: 366-68; III: 333
Petersburg (Va.), IV: 472; V: 488,
499; VI: 535n; VII: 301n, 393n,
399, 484n, 547; VIII: 76, 274,
278-79, 324, 377, 379-84, 385,
396, 399, 410
Peterson's Magazine, IV: 526n
Petigru, James Louis, VIII: 302n
Petrikin, Benjamin Rush, IV: 167
Pettis, Solomon Newton, IV: 184,
294; V: 256, 309; VI: 86; VII:
317n, 531n; VIII: 14n, 17n, 103n
Pettis County (Mo.), VI: 402n

Pettit, John, II: 275, 283; III: 205,
301; IV: 115
Pettyjohn, John, I: 2
Petz, Weldon, IV: 524n
Peugnet, Ernest, VI: 149n
Peugnet, Louis, VI: 149n
Peyton, Bailie, VIII: 58-72
Peyton, Jesse E., VI: 44, 50
Pfau, John L., IV: 527n
Phares, Allen W., II: 389n
Phelps, ———, (Conn.), VII: 82-
83
Phelps, ———, (Ill.), II: 208
Phelps, E. P., IV: 542n
Phelps, Edward Elisha, V: 67
Phelps, George, II: 445; IV: 467n
Phelps, George D., II: 198
Phelps, John Elisha, V: 217n
Phelps, John Smith, IV: 475-76;
V: 82n, 342-43, 463, 500; VI:
221
Phelps, Justus McKinstry, V: 379
Phelps, Salmon A., II: 425; III:
493n
Phelps, William J., I: 215n
Phi Alpha Society of Illinois College, III: 356n
Philadelphia (Pa.): banks' suspension of specie payments (1837,
1839), I: 193; Springfield Whig
meeting replies to charges of
responsibility for 1844 riots in,
337-38; L.'s reply to invitation
to attend a rally in support of
Taylor nomination for president, 449-50; L. mentions attend-
ing Whig National Convention
at, 476-78; L.'s speeches en route
to his inaugural, IV: 216, 238-
42; appointments, 327, 329, 337-
38, 342, 444; Small's regiment
from, 380-81; L. commends volunteer work for soldiers in
transit through, V: 217-18, 394;
Chase visits to (May '62, Apr.
'63), 219n, VI: 180n; fear of enemy capture (Sept. '62), V:
409n, 411-12, 417-18, 501; and

proposed tests of new weapons, VI: 3n, 145, 163; mention of Christian Commission public meetings, 115n Letters addressed to Mrs. L. at, VI: 256, 260, 277, 283, VII: 106, 112, VIII: 174-75; Cadwalader to command in, VI: 279n; enlistment of Negroes in, 292; courts-martial and discharges, 364, VII: 335, VIII: 249; L. accepts honorary membership in the Union League, VI: 533-34; mention of Freedmen's Aid Society, VII: 76; state militia paid by citizens of, 178n; mentioned delivery of Absterdam projectiles to, 236n; L.'s attendance at the Great Central Fair, 187n, 324n, 365-66, 390n, 394-98 (texts of his speeches), 442n, 529n; and the draft, 299-300, VIII: 48, 311-13; postmaster accused of exercising political pressure on post office employees in senatorial campaign, VII: 452, 480-81; L. presented with a cane manufactured in, 457-58; women arsenal workers protest low wages, 466-67; firing of victory salute ordered (Sept. '64), 532; L. acknowledges gift to soldiers' hospital, VIII: 204-205; L. replies to gift of "vase of skeleton leaves, gathered from . . . Gettysburg," 236; loans fire engine to Washington, 319n; mention of documents owned by institutions and persons in, V: 341n, VII: 529n; mentioned also, IV: 166, 181n, 311, V: 207n, 241, VI: 324n, 325n, 533n; see also Pennsylvania

Philadelphia (steam tug), VII: 258n

Philadelphia in the Civil War 1861-1865 (Taylor), V: 218n

Philadelphia Inquirer, IV: 216n, 219n, 220n, 232n, 239n, 240n, 241n, 242n, 274n; VII: 20n, 21n, 396n

Philadelphia Mercury, IV: 181n

Philadelphia Press, III: 495n; VI: 62, 214n; VII: 396n, 397n, 398n, 469n

Philadelphia, Wilmington & Baltimore Railroad, V: 24

Philippi (W. Va.), IV: 451n

Philips, James M., VII: 427

Philips, John F., VI: 402n

Philips, Maria [alias], see Coffman, Maria

Phillips, Alexander, I: 249

Phillips, Charles, II: 281

Phillips, David L., III: 116, 516n, 520-21; IV: 81, 136; V: 59n; VI: 63n

Phillips, Edward, VIII: 118n

Phillips, Isaac Newton, VI: 198n, 232

Phillips, James, VI: 351-52

Phillips, John, VIII: 118, 269n

Phillips, P. T., VIII: 69

Phillips, Philip, VIII: 245-46

Phillips, Richard, VIII: 69

Phillips, Thomas A., IV: 187

Phillips, Wendell, III: 263; VII: 81

Phillips Exeter Academy (Exeter, N. H.), III: 555n; IV: 87n, 443

Phillips' Illinois Battery, VII: 6n

Phillips Island (S. C.), VI: 455

Phipps, George W., VI: 114, 131n

Phipps, L. H. [S. H.?], VI: 131

Phipps, Mrs. L. H. [S. H.?], VI: 114n, 130-31

Phoenix, John, III: 74

Phoenix Bank (N. Y.), I: 187

Phoenix Hall (Bloomington, Ill.), IV: 41

Photographs and portraits of L., IV: 30, 39-40, 76n, 89, 102, 114, 122, 127, 145, 546; VI: 118, 125; VII: 106n, 187n, 392; VIII: 92-93, 191-92

Piankashaw Indians, V: 147

Piatt, Abraham Sanders, III: 513
Piatt, Donn, IV: 136, 143n; VI: 139n, 309n, 529; VII: 60n
Piatt, Mrs. Donn, see Piatt, Louise
Piatt, John James, VIII: 337
Piatt, Louise (Kirby), IV: 143n
"Picayune Butler" (song), VII: 549-50
Pickaway County (Ohio), II: 161n
Pickens, Francis Wilkinson, IV: 322-24, 409, 425
Pickens, William, VIII: 68
Pickering, Catherine, IV: 550n
Pickering, John, IV: 38-39
Pickering, Martha, IV: 550n
Pickering, William W., II: 75; IV: 39n, 509n, 550; V: 257n; VII: 544; VIII: 310
Pickett, George Edward, VI: 249n, 476; VIII: 380n
Pickett, Thomas Johnson, III: 356n, 377; IV: 297; VI: 161n, 182, 196; VII: 371
Pickrell, Harry E., III: 493n
Pickrell, Jesse A., II: 442; III: 493
Pickrell, William S., I: 398, 405; III: 493
Pico, Andreas, IV: 519
Pico, Antonio María, IV: 305
Pictorial History of the Civil War (Lossing), VI: 30n
Pieper, Frederick, VII: 177
Pierce, Byron R., VII: 75
Pierce, Calvin, I: 11
Pierce, Carlos, VIII: 96n
Pierce, Charles, I: 12
Pierce, Edward Lillie, V: 132; VIII: 364n, 372n
Pierce, Elijah, I: 11
Pierce, Franklin, II: 135-57, 158, 235, 321n, 333, 353-54, 364, 367, 371, 384-85, 463, 465-66, 539; III: 20, 34-35, 68-69, 85, 124, 162, 166-67, 170, 195, 259; IV: 141n, 420, 505, 544n; VI: 51n; VII: 128, 169n
Pierce, Henry Lillie, III: 374-76
Pierce, John, V: 485
Pierce, Lewis B., VI: 322

Pierce, Thomas, I: 11
Pierce, William, IV: 113n
Pierpoint, Francis Harrison, see Peirpoint, Francis Harrison
Pierpont Morgan Library (N. Y.), II: 453n, 552n
Pierson, Edward L., I: 67
Pigeon Point (S. C.), VI: 455
Pike, Bennett, VIII: 242n
Pike, Edgar M., VI: 279
Pike, James Stephen ("Particular Pike"), V: 181
Pike, William S., VIII: 244n
Pike County (Ill.), I: 157
Pike County Free Press [Pittsfield, Ill.], II: 410n
Pike House (Bloomington, Ill.), II: 340
Pilcher, Moses, I: 206
Pilgrims, landing of the, VIII: 170
Pillow, Gideon Johnson, IV: 413n
Pillsbury, Josiah, VII: 105n
Pinckney, Charles, III: 525n, 529-30, 534n
Pinckney, Charles Cotesworth, III: 531n, 545n
Pinckney, Daniel J., II: 298, 303; III: 65; VIII: 343
Pinckneyville (Ill.), I: 147
Pine [Vine] Street Presbyterian Church (St. Louis), VI: 20n; VII: 85-86
Pineville (Ark.), V: 456n
Pinkerton, Allan, IV: 353
Pinney, George M., VII: 206-207, 215
Pioneer Fire Company (Springfield), II: 483
Piotr [Pierre] Nikolaievich, Grand Duke of Russia, VII: 296
Piper, Edward, Count, V: 17-18; VI: 539n; VIII: 228
Piper, Israel S., II: 455-56
Piqua (Ohio), I: 513
Pirsson, ———, VII: 127
Pitcher, John, I: 342n
Pitman, John T., Jr., VI: 461
Pitts, Edward P., VII: 203

Pittsburg Landing (Tenn.), V: 200n, 203, 210, 283; *see also* Shiloh, battle of
Pittsburgh (Pa.), IV: 208-15; V: 81n, 108n, 110; VI: 193n, 195n, 246n, 285n, 286, 324n, 325n; VII: 395, 532
Pittsburgh Dispatch, IV: 209n, 210n, 213n
Place, Charles A., IV: 474n
Plainville (Ohio), III: 336n
Planck, Jacob C., II: 188
Plan-doo-ta (Indian), V: 542
Plant, George H., VII: 318
Plant, Pascal, V: 156n
Planters' House (St. Louis), I: 303
Plaquemines Parish (La.), VI: 29
Plaster, John, I: 11
Plaster, Michael, I: 12
Plato, III: 357
Platt, Charles F., VI: 520n
Platt, Edwin F., VI: 520
Platt, Elizabeth J., VI: 520
Platt, Obadiah Henry, VIII: 425n
Platt, Orville Hitchcock, VIII: 425n
Platt, P. W., III: 126
Platte County (Mo.), VI: 489, 544n; VII: 337; VIII: 166
Platte River, IV: 306; VIII: 225n
Pleadwell, Frank L., V: 478n; VII: 172n; VIII: 149n
Pleasant Hill (Ind.), II: 394n
Pleasant Hill (La.), VIII: 48n
Pleasant Point (S. C.), VI: 456-57
Pleasants, James Snowden, VI: 148
Pleasants County (W. Va.), V: 298
Pleasonton, Alfred, V: 410n, 412n, 474n, 477n, 481n; VI: 257n, 273n, 318, 342n, 450n, 509; VII: 337n, 407n
Plum, William Rattle, V: 6n
Plumb, Edward L., V: 357n
Plumley, Benjamin Rush, VII: 114n
Plunkett, Robert S., I: 12
Plymouth (Mass.), VIII: 170
Plymouth (N. C.), VIII: 94, 133-34, 396

Plymouth Church (Brooklyn), III: 494n
Pocahontas (steamer), IV: 301, 351n
Podell, Jacob J., V: 153n
Poe, Edgar Allan, I: 377
Poems, *see* Verses composed by L.
Pohlman, H. N., V: 213n
Point Isabel (Tex.), II: 84; VIII: 396
Point Lookout (Md.), VI: 355n; VII: 80n, 87, 91, 95n, 103, 139n, 293n, 297n, 362n, 406, 419, 524n; VIII: 123n, 124n, 314n, 373n, 412n
"Pole-Cat, The" (poem), I: 377n
Poles, IV: 374
Political acclaim, L. on, IV: 91
Political campaigns, *see* Political parties; *and under* Lincoln, Abraham, political career of
Political Debates between . . . Lincoln and . . . Douglas . . ., III: 510n
Political History of the United States during the Great Rebellion . . ., A (McPherson), V: 216n; VI: 245n; VII: 179n, 183n
Political institutions, the preservation of, I: 8, 108-15
Political parties, L. on: vote of opposition on party measures, I: 237-38; struggles between candidates within a party, 364-65; the role of young men in, 490-91, 497-99; adherence to party platforms, II: 2-3, III: 394, 433-34, IV: 119, 125, 201, 211-12, 223-24, 227-28, 249-50, 263; a natural division of opinion among party members, II: 126, III: 366; sacrifice of belief to party necessity, II: 322; use of money in campaigns, IV: 32; and welfare of the country, 192, 197, 199
Political prisoners, *see* Military arrests
Politicians, L. on: the general

character of, I: 65-66; and
slavery, III: 310-11; warnings
against pressure from, IV: 78,
81, 88, 92, 114, 122; and the will
of the people, 194, 197, 211, 215-
16; and office seekers, VII: 303

Polk, James Knox, I: 336n, 417-19,
420-23, 432-41, 446-48, 451-53,
457-58, 463, 476, 480-81, 485-89,
501n, 506, 508
    II: 12-13, 14, 39-41, 49, 125,
145-46, 237, 252; III: 17, 162,
183; IV: 66, 420

Polk, Leonidas, V: 31n, 458n; VII:
329n

Polk County (Tenn.), VIII: 68

Pollard, Emanuel, VII: 278

Pollock, James, IV: 165, 167, 485-
86; VII: 397n; VIII: 192n

Pollock, William, VI: 285n

Polly's Grove (S. C.), VI: 457

Polygamy in Utah, L. on, II: 399;
IV: 41-42

Pomeroy, George S., V: 68

Pomeroy, Isaac, III: 554

Pomeroy, John Means, IV: 84n,
103-104, 113n

Pomeroy, Samuel Clarke, IV:
312n, 346n, 483; V: 94, 107, 164,
193n, 371n, 414n; VI: 50n, 144n,
179, 343; VII: 4-5, 200-201, 213,
222-23, 261n, 338; VIII: 291n,
355

Pomeroy, Theodore Medad, V:
383

Pomroy, George King, V: 326-27

Pomroy, Rebecca R., V: 326-27

Ponca Indian Agency, IV: 303;
VIII: 359n

Ponca Indians, V: 106-107

Pond, Daniel B., V: 54

Pond, Fern (Nance), I: 38; II:
133n

Poolesville (Md.), IV: 560; V:
410n, 412n; VII: 294

Poor Bear (Indian), VI: 153n

Poor-House Prison (Charleston,
S. C.), VIII: 131

Poorman, Allison C., VII: 342

Poorman, Mrs. Allison C., see
Poorman, Amanda

Poorman, Amanda (Hanks), VII:
342n

Pope, Alexander, III: 472

Pope, John (1770-1845), V: 69n

Pope, John (1822-1892), IV: 327n,
344-45, 407, 411, 461, 463, 553;
V: 142, 186-87, 259n, 287, 290,
334n, 344, 366, 395, 397, 399-
400n, 402n, 403, 455n, 486n, 493,
550
    VII: 84, 235; VIII: 17n, 292-
93, 297-98, 300, 316, 320n, 342-
43, 351n, 365-66

Pope, John (b. 1830 as John Pope
Cocke), V: 68-69

Pope, Nathaniel, II: 29-30, 53-54,
72n, 78-79; IV: 327n

Pope, William, I: 393

Popular sovereignty, L. on the
doctrine of, II: 235, 238-41, 250,
265-70, 275, 399-400, 451-52,
454, 462, 486-89, 507-508, 519,
525-26
    III: 18-19, 23, 82, 86, 89-95,
276, 279, 394-95, 404-13, 416,
418, 420-30, 446-47, 457-58, 465-
69, 482-86, 488, 499-500, 538,
552; IV: 18, 21, 27, 41-42, 149-
51, 154-55

Population: mention of census
(1840, 1860), I: 258, V: 68;
Negro population, (1850 cens-
sus) II: 262, 265, (1862 ratio to
whites) V: 535; statistical report (1790-1860) with predictions through 1930, V: 533

Port Angeles (Wash. Terr.), VI:
144n

Port-au-Prince (Haiti), VIII: 167

Port Gibson (Miss.), VI: 226n, 326

Port Hudson (La.), VI: 71n, 244n,
247, 252, 254, 363-64; VII: 507;
VIII: 196

Port Leon (Fla.), VIII: 396

Port Royal (S. C.), IV: 517n, 528n,
545n, 557n; V: 26-27, 50, 70n,
127, 132, 210, 315, 389n, 445-46;

VI: 160; VII: 538n; VIII: 20, 201n, 396

Port Royal (Va.), V: 514

Port Royal Islands (S. C.), VI: 455-57

Port Townsend (Wash. Terr.), VI: 214n

Port Walthal Junction (Va.), VIII: 377n

Portage (Ohio) *Sentinel,* IV: 217n

"Porte Crayon" [pseud.], *see* Strother, David H.

Porter, (Miss), VIII: 36n

Porter, Albert Gallatin, IV: 539

Porter, Andrew, V: 82, 162n

Porter, C. L., II: 411n, 534n

Porter, David Dixon, IV: 313-15, 319-20, 351n, 366-67; V: 215, 316, 490, 509; VI: 82, 112; VII: 56-57, 63n, 242n; VIII: 187n, 285

Porter, Fitz-John, IV: 409n, 411n; V: 5n, 208-209, 244-45, 248, 292, 311-12, 370n, 385n, 398n, 407n, 415, 448, 481n, 485; VI: 54, 67; VII: 549

Porter, Frank E., Jr., II: 533n

Porter, Horace, VIII: 380n

Porter, J. & R. H., V: 451n

Porter, John F., IV: 304

Porter, Lyman, II: 411n, 534

Porter, Lyman, & Company (Mackinaw, Ill.), II: 411

Porter, Mortimer, II: 308

Porter, Reyburn, IV: 299n

Porter, William, I: 258, 264n; II: 55-57

Portland (Me.), VI: 540-41; VII: 172, 276n, 520n; VIII: 45n

Portland (Oreg.), IV: 90n

Portsmouth (N. H.), V: 13n; VII: 529, 531

Portsmouth (Va.), VI: 26n, 29, 371; VII: 135, 232n, 289n, 292

Portugal, IV: 73n; V: 141, 521; VII: 181

Portuguese, II: 225n, 298

Post, John P., V: 471n

Post, Philip Sidney, VIII: 175

Post, William B. [J.], VII: 372-73

Post Office Key . . ., III; 336n

Postlethwaite, William H., VII: 357n

Postoffice Department: L. claims (1839) misrepresentation of operating costs, I: 175-77; postal contracts, 423-30, 442-43, 455; salary of Springfield postmaster, 444-45; report on a postoffice destroyed by fire, 456-57; establishment of certain postal routes, 500; flag-raising at General Post Office Building (May '61), IV: 382-83; postal conventions with Mexico and Costa Rica, 467, V: 189-90, 312, 521; and the Chiriqui project, IV: 561; annual reports, (*1861*) V: 44-45, (*1862*) 524-25, (*1863*) VII: 45-46, (*1864*) VIII: 145; appointments, IV: 297, 303-307, 310-11, 342, 363-65, 502, V: 197, VI: 128, 137-38, 346, 425, VIII: 261-62, 330; *see also* LINCOLN, ABRAHAM, postmaster

Postoffice Mistake, The (play), VI: 559n

Poston, Charles DeBoille, VIII: 214n

Postville (Ill.), I: 130

Potawatomi Indian Agency, IV: 306

Potawatomi Indians, V: 89, 101-102; VI: 109

Poteet, ———, VII: 75

Potomac, Department of the, V: 155, 164n

Potomac Home Brigade (Md. Inf.), IV: 494n; VII: 134n, VIII: 82n

Potomac River, IV: 343, 348, 455n, 539; V: 4, 31, 34, 45, 120n, 121n, 122n, 130n, 151, 157, 184, 220n, 231, 236, 271, 284n, 293, 305, 412n, 417-18, 427n, 452n, 460-61, 477, 479, 481n

VI: 15n, 36, 47n, 218n, 250n, 257, 276, 282n, 284n, 293n, 317-

19, 321-23, 327-28, 341-42, 354, 355; VII: 238n, 285, 291n, 438, 472n; VIII: 163n, 344n
Potter, F. W., VIII: 338
Potter, Howard, VIII: 327-28
Potter, James Brown Mason, IV: 399, 403; V: 172-73
Potter, Joel A., VIII: 359n
Potter, John, I: 18
Potter, John Fox, IV: 404n, 462n, 531n, 556n; V: 25n; VI: 70; VII: 371n, 372
Potter, Joseph Adams, VI: 516
Potter, Platt, IV: 224
Potter, Royal, I: 12
Pottstown (Pa.), II: 446n
Poughkeepsie (N. Y.), IV: 228-29; VIII: 331n
Powell, ———, VI: 252
Powell, Elihu N., II: 78-79, 289, 331-32
Powell, Lazarus Whitehead, V: 127, 300; VI: 50, 85, 87; VII: 149; VIII: 219n
Powell, Lorenzo, VII: 537n
Powell, William Henry (Ill.), II: 345; III: 389
Powell, William Henry (W. Va.), VII: 537
Power, the utilization of, II: 441-42
Power, George, I: 298
Power, John Carroll, I: 116n
Powers, D. J., III: 397
Powhatan (steamer), IV: 313-15, 320n, 351n, 366
Practical Handbook for Miners, Metallurgists and Assayers (Silversmith), VII: 323n
Prairie Beacon [Paris, Ill.], II: 312n, 359n, 483
Prairie City (Ill.), II: 193n
Prairie Grove (Ark.), VI: 2n
Prairie Grove (Iowa), VI: 40n
Prall, John A., VIII: 79
Prather, Henry, II: 118-19
Prather, William, II: 119
Pratt, Alonzo D., VIII: 19n
Pratt, Harry Edward, I: vii; see

Personal Finances of Abraham Lincoln, The
Pratt, Henry S., VI: 533n
Pratt, Marion Dolores, I: xv
Pratt, Seth, I: 19n
Pratt, William H., IV: 305
Pray, ———, II: 308
"Prayer of Twenty Millions, The" (editorial), V: 388-89
Preble, George Henry, V: 215; VI: 102
Prentice, Charles, I: 67
Prentice, Clarence J., VI: 219-20; VIII: 302n
Prentice, George Denison, IV: 134-35, 184, 534n; V: 14-15, 60-61; VI: 219n; VIII: 302, 337n
Prentice, Mrs. George Denison, see Prentice, Henrietta
Prentice, Henrietta (Benham), VI: 220n
Prentiss, ———, VI: 72
Prentiss, Benjamin Mayberry, IV: 395-96, 461, 463n; V: 471n, 501n; VIII: 593-94
Prentiss, Charles W., VI: 207n
Prentiss, William, I: 211n
Presbyterians, I: 320; II: 452; III: 84, 87, 310; V: 7, 327; VII: 244-45, 531-32, 535-36; VII: 427-28
Prescott, G. L., VI: 336n
Prescott House (N. Y.), IV: 367n
President, office of: Whig proposal to limit to one term, I: 339; cost of compared to price of coal, 484; "no bed of roses," II: 89; military men not disqualified for, 146-48; and sectional candidates for, 349-52; relation to cabinet, IV: 316-17; see also President, powers of
President, powers of: and declarations of war, I: 451-52, II: 153; and legislation, I: 454, 504-505, II: 2, 5, IV: 214-15, 532; and patronage appointments, II: 60, V: 66; and acquisition of territory, III: 235; and suspension of writ of habeas corpus, IV: 390; and

promotion of generals, 411; to appoint naval academy cadets, V: 66, VI: 385-86; and settlement of land claims, VI: 402; "the law of war in time of war," 408; terms of pardons and restoration of forfeited rights, VII: 51; and Constitutional amendments, VIII: 253n; canvassing or counting electoral votes, 270-71; see also Veto power

"President Lincoln and His Happy Cabinet" (editorial), V: 225n

"President Lincoln's Visiting Card" (art.), VIII: 296n

"President's Last, Shortest, and Best Speech, The," VIII: 154-55

President's Orders: general order on rank of flag officers (Oct. '61), IV: 548; general war order no. 1 (Jan. '62), V: 111-12; special war order no. 1 (Jan. '62), 115; general war orders nos. 2 and 3 (March '62), 149-51; war order no. 3 (March '62), 155

"President's Policy, The" (art.), VII: 132-33

Press, L. and the, see Newspapers, L. and the

Preston, Finney D., II: 298

Preston, John, VIII: 68

Preston, Margaret (Wickliffe), V: 386

Preston, Samuel W., V: 389n

Preston, William Ballard, I: 517; II: 42-43, 48-49, 50, 56, 66; IV: 329-31

Preston, William C., V: 386n; VI: 265, 480

Preston, Mrs. William C., see Preston, Margaret

Preston County (W. Va.), V: 298

Prettyman, Benjamin S., II: 411

Prettyman, James S., IV: 300n

Pretzel, Nicholas, V: 261n

Price, ———, II: 410

Price, Edwin R., V: 501n; VI: 211n

Price, Margaret C., VIII: 79

Price, Philemon B., VIII: 79

Price, Sterling, IV: 538n; V: 1-2, 501n; VI: 211, 360; VIII: 57, 94, 320n

Price, Thomas Lawson, V: 543; VII: 463n

Price, Thomas W., VII: 452

Price, William M., I: 166, 177

Price, William P., VI: 2n; VIII: 73, 220n

Price, Winfred E., VIII: 234

Prichard, Frank, VI: 456

Prichard, Jane, VI: 456

Pricked Forehead (Indian), VI: 153n

Prickett, David, I: 152-53, 198n; II: 159

Priest, John W., I: 405n, 420

Priest's Oil Factory (Springfield), I: 405n

Prime, Samuel Irenaeus, V: 391

Prince, David, IV: 393

Prince, Henry, V: 410n

Prince George's County (Md.), V: 224n; VIII: 323n

Prince's Mill [now Princeville] (Ill.), I: 69

Princess Anne (Md.), VIII: 167n

Princess Anne County (Va.), VI: 26n, 29

Princess Anne election district (Md.), VII: 9n

Princeton (Ill.), II: 346-47

Princeton (N. J.), VI: 310n

Princeton University, see New Jersey, College of

Pringle, Andrew, I: 405n

Printing, L. on; expediency and costs of public printing, I: 44, 56-57, 212, 221-24, 241-42, 474, 517; one of the basic "inventions," III: 361-63

Printing office, government, V: 370n; VII: 12n

Prisoners-of-war, V: 86, 260, 264-65, 324, 332-33, 344, 369, 376-77, 381n, 403, 429-30, 432, 449, 484n VI: 99n, 202-203, 207n, 219-20, 241, 293n, 316n, 323-25, 337,

353, 357, 394, 398-99, 422, 427n, 429, 436-37, 451-52, 470n, 473n, 474n, 476n, 507-508, 510n, 513-14, 520, 522, 532, 562
  VII: 7, 12n, 30n, 34, 42, 55, 66n, 80, 87, 89, 91, 94-95, 97, 100, 103, 119-20, 129, 136, 139, 168, 171, 172n, 188, 195, 197n, 204, 244-45, 252, 254-55, 257, 260, 265, 269-70, 273, 274, 288, 289n, 291, 294, 297, 309-10, 322n, 325, 345-46, 362, 373, 391n, 406, 419-20, 425, 430, 446n, 502, 524, 530-31, 538
  VIII: 9n, 10, 13n, 14, 16, 17-18, 29n, 30, 36-37, 40, 51, 79, 82, 86, 94-95, 103, 112, 116n, 117n, 123-25, 127, 131, 133, 154-55, 160, 162-63, 165, 169n, 185, 192, 204, 218, 220, 223n, 224n, 238n, 241, 244, 259, 263-64, 287-88, 293-94, 296, 300, 302-304, 310n, 311, 314-15, 317, 322-24, 331n, 347-48, 357, 363-64, 368, 374, 377n, 380n, 382-85, 389-90, 412n, 423
Prisons, L. on: imprisonment and crime prevention, I: 169-70; interpretation of involuntary servitude, II: 22
Private and Official Correspondence of Gen. Benjamin F. Butler, cited, IV: 519n; V: 472n, 487n; VII: 203n, 207n, 289n, 292n; VIII: 163n, 174n, 186n, 368n, 395n
Privy Council for Trade, British, VII: 198
Proceedings of a General Court Martial . . . for the Trial of Brevet Major John C. Henshaw (pamphlet), IV: 287n
Proceedings of the First Three Republican National Conventions, II: 346n
Proceedings of the Massachusetts Historical Society, III: 555n
Proceedings of the National Union Convention . . ., VII: 381n
Proctor, William, II: 534

"Prophet, The" (Indian), *see* Tenskwatawa
Protective War Claim Association (U. S. Sanitary Commission), VIII: 327
Proud, Robert G., VIII: 411n
Providence (R. I.), III: 550-51, 554; IV: 352-53, 365; V: 165-66
Providence Journal, III: 551n
Providence Post, III: 550
Providence Press, III: 550
Providencia, V: 109-10
Provost, Joseph, VIII: 22-23
Prunk, Daniel H., IV: 541-42
Prussia, IV: 278n; V: 66, 102, 520, 521; VII: 72; VIII: 227n
Pruyn, Robert H., VI: 95n; VII: 39; VIII: 132n
Pryor, J. W., VII: 322
Pryor, Pleasant, VIII: 68
Pryor, Roger Atkinson, III: 431, 451-52; IV: 6-7, 23; VI: 84; VIII: 314-15, 317
Pryor, William, VIII: 68
Pryor, William S., VI: 50
Public lands: purchase of and revenue from sale of, I: 32, 48, 50n, 132-38, 147-48, 163-64, 174, 181, 307, 312-14, 329-30, 339, 469-71, II: 134-35, III: 348-49, 352-55, IV: 128-29, V: 45, 511-12, 525, VII: 46-47, 300, 515-16, VIII: 146; pre-emption, I: 308n, II: 333-35, VII: 99; military bounty claims, I: 422, 442, 446, 453, 460-61, 464, II: 27-28, 223-24, 312n, 319; school lands, I: 461, 478-79
  Use in the construction of railroads and canals, II: 26-27, 162-87, 333-35, VI: 227-28, VII: 47, VIII: 146; L.'s candidacy for land office commissioner, II: 28-29, 41, 43-44, 48-60, 67-68, 91-93, VIII: 414; procedure for procuring patents, II: 397; swamp lands, III: 352-55; canal scrip fraud, IV: 128-29; the Homestead Law, 202-203, VII: 46, VIII: 146; formation of Yank-

ton land district, IV: 325; Ill. claim to two per cent fund, V: 153-54, VI: 85, 90, 96n, 403-405, 411-12, 463; unsettled (1851) claim of land officers, V: 541-42; land grants for colleges, VI: 123-24; extent of President's duty in contested land titles, 242, 402; mentioned also, VIII: 196n
    Land office appointments: III: 107, IV: 83, 303-304, 306-308, 310, 322, 325, 349, 442, V: 316, 474n, 500, VIII: 355-56, 358-59, 363
Public office, candidates for, L. on: fitness for role of public official, I: 48-49, 167, 316, 382, 507, II: 28-29, 89, VII: 266; members of Ill. legislature not allowed to hold federal office, I: 138; election not necessarily a blanket endorsement of candidate's opinions, 504-505; effect of candidate's private business on eligibility for office, IV: 180-81, 326n, 373
Public opinion, L. on, I: 246; II: 385; IV: 3-4, 9-10, 17, 202-203, 432-33
Public Reaper [Farmer City, Ill.], II: 381n
Puckett, ——, VII: 106, 109
Puerto Rico, VI: 110n

Puget Sound Agricultural Company, VII: 76, 246-47; VIII: 140
Puget Sound District, VI: 202, 209-10, 213
Puget Sound Indian Agency, IV: 308
Pugh, Isaac C., I: 2; V: 491n
Pulaski (Ill.), *see* Mount Pulaski (Ill.)
Puleston, J. H., VII: 97n
Pulizzi, Venerando [O. Pullizi], IV: 366
Purdy, Charles A., II: 397
Puritans, Church of the (N. Y.), VI: 239n
Purnell, William H., IV: 304, 328; V: 183n; VIII: 111, 114n
Purple, Norman Higgins, I: 214-15, 327; II: 79n, 482-83; III: 325
Pursley, James M., II: 298
Purviance, Samuel Anderson, IV: 158n
Putnam, Balie, VIII: 68
Putnam, Charles, Jr., IV: 517n
Putnam, George Haven, IV: 59n, 119n
Putnam, James O., II: 249n; IV: 57, 83-84, 89, 115, 312n
Putnam, L. H., VII: 295
Putnam County (Ill.), I: 358n
Putnam County (Tenn.), VIII: 69
Putnam County (W. Va.), V: 298
Pyle, George Washington, VII: 210, 235n

Q

Quaker City (steamer), VI: 79n
Quaker Road (Va.), VIII: 377n
Quakers, II: 299; IV: 243; V: 92, 165-66, 278-79, 478; VI: 39-40; VII: 535-36; VIII: 35n, 72-73, 76, 124-25, 290, 322n
Quanders, Lawrence, VIII: 179
Quantrill, William Clarke, VI: 416n
Quapaw Indians, VIII: 399n

Queen, Walter W., V: 215
Queenstown (Canada), II: 159
Quincy, Josiah, VI: 443
Quincy (Ill.), I: 34-35, 138n; II: 284-86; III: 245-83, 298, 315; IV: 85-86; V: 540n; VI: 2n; VII: 373
Quincy Republican, IV: 348n
Quincy Whig, II: 317; cited, I: 138n, 146n, 149n, 159n, 213n, 308n, 309n, 340n, 371n, 377n, 378n, 385n, 392; II: 286n; III: 333n
Quincy Whig & Republican, V: 540n
Quinn, Martin, VII: 216
Quinton, Richard, I: 298
Quisenberry, Roger X., VIII: 86
Quitman, John Anthony, I: 450-51
Quito (Ecuador), VII: 247

R

Raaslöff, Waldemar Rudolph de, V: 162
Rabé, William, IV: 304-305
Racey, John, VII: 131
Radford, Reuben, I: 15-16, 20, 96
Rafael repeater gun, V: 365
Rafter, Lizzie L., VII: 275n
Rail, Charles E., IV: 494n
Railey, Elise C., IV: 546n
Railroads: costs and expediency of construction in Ill. (1832-1836), I: 5-6, 48, 54, 251; railroad and fund commissioners (Ill.), 122-23; and transportation of the mail, 423-30; and public lands, II: 26, 333-35, IV: 400-402, VII: 46-47, 264; Ill. law (1854) on incorporation of railroad companies, II: 212-16; proposed construction (1863) of roads concentrating on Washington, D. C., VI: 68-69; consolidation of, 287n; *see also names of individual railroads*
Railsplitter, The [Cincinnati], II: 544n
Railsplitting, L. and, IV: 48, 63, 100n

Rainese, John [alias George Rionese], VI: 414-15
Rains, James E., VI: 39n
Rains, James S., IV: 538n
Raleigh (Ill.), II: 106n
Raleigh (N.C.), V: 122n
Raleigh County (W. Va.), V: 298
Ralston, Robert, VIII: 68
Ramsay, Alexander B., *see* Kinney, Alexander B.
Ramsay, David, III: 526n
Ramsay, George Douglas, IV: 530-31, 551, 556; V: 9, 85, 172; VII: 100n, 216n, 229, 236-37
Ramsay, William, I: 254
Ramsdell, Robert A., IV: 54n; VII: 343n
Ramsey, Mrs., V: 450n
Ramsey, Alexander, V: 59, 396-97, 432n, 493n; VII: 48n, 116-17
Ramsey, Anna Maria (Breck), VII: 219-20
Ramsey, F. A., VII: 219n
Ramsey, Mrs. F. A., *see* Ramsey, Anna Maria
Ramsey, Robert Hampton, VII: 3n
Rand, Charles W., IV: 301; VI: 205-206, 322n, 333n

Randall, Alexander Williams, V: 513n; VII: 11n, 499, 501n, 506-508, 529n
Randall, Charles, VIII: 80n
Randall, James Garfield, I: xiv, xvii; V: 64n
Randall, Jonathan G., I: 210
Randall, Richard, I: 210
Randall, Samuel Jackson, VIII: 312n
Randall, William, VIII: 301, 305
Randall, William Harrison, VII: 187n, 219n, 256n, 274, 280, 291; VIII: 165, 290n
Randles, James D., VI: 23n
Randolph, Edmund Jennings, I: 502; III: 415, 523n, 526n
Randolph, George W., IV: 329-31
Randolph, John, VI: 107-108
Randolph, Willard M., VII: 221-22, 226, 253
Randolph County (N.C.), VIII: 124n
Randolph County (W.Va.), V: 298
Raneer, James, VI: 544
Rankin, David, I: 11, 19
Rankin, Henry Bascom, II: 435
Rankin, Ira P., IV: 305, 323, 345n
Rankin, J. Duffell, VIII: 68
Rankin, Nicholas A., I: 43
Rankin, William, I: 46
Ranking, James, V: 205n
Ranney, Nathan, VII: 85-86
Ransdell, Wharton, I: 122, 256
Ransom, ———, I: 324
Ransom, George Marcellus, V: 215
Ransom, Thomas Edward Green, V: 457
Rapidan River, VI: 175, 190n, 354n, 450n, 467n, 535n
Rapides Parish (La.), VIII: 14-15
Rappahannock, Department of the, V: 220n, 226n
Rappahannock River, and military operations: (spring '62), V: 118, 123n, 184, 195, 220n, 254n; 312, 382; (fall '62), 443n, 514-15; (spring '63) VI: 31, 47n, 125-26, 164, 169n, 175n,
199-200, 216, 217, 249-51, 257-58, 280n, 282n, 354n; (fall '63) 450n, 509n, 528, 535n, VII: 6-7
Rappahannock Station (Va.), V: 397n; VI: 175n, 354n, 418; VII: 6, 7n
Ratcliffe, ———, VIII: 427
Ratcliffe, Charles T., VII: 62
Rathbone, Henry Riggs, VIII: 14n, 40
Rathbone, Jared Lawrence, IV: 387n
Raub, John, I: 417n
"Raven, The" (poem), I: 377
Ravenna (Ohio), IV: 217
Rawalt, Jonas, I: 76
Rawlings, F. M., II: 298
Rawlins, John Aaron, VI: 226n; VII: 469n; VIII: 208n, 226n
Ray, Charles Henry, II: 303, 304, 444, 474n; III: 341-43; VIII: 288-89, 299
Ray, John, VII: 213
Ray, W. D., VIII: 310n
Ray County (Mo.), VII: 152n
Raymond, George B., VI: 194n
Raymond, Henry, VIII: 179
Raymond, Henry Jarvis, IV: 145-46, 156, 397; V: 152-53, 544-45; VI: 30n; VII: 490n, 494-95, 515n, 517-18, 526-27; VIII: 39-40, 87-88
Raymond, W. G., VI: 212n
Raymond (Miss.), VI: 226n
Raynor, Kenneth, IV: 164
Rda-in-yan-kna (Indian), V: 542
Rea, ———, VII: 433n
Read, George, III: 527-28, 530
Read, John M., IV: 71, 102, 127
Read, Thomas S., II: 195n
Read, William Brown, IV: 70
Reade, Philip, VI: 99
Reading (Pa.), VI: 217n, 322n
Ready, Simon, VIII: 22
Reagan, Jacob, VIII: 68
Ream's Station (Va.), VIII: 32n
Reaney (ship), VII: 37n
Reavis, C. Frank, II: 327n
Reavis, Isham, I: 83n; II: 327

"Rebecca" letters, I: 89n, 291-97, 299-301

Recollections of Abraham Lincoln (Lamon), VI: 2n; VII: 549n

Recollections of Alexander H. Stephens (Avary), IV: 160n

Reconstruction, *see* Movements to reorganize state governments *under* LINCOLN, ABRAHAM, President (1861-1865)

Record of Connecticut Men in the War of the Rebellion, VI: 232n

Record of Services Rendered the Government by B. H. Grierson in 1865, VIII: 418n

Records of Columbia Historical Society (Bacon-Foster), VIII: 423n

Recruitment, *see* Troops, mobilization and equipment

Rector, William H., IV: 407n

Rectortown (Va.), V: 251-52

"Red Jacket" (poem), IV: 48

Red Lake River (Minn.), VII: 116

Red River, II: 84; VII: 63, 213-14, 335n, 348n, 358n; VIII: 14-15, 177n, 178, 196, 595n

Red River of the North, VII: 160n

Reddick, William, II: 171, 183; III: 125

Redfield, Alexander H., V: 23

Redman, George, I: 150-51

Redmond, Charles P., VIII: 242n

Redpath, William G. L., VII: 187n

Redson, Stephen, VII: 82n

Redwood, William H., Jr., IV: 417

Reed, ———, V: 228n

Reed, Aaron, II: 167

Reed, Alexander, VI: 114-15

Reed, Amos, IV: 556n

Reed, Henry J., II: 165-68

Reed, Horatio Blake, IV: 409-10

Reed, James H., IV: 124-25

Reed, John, V: 347

Reed, John F., VI: 431n; VII: 91n

Reed, John W., I: 3

Reed, Philo E., III: 244

Reed, Robert W., VIII: 91

Reed, Silas, I: 252-53

Reeder, Andrew Horatio, II: 321; IV: 71, 167; V: 362n

Reep, Thomas P., I: 10n

Reese, A. A., V: 215-16

Reeside, James, I: 176, 443

Reeves, James H., VIII: 68

Reeves, Timothy, VIII: 102n

"Reflection" (poem), I: 378-79, 392n

Register, John, VI: 544

Register, Joseph, VI: 544

Register of Officers and Agents, Civil, Military, and Naval, in the Service of the United States [U. S. Official Register], cited in the footnotes on the ff. pages:
IV: 277, 349, 360, 441, 448, 456, 460, 462, 471, 474, 483, 485, 493, 494, 498, 502, 509, 517, 527, 528, 537, 553
V: 12, 13, 56, 93, 115, 197, 353, 370, 396, 447, 464, 472; VI: 1, 16, 21, 90, 94, 118, 120, 123, 134, 142, 214, 216, 224, 232, 233, 247, 284, 312, 313, 351, 361, 363, 425, 436, 507
VII: 166, 220, 333, 338, 392, 420, 496; VIII: 8, 157, 159, 180, 214, 215, 262, 325, 348, 355, 356, 358, 363, 370, 408, 411

Regnier, Felix, I: 150-51

Regnier, Francis, I: 151n, 322n, 348

Rehm, Charles, V: 125

Reid, Mrs. J. R., VII: 240; VIII: 57

Reid, Whitelaw, VII: 377n

Relations of the Government to the Revolted Citizens, The, V: 382n

Relay House (Md.), IV: 479

Religion, L. and: the importance of education, I: 8; his church attendance, 78, 320, 382-84: "a sacred legacy," 108; the Bible "the best cure for the blues," 261; our constitutional "guarantee of the rights of conscience," 338; replies to charges

of infidelity, 382-84; divine law and duty, II: 3; and his father's last illness, 97; the choice between good and evil, 278; Bible gives us the standard "of moral perfection," 501; pro-slavery theology, III: 204-205; applicability of Bible maxims, 462; religion and the armed forces, IV: 381-82, V: 497-98, VI: 114-15; arranges to hear a recommended sermon, IV: 445-46; "the supreme government of God," 482; "fear of the Lord is the beginning of wisdom," 482; meditation on the Divine will, V: 403-404; the "precious birthright of civil and religious liberty," VI: 39-40; "we have forgotten God," 155-56; "often wished that I was a more devout man," 535; mention of L.'s attendance at a Washington church, 536n; the Bible "the best gift God has given to man," VII: 542-43; "the sort of religion" by which people cannot "get to heaven," VIII: 154-55; see also Baptists; Bibles, L.'s; Catholics; Churches; Congregationalists; Jews; Methodists; Presbyterians; Quakers; and Unitarians

Religio-Philosophical Society of St. Charles, Ill., VIII: 103n

Remann, Frederick, II: 52

Remington, Joseph, VI: 150n

Reminiscences (Haupt), V: 400n, 401n, 402n

Reminiscences and Incidents of a Long Life (Teasdale), VIII: 363n, 365n

Reminiscences of Abraham Lincoln (Rice), IV: 76n; VI: 135n

Reminiscences of Carl Schurz (Schurz), VIII: 258n

Remount Camp (Shenandoah Valley), VIII: 317n

Rencher, Abraham, V: 354

Reninger, Mrs. H. A., III: 487n

Reno, Jesse Lee, V: 334n, 399n, 407n, 510-11

Renshaw, J. M., VIII: 395

Renshaw, William Bainbridge, V: 215

Renwick, G. W., III: 125

Reply to Breckinridge (Baker), V: 382n

Report of the Joint Committee on the Conduct of the War, cited in footnotes on the ff. pages: VI: 125, 135, 209, 244, 280

"Report on the Transportation, Settlement, and Colonization of Persons of the African Race" (Smith), V: 48n

Republican, The (Jarvis), II: 516

Republican Party: L. deterred from joining, II: 288; call for county conventions (1856, 1857), 340, 424-25; fragment on the foundation of, 391; and apportionment bill, 504-505; the essential "difference" between Democratic and Republican parties, III: 91-93; call for Springfield convention and meeting (1859), 372, 377; the "original and chief purpose of," 404, 425, IV: 256-57; first known use of elephant symbol, IV: 91n; estimated electoral vote (1864), VIII: 46; see also LINCOLN, ABRAHAM, political career of; and Abolitionism

Requa, Abram, VI: 562

"Return, The" (poem), I: 378-79, 385-86, 392n

Retz, Charles, VI: 137n

Retz & Storm, catalog cited, VIII: 191n

Revenue Act of 1852, V: 333n

Revenue and expenditures (Ill.): charges of wasteful expenditures (1834), I: 31; sale of public lands, 32, 47, 48, 50, 132-38, 147-49, VI: 85, 90, 96n, 403-405, 411-12, 463n; on expendi-

tures for public printing, I: 44, 212, 221-24; estimated state budgets (1836, 1837), 45, 74; on public depositories, 134; on new revenue law, 147-49; payment of state debt, 215-21, 243, III: 381-83, 392; sale of state bonds, I: 238; the "Rebecca" letter, 291-97; mobilization and recruitment (1861-62), V: 153-54

Revenue and expenditures, national: L. charges Van Buren administration with extravagance, I: 172-79; use of tonnage duties for improvement of harbors, 486-87; analysis of government expenditures for 1850 and 1851, II: 154-56; offshore collection of duties (1861), IV: 290, 292-93; reports in annual messages, *(1861)* V: 39-40, 44-45, *(1862)* V: 522-24, *(1863)* VII: 41-42, *(1864)* VIII: 142-44; foreign loans, V: 73-74, 109, 281-82, VII: 285, 347; transmits to Congress report on foreign systems of finance, V: 181; on Congressional resolution to issue additional U. S. dollars, VI: 60-62; *see also* Bank, national

Revenue Law of 1839 (Ill.), I: 147-49

Revolution, American, I: 112, 114-15, 181-82, 278-79; II: 115-16, 370-71; IV: 433-35; V: 373, 502-503; VII: 337n; VII: 147, 222n

Revolution, the right of, L. on, I: 114-15, 278, 438-39; II: 115-16, 153

Reynolds, Edward M., VIII: 170

Reynolds, Francis, V: 79n

Reynolds, George A., VIII: 355n

Reynolds, Hugh W., II: 396

Reynolds, James, I: 249

Reynolds, John, I: 10n, 149n, 233, 314; III: 105, 122, 172, 175

Reynolds, John Fulton, IV: 494; VII: 88

Reynolds, Joseph Jones, IV: 404-405, 463; V: 481n; VIII: 228-29, 288n

Reynolds, Thomas, IV: 182

Reynolds, William M., III: 394-95

Reynoldsburg (Tenn.), VII: 478n

Rhea County (Tenn.), VIII: 68

Rheim, William C., VII: 371

Rhett, Robert Barnwell, I: 489

Rhine (French steamer), VIII: 259

Rhoads, Calvin B., VII: 216

Rhoads, Franklin L., I: 418-19

Rhode Island, IV: 352-53; V: 361; VIII: 100n, 129-30, 150, 153

Rhodes, ———, VII: 540n

Riblett, Henry, II: 298

Rice, Alexander Hamilton, VIII: 95-97, 352n

Rice, Allen Thorndike, see *Reminiscences of Abraham Lincoln*

Rice, Clement T. [W.], V: 316n; VII: 371

Rice, Clement W., VII: 371

Rice, Clinton, VII: 314

Rice, E. C., II: 357n

Rice, Elliott Warren, VII: 379

Rice, Henry Mower, IV: 446; V: 55, 455; VIII: 121

Rice, John F., VII: 274

Rice, John Hovey, VII: 92

Rice, Thomas, VIII: 165

Rice, William C., II: 298

Rice, William T., IV: 460n

Richard III (play), VI: 392

Richards, ———, I: 284

Richards, Guy, II: 198

Richards, Nathaniel, II: 198

Richardson, A. D., VI: 241

Richardson, Cornelia (Sullivan), I: 495-96

Richardson, George H., VIII: 372n

Richardson, Harriet F., I: 455n

Richardson, Hiram, VII: 536n

Richardson, Israel Bush, IV: 499; V: 70n, 159, 256n, 360, 510-11; VII: 454, 549

Richardson, James Daniel, see *Compilation of the Messages*

and Papers of the Presidents,
1789-1897
Richardson, John M., IV: 283
Richardson, Joseph, VII: 96, 104
Richardson, Oliver Hazard Perry,
IV: 349
Richardson, Orla [Orlu] Col-
burn, VIII: 191n
Richardson, William, VIII: 168n
Richardson, Mrs. William, VIII:
168
Richardson, William Alexander,
I: 417, 432, 438, 447-48, 495-96;
II: 405; IV: 86, 505
Richardson, Mrs. William Alex-
ander, *see* Richardson, Cornelia
(Sullivan)
Riché, George Inman, VII: 430
Richland (Ill.) I: 10n
Richland Creek (Ill.), I: 39, 85
Richmond, Dean, VI: 552n
Richmond, Henry, II: 298
Richmond, James Cook, VI: 226-
27
Richmond, John P., II: 298, 303
Richmond, Thomas, II: 298
Richmond, William B., IV: 313,
397n, 478, 498n
Richmond, William W., IV: 313n,
397, 478n, 498
Richmond (Ill.), I: 82
Richmond (Ky.), V: 401-402;
VII: 219-20
Richmond (Me.), VIII: 411n
Richmond (Va.): L.'s objections
(1848) to contract for transporting mail to Washington, I:
423-29; references to 1852
speech of Douglas in, II: 135,
138, 141, 144, 154, 156; mentioned as the Confederate capital, IV: 427; arrests of loyalists, 469n, V: 221, VI: 128n,
241, VIII: 162n, 182n, 216; Villard offers to bring information
from (Aug. '61), IV: 484n;
prisoners-of-war in, 492, V:
86n, VII: 119-20, 244-45, 252,
257, 310, 502, VIII: 16n, 117n,
185n; requests for passes and
communication with, IV: 525n,
VII: 525n, VIII: 161, 185n, 198,
200n, 292n, 395, 409-410, 416;
and L.'s and McClellan's plans
for the Army of the Potomac
(Dec. '61, Feb. '62), V: 34, 122n,
123n
  Military operations: *(spring
'62)* V: 184, 210, 216, 219n,
226-27, 231-33, 236, 240, 244-45,
249, 269, 271, 276-78, 284n,
287-93, 295, 301, 304, 305,
307n, 311, 322-23, 355-56,
360; *(fall '62)* 460-61, 499,
514-15; *(spring '63)* VI: 164-66,
169n, 173n, 175n, 190n, 198,
202-203, 207, 218n, 233, 249n,
257-58, 285n, 293, 354n; *(fall
'63)* 399n, 466-68, 476, 510n,
529n, 534-35; *(spring '64)* VII:
222n, 393n, 396, 406n, 453n,
456n; *(fall '64)* 521-22, 547,
VIII: 29n; *(spring '65)* 377n,
378n, 384-86
  City newspaper reports on
action at Vicksburg, VI: 43, 83,
210, 226; capture of city not as
important as destruction of
Lee's army, 47n, 257, 467; report of visit of French minister
to (Apr. '62), 99; city newspaper scorns "Lincoln's cow-
ardice," VII: 303; unofficial
peace missions to (July '64),
429n, VIII: 188n, 275; city
newspapers' report of U. S.
naval expedition to Florida
(Oct. '64), VIII: 94; mention
of delegation to Hampton
Roads conference, 286n; Grant
reports on city newspaper bulletins (Mar. '65), 329; and
suspension of Treasury trade
permits, 343-45, 353n; L.'s
visit to (1865), 374n, 387-88,
413n
  L. on the possible assembly
of Va. legislators (Apr. '65),

VIII: 389, 405-408; blockade lifted, 396; mentioned in L.'s last public address, 399; resumption of church services (Apr. '65), 405-406; L. orders special boots for wounded Confederate soldier, 425

Richmond & Fredericksburg Railroad, V: 219n, 227n, 244, 249; VI: 468n

Richmond Dispatch, VI: 252

Richmond Enquirer, II: 364, 369, 385; III: 205, 431, 451, 549n; IV: 6, 23; VI: 247n

Richmond Examiner, V: 308; VI: 43n; VIII: 163n, 200n

Richmond, Fredericksburg and Potomac Railroad, I: 423n

Richmond Sentinel, VI: 247; VII: 226, 522n; VIII: 183n

Richmond Whig, VI: 166-67; VIII: 216n

Richstein, William F., V: 394

Rickard, John, I: 206

Rickard, Noah M., I: 206, 267

Rickard, Sarah A., I: 258, 267n, 268, 282

Ricketts, James Brewerton, VII: 437

Riddell, John L., VII: 71n, 186n

Riddle, Albert Gallatin, VIII: 224n

Riddle, George Read, VIII: 292n

Ridgefarm (Ill.), VIII: 290n

Ridgely, Charles, IV: 139-40

Ridgely, James L., IV: 523; VII: 75-76; VIII: 348

Ridgely, Nicholas H., I: 400, 420, 491n; II: 340, 411n, 425n, 434-35; IV: 139-40

Ridgely, Reddick, I: 491

Ridgeville (Md.), V: 412n, 481n

Ridgeway, Charles S., IV: 362

Ridgeway, Elizabeth, *see* Corneau, Elizabeth

Riell, Robert, VI: 432n

Rienzi (Miss.), V: 546n

Rifferd [Rifford, Riffert], Emanuel, V: 202n, 211n

Riggs & Company (Washington), V: 154; VI: 380

Rightmyer, J. L., IV: 167

Riker, John L., IV: 406

Riley, Edward, II: 320n

Riley, Hugh F., VIII: 274

Riley, John C., I: 67

Riley, Joseph [alias], *see* McNulty, John

Riley, Lawrence, VI: 279

Riley, Matthew, VII: 306n

Riley, William H., VII: 133n

Riney, Zachariah, IV: 61

Ringgold, James, VII: 74n

Ringgold, Samuel, II: 85

Ringgold, William, VI: 195n

Ringgold (Ga.), VII: 540n; VIII: 262n

Ringgold Barracks (Tex.), VII: 90n

Ringo, Alvin, I: 52-53

Rio de Janeiro (Brazil), IV: 310; V: 162

Rio Grande del Norte, I: 421, 433-38, 446, 473, 494; II: 84; IV: 66; V: 357, 358n; VI: 355n, 366n; VII: 90n

Rionese, George [alias], *see* Rainese, John

Riotte, Charles N., IV: 397n

Ripley, George B., V: 17n, 366

Ripley, James Wolfe, IV: 362, 415-16, 419, 505n, 520, 530, 540; V: 18, 75-76, 172n, 189, 192, 196-97, 219n, 225n, 257; VI: 343n

Ripley (Ohio), VII: 314n

Risley, Hamilton D., II: 113-14

Risley, Hanson A., VIII: 88, 110, 185-86, 199-200, 209-210, 221, 300, 330, 337, 354n

Ritcher, ———, V: 473

Ritchie, Margaret, *see* Stone, Margaret

Ritchie County (W. Va.), V: 298

Ritter-Hopson Galleries, V: 483n; VI: 462n

Rivas, José María, V: 475

Rivas, Rafael, VI: 57

River and Harbor Convention, (Chicago), I: 395
River Queen (steamboat), VIII: 283-84, 286n, 372n, 373n, 375
Rives, George W., II: 46, 69, 443
Rives, John C., I: 38; V: 405
Rives, William Cabell, I: 165
Rives, Wright, V: 405
Roads (Ill.): establishment of, I: 17, 21, 24, 26, 32-36, 39-40, 42, 45-46, 52-54, 60, 69-72, 79, 82-83, 85-87, 93, 182-83; road tax (1836), 50-51; procurement of road scrapers, 50-51; Springfield and Alton Turnpike Company, 250-52
Roaman, John Henry, VII: 513
Roane County (Tenn.), VIII: 68
Roane County (W. Va.), V: 298
Roanoke Island, V: 132n, 134, 305n
Robb, Allen, VIII: 68
Robbins, Silas W., II: 310
Robbins, Z. C., II: 32, 36
Robert Henry Hendershot; or, The Brave Drummer Boy of the Rappahannock (Dodge), VII: 249n; VIII: 195n
Roberts, Arch W., II: 374n
Roberts, Benjamin, I: 211
Roberts, Benjamin Stone, V: 283, 340; VI: 195n
Roberts, D. L., II: 180
Roberts, E., II: 374n
Roberts, Edmund, I: 67
Roberts, Mrs. Isaac G., VII: 187n
Roberts, James (Ill.), II: 411
Roberts, James (Tenn.), VIII: 70
Roberts, Joseph, VII: 341, 344, 357-58, 359-60; VIII: 34, 162-63
Roberts, Joseph Jenkins, V: 373
Roberts, M. J., VI: 155n
Roberts, Marshall O., VI: 112n; VII: 363
Roberts & Company, II: 184
Robertson, Benjamin C., VII: 130
Robertson, George, II: 317-19; V: 104n, 502-503, 512-14

Robertson, Mrs. Max, V: 200n
Robertson, Richard, IV: 445n
Robertson County (Tenn.), VIII: 69
Robinson, A., VII: 193-94
Robinson, Arnold R., I: 490
Robinson, Charles, V: 71n
Robinson, Charles D., VII: 499-502
Robinson, Christopher, IV: 396-97
Robinson, Daniel, I: 52
Robinson, Edward, I: 298
Robinson, Mrs. F. de L., II: 59n
Robinson, Gilbert P., VIII: 76
Robinson, James Carroll, VII: 202n
Robinson, James F., V: 384n, 387n, 419n, 426n, 513n; VI: 42, 141n, 147n, 200n
Robinson, James T. [F], VII: 265
Robinson, John Cleveland, V: 187
Robinson, John M., VI: 37
Robinson, John McCracken, I: 221n
Robinson, Richard M., IV: 542n
Robinson's Mill (Sangamon County, Ill.), I: 82
Roby, Charles, VI: 513n
Roby, Charles O., VI: 513
Roche de Boeuf (Kans.), V: 288
Rochester, William Beatty, V: 385n
Rochester (Ill.), I: 85
Rochester (N.Y.), IV: 222
Rochester (Pa.), IV: 208
Rock, George [alias], *see* Brown, George
Rock County (Wis.), III: 484
Rock Creek (Sangamon County, Ill.), I: 44, 128
Rock Island (Ill.), II: 105, 314; III: 377, 544n; IV: 297; VI: 161n, 182, 386; VII: 172n, 274, 288, 530-31; VIII: 14n, 17n, 40, 127n, 165, 191n, 348n, 359
Rock Island & Alton Railroad, II: 521n
Rock Island Argus, VI: 162n

Rock Island Bridge case, II: 413, 415-22
Rock Island Railroad, II: 189-90, 521n
Rock Island Register, III: 377n
Rock River (Ill.), II: 337
Rock River Seminary (Mt. Morris, Ill.), VIII: 343n
Rock Spring (Ill.), I: 472
Rock-a-to-wha (Indian), IV: 401
Rockcastle Hills (Ky.), V: 22n
Rockefeller Foundation, I: xiv
Rockford (Ill.), II: 315; III: 58-59, 239, 258; VI: 346n; VIII: 330n
Rockhill & Wilson (Philadelphia), VII: 442
Rockingham County (Va.), I: 456, 459; II: 218; III: 511; IV: 37, 60, 117; VII: 295
Rockport (Ind.), I: 341-42; IV: 85
Rockport Herald, I: 342n
Rockville (Md.), V: 410, 412; VII: 438
Rockwell, John A., II: 189-91
Rockwell (N. J.), I: 359
Rocky Mountains, VII: 122n; VIII: 146
Roden, George, IV: 552-53
Roden, Hugh, IV: 552-53
Rodes, Robert E., V: 120n
Rodgers, Harris G., IV: 555n
Rodgers, James B., VII: 65
Rodgers, John, V: 207n; VII: 57
Rodgers, John B., V: 333
Rodgers, William H., VII: 522n
Rodgers, William, & Company (Knoxville, Tenn.), VII: 409
Rodman, Thomas Jefferson, IV: 520n
Roe, Edward Reynolds, II: 75; VIII: 88
Roe, Francis Asbury, VII: 360
Roescher, Charles, VI: 336n
Rogers, ―――― (Md.), VIII: 158
Rogers, ―――― (Tex.), V: 492n
Rogers, Alfred, VI: 544
Rogers, Andrew F., VII: 260

Rogers, Anthony Astley Cooper, VII: 199n, 334-35; VIII: 324
Rogers, C. M., V: 195n; VIII: 311n
Rogers, Cannady, VIII: 68
Rogers, Henry Munroe, V: 480
Rogers, John, VII: 389
Rogers, Newton, VI: 544
Rogers, Reuben, VIII: 68
Rogers, S. W., VIII: 179
Rogerson, William, VIII: 309n
Rogersville (Tenn.), VII: 5-6, 520n
Rohrer, ――――, VII: 456
Rohrer, Daniel, III: 397
Rolla (Mo.), IV: 513n, 563n; V: 1-2, 314-15, 351n, 459n; VI: 106n, 218n; VII: 224, 237
Rollin, Frank A., VIII: 273n
Rolling Fork (Ky.), IV: 61
Rollins, ――――, II: 207-208
Rollins, Edward Henry, IV: 516; VII: 322; VIII: 413
Rollins, Hiram, VI: 352n
Rollins, James Sidney, IV: 473n; V: 152n, 391n; VI: 37-38, 51n, 100, 133-34, 360; VII: 189n
"Romance of Reality, A" (art.), IV: 104n
Rombauer, Sophie, II: 503n
Rome (Ga.), VI: 214n; VIII: 10n, 27n, 120n
Rome (Papal States), IV: 293; V: 521
Romero, Matías, IV: 177-78; VI: 66n, 548-49
Romney (W. Va.), V: 234n, 247n
Ronckendorff, William, VIII: 133
"Ronins" (Japanese revolutionary faction), VIII: 45n
Rooks, Elizabeth, VI: 443
Roosevelt, Robert Barnwell, VII: 4-5
Roosevelt, Theodore, Sr., VIII: 327-28
Roorke, Barney, *see* Rourke, Barney
Root, Adrian Rose, VI: 88
Root, James P., III: 202n
Root, Newell W. [alias George H. Harris], VIII: 235, 237

Root, Thomas M. [J. M.], VIII: 324-25, 347n

Rose, David G., V: 275n

Rose, Edward W., VIII: 69

Rose, Hiram, II: 481

Rose, Joseph Holt, V: 22n; VII: 294n; VIII: 303n

Rose, Randolph, I: 2

Roseburg Land Office, IV: 407n

Rosecrans, William Starke: appointed Brigadier General, IV: 407, 463; reports lack of officers to train raw troops (1861), 481n; and appointments, 492, VI: 117, 138-40, 148-49, 393n, 428; and duty assignments, IV: 560n, VI: 104, 136-37, 168n, 229, VII: 198; arrests, courts-martial and dismissals, V: 69n, VI: 224-25, 296, 297, 324, 442, VII: 252, 354, VIII: 4-5, 102, 116, 122, 159-60

Military operations: *(fall '62)* V: 478, 483-84, 497n, 545n; *(Jan.-Mar. '63)* VI: 39, 101, 108-109, 142n, 147n; *(May-July '63)* 233, 236, 331n, 350n, 352n; *(Aug.-Oct. '63)* 373, 377-78, 394n, 424-25, 462, 469-76, 478, 480-81, 483-86, 494n, 498, 503, 505, 510-11, 528; *(fall '64)* VIII: 57, 97

Assumes command of the Department of the Cumberland and the Fourteenth Corps, V: 501n; appointed a Major General, VI: 138-40; complains of criticism of his army policy in Tenn. (Apr. '63), 186; ordered to take Vallandigham beyond military lines, 215n; endorses clergyman's proposed peace mission to the South, 225, 236; and pressure for a command for Frémont (May '63), 230; mention of Ohio as his home, 304n; requests publication of his report on battle of Chickamauga, VII: 14; replaces Schofield in command of the Department of Missouri, 14n, 78, 84n, 157-58; and disturbed conditions in Mo. (1864), 179n, 182-83, 283-84, 310-11, 337, 407, VIII: 156n; and the use of colored troops, VII: 198n, 284; and expediency of constructing railroad from Rolla to Springfield (Mo.), 224, 237-38; warns L. of plot to overthrow the government, 379, 386-88, 436; and election (1864) in Mo., VIII: 24-25; relieved of command of Department of Missouri, 166n; mentioned also, VII: 206

Rosenbach Company, The, I: xiv; MSS owned by, noted in footnotes on the ff. pages: I: 156, 209, 452, 456, 460; II: 41, 43, 49, 56, 69, 78, 120, 357, 391; III: 349, 379; IV: 58, 69, 115, 147, 280, 333, 337, 340, 361, 364, 396, 408, 464, 477, 503, 545; V: 70, 143, 221, 338, 447; VI: 247, 361, 376, 461; VII: 122, 303, 386, 455, 534; VIII: 108, 136, 236, 335, 380, 388; see also *The History of America in Documents*

Rosenberg, ——, VI: 180

Rosengarten, J. G., VIII: 312n

Rosenkrans, Omar L., VIII: 368n

Rosette, John E., II: 389-90

Ross, ——, V: 473

Ross, Frederick A., III: 204-205

Ross, G. W., VIII: 68

Ross, John (chief of Cherokees), V: 415-16, 439-40, 456; VII: 196n

Ross, Lewis, VII: 196n

Ross, Lewis Winans, I: 230-32; II: 192-93; III: 515

Ross, William, I: 146n; II: 410, 434

Ross, William A., III: 372-74

Ross, William J., IV: 356n, 358

Ross, William W., V: 89, 101-102; VI: 109

Rosser, C. P., II: 107

Rossiter, Luther, VII: 28n

Rouke, *see* Rourke, Barney
Round Valley Indian Reservation (Calif.), IV: 326n
Rourke, Barney, VIII: 240-41
Rouse's Point (N. Y.), V: 503
Rousseau, A. V. D., II: 192n
Rousseau, Lovell Harrison, IV: 411, 499; V: 283; VI: 352n, 394-95; VII: 242n, 288n; VIII: 259n
Routt, John L., VI: 352n
Rowan, Stephen Clegg, V: 316; VI: 112
Rowland, Smith & Company, I: 335
Rowley, George Augustus, V: 362, 369-70, 457-58
Roxbury (Mass.), V: 406
Royal College of Surgeons (Dublin), V: 79n
Rubery, Alfred, VII: 71-72
Ruby, Joseph, VII: 216
Ruby Valley (Nev.), VII: 112
Ruckel, Daniel E., II: 109, 188, 201, 422; V: 157
Ruckel, Jacob, II: 422-23; IV: 189
Ruckel, Mrs. Jacob, *see* Ruckel, Laura A.
Ruckel, Laura A., II: 422-23
Rucker, Daniel Henry, V: 390n; VI: 197n; VIII: 75
Rucker, G., II: 310
Ruff, Charles Frederick, IV: 551-52
Rugg, George H., II: 382n, 426-27, 436-37; III: 384-85
Ruggles, James Monroe, II: 296, 380
Ruggles Mills (Ky.), VI: 225n
Rumsey, John, II: 173
Runk, Charles M., VII: 371
Rural Hotel (Springfield, Ill.), I: 87n
Rush, Richard, II: 351
Rush Medical College (Chicago), II: 24n
Rushville (Ill.), III: 329
Rusk, Thomas Jefferson, I: 435n
Rusling, Robert, V: 376n
Russell, Abraham D., V: 5

Russell, Alexander L., V: 414-15
Russell, Alfred, VI: 119-20
Russell, Caleb, VI: 39-40
Russell, Charles G., VII: 321-22
Russell, Charles H., IV: 375-76
Russell, Ira, V: 15
Russell, John Henry, V: 215
Russell, John L. [T.], IV: 349
Russell, Lord John, IV: 376-77; V: 62-64, 115; VI: 89n; VIII: 373-74
Russell, Mary Todd, *see* Wickliffe, Mary Todd
Russell, Tip, VI: 544
Russell, William H., V: 73
Russell, William Hepburn, IV: 281
"Russell fraud," IV: 281; VII: 246
Russell, Majors & Company, IV: 281n; VII: 246n
Russellville (Ill.), I: 85-86
Russellville (Tenn.), VIII: 111n
Russia, II: 115; IV: 293, 310, 347n, 348, 378; V: 23, 96-97, 114n, 137, 240n, 368, 425n, 521; VI: 104n; VII: 39n, 93; VIII: 138, 181n
Ruth, Reuben Francis, II: 188
Rutherford, ———, IV: 496
Rutherford County (Tenn.), VIII: 69
Rutledge, Anna Mayes, I: 60n; IV: 104n
Rutledge, David Ham, I: 12, 16-17; II: 108
Rutledge, Mrs. David Ham, *see* Rutledge, Elizabeth
Rutledge, Elizabeth, II: 108n
Rutledge, James, I: 4, 13-14, 17-18
Rutledge, John, III: 531-32
Rutledge, John M., I: 12
Rutledge, Mary Middleton, *see* Fogg, Mary
Ruwitch, R. S., IV: 496n
Ryan, ———, I: 290; II: 92
Ryan, Daniel Joseph, III: 437n
Ryan, J. W., VII: 322n
Ryan, Maggie K., VIII: 15-16
Ryder, Simeon, I: 332
Ryerson, Henry O., VII: 159

S

S. B. Carson (steamboat), II: 419, 421

Sabine (steamer), IV: 424, 465n; V: 154n; VII: 520n

Sabine Cross Roads (La.?), VIII: 48n

Sabine Lake, VI: 366n

Sabine Pass (Tex.), VI: 366n; VII: 489; VIII: 103

Sabine River, I: 434; II: 84

Sac and Fox Indian Agency, IV: 306; VII: 69; VIII: 339n

Sac Indians, I: 152; II: 319; V: 189, 307; VII: 69-70

Sack, Christiana A., VII: 356

Sack, Henry, VII: 356-57, 359-60

Sacket, Delos Bennet, IV: 489

Sacramento (Calif.), IV: 304; VIII: 146

Sacramento Valley, VII: 122

Saeger, Henry J., VII: 369n

Saginaw (Mich.), VIII: 220

Sailor's Creek (Va.), VIII: 390-91

St. Albans, Duchess of, II: 482n

St. Albans (Vt.), VIII: 141n, 208-209

St. Augustine (Fla.), V: 167; VIII: 396

St. Bernard Parish (La.), VI: 29

St. Charles Hotel (New Orleans), VI: 288n

St. Charles Parish (La.), VI: 29

St. Domingo, see Santo Domingo

St. Elizabeth Hospital (Washington), VI: 227n

St. Francis River, VI: 340n; VIII: 288n

St. Helena, IV: 509; V: 85n

St. Helena (Ark.), see Helena (Ark.)

St. Helena (S. C.), VI: 453-59

St. Helenaville (S. C.), VI: 455

St. Helenaville County (S. C.), VI: 455

St. James Parish (La.), VI: 29

St. John's (Fla.), VIII: 396

St. John's College, VII: 462n

St. John's Parish (La.), VI: 29

St. Joseph (Mo.), III: 506; VI: 543-44; VII: 78, 337n; VIII: 176, 205, 210n

St. Joseph Free Democrat, III: 506n

St. Joseph Tribune, VII: 197

St. Leonard's Landing (Md.), VI: 530n

St. Louis (Mo.): mention of circuit court, I: 88; L. describes (1838) rule by mob law in, 109-10; competition with Alton lead trade, 190-91; effect of Springfield and Alton R. R. on costs of trade with Springfield, 396-97, 403; mention of Whig speech on Mexican War, 447; mention of an old French settlement near, II: 231; the original territory of, 235, 250; L. describes his steamboat trip (1841) from Louisville to, 320; Chamber of Commerce promotes case against Rock Island Bridge Co., 415n; troubled conditions in, IV: 369n, 372, 485, 529-30, 550n, V: 502, VI: 218, VII: 84; Congressional committee investigates war contracts in, IV: 560, V: 20; Halleck assigned to, V: 21-22; martial law authorized, 27; settlement of claims against and military seizure of bank funds, 57-58; transfer of an officer and regiment from, 177-78, VII: 11n; control of churches and loyalty of ministers, VI: 20n,

VII: 85-86, 178-80, 182-83;
Herndon offered "job of about a
month's duration" in, VI: 111;
L.'s memo on patronage in, 178;
banishment of persons from,
219, 223, VII: 310-11, VIII: 351;
and the cotton trade, VI: 307n,
VII: 78; courts-martial, VI:
392, 562n; hospital chaplaincy
vacant at, VI: 421n; newspaper
publication of L.'s letter to
Conkling "botched up," 430n;
lithographer sends L. example
of his work, VII: 106n; recognition of Belgian consul with-
drawn, 352; Hay receives report of Vallandigham case at,
386-88; salute to victories ordered at, 532; Third Na-
tional Bank authorized to receive subscriptions to Union
Pacific R. R. stock, VIII: 192-93;
Ewell's wife detained in, 372;
mentioned also, I: 303, V: 411n,
VIII: 57, 78, 292; *see also* Mis-
souri; *and* Mississippi Valley
Sanitary Fair
St. Louis County (Mo.), VI: 37;
VIII: 297-98, 342-43
St. Louis Intelligencer, II: 212n;
III: 433
St. Louis Republican, see *Mis-
souri Republican*
St. Mark's (Fla.), IV: 389; VIII:
396
St. Martin Parish (La.), VI: 29
St. Mary's (Fla.), V: 167
St. Mary's (Ga.), VIII: 396
St. Mary's County (Md.), VI:
530n
St. Mary's Parish (La.), VI: 29
St. Matthew's Academy, VII: 309n
St. Matthew's Colored Sunday
School (Washington), VII: 419n
St. Nicholas Hotel (N. Y.), VI:
552
St. Paul (Minn.), IV: 87n; V:
397n, 551
St. Paul Pioneer Press, V: 288n

St. Paul's Church (New Orleans),
VII: 247-48
St. Paul's Episcopal Church
(Springfield), I: 331n
St. Peter Land Office, VII: 515;
VIII: 363n
St. Petersburg (Russia), V: 240n,
425n; VII: 93n
St. Thomas (Danish West Indies),
VI: 349; VIII: 271n
Ste Genevieve (Mo.), III: 456
Salem (Ill.), I: 146
Salem (Mass.), IV: 123n
Salem (Oreg.), IV: 90n
Salem (Va.), VI: 441-42
Salem (Ohio) *Republican*, IV:
215n
Salesbury, *see* Salisbury, S. John-
son
Salgar, Eustorgio, VII: 37n; VIII:
6-7
Saline County (Ill.), II: 106
Salisbury, A. J., *see* Salsbury, A. J.
Salisbury, David L., VI: 246n
Salisbury, S. Johnson, VI: 194
Salisbury (Ill.), I: 206-207
Salisbury (Md.), VII: 10n
Salisbury (N. C.), V: 429; VIII:
117n
"Sally Brown" (song), II: 157
Salmon, Alexander, IV: 553n
Salm-Salm, Félix, Prince de, IV:
524n
Salomon, Frederick, V: 221
Salsbury, A. J., VI: 422n
Salt Creek, I: 21, 24, 28-29
Salt Lake City (Utah Terr.), II:
398n; IV: 558; VI: 518n, 526n
Salt Lake Land Office, IV: 308
Saltillo (Mexico), II: 86
Saltmarsh, Orlando, I: 442-44
Salvador, *see* El Salvador
Sambo (slave), III: 204
Samnites, V: 122n
Sampson, George R., VIII: 137n
Sampson, William, I: 9
"Sampson's Ghost" [pseud.], I:
89n, 100
Sams, Thomas M., II: 298

Samuel, Mrs. Dillard Estep, I: 4n
Samuels, Abraham, VIII: 162-63
San Diego (Calif.), IV: 305
San Domingo, *see* Santo Domingo
San Francisco (Calif.), IV: 305, 363, 386n, 500; V: 521; VI: 206n, 325n, 333; VII: 71n, 158
San Jacinto (steamer), V: 64n, 82, 115, 137, 154n, 539
San Joaquín (Calif.), IV: 304
San José (Costa Rica), V: 312
San Juan (Nicaragua), VIII: 137
San Juan River, VIII: 137
San Marino, Republic of, IV: 360
San Pedro (Calif.), IV: 305
San Román, Miguel [de], VI: 124, 213
San Salvador, *see* El Salvador
Sanborn, Anson L., VI: 362n, 505
Sanborn, John Benjamin, VI: 493n, 495n
"Sandbar case," II: 430-31
Sandburg, Carl, VI: 227n; see also *Abraham Lincoln: The War Years;* and *Mary Lincoln, Wife and Widow*
Sanders, Alvin, *see* Saunders, Alvin
Sanders, George N., VII: 436n, 441n, 443n
Sanders, Rufus K., V: 543
Sanderson, John Philip, IV: 166, 174; VII: 198, 386n
Sandford, Charles W., IV: 385n; VI: 453n
Sandford, D. R., II: 312-13
Sandford, James S., II: 308
Sandford, Sylvanus, II: 312-13
Sands, Alexander C., VI: 376
Sands, George W., VIII: 348
Sands, Nathaniel, VII: 5
Sands, Thomas, VI: 548
Sandusky (Ohio), V: 300; VII: 171; VIII: 259n
Sandwich Islands, *see* Hawaiian Islands
Sandy Hook (N. J.), VII: 264n, 424

Sanford, Edward Sewall, V: 290n; VI: 389-91
Sanford, Henry S., IV: 138-39; VI: 271; VII: 87
Sanford, James T., VI: 112n
Sangamo Journal [Springfield, III.], I: 5n, 22, 25, 31n, 47-48, 50n, 61n, 80, 87n, 88n, 89n, 93, 95n, 101-106, 108n, 123n, 127n, 149n, 153n, 156n, 158n, 159n, 197n, 201n, 203n, 207n, 208n, 210n, 212n, 215n, 219n, 225n, 228n, 229, 230n, 231n, 232n, 239n, 240n, 241n, 242n, 244n, 259n, 262n, 264n, 269n, 271n, 282, 290, 291n, 292n, 299n, 300n, 302n, 309n, 318, 322n, 326n, 333n, 335n, 337n, 338n, 341n, 353-54, 358n, 359, 363, 371n, 393n, 395n, 405n, 492n; III: 203n; see also *Illinois State Journal*
Sangamo Town (Ill.), I: 26; IV: 63
Sangamon & Morgan Railroad, I: 399-400; V: 386n; *see also* Northern Cross Railroad
Sangamon County (Ill.), I: 48-50, 55-60, 72, 120, 139n, 142, 144, 148-51, 155, 209, 213, 287, 297-99, 357-58; II: 340, 424-25; III: 381; IV: 63, 64; VIII: 429
Sangamon County Commissioners' Court, I: 3, 17-18, 21, 24-26, 47, 50-54, 79, 116
Sangamon Fire Insurance Company, I: 43-44
Sangamon River, I: 6-7, 13n, 35, 40, 85; IV: 63, 64
Sangster, George, VI: 136
Sangster's Station (Va.), V: 120n, 121n, 399n
Sanitary Commission: references to the work of, IV: 469, VII: 167, 362n, VIII: 54-55, 298n, 327; fund drive for, IV: 543; L. donates autographs and copies of addresses and Proclamations for sale at fairs, V: 341n, 433n,

VI: 30n, 497n, 539-40, VII: 21n, 22n, 53n, 135n, 220, 343, 369; replies to invitations to attend fairs, VI: 539-40, VII: 323-24, 353, 354, 365-66, 390, VIII: 171; gifts sent to L. from fairs, VII: 75, 258n, 278n, 442, 458, 529; L.'s remarks at fairs, 253-54, 301-303, 394-97; mentioned also, V: 201, 512n, VI: 53n, 394n, VII: 12, 316n, VIII: 106n, 122n

Santa Anna, Antonio López de, I: 434-36; II: 86

Santa Barbara (Calif.), IV: 304

Santa Clara County (Calif.), VI: 205-206

Santa Fé (N. M. Terr.), IV: 307, 349; V: 475n; VI: 124n

Santa Fé Indian Agency, IV: 307, 349

Santa Rosa Island (Fla.), IV: 315, 365

Santiago (Chile), VII: 143

Santo Domingo, III: 540n; IV: 316, 318n, 446; VI: 110n; VII: 164; VIII: 138

Saratoga Springs (N. Y.), VI: 402n; VII: 474

"Saratoga Water Cure," VIII: 98n

Sar-cox-ie (Indian), IV: 401

Sarcoxieville (Mo.), IV: 400

Sardinia, Kingdom of, see Italy

Sargent, Aaron Augustus, V: 500n

Sargent, Horace Binney, IV: 186

Sargent, Josiah M., VII: 67n

Sargent, Nathan, I: 417; III: 387-88; IV: 117, 137, 363-64; V: 89, 451n

Sargent, Porter, II: 298, 303; III: 65

Sarragossa, see Zaragoza (Spain)

Sartain, John, IV: 102n, 127n

Sartori, Edmund, VI: 92

Sassacus (ship), VII: 360

Satterlee, John, IV: 296, 302n

Saulsbury, Willard, VIII: 292n

Saumenig, Charles, VIII: 76

Saunders, Alvin, IV: 298, 337n

Saunders, Charles R., IV: 488, 501-502

Saunders, E. D., VIII: 252n, 312n

Saunders, J. R., II: 71

Saunders, James, VI: 336n

Saunders, Presley Asbury, I: 297

Savage, George, VII: 318

Savage, Joseph L., VII: 318n, 409-10

Savage, Thomas, VII: 399-400

Savannah (Ga.), IV: 479n; V: 50; VIII: 51n, 181-82, 201n, 227, 238, 290, 321n, 331, 344n, 396

Savitz, George F., IV: 547

Sawyer, ———, VII: 355

Sawyer, Llewellyn, VIII: 233n

Sax-cox-ie, see Sar-cox-ie

Saxcoxieville, see Sarcoxieville

Saxton, Rufus, V: 227n, 234, 237-38, 245, 247, 250-52; VI: 98, 150n, 208n; VII: 385-86; VIII: 273n

Sayers, Charles, VIII: 69

Scal, J. Coleman, VI: 430n; VII: 118n

Scally, John, VIII: 76n

Scammon, Eliakim Parker, V: 398n

Scammon, Jonathan Young, I: 340n; II: 383n; III: 381n

Scates, Walter Bennet, VI: 44n, 48-49; VII: 277; VIII: 369-70

Scayne, William, VIII: 70

Schaadt, David, VI: 191-93

Schaefer, Louis, VI: 300-306

Schaerff, John W., VII: 105-106

Schalowsky, Peter, VI: 356

Schaffer, see Shaffer, Simon J.

Scheil (Scheel), see Schiel

Scheldt dues, VII: 37, 87; VIII: 203-204

Schell, Augustus, V: 70

Schell (John or Frederick), see Schiel

Schenck, James Findlay, VI: 299n

Schenck, John S., VI: 59n, 537n

Schenck, Robert Cumming, II: 53, 77-78; IV: 43, 99-100, 136, 449-50, 463; V: 271-72

VI: 86, 90, 195, 203n, 233-34, 238-39, 251n, 253n, 259n, 274, 299, 308-309, 317, 323-25, 329, 345-46, 378, 427n, 434-35, 437, 461-62, 482, 529n, 530, 532, 541-42, 555-58
VII: 4n, 9n, 26-27, 88, 197n, 262, 276-77, 319, 321n, 326-27; VIII: 360n, 408-409

Schenectady (N. Y.), IV: 224

Schenectady Evening Star, IV: 224n

Schermerhorn, Mrs., V: 106n; VII: 278

Schermerhorn, F. Augustus, V: 106n; VII: 278

Schermerhorn, Isaac M., VII: 546; VIII: 1-2

Schiel, Frederick E., VII: 177n

Schiel, John, VII: 177n

Schlater, C., II: 19

Schleich, Newton, IV: 451n

Schleidu, R., VI: 51n

Schley, Frederick, IV: 304; VII: 477n

Schley, James M., VII: 477n

Schmedding, Felix, VII: 354

Schmolz, William, IV: 305

Schneider, Isaac, V: 429

Schoepf, Albin, V: 21-22

Schofield, John McAllister, V: 61-62, 203, 347, 548
VI: 210, 218n, 234, 253, 289, 291, 325n, 326-27, 338, 343-44, 396n, 402, 415-16, 418, 423-24, 489, 492-93, 495, 498-503, 526-28, 543-45, 546n, 556n
VII: 8, 10, 61-62, 78-79, 84-85, 161, 172n, 409n; VIII: 24-25, 35n

Schools, land grants for, I: 461, 478-79; VI: 123-24

Schouler, James, I: 519n; III: 555n

Schouler, William, I: 516, 518-19; II: 25; IV: 370n; VIII: 116

Schramm, John H., VIII: 127

Schroeder, Herman, II: 444n

Schuckers, Jacob W., VII: 201n

Schufeldt, ———, IV: 310

Schumacher, John, VII: 468

Schurz, Carl, IV: 50, 78-79, 88, 144, 280, 293, 367-68, 371-72, 388, 406; V: 274-75, 493-95, 509-11; VI: 5, 43n, 55, 79-80, 93, 168; VII: 243-44, 262-63, 466; VIII: 257-58

Schurz, Mrs. Carl, *see* Schurz, Margarethe (Meyer)

Schurz, Margarethe (Meyer), V: 493

Schuyler, Phillip C., VIII: 339

Schuyler Citizen [Rushville, Ill.], II: 538n, 541n; III: 329n

Schuyler County (Ill.), I: 31, 34-35, 41-42

Schwartz, Adolph, VI: 44n

Schwartz, Jacob, VI: 519

Schwinge River, V: 132n

Sconce, J. A. D., II: 210

Sconce, Mrs. J. A., II: 210

Sconce, Lafayette H., II: 430n

Scotia (steamer), VII: 468n

Scott, Alpheus, VI: 336n

Scott, Charles H., VII: 375

Scott, Dallas, I: 85-86

Scott, Dred, *see* Dred Scott case

Scott, Mrs. Dred, *see* Scott, Harriet

Scott, E. R., VIII: 285

Scott, Edward, VIII: 80n

Scott, Harriet, III: 544n

Scott, John M., III: 374

Scott, John S., IV: 326-27

Scott, Joseph R., V: 546n

Scott, Otho, IV: 356n, 358

Scott, Robert E., IV: 155n

Scott, S. E., III: 520-21

Scott, Thomas A., IV: 464n, 471, 476n, 525, 537n, 557n; V: 6n, 28-29, 99, 231, 382n; VI: 493-94

Scott, W. T., V: 142n

Scott, William Henry Harrison, VI: 444

Scott, Winfield: and the Mexican War, I: 381, 441, 457; support for his presidential nomination

(1848), 467; presidential candidate (1852), II: 135-59, III: 78, 85, 119, 170, IV: 67; and military action in the event of secession and seizure of Southern forts, IV: 137, 157-59, 172-73, 175, 277, 279-80, 285n, 331, 423-24; mentioned for L.'s cabinet, 155n; arrests, courts-martial, leaves of absence, and discharges, 286, 372n, 373n, 503, 529, 554, VI: 442n; and appointments, IV: 287, 304, 356, 362n, 389, 394-95, 398n, 404n, 407, 411-12, 451, 472n, 480n, 489, 511, V: 12, VIII: 416; and the Fort Pickens expedition, IV: 315n, 320n, 465n

L. asks for daily reports from (1861), IV: 316, 338, 348; his opinion on appointment of a commanding officer for the D. C. militia, 334-35; and the movement of troops through Baltimore (1861), 340-41; his instructions from L. on the expected assembly of the Maryland legislature (Apr. '61), 344; authorized to suspend the writ of habeas corpus, 347, 414, 419, 429, 554; suggests Potomac R. patrol for protection of the White House, 348; and mobilization and recruitment, 355, 370n, 375, 500, 525; L. suggests a proclamation of reassurance to people of Alexandria and Arlington, 385; L. asks his cooperation in removing Cameron's objections to Meig's appointment as quartermaster general, 394-95; his opposition to a command for Hooker (1861), 412-13; and Frémont's assignment to command in the West, 420; reports action near Martinsburg (July '61), 419; L. introduces to crowd at a review of N. Y. regiments, 441-42; not enthusiastic over use of balloons for military observation, 460; orders arrest of Baltimore police commissioners, 462n, 523

Suggests assignment of Wool to Fort Monroe (Aug. '61), 478; Villard recommended to him by L., 484; and Frémont's requests for men and arms (Aug.-Sept. '61), 485n, 510; replies to complaints of atrocities committed by Union marauders, 502; Hunter relief of Frémont in Western command, 513n, 549n, 562n, V: 2n; receives report on number and placement of Frémont's forces, IV: 524; requested by L. to suggest a form of recognition for gallantry in the battle of Springfield, Mo., 526-27; and Va. loyalists appeal for salt, 536; receives report of Zollicoffer at Cumberland Gap, 541; L. commends work of Sanitary Commission to, 543; his retirement, V: 9-11, 50-51; declines appointment as additional minister to Mexico, 138; report of West Point conference (June '62) with L., 284; asked to preside at N. Y. meeting honoring Grant, VII: 374n; his nephew paroled in his custody, VIII: 285, his promotion of employment for disabled and discharged war veterans, 327-28

Scott County (Ill.), I: 354, 357-58, 380
Scott County (Tenn.), VIII: 68
Scott's Dam (Va.), VI: 200n
Scott's Infantry Tactics, II: 149
Scovel, James M., VI: 191n, 425n; VII: 238; VIII: 113, 329
Scrapbook, L.'s, III: 347, 372-74, 510n; IV: 88

Scrap Book on Law and Politics, Men and Times (Robertson), II: 319n

Scribner, Benjamin Franklin, VII: 144n

Scribner's Magazine, VII: 102n

Scribner's Sons, Charles (N. Y.), V: 352n

Scripps, John Locke, II: 471; III: 330, 332; IV: 60-67, 77; VII: 104, 423-24, 453

Scroggin, John, I: 206

Scroggin, Thomas J., I: 206-207

Scroggs, Gustavus Adolphus, IV: 471; VII: 170-71

Sealey, George H., VI: 75n

Sears, Henry, I: 150

Seaton, William W., II: 24; V: 306n

Sebastian, William King, VI: 358-59; VII: 335n

Sebastian Gabriel, Infante of Spain, V: 133

Sebastopol (Russia), II: 485-86

Sebring, William H., VI: 562

Secession, L. on: pre-inauguration warnings (1861) of the threat of, III: 351n, IV: 137, 139-42, 150n, 151n, 155n, 163n, 175n; the right of a state to secede from the Union, IV: 154, 158, 232-33, 240-41, 252-59, 264-65, 267-70, 287, 345, 355-56, 422-23, 426-28, 432-37, VI: 27-28, 263; "the proper mode of dealing with," IV: 164-65, 195, 208, 254-55, 329-31, 387, 407n; the Constitution and the Union, 168-69; the impossibility of compromise, 175-76; removal of secessionists from government employ, 333; the legality of the Secession Act, VII: 6-7, 55, 132

Secessionville (S. C.), VI: 35n

Secor & Company (N.Y.), VI: 112n

Sectionalism, L. replies to accusations of, II: 138-40, 344-45, 349-54, 359, 364-65, 367, 371-72, 450, 513, 526; III: 224-26, 396, 535-50, 551-54; IV: 1, 7-8, 26-28, 82, 274-75, 288-90

Sedalia (Mo.), IV: 563n; V: 1-2

Sedgwick, Charles Baldwin, VII: 369

Sedgwick, John, IV: 505n; V: 256n; VI: 196, 198, 200n, 342n; VII: 7, 133, 140, 152, 159, 174, 178

Seehorn, Eli, II: 298

Seeley, Aaron, VI: 452-53

Segar, Joseph Eggleston, V: 507-508; VI: 132, 186-87, 419, 434

Seidel, Gustavus A., V: 257n

Seine, La (French ship), VI: 105n

Select Papyri in the Hieratic Character, VI: 10n

Selkirk & Sons, Benjamin J., V: 22n

Sells, Elijah, VIII: 325n

Selma (Ala.), VII: 89n; VIII: 336

Selvage, Edwin, VI: 452

Seminole Indian Agency, VIII: 355n, 398n

Seminole [Florida] War, I: 174-75; II: 84; IV: 448; V: 455n

Semple, James, I: 381

Semple, O. P., VII: 321n

Senate: L. convenes special sessions of, *(Mar. '63)* VI: 111n, 120-21, *(Feb. '65)* VIII: 304; and rejection of nominations made by the Chief Executive, VI: 158-59; *see also* Congress

Senate, L. runs for, see *Campaign of 1854* and *Campaign of 1858* under LINCOLN, ABRAHAM, political career of

Senate, messages to, reporting or transmitting reports on: Fort Sumter, IV: 299; instructions to U. S. ministers on the rebellion, 462; imprisonment of a navy lieutenant, 465; determining military rank by lottery, 470; brigadier general appoint-

ment for Lane, 473-74; courts of inquiry reports, V: 70, 198-99, VIII: 324; arrest of slaves in D. C., V: 72; foreign intervention in Mexico, 109, 234, VI: 66-67, 105, VII: 265-66, 365, 394, VIII: 259-60; navy promotion, retirement, and commendations, V: 127-28, VI: 91, 111-12, 116-17, VII: 56-57, 360, VIII: 133-34, 345; presentation of Americans to the French Court, V: 130; withdrawal of Scott's diplomatic appointment to Mexico, 138; New Granada claims, 140-41, VII: 415; Paraguay claims, V: 144, 161, 260; French railroad system, 156-57; imprisonment of Stone, 201, 204; claims from Indian uprisings, 204-205; Ky. arrests, 227, VIII: 250

Circulation of bank notes in D. C., V: 282-83; army medical service, 302; postponement of adjournment (1862), 325-26; seizure of French minister Fauchet, 547-48; Indian uprising in Minn., 550-51; navy dismissals, VI: 1, 102-103; seizure of foreign consul's property in New Orleans, 16; blockade runners, 79, 102; Japanese contracts for war materiel, 95-96; death of American general in China, 96; French ambassador's visit to Richmond, 99; foreign proposals for ending the Civil War, 101-102; number of quartermasters and paymasters in Volunteer force, 116; correspondence with workingmen in England, 121; national fast day (1863), 155-57; a contested seat, 358-59; civilian government employees, VII: 70; Confederate prisoners-of-war, 123; help of U. S. citizens in Chilean disaster, 143; pursuit of hostile

Indians, 160; prisoner-of-war exchange, 168; prohibition of slavery, 172n; construction of the Union Pacific R.R., 233-34

Negro colonization, 241, 417-18; sale of Indian lands, 246; Hampton Roads conference, 286-87; appointment of generals, 311; territorial development, 322-23; Negro soldier rights, 332; Bolivia-Chile war, 338-39; Kans. Indian refugees, 341-42; organization of a free state government in Ark., 388n; trial of William Yocum, 389-90; appointment of a D. C. judge, 408-409; maltreatment on ships between N. Y. and Aspinwall, 415; recruitment of U. S. troops in foreign countries, 415-16; slave trade, 422; nomination of Chase for Chief Justice of the Supreme Court, VIII: 154; British aid to Confederates, 157-58; Navy defense of lakes, 206; judiciary appointments, 242-43; regulations for compensated plantation labor, 317; "in relation to certain railroads," 346; appointment of a N. Y. revenue collector, 350-51; see also Congress, messages to; Treaties and agreements; and Treaties with Indian tribes

Senate Executive Documents, cited in footnotes on the ff. pages: IV: 462, 465, 467, 474; V: 35-40, 44-45, 47-48, 54, 70, 83, 96, 102, 130, 137, 141, 151, 157, 171-72, 193, 197, 204, 214, 215, 227, 240, 265, 283, 328, 331, 419, 548, 551; VI: 16, 19, 65-66, 76, 79, 89, 95, 102, 121; VII: 59, 77, 123, 143, 148, 160, 168, 187, 199, 323, 365, 390, 394, 422; VIII: 158, 260, 287, 296-97, 317, 332

Senate Executive Journal, cited in footnotes on the ff. pages: IV:

288, 299, 313, 395, 445, 453, 470;
V: 109, 138, 141, 143, 144, 219;
VI: 1, 91, 93, 94, 102, 103, 112,
116, 117, 135, 231; VII: 68, 69,
70, 113, 117, 215, 261, 284, 299,
311, 345, 360, 389, 403, 407, 408;
VIII: 133, 134, 167, 220, 242,
322, 345, 351
Senate Journal, cited, V: 72n,
234n; VII: 246n, 415n; VIII:
153n, 414n
Senate Reports, cited, IV: 485n,
495n, 499n, 533n; V: 158n,
395n, 399n
Seneca Indians, VII: 27n
Sengstack, Charles P., IV: 555n
Sennitt, S., I: 2
Senter, George B., IV: 188; VIII:
347n
Sequatchie County (Tenn.), VIII:
68
Serrell, Edward Wellman, VII:
221
Servant, Richard B., I: 60-61,
146n, 253; II: 42
Seven Days' Battle, V: 381n; VII:
166n
Severson, B., V: 177n
Sevier County (Tenn.), VIII: 68
Sewall, Hartley W., VII: 497n
Seward, Anna M. (Wharton),
VIII: 334n
Seward, Clarence A., IV: 525
Seward, Frederick William, IV:
262n, 317n, 421n, 504; V: 299,
383n, 433n; VII: 296, 400n,
537n; VIII: 195n, 412n
Seward, Mrs. Frederick William,
see Seward, Anna M.
Seward, William Henry: and L.'s
candidacy for General Land
Office commissioner, VIII: 414;
Democrats attack his position
on the slavery question (1852-
1860), II: 136, 140-41, 156-57,
345, III: 53, 170, 321, 406, 408,
426-27, 431, 438-39, 451, 464,
(*see also* the "irrepressible conflict" *infra*); his candidacy for
Republican nomination for
president (1856), II: 342-43;
his attitude toward L.'s candidacy for the Senate, 457; his opposition to the Toombs bill, III:
198-99; his candidacy for Republican nomination for president (1860), 434, 517, 542n,
IV: 36, 44-47, 50n, 55, 57n, 58n,
78; the "irrepressible conflict,"
IV: 3, 6, 9, 12, 17, 23, 50; visits
L. in Springfield (May '60),
57n, 71n; and his 1860 campaign speeches in the West, 86-
87, 126-27

The formation of L.'s cabinet
and his appointment as Sec.
of State, IV: 147-49, 164, 170-
71, 173, 176, 180, 248, 273; his
proposed legislation to enforce
the Constitution's fugitive slave
clause, 157n, 158-59, 176n; in-
forms L. of rumored plot to
seize Washington before 1861
inauguration, 170-71; advised of
L.'s position on extension of
slavery (Feb. '61), 183; requested by L. to oppose appointment of a military commander
for Tex. (Mar. '61), 248; his
suggested revisions of L.'s first
inaugural address, 249-62,
271n; on expediency of attempt-
ing to provision Fort Sumter,
284-85; and the Fort Pickens
expedition, 302n, 314n, 315, 320;
"Some Thoughts for [L.'s]
Consideration," 316-18; and
Weed's complaints of being in
L.'s disfavor, 337; replies to
Baltimore complaints of passage
of Union troops through the
city, 341n; and proffered services of a Pinkerton detective,
353; his instructions to Adams
on U. S. position toward foreign
recognition of the Confederacy,
376-80; concurs with L.'s request for legal opinion on exec-

utive power to suspend writ of habeas corpus, 390, VI: 368-69, 444n; mobilization and recruitment, IV: 398, 459n, V: 291-94, 297n, 338n, VII: 416n; asked to attend conference on assignment for Frémont (July '61), IV: 419-20; his revisions of L.'s special message to Congress (July '61), 421-41; visits Fort Corcoran (July '61), 458; reinstates arsenal employee listed as disloyal by Congressional investigating committee, 530-31; L. suggests release of imprisoned Ky. Governor Morehead, 549, V: 81; expresses L.'s thanks for Presbyterian support, V: 7n; and spy cases, 8, VIII: 226n; and compensation for seizure of British ship *Perthshire*, V: 38; and the arrest of Vallandigham, 66, VI: 215; and a proposed scheme to offset British demand for the surrender of Mason and Slidell, V: 83; advised by L. not to show Illinoisans any special considerations, 102

And N. Y. *Herald* speculation on cabinet reception of Hunter proclamation (May '62), V: 225-26; authorizes arrest of Md. judge, 285n; military bulletins from L. addressed to him at N. Y. (June '62), 291-96; drafts call for troops following N. Y. conference with Union Defense Committee (June '62), 294n, 297n; and the Emancipation Proclamation, 337n, 433n, VI: 24n, 26n, 30n, 120n; and the draft, V: 338n, VI: 444n; furnishes L. with translation of Count Gasparin's letter supporting administration policies, V: 356n; recommends sending "paroled troops" to Utah, 432n; and the removal of McClellan from command of the Army of

the Potomac, 485n; L. refuses to accept his resignation, VI: 9n, 11n, 12-13; supports admission of W. Va. to the Union, 17n; suggests legislation authorizing appointment of "consular pupils," 19; advises L. on executive power to appoint acting heads of departments, 35n; and proposed contracts for the Isle à Vache colonization of Negroes, 41-42, 178-79; transmits to L. British workingmen's resolutions supporting administration's policies, 65n, 89n

And unauthorized peace missions, VI: 99n; opposes calling extra session of Senate (Feb. '63), 110; and 1863 elections in N. H. and Conn., 112n; supports marque and reprisal bill, 126; attends L.'s interview with Indian chiefs, 152n; disagrees with Welles on question of opening mail found on captured vessels of neutral powers, 183-84; and the reestablishment of state government in La., 289n; and the question of receiving Stephens as an emissary from Jefferson Davis (July '63), 315n, 317n; and Welles' criticism of his policy toward Britain and prize courts, 342, 349, 378-80; alarmed by French "effort to get Texas," 355n; military bulletins from L. addressed to him at Auburn, N. Y. (Nov. '63), 554, 562; estimates Republican strength in N. Y. state, 562n; export of tobacco dependent upon his regulations, VII: 8; communications from L. reporting military action (Nov. '63), 29-30; requests report of losses from fire in American embassy in Japan, 39n; receives report of discovery of gold in Ariz., 40n

His nephew accused of involvement with blockade runners, VII: 87n; and order for observance of mourning for Caleb Smith, 118-19; receives plea of Miss. woman for protection of her property, 131n; application for a passport, 167; Swayne bas-relief heads of L. and cabinet members donated to Christian Commission Fair, 187n; and L.'s request for a pardon for William Yocum, 256n; charged by Cameron with presidential ambitions, 289n; military bulletin from L. addressed to him at N. Y. (Apr. '64), 294; his position on retaliation of Fort Pillow massacre, 329n; receives letter on Ark. politics (May '64), 334; spurious L. proclamation published in N. Y. newspapers purported to be countersigned by him, 348; Welles discounts charges of a political conspiracy with Weed, 410n; and the reestablishment of telegraphic communication with Sandy Hook (July '64), 429; approves deposit of appropriations to encourage immigration, 489n; and the 1864 elections, 514n, VIII: 43n, 49n, 52, 102

And Henry J. Raymond's plans for a peace conference, VII: 517n; receives Washington serenade, VIII: 4n; the resolution of Navy and War Departments' difficulties over exchange of naval prisoners, 37n; and plan for government purchase of American-built Japanese gunboats, 45n, 132n; military bulletins from L. addressed to him at Auburn, N. Y. (Nov. '64), 91, 94, 97; Welles' report of his position on L.'s order re cotton trading, 93n;

favors suggestion for U. S. purchase of controlling interests in Southern newspapers, 114; L.'s summary of his report on foreign affairs (Dec. '64), 136-39; appeal from wife of Belgian consul at Atlanta for help in communicating with her husband, 244; and the Hampton Roads peace conference, 250-52, 256, 265, 279-84, 286-87; and amnesty oath records, 270; and special parole for a prisoner-of-war, 302n; his attendance at the inaugural ball (1865), 334n; request for a pass, 354; visits City Point, 379; military bulletin from L. addressed to him at Fort Monroe (Apr. 1, '65), 380-81; suggests bringing government papers to L. at City Point (Apr. '65), 387; injured in riding accident, 388, 389n, 412n

Communications referring matters to his attention and routine departmental business, IV: 276-77, 355, 419, 454, 466, 511, 540, 551, V: 73, 144, 167, 188, 335, VI: 93, 258, 294, 459, VII: 471, VIII: 168, 251, 354; calls for cabinet meetings, IV: 416, 419, V: 144, VI: 110-11, VII: 330, VIII: 412; presents foreign ministers to L., V: 17, 18n, VI: 549n, VII: 383n, 474n; absent from cabinet meeting, V: 486n

See also Seward, William Henry, and appointments; Seward, William Henry, documents countersigned by; and Seward, William Henry, and L.'s replies to Congressional resolutions requesting documentation on

Seward, William Henry, and appointments: IV: 57, 71, 276, 280-83, 292-93, 297-98, 302-303, 310-

11, 334n, 336-37, 347-48, 357-59, 362, 397, 418, 445, 447, 460, 471, 475, 478, 481, 483, 490-91, 493-94, 504, 509, 511, 514, 521, 525, 527-28, 536-38, 540, 547, 551, 553, 559

V: 5, 8, 12-13, 27, 32, 56, 62, 73, 76, 85, 97-98, 106n, 107, 114, 147, 158, 161, 173-74, 178-79, 182, 187, 339, 366-67, 383, 391, 394n, 403, 405, 411n, 447n, 451, 467, 476, 491n, 492

VI: 51-52, 58, 69, 77, 92, 173n, 174, 195, 429, 494, 507

VII: 166, 188, 238, 356-57, 370-71, 375, 403, 407, 408-409, 498, 511n

VIII: 181, 195-96, 247, 337, 360, 416-17, 426

Seward, William Henry, documents countersigned by: IV: 332, 339, 347, 354, 360, 365, 414, 417, 419, 468, 483, 488, 490, 546, 552, 554

V: 6, 19, 35, 75, 105, 118, 126, 128, 133, 136, 186, 199, 211, 223, 341-42, 363, 392-93, 436-37, 440, 449, 470, 483

VI: 19, 30, 45, 95, 121, 124, 136, 156, 160, 162, 171, 179, 181, 183, 204, 213, 222, 260, 272, 278, 333, 358, 388, 452, 479, 497, 524

VII: 56, 73, 110, 111, 165, 193, 231, 270, 283, 337, 352, 373, 427, 432, 434, 449, 475-77, 479, 494, 504, 551

VIII: 53-57, 84, 115, 172, 209, 304, 350, 360, 397-98

Seward, William Henry, and L.'s replies to Congressional resolutions requesting documentation on: Spanish conquest in the Dominican Republic, IV: 446n; London International Industrial Exhibition, 450-51, V: 47, 88; development of northeastern fisheries, IV: 453-54; position of foreign powers on maritime rights and the insurrec-tion, 459-60, 462; Confederate imprisonment of loyalists, 469; trade with foreign countries and the blockade, V: 55-56, 109-10, 162, 199, 520, 539, 547-48, VI: 79, VII: 187-88, VIII: 140n; foreign intervention in Mexico, V: 61, 188, 230, 234, 257, 281-82, VI: 38-39, 66-67, 90, 105, VII: 359, 365, 394, VIII: 259; fortification of north-east seacoast and lakes, V: 74; coolie trade, 79; the *Trent* af-fair, 82, 95-96, 102, 115, 137, 141; a postal convention with Mexico, 113; presentation of American citizens to the court of France, 130; settlement of Granadian claims, 140-41; Portuguese plans to increase cotton culture in Africa, 141; analysis of French railroad sys-tem, 156-57; salaries of territo-rial officials, 171; commerce treaty with the Ottoman Em-pire, 176; treaty with Britain for suppression of slave trade, 186, 265; arrest of Cameron, 193-94; maltreatment of Amer-ican missionaries in Egypt, 229; claims of U. S. citizens on Paraguay, 260

Status of U. S. relations with foreign powers (July '62), 319; arrest of Confederates in Tan-gier by U. S. consul, 549; Library of Congress acceptance of British Museum gift of books, VI: 9-10; "the subject of Con-sular Pupils," 19; regulations for consuls assigned to Turkey, 76; construction of Japanese warships in the U. S., 95-96; reports death of American general in China, 96n; visit of French minister to Rich-mond, 99; foreign proposals for ending the war, 101-102; ex-pression of gratitude for relief

to "distressed operatives in Blackburn, England," 121-22; regulation of diplomatic and consular systems, VII: 59, VIII: 331-32; number and salaries of civil employees of the government, VII: 70; extinguishment of Scheldt Dues, 87; Peruvian claims, 88; report of American visitor to Hamburg International Agricultural Exhibition, 140; help of Americans in Chilean church fire, 143; control of hostile Indians on Canadian border, 160; reciprocity treaty with the Sandwich Islands, 169

British gift in gratitude for American sea rescue, 198; rumored plan for establishment of monarchical governments in Central and South America, 265-66, 359, 365; acceptance of British naval officers' gift in gratitude for medical treatment in U. S. naval hospital, 311; condition of affairs in Nev. Terr., 322-23; Bolivia's declaration of war upon Chile, 338-39; delivering up Spanish fugitives from justice in the absence of extradition treaty, 370, 399-400; appointment of a D. C. justice of the peace, 408-409; maltreatment of persons aboard ships plying between N. Y. and New Granada, 415; foreign recruitment for U. S. military services, 415-16; slave trade, 422; aid furnished rebellion by British subjects, VIII: 157-58; "Naval armament on the Lakes," 206; "case of the French war transport steamer *Rhine*," 259-60; acceptance of British gift in gratitude for aid to disabled vessel, 271; the Hampton Roads peace conference, 286-87; Norwegian and Portuguese International Expositions, 296

Seward, William Henry, Jr., VI: 562n

Sewell's Point (Va.), V: 209n

Sexton, Orville, II: 469

Seymour, Mrs. Arthur, II: 224n

Seymour, Edward, II: 224

Seymour, Horatio, V: 491n; VI: 145-46, 184, 211, 256-57, 282-83, 331n, 361-62, 369-70, 381-82, 389-92, 412-13, 416-17, 435, 508, 533, 551-52; VII: 32, 210, 274, 332n, 424n; VIII: 109, 226n, 321n

Seymour, L., VIII: 185-86

Seymour, Thomas H., VI: 113n

Seymour, Truman, VIII: 391-92

Shackelford, James M., IV: 498; V: 142n; VI: 346n, 470n

Shaffer, Hamel, VIII: 239, 263n

Shaffer, Mrs. Hamel, *see* Shaffer, Nellie O.

Shaffer, John Wilson, IV: 55, 553, 563n; V: 428n, 487n; VII: 59n, 207

Shaffer, Nellie O., VIII: 239n

Shaffer, Simon J. [alias Samuel Jefferson], VIII: 263

Shaffer, T., VII: 457

Shaffer, William F., IV: 294; VI: 197-98; VII: 371

Shakers, VII: 485-86

Shakespeare's plays, L. on, II: 384; VI: 392-93, 558-59

Shaler, Alexander, V: 60

Shandy, ———, VIII: 421

Shanghai (China), V: 38n

Sharp, B. W., VI: 359n

Sharp, Miss E., VII: 305

Sharp, Edward Everett, IV: 473; V: 152

Sharp, Granville, II: 482

Sharp, Solomon, VII: 311

Sharp, William H. [N.], IV: 305; VII: 497n; VIII: 242n

Sharp, William S., V: 376n

Sharpe, George H., VI: 534-35

Sharpe, H. D., III: 344

Sharpe, Kate, VI: 444

Sharps' rifles, VI: 395n
Sharpsburg (Md.), V: 427, 442
Sharpshooters, V: 431; VI: 97n; VIII: 100n
Shaw, Calvin P., VII: 314n
Shaw, George W., II: 310
Shaw, Hiram, IV: 557
Shaw, Hiram, Jr., VII: 136n, 169n
Shaw, Josiah, VIII: 42
Shaw, M. C., I: 2
Shawnee and Wyandot Indian Agency, IV: 306
Shawnee Indians, VII: 261
Sheahan, James Washington, III: 515; VI: 251-52
Shear, Lorenzo C. [alias], *see* Stewart, Lorenzo C.
Sheehan, James A., IV: 368
Sheffield, Alonzo, VII: 328
Sheffield, Mrs. Alonzo, *see* Sheffield, Mary
Sheffield, Mary, VII: 328n
Shelby, Alfred, VI: 148n
Shelby, Isaac, VI: 148n
Shelby, Joseph O., VIII: 220
Shelby, Susan, *see* Grigsby, Susan
Shelby County (Ill.), I: 72, 140, 146
Shelby County (Ky.), VI: 428
Shelby County (Tenn.), VIII: 70
Shelbyville (Ill.), I: 324; II: 359
Shelbyville (Ky.), I: 495
Shelbyville (Tenn.), VII: 242n, 288n
Sheldon, George D., VIII: 93n
Shelledy, Garland B., I: 271n
Shelledy, Garland B. (1842), I: 270-71
Shelton, Charles M., VII: 138-39
Shelton, Philo S., VIII: 137n
Shenandoah, Department of the, V: 287
Shenandoah River, V: 236, 258n, 264, 267, 269
Shenandoah Valley, V: 230-40, 244-58, 264, 267-75, 409-10, 452n, 460; VI: 309n, 509n; VII: 445, 466n, 472n, 476n, 547, 548n; VIII: 74, 82n, 316-17

Shepard, John B., VII: 213
Shepherd, Annie P., VII: 419-20
Shepherd, Frank P., VII: 419
Shepherd, James, I: 298
Shepherd, Oliver Lathrop, IV: 409
Shepherdstown (Va.), V: 249n
Shepley, George Forster, V: 342-43, 462-63, 504-505; VI: 365, 405; VII: 1, 89-90, 114n, 248n, 416; VIII: 34n, 245, 255, 400n, 406n
Shepley, John R., V: 177
Sheppard, Justus B., VI: 554
Sheppard, S. R., I: 2
Shepperd, A. H., I: 497
Sherberne, William L., *see* Shurburne, William L.
Sherburne, John P., V: 320
Sherer, Edward, VI: 403
Sherfy, C. M., III: 203n
Sheridan, Philip Henry, VII: 439, 476, 537n, 548; VIII: 13, 29, 50, 58, 73-74, 297-98, 300-301, 316-17, 320, 376n, 379-83, 385-87, 389, 392
Sherman, Charles E., VII: 376n
Sherman, Charles T., VII: 451; VIII: 39
Sherman, D., III: 399
Sherman, Francis Cornwall, III: 125; VI: 417-18, 435-36
Sherman, Henry, VIII: 82n
Sherman, John, IV: 248; V: 76-77; VI: 19; VII: 53n, 84n, 131n; VIII: 347n
Sherman, Robert, VII: 219n, 225
Sherman, Roger, III: 524, 527, 530, 546n
Sherman, Thomas West, IV: 528, 545n, 557; V: 122n; VIII: 593-94
Sherman, William Tecumseh: and military operations, *(fall '61)* IV: 542, 544-45, V: 14n; *(spring '63)* VI: 142n, 254, 380n; *(fall '63)* 480, 510-11, VII: 30n; *(spring '64)* VII: 308n, 355-56, 444-45; *(fall '64)* 478n, 499n,

VIII: 9-10, 27, 33, 97, 148, 154, 171; (*Jan. '65*) 201; (*spring '65*) 329n, 376n
Recommended for commands in Tenn. and in Ky., V: 21-22, 31, 84; and appointments, VI: 126n, 340n, 555, VIII: 376; correspondence of Grant, Sherman, and L. on arrest of N. Y. *Herald* correspondent for violation of his orders, VI: 142-43; his action at Vicksburg commended by L., 230-31; his appointment as brigadier general, 231n; reported wounded (June '63), 254n; and courtsmartial, VII: 104n; assigned to command the Military Division of the Miss., 240; and Blair's assignment to command of the Fifteenth Corps, 248n, 319-20; and Hurlbut's demand for a court of inquiry, 327-28; complaints against his order prohibiting issuance of provisions to Tenn. citizens at military posts, 330-31

Contradiction of his and Hurlbut's orders concerning rights of possession of Memphis church, VII: 427n; and the question of recruitment by state agents in areas under his military command, 449-50; his objections to Osterhaus promotion to Major General, 463-64; L. requests his opinion on expediency of using railroad transportation for government purchase of cotton, 495-96; dismissed officer seeks reinstatement, 524n; orders for thanks and celebration of his capture of Atlanta, 532, 533; and disbandment of Ga. militia "to gather the corn and sorghum," VIII: 9-10; his opinion on importance of the draft, 11; advised by L. of importance of

allowing Ind. soldiers leave to go home and vote in state elections (Oct. '64), 11-12, 46-47; duty assignments and leaves of absence, 91, 105; and the capture of Savannah, 181-82, 201, 331
Shields, Ben, *see* Nields, Ben
Shields, James, I: 62, 292-96, 299-302, 323n, 381; II: 23, 149, 304-305, 405; III: 3, 7, 13, 62-63, 104, 107-108, 171-72, 388n
IV: 418, 492; V: 150, 219n, 231-33, 235-36, 246n, 248n, 251n, 254-55, 258, 269n, 272, 274-75, 280
Shieldsborough (Miss.), VIII: 396
Shiloh (Tenn.), *see* Pittsburg Landing (Tenn.)
Shiloh, battle of, V: 457, 511n; VI: 67n; VII: 322n; VIII: 330n
Shindel, Jacob A., VIII: 91
Ship Island, V: 50
Shipley, Enoch, VIII: 68
Shipley, Nathan, Jr., VII: 372
Shipley, Reason, survey for, I: facing p. 20
Shippensburg (Pa.), VI: 310n
Shoaff, James, II: 112
Shoe strike (Mass.), L. on, IV: 1, 7-8, 12, 24-25
Shoemaker, Thomas C., II: 341
Sholes, Christopher Latham, VI: 138n
Shore, John C., VI: 253n
Short, Allen, I: 51
Short, Chloe, *see* Thomas, Chloe (Short)
Short, Elizabeth (Short), I: 51
Short, James (son of Joshua), I: 51
Short, James (son-in-law of Joshua), I: 20n, 51, 321; IV: 326
Short, Mrs. James II, *see* Short, Elizabeth
Short, John, I: 51
Short, Joseph, I: 51

Short, Joshua, I: 51
Short, Mrs. Joshua, *see* Short, Parthena
Short, Levi, V: 181-82; VI: 145n
Short, Parthena, I: 51
Short, Sarah, *see* Bennett, Sarah (Short)
Short, William, I: 51
Shoshone Indians, VII: 112-13
Shoshone River, VII: 113
Shoup, Samuel N., II: 456
Shriver, Mary L. (Hanks), VII: 342n
Shriver, William F., VII: 342
Shriver, Mrs. William F., *see* Shriver, Mary L.
Shufeldt, Robert W., V: 539
Shultis, Peter L., VII: 538n
Shultz, Reuben, VII: 218n
Shurburne, William L., VII: 350
Shurtleff, Benjamin, II: 121n
Shurtleff, Milton, II: 121n
Shurtleff College (Alton, Ill.), II: 121n
Shutes, Milton H., IV: 501n; VI: 133n; VIII: 175n, 257n, 365n
Shutt, George W., II: 310
Siam, V: 125-26, 137
Siberia, VIII: 138
Sibley, Ebenezer Sprote, V: 75n; VI: 105n; VII: 443n
Sibley, Henry Hastings, V: 542-43, 551; VI: 6-7
"Sibley Tent Royalty papers," VII: 443n
Sicily, VI: 18
Sickles, ———, V: 33-34
Sickles, Daniel Edgar, IV: 504-505; V: 12; VI: 55, 322-23, 402; VII: 160, 176, 180, 185, 204-205, 235n, 250, 273n
Siefke, John J., VII: 318
Sierra Leone (Africa), V: 265n
Sierra Nevada, VII: 122n; VIII: 146
Sigel, Franz, IV: 463n; V: 100n, 101n, 106n, 117, 142, 255-56, 268-72, 277-78, 398n, 405, 415, 446n, 472n

VI: 5-6, 43, 55, 79-80, 93, 147n, 168n, 180, 196, 216-17, 230-31, 282-83, 383; VII: 129, 199, 244n, 263n, 424, 521; VIII: 8-9, 593-94
Siletz Indian Agency, IV: 308
Silliman, Benjamin, II: 452, 463
Sills, Elijah, VII: 392
Silver Spring (Md.), VII: 440n
Silverman, Frank, VIII: 335-36
Silverman, Lion, VIII: 335-36
Silversmith, Julius, VII: 323
Silverwood, William, VII: 97
Silvester, Peter Henry, IV: 160
Silvey, William, III: 554; VII: 241
Sim, Thomas, VI: 55
Sim, Mrs. Thomas, VI: 55
Simerly, Elijah, VIII: 68
Simmons, Charles, I: 52
Simmons, Isaac R., VIII: 219n, 294n
Simmons, James, I: 11
Simmons, James Fowler, IV: 97, 248, 293, 313, 365n, 396, 478, 498; V: 228
Simmons, Julius, I: 52
Simmons, Pollard, I: 25
Simmons, R., I: 52
Simmons, Sam R., Jr., V: 228n
Simmons, Samuel, IV: 474n
Simmons, Walter C., IV: 365
Simmons, William T., VIII: 86
Simms, Chattam, I: 354, 455n
Simms, Ignatius R., I: 455
Simms, John H., VII: 318
Simons, Charles J., IV: 443
Simons, Emery R., VII: 294n
Simonton, J. W., IV: 302n
Simpson, Josiah, V: 467n
Simpson, Matthew, IV: 550; V: 12-13; VIII: 264n, 595
Sinclair, Samuel, VII: 485n
Sinco, Henry, I: 20
Singleton, James Washington, II: 113-14, 342-43; III: 213, 320-21; VIII: 200-201, 267, 343-44, 353n, 410
Singleton, Milton R., VI: 544

Sintz, Nicholas, I: 148
Sioux Indians, V: 397n, 455n, 493n, 525-26, 542-43; VI: 6-7; VII: 160, 325-26; VIII: 225n
Sister's Ferry (Ga.), VIII: 201n
Sisters of Charity of Nazareth (Ky.), VIII: 219
Sisters of Mercy (Chicago and Washington), VIII: 428
Sitana (Peru), VII: 37
Sitton, James O., IV: 392n
Six Months at the White House (Carpenter), V: 337n; VII: 34n
"Sketch of the Dubois Family, Pioneers of Indiana and Illinois, A" (art.), VIII: 422n
Skinner, Charles, VII: 419
Skinner, John J., VII: 543n
Skinner, Samuel P., VI: 294n
Skinner, Thomas R., I: 183
Skivving, James, VII: 318
Skoon-ka-ska [White Dog] (Indian), V: 542
Skurlock, T., VIII: 70
Slack, William B., VII: 353
Slack, William D., IV: 445
Slade, William, IV: 538
Slaght, James C., IV: 504n
Slater, E. F., IV: 516n
Slaughter, Mrs. John F., *see* Slaughter, Mary
Slaughter, Mary, VIII: 302-303
Slave trade, L. on: bill to abolish in D. C., II: 20-22; Washington's "Georgia Pen," 237-38, 253; prohibited in D. C., 243; and the Douglas doctrine of popular sovereignty, 245, 256, 259, 263-64, 267-69, 275-76, 278-79, 298-301, 449, 467-68, 492, 496, 546, III: 15, 40, 42, 77-79, 88, 276, 304-307, 388, 394-95, 403-405, 413, 421-23, 425-27, 429, 435, 446-60, 464-65, 498-500, 526n, 531, 537, 545n, 552, IV: 6, 11, 22, 27, 258-59, 269; attitude toward domestic slave trade, IV: 183; "suppression . . . recently attended with unusual

success [Dec. '61]," V: 46-48; convictions and pardons of slave traders, 57, 128-29, VI: 294n, VII: 256n, 357n, VIII: 324n; 1862 treaty with Great Britain to suppress trade, V: 186, 265, 339n, 367n, 403n, 519, VI: 110, VII: 36; transmits report to Senate, VII: 422; gives gunboat to Liberia to aid in arresting trade, VIII: 138; recommends exclusion of foreign slave traders from U. S., 140
Slaveholders, L. on: II: 130, 230-31, 255, 322; IV: 3, 16
Slavery, L. on: protest and remarks in Ill. legislature, I: 74-76, 126, IV: 104-108; description of slaves on a Mississippi R. steamboat, I: 260, II: 320; and attitude of Whig abolitionists, I: 347-48; effect of Negro population on state representation, 450, II: 246, 268-69, 279, 363, III: 307; and support of Taylor in 1848 political campaign, I: 454, 505, II: 3, 5, 7-9, 11, 14; and Henry Clay, II: 121-32, III: 29, 37-38, 89, 93-94, 233-34, 250, 280, 300, 302-305, 314, 327-29, 333, 424, 484; and support of Scott in 1852 political campaign, II: 125, 127-31, 136-40, 156-57; fragments (1854) on the moral wrong of, 222-23; and 1854 Ill. political campaign, 226-86, 288; editorial (1854) in the *Ill. Journal*, 229-30; the doctrine of necessity, 274-75, 501, 520-21, III: 327, 334-35, IV: 101; historical outline of slavery in the U. S., II: 298-99; resolutions drafted for Kansas-Nebraska Act, 300-301; letters (1855) on the "abstract wrong" and the "political problem" of slavery, 316-18, 320-23; and 1856 political campaign, 341, 344-47, 361-73, 375, 379, 384-85

Fragment on sectionalism (July '56), 349-53; fragment on Dred Scott case, 387-88; and the formation of the Republican party, 391; Springfield (1857) speech, 398-410, V: 278; "House divided" speech, II: 446, 448-54, 461-69 (text of speech), 471, IV: 147; and religion, II: 452, III: 84, 204-205, IV: 3, VII: 368, VIII: 154-55; and 1858 Ill. political campaign (inc. debates with Douglas), II: 486-502, 507-508, 513-16, 518-21, 526-27, 530, 536, 538-41, 543-48, 551, 553, III: 14, 30, 38-49, 70-101, 116-33, 144-46, 178-81, 205, 220-37, 245-57, 275-83, 297-318, 328-29, 333-35; and the definition of democracy, II: 532

"Substance of all I have ever said about negro equality [is] . . .," III: 326-28; in letters and speeches (Nov.'58-Nov.'60), 339-40, 342, 344, 349, 351, 366-70, 376, 378-79, 384, 394-470, 482-89, 493, 495-504, 519-20, 522-54, IV: 2-30, 41-42, 67n, 77, 82, 93, 95-97, 101, 104-108, 112n, 115 123-24, 130-33; estimated property value of slaves, IV: 3, 9, 15-16, V: 62; compared to rattlesnakes and wens, IV: 5-6, 10-11, 18, 25, V: 327; as President-elect opposes any compromise on extension of slavery, IV: 140, 149-56, 163-64, 172, 183, 245, 250-51, 255-56, 259; the "substantial difference" on the slavery question, 160, 258; the "artificial crisis," 211, 215-16, 238-39; and first inaugural address, 262-63, 268-69, V: 527; refusal of troops to catch runaway slaves, IV: 287n; liberation of slaves by military unlawful, 506-507, 531-33, VI: 67n

As a Civil War issue, V: 26n, 52-53, 152-53, 169, 192, 195, 328-

31, 343n, 388-89, 424, 545n, VI: 176, 210n, 330n, 500, VII: 172-73, 259, 381n, 507, VIII: 332-33, 387; the holding of slaves in D. C. jails, V: 72; reiterates views on slavery (1862), 327, VII: 260; and acceptable peace terms, VI: 330n, 410-11, VII: 435, 451, 459-60, 499-502, 515n, 518n, VIII: 63, 152, 279, 286n, 386-87, 407n; "I have done no official act in mere deference to my abstract judgment and feeling on slavery [Apr. '64]," VII: 281-82; reply to Concord (Mass.) children's petition to free all slave children, 287; reply to a letter on white supremacy, 483; "[When I] hear any one, arguing for slavery I feel a strong impulse to see it tried on him personally [Mar. '65]," VIII: 360-62

See also Abolitionism; Colonization of Negroes; Dred Scott case; Emancipation; Fugitive slaves; Kansas-Nebraska Act and repeal of the Missouri Compromise; Mulattoes; Negroes; Secession; Slaveholders; Slave trade; and Thirteenth Amendment to the Constitution

Slavery and Freedmen, Committee on (U. S. Senate), VII: 241n

Slavery Ordained of God (Ross), III: 205n

Slemmer, Adam Jacoby, IV: 409, 418

Slemmer, Mrs. Adam Jacoby, IV: 418

Slicer, Henry, I: 474-75

Slidell, John, II: 377-78; V: 26, 64n, 83n; VIII: 107

Sloan, ———, IV: 228

Sloan, Andrew Scott, IV: 481

Sloan, George W., VII: 320

Sloan, Joshua, IV: 305

Slocum, Henry Warner, VI: 43,

295, 342n, 486n, 524; VII: 378-79

Slocum, Joseph Jermain, V: 89n

Slocum, Willard, IV: 496

Sloo, Thomas, VII: 247n

Slough, John P., VII: 544; VIII: 9

Small, William F., IV: 166, 380-81

Smalley, ———, IV: 416n

Smallwood, Parmenius, I: 2

Smart, John C., VII: 215

Smead, Alexander Dallas Bache, VII: 143

Smedberg, William Renwick, VII: 357

Smedes, William C., IV: 156

Smedie, John, VI: 544

Smiley, Mrs. M. E., VI: 443

Smith, ———, V: 249; VII: 106, 109

Smith, A. C., VI: 98

Smith, Abraham D., VI: 453-59

Smith, Abraham Lincoln, VI: 511

Smith, Albert N., V: 215

Smith, Alexander, VIII: 328n

Smith, Alice C., VI: 511

Smith, Alice Orme, VI: 17n

Smith, Allen Hall, VI: 464n

Smith, Andrew Jackson, VII: 308n, 479n; VIII: 193

Smith, Andrew W., I: 2

Smith, Ann (Todd), III: 491n

Smith, Annie M., VI: 346n; VIII: 330n

Smith, B. F., VIII: 68

Smith, Benjamin Franklin, V: 180n

Smith, Benjamin G., VII: 523n; VIII: 240n, 364

Smith, C. DeWitt, VII: 371

Smith, C. T., VIII: 127

Smith, Caleb Blood: and appointments, I: 418n, II: 46, IV: 296-98, 303, 348-49, 356, 389n, 391, 406-407, 442, 456, 490n, 498, 537, 551, 554, 561, V: 28, 68, 78, 262, 316, 500, VI: 21, 153n, VII: 128n; serves as chairman of House committees (1848), I: 429-30,

469; on appropriations of lands to states and the admission of Wis., 469-71; and Taylor candidacy for president (1848), 504, 517-18; appointed to board investigating claims of American citizens against Mexico, II: 46n

And elections (1860), IV: 55, 87-88; a reporter's comment on L.'s attitude toward, 276n; his appointment to L.'s cabinet, 278; his opinion on the provisioning of Fort Sumter, 285n; and the Fort Pickens expedition, 302n; receives L.'s order on lodgings and subsistence for political prisoners, 466; and loyalty cases of federal employees, 526, 556; recommends establishment of Indian reservation in Utah, 548; and the Chiriqui colonization project, 561-62, V: 2-3, 48n, 414, 418-19; L.'s summary of his report in 1861 annual message, V: 45-48; L. transmits to Senate his reports on Indian treaties, 89, 101-102, 106-107, 147, 189, 287-88, 307; appeals for bettering conditions of Indians, 173, 415-16; directed to turn over Washington penitentiary to War Department, 429-30; supports removal of McClellan from command of the Army of the Potomac, 485n; his resignation from the cabinet and appointment to a judgeship, 492n, VI: 35n; and clarification of reported income from the sale of public lands (1862), V: 511-12, 525; L.'s summary of his report in 1862 annual message, 525-26; his report on Indian barbarities in Minn., 540-41, 550-51; authorizes foreign purchase of seeds, VI: 49-50; national mourning at his death, VII: 118-19; and erection of

the Capitol extension and new dome, 267n
Smith, Calvin, VIII: 68
Smith, Charles, VII: 420; VIII: 207n
Smith, Charles Ferguson, IV: 326; V: 142
Smith, Charles L., VIII: 594
Smith, Chauncey, VII: 211n
Smith, Clark Moulton, II: 424-25; III: 346, 491n, 513n; VI: 464-65
Smith, Mrs. Clark Moulton, see Smith, Ann (Todd)
Smith, David Allen, I: 416; II: 100, 104-105, 197-98, 287n
Smith, Delano T., IV: 452n; V: 21
Smith, E. A., VII: 29-30, 168n, 275; VIII: 323n
Smith, E. B., VI: 442n
Smith, E. Delafield, IV: 231n, 334; VI: 183n, 207n, 321
Smith, Edmund Kirby, V: 409n, 416n, 419n; VI: 254, 293, 529n; VII: 62; VIII: 178n, 595n
Smith, Edward, I: 87, 124
Smith, Edward Jacquelin (Clark Co., Va.), VI: 442n
Smith, Mrs. Edward Jacquelin, VI: 442n
Smith, Edward Jacquelin (Fauquier Co., Va.), VI: 441-42, 452
Smith, Edward Worthington, V: 222
Smith, Elizabeth, IV: 389
Smith, Enos W., III: 125-26
Smith, Franklin W., VII: 523n; VIII: 240n, 364
Smith, G. Rush, IV: 166-67
Smith, George (Cook Co., Ill.), II: 174
Smith, George (Madison Co., Ill.), I: 123n
Smith, George H., VII: 353n
Smith, Gerrit, V: 433n
Smith, Gilead, IV: 512-13
Smith, Giles Alexander, VI: 126n
Smith, Goldwin, VIII: 97n, 371

Smith, Green Clay, VI: 366n, 372, 414; VII: 29, 34, 127-28, 146n, 187n, 256n, 309, 375n; VIII: 104n, 197n, 311n, 425n
Smith, Greenberry, I: 206
Smith, H. D., VI: 157n
Smith, H. G., IV: 179, 181n
Smith, Henry, II: 178-79
Smith, Herman, VIII: 5n
Smith, Hugh, VI: 51n, 58n
Smith, I. L., II: 33
Smith, Ira, VII: 152
Smith, Isaac, II: 425n
Smith, Israel S. ("Ichabod"), IV: 311, 340
Smith, J., I: 287-88
Smith, J. C. (Ill.), V: 351n
Smith, James (Ill.), II: 188; VI: 51-52, 58
Smith, James (Va.), I: 518n
Smith, James (Tenn.), VIII: 70
Smith, James W., VIII: 133n
Smith, James Youngs, VI: 553; VII: 241, 545; VIII: 109
Smith, John (La.), VIII: 179
Smith, John (Mo.), VI: 544
Smith, John A., II: 425n
Smith, John C., V: 27n, 54, 149n
Smith, John Condit, V: 168-69
Smith, John Gregory, VI: 549; VIII: 109, 271-72
Smith, John M., I: 340n
Smith, John T., IV: 189n
Smith, John W., II: 424-25; VI: 238n
Smith, Jones, VIII: 68
Smith, Joseph (Mormon prophet), I: 206-207
Smith, Joseph (naval construction commissioner), V: 174
Smith, Joseph (Springfield, Ill.), II: 301-303
Smith, Joseph Lee Kirby, IV: 500n
Smith, Joseph Rowe, V: 206n, 451
Smith, Joseph S., VI: 461
Smith, Lewis B., VIII: 3
Smith, Mary Rebecca Darby, IV: 339

Smith, Melancthon (Ill.), VI: 346n
Smith, Mrs. Melancthon, *see* Smith, Annie M.
Smith, Melancthon (Navy), V: 215; VIII: 37n
Smith, Micajah, II: 302
Smith, Noah, IV: 110
Smith, P. Frazer, VII: 375n
Smith, Preston, VI: 480
Smith, Richard, V: 516n; VI: 366n
Smith, Richard B., VII: 531n
Smith, Richard M., VIII: 410n
Smith, Robert (Ill.), I: 211, 416n; II: 212-16; VIII: 419n
Smith, Robert (Tenn.), VIII: 68
Smith, Samuel (Ill.), I: 349
Smith, Samuel (Tenn.), III: 269
Smith, Samuel J. [alias William Jones], VIII: 88-89
Smith, Samuel Lisle, II: 43-44
Smith, Sheriff, VIII: 68
Smith, Simeon, IV: 319-20, 452n, 480
Smith, Stephen B., V: 376n
Smith, Theophilus Washington, I: 64
Smith, Thomas Alexander, VIII: 411n
Smith, Thomas R., V: 470
Smith, Thomas W., II: 24n, 198n
Smith, Timothy C., IV: 348
Smith, Truman, I: 517; IV: 133n, 138-39, 281; V: 339n
Smith, Victor, IV: 308; VI: 144, 202, 209-10, 214n, 215
Smith, Walton J., IV: 554n
Smith, Watson, V: 215
Smith, William (S. C.), III: 534n
Smith, William (Va.), VI: 535n
Smith, William C. S., VIII: 408
Smith, William F. (N. Y.), VI: 366-67
Smith, William Farrar, IV: 483; VI: 15-16, 75n, 129-30, 327-30; VIII: 161-62
Smith, William T., VI: 442n
Smith, Willie, VII: 202

Smith Brothers (Boston), VII: 523n; VIII: 240, 364
Smith County (Tenn.), VIII: 69
Smith, Edwards & Company (Springfield), IV: 188-89
Smith, George, & Company (Chicago), II: 314
Smith Island (Va.), VI: 427, 434-35, 472
Smith, Wickersham & Company (Springfield), IV: 189n
Smithfield (Va.), VI: 274
Smithson, William T., VI: 361; VII: 257; VIII: 119
Smithson, Mrs. William T., VII: 257
Smoot, Coleman, I: 54n
Smyrna (Turkey), IV: 481n
Sna-ma-ni (Indian), V: 542
Snead, Edward K., VII: 481, 488n, 508
Sneed, Alexander H., V: 464n
Snell, Asa, II: 330n
Snell, Jason D., VII: 322
Snethen, Worthington G., VII: 73
Snicker's Gap (Va.), V: 461
Snickersville (Va.), V: 235n
Snider, Joseph, VI: 130
Snider, William O., VII: 457n, 460
Snodgrass, Miss E., VIII: 351
Snow, G. C., VIII: 398n
Snow, J., VII: 334-35
Snow, William D., VII: 334-35, 519n
Snyder, ———, VIII: 427
Snyder, A. J., IV: 305
Snyder, William Henry, II: 75
Snyder's Bluff (Miss.), VI: 43n
Soda Springs (Idaho Terr.), VII: 113
Solano County (Calif.), IV: 323n
Soldier vote (1864), V: 453-54; VII: 233; VIII: 11, 24-25, 38, 43, 46, 48n, 67, 75, 89, 100, 130, 150-51, 321n
Soldiers' Homes: in Washington,

V: 484, 492, VI: 314n, VII: 417n, 544n; in other cities, VI: 90n, VII: 135n, 167, 291n, 316 "Solidified Greek Fire" (weapon), VI: 145n

Somdetch Phara Paramendr Maha Mongut, Major King of Siam, V: 125-26, 137

Somers, James W., II: 469-70, 474-75; IV: 33, 35, 79; VIII: 424n

Somers, Richard, VII: 26

Somers, William D., II: 469-70

Somers, Winston, VIII: 210

Somerset (Ky.), VII: 331n

Somerset County (Md.), VII: 9n, 374n; VIII: 167n, 198n

Somes, Daniel E., VII: 371

Sommers, Miss A. E., V: 472

Sommers, John, IV: 507n

Sonoma (Calif.), IV: 304

"Sons of Liberty" (Copperheads), VIII: 123n

Sons of Temperance, VI: 486-90

Sothoron, John H., VI: 530n, 532n; VII: 28, 255

Soto, ———, II: 299

Soulé, H. D. B., II: 342n

Soulé, Joshua, VIII: 264n

Souter, Louis B., VII: 216n

South, Department of the, V: 222; VI: 310, 490n; VII: 81n; VIII: 187n

South, The [Baltimore], IV: 341n, 342n

South America, V: 318; VII: 265-66

South Anna River (Va.), V: 245n, 248n, 249n; VI: 207

South Carolina, II: 246, 269, 363; IV: 195, 324n, 437; V: 122n, 193n, 222, 298; VI: 98, 247n, 250n, 453-59; VII: 98-99; VIII: 201n, 344n, 407n; see also Nullification

South Mountain (Md.), V: 426n, 511n; VI: 88; VII: 549

South West, Army of the, V: 441n; VI: 72n

South Western Telegraph Company, VII: 59

Southampton (Va.) slave insurrection, III: 540

Southard, Samuel Lewis, II: 355n

Southern, see Sothoron, John H.

Southern Advocate [Richmond, Va.?], VII: 102n

Southern Illinoisan [Shawneetown, Ill.], II: 469n

Souvenir of Abraham Lincoln, A (Whitney), II: 535n

Soward, Richard, I: facing 20

Sowers, George, VII: 159

Spaight, Richard Dobbs, III: 531n

Spain, I: 421; II: 153, 251, 298-99; IV: 280n, 281n, 317n, 446; V: 61n, 100n, 109-10, 383, 520-21; VI: 332n; VII: 37, 339n, 370n, 399-400; VIII: 138

Spalding, R. D., VI: 529n

Spalding, Rufus Paine, VIII: 347n

Spane, J. S., VIII: 69

Sparks, Josiah C., V: 376n

Sparta (Tenn.), V: 410n

Sparta (Va.), II: 218; IV: 37

Spaulding, Benjamin J., VIII: 88n

Spaulding, Elbridge Gerry, IV: 94-95; VI: 88n

Spaulding, Mrs. Elbridge Gerry, VI: 88

Spaulding, Robert R., VII: 151n

Spaulding, William E., VII: 318

Spear, David, II: 114, 188

Spear, Isaac P., II: 114

Spear, Samuel Perkins, VIII: 193

Spears, George, I: 121

Spears, George C., I: 25

Speech, the "first invention," III: 359-63

Speechmaking, L. and: comment on his delivery of speeches, I: 49-50, 157-58, 209-10, 333-35, 341-42, II: 1-2, 5-7, 11, 13, 227, 229, 285-86, 344-45, 348-49, 359, 373, 375-76, 378, III: 373, 489, IV: 38-39, 50, 84n, 241, 276n; L. on, I: 430, 448, II: 81, 126-27,

248, 283, 512-13, III: 300, 397, 400-401, 555, IV: 204-205, 218, 224, 241-42, 441, VIII: 154

Charged with plagiarism, II: 367; notes for a speech (1860), IV: 1; "not a professional lecturer," 39-40; no desire to obtain a reputation as a talker, 221, V: 358; "not accustomed to the use of the language of eulogy," VII: 254; see also Editorial revision, L. on

Speed, Eliza Davis, I: 261n

Speed, Emma (Keats), I: 261n

Speed, Fanny (Henning), I: 261, 266-70, 280-83, 285, 289-90, 303, 325, 328, 391; II: 17, 29, 323, 328; IV: 141, 521; VI: 459

Speed, James: mentioned in letters to his brother Joshua (1843), I: 305-306, 328; and the military situation in Ky. (1861), IV: 369n, 499n, V: 14-15; protests Frémont proclamation of Aug. 30, 1861, IV: 506-507; arrests and pardons, 549, VI: 223n, VII: 136n, 177n, 446-47, VIII: 127, 177, 193, 196, 205n, 290, 298, 309, 317, 323-24, 369-70, 398-99; reports to L. on loyalty conditions in Ky., V: 113; L. requests military appointment of his son, 552

And appointments, VI: 428, VIII: 158, 212, 214, 222, 242-43, 287, 324-25, 349, 355, 368, 410, 412; appointed Attorney General, VIII: 126-27, 160, 168; L. requests his opinion on release of navy files of court-martial cases, 190-91, and violations of Enrollment Act, 245; member of Board to examine draft quotas, 264-65; interprets property rights of Va. loyalist, 268; mentioned in L.'s request for band to play "Dixie," 393

Speed, John (father of James), I: 259n, 261n

Speed, John (son of James), V: 552

Speed, Mrs. John, see Speed, Lucy G.

Speed, John Smith, VI: 140n

Speed, Joshua Fry: and appointments, I: 121, IV: 294, 393n, V: 71n, VI: 10n, 83, 428; note concerning remittance to Bohannon, I: 153; note on his friendship with L., IV: 546n; mentioned in letter to Stuart on 1840 election campaign, I: 206; correspondence with L. on mental health and marital affairs, 228n, 265-70, 280-83, 288-89, 303, 391; letter from L. describing the Trailor murder case, 254-58, 371n, 377n; description of his river trip with L. from Louisville to St. Louis, 259-60; letters from L. on legal and business affairs, 284-85, 289-90, 305-306, 319, 323-24, 328-29, 389-90, II: 17, 328

Letter from L. on threatened Shields-Butler duel, I: 302-303; letters from L. on Ill. Congressional election (1844), 319, 324-25, 391; letter from L. on political affairs (Feb. '49), II: 28-29; letters from L. on slavery and Kansas-Nebraska Act (1855), 320-23; Chicago meeting with L. on formation of cabinet (1860), IV: 141; and assignment of arms and men to Ky., 368-69, 499n, 559n, V: 31n, 147n; pardons, arrests, and prisoner exchanges, V: 258n, 426n, VI: 140, 223n, VIII: 120n, 127, 314n; recommends a hearing for Rousseau, V: 283n; L. introduces to Weed, VII: 77

One of the signers of: letter to Chicago American (1839) on illegal voters, I: 151; Whig campaign circulars (1840), 203;

Communication to the Readers of *The Old Soldier*, 205n; calls for Whig state convention, 261-62

Speed, Mrs. Joshua Fry, *see* Speed, Fanny (Henning)

Speed, Lucy G., I: 265; IV: 546

Speed, Mary, I: 259-61, 281n; II: 320n

Speed, Philip, I: 261n

Speed, Mrs. Philip, *see* Speed, Emma (Keats)

Speed, William, I: 265, 280, 306

Speed, Mrs. William, I: 265

Speed, William Pope, I: 390

Speer, William S., IV: 130

Spence, Paul H., VII: 422n

Spence, William, VIII: 69

Spencer County (Ind.), I: 1n, 378n; II: 536n; III: 463, 511; IV: 37n, 61, 116n, 131n

Spencer's Landing (Md.), VI: 530n

Spencer's rifles, VI: 395n

Sperry, Mrs. Ben, V: 161n

Sperry, Lewis, IV: 305

Sperry, Nehemiah Day, IV: 121-22

Sperry, Robert J., VI: 376, 386n, 403n

Sperry, S. W., IV: 304

Spezia (Italy), IV: 460

Spicer, John, IV: 553; VII: 448

Spiegel, Solomon, VIII: 212

Spies, IV: 372n; V: 8, 475; VI: 225, 227, 229, 236, 263, 296n, 337n, 442n, 451; VII: 26n, 136, 172, 205-206, 322, 356, 393, 425, 493, 502, 522n, 526-27, 536; VIII: 123, 226n, 291-92, 309-10, 357

Spinner, Francis Elias, IV: 88, 120-21; VI: 125; VII: 249n; VIII: 195n

Spiritualism, VII: 133n

Spofford & Tileston (N. Y.), VI: 112n

Spooner, John Alden, VII: 293n

"Spot Resolutions," I: 420-22, 438

Spotswood House (Richmond, Va.), VIII: 198

Spotsylvania Court House (Va.), V: 254n; VII: 334n, 373n, 506n; VIII: 170n, 311n

Spotted Wolf (Indian), VI: 153n

Spottswood, George W., I: 228n, 343

Spottswood's Rural Hotel (Springfield), I: 87n

Sprague, Charles, II: 521

Sprague, Edwin, VIII: 306

Sprague, William, IV: 365, 399n, 403; V: 166n, 297n, 308, 377n, 431; VI: 552-53; VIII: 9, 288

Sprigg, Ann G., IV: 391n; VII: 454n

Sprigg, Benjamin, IV: 391n

Sprigg, Mrs. Benjamin, *see* Sprigg, Ann G.

Spriggs, John S., V: 278

Sprigg's Ford (Va.), V: 120n

Spring, Sydney, II: 470

Spring, Sydney T., II: 470n

Spring Creek (Ill.), I: 255-56

Spring Hill (Tenn.), VI: 233n

Springer, Francis, III: 372, 399; VI: 171, 237-38

Springfield (Ill.): the construction of railroads to, I: 5, 233, 395-405; the construction, relocation, and repair of roads, 35-36, 42, 45-46, 70-72, 85-87, 250-52; election returns (1836), 48n; L. comments on social life in, 78; extension of corporate powers of city officials, 81-82; toasts offered by L. at public dinners, 87, II: 483; incorporation and mention of Mechanics Union, I: 158, 464n, II: 19n; location of Whig conventions (1839, 1856), I: 201n, II: 340; and support of Harrison (1840), I: 206; incorporation of city, 238-39; invitation to Clay to speak in city, 297; mention of Clay Club, 297, 326, 341, III: 203n; Whig meeting resolu-

tions (1843, 1844), I: 325-26, 337-38; mention of Democratic Association, 326; purchase of L.'s home, 331; Clay Club resolutions on the death of John Brodie, 341; appointments of postmasters, 342-43, IV: 303; mention of Scott Club, II: 135

Mentioned in L.-D. debates as location of 1854 convention to form the Republican Party, III: 3, 13, 31, 33, 43, 44, 56-58, 119, 227, 228, 239-40, 251, 257-58, 282; Douglas mentions 1854 visit to, 30; mention of Republican Club, 203; mention of Library Association, 356n; calls for meetings of city Republicans (1859), 372, 377; call for old settlers meeting, 381; mentioned in L.'s autobiography, IV: 63, 65, 67; mention of Marine Bank, 189n; assignment of a quartermaster to, 538n, V: 277n, VI: 237-38, 516; L. harassed by appointment difficulties with his old friends, VI: 275-76; his letter to Conkling and mass meeting of Union men (Sept. '63), 399, 406-10, 420, 430n; L. authorizes site for Soldiers Home, VII: 167; L. asked to invest in First National Bank, 316n; Nicolay reports on Mo. affairs from, VIII: 57n; *see also* Illinois, capital of

L.'s speeches at: 1836 political rally, I: 49-50; before Young Men's Lyceum (1838), 108-15; in debate with Douglas (1839), 157-58; on the subtreasury system, 159-79; eulogy on Benjamin Ferguson, 268-69; temperance address (1842), 271-79; eulogy on Henry Clay, II: 121-32; address to Scott Club (1852), 135-59; report of speech (Sept. 9, '54), 229; speech of Oct. 4, '54, 240-47,

276; speech of June 10, '56, 344-45; speech of June 26, '57, 398-410; "A House Divided" speech, 461-69, III: 35, 259; speech of July 17, '58, II: 504-21, VIII: 415; response to a serenade (Sept. '58), III: 203; speech of Oct. 30, '58, 334-35; on Discoveries and Inventions, 356-63; speech of Oct. 15, '59, 489; response to a serenade (May '60), IV: 50-51; 1860 political rally, 91-92; remarks of Nov. 20, '60, 142-43; farewell address, 190-91, V: 278

Springfield (Mass.), IV: 94, 99, 311; VIII: 171

Springfield (Mo.), IV: 527n; V: 84-85, 114, 314, 459; VI: 53n, 66, 221; VII: 224, 237

Springfield (S. C.), VI: 456-57

Springfield & Alton Railroad, I: 233, 395-405

Springfield & Alton Turnpike Company, I: 250-52

Springfield & Meredosia Railroad, *see* Sangamon & Morgan Railroad

Springfield & Terre Haute Railroad, II: 133

Springfield Republican, II: 389-90, 425n

Sprouce, William T., I: 12

Squakson Indian Agency, IV: 308

Squatter Sovereign [Atchison, Kans.], II: 322n

Squatter Sovereignty, *see* Popular Sovereignty

Stabler, William H., VIII: 322n

Stackpole, Joseph Lewis, VIII: 30n

Stackpole, Thomas, V: 447; VII: 417n

Stacy, Matthew, II: 188

Stade or Brunshausen dues, V: 58, 131-32, 519

Stafford, Daniel, Jr., I: 267

Stafford, Daniel Sattley, I: 267n

Stafford, E., IV: 33

Stafford, Spencer H., VI: 59
Stager, Anson, V: 6n, 92n, 499n; VI: 228-29
Stager, Samuel, VIII: 595n
Stagg, James H., VIII: 125n
Staghound (ship), V: 79n
Stahel, Julius [H.], V: 272n; VI: 5-6, 43n, 55, 79-80, 93, 135, 280n; VIII: 195
Stamps, John, VIII: 69
Stanbery, Henry, VIII: 161-62
Standing Water (Indian), VI: 153n
Stanford, Joshua R., II: 194
Stanford, Leland, IV: 302n, 304; VI: 422n, 550
Stanley, Luther, V: 360n
Stanley, William [alias], see Judd, Frank Rossiter
Stanly, Edward, V: 259-60, 354n, 445, 451n; VI: 184; VII: 158
Stansbury, E. A., VII: 357
Stansbury, Howard, IV: 554
Stanton, Edwin McMasters: snubs L. while both were serving as attorneys in patent infringement case (1855), II: 315n; appointed Sec. of War, V: 96n; rejection of his plan for Adjutant General's personal attendance of L., 108; distribution of arms and war supplies, 110, 151-52, 225, 506n, VIII: 112, 427; recommends changes in the Bureau of Ordnance, V: 110; and the President's General War Order No. 1, 111-12; and Lane's objections to assignment under Hunter, 115-16, 131n; directs payment of Sigel's staff, 117; receipt of McClellan's report following L.'s Special War Order No. 1, 119n, 124n; correspondence with McClellan on the formation of army corps, 150n, 208-209; checks on McClellan's compliance with L.'s order to keep Washington "entirely secure," 151n, 164n; his preliminary

draft of President's War Order No. 3, 155n
And government contracts for war materiel and supplies, V: 163, 165, 172, 197n, 271, VI: 122; McClellan's command of Fort Monroe (Mar.-Apr. '62), V: 164; Greeley comments on his differences with Frémont, 169n; Meigs recommends return to their rightful owners of boats used in repairing the Chesapeake and Ohio Canal, 191; claims for recruitment expenses, 194, 257; authorization to raise a temporary force to protect mail and telegraph routes from hostile Indian attacks, 200; L. replies to N. Y. *Herald's* speculations on cabinet division over Hunter proclamation (May '62), 225-26; "this note . . . attempts to incite me against the Secretary of War, and therein is offensive to me," 229; and proposed exchange of secessionist and loyalist prisoners, 260n, 332-33, 344; and recruitment, 267, 294, 304n, 334, 335, 337n, 347, 349-50, 365, 406, 411, 431, 456-57, 469n, 482-83, 516, VI: 44, 50, 59, 134, 141, 171, 212, 279, 285, 292, 317n, 335, 342, 471n, VII: 57-58, 206, 241, 249, 295, 308, 312-13, 340n, VIII: 189
Treatment of captured guerrillas, V: 278n; L. recommends Rousseau hearing on the Army of the Ohio, 283; "holds a pretty tight rein on the Press . . . ," 284; a chaplain complains of not receiving pay, 297n; his order authorizing confiscation of property and Negro recruitment, 337n; and the draft, 338-39, 349n, 359n, 362-63, 366, 378-79, 384, 386-87, 397n, VI: 299-300, 337-39, 347-48, 352, 390n,

412-13, 416-17, 444n, 477-78, VII: 164n, 210-11, 272, 347, 380, 393n, 534, VIII: 11-12, 84-85, 168, 194, 232, 257, 258n, 290, 311-13

Requested to help Robert L. find "John Reed," V: 347; Christian Commission granted transportation for distributing hospital supplies, 348-49; and a proposal to rearm Tex. Unionists, 357; a "wide-spread attempt to have a quarrel" between him and McClellan, 358-59; and new types of war materiel and supplies, 365, VI: 59, 105, 107, 342-43, 367, VII: 510; invitations to White House dinners, V: 380-81, VII: 235n; orders Halleck to "immediately commence . . . to organize an army for active operations [Sept. 3, '62]," V: 404; report of troops arriving in Washington (Sept. '62), 413-14; Belmont recommends his replacement by Halleck, 416n; prevents shipment of gunpowder purchased in N. Y. by Chinese government, 430; and use of paroled prisoners to subdue Minn. Indians, 432; evacuation of wounded and removal of bakeries from Washington (Sept. '62), 443; commends military governor of N. C., 445n; his attention called to discord among religious denominations ministering to colored people about Port Royal, 445-46; on the right to use paroled prisoners in military operations against the Indians, 449n

His power in respect to war accounts and expenditures, V: 451n; and 1862 elections, 453-54, 504-505; report of impending troubles with Sioux and Chippewa Indians (Oct. '62),

455; and cotton trading, 472, 540, VIII: 22, 93n, 267n, 368n; and the Emancipation Proclamation, V: 476-77, VI: 24n; and McClellan's removal from command of the Army of the Potomac, V: 485n; opposes transfer of Mississippi R. war vessels to the Navy, 490n; L.'s order prohibiting export of arms and munitions, 503, VI: 432, VIII: 25; annual reports, (1862) V: 524, (1863) VII: 42-43, (1864) VIII: 144, 328, 329; supports bill for admission of W. Va., VI: 17; parole of Ohio and Ill. regiments captured at Hartsville, Tenn., 20; Halleck's letter of resignation, 32n; appeal of Washington woman against military confiscation of her home, 33; approves revocation of Benham's appointment as Brigadier General, 35n, VII: 174; Hurlbut's proposed visit to Washington (Jan. '63), VI: 70; suggested reassignment of Butler to New Orleans (Jan. '63), 76-77; Burnside replaced by Hooker in command of the Army of the Potomac, 77-78; request of English author to visit the army, 80-81; protested omission of Keyes name from list of promotions to Major General, 82; L. endorses agent to settle Ill. claims, 90

Sigel's protest against a subordinate command, VI: 93n, reported danger of insurrection in Ill. (Feb. '63), 97, 99-100; charge against Warren of fraud in payment of a regiment, 106; and L.'s suggestions to Rosecrans on counteracting enemy raids, 108-109; proposed new command for Frémont (Mar. '63), 127; orders Sumner to relieve Curtis in command of the De-

Stanton, Edwin McMasters (*continued*):
partment of the Missouri, 131; countersigns amnesty proclamation, 133; accused by Rosecrans of neglecting to give his promised attention to requests, 138-40; Ky. request for federal funds to recruit new troops, 147; and N. Y. *Mercury's* false announcement of successful use of canal to bypass Vicksburg fortifications, 155; and L.'s memo on harbor defenses, 163; leaves Washington to attend funeral of brother-in-law (Apr. '63), 165

Orders defining Johnson's authority as military governor of Tenn., VI: 187, 465, 469; proposed enlargement of the Department of the Ohio to include parts of Ky., 200; relief of Curtis from his command in Mo. (May '63), 210; employment of disabled veterans, 212, 419; the Vallandigham case, 215-16, 248, VII: 387n; Herron's threat to resign rather than serve under Schofield, VI: 218n; settlement of accounts with the *National Republican* for printing official government notices, 221; settlement of Ill. Central R. R. claims, 227-28; need of cavalry to protect Baltimore and Ohio R. R., 238-39; revocation of order suspending the Chicago *Times*, 248; cancellation of L.'s visit to Hooker, 271n; mention of his corrections to draft of proclamation calling for 100,000 militia (June '63), 278n

Authorizes issuance of U. S. supplies to Pa. state troops, VI: 298; proposed Stephens peace mission (July '63), 315n, 317n; receives protest against Scho-

field's arrest of *Missouri Democrat* editor, 325; suspends military occupation of the New Almaden mine, 333n; promotion of Mott to Major General, 334, VII: 491-92; troubles between military and civil authority in Kans. (July '63), VI: 339-40; formation of a cavalry force under Rousseau, 352-53, 394-95; request of family to assume care of their son wounded at Gettysburg, 353; and proposed expedition to western Tex., 354-55; Hurlbut's resignations and demands for a court of inquiry, 358, VII: 327-28; request for relief for contrabands working on Washington roads, VI: 362-63; authorized to control appropriation for effecting habeas corpus act, 370-71

McClernand's request for a court of inquiry after being removed from command, VI: 380, 383n; city of Rock Island, Ill., asks permission to build bridge to U. S. island by same name, 386; "An act . . . for the better Organization of the Military Establishment," 386; War Department possession of Washington school building relinquished to school authorities, 397-98; his opinion on release of prisoners-of-war, 398; amnesty difficulties in Eastern Va., 401, 427, 434-35; tries to locate reference to act of Congress on House organization, VI: 405-406; naming of hospital for Gov. Harvey of Wis., 437; Hamlin's son reports on difficulties of his regiment of colored troops, 440n; emancipation in Tenn., 440n; Naglee's relief from duty in the Department of Va. and N. C., 482-83;

Stanton, Edwin McMasters (*continued*):
and facilities for soldier membership in the "Sons of Temperance," 489-90; wounded officer's protest against reassignment with lowered rank, 490; and complaints against enlistment of Md. Negroes, 491n

And 1863 elections, VI: 515n, 554, VII: 10; Hardie designated to act as temporary Sec. of War (Oct. '63), VI: 521; Watson designated temporary Acting Sec. of War, VI: 529, VII: 30; receives plan "for making condemned government horses useful," 537; settlement of an officer's pay claim, 561; and formation of a new state government in La., VII: 2n; and the Western Sanitary Commission, 12; arranges for L.'s trip to Gettysburg, 16; request for release of Seneca Indians unlawfully enlisted, 27; requested by L. not to accept Palmer's resignation, 61; New Bedford (Mass.) complains of "promises made to them, that had been broken," 77; relief of Schofield from command of the Department of the Missouri and suggested commands for Rosecrans and Curtis, 78-79, 84-85, 100; visits Point Lookout with L. (Dec. '63), 95; employees at Watertown (Mass.) arsenal complain about working hours, 100; complaints of corruption from Memphis, 104; and extension of law authorizing bounty payments to veteran volunteers, 107-108; request for a court of inquiry for Crittenden, 108; Harrow ordered to report to Grant, 113-14

Resignation of Boyle, VII: 121-22; Crittenden granted permission to visit N. Y. (Jan. '64), 127; and relinquishment of Smith's military commission while occupying a seat in Congress, 127-28; Sigel assigned to command of the Department of W. Va., 129, 199; Peirpoint complains of bank investigations at Norfolk and Portsmouth, Va., 135-36; arrangements for return of Negro colonists from Isle à Vache, 164-65; and L.'s opinion on loyalty oaths, 169-70; and proposed distribution of copies of amnesty proclamation behind enemy lines, 176-77; and U. S. reimbursement to Pa. for military expenditures, 178n; L. disapproves his order giving church authorities control and possession of Southern churches, 178-80, 182-83, VIII: 264n; requested to meet with friend of Blair, VII: 189; and Mass. recruiting of colored troops in Va., 190-91, 204; and lifting of the blockade of Brownsville, Tex., 192-93; questioned use of *St. Joseph* (Mo.) *Tribune* for government advertising, 197n

Order commuting sentence of deserters, VII: 208; Thomas sent to Mississippi R. area to control contrabands and plantation leasing, 212; denies Serrell permission to go to Washington, 221; deems it inexpedient to allow steamboat run to Mount Vernon, 225; directed to satisfy a rental claim for government use of private property, 229-30; letter introducing Gov. Hall of Mo., 230; and Grant's assignment to command the armies of the U. S., 234n, 236n, 239-40; letter from L. on policy toward prisoners-of-war, 254-57; request of N. J.

Stanton, Edwin McMasters (*continued*):
railroad to run a track through government land, 263-64; Pa. school teachers express administration support, 271; Townsend requests court of inquiry into his conduct at Gettysburg, 273; arrest of Stone, 285-86; Tenn. protest against rumored assignment of Buell to Knoxville (Apr. '64), 287-88; and question of Blair's holding a military commission while in Congress, 307, 312, 319-20, 326-27; arrangements for the enlistment of 100-day troops, 308, 312-13; Grant expresses gratitude for his cooperation, 325n

His opinion on retaliation for Fort Pillow massacre, VII: 328-29, 345-46; directed to "relax" order prohibiting export of horses, 331; press release disclaimed by L., 332; complaint against soldiers in Kans. "pressing hay and corn," 343; spurious proclamation published by N. Y. newspapers (May '64), 348n, 512-13, VIII: 13-14; refuses to approve pass for N. Y. *Times* correspondent, VII: 360-61; and reimbursement for expenditures made under his orders, 362; requested by L. to investigate charges of impressment of Negroes by recruiting parties, 363; and termination of officers' pay in cases of resignations, 368-69; the protection of a Department's commanding general not limited by considerations of color or age, 374; and status of 3-year men enlisting after mustering in of regiment, 376; recommends repeal of the $300-clause of the enrollment act, 380; Hobson's defeat and capture near Cythiana, Ky., 391-92; mistakenly announces capture of Petersburg, Va., 399n; urged to authorize resumption of assessments in West Ky., 400; interpretation of the law in respect to pay, bounty, and clothing for colored soldiers, 404n, 440; L. rejects his suggestion of a bodyguard, 423

Complaints against commissioners examining claims of Md. owners of slaves enlisted in the army, VII: 432-33; and Grant's request for the release of Dr. Barrett, 436; letter from L. on Blair's reported offensive remarks about military officers in Washington, 439-40; women arsenal workers' petition for a pay increase, 466; Halleck placed in command of combined Department of Susquehanna, Washington, Middle and West Va., 470n; and Hunter's order removing or imprisoning some citizens of Frederick, Md., 477-78; and military possession of the Northwestern R. R., 478; arranges meeting with Grant and L. (Aug. '64), 482; agrees with with L. on advisability of a Grant-Lee conference for mutual discontinuance of destruction of private property, 493; Owen requests court-martial trial, 505-506; and Raymond's peace mission, 518n; Ark. requests U. S. aid in driving rebels from state, 519; Sigel requests court of inquiry, 521; checks Richmond newspaper report of Union possession of Fort Morgan, 522n; and enlistment of prisoners-of-war, 530n, VIII: 14, 17

Order for celebration of victories at Atlanta and Mobile,

Stanton, Edwin McMasters (*continued*):
VII: 532; L. helps boy obtain interview with him, 534; Washington newspapers complain of necessity of getting War Department news from N. Y., 546; orders of thanks for 100-day troops, 547, VIII: 33-34; and the 1864 election, VIII: 11-12, 41, 46-47, 89, 91-92, 100n; objects to proposed Treasury order in relation to freedmen and plantations, 31; army officer protests order disgracing his regiment as a result of capture of regimental colors, 32; and exchange of naval prisoners through army lines, 37n; his permission to Sanitary Association agent to visit sick and wounded soldiers, 55n; a scheme to convert rebels through cotton trading contacts, 93n; and attempt "to devise means of pacification" for Ky. (Nov. '64), 120; Banks' dissatisfaction at his failure to receive military command of the Department of the Gulf (Nov.-Dec. '64), 121, 131n; complaints against Commission investigating loyalty cases in Md., 158; order appointing commissioners to investigate military division west of the Mississippi R., 161-62; and trade regulations between Ky. and Ohio, 197

Directed by L. to urge Sherman to move quickly (Jan. 5, '65), VIII: 201; Butler requests permission to publish his report on "the Wilmington expedition," 207-208; Hovey's interpretation of his instructions in respect to pardons, 211n; requests L. audience for N. Y. commissioners concerning imprisoned citizens, 212n; L. requests Brown's report of Shelby's raid (fall '64), 220; and the Hampton Roads peace conference, 246-47, 265, 269-70, 274-85; complaints against forcing Ky. Negroes into military service, 268; proposed Negro officering of colored troops, 272-73; draft of West Tenn. proposals concerning reestablishment of state government, 295n; designation of military prisons, 300; reorganization of First Army Corps, 307; objects to release of Pryor, 314n; capture of Robert Breckinridge with orders for Confederate officers and men in Ky., 315n; directs Grant to have no conference with Lee except on strictly military matters (Mar. '65), 330-31; and the question of assessments in St. Louis County, Mo., 342n; reported use of Treasury trade permits to deliver supplies to rebel army, 343-45; protest against Grant's destruction of tobacco purchased under a trade permit, 353n; requested to see new Representative from Ill., 366; Crook relieved from command of the Department of the Cumberland, 371n; orders arrest of Mrs. Ewell, 372n; communications to and from L. during L.'s visit to City Point, Va. (Mar. 25-Apr. 7, '65), 372-92; arranges for Fort Sumter flag-raising, 375-76; cautions L. against exposing himself to enemy fire, 384n; receives reports from Dana on reinstatement of Va., 387n; reports on progress of Seward's recovery (Apr. '65), 389n; crowd at peace demonstration call for his appearance, 393n; L. requests flags for son Tad,

395; his opinion on reopening of Richmond churches, 405n; starts process of demobilization (Apr. 13, '65), 409n

And military operations: *(spring '62)* V: 157-59, 179, 182n, 200n, 203n, 207, 209n, 210n, 216, 219n, 230n, 233n, 240n, 243n, 245n, 246, 247n, 248n, 251n, 254n, 255-56, 259, 264n, 268n, 272, 273n, 274n, 276n, 280, 281n, 286n, 288n, 289n, 290n, 293n, 294n, 295n, 298n, 300, 305n, 306n, 308, 310n, 314n, 321n, VIII: 426; *(fall '62)* V: 452n, 469n, 478; *(spring '63)* VI: 196n, 197n, 201, 210, 273n, 321-22, 350, 373, 377; *(fall '63)* 399-400, 436, 471n, 525n, 554n; *(spring '64)* VII: 359, *(summer '64)* 424n; *(Feb. '65)* VIII: 316-17; *(spring '65)* 373-92

Assignments to duty, transfers, and leaves of absence, V: 103, 180n, 262-63, 271n, 360, 367, 406, 425, 428-29, 469, 488, 499n, 506, 541; VI: 93n, 97, 113, 141, 154, 235, 312, 372-73, 382-83, 552; VII: 11, 113-14, 119-20, 217, 277, 464, 509-10, 513; VIII: 91

Requests for passes and permission to travel to and from the South, V: 354; VI: 421-22, 553; VII: 4, 27, 74, 84, 136, 287, 354, 360-61, 408n, 525; VIII: 38, 119, 238, 321n, 351, 409n, 427

Arrests, paroles, pardons, discharges, resignations and dismissals, V: 163, 176, 183, 188n, 249, 285-86, 300, 370, 403, 408, 426-27, 429, 458, 493n, 538-39; VI: 1-2, 18, 55, 60, 63, 67, 86, 114, 126-27, 144, 148, 153, 158, 161-62, 169, 179, 184, 208, 219-20, 223, 242, 258-59, 286, 294, 309, 312-13, 324, 351, 384, 392, 394, 398, 399n, 426-27, 429, 431-32, 436, 438, 441, 452, 462,

465, 504, 507-508, 513, 516, 520, 532-33, 536-37, 545; VII: 2, 11-12, 34, 65-66, 80, 89, 94-95, 97, 100, 103, 158, 171-72, 188, 194, 195, 199, 204, 208, 230-31, 238, 250, 254-57, 285-86, 289n, 293, 298n, 309, 323, 330n, 358, 362, 372-73, 375, 393-94, 421, 427, 430, 454-55, 474, 486, 505-506, 524-25; VIII: 10n, 48, 74, 81, 119, 125, 193, 198, 204n, 211n, 229n, 234, 236-37, 240n, 291, 293, 303n, 307, 322, 347-48, 372n, 417

Mentioned also, V: 480; VI: 137, 216, 221, 232, 295, 310n, 339, 385, 400, 431, 542; VII: 127, 181-82, 276-77, 279n, 291, 310, 335, 443, 450, 468n; VIII: 40, 90, 114n, 173, 220, 309n, 413n, 419

See also Stanton, Edwin McMasters, appointments and promotions; *and* Stanton, Edwin McMasters, reports transmitted to Congress on

Stanton, Edwin McMasters, appointments and promotions: V: 79n, 101, 102-104, 107-108, 111, 114, 126, 129-31, 135, 138-40, 142-43, 148, 156, 159, 164, 167-75, 177, 179-83, 187, 191-93, 196, 201-202, 205-207, 211n, 216-17, 221, 224, 229-30, 253, 261-63, 266, 271, 283, 299, 304, 316-17, 320, 326-27, 332, 334, 340, 342, 348, 351, 361, 365-67, 377, 379, 381, 384, 391, 394-95, 398, 405, 410-11, 426, 430, 437, 441, 446, 455-56, 458, 466, 470-72, 475, 501, 539-40, 543, 552

VI: 5, 10, 18-19, 44, 50, 55, 63, 81n, 83, 94, 96, 98, 100, 107, 114, 126, 130, 147, 149, 153, 154, 161, 163-64, 177, 180-82, 185, 191n, 194, 208, 228, 232, 235, 236-37, 254-55, 258-59, 291-92, 334, 351, 352, 386, 413, 419-20, 428, 443, 452-53, 477, 480, 490, 509, 528, 533

VII: 3, 11, 27-28, 74, 88, 92,

97, 101, 102, 114, 117, 119, 121, 133, 137-38, 141-44, 154n, 174, 203, 230, 249, 253n, 260-61, 277, 279, 289, 307, 311, 345, 357-58, 374, 375n, 379, 400, 418, 430, 439, 443-44, 450, 452, 484, 491-92, 496, 502, 509, 513, 537-38, 545 VIII: 35, 44, 76, 78-79, 102-103, 118-19, 127, 175, 184n, 189, 191, 197, 214, 225, 255, 316, 334, 349, 362-63, 373n, 405, 417-18, 426, 594

Stanton, Edwin McMasters, reports transmitted to Congress on: arrests in Ky., V: 227; education of Negro and white children in N. C., 259-60; reorganization of medical department, 275; on number of paymasters, commissaries, and quartermasters, VI: 116; alleged Confederate execution of prisoners-of-war, VII: 123; exchange of prisoners-of-war, 168; reenlistment of veteran volunteers, 214; assignment of McLean to Vancouver, 290; appointment nominations (Apr. '64), 311; the $300-clause of the enrollment act, 380; trial of William Yocum, 389-90; reported enlistment of men in Ireland or Canada, 415-16; arrest of Ky. lieutenant governor and presidential elector, VIII: 250; Banks' order concerning compensated plantation labor, 317; explosion of a mine in Petersburg, 324

Stanton, Mrs. Edwin McMasters, see Stanton, Ellen M.

Stanton, Ellen M. (Hutchinson), VIII: 373n

Stanton, Frederick Perry, I: 502; IV: 167; V: 451n; VI: 395

Stanton, Henry B., IV: 307, 334

Stanton, Robert L., VII: 345

Stanton Hospital (Washington), V: 465n; VII: 496

Staples, D. J., IV: 301

Stapp, James T. B., I: 116; II: 52

Star (steam tug), VII: 457n

Star of the West (steamer), VIII: 1

Starbuck, C. L., II: 186

Stark County Democrat [Canton, Ohio], IV: 215n

Starks, Joseph, VIII: 69

Starkweather, William A., IV: 406n; VIII: 359n

Starr, John Farson, VI: 191

Starr, Samuel Henry, IV: 500n

Statement of the Causes Which Led to the Dismissal of Surgeon-General William A. Hammond, A (Hammond), VII: 475n

States rights, L. on, I: 75, 126, 348; II: 238-39, 267, 345-47, 451, 494; IV: 162, 195-96, 251, 263-68, 433-37; V: 145; VI: 331n; see also Popular sovereignty

Staunton (Va.), VI: 115, 354n

Stead, Samuel, I: 405n

Steadman, see Steedman, James Blair

Steampower, L. on, III: 358-59, 476-77

Stearns, ——— (CSA), V: 402n

Stearns, William K., VII: 206

Stebbins, Henry, III: 392; V: 548; VII: 278

Steck, Michael, VII: 70; VIII: 157

Stedman, Griffin Alexander, Jr., VII: 484n

Steed, John [Jonas], VIII: 16-17

Steedman, James Blair, VIII: 7

Steel & Aymer, II: 180, 184

Steele, A. A., VIII: 69

Steele, Ella, VII: 295; VIII: 309

Steele, Frederick, V: 463, 500; VI: 72-73, 226n, 230, 503; VII: 108-109, 141-42, 144, 154-55, 161, 173, 180, 185, 189, 190-91, 199, 204-205, 208n, 221-22, 253, 318n, 398, 418; VIII: 35n, 109-10

Steele, George, II: 179-82

Steele, James, II: 389
Steele, John, VI: 286; VII: 314n, 525n
Steele, John Benedict, V: 383, 490-91; VII: 180, 538
Steele, William, VII: 524n
Steele, William Gaston, V: 20n
Steele, William W., VI: 72n; VII: 109n, 142n, 155n, 161n
Steele's Bayou (Miss.), VI: 142n
Stegall, John, VIII: 70
Steinwehr, Adolph von, VI: 168n
Stellwagen, Henry S., VIII: 271
Stembel, James McBride, V: 387-88
Stembel, Roger N., VII: 199-200
Stéphanie Clotilde Louise Herminie Marie Charlotte, Princess of the Belgians, VII: 477
Stephens, Alexander Hamilton, I: 448; II: 2n; III: 269, 295, 423; IV: 146, 155, 160-61, 169n; VI: 314-17; VII: 441n, 483n, 489-90; VIII: 9n, 27, 246-48, 250, 258-59, 269, 276-88, 388
Stephens, James L., VI: 37
Stephens, John A., VIII: 259, 287-88
Stephens, Robert Allan, I: 519n
Stephens, Robert G., VIII: 287n
Stephens, Thomas, VIII: 68
Stephens, William N., VI: 425-26, 428
Stephens, Douglass & Norton, II: 181
Stephenson, Benjamin Franklin, VIII: 316
Stephenson, James W., I: 121
Stephenson, John G., IV: 537
Stephenson, Luther J., VI: 337n
Steptoe, George W., VIII: 179
Steptoe, R. H., VIII: 179
Sterling, ———, VI: 334n
Sterling (Ill.), VIII: 261n
Stern, Alfred Whital, I: xxii; II: 208n; IV: 451n, 559n; V: 340n; VI: 53n, 79n, 393n, 559n
Sternberg, L., V: 213n
Sternbergh, Thomas, VII: 338n

Sterry, Mrs., VII: 245n
Stetler, John K., VIII: 104
Steubenville (Ohio), IV: 206-207; VI: 347n; VIII: 25n
Stevens, Buel, I: 2
Stevens, David H., I: xiv
Stevens, Henry, VI: 137
Stevens, Isaac Ingalls, IV: 504; V: 510-11
Stevens, John A., Jr., V: 357n
Stevens, Joseph, I: 2
Stevens, Lucian, VII: 314n
Stevens, Mary A., VIII: 108
Stevens, Robert J. [I.], IV: 301n, 305; VI: 128-29
Stevens, Thaddeus, II: 1; IV: 509; V: 202-203; VI: 129, 172n; VII: 216, 491; VIII: 50n, 275n, 286n
Stevens, William H., IV: 301
Stevensburg (Va.), V: 397n; VI: 535n
Stevenson, Adlai Ewing, I: xvii
Stevenson, John Dunlap, VIII: 305, 325
Stevenson, William, VIII: 133n
Stevenson (Ala.), VI: 486n
Stewart, ———, VIII: 305
Stewart, ——— (Ga.), VIII: 120n
Stewart, Alexander Turney, VI: 112n
Stewart, Andrew, I: 474
Stewart, Charles D., VII: 541-42
Stewart, D. H., I: 2
Stewart, J. R., VII: 496n
Stewart, Mrs. James A., VII: 541n
Stewart, Joseph J., VII: 76, 97; VIII: 348
Stewart [alias Shear], Lorenzo C., VII: 227n, 313-14
Stewart, Middleton, VI: 455-57
Stewart, Richard D., IV: 399n
Stewart, Robert, I: 2
Stewart, Watson, VIII: 356n
Stewart, William D., VI: 312-13
Stewart, William Morris, VIII: 358n
Stewart County (Tenn.), VIII: 69
Stice, Charles, I: 255n, 257

Stickney, Lyman D., II: 63; V: 167n; VI: 150n
Stiles, John Dodson, VII: 92, 148n
Stillman, Isaiah, I: 509-10
Stillwater (Minn.), II: 55
Stimson, H. Warren, VIII: 85
Stineburgh, see Sternbergh, Thomas
Stipp, George W., II: 192-93
Stipp, George Winfield, V: 358, 451; VI: 235, 294
Stirling, Archibald, Jr., VII: 97; VIII: 251n
Stockton, Esther, VII: 117
Stockton, Joseph, VII: 117n
Stockton, Mrs. Joseph, see Stockton, Esther
Stockton, Thomas Baylies Whitmarsh, IV: 405
Stockton Hall ' (Leavenworth, Kans.), III: 497n
Stockton (Calif.) Land Office, IV: 305
Stoddard, William, VI: 197n
Stoddard, William Osborn, V: 54n; VIII: 242n
Stoeckl, Edouard de, V: 137
Stokes, Jordan, VIII: 28n
Stokes, William B., VIII: 125-26
Stone, Asahel, III: 399
Stone, Charles Pomroy, IV: 335n, 411n, 560; V: 167n, 201, 204; VII: 285-86
Stone, Daniel, I: 74-77, 108n, 140-41, 298; IV: 65, 105-106
Stone, Edward C., I: 418n, 465n; IV: 109n, 161n, 442n, 528n; V: 78n, 321n; VI: 171n, 248n, 284n, 400n, 412n, 523n, 561n; VII: 133n; VIII: 85n, 258n
Stone, Margaret (Ritchie), VI: 295; VIII: 161
Stone, Robert K., V: 228-29; VI: 295; VIII: 161, 179
Stone, Mrs. Robert K., see Stone, Margaret (Ritchie)
Stone, William Milo, VII: 308, 312-13, 356, 392; VIII: 33, 109
Stone, William S., I: 153n

Stoneman, George [H.], IV: 483, 519, 524n; V: 226n, 245, 289, 294, 481n; VI: 173n, 175-76, 190n, 196, 198-99, 203, 217n, 360, 537n, 551
Stone's River, battle of, VI: 104n, 117n, 138-40, 203n, 377; see also Murfreesboro (Tenn.)
"Stonewall Jackson" (editorial), VI: 214
Stony Creek (Tenn.), VIII: 68
Stookey, Daniel, I: 14
Store Chat, VIII: 373n
Storer, Bellamy, IV: 478n
Stork, Henry, VIII: 212-13
Storm, Sigurd S., VIII: 170n
Storrs, C., Jr., III: 516
Story, Joseph, I: 486; III: 525n
Story-Life of Lincoln, The (Whipple), VIII: 319n
Story's Equity, III: 344; IV: 121
Stoughton, Edwin Henry, VI: 129n
Stout, Ebenezer, I: 420
Stout, Huldah (Briggs), II: 73; VIII: 592
Stout, Nathan W., VII: 292-93
Stout, Ingoldsby & Company, I: 267
Stover, H. D., IV: 412
Stover, John Hubler, VIII: 41n, 44
Stowits, George H., VII: 171n
Strabridge, Hines, VIII: 192n
Strang, Peter O., IV: 129
Strange Affair, A (Barrett), I: 376n
Strasburg (Va.), IV: 457-58; V: 184, 235-36, 247-48, 250-52, 254-56, 264, 269, 271, 274n; VII: 456n
Strathdee, George, VI: 297n
Stratton, John Leake Newbold, IV: 391, 493
Straughn, Lev. E., VII: 432n, 482n; VIII: 158
Strawberry Plains (Tenn.), VIII: 111n
Strawbridge, James, I: 26

Strawn, David, II: 298
Streeter, Henry W., VI: 12, 185-86
Streeter, Joseph E., IV: 452, 548
Streever, Mary (Pickering), IV: 550n
Streight, Abel D., VI: 213-14
Stretch, William, VIII: 87
Strickland, Jesse H., V: 546
Striker, Ambrose K., II: 308
Stringer, Daniel, I: 332
Stringfellow, Benjamin F., II: 322n
Stringfellow, John H., II: 322n
Stringfield, John W., I: 453n
Stringham, Silas Horton, IV: 285n, 318-19, 324; V: 316
Strode, James M., III: 126
Strohm, John, IV: 167
Strong, George P., VI: 33-34, 37n
Strong, Matilda (Edwards), I: 466
Strong, Mrs. Newton D. [William], see Strong, Matilda (Edwards)
Strong, Schuyler, I: 210-11
Strong, William, I: 466
Strong, William Kerly, V: 12-13; VI: 392, 395, 402; VIII: 87-88
Strother, David Huner ("Porte Crayon"), VII: 392n
Strunk, John, II: 304-305
Struthers, Mrs. John, VI: 462
Struthers, John S., VI: 462
Stuart, Alexander Hugh Holmes, II: 93n; IV: 329-31
Stuart, Bettie, I: 159
Stuart, Charles Beebe, IV: 460n; VI: 508; VII: 274
Stuart, Charles Edward, III: 25
Stuart, George Hay, V: 67; VI: 115n; VIII: 241n, 245-46
Stuart, James Ewell Brown ("Jeb"), V: 412n, 449, 474n, 477, 481n; VI: 292
Stuart, John Todd: his legal and business affairs and references to his law partnership with L., I: 20n, 90, 92, 106-107, 116,
119-20, 122, 143, 145-46, 148, 152-53, 158, 195, 200, 207n, 208, 209, 229-30, 264, 267, 271n, 288n, II: 63, 134-35, 203-204, 212-16, 397-98, IV: 65, VIII: 337
Mention of his introduction of bills in Ill. legislature, I: 28n, 33n; his corrections to L.'s draft of a road bill, 46n; bills opposed by him in Ill. legislature, 56n, VIII: 429; co-author of Sampson's Ghost letters, I: 89n; co-founder of Springfield's Young Men's Lyceum, 108n; and threat of Douglas' contest of his Congressional seat, 151-52, 154, III: 85
Letters from L. on political affairs (1839-1841), I: 154, 158-59, 181, 184, 195, 200, 206-208, 221, 228-30, 233, 253; memo on L.-Stuart bank account, 267; listed in Sangamon County election returns (1832, 1834), 298; his Congressional speech on the tariff quoted by Cavarly in debate with Calhoun, 334-35; co-signer of pardon petitions, 346-47, II: 394-95; L.'s informant on newspaper gubernatorial election support (1845), I: 350, 363; on choice of place of holding Whig district convention (1846), 354
Co-signer of open letter and report on construction of Springfield and Alton R. R., I: 395-405; L.'s informant on Congressional legislation concerning stockholders of corporations, II: 99; co-signer of call for Whig convention (1851), 113; endorses temperance lecture, 188; member of committee to draft resolutions on death of Ill. lawyer, 289-90; bond as bank receiver, 291-92; and nomination of a Whig candidate for president (1856),

342-43; mention of his preservation of L.'s notes on a debate, III: 101n; letter from L. on Springfield post-office appointment (1861), IV: 303; L. helps his Ark. cousin to reoccupy her plantation (1863), VII: 83-84
And appointments, I: 122, II: 48n, 64, 77, 103, 310, IV: 303
Stuart, Mrs. John, see Stuart, Mary Virginia
Stuart, Joseph J., see Stewart, Joseph J.
Stuart, Mary Virginia (Nash), I: 154, 159; VII: 83n
Stuart, Middleton, see Stewart, Middleton
Stuart, Robert, I: 76
Stuart, William (Ill.), I: 152n
Stuart, William (N. Y.), IV: 311n
Stuart & Dummer (Springfield), I: 20n
Stubblefield, J., VIII: 69
Sturgeon (Mo.), IV: 466n
Sturges, Burton, IV: 44n
Sturges, Russell, VI: 112n
Sturges, Solomon, IV: 44, 394
Sturges, William, IV: 394n
Sturges Rifles, IV: 394n
Sturgis, Samuel Davis, V: 114, 168n, 287; VI: 75n
Sturtevant, Julian [John] Monson, II: 378-79; VI: 160-61; VII: 388
Sub-treasury system, L. on, I: 143, 157-79, 184, 200, 209-10; see also Bank, national
Suddards, William, VIII: 236n
Suddarth, Samuel G., VIII: 120
Suffolk (Va.), VI: 173n, 238n, 295
Sugar Creek (Ill.), I: 334
Sugar Grove (Ill.), I: 53, 130
Sugar Loaf Mountain (Md.), V: 412n
Sulgrove, James, IV: 181-82
Sullivan, Charles, I: 11
Sullivan, Daniel, VI: 478, 481-82
Sullivan, Ep., I: 11

Sullivan, Eugene, V: 206
Sullivan, Eugene L., IV: 304, 335n
Sullivan, George W., V: 266n
Sullivan, Henry V., II: 298; IV: 348
Sullivan, Jeremiah Cutler, VII: 102-103, 134
Sullivan (Ill.), III: 201
Sullivan County (Tenn.), VIII: 68
Sullivan House (Sullivan, Ill.), III: 202n
Sullivan's Island, VI: 173
Sully, Alfred, VIII: 116, 269, 298-99, 305, 309
Sulphur Springs (Va.), VI: 250n
Sum book, L.'s, I: 1-2, and facsimiles immediately preceding page 1
Summers, Alfred, I: 150n
Summers, Charles, II: 389
Summers, Conrad, II: 28
Summers, Levi, I: 15, 18, 121, 150n
Summit County Beacon [Akron, Ohio], IV: 218n
Sumner, Charles, II: 345, 514; III: 117; IV: 76, 288n, 454n; V: 39n, 43n, 107, 109n, 141n, 191n, 228; VI: 93n, 134, 157n, 176n, 185, 242-44, 248n
VII: 72n, 85n, 199n, 287-88, 293, 311n; VIII: 138n, 194n, 266n, 274n, 286n, 334, 337, 352n, 364n, 371
Sumner, Edwin Vose, V: 150, 159, 179, 184, 208-209, 226n, 256n, 310, 312, 325n, 448; VI: 77n, 82n, 131, 185, 236n; VII: 548
Sumner, G. Lynn, V: 228n
Sumner County (Tenn.), VIII: 69
Sumner (Kans.) *Gazette*, IV: 54n
Sumter (brig), V: 549
Supreme Court (Ill.): and constitutionality of the state bank, I: 62-64, II: 552; Whig opposition to reorganization, I: 234-37, 244-

49; and power of governor to remove the Sec. of State, III: 28, 232, 278, 450-51; and interpretation of an election law, 326; mentioned also, I: 239, 291n, 304, 305n, 342, 344n, 352, 354, 370-71, 394, II: 198n, 460n, 526

Supreme Court (U. S.): establishment of a national bank, I: 171, 312, II: 402-403, 496, 526, 551-52, III: 28, 232; adoption of new regulations (1842), I: 285-86; and Ill. property laws, 335

And the slavery question: II: 343n, 355, 387-88, 400-405, 463, 465-67, 487-88, 495-96, 508, 516-18, 526, 541, 548-53; III: 9, 27-29, 43, 46, 48, 51-53, 68, 78, 89, 99-101, 112, 114, 129-30, 132-33, 142-44, 179, 230-33, 242-43, 245, 250-51, 259-60, 267-68, 270, 277-78, 282, 295, 298, 316, 404, 414, 419-20, 431, 449-51, 500, 533, 543-44, 548n; IV: 67, 155, 257n, 268; VII: 54

Vacancies in (1861), V: 41; allotment of judges to circuits, 42, 465-66, 480-81, VI: 290; right of appeal to, V: 44; and the New Almaden mine case, VI: 205-206, 322, 333-34, 393-94, 422; and the draft law, 370; a petition to, VIII: 98n; Chase nominated for Chief Justice, 154; decision on president's power concerning constitutional amendments, 253n; recommended Associate Justice appointment (1865), 302n; mentioned also, I: 429

Susquehanna, Department of the, VI: 93n, 130n, 293n; VII: 157n, 469n

Susquehanna River, VI: 310, 330n; VIII: 346n

Sutherland, Joseph, VII: 32

Sutherland's Station [Southerland, Sullivan Station] (Va.), VIII: 383-85

Sutphin, Hugh L., II: 296, 481

Sutton, Goyn A., II: 434

Sutton, Robert, VI: 340

Sutton, Robert M., VIII: 303n

Suydam, Charles Crooke, VI: 82n

Swain, James B., IV: 501n

Swain, Robert B., VI: 129n

Swain, Seth M., IV: 304

Swallow, John D., II: 219

Swallow (steamboat), IV: 352n

Swan, Hurlbut, II: 298, 303; III: 65

Swan, Joseph R., III: 394-95

Swan, Press, VIII: 68

Swan, Thomas B., VIII: 68

Swan Creek (Mich.), VII: 215; VIII: 220

Swaney, James, IV: 62

Swann, Thomas, IV: 328; VI: 542-43, 558n; VII: 437-38; VIII: 348, 369, 411

Swann Auction Galleries, VII: 399n; VIII: 428n

Swartwout, Samuel (N. Y. collector under Jackson), I: 166, 177

Swartwout, Samuel (naval officer), V: 215

Swayne, Noah Haynes, V: 481; VI: 215-16, 268; VII: 534-35; VIII: 20n

Swayne, W. Marshall, VII: 187

Sweany, Dennis S., VII: 371

Sweatman, Anne, VIII: 37n

Sweatman, Robert, VIII: 37n

Sweatman, Mrs. Robert, *see* Sweatman, Anne

Sweden and Norway, IV: 283, 287; V: 17-18, 521; VIII: 228

Sweet, Benjamin Jeffery, VIII: 123n

Sweet, Forest H., catalogs cited, II: 18n; VII: 80n

Sweet, Martin P., II: 29, 303; III: 124, 144; VI: 495

Sweney, Thomas William, V: 168; VI: 520-21, 531

Swetland, S. H., V: 259n

Swett, Leonard, II: 218, 294, 340, 347; III: 489n, 513; IV: 55, 57,

83-84, 174, 287n, 495n, 529, 562n; V: 14, 353-54; VI: 94, 167n, 206, 322, 333-34, 422; VII: 376-78, 515n, 518n; VIII: 7n, 102 420

Swift, F. B., VII: 314

Swift, Mrs. George W., VIII: 77

Swift, Henry A., VIII: 363n

Swift, John C., VII: 361-62

Swift, Joseph Gardner, IV: 297

Swift, William Henry, IV: 343

Swigert, Samuel Miller, VI: 443n

Swinburne, John, VI: 211

Swingle, B. F., VIII: 68

Swinton, William, VI: 331n; VIII: 26n

Switzerland, IV: 287-88

Switzler, William F., V: 391n

Swords, Thomas, V: 192n

Sydney (Australia), IV: 362n

Sykes, George, V: 370n; VI: 342n

Syles, John R., see Lyle, John R.

Sylvan County (Tenn.?), VI: 470n

Sylvester, H. H., II: 36

Symington, John, V: 110n

Symington, Mrs. John, VIII: 185n

Symington, William N., VIII: 185

Sympher, ———, VI: 332n

Sympson, Alexander, II: 538; III: 332, 346; IV: 43, 456n

Sympson, Coleman C., IV: 456n

Sympson, Samuel A., IV: 456n

Syms, J. G., IV: 399n

Syracuse (Ill.), I: 70

Syracuse (N. Y.), IV: 222; VI: 420

T

Tabequache band of Utah Indians, VII: 70

Tabor, Stephen J. W., VI: 118n

Tad Lincoln's Father (Bayne), VIII: 421n, 425n

Taft, Halsey, V: 28n

Taft, Horatio Nelson, Sr., IV: 441; V: 28

Taft, Horatio Nelson, Jr., IV: 441; V: 28n; VIII: 421n

Taggart, David, IV: 111, 167

Tahiti, IV: 536-37, 553n

Tahohpi Wakan (Indian), VII: 325-26

Tahokaye (Indian), VII: 325-26

Tah-ta-kay-gay (Indian), V: 542

Tai-ping Rebellion (China), VI: 96n; VIII: 139n

Talambo ("Spanish settlement"), VIII: 138n

Talbot, John, VIII: 341

Talbot, Theodore, IV: 322, 324n, 409

Talbot, William, VI: 522n

Talbot, William K., VI: 58n

Talbot County (Md.), V: 285n

Talbott, Benjamin, I: 90-93, 95-100, 102-106

Talbott, John B., VII: 291

Talcott, Wait, II: 296, 303, 480; III: 371n; V: 379, 397

Talisman (steamboat), I: 13n

Tallmadge, ———, VII: 406

Tallmadge, Nathaniel Pitcher, V: 447

Tallula (Ill.), I: 23n

Tampa Bay, V: 167n

Tams, G. Yoke, IV: 119

Taney, Roger Brooke, II: 400, 403, 405, 465-66, 539, 549; III: 20-

22, 34-35, 79, 112, 114, 143, 217, 242, 259, 269, 295, 304, 322, 524n, 543n, 544n; IV: 4, 19; V: 481; VIII: 154
Tangier (Morocco), IV: 514; V: 549
Tangier election district (Md.), VII: 9n
Tanner, Henry, IV: 501
Tanner, T. B., II: 298
Tapeta Tanka (Indian), VII: 325-26
Tappahannock (Va.), VIII: 396
Tappan, Henry P., VI: 17-18
Tappan, Lewis W., VIII: 137n
Tarbell, Ida Minerva, see *The Life of Abraham Lincoln*
Tariff: L. on, I: 287, 307, 309-13, 329-30, 333-36, 339, 341, 381-82, 407-16, 454, 503-507, II: 7, 158, III: 486-87, IV: 14, 49, 119, 125, 211-15; Douglas on, III: 292-93
Tasker, Thomas T., VII: 470n
Ta-tay-hde-don (Indian), V: 542-43
Tate, Fleming, VI: 544
Tate Ibomdu (Indian), VII: 325-26
Tate Sica (Indian), VII: 325-26
Ta-te-mi-na (Indian), V: 542
Tattnall, Josiah, IV: 479n
Tatum, John W., VIII: 124-25
Tatum, Joseph, VIII: 124-25
Taunton (Mass.), II: 6-9
Taunton Daily Gazette, II: 6n
Taxation: L. on, I: 48, 147-48, 307, 309-12, II: 209-10, IV: 211, 213, VI: 448-49, VII: 505; Ill. road tax (1836), I: 50-51; collection of taxes in new (Ill.) county, 155, 198-99; share of county taxes by incorporated towns, 183-84; and Ill. state debt, 215-21; of doctors and lawyers, 252; Ill. poll tax, 394; and Ill. two-mill tax, II: 209; collection of taxes in rebellious states, V: 298-99, 502, 507-508; and in-

comes of consuls from foreign countries, VII: 41
Tayler, Robert Walker, VI: 312n
Taylor, Mrs. Albert, *see* Bledsoe, Harriet (Coxe)
Taylor, Arthur, VIII: 112
Taylor, Bayard, VII: 93
Taylor, Caleb Newbold, IV: 327
Taylor, Daniel Morgan, VIII: 291
Taylor, Edmund Dick, I: 67, 154n, 208, 298
Taylor, Edward, I: 336
Taylor, Edward B., VII: 264n
Taylor, Frank Hamilton, V: 218n
Taylor, George R., VII: 237n
Taylor, George William, V: 480
Taylor, Hawkins, III: 399-400; IV: 43, 45; V: 348
Taylor, Mrs. Howard, II: 51n
Taylor, J. N., VII: 291
Taylor, Jackson, VIII: 69
Taylor, James, VII: 172
Taylor, James (deserter), VII: 172n, 174, 180, 182
Taylor, James (N. Y.), IV: 334
Taylor, John (Sangamon Co., Ill.), I: 43, 54-55, 67, 139; II: 70
Taylor, John, Sr. (Schuyler Co., Ill.), I: 34
Taylor, Joseph Hancock, VI: 75n
Taylor, Joseph Pannel, V: 219n, 317n; VI: 86, 94, 185, 403
Taylor, Marble N., V: 3n, 26n
Taylor, Moses, V: 110n, 162n
Taylor, Nathaniel Green, VI: 525, VIII: 7n
Taylor, Richard, II: 83
Taylor, Robert F., VII: 460-61
Taylor, Robert M., VII: 521
Taylor, Samuel Staats, II: 172-73
Taylor, T. P., II: 201
Taylor, Thomas G., II: 310
Taylor, Thomas M., II: 188
Taylor, William B., IV: 334n
Taylor, Zachary, I: 381, 416n, 419, 422, 439n, 441n, 448-50, 452-54, 457-58, 463, 467-68, 472, 476-77, 479, 491-92, 498, 501-17; II: 1-9, 11-14, 17-18, 30, 39-

44, 46-51, 54, 55n, 57-58, 60, 71-72, 77-78, 82-91, 125, 144-45, 148, 150, 156, 377; III: 78, 85, 162-63, 320-21; IV: 36, 66-67, 139n, 239, 403, 420; V: 541
Taylor County (W. Va.), V: 298
Taylorville, *see* Tolersville (Va.)
Tazewell County (Ill.), I: 120, 290, 354, 357-58; II: 194n
Tazewell Mirror [Pekin, Ill.], II: 79
Tazewell Whig [Tremont, Ill.], cited, I: 349n, 351n, 353-54, 356n, 359, 383n
Tazoo (Indian), V: 542
Teasdale, Thomas C., VIII: 363, 365
Teche (La.), VII: 90n; VIII: 396
Tecumseh (Indian), II: 84
Te-he-hdo-ne-cha (Indian), V: 542
Tejon Indian Agency, IV: 306
Telegraph: message sent from a balloon, IV: 460n; completed to Salt Lake City, 558; protection against hostile Indians, V: 200n; proposed extension to Europe, V: 521, VII: 39, VIII: 138-39, 146; completed to Washington Terr., VII: 544n
Telegraph, military, V: 6n, 92n, 234n, 499n; VI: 322; VII: 205; VIII: 313n
Temperance, L. and: Springfield address, I: 271-79 (text of speech), 282-83, 290, II: 188; requests use of Hall of Representatives (Ill.) for a lecture, I: 343; on his personal habits, IV: 75, 420, VI: 487; endorses work among soldiers, IV: 451, VI: 486-90
Temple, John B., V: 262n, 370n
Templeton, Isaac F., VI: 295, 297n
Ten Bears (Indian), VI: 153n
Ten Eyck, John Conover, VII: 257n, 310, 502n, 525, 540n; VIII: 12, 26

Ten Eyck, Mrs. John Conover, VII: 540
Ten Eyck, Tenodor, VII: 257, 310
Tennessee: L. supports presidential candidacy of Senator White (1836), I: 48; admission to the Union, II: 231; position as a border state, IV: 351-52, 427, 437, V: 50, 302-303; and L.'s memo of military policy (July '61), IV: 458; and L.'s memo for a plan of campaign (Oct. '61), 544-45; Holt recommends command for Sherman in (Nov. '61), V: 22n; L. on importance of rail connection between East Tenn. and other loyal sections of the Union, 37, VII: 321; and McClellan's plans for the Army of the Potomac (Feb. '62), V: 122n; Johnson proposes exchange of secessionist prisoners for East Tennesseans held by the Confederacy in Mobile, 260, 264-65, 344n; and L.'s "view of the present [June '62] condition of the War," 291-92

Declared an insurrectionary state in proclamation concerning taxes (July '62), V: 298-99; recruitment, 302-303, VI: 393n, 471n, 521-22, 525; reestablishment of state government, V: 303, 462-63, 470-71, 489-90, VI: 187, 440-41, 462-63, 465, 468-69, VII: 144, 183-85, 196, 205, 209-10, 351-52, VIII: 148-49, 216-17, 294-96; Johnson opposes Buell command, V: 303n; appointments, 333n, 501n, VI: 137, 393n, VIII: 418n; plan for holding elections (1862), V: 470-71; Rosecrans replaces Buell in command of the Department of the Cumberland, 501n; definition of Johnson's authority as military governor, VI: 187n; trade and protection

of property in, 340n; L.'s reply to East Tenn. loyalists' petition for military protection (Aug. '63), 373-74; and the Emancipation Proclamation, 428-29; L. reports "All Tennessee is now cleared of armed insurrectionists [Sept. 11, '63]," 440 Loyalists' appeal not to withdraw U. S. forces from state, VI: 525; L. requests personal Washington consultation with Gov. Johnson, 543; L. replies to charges of federal and state arming of disloyal persons and disarming of loyal persons, 543-45; announcements of Union success in clearing state of insurgent forces, VII: 35, 49, 58; L. commends Grant's success at Chattanooga and Knoxville, 53; and amnesty oath, 130-31, VIII: 7; objections to new oath of office disqualifying loyalists previously forced to take Confederate oath, VII: 169n; opposition to rumored plan to reassign Buell to command at Knoxville, 287n; requests for Rousseau visit to deliver speeches on Negro question, 287n; protest against Johnson's proclamation concerning holding of 1864 national elections, VIII: 58-72; Johnson commends Mrs. Stevens for kindness and hospitality to Union refugees, 108n; election returns (1860, 1864), 129-30; "produced reasonably fair crops" in 1864, 148; "The President's Last, Shortest, and Best Speech" about two Tenn. ladies requesting release of their prisoner-of-war husbands, 154-55; abolishment of slavery, 216n

Military operations: (1861) IV: 524n, V: 31n, 54n, 60n; (Jan. '62) 90-91, 98-99; (spring '62) 200, 276, 295, 305n, 313, 409n; (fall '62) 483-84, 497, VII: 288n, VIII: 426; (spring-summer '63) VI: 53, 238n, 377-78; (fall '63) VI: 436, 439, 450n, 469-76, 478, 480, 483-84, 493n, 498, 505, 510-11, 522n, 525, 534-35, VII: 14, 29, 30-31, 35; (fall '64) 520, VIII: 27n, 111n, 201n

Tennessee, Department of the, VI: 241n; VII: 14n, 179n, 240, 248n; VIII: 74n, 136n

Tennessee River, V: 108n, 156n, 421; VI: 481, 483n; VII: 6n, 14n; VIII: 94

Tenney, Amos, VII: 416

Tenney, Horace Addison, V: 320n

Tenskwatawa ("the Prophet") (Indian), II: 84

Terence, L. quotes from, I: 489

Terrebonne Parish (La.), VI: 29

Terrell, Charles Milton, VI: 139n

Terrill, William Rufus, V: 458n

Territories: reports in annual messages, (1861) V: 45, 47, (1862) V: 521-22, (1863) VII: 40, (1864) VIII: 145; see also Kansas Nebraska Act and repeal of the Missouri Compromise; and Congress, the slavery question and

Appointments: IV: 293-95, 298, 303-308, 336-37, 347, 366, 391, 406-407, 447-48, 509, 550; V: 107, 171, 173-74, 178-79, 182, 256, 265, 354, 391, 467; VI: 113, 231-32, 255, 494-95; VII: 163, 166, 188, 194, 206-207, 215, 238, 264, 266, 280, 355-57, 371-72, 402-403, 428, 480, 483-84, 490; VIII: 82, 157, 168, 214, 242n, 356, 368, 410, 412; see also under Public lands and names of individual Territories

Terry, Alfred Howe, IV: 349n

Terry, Henry Dwight, VII: 171, 205

Terry, Lucius H., VIII: 341-42
Terry, P. L., VIII: 102n
Terwilliger, Eli D., V: 490-91
Teter, Abigail, *see* Eastep, Abigail (Teter)
Teter, Abraham, I: 3-4
Teter, Solomon, I: 3
Tevis, Joshua, VI: 202, 286-87; VII: 77; VIII: 23n
Texas, I: 4n, 177, 336-37, 347-48, 382, 421, 431, 433-39, 464, 468-69, 493-94; II: 9, 237-38, 243, 251, 253-54, 259, 346-47, 536
 III: 86, 111, 121, 123, 125, 137-38, 180, 224-25, 261, 271, 289, 310; IV: 66, 426, 433-34, 436, 503n
 V: 41, 123n, 298, 357; VI: 74, 77, 100n, 354-55, 364, 366n, 374-75, 465-66; VII: 90, 124n, 148n, 171; VIII: 104n
Thacher, George H., IV: 224
Thames, battle of the, I: 509
Thanksgiving proclamations, V: 32, 185-86; VI: 332-33, 496-97; VIII: 55-56
Thayer, Asahel, II: 25
Thayer, Edward R., II: 388n
Thayer, Eli, IV: 151, 154, 535n; V: 85; VI: 108n
Thayer, John Milton, VI: 142-43; VII: 185-86
Thayer, Joseph, II: 25
Thayer, Martin, II: 25
Thayer, Martin Russell, VII: 137; VIII: 312n
Thayer, William S., IV; 552; V: 229; VI: 105n; VIII: 139n
Theaker, Thomas Clarke, IV: 295
Theobald, Edward S., VI: 141, 147n
Thérèse Amélie Caroline Josephine Antoinette, Princess of Saxe-Altenburg, VII: 475
They Knew Lincoln (Washington), VI: 9n; VII: 157n
Third Avenue Railroad Company (N. Y.), V: 296n
Thirteenth Amendment to the Constitution, V: 529-32; VII: 172-73, 380-82, 411n, 433; VIII: 149, 253-54, 260-61, 289n, 403-404
"Thirty-Ninth Rebel Regiment," VI: 427n
Thomas, ———, VIII: 69
Thomas, Benjamin Platt, I: vii, xiv, xvii
Thomas, Charles, IV: 394n
Thomas, Charles G., II: 36-37; VIII: 415
Thomas, Chauncey Boardman, VI: 313n
Thomas, Cheney, I: 129
Thomas, Chloe (Short), I: 51
Thomas, Daniel G., IV: 167
Thomas, Edward M., V: 370-71, 375
Thomas, F. W., IV: 166
Thomas, Francis, IV: 455n, 486, 494; VI: 239
Thomas, Frederick A., I: 285-86, 290
Thomas, G. L., II: 536n
Thomas, George Henry, IV: 491-92, 544-45; V: 79n, 135, 321n, 546n; VI: 474-76; VII: 14n, 30n, 80n, 122, 211, 244n, 288n, 316-17, 327, 503n; VIII: 74, 97, 111-12, 135-36, 169, 171, 180-82, 217n, 372n
Thomas, H. S., II: 188
Thomas, Jack, IV: 56
Thomas, Jesse Burgess, Jr., I: 34n, 107n, 121
Thomas, John F., VIII: 69
Thomas, Joseph, I: 90, 92
Thomas, Lorenzo: and appointments, IV: 254n, 395, 413, 472n, 474n, 479-80, 484, 489, 491, 493, 498, 503, 511, 513, 529n, 530n, 551-52, V: 25, 79, 206n, 211, 217n, 277, 320n, 321, 382n, VI: 18n, 254n, 259, 452-53, VII: 3n; report received from Anderson at Fort Sumter (Apr. '61), IV: 322n; promoted to Adjutant General, 366n; army

reinstatements, 366, V: 400; letter to Harney on maintaining government authority in Mo., IV: 373n, 387; and mobilization and recruitment, 388, 390, 454, 460, V: 200n, 431, 432n, VI: 44n, 342, 374-75, 494n, 530n, VII: 212, 390

Writes Cameron on distribution of copies of Frémont proclamation, IV: 518n; requested to assign an aide to McClernand, 527; receives appeal for alleviating conditions at Camp Denison, Ohio (Sept. '61), 535; and McClellan's request for more information on maintaining martial law in St. Louis, V: 27n; and newspaper publication of his report to Cameron on conditions in Mo. leading to the removal of Frémont, V: 65-66; arrest of Benham, 69n, VII: 174n; reassignments and promotions, V: 77n, 93n, 103n, 464, VI: 75n, 235n, 516n, 533, VII: 113n, VIII: 32; rejection of plan for his constant personal attendance of L., 108; and difficulties over Lane command under Hunter, 116n; directed to execute payment of Sigel's staff, 117n; L. submits to Congress his report on employment of army officers in the recruiting service, 140n; examines reports of McClellan's operations in carrying out L.'s order to keep Washington "entirely secure," 151n, 164n, 179n; and Stanton's preliminary draft of President's War Order No. 3, 155n; receives McClellan's report on action along James R. and need of reinforcements, 301n; leave of absence for Morrison, 342; requested to help Robert Lincoln "find . . . John Reed," 347n

Discharges, resignations, and suspensions from duty, 358, 465, VII: 455n; loyalty of his subordinates questioned by Schurz, V: 510-11; reports military operations near Harrisburg (July 8, '63), VI: 321-22; L. commends his work of recruiting Negro troops, 342; and Grant's removal of McClernand, 380n; Stanton proposes his assignment to accompany L. to Gettysburg, VII: 16n; and Mississippi woman's claim for government protection of her property, 131-32; assigned to control plantation leasing and employment of Negroes in Miss. area, 212, 217-18; and cases of persons resisting the draft, 393n, VIII: 418; directed to authorize equal pay for colored and white troops, VII: 406n; and claims for supplies taken by the army from La. citizens, 492n; instructed to release two prisoners from Albany (N. Y.) Penitentiary, VIII: 119n; L. submits to Congress his report on exchange of prisoners-of-war, 204; and pardons, 357; mentioned also, V: 167n, VI: 537n

Thomas, Martin, IV: 512

Thomas, Richard Symmes, Jr., I: 307, 309, 332, 422-23, 455, 461, 478-79; II: 73, 80-81, 226

Thomas, Scott, I: 290n

Thomas, Stephen, VIII: 255

Thomas, William, I: 61, 445-47; II: 75; IV: 459n, 538n

Thomas, William (McLean County, Ill.), III: 518

Thomas, William B., IV: 167, 329n, 362, 486n; VI: 145n, 525

"Thomas à Becket" [pseud.], VIII: 136n

Thomas Collyer (steamboat), VII: 225

Thomasson, Charles L., IV: 393; VI: 10n

Thomasson, William Poindexter, IV: 521; VI: 83

Thompson, ———, II: 112; VI: 286

Thompson, Ambrose W., IV: 561n; V: 3n, 414; VI: 246n; VII: 285

Thompson, Ambrose W., Jr., V: 3n

Thompson, Charles H., II: 44n; VIII: 170

Thompson, Charles Manfred, I: 406n

Thompson, Clark W., IV: 288n; VII: 344-45

Thompson, David, II: 442-43

Thompson, Gideon W. [H.], VIII: 166

Thompson, Mrs. Gideon W., see Thompson, Nancy H.

Thompson, J. L., I: 298

Thompson, Jacob, VII: 443n

Thompson, Jared D., VII: 207n

Thompson, John [William], VI: 400

Thompson, John Edgar, IV: 513

Thompson, Joseph, VIII: 69

Thompson, Mrs. Lewis S., IV: 48n

Thompson, Nancy H., VIII: 166

Thompson, Newell A., IV: 334

Thompson, Philo Hale, I: 349; II: 44, 47n

Thompson, Richard Wigginton, II: 51, 56; IV: 54, 79, 82-84, 133; V: 351; VI: 259; VII: 364-65, 464-65; VIII: 287

Thompson, Richard Wigginton, Jr., VII: 364-65

Thompson, Robert Means, IV: 507n

Thompson, S. P., III: 333n

Thompson, Samuel M., I: 11; II: 108, 312, 319

Thompson place (S. C.), VI: 456

Thoms, Robert Scott, VI: 139-40

Thomson, Clifford, VI: 509

Thomson, William, VIII: 348

Thorek, Max, V: 135n; VIII: 162n

Thornburgh, Duff Green, VIII: 68

Thorne, Eileen, IV: 558n

Thorne, John C., VIII: 415n

Thorne, Mrs. R. M., VII: 525n

Thorne, Richard, II: 186, 381-82

Thornton, Anthony, I: 389; II: 161-62, 204n, 342

Thornton, H. W., I: 249

Thornton, James Shepard, VIII: 134

Thornton, James T., III: 344

Thornton, John P. M. [W.], VII: 137

Thornton, Joseph, I: 405-406

Thornton, Seth Barton, I: 473; II: 84

Thornton, Waterman, VIII: 203

Thornton, William Fitzhugh, I: 67, 124, 140, 146; II: 181-82, 184, 204; IV: 107

Thornton's Gap (Va.), V: 461

Thorntown (Ind.), IV: 192-93

Thoroughfare Gap (Va), V. 248n, 399n

Thoroughman, Thomas, VI: 1-2

Thorp, Albert Gallatin, VI: 331n

Threlkeld, Thomas, I: 249

Through Five Administrations, Reminiscences of Colonel William H. Crook, VIII: 328n

Tibbetts, Abner, VIII: 363n

Tibbs, Joseph, I: 11

Tibbs, Samuel, I: 11

Tichenor, Edward, VIII: 196n

Tiffin (Ohio), V: 197

Tilden, L. L., IV: 537n

Tillie, John, I: 51

Tillinghast, Charles H., IV: 382

Tillson, Davis, VII: 219n, 220

Tillson, John, Jr., I: 67; II: 73; VIII: 592

Tilton, J. E., IV: 75

Timberlake, Thomas Collins, V: 161n

"Times When Lincoln Remem-

bered Albion" (art.), IV: 39n; VIII: 310n

Timmons, Thomas, VII: 482n; VIII: 158

Tingley, George B., IV: 305

Tinker, Charles A., VI: 475n; VII: 210n

Tinkham, Edward I. [J.], II: 177-78

Tinkham, Melville A., V: 21n

Tinsley, Seth M., I: 92, 101, 104, 251, 331

Tioga (gunboat), VIII: 140n

Tippecanoe, battle of, VIII: 374n

Tippett, Samuel, VIII: 69

Tipton, Isaac H., VII: 100n

Tipton, John P., VII: 100

Tipton, Landon P., VII: 100n

Tipton County (Tenn.), VIII: 70

Tiskilwa (Ill.) *Independent*, II: 347n

Titusville (Pa.), II: 349n

"To the Electors of Tazewell County" (broadside), I: 329

Toasts by L., I: 87-88; II: 483

Tobey, Samuel Boyd, V: 165-66

Tobias, James, II: 396n

Tod, David, V: 369n, 432n; VI: 50n, 131, 287, 515n; VII: 94, 277, 420, 423n; VIII: 337, 347n

Todd, Ann, *see* Campbell, Ann (Todd)

Todd, Charles S., V: 22-23; VIII: 181

Todd, Charles S. (Capt.), VI: 22-23

Todd, Eliza (Parker), VI: 517, 537n, 553n; VII: 7

Todd, Elizabeth (Humphreys), VI: 517, 553n; VII: 7

Todd, Elizabeth J., *see* Grimsley, Elizabeth J. (Todd)

Todd, Emily, *see* Helm, Emily (Todd)

Todd, Frances J., *see* Wallace, Frances J. (Todd)

Todd, Henry B., VI: 208n

Todd, John, II: 62n, 317, 437n; IV: 323n

Todd, John Blair Smith, IV: 530; V: 364; VII: 139n

Todd, Katherine, VI: 529n

Todd, Lemuel, VIII: 84-85

Todd, Levi Oldham, II: 197, 200, 203-204

Todd, Lockwood M., IV: 323, 345

Todd, Lyman B., VI: 517, 553

Todd, Mary, *see* Lincoln, Mary (Todd)

Todd, Robert Smith, I: 465-66, 473; II: 195-97, 203, 205, 318n; IV: 65, 70

Todd, Mrs. Robert Smith, *see* Todd, Eliza

Todd, William B., VII: 318

Tolersville [Taylorville] (Va.), VI: 249n

Toles, William G., VII: 130

Tollefsen, Carl, VII: 2n

Tolono (Ill.), III: 91n; IV: 191

Tompkins, Charles Henry, V: 206n; VIII: 393n

Tompkins, Frederick, VIII: 321

Tompkins, George W. B., V: 167

Tompkins, Logan, VII: 307n, 312

Tompkins, Patrick Watson, I: 450, 497

Tompkinsville (Ky.), V: 402n, 409n, 417n

Tonica and Petersburg Railroad, III: 343n

Toombs, Robert, II: 2n, 377-78; III: 53, 74, 149-56, 159-65, 184-86, 188-93, 195-98, 242, 244-45, 548n

Toon-kan-e-chah-tay-mane (Indian), V: 542

Toon-kan-ka-yag-e-na-jin (Indian), V: 543

Toon-kan-shkan-shkan-mene-hay (Indian) V: 543

Topliff, E. C., VIII: 231n

Topographical Engineers, Bureau of, IV: 517n, 527n, 554n; V: 171n

Torbert, Alfred Thomas Archimedes, V: 480

Toro, Manuel Murillo, *see* Murillo Toro, Manuel
Torpedo (Confederate ship), VI: 315n
Torrey, E. C., I: 348
Torrey, Mrs. E. C., *see* Torrey, Eliza S.
Torrey, Eliza S. (Cabot), I: 348
Torrey, Joseph, & Company (Springfield), I: 286-87
Torsey, Henry P., VII: 216, 357n, 371-72
Tortugas, the, *see* Dry Tortugas Islands
Tosk, ———, V: 380n
Totten, George Mansfield, V: 388
Totten, Joseph Gilbert, IV: 285n, 297n, 350, 417, 517; V: 13, 58, 60-61, 81, 85, 103-104, 152, 176-77, 219n, 261; VI: 188, 193, 216, 461n; VIII: 265n
Touro, John, VII: 492n
Towers, John T., I: 468
Towers, Lemuel, I: 468n
Towers, Michael, VI: 545n
Townley, Wayne C., II: 289n
Townsend, Copeland, IV: 294-95; V: 265
Townsend, Edward Davis, IV: 500n, 562n; V: 385n, 404; VI: 248n, 294, 355n, 392n, 433n; VII: 33n, 95n, 177n, 179n, 183n, 208, 273, 326-27, 478n; VIII: 13n, 303n, 371n
Townsend, J. H., VI: 421n
Townsend, Jeremiah A., I: 251
Townsend, Martin Ingham, IV: 227
Townsend, William Henry, I: xvii, 20n, 466n; II: 195n, 200n; III: 202n, 336n; IV: 74n, 303n; V: 154n; VI: 508n; VIII: 86n, 292n, 410n
Tracy, Gilbert Avery, VIII: 413n; see also *Uncollected Letters of Abraham Lincoln*
Tracy, William R., VIII: 418
Trade with insurrectionary states,

see Cotton and other products, trade in
Trailor (Trailer) brothers (Archibald, Henry, and William), I: 255-57, 371-77
Train, Charles Russell, IV: 275n; V: 9, 158
Transactions of the Illinois State Historical Society, I: 210n; III: 352n, 515n; VIII: 427n
Trans-Mississippi Department (C.S.A.), VI: 31n
Transportation, L. on importance of, II: 439-40; IV: 192
Transylvania College, II: 319n
Trapp, A. H., II: 298, 305
Travis, Daniel, I: 354-55
Treason: L. on, VI: 262-65, VII: 54, 132; cases of persons charged with, IV: 414, VI: 118n, 360-61, 421, 425-26, 428, 482, VII: 105n, 156n, 348, 393
Treasury Department (U. S.): claims forwarded by L. to the third auditor of, I: 79-80, 100-101, 430; engraving of treasury notes, IV: 326; *see also* Revenue and expenditures (national); *and* Chase, Salmon Portland
Treasury notes, U. S., IV: 325-26; V: 282-83; VI: 60-62; VIII: 80n
Treat, Samuel, V: 501-502
Treat, Samuel Hubbel, I: 43, 122, 239, 344, 347, 349, 352; II: 79, 160; III: 393, 494n; V: 266n; VI: 62-63; VII: 422-23; VIII: 592
Treaties and agreements with foreign powers: boundaries (Great Britain), IV: 287-88; deserting seamen (Denmark), 447; postal conventions, (Mexico) 467, V: 113, 189-90, (Costa Rica) V: 312, 521; Brunshausen and Scheldt Dues (Hanover and Belgium), V: 58, 131-32, 519, VII: 37, 87, VIII: 203-204;

amity and commerce, (Bolivia) V: 72-73, (Salvador) 253, (Nicaragua) 190-91, VII: 37, (Ottoman Empire) V: 176, 521, (Liberia and Haiti) 521, 550, (Honduras) VIII: 167; loans (Mexico), V: 73-74, 281-82; extradition, (Mexico) V: 113, 189-90, (Cuba) VII: 370n, 399-400, (Haiti) VIII: 166-67; suppression of slave trade (Great Britain), V: 186, 265, 339n, 367n, 403n, 519, VI: 110, VII: 36; settlement of various claims, (Granada) V: 521, VI: 56-58, VII: 37, 389, (Ecuador) VI: 35-36, VII: 247, (Peru) VI: 92-93, VII: 37, 88, (Great Britain) VII: 36-37, 76, 246-47, VIII: 140; trade (China), VII: 147-48; reciprocity (Sandwich Islands), VII: 169

Treaties with Indian tribes: Delaware, IV: 453, 455, 476-77, 540, VII: 403; Arapahoe and Cheyenne, IV: 464; Pottawatomie, V: 89, 101-102, VI: 109; Poncas, V: 106-107; Kaskaskia Piankeshaw, and Wea, 147; Sac and Fox, 189, 307, VII: 69-70; "Kansas tribe," V: 218-19, VII: 407; Ottawa, V: 287-88; Kickapoo, 315; Cherokee, 439-40; Chippewa, VI: 135, VII: 116-17, 215, 299, 344-45, VIII: 219-20; Comanche, Kiowa, Apache, and Osage, VII: 68; Creek, 69; Tabequache, 70; Shoshone, 112-13; Shawnee, 261; Nez Percé, 284; Klamath and Modoc, VIII: 322

Tremain, Lyman, V: 473n

Tremble, see Trimble, Isaac Ridgway

Tremont (Ill.), I: 120, 154n, 209-10, 299, 318, 329, 354-55, 377, 384; III: 76-77

Tremont House (Chicago), IV: 145n

Trent, Alexander, I: 4, 11, 16-17
Trent, Henry, I: 18
Trent, Martin S., I: 16-18
Trent, Williamson, I: 18, 47
Trent affair, V: 26, 62-64, 82-83, 92, 95-96, 102, 115, 137, 141, 166n
Trenton (N. J.), IV: 235-38; VII: 397n, 458
Trenton House (Trenton, N. J.), IV: 237-38
Trevelyan, George Macaulay, VII: 71n
Tribune Association of New York, VII: 249n
Tribune Tracts No. 4, III: 522n
Tribune Tracts No. 6, IV: 60n
Trimble, ———, IV: 74
Trimble, Isaac Ridgway, VI: 274n, 324-25, 557; VII: 119-20
Trimble, L. T., IV: 558n
Trinidad (British West Indies), IV: 447
Trinidad (Cuba), V: 73n
Triplett, Marshall, V: 278
Tripp, Hamilton, VI: 456
Tripp, Oliver, VI: 456
Tripp, Thomas James, VI: 456
Trist, Nicholas P., IV: 502n
Triton (slave ship), V: 47n
Troops, equipment and supplies for: new type of tent, VI: 105n; proposed steam ram for harbor defense, 163; new types of clothing, 519, 523, VII: 416; proposed floating harbor obstruction, VII: 468; proposed fire protection for wooden buildings, VIII: 213; new types of guns and ammunition, IV: 399, 534-35, V: 4-5, 99, 181-82, 198, 257, 263, 354, 365, 385, 476, VI: 3-5, 59, 107, 145, 206, 255, 270, 342-43, 367-68, 484-85, 521, 530-31, 559-61, VII: 3-4, 127, 216n, 229, 236-37, 510, VIII: 3 Use of balloons, IV: 460; procurement, production, and government contracts, IV: 343-44,

400, 412, 415-16, 499-500, 509, 512-13, 515-16, 534-35, V: 20n, 33-34, 54, 60-61, 75-76, 85, 163, 165, 174, 189, 196-97, 230, VI: 59, 122, 298n, VII: 29-30, 168, 202, 275, 362, 421, 448, 522-23, VIII: 104, 178, 201-203, 323; procurement of boats and ships, *see under* Navy, U. S.; requests for and assignments of, IV: 374-75, 381, 395-96, 419, 443, 464, 485, 504, 510, 525, 529-30, 535-38, 541, V: 3n, 18, 20, 151-52, 156, 172, 182, 184-85, 203-204, 225, 430-31, VI: 59

Troops, mobilization and recruitment (1861-1865): Blair's opposition to War Department policies, IV: 369, 370n; conflict between state and federal authorities, 375-76, 382, 384, 402, 556-57, V: 15-17, 349n, 391-93, 515-16, 538; McClellan complains of lack of men and arms, V: 182, 184-85, VI: 59; recruiting reports requested from Union governors, V: 347; on the manpower situation (Aug. '62), 355; on status of U. S. Sharpshooters, 431; on protest of McClellan officer-recruiting order (Oct. '62), 482-83; memo (Apr. '63) on army strength, VI: 164; illegal enlistment of Indians, VII: 27; plan of Middle West governors to recruit 100-day troops, 308, 312-13; rumored recruiting in foreign countries, 415-16; conflict between civilian and military recruiting officers, 449-50; protested recruiting of prisoners-of-war, 530-31, VIII: 14, 17, 40, 359; *see also* Draft (1862-1865); *and* Negro troops

Proclamations calling for: 75,000 militia (Apr. '61) for 20-day service, IV: 330-33; 3-yr. volunteers (May '61), 353-54;

300,000 volunteers (June '62), V: 293-94, 296-97, 302-304; 100,-000 militia (June '63), VI: 277-78; 300,000 volunteers (Oct. '63), 523-24; 500,000 volunteers (July '64), VII: 448-49, 452-53; 300,000 volunteers (Dec. '64), VIII: 171-72

Responses to proclamations and receipts of troops, IV: 333-550 *passim*; V: 9, 14n, 15, 23, 27, 29n, 40, 71, 96, 163, 194n, 200, 257, 267, 283, 291, 334, 339, 347, 350, 365, 367-68, 391-93, 411, 413-15, 456-57, 468-69, 476, 483, 546; VI: 43, 59, 97n, 134, 141, 147, 171, 282-83, 285, 311n, 317; VII: 206, 241, 249-50, 319, 338, 340-41, 376, 388-89

Troops, specific artillery units:
Connecticut (heavy)
1st Regt., VIII: 235
Illinois (light)
1st Regt., IV: 457n
2d Regt., VI: 44n; VIII: 367n
Maine
1st Battery, VII: 271n
3d Battery, VII: 277n
5th Battery, VIII: 233n
Massachusetts (heavy)
1st Regt., IV: 404n; VIII: 117n
4th Regt., VIII: 189
New York
2d Regt., V: 193n; VII: 444n, 509n
3d Regt., VI: 127n, 147n
5th Regt., VI: 75n; VII: 17n
13th Regt., V: 25n
14th Regt., VII: 227n
16th Regt., VI: 257n
28th Independent Battery, VIII: 368n
35th Independent Battery, VI: 257n
New York (heavy)
2d Regt., VII: 526
4th Regt., VI: 211n
5th Regt., VIII: 300-301, 325n
7th Regt., VII: 298

Ohio (heavy)
2d Regt., VII: 314n
Pennsylvania
1st Regt., VII: 82
2d Regt., VII: 82; VIII: 32n;
  see also Pennsylvania
  Infantry, 112th Regt.
3d Regt., VII: 125
Pennsylvania (heavy)
2d Regt., VII: 444; VIII: 133n
3d Regt., VII: 341n; VIII: 163n
Rhode Island
5th Regt., VIII: 290n
Rhode Island (light)
1st Regt., V: 431n
Tennessee (light)
1st Regt., VIII: 60n
Wisconsin (heavy)
1st Regt., VIII: 102-103
United States
1st Regt., IV: 409; V: 211n; VI:
  127n; VII: 241n
1st (colored) Regt., VII: 212n
2d Regt., V: 156n, 159n; VII:
  176n
3d Regt., IV: 392n; V: 33n,
  426n; VI: 223n
5th Regt., IV: 410n, 494n; V:
  202n; VII: 92
TROOPS, specific cavalry units:
Colorado Territory
1st Regt., VI: 335n
Connecticut
1st Regt., VI: 232n
Illinois
1st Regt., V: 58n, 351n
4th Regt., V: 457n; VI: 17n;
  VII: 482n
5th Regt., IV: 461n; VI: 490n;
  VIII: 307n
7th Regt., VI: 7n
8th Regt., V: 321n, 540n; VII:
  15n, 28n; VIII: 190n
10th Regt., IV: 551n; V: 177-78
12th Regt., VI: 207n
16th Regt., VIII: 51n
17th Regt., VII: 15n
Indiana
1st Regt., VIII: 324n

2d Regt., V: 546n
5th Regt., VIII: 311n
Iowa
2d Regt., VII: 117, 279
3d Regt., VII: 117
4th Regt., VII: 525n
5th Regt., IV: 121n; V: 490n
6th Regt., VI: 336n
7th Regt., VI: 545n; VIII: 6n
Kansas
11th Regt., VI: 67n
14th Regt., VIII: 159n
Kentucky (U. S. A.)
1st Regt., IV: 524n; VII: 431n
3d Regt., IV: 477n; V: 11n,
  458n
4th Regt., IV: 464n; VII: 119n;
  VIII: 91n
5th Regt., VI: 225n, 229, 428n
9th Regt., V: 552n
11th Regt., VIII: 310n
Maine
(unspecified), VII: 155n
Maryland
1st Regt., V: 234n
3d Regt., VII: 9n, 27n
Massachusetts
1st Regt., V: 474n
2d Regt., VI: 335n
3d Regt., VII: 28n; VIII: 190n
Michigan
5th Regt., VII: 176n, 439n
9th Regt., VIII: 212
Missouri
2d Regt., VIII: 44n, 299n
4th Regt., VI: 63n
7th Regt., VII: 325
9th Regt., V: 517
10th Regt., V: 517
New Jersey
1st Regt., VI: 135n; VII: 298n,
  318
3d Regt., VI: 7n
New York
1st Regt., IV: 406n; VI: 509n;
  VII: 446n; VIII: 23n
1st (veteran) Regt., VII: 460,
  486n
2d Regt., VIII: 297n

2d (veteran) Regt., V: 103n
3d Regt., VI: 363n; VII: 367n
4th Regt., V: 382n
6th Regt., VII: 152, 158; VIII: 36
10th Regt., VI: 258n, 532-33
20th Regt., VIII: 30n, 34n
25th Regt., VI: 453n; VIII: 329n
Ohio
7th Regt., VII: 6n
10th Regt., VIII: 79n
Pennsylvania
1st (six-months) battalion, VII: 175n
3d Regt., VII: 543n; VIII: 214n
5th Regt., VIII: 212-13
7th Regt., VI: 168n
8th Regt., VI: 463-64; VII: 470n
11th Regt., V: 335n; VII: 142, 292n; VIII: 193n
12th Regt., VII: 25n
13th Regt., VI: 462
14th Regt., VII: 486n
15th Regt., VII: 353-54; VIII: 169n
17th Regt., VIII: 32n
18th Regt., IV: 517n; VI: 337n
Rhode Island
1st Regt., VI: 292n; VII: 241
3d Regt., VII: 241
Tennessee (East)
1st Regt., VIII: 418n
4th Regt., VII: 169n
5th Regt., V: 546n
Vermont
1st Regt., VI: 360; VIII: 176
Virginia (U. S. A.)
1st Regt., VI: 115-16
West Virginia
2d Regt., IV: 559n; VII: 537n
4th Regt., VII: 502n
Wisconsin
3d Regt., V: 23n
United States
1st Regt., IV: 501n; V: 175n, 263n; VI: 221n; VII: 88n
1st (colored) Regt., VII: 161n; VIII: 357
2d Regt., IV: 491; V: 93n; VI: 76

3d Regt., IV: 395n, 409n, 413n; V: 11n, 217n; VII: 307n
4th Regt., IV: 505n; V: 239n; VI: 86
5th Regt., V: 12n, 21n, 79n, 206n; VII: 241n; VIII: 37n
5th (colored) Regt., VI: 509
United States (Dragoons)
1st Regt., VIII: 417
2d Regt., IV: 505n
Reserve Corps (units unspecified), VI: 43, 55n, 80n
TROOPS, specific engineer units (New York):
1st Regt., VII: 221n
15th Regt., IV: 474n; VII: 376n, 538n; VIII: 88n, 240-41, 263, 301
50th Regt., IV: 460n; V: 149n; VIII: 315
TROOPS, specific infantry units:
Arkansas
1st Regt., VI: 146n
Connecticut
2d Regt., VII: 138n
5th Regt., V: 142n; VI: 524
7th Regt., V: 211n; VII: 450n
8th Regt., VII: 138
11th Regt., VI: 76n; VII: 138n, 484n; VIII: 189-90
19th Regt., VII: 323
21st Regt., VII: 114n, 367n
23d Regt., VII: 154n
Delaware
1st Regt., VIII: 226-27
2d Regt., V: 286n; VII: 58, 152
3d Regt., V: 378-79; VIII: 159n
4th Regt., V: 378-79; VI: 351
District of Columbia
1st Regt., V: 238n; VI: 433n; VII: 309n
2d Regt., V: 15n; VIII: 5n, 168n
2d Battalion, IV: 493n
Illinois
4th Regt., I: 395, 446, 453n
6th Regt., I: 395
7th Regt., IV: 413n; V: 180n, 348n; VI: 7; VII: 100n
8th Regt., V: 471n

TROOPS, specific infantry units (*continued*):

9th Regt., IV: 448n, 505n
11th Regt., IV: 461n; V: 457n
12th Regt., V: 142n; VI: 421n
13th Regt., VIII: 261n
14th Regt., IV: 466n, 548n; VIII: 316n
15th Regt., VIII: 330n
19th Regt., IV: 535n; VII: 538n
20th Regt., IV: 553n
23d Regt., IV: 538n; VI: 474n; VII: 484n
24th Regt., IV: 390n
25th Regt., IV: 477n
27th Regt., V: 21n
30th Regt., IV: 477n; V: 21n; VIII: 191n
31st Regt., IV: 392n, 477n; V: 21n
32d Regt., VIII: 110
33d Regt., VI: 231n, 340n
37th Regt., V: 196n, 267n; VI: 2n
38th Regt., VI: 117n
41st Regt., V: 139n; VII: 315n
44th Regt., IV: 456n
45th Regt., VI: 346n
46th Regt., IV: 473n
49th Regt., V: 342n, 486n
53d Regt., VIII: 35n
54th Regt., V: 80n, 495n, 540n; VI: 98n; VII: 174n, 422n
56th Regt., V: 202n; VI: 97n
59th Regt., VIII: 175n
68th Regt., V: 65n
69th Regt., V: 377n; VI: 110n
73d Regt., VI: 225n; VII: 429
74th Regt., VIII: 161n
76th Regt., V: 541n
77th Regt., VII: 102n
79th Regt., VI: 140n
80th Regt., VII: 260
83d Regt., V: 58n, 447n
85th Regt., VI: 462n
94th Regt., V: 354n; VI: 352n
97th Regt., IV: 448n
100th Regt., VI: 297n
104th Regt., V: 546n; VI: 20n

109th Regt., VI: 253n
111th Regt., VIII: 314n
112th Regt., VI: 12n
113th Regt., V: 512n; VI: 126n
114th Regt., VIII: 198n
127th Regt., VI: 279n
130th Regt., V: 257n
153d Regt., VII: 245n
Indiana
6th Regt., VII: 122
7th Regt., IV: 505n; VII: 160-61
9th Regt., IV: 505n; VI: 153
11th Regt., IV: 505n
12th Regt., V: 213
17th Regt., VII: 144n; VIII: 166n
19th Regt., IV: 542n
20th Regt., IV: 542n
22d Regt., VI: 148n
27th Regt., VII: 144n
32d Regt., V: 66n, 253n; VI: 280n
33d Regt., VIII: 224n
36th Regt., VII: 144n
37th Regt., V: 66n, 126n
38th Regt., VII: 144n
40th Regt., VI: 153
46th Regt., V: 14n
51st Regt., VIII: 224n
63d Regt., VI: 475n
65th Regt., VI: 85n, 87n
73d Regt., VIII: 224n
86th Regt., VI: 296n; VII: 235n
91st Regt., VI: 86n
129th Regt., VII: 358n
140th Regt., VIII: 360-62
Iowa
7th Regt., V: 142n; VII: 379n
10th Regt., V: 261n
12th Regt., VII: 321-22
14th Regt., VII: 104
16th Regt., VII: 279n
Kansas
2d Regt., VI: 149n
Kentucky
2d Regt., V: 262n; VI: 235n
5th Regt., IV: 393n, 478n; VI: 10n, 532n
6th Regt., VI: 48

Troops, specific infantry units (*continued*):
11th Regt., IV: 533n; VIII: 256n
13th Regt., IV: 481n
15th Regt., IV: 501n, 557n
17th Regt., VI: 67n
18th Regt., V: 402n
20th Regt., VI: 313; VII: 98, 106n
23d Regt., VI: 293n; VII: 229n
26th Regt., V: 205n; VI: 313
33d Regt., VI: 424n
37th Regt., VIII: 229n
37th Regt. (mounted), VIII: 88n
Maine
2d Regt., IV: 505n
3d Regt., IV: 505n; VII: 317n
4th Regt., V: 142n; VII: 64
6th Regt., VII: 92n
7th Regt., VII: 31, 33
10th Regt., V: 234n, 237n
12th Regt., V: 343n
20th Regt., VI: 297n
30th Regt., VIII: 306n
Maryland
1st Regt., IV: 354n; V: 324n
1st (Eastern Shore) Regt., IV: 508n
1st (veteran) Regt., VIII: 94n
1st (Potomac Home Brigade) Regt., IV: 494n; VII: 134n; VIII: 82n
2d Regt., IV: 396n
2d (Eastern Shore) Regt., IV: 508n; VI: 554n
3d Regt., V: 410n; VI: 400, 459, 461n; VIII: 76
4th Regt., VI: 472
5th Regt., VI: 431-32; VII: 60; VIII: 238n
8th Regt., VI: 171n
Massachusetts
1st Regt., IV: 370n
2d Regt., IV: 370n
6th Regt., IV: 340n, 544n; VIII: 84
7th Regt., IV: 370n; V: 228n
8th Regt., IV: 346
9th Regt., IV: 370n, 486

10th Regt., IV: 370n
11th Regt., IV: 370n; V: 15n, 347; VIII: 274
12th Regt., IV: 336n, 405n; VI: 259n; VII: 143
13th Regt., V: 400n; VI: 478, 481-82, 519n
14th Regt., IV: 404n
15th Regt., V: 15n; VII: 294n
16th Regt., VII: 545n; VIII: 19n
17th Regt., VI: 72, 94n
20th Regt., VIII: 117n, 219n
22d Regt., VI: 60n; VIII: 86n, 87
24th Regt., VII: 344
26th Regt., VIII: 233n
29th Regt., VII: 447n
32d Regt., VI: 336n, 337n; VIII: 117n
36th Regt., VIII: 229n
40th Regt., VI: 336n
42d Regt., VIII: 81n, 84
54th Regt., VII: 280n
56th Regt., VIII: 117n, 239, 245
58th Regt., VIII: 117n
Michigan
1st Regt., V: 187n, 381n; VII: 129, 152; VIII: 246n
2d Regt., IV: 499n, 529n
3d Regt., IV: 499n
4th Regt., IV: 479
5th Regt., VI: 548n
7th Regt., VI: 126n
8th Regt., VII: 249n
16th Regt., IV: 405n
27th Regt., VII: 334n
Minnesota
1st Regt., IV: 446, 511n; V: 78n
2d Regt., IV: 320n; V: 33n; VI: 442n
3d Regt., V: 200n, 432n
6th Regt., V: 543n
7th Regt., V: 543n
Missouri
6th Regt., VIII: 135-36
8th Regt., VI: 126n
12th Regt., V: 476n
18th Regt., VIII: 309n

TROOPS, specific infantry units
(*continued*):
21st Regt., VII: 307n; VIII:
299n
24th Regt., V: 517; VII: 430n
25th Regt., V: 512n; VII: 206n
27th Regt., V: 517
31st Regt., VII: 307n
32d Regt., V: 517
33d Regt., V: 411n
43d Regt., VIII: 176n
New Hampshire
2d Regt., IV: 516; VII: 96n,
520n
4th Regt., VII: 517n
5th Regt., VI: 133, 355
6th Regt., VII: 93, 96n, 106n;
VIII: 167-68
7th Regt., VIII: 243, 302
9th Regt., IV: 443n
10th Regt., IV: 516n; VII: 206,
297n, 298n
11th Regt., VI: 352n; VIII: 170
14th Regt., VII: 322n
New Jersey
1st Regt., V: 480n; VI: 478;
VIII: 90n
2d Regt., IV: 552-53; VII: 546n
3d Regt., VII: 150, 152
4th Regt., VI: 466n; VIII: 42n
6th Regt., V: 136n, 483n; VI:
460-61; VII: 133, 152
7th Regt., IV: 552-53; VI: 520
9th Regt., V: 136n; VII: 232n
10th Regt., VII: 159
11th Regt., VI: 461; VII: 152,
335
12th Regt., VI: 461n
14th Regt., VII: 502n
15th Regt., VII: 150n
21st Regt., VI: 270n
25th Regt., VI: 295
27th Regt., VI: 285n
28th Regt., VI: 126n
30th Regt., VII: 546n
New Mexico Territory
2d Regt., V: 340n
New York

1st Regt., IV: 516
5th Regt., V: 285n, 350n, 408n
6th Regt., VI: 254n; VII: 238
7th Regt., IV: 352n, 368n, 372n,
390, 398; V: 60
8th Regt., IV: 368n, 372n, 524n;
VI: 6n
9th Regt., V: 59n
10th Regt., VI: 184n, 453n
11th Regt., IV: 408n; V: 149n;
VI: 59n
14th Regt., VII: 313
15th Regt., V: 349n
19th Regt., IV: 525n
20th Regt., IV: 372n
24th Regt., VI: 189n
25th Regt., V: 300n; VII: 292n
26th Regt., VI: 257n
27th Regt., VI: 427n
30th Regt., V: 103n
40th Regt., V: 258n, 483n
42d Regt., V: 466
44th Regt., IV: 474n
45th Regt., VI: 356
46th Regt., VIII: 405n
46th (veteran) Regt., VIII: 313
48th Regt., VI: 339n
50th Regt., IV: 460n; VII: 288n
51st Regt., VII: 328n
52d Regt., VII: 304
53d Regt. (Zouaves), V: 132n
54th Regt., VI: 221
59th Regt., IV: 416n; VI: 507n
61st Regt., VII: 33n, 137
61st (veteran) Regt., VII: 294n
62d Regt., IV: 406n; VII: 436n
63d Regt., VIII: 255
65th Regt., V: 60n
66th Regt., VII: 25n
68th Regt., IV: 524n
69th Regt., IV: 418n, 419n, 458,
492n; V: 25, 348; VI: 336n;
VII: 293, 301
70th Regt., IV: 505n
71st Regt., V: 81n; VII: 140, 152
73d Regt. ("4th Excelsior"),
VI: 561n
76th Regt., VII: 31

TROOPS, specific infantry units
(*continued*):
77th Regt., VIII: 213n
78th Regt., IV: 471n; V: 506n;
   VI: 41
79th Regt. (Highlanders), IV:
   469n, 504n, 557n; V: 321n
80th Regt., VI: 193n
82d Regt., V: 167n; VII: 89
84th Regt. (formerly 14th N. Y.
   State Militia), V: 381n; VI:
   496; VII: 307n, 473n
85th Regt., VI: 241
88th Regt., VII: 315n
89th Regt., VI: 287n
94th Regt., VI: 88n
97th Regt., VI: 498, 504, 515
100th Regt., V: 429; VII: 171n
103d Regt., VIII: 106n
104th Regt., VI: 516
115th Regt., VII: 496n
118th Regt., VII: 138
119th Regt., V: 413
122d Regt., VII: 171
124th Regt., VII: 33
126th Regt., VI: 397
131st Regt., V: 408n
133d Regt., V: 413
139th Regt., V: 413
140th Regt., VI: 296n; VII: 378,
   385n
143d Regt., VI: 294n
145th Regt., VII: 139n
146th Regt., VI: 248n
153d Regt., VII: 271
169th Regt., VII: 232n
178th Regt., V: 483n
179th Regt., VIII: 203n
188th Regt., VIII: 105
189th Regt., VIII: 75
   Ohio
1st Regt., IV: 450n
2d Regt., VII: 516n
4th Regt., VII: 159; VIII: 27n
9th Regt., VII: 516n
11th Regt., V: 395n
22d Regt., VI: 19n
23d Regt., IV: 496n

26th Regt., IV: 462n; VIII: 173n
28th Regt., VIII: 10n
30th Regt., VIII: 346n
39th Regt., IV: 485n
41st Regt., IV: 511n
44th Regt., VI: 19n
46th Regt., VII: 276n
50th Regt., V: 509n
52d Regt., VII: 516n
59th Regt., VII: 130
60th Regt., V: 453n; VII: 513n
61st Regt., IV: 451n
63d Regt., VII: 539n
64th Regt., V: 77n
65th Regt., V: 77n; VII: 173n
69th Regt., V: 200n, 314n
71st Regt., V: 408n
89th Regt., VIII: 91n, 169n
92d Regt., VII: 175n
106th Regt., VII: 211
114th Regt., VIII: 72n
120th Regt., IV: 496n
124th Regt., VII: 112n
128th Regt., V: 4n
130th Regt., VII: 388-89
148th Regt., VII: 528-29
164th Regt., VII: 504-505
166th Regt., VII: 512
   Pennsylvania
5th Regt., VI: 129n
8th Regt., IV: 336n
11th Regt., VI: 548n
19th Regt., VI: 515
21st Regt., IV: 553n
23d Regt., V: 170n; VI: 118, 125
26th Regt., IV: 381n
27th Regt., IV: 386n; V: 111n
29th Regt., VI: 297n
30th Regt., VIII: 85n
34th Regt., VIII: 131n
39th Regt. (10th Pa. Reserves),
   VII: 60-61
46th Regt., VI: 295
47th Regt., VIII: 48n
49th Regt., VI: 561; VII: 2, 96,
   99n, 104
53d Regt., VII: 373n
57th Regt., V: 471n

59th Regt., IV: 517n
61st Regt., VII: 94
62d Regt., VII: 317n, 455; VIII: 12, 49n
67th Regt., VI: 522n; VII: 120n, 265, 297; VIII: 273
68th Regt., VIII: 88n
71st Regt. ("1st Calif."), IV: 560n; V: 60; VII: 140, 152
72d Regt., VI: 364, 384; VII: 320; VIII: 37n
76th Regt., VIII: 47-48
81st Regt., VII: 157
82d Regt., VI: 228, 336n, 516n; VIII: 252n
84th Regt., VII: 482n
90th Regt., VI: 492n, 548n; VIII: 32n
93d Regt., VIII: 235n
98th Regt., VI: 86n; VII: 152
99th Regt., V: 168n; VII: 31, 33n, 491n
101st Regt., VIII: 192n
104th Regt., IV: 327n
109th Regt., VII: 65n
110th Regt., V: 380n
111th Regt., VI: 464; VIII: 103n
112th Regt., VI: 292, 336n; VII: 305n
116th Regt., VI: 548n; VII: 219-20
118th Regt., VI: 415n, 548n
119th Regt., VI: 506, 510, 515-16; VII: 65
140th Regt., VII: 372
142d Regt., VIII: 85n
143d Regt., VI: 429; VIII: 10n
148th Regt., VII: 97n
150th Regt., V: 485n; VII: 531n
153d Regt., V: 400n
176th Regt., VI: 192n, 193n
183d Regt., VII: 217n, 320n, 465
184th Regt., VIII: 41n, 44n
186th Regt., VIII: 273
199th Regt., VIII: 307n
Rhode Island
1st Regt., V: 86n

3d Regt., VI: 157n
4th Regt., VII: 138
6th Regt. (Negro), V: 431n
11th Regt., VI: 461n
Tennessee
2d Regt. (mounted), VII: 6n
10th Regt., VII: 466n
Tennessee (Middle)
1st Regt., V: 501n; VI: 393n
Vermont
3d Regt., VIII: 232n
4th Regt., VII: 479n
5th Regt., VI: 292n
6th Regt., VII: 261n
8th Regt., VIII: 255n
11th Regt., V: 413
Virginia
2d Regt., VI: 419n
7th Regt., VI: 115-16, 130
West Virginia
4th Regt., VI: 137n
9th Regt., VI: 137n
15th Regt., VIII: 17n
Wisconsin
2d Regt., V: 149n; VI: 528n
6th Regt., V: 447n; VII: 244, 252
9th Regt., V: 221n
10th Regt., VIII: 95n
22d Regt., V: 512n
36th Regt., VIII: 32n
United States
1st Regt., IV: 467n; V: 83n, 465n
1st (colored) Regt., VI: 362n
1st (Sharpshooters) Regt., V: 431; VI: 97n; VIII: 100n
2d Regt., IV: 442, 453n; V: 22, 70n, 362, 370n
2d (colored) Regt., VI: 494n
3d Regt., IV: 409, 505n; V: 327n; VI: 169n
3d (colored) Regt., VI: 439n
4th Regt., V: 56n, 181n; VII: 139n
7th Regt., II: 83; V: 56n, 64n
7th (colored) Regt., VI: 530n
8th Regt., IV: 395n; VII: 375

9th Regt., VIII: 346n
10th Regt., IV: 442n, 480n; VI: 477n
10th (colored) Regt., VI: 59n
11th Regt., IV: 395n, 409n, 410n, 479n, 492n
12th Regt., IV: 382n, 484n, 514n; VI: 426; VII: 261n, 265, 521; VIII: 14n
13th Regt., IV: 442n, 472n; VII: 198n
14th Regt., IV: 453n, 486n, 494n; V: 370n; VII: 65, 137, 357; VIII: 122n
15th Regt., IV: 409, 413n, 417n, 474n
16th Regt., IV: 446n; V: 332n
17th Regt., IV: 409n, 548n; V: 4n, 464; VI: 426n; VII: 61, 155n, 235n
18th Regt., IV: 409n; V: 83n, 217n; VII: 257, 310
19th Regt., V: 131n
20th Regt., V: 332n
21st Regt., VII: 265
73d (colored) Regt., VI: 59n
79th (colored) Regt., VI: 188n
80th (colored) Regt., VII: 416n
104th (colored) Regt., VIII: 273n
120th (colored) Regt., VIII: 266n
127th (colored) Regt., VII: 317n
Troops, specific militia units:
  Kansas
3d Brig., IV: 476n
  Maryland
4th Div., IV: 511n
  Missouri (Cavalry)
1st Regt., VII: 12n
3d Regt., VIII: 102n
7th Regt., VI: 402n
9th Regt., VI: 134n
  Missouri (Infantry)
38th Regt., VIII: 156n
  New Jersey
4th Regt., IV: 508n

  New York
14th Regt., IV: 381n; VI: 496; VII: 307n, 473n
47th Regt., VI: 136n
69th Regt., IV: 389n
79th Regt., VII: 332n
  Pennsylvania
45th Regt., VII: 3n
Troops, specific reserve corps units:
  Missouri
2d Regt., V: 348n
  Pennsylvania
3d Regt., VII: 137
6th Regt., VII: 448n
9th Regt., VII: 88n
10th Regt., VII: 60-61
12th Regt., VI: 373n
  U. S. (veteran)
9th Regt., VIII: 18n
12th Regt., VIII: 234n
14th Regt., VIII: 393n
19th Regt., VII: 545n
26th Regt., VIII: 159n
  Cavalry Reserve Corps (unspecified), VI: 43, 55n, 80n
Troops, specific units (Confederate):
  Artillery
1st Regt. (Md.), VIII: 103
  Cavalry
1st Regt. (Va.), VII: 26n
2d Regt. (Ky.), VII: 136n
4th Regt. (Ky.), VIII: 310n
6th Regt. (Ky.), VI: 148n
9th Regt. (Tenn.), VII: 310
9th Regt. (Va.), VI: 337n; VII: 91, 98n
12th Regt. (Va.), VII: 80n
33d Regt. (Va.), VII: 26n
  Infantry
3d Regt. (Mo.), VII: 139n
8th Regt. (La.), VIII: 112n
18th Regt. (Miss.), VI: 353n
Troops, specific volunteer units:
  Missouri (Reserve corps)
2d Regt., V: 348n

South Carolina (Negro)
1st Regt., VI: 158n, 340n
2d Regt., VI: 158n
Troutman, Charles E., IV: 70
Trowbridge, John Townsend, IV: 75n
Trowbridge, N. C., VII: 87n; VIII: 8n
Trowbridge, Rowland Ebenezer, V: 360n
Troy, Daniel, I: 249
Troy (Kans.), III: 425n, 497n
Troy (N. Y.), I: 428; IV: 227; VI: 339
Troy (N. Y.) *Budget*, IV: 227n
Troy (N. Y.) *Times*, IV: 227n, 553n; VI: 339n
Truckee River, VIII: 146
True, F. G., VI: 98n
True, John W., V: 540n; VI: 98
True, William M., II: 173-74
Truesdale, Calvin, VI: 182
Truett, Henry B., I: 195, 200, 207n
Truett, Myers, I: 195, 200
Truman, Mrs. B. P. [nee Shaw], VII: 136n, 169n
Trumbo, Mrs. Adam, VIII: 198n
Trumbo, Charles Adam, VIII: 198
Trumbull, Benjamin M., IV: 303n
Trumbull, Julia Maria (Jayne), I: 292n; II: 14n; IV: 55, 143n
Trumbull, Lyman: in Ill. legislature (1841), I: 227, 232, 239; mention of his marriage, II: 14n; member of committee presenting resolutions of sympathy with the cause of Hungarian freedom, 115-16; elected to Congress from Ill. (1854), 287; elected Senator from Ill. (1855), 290, 304-306; represents complainants in law case, 332n; and the 1856 presidential election, 342-43, 359-60, 362, 463, III: 99; mention of political visit to Minn. (1857), II: 395; signs agreement to promote the circulation of the *Missouri Democrat*, 410; mention of publication of his Springfield speech (June '57), 412; letters from L. on a divorce case and Buchanan-Douglas dispute, 427-28; letter from L. on N. Y. *Tribune* support of Douglas (Dec. '57), 430

And the 1858 campaign following L.'s nomination for the Senate: II: 471-72, 490, 511, 523, 531-32, 536, 542-43; Douglas attacks and L. defends in debates, III: 3, 6-7, 13, 43, 45, 50, 53, 60-63, 104-10, 118-19, 121, 128-29, 138-201 *passim*, 215, 220, 228-30, 245, 252-53, 282, 304

L. supports his reelection to the Senate, III: 337, 355-56, IV: 95, 171; letters from L. and mentioned by L. in connection with party affairs (Nov. '58-Nov. '60), III: 337, 344-45, 351, 355-56, 376, 388n, 399n, 495, 505, 507, 509n, 512-13, IV: 31-32, 34, 40-41, 44-47, 55-56, 59, 71; passage written for his Springfield speech (Nov. '60) by L., IV: 141-42, 146; accompanies L. to Chicago (Nov. '60), 143n

And formation of L.'s cabinet, IV: 147-49, 162, 171, 248; correspondence with L. on Republican stand against compromise on slavery extension, 149, 153, 183; receives copies of L.'s confidential letters on current political questions, 155, 163; letter from L. on L.'s resolutions drawn up for Republican members of Senate Committee of Thirteen, 157n, 158-59; and appointments, 303, 321, 381, 457n, V: 173n, 179n, VI: 98n, VII: 177, VIII: 225-26

Receives report of disturbed conditions in Mo. (July '61),

IV: 466n; and recruitment, 466n, 476n, V: 9n; mentioned as member of Senate judiciary committee, IV: 502n, V: 43n, VI: 53n, VII: 399n; requests report on number of assistant paymasters, commissaries, and quartermasters in the Volunteer force, VI: 116n; signs petition for release of prisoner-of-war Henry Warfield, VII: 66n; receives recommendation for transfer of Scates, 277n; requests leave of absence for paymaster to recover lost or stolen funds, 358n; L. mentions being influenced by his position on revocation of Burnside's order suspending the Chicago *Times*, 361, 364; requests information on reorganization of state government in Ark., 398-99; introduces act on fees of U. S. marshals, attorneys, and clerks in D. C., 415n; urges L. to give McClernand permission to visit Washington (July '64), 473n; L. suspends execution of his friend's son, VIII: 189-90; and reorganization of state government in La., 206-207; asserts president "has nothing to do with the proposition or adoption of amendments to the Constitution," 254n; member of committee notifying L. of 1864 reelection, 326-27; mentioned also, 427

Trumbull, Mrs. Lyman, *see* Trumbull, Julia Maria

Trumbull, Walter, IV: 381

Trunnell, William, VIII: 34n

Tse-Kzi (China), VI: 96n

Tuck, Amos, IV: 51-52, 81, 161; V: 395n

Tuck, Edward, V: 395n

Tucker, ———, VII: 420

Tucker, H. A., III: 203n

Tucker, Henry Russell, VI: 110

Tucker, Joseph H., V: 377; VI: 110

Tucker, Lansing B., VI: 110n

Tucker County (W. Va.), V: 298

Tuckerman, Charles K., VI: 42n

Tufts, Gardiner, VII: 450n

Tuileries Palace (Paris), V: 130n

Tuilla Valley (Utah Terr.), VII: 113

Tully, Joseph B., V: 348

Tune, William T., VIII: 69

Tunis (Africa), IV: 313, 498n

Tunkan Canholiska (Indian), VII: 325-26

Tunkan Oyate Yanka (Indian), VII: 325-26

Tunkanhuamani (Indian), VII: 325-26

Tunstall, Robert B., VI: 443

Tunstall, Thomas T., V: 549n

Tunstall, Warrick, I: 465

Turchin, John Basil, IV: 535n; V: 406

Turkey, IV: 358-59, 397, 546; V: 28n, 176, 521; VI: 76; VII: 40

Turkey Island (Va.), V: 301n

Turkey Island Point (Va.), V: 295n

Turks Islands (Bahamas), V: 27n

Turley, George W., I: 139; II: 105, 160, 201-202, 206n

Turnage, Joseph, VII: 213

Turner, George, IV: 295

Turner, J. D., VI: 212n

Turner, J. Miller, VII: 274

Turner, James W., VIII: 68

Turner, Joe D., VIII: 68

Turner, John Wesley, VIII: 380n

Turner, Justin G., I: 1n; VII: 415n; VIII: 148n, 246n, 248n, 265n, 279n, 281n, 282n, 283n, 284n

Turner, Levi C., V: 442-43; VI: 286n

Turner, Nat, III: 540n

Turner, Oaks, I: 490

Turner, Reuben, VIII: 165

Turner, Thomas Jefferson, I: 474;

II: 72, 199-201, 206-208, 285, 292-93, 295, 298, 303; III: 39, 61-62, 65-66, 490; IV: 168; VII: 377n, 519; VIII: 8n, 415
Turner, Visesimus, IV: 537n
Turner, W. A., VII: 495n, 519n
Turney, Daniel, I: 219
Turney, Elias T., VIII: 427
Turney, James, I: 25
Turney, Leander Jay S., IV: 308; V: 467n
Turnham, David, IV: 130-31
Tuscaloosa (Ala.), VII: 170n
Tuscumbia (Ala.), V: 276n, 321; VI: 213n
Tustin, Septimus, VI: 536n
Twichell, Ginery, V: 406-407
Twiggs, David Emanuel, IV: 248; V: 552-53

Twilley, Benjamin F., VIII: 412
Twiss, Stephen P., VII: 371
Twitchell, Norton, II: 183
Twitchell, Mrs. W. R., VII: 222n
"Two-Year Amendment" (Mass.), III: 377n, 380
Tybee Island, V: 50
Tyler, Daniel, IV: 449-50; V: 143; VI: 253, 273, 275, 278, 280, 283
Tyler, Erastus Barnard, V: 385n; VI: 221, 494
Tyler, John, I: 253, 295, 317, 337, 477; II: 49, 351, 354; III: 78, 162; IV: 420
Tyler, Samuel, VII: 150, 152
Tyler, W. H., VI: 108
Tyler County (W. Va.), V: 298
Tyson, James W., VII: 542n

U

Uintah Valley Indian Reservation, IV: 548n
Ullmann, Daniel, IV: 183-84, 334; V: 506; VI: 41, 134n, 154-55, 439-40
Ullmann, John J., IV: 334n
Ulmer, Leonard, IV: 167
Ulrich, Bartow A., VIII: 247
Ulrich, Sarah M., VI: 504n
Ulrich, William, VI: 504n
Ulrich, Mrs. William, see Ulrich, Sarah M.
Ulster County (N. Y.), V: 383
Umpqua Indian Agency, IV: 308
Uncollected Letters of Abraham Lincoln (Tracy), I: viii
  Cited in the footnotes on the ff. pages: I: 307, 352, 405; II: 60, 93, 96, 202, 206, 315, 325, 333, 357; III: 371, 380, 513

IV: 36, 39, 48, 59, 69, 75, 88, 111, 113, 291, 342, 349, 360, 388, 390, 471, 478, 496, 544, 561; V: 9, 17, 70, 81, 108, 189, 205, 218, 257, 348, 361, 488, 490
  VI: 188, 201, 229, 355, 368, 422, 428; VII: 34, 77, 117, 182, 258, 261, 315, 355, 429; VIII: 35, 94, 119, 126, 155, 232, 427
Underwood, John C., III: 344-45; IV: 360n, 452n; VII: 251n, 295
Underwood, John R., VII: 421; VIII: 77-78
Underwood, John R., Jr., VII: 421n
Underwood, William Henry, II: 332n
"Union" [pseud.], see Bailey, J. W.

"Union" (locomotive), IV: 227
Union Aid Society (St. Louis), VII: 311n
Union Bethel Church (Washington), V: 371n
Union City (Tenn.), V: 540n
Union County (Ky.), VI: 85
Union County (Tenn.), VIII: 68
Union League of America, V: 454n; VI: 118n, 212n, 533-34; VII: 216-17, 324n, 383-84, 397, 517n; VIII: 8n, 97n
Union List of Serials . . . , VII: 392n
Union Mills (Va.), V: 120n
Union Pacific Railroad, VI: 68, 491, 497, 504-505, 518-20, 525-26, 545n; VII: 16, 48, 122, 228, 233-34, 382n, 412n, 451-52, 464-65; VIII: 38-39, 89, 146, 192-93
Union Place Hotel (N. Y.), V: 32n
Union Square (N. Y.), VII: 374n
Union Station (Tenn.), VI: 470n
Union Theological Seminary (N. Y.), IV: 446n
Uniontown (Pa.), VI: 189n
Unitarians, II: 452; III: 310; V: 464
United Mining District, Rocky Mountains, IV: 295n
Union Party, *see* Republican Party
United Press, VIII: 409n
United States Express Company, IV: 35n
United States Ford (Va.), VI: 190n, 197n
United States Official Register, see *Register of Officers and Agents* . . .
United States Statutes at Large, IV: 328; VI: 133n
United Turner Rifles (N. Y.), IV: 368n
Universalists, I: 475
Updegraff, W. W., IV: 476
Upham, William Henry, V: 149, 152
Upper Missouri Indian Agency,

IV: 306; VI: 356n; VIII: 358n
Upper Platte Indian Agency, IV: 306; VIII: 225
Upperville (Va.), V: 481n
Upshur, Abel Parker, VII: 74
Upshur, Mrs. Abel Parker, *see* Upshur, Elizabeth A. B.
Upshur, Elizabeth A. B., VII: 74
Upshur, John H., VII: 360
Upshur, Sally, VII: 74n
Upshur County (W. Va.), V: 298
Upton, Miss, VI: 146
Upton, Charles Horace, V: 45n
Urbana (Md.), V: 412n
Urbana (Va.), I: 518n; V: 118, 123n
Urbana (Ill.) *Union*, III: 37n
Uruguay, VII: 493-94
Usher, John Palmer: mentioned in letter to Allen (May 2, '60), IV: 47; mentioned as attorney for the Indians in preparation of a treaty with the Delawares, 540; supports Wright for Congressman from Terre Haute (1862), V: 351; appointed Sec. of the Interior, 492n, VI: 35n; persons referred by L. for conference with, VI: 111, 172, VII: 180, 456; his opinion on whether L. should accept an invitation to preside at a religious meeting (Feb. '63), VI: 111n; protest from Rock Island agent removed on charges of graft, 161-62; and arrest of Milroy, VI: 308n; and the New Almaden mine case, 333n, 394; and extension of Gen. Logan's leave to make speeches in Ill. (Aug. '63), 382n; and Ill. two-percent claim on sale of public lands, 404-405, 411-12, 463n; opinion on the draft, 444n; mention of conference on release of Indians unlawfully enlisted, VII: 27; and naturalization of foreigners, 38; annual reports, (*1863*) 46-47, (*1864*)

VIII: 145-47; and relief for friendly refugee Indians, VII: 196n, 341n; and bill enlarging power of Commissioner of Public Works, 266-67; authorized to add certain public lands to Little Traverse Indian Reservation, 300; his opinion on retaliation for Fort Pillow massacre, 328; receives protest of West Point professor's dismissal, 496; requested to investigate a pension claim, VIII: 214; attends inaugural ball (1865), 334n; resigns his cabinet post, 347

Reports submitted to Congress on: Indian hostilities, VI: 104n; Indian treaties, 109, VII: 68-70, 112-13, 116-17, 261, 284, 299, 344-45, 403, 407, VIII: 219-20, 322; construction of Union Pacific R. R., VII: 233-34; expenditures for Negro colonization, 241, 417-18; investment of funds received from sale of Wea lands in Kans., 246; failure to return refugee Indians in Kans. to their homes, 341-42

And appointments, V: 354;

VI: 69, 134, 142, 208-209, 355-56, 494-95, 497, 507, 545; VII: 128, 225, 266, 521; VIII: 225-26, 325, 339, 355-56, 358-59, 363, 370

Usher, Mrs. John Palmer, *see* Usher, Margaret

Usher, Margaret (Patterson), VIII: 333n, 334n

Usher, Nathaniel, VII: 490

Usury, L.'s recommendations for limiting interest rates, I: 7-9, 66, 200

Utah Indian Agency, IV: 307; V: 354n

Utah Indians, VII: 70

Utah Territory, II: 232, 238, 243, 252-54, 259-60, 279-81, 347, 398-99; III: 224-25, 271-72; IV: 41, 308, 391, 462n, 554n; V: 432n, 485n; VI: 62n; VII: 113, 153n, 266n

Utica (N. Y.), IV: 223

Utica & Schenectady Railroad, II: 171

Utica Telegraph, IV: 223n

Utley, William L., V: 512-14

Utz, John H., VI: 544; VIII: 176, 205-206, 210

V

Vache Island, *see* Isle à Vache

Vahort, John, II: 167

Vaile, H. M., IV: 294

Vallandigham, Clement Laird, V: 66n; VI: 215n, 235n, 237, 248n, 266-69, 300-306, 445n; VII: 208n, 386n, 402

Valley Railroad, VI: 451n

Valparaiso (Chile), VI: 167n

Valverde (N. M.), V: 283

Van Alen, James Henry, IV: 157n; VI: 363; VIII: 413

Van Alstine, Buck, II: 183

Van Antwep, Verplanck, V: 56

Van Arsdale, Cornelius C., VIII: 241

Van Bergen, Peter, I: 20n, 290n, 305-306, 324, 328-29, 340

Van Buren, ·Daniel Tompkins, VII: 328n

Van Buren, Martin, I: 48n, 50, 161, 172-78, 184, 210, 336, 432, 507-508, 512; II: 3-6, 9, 12, 14, 154, 156, 159; III: 162, 195; IV: 420; V: 340-41

Van Buren, Thomas Brodhead, VIII: 231n

Van Buren County (Ill.) [proposed], I: 57-60

Van Buren County (Tenn.), VIII: 69

Vance, Deziah, IV: 74

Vance, John C., I: 38

Vance, John Wilson, I: 340; IV: 74

Vance, Mrs. John Wilson, see Vance, Deziah

Vance, William L., V: 507

Vance, Zebulon Baird, VI: 330-31

Vancouver Island, IV: 287

Vandalia (Ill.), I: 30-31, 73n, 76n, 78n, 118, 126-27, 146; II: 23, 52, 377-78, 383n; V: 541

Vandalia (sloop of war), VI: 103

Vandalia Free Press, cited, I: 61n, 123n, 126n, 127n, 132n, 144n

Van Dalsan, William, VIII: 351

Vandegrift, Lewis F. L., VII: 242n

Vandenburg, J. V. W., VII: 292n

Vanderbilt, Cornelius, V: 331-32; VI: 112n, 331n, 432

Vanderbilt, Cornelius, Jr., VI: 432-33

Vanderbilt (steamer), V: 331, 498

Van Deren, Archibald J., II: 424-25; IV: 188-89

Van Deren, Cyrus W., II: 480; IV: 188-89

Van Deren, John M., IV: 188-89

Vanderslice, Daniel, V: 189

Vandeveer, Aaron, I: 298

Vandeveer, Horatio Middleton, I: 336

Vandeventer, Jacob, I: 31n, 34n, 35n, 42n

Vandever, William, IV: 445n; V: 95

Van de Water, Frederic F., VIII: 112n

Van Duyn, G. A., VII: 178

Van Duyn, G. A., & Company (Springfield), VII: 178n

Van Duzer, Charles F., IV: 514

Van Duzer, Selah, IV: 514n

Van Dyke, John, II: 346; IV: 119-20, 235n, 405

Van Dyke, Mrs. John, II: 346; IV: 119

Vanhoff, Henry, II: 188

Van Horn, J. C., IV: 310

Van Horn, Robert Thompson, VII: 206, 371

Vanmeter, ———, IV: 74

Van Renssalaer, Stephen, IV: 399n

Van Riswick, John, IV: 319

Van Santvoord, Cornelius, VI: 193-94

Van Tine, Frederick, V: 408

Van Valkenburgh, Robert Bruce, VII: 288

Van Vliet, Stewart, VI: 292; VII: 164n

Van Wyck, Charles Henry, IV: 409-10

Varner, Jacob, VI: 240n

Vaughan, John C., III: 497n

Vaughan, John M., V: 18n

Vaughan, Richard C., V: 18; VI: 423n; VII: 12

Veatch, Harry, VI: 161n

Veatch, James Clifford, VI: 161n

Vedder, Nicholas, IV: 493

Veil, Charles Henry, VII: 88n

Velasco (Tex.), I: 436n

Veluzat, Joel S., IV: 481

Venable, ———, V: 503n

Venango County (Pa.), VIII: 204n

Venezuela, IV: 397; V: 3n; VII: 536-37; VIII: 137

Venice (Italy), IV: 483

Veracruz (Mexico), I: 436n; IV: 284n, 318-19

Vergel, Juan del Carmen, VII: 88n

Vermilion County (Ill.), I: 87n

Vermillion (Dakota Terr.), IV: 325

Vermillion Coal & Manufacturing Company, II: 189-91

Vermont, II: 4; III: 127, 140-41; IV: 276n; V: 67, 360; VIII: 4, 100n, 129-30, 150, 153, 271-72

Verree, John Paul, IV: 447; V: 129

Versailles (Ill.), I: 322n

Versailles (Ky.), VIII: 315n

Verses composed by L.: copybook verses, I: 1-2; "My Childhood Home I See Again," 367-69, 378-79; "The Bear Hunt," 367n, 386-89; "The Maniac," 384-86, 392; to Rosa and Linnie Haggard, III: 203-204

Vestal's Gap (Va.), V: 461

Veto messages, V: 282-83, 302, 328-31

Veto power, L. on, I: 339, 454, 476, 501-505; II: 2, 5, 7, 11-14; III: 364-65; VII: 414-15

Vickers, George, VI: 494n

Vicksburg (Miss.), I: 110; V: 469n; VI: 43, 71n, 83, 142-43, 155, 210, 226n, 228, 230, 241, 247, 252, 254, 293, 319, 321, 326, 346n, 350, 356n, 374n, 377, 380n, 398n, 415n, 503, 537; VII: 56, 131, 146n, 149n, 185, 218n, 378n, 464n, 483n; VIII: 7-8, 299n, 396

Vicksburg, District of, VI: 486n

Victor Emmanuel II, King of Italy [Sardinia], III: 391n; IV: 300; V: 141; VII: 473-74

Victoria, Queen of Great Britain, IV: 417, 450; V: 117-18, 186, 265, 363; VI: 64, 222; VII: 36, 231

Victoria Adelaide Maria Louisa, Princess Royal of Prussia, V: 448; VIII: 56

Vienna (Austria), IV: 418

Vienna (Va.), IV: 449-50

"Views Suggested by the Imminent Danger of a Disruption of the Union by the Secession of One or More Southern States" (Scott's MS memo.), IV: 137n

Vigal, William W., II: 330-31

Villard, Harold Garrison, IV: 191n

Villard, Henry, IV: 191n, 276n, 484; VII: 222-23

Villard, Oswald Garrison, IV: 191n

Ville de Malaga (French ship), V: 549n

Villiers, George C., V: 225n

Villiers, Mrs. George C., see Villiers, Sarah Sophia

Villiers, Sarah Sophia (Fane), V: 225

Vincent, Thomas McCurdy, VI: 228n, 242n, 258n, 433n, 490n; VII: 92n, 250n

Vindication of Brig. Gen. J. McKinstry . . ., IV: 516n

Viney, William S., II: 324-25

Vineyard, Mrs. George H., I: 79n

Vineyard, James G., I: 55n

Vinton, Samuel Finley, I: 489, 501; II: 27; VIII: 419n

Virden (Ill.), VI: 561n

Virginia: and interchange of state resolutions on slavery (1837), I: 75n; L. on exclusion of slavery from lands ceded to federal government as the Northwest Terr., II: 231, 248-49; mention of introduction (1620) of slavery, 299; L. cites state Supreme Court ruling on inheritance of slaves as property, 515; Patrick Henry on federal control of slavery in territories (1787), III: 526n; as a border state, IV: 329-31, 341, 343, 426-28, 437; and the blockade, 346-47, VI: 479; recruitment, IV: 355n, 359, 395n, 416n, VII: 191, 204; Western section appeals for arms, troops and trained of-

ficers, IV: 443, 464, 481n, 491n, 511n; and L.'s memo on military policy (July '61), 457-58 L. recommends regaining portion of D. C. retroceded (1846) to Va., V: 45; L. reports Unionists in western section "masters of their own country" (Dec. '61), 50; restoration of state government, 166, 476-77, VI: 26, VII: 83n, 487, VIII: 174, 186, 387-89, 399n, 405-408; proclamation concerning taxes in rebellious areas, V: 298-99; appointments, 465n, 473n, 497n, VII: 416n; and the Emancipation Proclamation, VI: 24-25, 29, 30n, 186-87, 428; L. suggests military aid for removal of refugee families and their property, 36; and amnesty, 401, 427, 434-35, 461-62, 472, VIII: 203; assessment of Confederate sympathizers, VIII: 77-78; and suspension of Treasury trade permits, VIII: 344n; *see also names of individual towns*

Virginia, Department of, V: 164n, 273n
Virginia (Ill.), I: 332-33; II: 70n
Virginia and North Carolina, Department of, VI: 77n, 483n; VIII: 207n
Virginia Central Railroad, V: 240n, 244-45; VII: 476n
Virginia Partisan Rangers (C.S.A. guerrillas), V: 278n
Visalia Land Office, IV: 305
Vliet, G. L., IV: 167
Vogdes, Israel, IV: 465n
Volk, Leonard Wells, IV: 114-15
Voltaire, François Marie Arouet de, II: 130
Volunteer (boat), VII: 242n
Von Gernsbach, Weil, V: 106n
Von Heinecke, Edmund W. [alias], *see* Barber, Herman
Von Horn, John, IV: 390
Voorhees, Daniel Woolsey, V: 352n
Voss, Arno, III: 125
Voting in the Field (Benton), VIII: 321n
Vyacheslav Constantinovich, Grand Duke of Russia, V: 440

W

Wabash River, I: 32-33, 213
Wachusett (steamer), VIII: 97, 140n
Wackerle, William J., III: 329
Waddel, Martin, I: 18
Waddell, Asbury, VI: 171
Wade, Benjamin Franklin, II: 348; III: 401; IV: 55, 71n, 153, 278-79, 282, 294; V: 4n, 12n, 88n, 198n, 455n; VI: 128, 177n; VII: 121, 329n

Wade, Henry Parsons, VII: 121
Wade, Melancthon Smith, IV: 539; V: 183n
Wade, Owen, VIII: 359
Wade-Davis Bill, VII: 433-34
Wadford, Stewart L., IV: 272n
Wadsworth, Mrs. James, VII: 435n, 442n
Wadsworth, James Samuel, IV: 325; V: 150, 179n, 224, 263n, 296, 302n, 320, 398, 473n, 491n;

VI: 312n, 330n, 342n; VII: 101-
102
Wadsworth, William Henry, V:
225
Wager, Barnet, VI: 413n
Wager, David Collin, V: 99n; VI:
413n
Waggoner, Wilkins, VIII: 69
Wagley, William C., III: 277, 332
Wagner, Joseph H., II: 163-65,
168-71
Wagonsella, ———, IV: 165
Wa-he-hud (Indian), V: 542
Wahlstrom, Carl E., V: 471n; VI:
150n
Wah-pay-du-ta (Indian), V: 542
Wainwright, Jonathan Mayhew,
V: 215; VI: 102
Wainwright, Richard, IV: 507n;
V: 215
Wait, William Smith, I: viii, 147-
49
Waite, Charles B., II: 396-97
Waite, Otis Frederick Reed, VI:
355n
"Waiting for the Hour" (paint-
ing), VIII: 266
Wakan Inapedan [alias Muza
Kiyemani] (Indian), VII: 325-
26
Wakanhotito (Indian), VII: 325-
26
Wa-kan-tan-ku (Indian), V: 543
Wakeman, Abram, IV: 307,
334; V: 554n; VI: 552n; VII:
460n, 461; VIII: 239-40
Wa-kin-yan-na (Indian), V: 543
Walborn, Cornelius A., IV: 342;
VII: 365-66, 400, 402, 452-53,
469n, 480-81
Walbridge, Alonzo, II: 186
Walbridge, Hiram, IV: 384, 408;
V: 27, 403n; VI: 21-22
Walbridge, Mary, II: 186
Walbridge, Washington [Wil-
liam] Hunt, VI: 185-86
Walcott, C. P., VI: 165n
Walcott, Christopher C., VI: 185-
86

Waldron, George B., VII: 115n
Waldron, George P., V: 200n; VII:
207n
Waldron, Lulu, V: 200
Walker, Albert Galiton, see Wat-
kins, Albert Galiton
Walker, Alvin, IV: 493n
Walker, Anderson W., VIII: 68
Walker, Benjamin P., V: 538-39
Walker, Cyrus, I: 122
Walker, Dave, III: 388
Walker, George (Ill.), II: 298
Walker, George (Mo.), VIII:
290n
Walker, Harvey, VII: 463n
Walker, Isaac Pigeon, I: 134n,
291
Walker, J. B., VIII: 68
Walker, J. C., VIII: 69
Walker, John George, V: 488
Walker, John M., II: 386
Walker, Lucius C., V: 397n
Walker, Newton, I: 129
Walker, Pinckney H., II: 309
10
Walker, Robert James, V: 451
Walker, S. B., VI: 387n
Walker, Samuel J., IV: 549
Walker, Samuel P., VIII: 336
Walker, W. D., VII: 139
Walker, W. E., VIII: 256, 289
Wallace, ———, II: 96
Wallace, Adam, VII: 374n
Wallace, Edward, III: 486-87; IV:
49, 337-38
Wallace, Frances J. (Todd), II:
195n
Wallace, James, V: 163n
Wallace, John M., IV: 472
Wallace, John Winfield, IV: 167
Wallace, Joseph, VIII: 429n
Wallace, Lewis, IV: 505; V: 142;
VI: 46n; VII: 241, 258-59, 275-
77, 335-36, 339-40, 356, 363n,
396n, 434n, 437, 440n, 522, 531;
VIII: 163n, 167, 172-74, 198,
229-30, 232, 251
Wallace, William (Ind.), IV: 181-
82

Wallace, William (Tenn.), VIII: 295n

Wallace, William Henson, IV: 308, 550n; V: 78n, 467n; VII: 163-64, 188; VIII: 412n

Wallace, William Hervy Lamme, IV: 461; V: 142, 457

Wallace, William S., I: 325; II: 45, 64; III: 486; IV: 49, 303

Wallace, Mrs. William S., see Wallace, Frances J.

Wallach, Richard, VIII: 126, 169n

Wallen, Henry Davies, V: 56, 103

Wallen, Henry Davies [Davis], Jr., IV: 530; V: 103-104, 152

Wallen, Mrs. Henry Davies, see Wallen, Laura L.

Wallen, Laura L., IV: 530n

Waller, Royal Hiram, IV: 305

Waller, W. E., see Walker, W. E.

Waller, William, VI: 295-96

Wallis, S. T., IV: 341n

Walnut Grove (Ill.), see Eureka

Walpole Galleries, VI: 437n

Walter, Charles [alias C. Zene], VI: 414-15

Walters, ———, VI: 144n

Walters, Green Berry, V: 491n

Walters, Harry, VIII: 169n

Walters, James W., V: 491.

Walters, S. H., IV: 167

Walters, William, I: 290n, 305-306, 319, 324, 328

Walthall, Edward Cary, VI: 480

Walton, John, VI: 136

Walworth, Reuben Hyde, III: 533n; VIII: 426n

Walworth, Mrs. Reuben Hyde, VIII: 426; see also Hardin, Sarah Ellen (Smith)

Wamne-omne-ho-ta (Indian), V: 542

Wampole, Elias, IV: 485-86; V: 6-7, 102-103, 114

Wann, Daniel, I: 67

Waples, Rufus, VI: 224n; VIII: 242n

War, Albert C., VI: 89n

War Bonnet (Indian), VI: 153n

War of 1812, I: 154n, 172-73, 184, 205, 210, 226, 460; II: 83-84, 124, 127; III: 321; V: 306; VI: 268; VII: 337n; VIII: 222n, 408

War of the Rebellion. A Compilation of the Official Records of the Union and Confederate Armies (OR), cited *passim* in footnotes throughout volumes IV-VIII as source references; cited in footnotes on the ff. pages as source for L. documents: IV: 315, 333, 344, 388, 405, 414, 415, 454, 455, 459, 485, 489, 500, 508, 524, 525, 534, 549, 554, 557, 560; V: 15, 27, 54, 80, 84, 86-87, 95-96, 100, 153, 167, 203, 218, 235, 237, 246, 254, 267, 272, 280, 286, 294, 297, 323, 415, 418, 429, 468, 470, 479, 538; VI: 35, 54, 169, 173, 188, 196, 199, 215, 233, 240, 248, 253, 270, 273, 274, 289, 290, 297, 318, 319, 325, 344, 423, 505, 554; VII: 7, 119, 164, 209, 236, 300, 440, 502; VIII: 8, 10, 14, 32, 34, 40, 90, 162, 262, 285, 378, 382, 383, 384, 385, 387, 389, 392

War Powers of the Government, The, V: 382n

Warburton, George, I: 12

Ward, Mrs., VII: 288n

Ward, Mrs. [nee Weimer], VII: 310-11

Ward, E., IV: 167

Ward, Elijah, V: 483n

Ward, Frederick B., VII: 238n

Ward, Frederick Townsend, VI: 96

Ward, George, VII: 304n

Ward, Henry G., V: 430

Ward, James Harman, VII: 238

Ward, Mrs. James Harman, VII: 238

Ward, John, IV: 349

Ward, John H., IV: 369n

Ward, John S., VIII: 33

Ward, Marcus Lawrence [C.], VI: 429n, 461

Ward, Mrs. R. I., VIII: 221

Ward, Reuben C., VII: 288
Ward, W. C., VIII: 33n
Ward, William, IV: 367
Ward, William Hayes, IV: 544n
Wardan, Phebe (Lawrence), III: 336n
Warden, Robert Bruce, see *Account of the Private Life and Public Services of Salmon Portland Chase*
Wardensville (Va.), V: 247n
Ware, Eugene Fitch, VIII: 214
Ware, G. B., VIII: 70
Wareham (Mass.), VII: 190n
Warfield, Henry M., VII: 120
Warfield, Henry N., VII: 65-66
Warfield, Rebecca P., *see* Brown, Rebecca P. (Warfield)
Wariner, Richard O., I: 129, 131
Waring, Alice Maria, VII: 491
Waring, John H., VIII: 119
Warner, Adoniram Judson, VIII: 177, 192, 194
Warner, Freeman, VII: 205n
Warner, Jacob, II: 395-96
Warner, Nicholas, VIII: 23n
Warnsing, John W., I: 100-101
Warren, Mrs., IV: 529
Warren, Fitz-Henry, VI: 106
Warren, Gouverneur Kemble, VI: 342n, 450n, 528; VII: 307; VIII: 377n, 379-80
Warren, Henry A., II: 330n
Warren, James, VIII: 69
Warren, Louis Austin, IV: 57n
Warren, Peter, I: 77
Warren, William Barton, II: 41-42, 75, 454
Warren County (Ill.), I: 255-56, 371-72, 375
Warren County (Tenn.), VIII: 69
Warrensburg (Mo.), VII: 12n; VIII: 203
Warrenton (Ga.), I: 442
Warrenton (Va.), V: 235n, 398, 488; VI: 47n, 169n, 250n, 437, 459
Warrenton Junction (Va.), V: 397-99

Warwick River (Va.), V: 182
Wash, Milton H., I: 294
Washburn, Cadwallader Colden, VI: 540-41; VII: 148, 215, 427-28; VIII: 74
Washburn, Charles Ames, IV: 397n
Washburn, Henry, VII: 314n
Washburn, Israel, Jr., III: 351-52; IV: 110, 114; V: 14n, 74; VI: 540-41; VII: 172
Washburne, Clarke, IV: 151n
Washburne, Elihu Benjamin: and political campaign of 1848, I: 467; signs call for Whig convention (1851), II: 113-14; and elections (1854), 287, 292-93, III: 58, 61; letters from L. on L.'s candidacy for the the Senate (1855), II: 295, 303-306; mention of his speeches at Bloomington, Ill. (May '56), 340-41; and elections (1858), 443-47, 455, III: 58-59, 61, 140, 144-45, 176, 241; letter from L. on Israel Washburn's House speech on the Republican party (Jan. '59), III: 351-52; L.'s reply to his congratulations on 1860 nomination, IV: 56; plans conference with L. in Springfield (summer '60); 77; letter from L. on election predictions for Maine (1860), 113-14; correspondence with L. on secession and threat to Charleston forts (Dec. '60), 151, 159; requested to make Washington hotel arrangements for the Lincolns (Feb. '61), 217; reports conditions in St. Louis as member of investigating committee (Oct. '61), 560, V: 20, VII: 79n; and appointments, V: 253, 265n, 397, VIII: 261-62, 594n
   Hurlbut requests his influence to obtain orders to report to L. in Washington, VI:

70; letter from Grant supporting promotion for Steele, 73n;
correspondence with L. on an
appointment for his brother
and L.'s candidacy for reelection, 540-41; signs petition for
release of Henry Warfield, VII:
66n; sponsors presentation of
gold medal and resolutions of
thanks to Grant, 79; requests
authority for his brother to
visit Washington and report
on affairs in Tex., 148; on
Ill. support of L.'s reelection,
518n; asks for Blair's return
to Washington to relieve Randall for political campaigning
in the West, 529n; his reelection to Congress, VIII: 102;
facilitates Logan conference
with L. in Washington, 105;
introduces Congressional bill to
encourage immigration, 141n;
L.'s note forwarding draft of a
pension, 423
Washburne, Hempstead, III:
145n; IV: 56n, 77n, 114n; VI:
540n
Wa-she-choon (Indian), V: 542-
43
Washington, George, I: 115, 170,
172-73, 279, 312, 333, 439, 502;
II: 127, 283, 340, 378; III: 8, 12,
18-19, 111-12, 116, 162, 178, 195,
220, 453, 484, 498, 502, 524n,
527, 537, 550-51; IV: 6, 11, 23,
26-27, 30, 144n, 160, 190-91, 199,
204, 235, 244, 262n, 341, 438-39;
V: 136-37, 373, 498; VI: 106,
114-15; VII: 225n, 397n, 406n,
458n, 459; VIII: 118n
Washington, Harriet, VII: 406n
Washington, John E., VI: 9n; see
also *They Knew Lincoln*
Washington, Peter G., IV: 334-35
Washington (D. C.): L.'s remarks
in Congress on railroad contracts for transporting mails to
and from Richmond, I: 423n,

427-29; L. describes his attendance at a concert on the
Capitol grounds (July '48),
495-96; L.'s reply to Mayor's
welcome and a serenade (Feb.
27-28, '61), IV: 246-48; munici-
pal authorities proclaim Thanksgiving day (Nov. '61), V: 32;
concerning construction and extension of Capitol and dome,
V: 149, 177n, VII: 266n; settlement of claims in connection with the building of the
Washington Aqueduct, V: 238n;
L.'s address to a Union meeting in front of Capitol (Aug.
'62), 358-59; mention of "Old
Capitol Prison," 413n, VI: 536,
VII: 208; requisition of penitentiary for use as an arsenal, V:
429-30; temporary requisition
of Capitol for use as a hospital,
443n; removal of bakeries from,
443n, 463; proposed construction of railroads concentrating
upon the city, VI: 68-69; Capitol policeman fined for arrest
of persons in House lobby, 106-
107; proposed public meeting
of U. S. Christian Commission,
115n

Employment of contrabands
in building roads and fortifications, 246n, 362n; L.'s response
to serenade (July '63), 319-20;
theatre performances (1863),
392-93, 559n; requisition of
schoolhouse for a "Medical
Museum," 397n; mention of
Presbyterian Synod meeting,
532n; L. orders Executive
buildings draped in mourning for Caleb Smith, VII:
118-19; mention of smallpox
epidemic, 137; Isle à Vache
colonists returned to camps
around the city, 164; Mount
Vernon Association requests
permission to run steamboat to

Washington's home, 225n; L.'s remarks at Sanitary Fair, 253-54; celebration of Grant's victory (May '64), 334n, 384; newspapers protest necessity of obtaining War Department news from N.Y., 546; L.'s responses to serenades, (Sept.-Dec. '64) VIII: 4, 52-53, 57-58, 96, 100-102, 154, (Feb.-Apr. '65) 254-55, 331, 393-95; coal shortage, 208; arrest of merchants for illicit trading, 303-304; L.'s last public address, 399-405

Military threat to, IV: 341-43, 346, 348-49, 352, 541; V: 10n, 115, 120n, 122n, 149, 151, 157, 164n, 179, 184, 195n, 219-20, 226n, 235-36, 241, 244n, 273n, 284n, 287, 289-94, 301, 307, 343, 399n, 402n, 404, 452, 461, 469, 486n; VI: 15, 47n, 164, 169n, 218n, 250n, 258n, 277n, 282n, 285, 318, 467, 525; VII: 424n, 437-38, 440n, 476n; VIII: 189

See also District of Columbia; Washington Arsenal; and Washington Navy Yard
Washington (Ill.), I: 379-80
Washington (N.C.), VI: 184; VIII: 396
Washington (Pa.), VII: 372
Washington (Tenn.), VII: 6n
Washington, Department of, IV: 326n, 385n; VI: 363n; VII: 60n, 423n, 469n; VIII: 43n
Washington Agricultural Literary Society (Farmer's High School, Pa.), IV: 70
Washington Arsenal, IV: 530-31, 551n; V: 4, 9; VI: 255n; VII: 216n, 532; VIII: 373n, 381
Washington Chronicle, VI: 59-60, 152n, 214, 251-52, 401n, 430n; VII: 254n, 351n, 429n, 537n, 542n, 543n; VIII: 58n, 114n, 155n, 179n, 226n, 228n, 236n, 355n, 393n

Washington Constitution, IV: 146
Washington County (D.C.), VII: 64, 408
Washington County (Ill.), I: 147
Washington County (Ky.), I: 461; V: 57
Washington County (Oreg.), V: 163n
Washington County (Pa.), VIII: 418n
Washington County (Tenn.), VIII: 68
Washington Globe, I: 336n; VI: 106n
Washington Intelligencer, see National Intelligencer
Washington Navy Yard, IV: 342, 384n; V: 34n, 464, 473; VI: 272; VII: 118n, 532; VIII: 393n
Washington Republican, see National Republican
Washington Rifles (N.Y. Infantry, 11th Regt.), IV: 408n; V: 149n; VI: 59n
Washington Star, IV: 249n, 272n, 274n, 275n, 281n, 390n; V: 116n; VI: 60n, 245n; VII: 254n, 454n; VIII: 237n
Washington States, III: 431, 452; IV: 23, 469n
Washington Temperance Society, I: 268-69, 271-79
Washington Territory, II: 280-81, 347; III: 137; IV: 308, 322n, 389, 403, 447-48, 504n, 509, 550; V: 78n, 204n, 467n; VI: 111n, 119n, 144n, 432; VII: 36-37, 188, 290n, 544; VIII: 368
Washington Times, VII: 332n
Washington Union, I: 510; II: 154, 471, 507; III: 24-26, 49, 53, 68-70, 73-76, 242, 270-73, 277, 294
Washingtonian Hall (Boston), II: 5
Watauga River (Tenn.), II: 217; IV: 61; VI: 470n; VII: 6n
"Watch Night—or, Waiting for

the Hour" (painting), VIII: 266

Waterbury, Nelson J., VI: 361n, 381-82

Waterloo (Belgium), IV: 23

Waterloo (Ill.), III: 106, 121, 175

Waterman, Henry, II: 113-14

Waters, Charles E., VIII: 251

Waters, George W., I: 249

Waters, Levin L., VIII: 167, 172-73, 198, 229-30, 232, 251n

Waters, William, VIII: 69

Waters, William J., VIII: 69

Watertown (Mass.), V: 406

Watertown Arsenal, IV: 520n; V: 458n; VII: 100n

Watertown (N.Y.) *Times,* V: 509n

Watkins, Albert Galiton, VII: 520n

Watkins, Joseph E., I: 77

Watkins, Nathaniel W., VI: 6

Watkins' Mill, I: following 48, 52

Watrous, Charles, IV: 302n

Watseka (Ill.), IV: 38n

Watson, Abner M., II: 223, 424

Watson, Benjamin A., VI: 237-38; VII: 252-53

Watson, Benjamin Franklin, IV: 543-44

Watson, Gillet F., V: 387

Watson, Jacob [alias], *see* Gallagher, John

Watson, Peter H. [G.], II: 314-15, 325; III: 370-71, 380; V: 432n, 458n; VI: 107n, 127n, 165, 187n, 188-89, 206, 209, 480, 529; VII: 30

Watson, William D., II: 296, 480

Watson, William W., I: 207, 239

Watson, W[illiam] W., & Son (Springfield), VII: 253n

Watt, Harold L., VII: 172n

Watt, John, V: 25; VI: 49-50

Watts, J. T., V: 283

Watts, John Sebrie, IV: 349n; V: 340n; VI: 113; VII: 480

Watts, Robert, VIII: 290n

Watts, Thomas M., VII: 213

Wauhatchie (Tenn.), VI: 554n

Waukegan (Ill.) *Gazette,* V: 353n

Waverly (Ill.), I: 182-83

Way, George W. [A.] [alias], *see* Bixby, George W. [A.]

Way, John H., *see* Utz, John H.

Wayman, A. W., VII: 543n

Wayne, James Moore, III: 543n; V: 481

Wayne County (Tenn.), VIII: 69

Wayne County (W. Va.), V: 298

Wea Indians, *see* Ouiatenon Indians

Wead, Hezekiah Morse, I: 391; II: 117-18, 415-16

Weakley County (Tenn.), VIII: 70

Weather, L. and the: effect on the nervous system, I: 265; describes Springfield storm, IV: 90; an opinion on forecasters, VI: 190-91

Weathers, Susannah (Crume), V: 57

Webb, ———, V: 73

Webb, Alexander Stewart, VIII: 390

Webb, David, IV: 371

Webb, Edwin B. ("Bat"), I: 61, 156-57, 233, 237, 249, 253; II: 63, 470

Webb, Ezra, VI: 177n

Webb, Henry Livingston, I: 496

Webb, J. S., VIII: 69

Webb, James Watson, IV: 164-65, 358-59, 397

Webb, Moses F., IV: 405

Webb, Timothy U., II: 388

Webber, Charles M., II: 202n

Webber, Jonathan R., VII: 418

Webber, Thomson R., II: 202; V: 398; VIII: 210n

Webber's Falls (Indian Terr.), IV: 476n

Weber, George Richard, I: 158; III: 339-40; VI: 237-38, 290n

Weber, John B., III: 339-40

Weber, Louvenia Elizabeth (Adams), I: 98n
Weber, Peter S., I: 98-100
Weber, Mrs. Peter S., *see* Weber, Louvenia Elizabeth
Webster, Bela C., I: 398; II: 331
Webster, B[ela] C., & Company (Springfield), I: 323, 325, 328
Webster, Daniel, I: 515; II: 137-38, 282, 367, 370, 372-73, 383, 519, 545; III: 2, 61, 77, 102-103, 168-70, 270, 273; IV: 230-31, 336n, 405; VII: 303
Webster, Daniel Fletcher, IV: 336, 405
Webster, Edwin Hanson, VII: 75-76, 427, 511n; VIII: 348, 409n, 411n
Webster, George, V: 458n
Webster, George D., IV: 305
Webster, Joseph Dana, V: 526; VII: 104
Webster, Noah, III: 360
Webster, Thomas, V: 411-12; VII: 390
Webster, Thomas, Jr., IV: 329
Webster, Timothy, IV: 353n
Webster, Warren, V: 429n
Webster County (Ky.), VI: 85
Webster County (W. Va.), V: 298
Webster-Ashburton Treaty, II: 146n
Weed, Harriet A., VI: 112n
Weed, John J., VII: 468; VIII: 243n
Weed, Thurlow, IV: 57, 71, 97-98, 154, 157-59, 164n, 185-86, 334n, 337, 361-62; V: 350-51, 365n, 383, 408n; VI: 83-84, 96n, 112-13, 513-14, 525n; VII: 23-24, 77, 268-69, 289n, 410n, 461n, 511n, 514n, 526-27; VIII: 45n, 88n, 114n, 132n, 356
Weehawken (ironclad), VI: 84n; VII: 57
Week by Week in Springfield (periodical), cited, II: 292n; VI: 193n, 550n; VII: 439n

Weeks, William F., VI: 506-507
Weems, Mason Locke, IV: 235
Weer, William, Jr., II: 198-99
Weik, G. [alias], *see* Kuhne, George
Weik, Jesse William, II: 47n; IV: 126n; VIII: 420n
Weimer, John M., VII: 310
Weirman, Miss, VII: 129
Weisenfeldt, Moses, VIII: 304n
Weiss, Bernhardt, VI: 98n
Weitzel, Godfrey, V: 428n; VIII: 187n, 377, 385, 387n, 389, 405-408
Welch, Benjamin, Jr., IV: 307
Welch, James, VIII: 112n
Welch, John A., VII: 28-29, 59
Welch, William, VI: 118n
Welch, William G., VI: 118
Welcome to Goldwin Smith, VIII: 97n
Weld, Lewis L., IV: 294; V: 179n, 182
Weldon, Lawrence, II: 475; III: 81n, 489n; VI: 63n
Wellers, Samuel, VI: 561; VII: 2
Welles, Charles R., II: 29-30, 159, 289-90
Welles, Gideon: and appointment to L.'s cabinet, IV: 147n, 161; matters referred to his attention by L., 248, VI: 422, 483, VII: 292, 366, 390, 479, 532, VIII: 428; summoned by L. for conference, IV: 280, 338; and relief for Fort Sumter, 285n, 321, 324, VIII: 427; L.'s servant recommended to him for employment, IV: 288; and assignment of naval vessels for revenue service, 293; expedition to Fort Pickens, 301-302, 366-67, 465n; L. requests home squadron remain in observation at Veracruz (Apr. '61), 318-19; L. requests identity of vessels seen near Wilmington Navy Yard, 342; L. suggests Potomac patrol

for security of White House, 348-49; new inventions for military use and procurement of boats, 370, 412, V: 33-34, 354, 489, 498, VI: 107, 272, 342-43, 367-68, 521, VII: 510; use of naval vessels for transporting refugees, IV: 389, VI: 36, VII: 27n; reported Confederate foreign purchase of ships, IV: 397; L. requests report on number of vessels and seamen (June '61), 415

Annual reports, *(1861)* IV: 431, V: 40-41, *(1862)* 524, *(1863)* VII: 43-45, *(1864)* VIII: 144-45; reported Confederate plan to attack blockading fleet, IV: 478-79; appointment of Acting Sec. Fox, 507; Port Royal expedition, 528; N. Y. *Herald* reporter protests refusal of permission to accompany naval vessel down the Potomac, 539; and the Chiriqui project, 561-62, V: 2-3; and the President's General War Order No. 1, V: 111-12; and a Congressman's complaint against Philadelphia naval agent, 129; correspondence on the *Monitor*, 154, VI: 165-66; Foote requests equipment for captured gunboat, V: 156; N. Y. *Herald* speculates on cabinet division over Hunter proclamation, 225n; a review of his instructions from L. immediately following outbreak of armed hostilities, 241-42

And military operations, *(spring '62)* V: 294n, *(fall '62)* 489, 498, *(spring '63)* VI: 165-67, 174n; and the Emancipation Proclamation, V: 433n, VI: 24n; and McClellan's relief from command of the Army of the Potomac, V: 485n; and Stanton's objections to transfer

of Mississippi R. war vessels to the navy, 490n; on constitutionality and expediency of bill to admit W. Va. to the Union, VI: 17; favors standard gauge track for Union Pacific R. R., 68n; and patrol of rivers, 101; opposes L.'s acceptance of an invitation to preside at a religious meeting, 111n; notes Weed's presence in Washington in connection with N. H. and Conn. elections (1863), 112n; reports conference with Conn. Senator on an internal revenue appointment, 122n; opposes Marque and Reprisal bill, 126n; attends L.'s audience to Indian chiefs, 152n; and L.'s memo on harbor defenses, 163; disagreements with Seward, 183n, 349n; and question of government right to open mail of neutral powers found on vessels captured in breach of blockade, 183-84

And trade with insurrectionary states, VI: 207n, 212, VIII: 22, 93n, 103n; and the Vallandigham arrest, VI: 261n; and the Stephens peace mission, 315n, 317n; and protection of northeast coastal waters, 320-21; and L.'s instructions on conduct of naval officers in foreign ports in respect to neutral vessels, 342-43, 348-50, 378n; and plan to organize force to go to Tex., 354-55; and the draft, 444n, VII: 519-20, 534, VIII: 86-87; and postponement of joint army-navy movement against Charleston, VII: 81, 84; captured letters intimate Seward's nephew connected with blockade running, 87-88; L. suggests Congressional vote of thanks for Stembel, 199-200; and seizure of privately owned

boat on charges of illicit trading, 242; criticized by Weed,
268n; and retaliation for Fort
Pillow massacre, 328-29; and
court-martial of Rear Ad-
miral Wilkes for unauthorized
publication of official letters,
343n, VIII: 182; request of
Mare Island Navy Yard em-
ployee for reimbursement of expenses, VII: 401; N. Y. *Evening
Post* publisher charged with
government frauds, 409-10; and
the appointment of a successor
to Chase, 420n

And L.'s memo on probable
reelection failure, VII: 514-15;
charges against Smith brothers
for alleged fraudulent deliver-
ies under contract, 522-23,
VIII: 240, 364n; and difficulties
over exchange of naval prisoners through army lines, VIII:
36-37; and the sailor vote, 43;
and recommended U. S. purchase of American-built Japanese war vessel, 131-32; and the
release of files of court-martial
cases, 190-91; and L.'s proposal
concerning compensation to rebel states for war expenses,
261n; L. recommends government advertising in N. Y.
French newspaper, 343; mention of peace parade to his
home (Apr. 10, '65), 393n; L.
requests navy sword for son
Tad, 395

Appointments and promo-
tions, IV: 297, 310, 335, 337-38,
340, 356, 363, 381, 411, 444, 447,
494, 507, 526; V: 23, 59, 66, 148,
161, 387-89, 395, 447, 480; VI:
52, 107, 122n, 154, 376n, 432,
511; VII: 82-83, 315, 450, 456,
484n, 491, 513; VIII: 215, 291

Duty assignments, IV: 320, V:
13, 70, 242; dismissals, discharges, resignations and retire-

ments, IV: 343, 361; V: 59, 101,
199n, 335-36, VI: 376n, VIII:
170, 427; arrests, VI: 194n, 385,
VII: 409-10, 522-23

Reports transmitted to Congress on: disobedience of *Sabine*
commander in Fort Pickens expedition, IV: 465; rank of navy
officers, 470; seizure of foreign
vessels, V: 109-10, 162; courts
of inquiry, 198-99; alleged U. S.
recruitment in foreign countries, VII: 415-16

His *Diary* cited in footnotes
on the ff. pages, V: 144, 198,
433, 490; VI: 68, 111, 113, 122,
183, 207, 261, 315, 317, 321, 349,
355, 378, 444; VII: 87, 343, 410,
420, 522; VIII: 37, 93, 132, 261,
364, 412, 425

Welles, Mrs. Gideon, *see* Welles,
Mary Jane

Welles, Lemuel A., V: 4n

Welles, Mary Jane (Hale), VIII:
131

Welles, Thomas Glastonbury,
VII: 484n

Welling, James Clarke, V: 341n;
VII: 462-63

Wellington, Arthur Wellesley, 1st
Duke of, VI: 332n

Wells, Alfred, IV: 307

Wells, Charles, VI: 138n

Wells, Franklin, VIII: 270

Wells, Gabriel, VIII: 159n

Wells, Hezekiah G., II: 358-61;
IV: 397n

Wells, T. M., VII: 420

Wells, W. H., III: 349

Wellsville (Ohio), IV: 207-208

Welsh, ———, VII: 341

Welsh, John, VII: 366n

Welsh, Robert, VI: 477n

Welte, M., und Söhne, II: 524n

Welton, Louis A., VII: 393, 493n,
526-27; VIII: 187-88

Wendell, Arthur, VI: 206n; VIII:
333n

Wendell, Mrs. Arthur, VII: 351n

Wendell, Cornelius, III: 69

Wendt, Henry, II: 475

Wentsel, Mrs. Karl, VIII: 261n

Wentworth, John, I: 493-94, 506; II: 12-13, 20, 293, 340, 367, 429, 444n, 457, 472; III: 7, 61, 105, 109, 139, 174, 202, 356n, 506n; VII: 424n; VIII: 419n

Wessells, Henry Walton, Jr., V: 388

Wessels, Leverett W., VII: 133n

Wesson, William, VIII: 69

West, John, V: 327

West, Joseph Rodman, VII: 159

West, Nathaniel T., VI: 116-17

West, Department of the, IV: 373n; V: 1-2, 7, 13, 15, 22n, 57-58; VI: 228n; *see also* Western Department

West Point: commanding officers and faculty at, IV: 350n, V: 390, VI: 107n, VII: 496, VIII: 405; L. urges expansion of, V: 40; comment on officers trained at, 187, VI: 7, 169n, 249n, 308, VII: 400; L. and Scott conference at, V: 284; appointment to Board of Visitors, VII: 345

Cadet appointments, I: 466; IV: 382, 387, 392, 398, 417, 443, 448, 473, 486, 530; V: 9, 13, 33, 58, 75, 103-104, 106, 139, 149, 152, 161, 261, 288, 296, 473, 549; VI: 12, 60, 75-76, 88-90, 99, 110, 119-20, 132, 144, 162, 177, 185-86, 216, 362, 366-67, 399, 403, 411, 413, 428, 433, 443, 461, 463, 480; VII: 26-28, 58, 110, 121, 139, 143, 154, 210, 231-32, 235-36, 246, 249, 278, 353-54, 367, 375, 454, 458-59, 470, 509, 511, 545; VIII: 6, 85, 156, 184-85, 190n, 194-95, 232-33, 291, 334, 346

West Point (Va.), V: 123n, 195n, 220n, 244; VI: 218n

West Tennessee, District of, VIII: 74n

West Union (Ohio), VII: 28

West Virginia, IV: 451n; VI: 17, 24, 26-29, 115-16, 130n, 137, 160, 181, 238n, 277; VII: 129, 166n, 199, 319, 487; VIII: 46, 100n, 129-30, 150, 153; *see also* Virginia

West Virginia, Department of, VI: 311n; VII: 129n, 244n, 445-46, 469n, 478n; VIII: 82n, 371n

West Virginia and East Tennessee, Department of (C. S. A.), VIII: 310n, 315n

Westcott, Edward J., VI: 150

Western, John, *see* Weston, John

Western Academy of Art (St. Louis), VII: 106n

Western Characters or Types of Border Life (Mc Connel), II: 75n

Western Department, IV: 420n, 562n; V: 84; *see also* West, Department of the

Western Reserve (Ohio), I: 518

Western Union Telegraph Company, IV: 534n, 537n, 541n; V: 6n

Western Virginia, District of, V: 497n; VII: 365n

Westfield (N. Y.), IV: 219

Westheimer, Irvin F., V: 453n; VII: 464n

Westlake, Benjamin F., VI: 197

Westminster (Md.), V: 418n

Weston, Charles, IV: 520, 530, 540n; V: 458n

Weston, George M., IV: 520n, 540

Weston, John, IV: 514-15

Westville (N. J.), VII: 3n

Wetherill, Charles M., V: 354, 385; VI: 3n, 163, 343, 367, 560n; VII: 3-4

Wetherill, John W., VI: 228

Wetherland, R. G., VIII: 68

Wetmore, James C., VII: 505n

Wetmore, Prosper M., VI: 312n; VII: 32

Wetmore, Titus C., IV: 294-95

Wetterstedt, Nicholas G., Baron de, VIII: 228

Wetzel County (W. Va.), V: 298
Weyer, Josiah S., V: 8
Whaley, Kellian Van Rensalear, VI: 137; VII: 289, 309n; VIII: 160
Whary, David, I: 18, 24
"What's in the Wind?" (editorial), II: 355-56
Wheat, James S., IV: 443
Wheaton, Frank, VI: 437, 439; VIII: 391-92
Wheelan, James, VII: 219-20
Wheeler, Alanson, II: 298, 304
Wheeler, Alpheus, I: 227n
Wheeler, B. G., II: 113-14
Wheeler, David H., IV: 445
Wheeler, George Augustus, VIII: 136n
Wheeler, Joseph, VII: 520n
Wheeler, L. D., VIII: 69
Wheeler, Oliver B., VIII: 135-36
Wheeling (W. Va.), IV: 464, 511n; V: 418; VI: 189n, 249n
Wheler, Charles L., II: 148n
Wherry, Jesse, IV: 325
"Whig, A" [pseud.], see Henry, Anson G.
"Whig Junto," I: 288n
Whig Liberty Pole, I: 341
Whig Party: election returns (1836), I: 48n; support of Clay land bill, 50n; the committee of nine (1839), 146, 227-28; Whig newspapers, 151, 493, 498; resolutions (1839) inviting opposition debate of issues, 155-56; debate sub-treasury issue, 159n, 160-61; Congressional strength (1838), 173-74; "the difference between the Van Buren party and the Whigs is . . . ," 177-78; plan of campaign (1840), 180-81; campaign circular (1840), 201-203; an incident at the Whig (1840) convention, 210; protest against judiciary bill (1841), 234-37, 244-49; the adoption of a convention system, 261-62, 264, 308-309, 314-16, 318-19, 325-26, 353-58; nominations of Whig county convention (1842), 284-85; and effect of ambiguity in apportionment bill, 287-88; position of state bank currency, 293n, 295-96; resolutions (1843) on current issues, 307-308, 329-30; campaign circular (1843) 309-18; resolution (1843) recommending Baker for Congress, 322

Blamed for Philadelphia riots (1844), 337; state convention (1844) endorses Clay for President, 338-40; effect of vote of abolitionist element, 347, 458, II: 492; charged with abolitionism, I: 347, 458, II: 157, 228-29, 322-23, III: 206; organization (1847) in Congress, I: 417; national convention (1848), 476, 477, 478; Whig chances in 1848 election, 490-91; position on Mexican War, 447-48, 514-16; campaign duties of executive committee (1848), 517-18; compared to Free Soil party on slavery question, II: 3-14 passim; speaks at Boston Whig Club (1848), 5; plan to develop party strength in Calif. (1849), 38; government advertising (1849) in Democratic papers, 42-43; state and national conventions (1852), 113-14, 232, 254; call for Springfield meeting (1852), 120; position on Missouri Compromise, II: 232, 237, 254; L. charged with "selling out" at formation of Republican party, III: 12-14, 76-77, 85-86, 118-19, 121-27, 181-88; L. belonged to "from it's origin," IV: 70
Whipple, Amiel Weeks, V: 171; VI: 216n
Whipple, Charles William, VI: 216; VII: 235

Whipple, Henry Benjamin, V: 173, 455n; VII: 275
Whipple, S. M., I: 467n
Whipple, Wayne, VIII: 319n
Whipple, William Dennison, V: 259n; VII: 3, 235n
Whistler, Garland Nelson, VII: 509
Whistler, Joseph Nelson Garland, VII: 509
Whitaker, ———, VII: 2n
Whitcomb, Lot, II: 183
White, ———, II: 418; VIII: 302n
White, A. W., VIII: 95
White, Albert Smith, IV: 405n; V: 324n, 492n; VI: 53n; VII: 128; VIII: 47n, 158n
White, Charles, VIII: 70
White, Chilton Allen, V: 454n; VI: 300-306
White, Eben, VI: 530n; VII: 28, 255
White, Ebenezer, V: 9n
White, Frank J., VIII: 34n, 186n
White, Harry, VI: 522n; VII: 120
White, Horace, II: 538n, 544n; III: 519
White, Hugh, I: 497
White, Hugh Lawson, I: 48; III: 78
White, Isaac C., VII: 32-33
White, James, I: 13
White, James B., II: 310
White, James W., V: 325, 349n
White, John, VIII: 421
White, Joseph Worthington, VI: 300-306
White, Julius, IV: 43; V: 196, 267
White, Katherine (Dresser), I: 331n
White, Leonard, I: 14
White, Martin, I: 239
White, Wharton, V: 332n
White, William W., VII: 329-30
White & Wright, III: 521
White Bull (Indian), VI: 153n
White County (Tenn.), VIII: 69
White Dog (Indian), see Skoonka-ska

White Hall (S. C.), VI: 455-57
White House: Washington Mayor calls on Buchanan (Feb. 27, '61), IV: 247n; wartime protection, 348-49; refurnishing, 407, 528, 557-58, VII: 65; mention of staff, V: 25, 143-44, 263, 447, 491, 492, VI: 175, 436n, VII: 128, 417, VIII: 345; L. receives Negro committee (Aug. '62), V: 370; entertaining, V: 380-81, VI: 185, VII: 234n, 235, 241, 262; purchase of books for, V: 394; L. receives wounded veterans, VI: 227n; Emily Helm's visit to (1863), VII: 63n; Negro celebration on the adjacent grounds, 419n; workmen celebrate L.'s reelection, VIII: 98
White House Landing (Va.), IV: 348; V: 240n, 289, 292-96, 499n
White Mountains, VI: 399n
White Oak Road (Va.), VIII: 378-80, 383
White Oak Swamp (Va.), V: 66n, 126n
White Plains (Va.), V: 235, 240n; VI: 289
White River (Ark.), VII: 464n; VIII: 288n, 335
Whitehead, P. T., VIII: 235n
Whitehill, John, VII: 86n
Whiteley, L. A., VI: 551n
White's Ford (Va.), V: 481n
Whiteside, James A., I: 77
Whiteside, John Davis, I: 299-303
Whiteside, Samuel, I: 10, 80; II: 312
Whiting, Elbridge, III: 393n
Whiting, Riley, VIII: 316
Whiting, William, VII: 92n, 523n; VIII: 373-75
Whiting, William Danforth, VIII: 134
Whiting, Mrs. William F., IV: 540n
Whitlock, Charles, VIII: 395
Whitly, Simeon, VII: 70
Whitmarsh, Warren, VI: 232

Whitney, Alfred, IV: 145
Whitney, Mrs. Alfred, *see* Whitney, Lucinda
Whitney, Daniel H., II: 303-304
Whitney, Henry Clay, II: 313, 328, 341n, 347, 428-29, 472, 534-35; III: 343, 347, 378; IV: 33n, 35n, 79n, 145, 543; V: 433n; VII: 120
Whitney, Mrs. Henry Clay, IV: 145
Whitney, Jonas, I: 207-208
Whitney, Lucinda (Ring), IV: 145
Whittingham, William Rollinson, VII: 335-36
Whittington, George T., VIII: 416-17
Whittlesey, Elisha, IV: 384, 454-55; V: 73n
Wholihan, John W., IV: 374n
Whray, David, *see* Whary, David
Wick, Cyrus, VIII: 166
Wick, William Watson, I: 468
Wickersham, D., III: 399
Wickersham, Josiah, I: 255
Wickes, William H., VII: 232n
Wickizer, John H., V: 472n; VII: 513
Wickliffe, Charles Anderson, IV: 369n, 464n; VI: 372
Wickliffe, Mary Todd (Russell), I: 466n
Wickliffe, Robert, I: 465-66; II: 318n; V: 386n
Wickliffe, Mrs. Robert, *see* Wickliffe, Mary Todd
Widmer, John H., III: 344
Wiegand, Charles, VI: 146-47
Wiegand, Conrad, IV: 305
Wiegand, Dill, *see* Wigand, H.
Wiel, Samuel Charles, VI: 206n
Wigand, H., IV: 94
Wigeon, Margaret E., VI: 443
Wiggins, Samuel, I: 64, 187-88
Wiggins loan, I: 45, 69; VIII: 429
Wight, A. G. S., I: 67
Wightman, Joseph M., V: 384n
Wigle, John, I: 35n

Wigwam (Peoria, Ill.), IV: 137n
Wigwam (Springfield), IV: 143n
Wigwam (newspaper), II: 544n
Wikoff, Henry ("Chevalier"), IV: 539
Wilberforce, William, II: 482
Wilcox, Cadmus Marcellus, VIII: 383
Wilcox, Elijah, III: 125
Wilcox, Nathaniel Green, II: 37, 55; VI: 109-10
Wilcox, Nathaniel M., VIII: 86-87
Wilcox, William, I: 467n
Wild, George W., VIII: 317n
Wilder, Abel Carter, IV: 476; VI: 334n, 415n, 418; VII: 119n, 338n
Wilder, Daniel W., III: 506; VI: 507
Wilder, John Thomas, VII: 144n
Wilderness, battle of the, VII: 102n, 159n, 334n, 340n, 357n, 406n
Wildman, Frederick S., V: 375
Wiley, Benjamin L., II: 469; III: 521n
Wiley, Edmund R., I: 158
Wilhelm August Karl Joseph, Hereditary Prince of Hohenzollern-Sigmaringen, VII: 478-79
Wilkes, Charles, V: 64n, 82, 95, 102, 141; VII: 343n; VIII: 182
Wilkins, R. S., I: 430n
Wilkinson, Ira O., VI: 386n
Wilkinson, Jarvis, III: 384n
Wilkinson, Joab, I: 496; IV: 513n
Wilkinson, Mahlon, VI: 134n
Wilkinson, Morton Smith, IV: 276n, 513n; V: 397n, 493n; VII: 403
Wilkinson, Samuel, II: 458
Willard, Ashbel P., III: 469
Willard, Peter H., I: 354-55
Willard & Zimmerman (Springfield), III: 399
Willard's Hotel (Washington), IV: 247n, 248n; VI: 85n, 508n; VII: 3n, 230n; VIII: 15n, 114n
Willcox, Orlando Bolivar, V: 381,

485n; VI: 488; VII: 29n, 30; VIII: 276

Willey, Waitman Thomas, V: 319n; VI: 132; VII: 502n

William (Negro servant), see Johnson, William H.

William, Landgrave of Hesse, VII: 336

William, Prince of Baden, VI: 171

William I, King of Prussia, V: 102, 448-49; VII: 478-79; VIII: 56-57

William III, King of the Netherlands, IV: 287

William Lee (whaling ship), VI: 92

Williams, ———, IV: 248

Williams (Ky. judge), V: 503

Williams, Miss, VIII: 123n

Williams, A. F., VII: 371n

Williams, Amos, II: 14-15

Williams, Archibald, I: 125n, 132n, 146n, 344, 367, 392, 467-68, 477n; II: 31, 78, 115-16, 284, 287, 293-94, 315n, 317, 386, 483n; III: 7, 109, 174; IV: 401, 455; VI: 179, 507n

Williams, Barney, VIII: 424

Williams, Barney [Bernard O'-Flagerty], VI: 120

Williams, C. C., VI: 107n

Williams, Cecilia, V: 8n

Williams, Charles W., VI: 472n

Williams, David F., IV: 337n

Williams, E. B., III: 125

Williams, George, V: 181n

Williams, Harvey, VIII: 257

Williams, Henry (Tenn.), VIII: 68

Williams, Henry (U. S. Sharpshooters), VI: 97-98

Williams, Henry H., VI: 548

Williams, Isaac, I: 379-80

Williams, James E., VII: 486

Williams, James Monroe, VI: 188

Williams, James Seymour, VIII: 369n

Williams, Jesse Lynch, VII: 451; VIII: 39

Williams, John (Ill.), I: 43, 79, 398, 405; II: 188, 410, 424; VI: 237-38; VII: 316; VIII: 198

Williams, John (Tenn.), VI: 525; VIII: 58-72

Williams, John, Jr. (Va.), V: 8n

Williams, Mrs. John, Jr., see Williams, Cecilia

Williams, John Benson, VI: 169

Williams, John H., VI: 472

Williams, John J., V: 376n

Williams, Mrs. John J., see Williams, Virginia

Williams, John W., VII: 289n, 292n

Williams, Joseph J., V: 369, 376-77

Williams, Joseph Lanier, IV: 408

Williams, Lewis O., II: 374n

Williams, Michael, II: 182-83

Williams, Nancy Jane, see Johnston, Nancy Jane

Williams, Overton, I: 445

Williams, Philip D., I: 2-3

Williams, Pleasant, VIII: 68

Williams, Robert, V: 474n

Williams, Robert E., II: 91n, 413; III: 378

Williams, Rufus King, VII: 400, 495n, 519

Williams, Seth, V: 93-94; VII: 92n

Williams, Thomas (Ill.), II: 182, 186

Williams, Thomas (Pa.), VII: 486n

Williams, Virginia (Noll), V: 376n

Williams, Mrs. W. C., VIII: 428

Williams, William, VII: 358n

Williams, William R., IV: 528

Williams College, VIII: 352n

Williamsburg (Va.), V: 207, 294-95, 387n; VI: 60n, 82n, 236n

Williamson, Alexander, VI: 144-45; VIII: 237n, 313n

Williamson, Anne, VII: 471

Williamson, Elizabeth, I: 281
Williamson, Hugh, III: 524, 546n
Williamson, John, I: 281
Williamson, Thomas S., VII: 326n
Williamson, William B., VIII: 313
Williamson County (Tenn.), VIII: 69
Williamsport (Md.), IV: 416n; V: 237n, 239, 247, 249, 254, 417-18, 427n; VI: 276, 278n, 317n, 319n, 321, 323, 354
Willich, August, V: 66, 253; VI: 202
Willis, Arthur G., IV: 508n
Willis, Henry, VIII: 53n
Willis, Nathaniel Parker, I: 377n
Willis, W. W., VIII: 68
Williston, J. P., VII: 215n
Williston, Lorenzo P., IV: 294-95; VII: 355n, 371-72
Willmann, Andreas, V: 106n; VII: 262
Wills, David, VII: 18n
Wilmington (Del.), I: 475-76; IV: 239-40; V: 163; VI: 351n, 459n; VIII: 251n
Wilmington (N. C.), V: 122n; VI: 330n; VIII: 28n, 187, 207-208, 235-36, 351, 396
Wilmore, ———, IV: 499
Wilmot, David, II: 237, 241, 252, 367; III: 6, 521; IV: 167, 327; V: 172n, 549; VI: 52, 167n
Wilmot, Thomas M., V: 549
Wilmot Proviso, I: 503, 505, 510-12; II: 7-8, 12, 232, 236-37, 252-53, 257-60, 323, 377; III: 6, 56, 64, 78, 105, 107, 126, 196, 321
Wilms, Mrs. Herman G., I: facing 20
Wilson, ———, II: 96
Wilson, Andrew J., I: 336n
Wilson, Mrs. Andrew J., see Wilson, Susan
Wilson, Charles G., IV: 114
Wilson, Charles Lush, II: 68n,

444-47, 455-57; III: 356n, 505-506
Wilson, Daniel M., V: 376n
Wilson, Edward M., I: 67
Wilson, Frederick A., VI: 209-10
Wilson, G. R., VIII: 87n
Wilson, George, IV: 210
Wilson, Harriet Malvina (Howe), VIII: 334n
Wilson, Henry, III: 53; IV: 109, 484n; V: 104n, 172n, 201n, 217-18, 420; VI: 115, 181-82, 208n; VII: 84n, 257; VIII: 334n, 352n
Wilson, Henry B., VI: 425
Wilson, Henry Clay, IV: 308; VI: 202, 209
Wilson, Isaac Grant, II: 329n; VIII: 405
Wilson, Jacob, VI: 154n
Wilson, James (Ill.), I: 416
Wilson, James (Mo.), VIII: 102n, 116, 223n
Wilson, James (N. J.), VIII: 26
Wilson, James, (Pa.), III: 526n, 531n
Wilson, James Falconer, VIII: 327n, 358n
Wilson, James Grant, IV: 48
Wilson, James Harrison, IV: 517n, 527n
Wilson, John (deserter), VII: 137, 140, 152
Wilson, John (Ill.), II: 135n; IV: 83, 456; VI: 113; VII: 392n
Wilson, John F., I: 83
Wilson, Mrs. John F., see Wilson, Martha (Hart)
Wilson, John L., II: 113-14
Wilson, Joseph Frye, V: 68n, 471
Wilson, Joseph J., VII: 516
Wilson, M. L., IV: 45n
Wilson, Martha (Hart), I: 83
Wilson, Mary S. (Davidson), I: 253
Wilson, Nathaniel G., IV: 295n
Wilson, Robert, VI: 115
Wilson, Robert L., I: 76-77, 298
Wilson, Singleton, VI: 398-99
Wilson, Susan, I: 336n

Wilson, William (Ill.), I: 253n
Wilson, William (N. Y.), VI: 254n
Wilson, Mrs. William, *see* Wilson, Mary S.
Wilson, William, Potter, VII: 97n
Wilson County (Tenn.), VIII: 69
Wilson's Creek, battle of, IV: 526; V: 114, 511n; *see also* Springfield (Mo.)
Wilton, Harry, I: 258-59; II: 306-307
Winant, John Gilbert, VIII: 415n
Winchell, James M., VII: 201n
Winchester (Ill.), II: 226-27; III: 5, 203-204
Winchester (Tenn.), VI: 352n
Winchester (Va.), V: 98, 184, 233-38, 246-47, 249-50, 252, 254-55, 264, 267, 269, 460-61; VI: 137, 273-74, 276, 278, 293n, 308-309, 522n, 541-42; VII: 102-103, 466n, 484n; VIII: 13, 74n, 297, 317n, 370-71
Windom, William, VII: 48n, 275; VIII: 363n
Windward Passage, VII: 164n
Winebiddle, Philip, V: 81
Winfrey, T. J., VIII: 69
Wing, W. W., VI: 26n
Wingle, Peter, *see* Fingle, Peter
Winham, Anderson, VIII: 68
Winnebago Indians, VII: 515-16; VIII: 370n
Winslow, J. F., VI: 112n
Winslow, John Ancrum, VIII: 135
Winston, ———, VI: 135; VII: 350, 354
Winston, Mrs. VI: 135
Winston, Frederick, V: 325, 498n
Winters, Gilbert E., VIII: 236-37
Wintersmith, Robert L., IV: 139
Winthrop, Robert Charles, I: 417
Winton, B., I: 52
Wippermann, Frederick, VI: 507
Wirt, William, V: 503n
Wirt County (W. Va.), V: 298
Wisconsin, I: 469-71, 478; II: 249; III: 397n, 463n, 471-82; IV:

296; V: 41, 332; VII: 312n, 356n; VIII: 33-34, 46, 100n, 129-30, 150, 153
Wisconsin Farmer & Northwestern Cultivator [Milwaukee], III: 397n
Wisconsin Magazine of History, III: 477n; VI: 437n
Wisconsin Territory, I: 184
Wisden, Robert, II: 309n
Wise, Charlotte Brooks (Everett), VI: 332n; VIII: 92-93
Wise, Henry Alexander, II: 377-78; III: 452, 496-97; IV: 159n; VI: 332n, 476
Wise, Mrs. Henry Alexander, *see* Wise, Charlotte Brooks
Wise, Henry Augustus, V: 108n, 112, 156n; VI: 272n, 530-31
Wise, James A., IV: 319; V: 352
Wise, William, IV: 319; V: 205
Wiseman, Benjamin, I: facing 48
Wisewell, Moses N., VI: 126n; VII: 371, 393, 479n
Witherill, Orlando Stewart, VII: 430n
Withey, George, IV: 90
Withey, Solomon L., VI: 117n
Withey, William H., IV: 90
Witt, Franklin, I: 60-61
Wittenmyer, Annie, VIII: 54-55
Wiyaka (Indian), VII: 325-26
Wiyuha (Indian), VII: 325-26
Wofford, William T., VI: 480
Wolf, Edwin, I: xiv
Wolf, Enoch O., VIII: 102, 116, 223
Wolf, Mrs. Enoch O. [alias], *see* Beattie, Kate
Wolf, Ezra, VI: 114n
Wolfe, Adam, VI: 482
Wolfe, John S., III: 384; VI: 197-98
Wolfe, William Vernon, IV: 557
Wolff, August L., IV: 298
Wolford, Frank L., VII: 430-31, 446-47, 480; VIII: 120, 183n, 250

Wolf's Run (Va.), V: 121n

Woman Surgeon, A (Morton), VIII: 303n

Women and marriage, L. and: woman suffrage, I: 48; the Mary Owens affair, 54-55, 78-79, 94-95, 117-19; "Whatever woman may cast her lot with mine, should any ever do so, it is my intention to . . .," 78; "I want in all cases to do right, and most particularly so, in all cases with women," 94; "others have been made fools of by the girls; but this can never be with truth said of me . . .," 119; "have now come to the conclusion never again to think of marrying . . . I can never be satisfied with any-one who would be block-head enough to have me," 119; L. deplores lack of feminine society in Springfield, 156-57; courtship and marriage advice to Speed, 265-70, 280-83, 288-90, 303; "nothing new here, except my marrying, which to me, is a matter of profound wonder," 305; "as to kissing a pretty girl . . .," 499; sewing as "woman's work," III: 360; source of the Ann Rutledge story, IV: 104n; "have never corresponded much with ladies . . . hence I postpone writing letters to them, as a business which I do not understand," 118; guarantees to pay freight charges for a lady, 131; remarks directed to the ladies in his audiences, 206, 218, 219, 223, 228, 234; "have never studied the art of paying compliments to women," VII: 254; subject of divorce, 296; no objection to appointment of a lady chaplain, VIII: 102-103; *see also* Lincoln, Mary Todd

Wood, ———, VIII: 38

Wood, Alfred M., V: 381

Wood, Bradford Ripley, VI: 69n

Wood, Bradford Ripley, Jr., IV: 474n

Wood, David, VI: 259

Wood, Erastus, IV: 372n

Wood, F. A., IV: 68

Wood, Fernando, IV: 232-33; V: 553-54

Wood, George, I: 158

Wood, George M., VI: 127n

Wood, George W., V: 83n

Wood, John (Ill.), II: 345n, 410; III: 389; IV: 73n, 86n, 92-93, 116, 168n; V: 18, 277

Wood, John, Jr. (Ill.), V: 381

Wood, John (Tenn.), VIII: 69

Wood, John D., I: 179, 195

Wood, John F., IV: 181-82

Wood, Oliver, VI: 19

Wood, Thomas John, IV: 542

Wood, William E., VII: 291

Wood, William P., IV: 319; VIII: 233n

Wood, William S., IV: 326, 528; V: 71n

Wood County (W. Va.), V: 298

Woodbury, Daniel Phineas, V: 182

Woodbury, Levi, I: 162n, 165

Woodbury, W. W. R., II: 210

Woodbury, William W., VI: 442n

Woodbury family (Danville, Ill.), II: 15

Wooden, Edward L., VII: 154

Woodford County (Ill.), I: 354, 358n, 360, 384n; II: 191n

Woodford County (Ky.), V: 507n

Wooding, Henry, VII: 138

Woodley, W. H., IV: 356

Woodman, C. & G. (N. Y.), VII: 148

Woodman, George, II: 6

Woodruff, ———, VI: 340n; VIII: 428

Woodruff, Isaac O., V: 18

Woodruff, Israel Carle, VI: 461n

Woodruff, James, VI: 197

Woodruff, Truman, VI: 178n

Woodruff, William E., V: 262;
VI: 235
Woods, Donald A., VII: 316n
Woods, George W., II: 524
Woods, John R., VII: 316
Woods, Samuel S., VIII: 5n
Woods, Thomas, VIII: 309n
Woodson, David Meade, I: 249
Woodson, Silas, VII: 280, 371-72,
428n
Woodstock (S. C.), VI: 456
Woodstock (Va.), V: 258n
Woodward, ——, I: 383-84
Woodward, Dillard, VI: 544
Woodward, Enos, VI: 544
Woodward, George Washington,
VI: 512n
Woodward, James H., VIII: 119n
Woodward, Wiley, VIII: 69
Woodworth, Mrs. J. B., II: 72n
Woodworth, James Hutchinson,
I: 179; II: 287
Woodworth, Selim E., V: 215
Wool, John Ellis, IV: 175, 178,
478, 525n; V: 3n, 10, 59, 164,
174, 182, 184-85, 206-207, 216,
255, 259n, 272-73, 301, 409, 432,
447, 455; VI: 184, 236, 335
Woolfolk, George, VI: 537
Woolford, see Wofford, William
T.
Woolsey, King S., VIII: 214n
Woonsocket (R. I.), IV: 13n
Worcester (Mass.), II: 1-5; IV:
535
Worcester & Albany Railroad, IV:
99n
Worcester County (Md.), VIII:
49n
"Word with a Congressman, A"
(editorial), III: 507n
Worden, John Lorimer, IV: 465;
V: 154, 547; VI: 91
Wording, William E., VI: 98,
453-59
*World's Sages, Infidels, and
Thinkers, The* (Bennett), VIII:
102n
Wormer, Daniel, VII: 421, 448

Wormley, William, VI: 195n
Worrell, Edward, VIII: 293
Worsley, Pardon, VIII: 224n,
251n, 303
Worster, J. Rutherford, VII: 416
Worster, R. J., VI: 208
Worth, William Jenkins, II: 87-
88
Worthington, ——, VIII: 68
Worthington, Morrison, II: 60n
Worthington, Thomas, VII: 276-
77, 523-24
Worthington, U. G., VIII: 358n
"Wounded Scout" (statuary
group), VII: 389
Wren, Aquilla, I: 67
Wright, ——, VI: 104
Wright, ——, (Ill.), I: 158-59
Wright, ——, (Md.), VII: 75
Wright, Alfred G. [alias], see
Lawrence, Alfred G.
Wright, Arthur S., II: 534n
Wright, Augustus Romaldus,
VIII: 10n, 27n, 119-20
Wright, Crafts James, VII: 114-16;
VIII: 15n
Wright, David M., VI: 362, 419,
437-38, 443, 505, 514, 522n
Wright, Mrs. David M., VI:
522
Wright, Edward, V: 317n
Wright, Edwin Ruthven Vincent,
IV: 355
Wright, Elisha M., VII: 371
Wright, Eliza Ann, see Hamilton,
Eliza Ann
Wright, Erastus, IV: 134n
Wright, George, VI: 322n, 324-25,
333n
Wright, George Washington, IV:
301
Wright, H. L., III: 371n
Wright, Henry Clay, VII: 81
Wright, Horatio Gouverneur, IV:
517; V: 402n, 410, 416-17, 419,
425, 428, 497n; VI: 19, 42n, 87n,
104; VII: 438, 445, 456, 472n;
VIII: 51, 381-82, 391-92
Wright, J. C., VII: 432n

Wright, Jacob Taylor [L.], VII: 454

Wright, James, I: 116, 122

Wright, James A., V: 174n

Wright, James E., VII: 156n

Wright, Joel, I: 92n, 103, 121

Wright, John, I: facing 49 and 139

Wright, John H., IV: 343

Wright, Joseph Albert, IV: 547; V: 152n, 205, 256n, 351-52, 516; VI: 206; VII: 140, 351n, 510n

Wright, Maria Jane, see Johnston, Maria Jane

Wright, Presco, II: 188

Wright, Silas, I: 161, 489

Wright, Thomas, I: 79

Wright, Thomas S., V: 370n

Writing, "the great invention," III: 359-63

Writings of Abraham Lincoln, The (Lapsley), I: viii; IV: 240n, 345n; V: 147n, 162, 384n; VI: 12n, 273n, 330n; VII: 254n, 334n; VIII: 49n

Wy-a-tah-to-wah (Indian), V: 542

Wyatt, John, I: 87n

Wyatt, Samuel, VI: 544

Wyche, James E., IV: 308; VIII: 368

Wyckoff, Samuel, I: 154, 326-27

Wydenbruck, Count, VIII: 355

Wylie, Andrew, VIII: 126, 160n

Wyndham, Percy, VI: 135n

Wynkoop, Alfred, VI: 285n

Wynkoop, George Campbell, VI: 167-68

Wynne, Lewis B., II: 133

Wynne, Thomas, I: 298

Wyoming County (W. Va.), V: 298

Wytheville (Va.), VIII: 315n

Y

Yadkin County (N. C.), VIII: 124n

Yale, Gregory, VI: 206n

"Yankee Doodle" (song), VIII: 394n

Yankton (Dakota Terr.), VII: 207n

Yankton Land District, IV: 325

Yankton Sioux Indian Agency, IV: 298n, 306; VIII: 358n

Yarbrough, T. J., VIII: 69

Yardley, James, I: 12

Yardley, Mahlon, IV: 327

Yardly, John, II: 13

Yates, Charles, VI: 322n

Yates, Edward, VI: 80-81

Yates, Frank, E., VI: 561n

Yates, Henry, I: 264

Yates, Richard (1818-1873): mention of letter from Boal on 1846 political campaign, I: 384n; mention of his law partner William Brown, 389; letter from L. on his claim against Douglas and Taylor's candidacy for president (Dec. '47), 419; his legal cases, 419, II: 27-28, 227-28, 425; appointments and promotions, II: 75, IV: 168n, 407, 411, 416n, 521-22, V: 148n, 186-87, 277, 351n, 377n, 512, VI: 171n, 229, 473n, 490n, VII: 253n, VIII: 175n, 191n

Fails to win reelection to Congress(1854), II: 226, 284-86, 289, 304, III: 31-32, 228,

IV: 67; supports Washington territorial law (1853), II: 280; against early announcement of Palmer's candidacy for Congressman (Aug. '56), 357; L. suggests he become candidate for Ill. legislature (Sept. '57), 424; elected governor of Ill., IV: 41n; mobilization and recruitment, 344-45, 374n, 459n, V: 267n, 365n, 391-93, 431n, VI: 97n; orders seizure of boat owned by Tenn., IV: 351-52; his support of a promotion for Pope, 407, 411, V: 186-87; requests arms and ammunition, V: 151-52, 172; requests leaves of absence, 342n, 541n, VI: 552; supports movement against dismissal of Turchin, V: 406n; rejoices at news of McClellan victory in Md. (Sept. '62), 426n; protests military assessments against St. Louis merchant, VI: 65n; and Ill. claim to two-percent fund, 96n; warns of danger of insurrection in Ill. (Feb. '63), 100n; his opposition to dismissal of McClernand, 383-84

And the draft, VI: 417n, 435n; supports parole of Warfield, VII: 66n; requests use of government lot in Springfield for a Soldiers Home, 167; recruitment of 100-day troops, 308, 312-13, 355-56, VIII: 33; recommends discharge of soldier in bad health, VII: 315n; informed of N. Y. newspapers' publication of hoax proclamation (May '64), 351; reports rumored Vallandigham conspiracy against the government, 386n; supports a prisoner-of-war exchange, VIII: 51n; L. requests report of state vote in 1864 election, 109

Yates, Richard (1860-1936), I: 419n; II: 226n, 285n

Yates, Robert, III: 523n, 525n
Yates, William, III: 513; VI: 237-38
Yazoo Pass (Miss.), VI: 142, 326
Yazoo River, VI: 43n; VIII: 288n, 299n, 335
Yeakle, Henry, II: 188
Yeaman, George Helm, VI: 104; VII: 91n; VIII: 181n, 244n
Yeatman, Cynthia Ann (Pope), II: 30n
Yeatman, James Erwin, II: 30n; VI: 34, 37n; VII: 459n; VIII: 102n, 373-76
Yeatman, Mrs. James Erwin, see Yeatman, Cynthia Ann
Yeatman, Lucretia (Pope), II: 30n; VII: 236n
Yeatman, Thomas, II: 29-30
Yeatman, Mrs. Thomas, see Yeatman, Lucretia
Yeaton, Charles C., IV: 491n
Yeaton, Franklin, VIII: 184-85
Yeddo (Japan), VII: 39
Yell, Archibald, II: 86
Yellott, John I., VIII: 82n
Yellow Banks (Ill.), see Oquawka (Ill.)
Yellow Buffalo (Indian), VI: 153n
Yellow Wolf (Indian), VI: 153n
Yocum, William, VII: 144, 167, 187, 256-57, 362, 389-90; VIII: 119
Yoncalla (Oreg.), VI: 433n
Yonge, Chandler C., VIII: 242n
York, Joseph S., IV: 474n
York (Pa.), VI: 299n, 310n, 324n; VII: 216-17
York County (Va.), VI: 29
York River (Va.), V: 118, 219n, 284n, 290
Yorke, Louis Eugene, IV: 442
Yorke At Lee, Samuel, V: 446-47; VI: 69
Yorktown (Va.), V: 182, 195, 202-203, 405n, 503n; VI: 15n, 56; VII: 297n; VIII: 396
Yost, Casper E., VIII: 349

Young, A. L., VIII: 179
Young, Ammi B., IV: 361-62
Young, Andrew White, II: 388n
Young, Bennett H., VIII: 141n
Young, Brigham, II: 398n; V: 200n; VI: 518n
Young, Francis G., IV: 560n; V: 60; VII: 294
Young, George I., VII: 452
Young, Henry W., VIII: 255
Young, John J., VIII: 345
Young, John Russell, VI: 62n; VII: 469n
Young, John S., Jr., VII: 502-503, 516; VIII: 180
Young, John S., Sr., VII: 516n
Young, Lawrence, II: 328
Young, Matilda, see Matthews, Matilda (Young)
Young, P. G., I: 220

Young, Richard Montgomery, I: 314, 453, 499-500; II: 135n; VIII: 307
Young, Solomon, VIII: 206
Young, T., I: 298
Young, William H., I: 453, 519; II: 411-12
Young & Brothers (St. Louis), II: 29
Young men, L.'s advice on: political activity, I: 490-91, 497-99, VII: 202; training for the law, II: 327; III: 344; IV: 121; unhappiness in school, IV: 87, V: 288; importance of outcome of Civil War, VII: 538-39
Young's Point (La.), VI: 143n
Youngstown (Ohio), VII: 420
"Your Mission" (hymn), VIII: 245-46

Z

Zabriskie, Christian B., I: 496n
Zabriskie, Elias Brevoort, I: 496
Zabriskie, George A., I: 496n
Zacharie, ———, VIII: 238
Zacharie, Isachar, V: 436; VIII: 12, 238
Zachringer, Conrad, V: 476
Zagonyi, Charles, V: 270, 272n
Zane, ———, VII: 236n
Zane, John Maxcy, II: 431n
Zane, John P., IV: 305
Zaragoza (Spain), VI: 167
Zeilin, Jacob, VII: 353n
Zene, C. [alias], see Walter, Charles

Zerman, Juan Napoleon, V: 28
Ziegler, Frederick, V: 472n
Zimmerman, David, VIII: 234-35
Zimmerman, J. H., VIII: 235n
Zinn, Peter, III: 400
Zinn, William P., III: 400n
Zollicoffer, Felix Kirk, IV: 541-42, 544-45
Zouaves (Anderson's), IV: 406; VII: 436n
Zouaves (Baxter's), VI: 364, 384; VII: 320; VIII: 37n
Zwisler, James, I: 491n
Zwisler, Louis, I: 491

INDEX TO

APPENDIX II, VOLUME VIII

Writings for which no text has been found, forgeries and spurious or dubious items attributed to Lincoln, certain routine communications issued on Lincoln's authority and routine endorsements. (Italic figures in parentheses indicate numbers of pertaining references on indicated pages.)

A

Abdul Aziz Khan, Padischah of the Ottoman Empire, 475
Abel, Oramel H., 576
Abingdon (Va.), 555
Abolitionism, 443, 445
Abraham Lincoln: A New Portrait (Hertz), 440, 448, 463, 466, 469, 524-25, 534, 546, 570, 588-91
Abraham Lincoln: The Prairie Years (Sandburg), 440, 459, 590
Abraham Lincoln: The War Years (Sandburg), 591
Abraham Lincoln and Men of War-Times (McClure), 460, 465
Abraham Lincoln by Some Men Who Knew Him . . . (Phillips), 453, 466
Abraham Lincoln in the National Capital (Clark), 590
Abraham Lincoln Quarterly, 591
Abraham Lincoln Tributes . . ., 474
Achá, José María de, 469, 515
"Adam and Eve's Wedding Song" (poem), 430
Adams, Augustus, 449
Adams, Charles Francis, 468
Adams, F. C., 520, 557
Adams, Green, 524, 555
Adams, Henry J., 481
Adams, James, 434
Adams, John Quincy, 544
Adams Bank, 450
"Adams Guards" (Sixth Auditor's office), 500

Addison, H., 498
Afflick, H. Malin, 585
African Colonization Society (Springfield), 450
Agassiz, Jean Louis Rodolphe, 511
Agriculture: act to incorporate societies, 439; state agricultural societies, 553
Aiken, William, 524
Albion (Ill.), 438
Albion (N. Y.), 582
Alden, Farrelly, 482
Alexander, W., 563
Alexander, William, 516, 569
Alexander II of Russia, 470, 489
Alexandria (Va.), 505, 531, 562, 567, 586
Allabaugh, William, 575
Allcock, Thomas, 560
Allen, Ada, 507
Allen, Charles H., 573
Allen, Cyrus McCracken, 581
Allen, David O., 493
Allen, George W., 578
Allen, Hiram L., 431
Allen, John B., 544
Allen, John M., 521
Allen, [Julian?], 481
Allen, Robert, Jr., 491
Allen, Robert B., 499
Allen, Robert H., 522
Allen, Susie P., 493
Allenton (Christian Co., Ill.), 433

Alling, Charles E., 462
Allison, William Boyd, 556
Alt, William, 447
Alton (Ill.), 432, 438, 451
Alton & Sangamon Railroad, 442
Alton Courier, 450
Alton Telegraph, 438, 440
Alvord, Benjamin, 527
Alvord, H. J., 530
"Am I for Peace? Yes!" (poem), 532
Ambos, Peter, 457, 460
Amboy (Ill.), 455
American Art Association, catalogs cited, 446, 462, 464, 468, 482, 589
American Art Association Anderson Galleries, catalogs cited, 470, 480, 483-86, 491, 493, 498-99, 502, 519, 524, 530, 541, 543, 547, 549, 557, 576, 585, 590
American Autograph Shop, catalogs cited, 537, 557
American Government, purported essay by L. on, 430
American Jewry and the Civil War (Korn), 466
American Knights, Order of, 551
Ames, Mrs., 518
Ames, Edward Raymond, 541
Amesbury, Henry M., 548
Amnesty, order of, 485
Anderson, Joseph, 434
Anderson, Larz, 533
Anderson, Lucian, 536, 545, 555
Anderson, Robert, 477-78, 550
Anderson, S. J., 477
Anderson Auction Company, catalogs cited, 442, 464, 511, 527, 530, 584, 590
Anderson Auction Company-Metropolitan Art Association, catalog cited, 465
Anderson, Bell & Company, 434
Anderson County (Ky.), 588
Anderson Galleries, catalogs cited, 451, 480, 487, 491, 496, 522, 528-30, 536, 575, 589-90
Anderson, Lamoreux & Company, 454
Andrew, John Albion, 476, 492, 505, 533, 569, 579
Andrews, Ferdinand, 538
Andrews, George Leonard, 533
Andrews, Timothy Patrick, 446
Angel, Benjamin F., 468
Angle, Paul McClelland, see *Lincoln 1854-1861*

Annapolis (Md.), *see* Naval Academy, Annapolis
Anno, Henry, 432
Annon, A., 516
Anonymous letters attributed to L., 432-36, 441
Anthony, Daniel Read, 495
Antonali, Geacomo, 518
Apel, ———, Baron von, 564
Apel, Philip von, 564
Appleton, John, 470
Apportionment of representation (Ill.), 432, 439
Aquia Creek, 502
Archer, William B., 449
Archibald, Albert W., 484
Argentina, 469, 487-88
Argosy Book Shop, catalogs cited, 483, 489, 515, 525, 545
Arizona Territory, 492
Arkansas, 548, 582
Armand, William, 515
Armour, Charles Lee, 581
Armstrong, H. B., 498
Armstrong, Hannah (Jones), 452
Army Corps (U. S.): *Fourth*, 493, 506; *Eighteenth*, 509
Army of the Potomac, 493, 496, 534-35
Army Orders (general): *AGO 1861*, 471, 477; Buford's, 539; District of Vicksburg, 554; Eighteenth Army Corps, 509; Fourth Army Corps, 493, 506; General War Order No. 1, 509; Hooker's, 560; McClellan's, 493; Pope's, 496
Army Orders (special): Army of the Potomac, 493; Department of the South, 545
Arthur, Frank, 550
Arthurs, S. C., 578
Arthurs, Mrs. S. C., 578
Ash, Annie L., 542
Ash, Joseph Penrose, 542
Ashburn, George W., 540
Ashmead, George L., 563
Atchison (Kans.), 459
Athens (Ill.), 433
Atkinson, Edward, 555
Atlanta (Ill.), 451-52, 458
Atwater, Mrs., 465
Auburn (Ill.), 443
Austria, 470, 474
Autobiography of Joseph Jefferson, 437

Autograph Album, The (Madigan), 465, 526, 536
Autographs, L. replies to requests for, 462 (*10*), 463 (*12*), 464 (*17*), 465

(*8*), 466 (*4*), 482 (*3*), 489 (*2*), 524, 528, 535, 548, 566, 581
Avandano, P., 559

B

Babbett, Robert, 533
Babcock, Horace G., 528
Babcock, James Francis, 556
Bache, Alexander Dallas, 473
Backus, Henry T., 584
Bacon, Wilbur R., 556
Bailey, B. S., 522
Bailey, E. C., 574
Bailey, Louis Cruger, 489
Bailey, T. C., 570
Bailhache & Baker (Springfield), 452
Baker, Edward Dickinson, 434, 437, 440, 469, 523
Baker, Francis P., 490
Baker, G. A., catalog cited, 472
Baker, Isaac, 545
Baker, John (Pa.), 527
Baker, Joseph F., 487
Baker, Reuben, 447
Baker, William C., 462
Balch, Mrs. T., 582
Baldwin, Alexander W., 584
Baldwin, Daniel Stevens, 551
Ball, George A., 536
Ballance, Charles, 529
Baltimore (Md.), 473, 483, 501, 525, 579-80
Baltimore & Ohio Railroad, 446
Baltimore Clipper, 444
Bane, Moses M., 527
Bangs & Company, catalogs cited, 478, 525
Banks, Eliza, 579
Banks, Nathaniel Prentiss, 458, 475, 478, 491-92, 505
Bannister, Rhett, 525
Baptiste Peoria (Indian?), 587-88
Baptists, 502
Barbados, 583
Barbier, Jean, 567
Barefoot, Sam [alias Eli Patterson] (Indian), 552

Baringer, Jacob, 467
Barker, Lucy A., 575
Barlow, Stephen S., 553
Barnes, George P., Jr., 516
Barnes, H., 575
Barnes, Joseph K., 528, 565, 572
Barney, Hiram, 471-73, 476-77, 530
Barnstoff, H., & Company, 586
Barnum, Philo F., 527
Barr, William, 488
Barrell, George, 474
Barret, John Richard, 531
Barrett,———, 586
Barrett, Oliver Rogers, 432, 452, 463, 471, 490, 500, 503, 524, 591
Barrett, Sallie A., 566
Barrett, William F., 525
Barrey, Alfred, 568
Barrow, Washington, 447
Barry, Alfred Constantine, 503, 553
Barrymore, John, 545
Bartell's farm, speech at, 435
Bartlett, Washington A., 471
Barton, Mary, 560
Barton, William Eleazar, see *Life of Abraham Lincoln*
Bascom, William T., 458-59
Batchelder, Albert M., 490
Bates, Calvin, 540
Bates, Edward, 466, 470-73, 475, 479-81, 483-84, 486-92, 494, 496, 499-501, 504-505, 507-13, 515, 519-20, 522-24, 526-38, 540-42, 544-45, 547-48, 550, 552-69, 589
Bates, George C., 489
Bates, Martin D., 586
Bates, Ralph O., 540
Bates House (Indianapolis, Ind.), 466
Bath (Ill.), 433
Batterton, William, 430
Bauer, Francis, 585
Bautz, Gideon, 570

Baxter, ———, 440
Beall, John Yates, 581
Beaman, Fernando Cortez, 544, 579
Beard, Henry, 481
Beardsley, W. C., 497
Beardstown (Ill.), 444, 451
Beardstown Gazette, 444
Beaty, John F., 565
Beaufort (N. C.), 505
Bebb, William, 469
Becker, Mrs., 512
Becker, George S., 512
Beckley, [Alfred?], 491
Becktel, T. Harry, 516
Bedford County (Pa.), 556
Beeson, John, 551
Behan, John H., 517
Belch, William B., 573
Belford's Magazine, 588
Belgium, 468
Bell, Charles, 431
Bell, Daniel D., 574
Bell, Joseph McClellan, 581
Belleville (Ill.), 438
Belleville Advocate, 438
Bellows, Henry Whitney, 549
Benedict, Kirby, 538
Benedict, L. S., 464
Benham, Henry Washington, 481, 510
Benicia (Calif.), 503
Benjamin, Park, 517
Benjamin, Reuben Moore, 589
Bennet, Hiram Pitt, 581
Bennett, John, 434
Bennett, William A., 509
Bennett, William W., 446
Bennett's Addition to Petersburg (Ill.), 434
Benton, Thomas Hart, Jr., 567
Benzinger Township (Elk Co., Pa.), 584
Berdan, Hiram, 473, 514
Berdan, James, 442, 444
Bergen, George S., 509
Berlin (Ill.), 433, 435
Berry, Joseph H., 445
Berry, Nathaniel Springer, 468
Berry, William Franklin, 431
Best, J. M., 584
Bettleheim, B. J., 532
Bierlien, Harmon, 545
Bigelow, John, 586
Bill, Earl, 584
Billinghurst, Charles, 461

Billy and Dick from Andersonville . . . to the White House (Bates), 540
Bingham, John Armour, 589
Bingham, Kinsley Scott, 465
Bingham, La Fayette, 488
Birch, John P., 579
Birch, Jonathan, 590
Birch, Joseph C., 579
Bird, Richard E., 489
Bishop, Jesse, 586
Bissell, William Henry, 452
Bitting, ———, 531
Bittner, Mark R., 464
Black, Alfred, 549
Black, Lawson, 549
Black, Samuel, 542
Black Hawk War, 431
Blades, Franklin, 453
Blair, Francis Preston, Jr., 459, 490, 506, 526, 572
Blair, Montgomery, 475, 480, 486, 492, 506, 509, 516, 519, 523, 526
Blake, William H., 541
Blakeman, Cyrus W., 502
Blakeslee, Francis D., 566
Blakeslee, George Harmon, 566
Blakey, George D., 491, 501, 522
Blanchet, Laurent, 556-57
Blankenship, Eli C., 464
Blatchford, Richard M., 502
Blatchford, Seward & Griswold, 453, 459
Blenker, Louis, 497
Bleyler, Peter A., 558
Bliss, Philemon, 511, 572
Block, Gordon A., 528
Blodgett, Henry Williams, 472
Blood, Caleb H., 480
Bloomfield, Ben, catalogs cited, 479, 488
Bloomfield (N. J.), 576
Bloomington (Ill.), 435, 444, 451
Bloomington Pantagraph, 435, 451-52
Blount, G. W., 495
Blow, Henry Taylor, 478, 495-96, 535
"Blubberhead, Johnny" [pseud.], 433
Blum, Herman, 507
Blumenberg, Rudolph, 519
Blunt, James Gilpatrick, 498, 507, 543
Blunt, Orison, 496
Boal, Robert, 447, 449
Bockman, William, 552
Boettig, T. G., 497

Boggs, H. A., 579
Boileau, Albert D., 510
Bolivia, 469, 493, 515
Bollman, Lewis, 524
Bombaugh, Charles C., 537
Bonham, Jeriah, 442
Bonham farm (near Henry, Ill.), 442
Bonifant, Washington, 479
Boone, Luke, 464
Boray, A. E., 506
Bordan, Daniel L., 572
Borden, James W., 469
Boston (Mass.), 444
Boston Atlas, 444
Boston Globe, 432
Bottles, William, 553
Botts, W. H., 471
Boughner, James Vance, 543
Bouligny, John Edward, 514
Bound, Franklin, 515
Bowen, C. H., 463
Bowen, Frank, 585
Bowen, James, 508
Bowen, Thomas Mead, 543
Bowie, George W., 581
Bowler, R. B., 490
Bowling Green (Ky.), 584
Bowman, Ezekiel, 445
Boyce, Joseph B., 585
Boyle, Francis E., 479
Bradbury, E. E., 463
Bradford, Allen Alexander, 574-75
Bradford, Augustus Williamson, 523, 544
Bradford, E. S., 463
Bradley, John H., 558, 564
Bradley, Joshua T., 503
Bradley, Thomas Henry, 503
Brady, ———, 511
Brady, John T., 512
Brady, Thomas Jefferson, 536
Brakeman, Nelson L., 526
Bramlette, Thomas E., 524, 551, 556, 562, 567
Branaugh, Malcolm H., 525
Branch, Phineas C., 572
Brandegee, Augustus, 528, 543
Brannan, John Milton, 505
Brantenburg, Joseph, 562
Brayman, Mason, 550
Brazil, 471
Breckinridge, John Cabell, 587
Breckinridge, Robert Jefferson, 587
Breese, James B., 472

Breese, Sidney, 457
Breneman, H. L., 568
Bressmer, McQuinton & Matheny (Springfield), 457, 460, 465
Brewster, Benjamin H., 494, 572
Brewster, H. A., 540
Brice, Benjamin William, 576
Bricer [?], ———, 520
Bridgeport (Conn.), 461
Bridges, Edwin T., 453
Brier, David, 483
Briggs, Charles C., 474
Briggs, G. H., 545
Bright, John, 555
Briscoe, Alexander, 478
Bristow, James H., 523
Brittenham, Sarah J., 451
Brittenham, T. A., 451
Britton, B. J., 519
Britton, J. Blodget, 481
Broadway, Jesse A., 563
Brocchus, Perry E., 583
Brockway, Laurel F., 497
Brooke, John Rutter, 528
Brooklyn (N. Y.), 461
Brooks, Albert I., 547
Brooks, Franklin, 547
Brooks, Harold C., 464
Brooks, Noah, 566
Brooks, Stephen, 472
Broomall, John Martin, 583
Brough, John, 524, 533, 536, 538, 553
Brower, Charles M., 497
Browers, S. E., 552
Brown, David P., 487
Brown, Egbert B., 579
Brown, George, 560, 573
Brown, James Nicholas, 500
Brown, James O., 524
Brown, Mary (Edwards), 452
Brown, Samuel Lockwood, 504
Brown, Uriah, 443
Brown, William (Fort Delaware prisoner), 585
Brown, William (Ill.), 453
Brown, William Gay, 489
Brown, William Hubbard, 458-59
Brown, William Young, 479
Browne, S. C., 545
Browne, Thomas C., 440
Browning, Ludwell Y., 538
Browning, M. D., 440
Browning, Orville Hickman, 440, 450, 464, 474, 478, 507-508, 538, 542, 581

Brownlow, William Gannaway ("Parson"), 491
Brown's Hotel (Washington), 442
Bruce, E. M., 538
Bruce, Mrs. E. M., 538
Bruce, Frederick A. W., 589
Bruce, Lizzie B., 552
Bruceville (Ind.), 441
Brum, J. D., 536
Bryant, Arthur Rush, 529
Bryant, J. W., 493
Buchanan, James, 467-68
Buchanan, James M., 470
Buchanan, Robert Christie, 483, 551
Buchrach, Mrs., 515
Buckalew, Charles Rollin, 469
Buckingham, William Alfred, 506, 580
Buell, Don Carlos, 482, 485-86, 503
Buford, Abra[ha]m, 583
Buford, Mrs. Abra[ha]m, 583
Buford, Napoleon Bonaparte, 521, 539
Buford, Thomas Jefferson, 521
Bull, Miss, 511
Bull, Luther, 511
Bullard, James, 546
Bullitt, Cuthbert, 559
Bullock, Jonathan R., 579
Bullock, Maria L., 452
Bundy, Hezekiah Sanford, 586
Bunker, Charles, 487
Bunn, Jacob, 452
Burbridge, O. M., 554
Burbridge, Stephen Gano, 552
Burdick, Raymond E., 477, 484
Burk, Eli, 537

Burke, Francis, 564
Burke, John, 484
Burke, Martin, 581
Burlingame, Anson, 473
Burlington (Iowa), 456
Burlington (N. J.), 499
Burlington (Iowa) Hawk-Eye, 438, 456
Burnham, Samuel, 541
Burnside, Ambrose Everett, 482, 484, 492, 494, 509, 515-16, 524-25, 532, 542
Burr, Maurice H., 572
Burrage, Henry S., 569-70
Burroughs, Edgar, 529
Burrows, Silas E., 529
Burt, ———, 575
Burt, Mrs., 575
Burt, John M., 462
Burtchill, Thomas, 586
Burtnete, D. Henry, 527
Burton, Allen A., 471, 518
Burton, Amos, 532
Buschrae, ———, 508
Buschrae, Margaret, 508
Bush, John M., 454
Bushnell, Mrs. Nehemiah, 557
Bushnell, Robert, 508, 557
Butler, Benjamin Franklin (1818-1893), 475, 477, 494, 511, 531, 551-52, 582, 588
Butler, Chester, 447
Butler, John George, 477
Butler, William, 434, 440, 462
Butterfield, Daniel, 515
Butterfield, Justin, 445-46

C

"C. N.," Miss, 539
Cabanis, Charles P., 431
Cabanis, George E., 431
Cadwalader, George, 549
Cain, James H., 512
Cairo (Ill.), 474, 485
Calahan, John, see Morris, John
Caldwell, George W., 471
Caldwell, Henry C., 542
Calhoun, John, 441
California, 445, 467, 494, 528, 535, 548

Callahan, A., 572
Calvert, Charles Benedict, 523
Cambridge (Mass.), 444, 590
Cameron, Simon, 461, 464, 467, 470-83, 489, 549, 553, 581, 589
Camp, Benjamin F., 520
Camp Chase (Ohio), 491, 537, 560, 563, 573
Camp Douglas (Ill.), 528, 554-55, 561
Camp Lookout (Md.), see Point Lookout

Camp Morton (Ind.), 558, 570, 572
Campbell, ———, 507
Campbell, James, 519
Campbell, James L., 541
Campbell, John, 556
Campbell, John Archibald, 471
Campbell, Julian R., 517
Campbell, Malcolm, 557
Campbell, Thomas, 433
Campbell, Thomas M., 445
Camron [Cameron], John Miller, 431
Canada, 546-47, 553, 556, 572, 583
Canals (Ill.), 432, 437-39
Canby, Edward Richard Sprigg, 516, 533, 538, 543, 549, 554
Canisius, Theodor, 465
Canley, R. S., 474
Carbery, Thomas, 473
Cardiff (Wales), 579
Cargon, Silas, 535
Carleton, James Henry, 528, 537
Carley, Mark, 453
Carlile, John Snyder, 473
Carlin, Delphy, 519
Carlin, William H., 457
Carlinville (Ill.), 438, 448
Carmi (Ill.), 438
Carnegie, Dale, 528, 543, 553-54
Carnegie Book Shop, catalogs cited, 471, 477, 486, 488, 497, 533, 584
Carney, Thomas, 529
Carney, U. P., 509
Carolin, Alexander, 484
Carr, Clark Ezra, 462
Carrera, Rafael, 468
Carrigan, Charles W., 574
Carroll, John, 552
Carryl, William H., & Brother, 472
Carson, George C., & Company, 538-39
Carter, Edward, 519
Carter, John, 531
Carter Township (Spencer Co., Ind.), 441
Carthage (Ill.) Republican, 456
Carther, Richard, 562, 574
Cartter, David Kellogg, 469
Casado, Galwey & Teller, 538
Case, Charles, 486
Case, J. I., 447
Casey, Silas, 489, 492
Casey (Ill.), 438
Cass County (Ill.), 433, 445
Cassidy, Mary, 482

Cassidy, Patrick, 482
Castilla, Ramón, 479
Castle, Samuel N., 495
Catalogue of Lincolniana, A (Madigan), 443, 486, 524, 591
"Cathleen" [pseud.], 440
Caton, John Dean, 480
Cavanaugh, Mrs., 524
Central Guard House (Washington), 544
Century Magazine, cited, 508, 532, 566
Chamberlin, Culver P., 548
Chambersburg (Pa.), 554
Champaign (formerly West Urbana) (Ill.), 452
Champion, Israel, 475
Champney, Benjamin C., 545
Chandler, L. H., 539
Chandler, Zachariah, 538, 580
Chapin, Gurden, 479
Chaplains, 500, 543
Chapman, ———, 587
Chapman, Augustus H., 587
Chapman, Julia A., 575
Charles XV, King of Sweden and Norway, 468, 470
Charles, Jonathan H., 473
Charleston (Ill.), 450
Charleston (S. C.), 565-66, 572
Charleston (S. C.), Mercury, 465
Chase, Charles D., 469, 491
Chase, Salmon Portland, 440, 470-74, 479, 481, 483, 492, 494-95, 497-98, 500, 508, 514, 521-22, 528, 530, 534-35, 538, 543, 587
Chaskay-don [alias Chaskay-etay alias Robert Hopkins] (Indian), 551
Checks, see LINCOLN, ABRAHAM, checks written by
Chelsea (Mass.), 444
Chester, A., 524, 526, 544
Chester, Elisha W., 524, 544
Chestnut Hill Hospital (Philadelphia), 565
Chetlain, Augustus Louis, 540
Chew, Henry, 457
Chicago (Ill.), 442, 444-45, 464
Chicago Book & Art Auctions, catalogs cited, 481, 499, 514, 580
Chicago Democrat, 456
Chicago Democratic Press, 450-51
Chicago Herald, 591
Chicago Journal, 451, 464

Chicago Press & Tribune, 451, 455, 458, 461
Chicago Tribune, 451, 491
Chickering, James W., 446
Children's Village, 463
Chile, 473
China, 473
Chiriqui project, 500
Chittenden, Lucius Eugene, 430, 506
Christian [formerly Dane] County (Ill.), 436
Christopher, J. M., 565-66
Christopher, John, 565-66
"Chronicles of Reuben," 430
Chumasero, William, 447
Church, R. B., 464
Churchman, James, 465
Cincinnati (Ohio), 440, 466-67, 531, 556, 566-67, 572
Cincinnati Commercial, 466
City Book Auctions, catalogs cited, 476, 502, 591
City Point (Va.), 529, 559
Clapp, Alfred, 551
Clapp, Daniel, 446
Clark, ———, 530
Clark, Albert, 576
Clark, Allen Culling, 590
Clark, Daniel, 575
Clark, David, 509
Clark, Francis D., 542
Clark, George F., 486
Clark, Henry Toole, 468
Clark, Joseph Claypoole, 560
Clark, K., 464
Clark, M. S., 576
Clark, Robert M., 584
Classmate (periodical), 590
Clay, Brutus Junius, 526
Clay, Cassius Marcellus, 462, 470, 483, 489
Clay, Henry, 435, 440-41, 448
Clay, John M., 587
Clay, Thomas H., 505, 514
Clay County (Mo.), 500
Clayton, John Middleton, 446
Clayton (Ill.), 588
Clemens, Sherrard, 492
Cleveland, Charles D., 465
Cleveland Plain Dealer, 467
Clinton (Ill.), 451
Close, James T., 537
Clume, Thomas, 575
Cluseret, Gustave Paul, 502

Coates, Henry T., 462
Cobb, Amasa, 546, 553
Cobb, George Thomas, 557
Cochran, H. P., 497
Cochran, Silas D., 545
Codwin, ———, 524
Coffey, George A., 470, 510
Coffin, Nathaniel, 448
Coffin, William G., 577
Coggswell, John B. D., 470
Cohez, S. N., 500
Colburn, William, 435
Colby, H. F., 497
Cole, William Hinson, 541
Coleman, Charles Hubert, 591
Coleman, Paul, 495
Colerick, William L., 517
Colfax, Schuyler, 488, 502, 555, 564, 588-89
Collamer, Jacob, 527
Collamore, John H., 542
Collector, The, 465-66, 508, 518, 542, 590
Collins, B. C., 448
Collins, James L., 499
Collins & Hughes (New York), 507
Collinsgrove, Spencer, 575
Colombia [New Granada], 471, 518
Colonization of Negroes, 448, 537; *see also* African Colonization Society
Colorado Territory, 488, 528, 536
Colt, Samuel F., 576
Columbia (S. C.), 573, 581
Columbus (Ohio), 459, 467
Commercial Gazette [Cincinnati?], 591
Conant, Augustus, Jr., 547
Conant, Horace Artemas, 479
Concerning Mr. Lincoln (Pratt), 460
Concord (N. H.), 461
Concord Independent Democrat, 461
Congregationalists, 494, 502
Congress: L. in, 442-45; L. and, 484, 493, 548, 572
Congressional Globe, 443-44
Conkle, William H., 550
Conkling, Clinton Levering, 489
Conkling, Frederick Augustus, 500
Conkling, James Cook, 464, 489, 497, 556
Conley, John, 567
Connecticut, 461
Connelley, John, Sr., 452
Connelly, Henry, 537

Conner, Monroe, 554
Conner, W. W., 554
Conness, John, 528, 530, 545
"Conservative," The" [pseud.], 435, 438
Constable, Charles Henry, 447
Constable, R. E., 493
Constables, bill on, 437
Constitution (U. S.), 468, 532
Constitutional Text-Book, The (Sheppard), 589
Conway, Martin Franklin, 457-58
Cony, Samuel A., 548
Conyers, George D., 494
Conyers, Vernon, 494
Cook, Burton Chauncey, 449, 459
Cook, J. W., 572
Cook, Mrs. J. W., 572
Cooper Institute (N. Y.), 459
Copperheads, 551, 561
Corcoran, Michael, 523
Corcoran & Riggs (Washington), 445
Corkran, Francis S., 510
Corneau, Stephen A., 450
Cornell, Charles M., 484
"Corporations Enthroned," 589
Corvin, Otto, 498
Corwin, Thomas, 459, 465, 469, 574
Corwin (Ohio), 467
Corwine, Richard M., 461-63, 526
Coryell, Ingham, 505
Coshocton (Ohio) Age, 467
Coskery, H. B., 574
Costa Rica, 468, 471
Cotton and other products, trade in, 549, 584, 587
Cotton Hill (Ill.), 433
Couch, Darius Nash, 549
Counterfeiters, 499, 582
Court of Claims, U. S., 511, 529
Covode, John, 505
Cowan, S. S., 458
Coyle, Andrew, 534
Craig, John Neville, 502
Cramer, James Lawrence, 498
Crampton, Rufus C., 500
Crawford, James A., 566
Crawford, Newton, 583
Crawford, R. Clay, 536
Creek Indians, 484
Cremin, James, 539

Creswell, John Andrew Jackson, 579
Crisfield, John Woodland, 456
Critchfield, L. R., 556
Crittenden, John Jordan, 460, 479
Crocker, Edwin B., 491
Crofut, Horace S., 517
Cromelien, R., 550
Crosby, Elisha O., 468, 494
Crosman, George Hampton, Jr., 476
Cross, Charles E., 496
Crossley, Thomas J., 563
Crossman, Delos W., 505
Croswell, Caleb, 502
Croswell, Edwin, 502
Crow, Tom, 558
Crowen, T. J., 497
Crowley, John C., 498
Crowley, Patrick, 469
Crump, Bina, 554
Crump, William D., 554
Cuba, 524, 538-39, 550, 586
Cull, James, 512
Cullom, Shelby Moore, 488
Culpeper County (Va.), 499
Culpeper Court House (Va.), 586
Culver, Erastus Dean, 497, 552
Culver, Frederick B., 482
Cummings, Alexander, 570
Cunningham, James T., 591
Cunningham, William A., 502
Cunnyngham, W. G. E., 555
Cuppy, Fletcher P., 468
Curran, Michael D., 552
Currey, Josiah Seymour, see Lincoln's Visit to Evanston
Currier, Joseph W., 501
Curry, George, 587
Curtin, Andrew Gregg, 468, 486-87, 501-504, 514, 526, 528, 536-37, 539, 546, 563
Curtis, Samuel Ryan, 505, 508-509, 532
Curtis, William Eleroy, see The True Abraham Lincoln
Cushing, Caleb, 524
Cushman, Joseph, 587
Cusick, Thomas, 540-41
Cutler, Abraham, 488
Cutler, George A., 484
Cutler, O. N., 504
Cuyler, John Meck, 524

D

D——, Barney, 590
Dabney, Mrs. L. B., 464
Daggett, Albert, 462
Dahlgren, John Adolphus, 493, 502, 516
Daily, Samuel Gordon, 536
Dain, Thomas, 567
Dakota Territory, 586
Dallas, George Mifflin, 468
Dallas City (Ill.), 456
Dana, Charles Anderson, 542, 547, 560, 562, 568, 575
Dana, Napoleon Jackson Tecumseh, 482, 554, 562, 568
Dane County (Ill.), see Christian County
Danforth, C. P., 457
Dannel, B. M., 586
Danville (Ill.), 450-51, 455
Darien County (Conn.), 554
Darling, Clarence, 474
Dart, Luther, 531
Dart, William A., 569
Davenport, B. M., 454
Davenport, W., 549
David, John, 553
Davidson, Alexander, 570
Davies, H., 480
Davies, Henry Eugene, Jr., 518
Davis, David, 445, 449, 453-54, 456, 460, 463, 499, 559
Davis, Edmund Jackson, 499
Davis, Evan, 571
Davis, Garrett, 485-86, 490
Davis, George M., 589
Davis, Henry C., 568
Davis, Mrs. Henry C., 568
Davis, Henry Winter, 570
Davis, James M., 446
Davis, Jefferson, 472
Davis, Oliver L., 453
Davis, Samuel J., 579
Davis, W., 490
Davis, William Watts Hart, 483, 485, 489, 507, 515
Day, Henry Martyn, 536
Day, Jeremiah, 590
"Day among the Quakers, A" (art.), 501

Dayton, William Lewis, 468
Deanes, Jason O., 550
Dearborn, Frederick M., 475, 533, 537
Death sentences, 505-90 *passim*
Decar, Jesse, 552
Decatur (Ill.), 430, 441, 450-51, 456, 466
Decatur Review, 466
Decker, Reuben [alias George Stephens], 486
Decline and Fall of the Roman Empire (Gibbon), 436
Dedham (Mass.), 444
DeFrate, Allie, 571
Defrees, John D., 564
Deitzler, George Washington, 545
Delafield, Richard, 573
Delahay, Mark William, 458-59, 461, 496, 498, 507
Delano, J. S., 499
Delano, Mrs. J. S., 499
Delavan (Ill.), 442
Delaware, 494
Delaware County (Ind.), 536
Delaware Indian Agency, 496
Delineator (magazine), 591
DeLong, James, 478
DeMott, W. H., 587
Denison, George W., 470
Denlinger, Henry, 535
Denmark, 470
Dennett, Tyler, see *Lincoln and the Civil War in the Diaries and Letters of John Hay*
Dennis, Edgar Whetten, 546
Dennison, William, 538, 568, 577, 580
Denny, Arthur Armstrong, 587
Denver Land Office, 490
DePuy, Henry W., 534
Derqui, Santiago, 469
Deserters, 513, 522, 530, 534, 544-45, 553, 560, 567-68, 570-71, 576
Desher, A. D., 551
DeStackpole, ——, 505
Devite, John, 568
Dewey, Chester P., 456
DeWitt Courier [Clinton, Ill.], 450
Dezeyk, Albert J., 475, 538
Dick, Franklin A., 500

Dicke, L. E., 474
Dickerson, ———, 549
Dickerson, Archer C., 501
Dickerson, Louise W., 549
Dickey, Theophilus Lyle, 458-59
Dickinson, Andrew B., 469, 514
Dickinson, Benjamin F., 441
Dickinson, Daniel Stevens, 551
Dickson, William M., 471
Dictionary of the United States Congress (Lanman), 457
Dike, John H., 490
Dill, Charles G., 464
Diller, Isaac Roland, 466, 516
Dilliard, Irving, 474
Dills, Harrison, 446
Dimitry, Alexander, 468
Dinkel, Barbara, 463
Discoveries and inventions, L.'s lectures on, 457, 460-61
District of Columbia, 434, 443, 445, 469, 589-90
Diven, ———, 503
Diven, Mrs. Alexander Samuel, 503
Diver, ———, 581
Dix, John Adams, 473, 487, 512, 526, 530, 553, 573, 581
Dixon, Archibald, 564
Dixon, James, 525, 527
Dixon, Joseph, 549
Dixon [Dixon's Ferry] (Ill.), 450
Dixon Telegraph, 451
Dobson, Joseph, 494
Dodds, Samuel, 447
Dodge, Grenville Mellen, 589
D'Oench, William, 578
Doherty, William Hugh, 508, 514
Dolan, John, 530
Dole, George Washington, 446, 459
Dole, William P., 495-96, 577, 588
Donaldson, James Lowery, 483
Donaldson, William D., 586, 588
Doniphan (Kans.), 459
Donn, Alfonso, 588
Donnelley, R. R., 464
Donnelly, Fannie, 558
Doolittle, James Rood, 472, 520, 522, 558-59
Dorchester (Mass.), 444
Dorsheimer, William, 553
Doss, N., 469

Doty, A. T., 567
Doubleday, Abner, 495
Dougherty, Betsy Ann, 590
Dougherty, John, 457, 526
Dougherty, P. A., 551
Douglas, Stephen Arnold, 436, 467
Douglass, John M., 462
Dovan, Robert E., 572
Dow, John W., 464
Dow, Neal, 520
Dow, Prentis, 464
Dowell, Thomas, 431
Dower, George, 484
Dowman, Mrs. M. E., 485
Downingtown (Pa.), 467
Draft (1863-65), 495, 499, 504, 515, 554, 564, 570, 580, 582, 584-85
Drake, A. T., 524
Drake, Daniel, 439
Dreer, F. J., 535
Dresser, Charles, 441
Dresser, Mrs. Charles, 577
Dresser, Thomas W., 577
Drew, Mrs. John, *see* Drew, Louisa (Lane)
Drew, Louisa (Lane), 545
Drummond, Josiah H., 522
Drummond, Thomas, 533
Dry Tortugas Islands, 505
Dryer, Thomas J., 485
Dubois, Jesse Kilgore, 448, 519, 537
DuBois, John Van Deusen, 560
Duell, Robert Holland, 563, 569
Duffy, Charles, 548
Duffy, Thomas, 588
Dugger, Jefferson L., 458
Dummer, Henry Enoch, 440, 454, 500
Dun & Bradstreet, 590
Duncan, Charles L., 449
Duncan, Mrs. Blanton, 529
Dungan, C. B., 541
Dunn, John P., 563
Dunning, George F., 545
Dunning, William B., 546
Dunshee, Spencer H. C., 588
Durand, Angelo, 556
Durant, Thomas J., 520
Durbin, J. P., 487
Durell, Edward H., 531
Duvall, William Penn, 564
Dwight, Chapman, 518

E

Easter, Hamilton, 570
Easton, Joseph G., 563
Eaton, John, Jr., 519
Ebaugh, Theodore O., 496
Ebert, B., & Sons, 570
Eccles, Joseph C., 453
Eccles, Joseph T., 446
Eckert, Thomas Thompson, 523, 542
Ecuador, 469
Eddy, Adelbert S., 517
Eddy, Asher Robbins, 483, 516
Eddy, Charles, 535
Eddy, Ellery, 475
Eddy, Henry, 446
Edgar County (Ill.), 443, 534
Edmiston, Franklin, 562, 565
Edmunds, Olivia S., 528
Edwards, Cyrus, 445-46
Edwards, J., 448
Edwards, James L., 446
Edwards, Ninian Wirt, 433, 436, 448,
    455-56, 476, 479, 485, 495
Edwards, William, 570
Eggleston, Robert D., 556
Egypt, 470, 542
Ekin, James Adams, 511
Elder, William Henry, 550
Eldridge, Charles Augustus, 534
Elections in Illinois, 436
Eliot, Charles, 577
Elkin, David, 430
Elkin, William F., 446
Elkin & Davis (Springfield), 464
Elliott, Charles W., see *Winfield Scott:
    the Soldier and the Man*
Elliott, John, 580
Elliott, Tobias M., 578
Ellis, Abner Yates, 431
Ellis, James Marsh, 570
Ellsworth, Elmer Ephraim, 471
Ellsworth, L. D., 493
Elmore, Johnson, 431

Elmore, Travice, 431
El Paso (Ill.), 455
El Salvador [San Salvador], 494, 514
Elwell, George H., 557
Ely, Alfred, 503
Ely, Alfred Brewster, 481
Ely, F. W., 463
Emancipation proclamation, 499, 507-
    508, 525
Emberet, John R. H., 554
Embree, Elisha, 443
Emily (ship), 563
Engineers, U. S. Bureau of, 583
Eno, Amos F., 511
Enos, Zimri Allen, 452
Enright, James, 547
Episcopalians, 506
Epler, John, 445
Epperson, G. T., 530, 534
Epping, J. P. M., 530, 534
Equality (Ill.), 438
Erie (Pa.), 563
Eustis, Isabella B., 465
Evans, Alexander, 447
Evans, John, 536
Evanston (Ill.), 461
Evansville (Ind.), 441
Evarts, William Maxwell, 527
Eve of Conflict, The (Milton), 471
Everett, David S., 568
Everett, Edward (Ill.?), 495
Everett, Edward (Mass.), 576
Ewing, Charles, 552
Ewing, Philomen, 501
Ewing, Thomas, 446-47, 465
Ewing, Thomas, Jr., 498, 501, 573
Exeter (N. H.), 461
Eyre, Severn, 557
Eyre, Wilson, 572
Eyster, Nellie Blessing, *see* "Day
    among the Quakers, A"; *and* "Mr.
    Lincoln and the 'Crazy' Quaker"

F

Fair, Agnes J., 480
Fair, Elisha Y., 468
Fair, John, 480
Fair, Mrs. John, *see* Fair, Agnes J.
Fairfax Court House (Va.), 512
Fairlamb, J. R., 564
Fairland, Remington, 481
Falcón, Juan Crisóstomo, 552
Fant, Hamilton G., 558
Fant Bank, 558
Farm & Fireside (periodical), 438
Farmer, Lewis W., 431
Farnham, W. B., 458
Farnsworth, Alfred Brush, 491
Farnsworth, George H., 565, 571
Farnsworth, John Franklin, 455, 466, 506
Farquhar, C., 586
Farquhar, Mrs. C., 586
Farragut, David Glasgow, 474, 549
Farragut, Loyall, 474
Farrar, Benjamin, 574
Farrar, W. H., 517
Farrell, James, 562
Farwell, Willard B., 469
Faulkner, Charles James, Sr., 468
Faxon, Henry, 465
Faxon, William, 543
Fay, Justus, 504
Fay, Theodore S., 467
Fell, Jesse Wilson, 435, 452
Fendall, W. Y., 565
Fender, Daniel, 552
Fenton, Reuben Eaton, 577, 580, 585
Ferguson, John, 431
Fessenden, William Pitt, 483, 528, 553, 559, 573-74
Feuerstein, Leopold, 549
Field, Jonathan E., 480
Field, Maunsell B., 543
Field, Richard, 509
Fielding, ———, 590
Fifty Years' Recollections (Bonham), 442
Filley, Oliver Dwight, 523
Fillmore, George Millard, 516
Fillmore, Millard, 448, 451
Findlay, John Van Lear, 520
Finkelheimer, John, 497

Finks, Morris [alias David Stocionski], 545
Finley, Martin, 517
Finney, Thomas M., 541
Fish, William S., 572
Fishback, William M., 453, 530
Fisher, Charles H., 464
Fisher, David, 457
Fisher, Elvira, 578
Fisher, George Purnell, 499
Fisher, R., 523
Fitch, Berry, 554
Fitch, Henry S., 457
Fitch Home for Disabled Soldiers and Their Orphans (Darien Co., Conn.), 554
Fitchett, E. B., 539
Fitchett, Mrs. E. B., 539
Fithian, William, 449
Fitzhugh, Harrison G., 560
Five Points House of Industry (Brooklyn, N. Y.), 461
Flanders, Benjamin Franklin, 507, 520
Fleming, A. L., 516
Florida, 506
Floyd, George P., 588
Flying Quill, The, 477
Flynn, John T., 529
Fogg, Frederick L. P., 550
Fonda, Cornelia, 485
Fonda, James, 466
Foot, Solomon, 527
Foote, Mrs. C. J., 563
Forbes, John Murray, 522
Ford, ———, 508, 510
Ford, George W., 536
Ford, Robert, 545
Forde, Lucy M., 569
Forgeries (*italic figures indicate number of references on page*), 431 (*3*), 432, 435, 438, 439 (*2*), 440 (*4*), 442 (*2*), 447 (*3*), 448 (*5*), 450 (*3*), 451, 452 (*2*), 453 (*2*), 455, 456 (*4*), 457, 459, 460 (*2*), 462, 463, 464 (*2*), 467 (*2*), 471, 478, 481, 485, 487, 489, 490, 492 (*2*), 493 (*3*), 494, 499 (*5*), 500 (*2*), 505, 506 (*4*), 507, 508, 509 (*2*), 512, 513, 514, 515, 517 (*2*), 518, 521,

523 (2), 525, 527, 528, 539, 544 (2), 546, 560 (2), 572, 576, 582, 591
Forney, John Wein, 519, 577, 584
Forquer, George, 433
Forsha, S. W., 511
Fort Delaware (Del.), 494, 555, 560, 563-64, 566, 568, 573, 585, 589
Fort Hatteras (N. C.), 475
Fort Lafayette (N. Y.), 574
Fort McHenry (Md.), 567-68
Fort Pillow (Tenn.), 540
Fort Smith (Ark.), 564, 577, 582
Foster, Charles H., 508
Foster, Lafayette Sabine, 526, 557
Foulke, J. Kenneth, 489
Fourbe, Mrs. M., 571
Fourbe, William, 571
Fox, Ann, 574
Fox, F. T., Jr., 488
Fox, Gustavus Vasa, 487, 505, 581
Fox, Mrs. T. A., 555
France, 468, 586
Francis, Simeon, 488
Franklin, John P., 575
Franklin & Company (Washington), 541
Franklin County (Pa.), 569
Franklin Institute (Franklin Co., Ill.), 436
Franz Josef I [Emperor of Austria-Hungary], 470, 474
Fraser, Philip, 496, 548
Frazear, James S., 461
Frederick VII [King of Denmark], 470
Frederick County (Md.), 582

Frederick Republican Citizen, 444
Freedmen's Aid Society, 555
Freedmen's Hospital (Washington), 568
Freeman, Samuel T., & Co., catalogs cited, 508, 510, 530
Freeport (Ill.), 451
Freese, Jacob R., 551
Frémont, John Charles, 474-75, 478, 490-93, 555
French, Benjamin Brown, 478
French, C. W. [alias J. W. Manning], 535
French, Ezra Bartlett, 520, 538
French, Fred W., 464
French, Harry B., 576
Friedberger, Alfred, 555
Friedberger, Julius, 555
Friends, Society of, *see* Quakers
Frisby & Metcalf[e], 438
Frost, George W., 551
Fry, James Barnet, 467, 508, 537, 558
Fryman, Eliza, 585
Fryman, Smith, 585
Fryman, Mrs. Smith, *see* Fryman, Eliza
Fuller, ———, 533
Fuller, Allen C., 492
Fuller, George F., 573
Fullerton, B. S. [S. B.], 476-77
Fulton, J. T., 568
Fulton, Sarah A., 524
Fulton Democrat [Lewistown, Ill.], 476
Fyler, John S., 493

G

Gadsby, Marion D., 569
Gage, George, 448
Gaggam, Audley W., 474
Gajerski, A. Ladico, 510
Galbraith, A., 568
Galbraith, S. G., 568
Galesburg (Ill.), 455
Gallatin County (Ill.), 439
Galloway, Samuel, 459, 523
Galt, Z. T., 479
Gamble, Hamilton Rowan, 475, 492, 559

Gampher, ———, 565
Gampher, John, 565
Gardner, Andrew, 474
Gardner, Michael, *see* Sullivan, George M.
Garfield, James Abram, 517, 558
Garlitztorf, Matthias, 554
Garlitztorf, Mrs. Matthias, 554
Garnett, Granville, 564
Garrard, Theophilus Toulmin, 485
Garret, H., & Company, 434
Garrett, John W., 579

Garrison, Jacob, 576
Gates, Benjamin, 504
Gatewood, William Jefferson, 439
Gaubert, Charles H., 482, 486-87, 524
Gaugan, Elizabeth, 578
Gearhart, ———, 559
Gearhart, J. S., 559
Geary, John White, 478
Geer, Nathan C., 454
Geneva (Ohio), 467
Gentryville (Ind.), 441
George, James, 509
Georgetown (D. C.), 480
Georgia, 558, 568, 574, 576, 582
Gerard, George, 478
Germans, 498, 505
Gettysburg (Pa.), 526
Gibbon, Edward, see Decline and Fall
    of the Roman Empire
Gibbon, John, 547
Gibbs, John W., 582
Gibney, William H., 545
Gibson, Charles, 464, 479
Gibson, George, 471, 475-77
Gibson, William, 526
Gideon, George S., 531
Gifford, Edmund, 506
Gilbert, Charles Champion, 501
Gilbert, F. B., 543
Gilbert, William Gates, 553
Gillespie, David, 458
Gillespie, Joseph, 458
Gillis, John P., 513
Gillmore, Quincy Adams, 478, 516, 527
Gilman, Samuel, Jr., 527
Gilmer, John Adams, 465
Gilmore, James Ross, 578, 591; see
    also Personal Recollections of Abra-
    ham Lincoln and the Civil War
Gilmore, Joseph Albree, 528, 573
Gilorley, John, 557, 561
Gilpin, Charles, 535
Glascock, E. R., 488
Glass, John P., 566-67
Glasscock, George, 590
Glover, Samuel Taylor, 463, 501
Glover, Cook & Campbell (Ottawa,
    Ill.), 460
Goddard, Mrs., 531
Godwin, Parke, 470
Goebel, C. H., 572
Goebel, F. C., 556
Goldsby, James, 431
Goldsmith, Middleton, 571

Gooden, ———, 449
Goodloe, William Cassius, 571
Goodman, ———, 491
Goodrich, Frank Chester, 505
Goodspeed's Book Shop (Boston), 463
Goodwin, Richard D., 499
Gorden, John, 461
Gordon, see Codwin, ———
Gordon, ———, 543
Gordon, Charles H., 456
Gordon, Nellie K., 587
Gordonsville (Va.), 496
Gorham, George Congdon, see Life
    and Public Services of Edwin M.
    Stanton
Gorman, Willis Arnold, 511
Goss, George Gideons, 477
Gould, John P., 504
Government, see American govern-
    ment
Grable, John Quincy, 559
Grandview (Ill.), 450
Granger, Gordon, 560
Grant, E. I., 551
Grant, Edward M., 519, 563
Grant, James, 534
Grant, Ulysses Simpson, 489, 509, 518,
    535, 539, 546-47, 583, 588
Grantsyn, William, 530
Granville County (N. C.), 521
Grassel, Waltam E., 431
Gratiot Street Prison (St. Louis), 562
Graves, William H., 530
Gray, James, 540-41
Gray, John P., 539
Great Britain, 468
Great Lakes, 443-44
Greeley, Horace, 454, 465, 508, 511,
    546
Green, Andrew J., 509
Green, Bowling, 439-40
Green, Duff, 447
Green, C. W., & Company, 460
Greene, Duane Merritt, 509
Greene, Elias M., 520
Greene, Oliver Duff, 560
Greene, William Graham ("Slicky
    Bill"), 432
Greenleaf, William C., 445
Greensburg (Ind.), 466
Greenwood, Aaron H., 463
Gregg, David McMurtrie, 504
Gregory, Dudley Sanford, 546
Grey, Benjamin E., 580

Grey, Mrs. Benjamin E., 580
Grider, Henry, 580, 584
Griffin, James, 579
Griffin, William, 492
Griffith, Thomas M., 514
Griggs, G. W., 501
Grigsby, Nathaniel, 441
Grigsby, Susan (Shelby), 588
Grimes, James Wilson, 529-30
Grimshaw, Arthur H., 502
Grimshaw, Joseph Jackson, 453, 507
Grimshaw, William A., 446, 456
Grindy, Robert G., 548
Grinley, Mrs. M. P., 585
Griswold, Albert E., 581
Griswold, John Augustus, 576
Gross, Anthony, see *Lincoln's Own Stories*
Groux, Daniel E., 497
Grove, Henry A., 449
Grover, William N., 572

Grow, Galusha Aaron, 510
Guatemala, 468
Guaymas (Mexico), 482
Guiney, Patrick Robert, 574
Gummere, Barker, 551
Gunn, John T., 571
Gunn, Lewis C., 528
Gunn, Thomas M., 571
Gunn, W. A., 571
Gunn, Winn, 516
Guppey, Joshua James, 570
Gurley, Emma Elizabeth (Brooks), 567
Gurley, Frank, 541-42
Gurley, John Addison, 478
Gurley, Phineas Densmore, 482, 517, 564, 567
Gurley, Mrs. Phineas Densmore, see Gurley, Emma Elizabeth (Brooks)
Gwin, William McKendree, 587
Gwinn, Charles J. M., 554

H

Hackett, H. B., 570
Haddam, Samuel, 501
Hagadorn, S., 485
Hagen, Erhard, 528
Hagerstown (Md.), 480
Hagerthy, Mrs., 506
Hahn, Michael, 507, 520
Hain, H. C., 583
Haines, Alfred, 456
Haines, H. L., 463
Haines, John W., 506
Haines, Jonathan, 456
Halbach, Thomas S., 457, 460
Haldeman, Jacob S., 468
Halderman, Mrs. R. B., 582
Hale, Charles, 542
Hale, George O., 526
Hale, John Parker, 525, 527
Hall, ———, 589-90
Hall, Allen A., 515
Hall, Benjamin F., 475
Hall, Henry C., 527
Hall, John P., 477
Hall, Nathan Kelsey, 447
Hall, Samuel, 518
Hall, Vincent, 588

Hall, Willard Preble, 560
Halleck, Henry Wager: communications to, 486, 490, 494, 498, 500, 502-505, 507, 520-21, 523, 526-34, 543, 590; writes for L., 503, 509, 514, 518
Haller, F. N., 498-99
Haller, G. O., 499
Hallin & Sander, 551
Halpine, Charles G. ("Miles O'Reilly"), 524
Ham, C. J., 532
Hamblin, Joseph E., 527
Hamilton, Alexander, Jr., 542
Hamilton, Andrew Jackson, 549
Hamilton, C. A., 492
Hamilton, Frank Hastings, 509
Hamilton, James A., 524
Hamilton (Ohio), 459
Hamlin, Hannibal, 506, 591
Hammond, N. W., 561
Hammond, P., 563
Hammond, William A., 492, 495, 510-11, 513, 518, 520, 522, 526
Hampshire County (W. Va.), 477
Hancock, F., 584

Hancock, John, 517
Hancock, John L., 565
Handlin, W. W., 559
Handy, ———, 564
Hanford, F. A., 586
Hanks, Dennis Friend, 492, 537
Hanks, John, 440
Hanna, John, 564
Hanna, William H., 456
Hannah, ———, 484
Hannibal (Mo.), 513
Hanson, William R., 473
Hardie, James Allen, 517-18, 529
Hardin, Charles, 453
Hardin, Martin Davis, 514
Harding, Belle (Boyd), 574
Harding, Chester, Jr., 479
Harding, Samuel, 574
Harding, Mrs. Samuel, see Harding, Belle (Boyd)
Harding, Sarah Anne M., 574
Harding, W. H., 576
Hardy, ———, 546
Harkins, Daniel H., 520, 524
Harkness, Bettie F., 567
Harkness, Robert, 567
Harkness, Mrs. Robert, see Harkness, Bettie F.
Harlan, James, 496, 542, 584, 586
Harlo, John L., 528
Harlow, William A., 565
Harmon, E., 513
"Harmon's Sandal Sock," 513
Harney, G. Julian, 495
Harper, William H., 550
Harper's Ferry (W. Va.), 513
Harper's New Monthly Magazine, 501
Harren [Warren?], W., 507
Harrington, George, 512, 525
Harris, Gibson William, 438
Harris, Ira, 500, 520, 527, 533
Harris, Isaac Newton, 511
Harris, Thomas, 582
Harris, Thomas Langrell, 450
Harris, Thomas Manley, 529
Harris, Townsend, 480, 486
Harrison, B. E., 496
Harrison, George M., 462
Harrison, John F., 432
Harrison, Mrs. John F., see Harrison, Parthena
Harrison, Parthena, 432
Harsha, D. A., 566
Hart, John P., 521

Hartford (Conn.), 503
Hartshorne, Louisa, 478
Harvard University, 462
Harvey, Cordelia A. P., 500
Harvey, Isaac, 501
Harvey, James E., 462, 469, 483
Harvey, Mrs. Louis P., see Harvey, Cordelia A. P.
Harvey, Samuel A., 453
Harvey Hospital (Madison, Wis.), 553
Haskin, Joseph Abel, 505
Haskins, Hugh, 519
Hassaurek, Frederick, 469, 557
Hatch, Ozias Mather, 455, 462, 519
Hatch, Reuben B., 488, 498
Hatton, William Henry Deacon, 583
Haupt, Herman, see Military Bridges
Havana (Cuba), 586
Haven, Luther, 575
Hawaiian [Sandwich] Islands, 469, 485, 512
Hawes, John, 451
Hawkes, E. S., 586
Hawkins, B. M., 515
Hawley, Joseph Roswell, 543
Hawley, Mrs. Joseph Roswell, 537
Hawley, Wait N., 503
Hawley, E[liphalet] B., & Company (Springfield), 465
Hay, C. D., 453
Hay, John Milton: 489, 518, 524, 542, 550, 563, 569; writes for L., 465, 471-73, 475, 478-86, 488-91, 494-98, 500-502, 506, 508, 510-13, 517-18, 520-23, 525-29, 537-39, 541-42, 544-46, 548-50, 557-59, 561-71, 573-74, 576-77, 586, 588-89
Hay, Nathaniel, 452
Hayes, Isaac Israel, 486
Hayes, John, 549
Hayner, Enoch, 537
Haynes, Gideon, 562
Haynes, John L. [P.], 499
Hays, Sallie H., 577
Haysleys, Robert, 556
Hazen, William Babcock, 577
Heard, Charles H., 460
Hearn, Samuel B., 554
Heartman, Charles F., catalog cited, 576
Heaton, David, 548
Hebron, Mrs. A. S., 541
Heintzelman, Samuel Peter, 518, 527-28

Heise, John, catalogs cited, 476, 521
Hellerson, Charles, 567, 589
Helm, Mrs. Ben Hardin, see Helm, Emily (Todd)
Helm, Emily (Todd), 528
Helper, Hinton Rowan, see Impending Crisis in the South and How to Meet It, The
Henderson, James G., 543
Henderson, John Brooks, 504, 507, 514, 555, 557, 574, 580
Henderson, Thomas Jefferson, 442, 579
Henderson, William D., 449, 454
Henkels, Stan. V., catalogs cited, 464, 475-76, 495, 512, 515, 528, 535, 538, 557-58, 571, 573, 588
Henkle, Rev., 533
Henkle, Mrs., 533
Hennepin (Ill.), 442, 444
Hennessey, James C., 553
Henry, Anson G., 441-42, 486, 511, 559, 566, 584
Henry, Guy Vernor, 501
Henry, I. N., 559
Henry, Joseph, 541, 543
Henry (Ill.), 442, 455
Henshaw, Edward C., 504
Henwood, Berryman, 561
Herbert, Edward, 575
Herbert, William, 562, 574
Herndon, Archer Gray, 434
Herndon, William Henry, 439, 450, 452, 457, 570
Herndon's Lincoln: the True Story of a Great Life, 430-31, 433, 435, 439, 450
Herrick, Anson, 547
Herrick, Edward, Jr., 462
Herron, Francis Jay, 516
Hertz, Emanuel, see Abraham Lincoln: a New Portrait; and The Hidden Lincoln
Heslope, ———, 500
Hester, Barbara, 568
Hewett, Josephus, 434
Hewins, Joseph S., 500
Hewlett, James W., 556
Hickling, Thomas, 481
Hickman, ———, 523
Hickman, Benjamin F., 523
Hickman, J. H., 588
Hickox & Brothers (Springfield), 443
Hicks, Russell F., 462
Hicks, Thomas Holliday, 471, 480, 522

Hidden Lincoln, The (Hertz), 441
Higgins, Jacob, 549
Higgins, Van Hollis, 460-61
Higgins, William T., 561
Higgins & Friehaus (Liège, Belgium), 479
Highland (Ill.), 455
Hileman, Bartholomew, 566
Hill, George H., 527
Hill, Mrs. H. C., 575
Hill, Ralph, 564
Hillsboro (Ill.), 441, 455
Hilton, Joseph H., 515
Hilton, Winthrop E., 545-46
Hines, ———, 580
Hines, Joseph, 580
Hirsch, Mrs. James L., 529
History of McLean County, Illinois (1879), 452
Hitchcock, Ethan Allen, 510, 523, 550, 553, 557, 563, 565, 571
Hitchcock, Peter, 447
Hitt, C. B., 453
Hobbies (periodical), 524
Hobbs, William C., 454
Hoblit, H. K., 450
Hobson, Atwood G., 580
Hobson, William E., 580
Hodges, Albert Gallatin, 530
Hodges, Henry Clay, 557
Hodges, William H., 520
Hoffman, John B., 470, 477
Hoffman, N. M., 543
Hoffmann, Ernest F., 492
Hoffmann, Francis Arnold, 580
Hoffmayer, ———, 547
Hoffmayer, Mrs., 547
Hogan, John, 532, 581
Hoge, Mrs. Abraham, see Hoge, Jane Currie (Blaikie)
Hoge, George Blaikie, 529, 534
Hoge, Jane Currie (Blaikie), 529, 534
Hogue, Eliza, 559
Hogue, Louis D., 559
Hogue, Mrs. Louis D., see Hogue, Eliza
Holbrook, Amory, 485
Holbrook, Frederick, 468, 527
Holland, George, 567
Holland, Samuel R., 556
Holmes, James H., 497
Holmes, S. N., 479
Holt, Joseph, 476, 494, 504, 508, 510, 512-19, 522, 525-26, 529-34, 536-56,

559, 562-67, 571-73, 575, 577-78,
  580-81, 583, 585-87
Holyoake, George J., 561
Honduras, 485, 514
Hood, George W., 578
Hood, Mrs. George W., 578
Hood, Thomas J., 503
Hook, R. B., 570
Hooker, Joseph, 511, 513-14, 520, 560
Hooper, ———, 568
Hooper, John, 568
Hopkins, Henry, 477
Hopkins, Robert, see Chaskay-don
Hopkins, Samuel A., 476
Hopkins, Hays, Palmer & Company,
  456
Hora, Mrs. J. K., 559
Horses and mules, export of, 524, 538,
  583, 586-87
Hoskins, Charles C., 473
Hostick, King V., catalog cited, 463
Houghton, Lawrence V., 546, 562, 568
House, Charles W., 464
House of Representatives, 442-45, 482,
  484, 486, 525
Houston, Albert, 519
How My Father Secured Lincoln's
  Autograph (Blakeslee), 566
Howard, Jacob Merritt, 582
Howard, John, 551
Howard, Samuel, 567
Howard, W. S., 463
Howe, Florin S., 544
Howe, N. S., 524
Howe, Timothy Otis, 472-73, 500, 506
Howell, William T., 584
Howells, William Dean, see Lives and

Speeches of Abraham Lincoln and
  Hannibal Hamlin
Howland, John D., 557
Howland, T. A., 454, 458
Howry, Samuel, 570
Hoyne, Thomas, 484
Hoyt, Mark, 579
Hsien Fêng, Emperor of China, 473
Hubbard, Gurdon Saltonstall, 459
Hubbell, J. M., 588
Huffman, John, 442
Hughes, A. M., Jr., 532
Hughes, James, 559
Hughes, John Joseph, 491, 517-18
Hughes, Robert H., 544
Huidekoper, Henry Shippen, see Per-
  sonal Notes and Reminiscences of
  Lincoln
Hull, George W., 566
Humboldt (Kans.) Land Office, 539
Humphrey, G. S., & Company, 474
Hunt, Henry Jackson, 502
Hunt, James H., 517
Hunt, Luther B., Jr., 512
Hunt, Thomas A., 575
Hunt, Woolman, 571
Hunter, Ann, 521
Hunter, David, 569
Hunter, William, 508
Hurlbut, Henry T., 523
Hurlbut, Stephen Augustus, 510, 522-
  23, 559
Hurst, Samuel, 434
Hutawa, Charles, 490
Hutchinson, C. G., 575
Hutchinson, Clinton C., 473
Hutchinson, John (Ill.), 452

I

"I Will Tell You a Joke about Joel
  and Mary" (poem), 430
Idaho: Six Months in the New Gold
  Diggings (Campbell), 541
Idaho Territory, 561
Ihrie, George Percy, 531, 548
Illinois, 451-52, 496, 538, 544
Illinois, Board of Public Works, 437-
  38
Illinois, capital of, 434

Illinois, elections in, see Elections in
  Illinois
Illinois Advocate, see Illinois State
  Register
Illinois Central Railroad, 442, 452
Illinois Gazette [Lacon], 440, 444, 457
Illinois legislature, 440, 466; L. in, 432-
  39
"Illinois Patriot" [pseud.], 433
Illinois Sanitary Commission, 565

Illinois School Fund, 436
Illinois Sentinel [Jacksonville], 455-56
Illinois Staats-Anzeiger [Springfield], 465
Illinois State Capitol, 441
Illinois State Chronicle [Decatur], 450
Illinois State Journal [Springfield]: 452, 466; cited, 432-42, 444, 448, 450-52, 455-56, 458-61, 463, 465, 506; see also *Sangamo Journal*
Illinois State Normal University (Normal), 452
Illinois State Register [Vandalia-Springfield], cited, 432-33, 436-41, 444, 448, 450-51
Illinois State University (Springfield), 448
Illinois Wesleyan Story, The (Watson), 589
Impending Crisis in the South and How to Meet It, The (Helper), 459
Indentures, 436, 440

Indest, Joseph, 564
Indian Department, 564
Indiana, 441, 466-67, 528, 568
Indianapolis (Ind.), 466, 511
Indians, 484, 503-505, 511, 551-52
Indis, ———, 521
Ingersoll, Ebon Clark, 545, 569
Ingersoll, Robert Green, 569
Ingham, Annette S., 548
Ingham, James, 548
Instructions for Officers on Outpost and Patrol Duty, 489
Interior, The (periodical), 435
Internal improvements, 444
Introduction to Algebra, An (Day), 590
Irwin, Edward, 584
Isaacs, Meyer S., 565-66
Isabel II (Queen of Spain), 468-69, 498
Isham, Henry, 543
Isherwood, Benjamin Franklin, 479
Italy, 470
Iyemoshi (Shogun of Japan), 480

J

Jackson, D. C., 470
Jackson, Floyd, 433
Jackson, Joseph Cooke, 512
Jackson, Joseph H., 461
Jackson, Lavinia (Hunter), 521
Jackson County (Mo.), 500
Jacksonville (Ill.), 437, 441-42, 448, 452, 455, 457, 460-61
Jacobs, Benjamin Franklin, 465
Jacobs, Mrs. Victor, 536
Jacoby, Jacob, 522
Jaeger, Victor, 563
James, Mrs. A. C., 582
James, Benjamin Franklin, 441, 446-47, 458, 573
Jamisson, Andrew, 531
Janney, Henry, 559
Janney, Joseph J., 559
Japan, 480, 486, 551
Jayne, Gershom, 434
Jayne, William, 522
Jefferson, Joseph, 437
Jefferson County (Ark.), 558
Jeffersonville (Ind.), 571

Jeffrey, James, 473
Jenkins, George Sumner, 518
Jenkins, Thornton A., Jr., 521
Jenks, ———, 541
Jenks, Henry C., 541
Jenks, Mrs. Henry C., 541
Jennings, Eli Fuller, 523
Jennings, F. A., 503
Jennings, Orville, 582
Jewell, J. Grey, 467
Jewett, Ashbury C., 565
Jewett, William Cornell ("Colorado"), 468
Jews, 566
Johns, ———, 475
Johns, Harvey C., 449
Johnson, ———, 537
Johnson, Andrew, 483, 492, 532, 554, 556
Johnson, Benjamin (Miss.), 496
Johnson, Emaline, 432
Johnson, Fielding W., 496
Johnson, Granville E., 516, 535
Johnson, Hugh Mortimer, 523

Johnson, John (Ill.), 438
Johnson, John M., 471
Johnson, John O., 450
Johnson, M. C., 490
Johnson, M. Y., 504
Johnson, Reverdy, 533-35, 554
Johnson, Richard W., 480
Johnson, S. H., 588
Johnson, Sophia, 531
Johnson, Thomas, 519
Johnson, Thomas W., 580
Johnson, William H., 471, 487, 526
Johnson's Island (Ohio), 549, 563, 565
Johnston, James D., 485
Johnston, William, 537
Joliet (Ill.), 451
Jonas, Abraham, 449, 461
Jonas, Benjamin F., 452
Jondreville de Villarceau, Comte de, 480
Jones, ———, 575
Jones, Albert G., 448
Jones, Alfred H., 475
Jones, Benjamin, 567
Jones, C. S., 473
Jones, Charles, 513
Jones, E., 502
Jones, Francis F., 478

Jones, H. G., 585
Jones, Henry L., 501
Jones, Horatio Morgan, 522
Jones, J. B., 457
Jones, J. Russell, 498
Jones, James G., 564, 578, 581
Jones, Jehu Glancy, 470
Jones, John, Sr., 431-32
Jones, Mrs. John, see Jones, Lydia
Jones, John, Jr., 432
Jones, John Albert, 446, 454
Jones, Llewellyn, 551
Jones, Lydia, 432
Jones, Newton F., 526
Jones, P. S., 569
Jones, Patrick Henry, 536
Jones, Stephen E., 494
Jones, W. P., 565
Jones, William (St. Joseph), 584, 586
Jones, William O., 533
Journal of the Illinois State Historical
Society, 442, 445-46
Juárez, Benito Pablo, 469
Judd, Frank Rossiter, 523
Judd, Norman Buel, 453, 458, 460, 463, 468, 523
Junction City (Kans.) Land Office, 571, 586
Justices of the peace (Ill.), 432

K

Kallman, H., 504
Kamehameha IV (King of Hawaii), 512
Kami, Ando Isvesimano, 486
Kämmerling, Gustav, 561
Kane, Thomas L., 566
Kannady [?], ———, 446
Kansas: 545, 571; legislature, 532
Kansas City Times, 582
Kansas River, 532
Kansas Territory, 451, 459
Kasmire, Franklin, 529
Kauffman, S. H., 482
Kearny, Philip, 478
Keel, George, 562
Keiley, Patrick, 452
Keller, G. H., 517
Kelley, Benjamin Franklin, 476

Kelley, Irad, 544
Kelley, William Darrah, 504, 511, 586
Kelley's Island, 544
Kellogg, Charles, 573
Kellogg, Francis William, 531
Kellogg, Mrs. R., 573
Kellogg, William, 454, 456
Kelly, Nancy, 546
Kelly, Nelson [alias Henry Mapes], 545
Kelly, Thomas, 546
Kelly, Thomas C., 553
Kendall, Amos, 432
Kendall, John, 527
Kennedy, John Pendleton, 513
Kent, John, Sr., 467
Kentucky, 482, 491, 495, 501, 506, 536, 545, 556, 578, 580-81, 587

Keokuk (Iowa), 550
Kerner, W., 491
Kerns, Wilson B., 585
Kerr, John Bozman, 480, 529
Kerr, Richard, 437
Ketcham, John L., 558
Ketcham, Hiram, 491
Ketcham, William W., 571
Ketcham, Howe & Company (New York), 459-60
Ketcham, Son & Company (New York), 461
Keys, W. J., 566
Killinger, Thomas J., 522
Kimball, Nathan, 526, 530
Kincheloe, Mrs. A. H., 578
Kincheloe, Burt, 578
Kindel, Mrs. Charles M., 570
King, A. P., Jr., 570
King, Edward, 529, 542
King, Hezekiah, 431
King, James, 558
King, James Smith, 584
King, John N., 482, 528
King, John Quincy Adams, 556
King, Preston, 472, 482, 487-88
King, Rufus (1814-1876), 470

King, Turner R., 446
Kinney, John F., 504
Kinsey, Mrs. John H., 527
Kinzer, G. W., 469
Kirk, Robert C., 485, 488
Kirkham, Robert, 476
Kirkham, Samuel, 591
Kirkham's Grammar, 591
Kirkman, Lewis [Louis], 536
Kirkwood, Samuel Jordan, 496, 511
Kleine, Louis, 589
Knapp, A. L., 447
Knapp, C. H., 447
Knox, James, 448
Knox, John T., 588
Knox, Joseph, 466
Knox, William, 591
Koerner, Gustave Philip, 452-53, 498, 513, 517, 565
Kohler, P., 481
Kohn, Abraham, 466
Korn; Bertram Wallace, see American Jewry and the Civil War
Kossuth, Lajos [Louis], 448
Krzyzanowski, Wladimir, 521
Kyle, A. A., 564

L

Labbez, David, & Company (Rheims), 497
Lacon [formerly Columbia] (Ill.), 451
La Harpe (Ill.), 456
Laidley, Theodore, 525
Lake Superior, 505
Lambert, Mary (Meagher), 477
Lamborn, Josiah, 438
Lamon, Ward Hill: 448, 481, 590; see also Life of Abraham Lincoln from His Birth to His Inauguration as President; and Recollections of Abraham Lincoln
Lander, Frederick West, 485
Landon, LaFayette, 541
Lane, Henry Smith, 564, 584
Lane, James Henry, 484-85, 488-90, 495-96, 543, 547-48, 571, 586
Lane, Ranson, 431

Langenbein, Charles, 545, 547
Langston, I. B., 583
Langston, J. W., 583
Langston, W. C., 583
Langston's Settlement (Ill.), 442
Lanigan, John, 479
Lanman, Charles, see Dictionary of the United States Congress
Lanman, George M., 488
Lansing, Jacob D., 510
Lapsley, Arthur Brooks, see The Writings of Abraham Lincoln
Larned, E. E., 498
Larned, Edwin C., 533
Larrabee, Charles Hathaway, 487
Latham, Henry Clay, 464
Latham, Philip C., 440
Latine, Alexander, 432
Law, John, 484
Lawler, Michael Kelly, 507

Lawless, Patrick, 545
Lawrence (Kans.), 457
Lawton, Bridget, 580
Lawton, William, 580
Layton, E. A., 535
Leach, DeWitt Clinton, 584
Lean, Thomas, 473, 544, 579
Leatherman, D. M., 577
Leavenworth (Kans.), 557
Lebanon (Ind.), 466
Lebanon (Pa.) *Reporter*, 566
Leber, Edward, 557, 561
Le Conte, Helen G., 510
Le Conte, John L., 510
Le Conte, Mrs. John L., *see* Le Conte, Helen G.
Lederer, Richard M., 581
Lee, John Fitzgerald, 481, 492-93
Lefferts, Marshall, 514
Leggatz, Andrew W., 442
Leggett, Mortimer Dormer, 544
Leggett, Wells Wilmer, 538, 544
Lehman, Michael, 590
Leib, Harrison, 525
Leitch, ———, 495-96
Leland, William W., 502
Leland & Company, 548
Lemen, James, 452
Leopold I, King of the Belgians, 468
Lesley, James, Jr., 581
Leslie, Charles P., 550
Leslie, Joseph L., 563
Leslie, William R., 501
Lessig, James C., 571
Lester, John H., 557, 575
"Let Auld Acquaintance Be Forgot" (poem), 430
Letters . . . of John Murray Forbes, 522
Levering, Lawrason, 446
Lewis, Alpheus, 539
Lewis, George W., 462
Lewis, James Taylor, 553
Lewis, Joseph J., 525
Lewis, Obed, 462
Lewis, S. D., 500
Lewistown (Ill.), 436
Lewistown Democrat, 476
Lexington (Ky.), 528
Libbie, C. F., catalogs cited, 465-66, 518, 534
Libby Prison (Richmond, Va.), 537
Liborius, Mrs. C. M., 551
Liborius, Ernest, 551

Lick Creek (Sangamon Co., Ill.), 433, 435
Life and Public Services of Edwin M. Stanton (Gorham), 489
Life of Abraham Lincoln (Barton), 461, 465-66, 590
Life of Abraham Lincoln (Tarbell), 439, 450, 525-26
Life of Abraham Lincoln (Whitney), 473
Life of Abraham Lincoln from His Birth to His Inauguration as President (Lamon), 431, 450, 483
Life of Cassius Marcellus Clay: Memoirs, Writings and Speeches . . ., The (Clay), 462
Life of Charles Sumner, 566
Life on the Circuit with Lincoln (Whitney), 448
Lime Point (Calif.), 482
LINCOLN, ABRAHAM, checks written by: 450, 452, 457-66, 471, 475-76, 487, 489, 515, 517, 537, 541, 563, 575, 579-81, 589; *see also* Autographs, L. replies to requests for
LINCOLN, ABRAHAM, commander-in-chief (Civil War), 467-591 *passim*
LINCOLN, ABRAHAM, his comments on: prosperity and thrift (spurious), 591; religion (purported essay on), 431
LINCOLN, ABRAHAM, communications attributed to (*italic figures indicate number of references on page*):
430 (*8*), 431 (*4*), 432 (*11*), 433 (*10*), 434 (*15*), 435 (*14*), 436 (*3*), 437, 438 (*4*), 439 (*3*), 440 (*8*), 441 (*7*), 442 (*3*), 443, 448 (*2*), 450 (*2*), 454, 457, 461 (*2*), 463, 465 (*2*), 466 (*3*), 467 (*2*), 471, 473, 476, 477, 480, 481, 483 (*3*), 489 (*2*), 491, 501 (*2*), 515, 518, 521, 524 (*4*), 525 (*2*), 528 (*2*), 529, 534, 539, 540, 541, 545, 551, 555, 570, 582, 588 (*2*), 589 (*9*), 590 (*15*), 591 (*10*); *see also* Forgeries
LINCOLN, ABRAHAM, lawyer, 439-40, 459-60, 528, 589-90
LINCOLN, ABRAHAM, political career of: *Campaigns of 1832-1838,* 431-35; *Campaign of 1840,* 437-38; *Campaign of 1844,* 440-41; *Campaign of 1846,* 441-42; *Campaign of 1848,* 443-44; *Campaign of 1852,* 448; *Campaign of 1854,* 448-49; *Campaign of 1855,* 450; *Campaign of*

1856, 450-52; *Campaign of 1858*, 453-56; *see also* Congress, U.S., L. in; *and* Illinois legislature, L. in
LINCOLN, ABRAHAM, postmaster, 432-33
LINCOLN, ABRAHAM, President (1861-1865), 467-591 *passim*
LINCOLN, ABRAHAM, President-elect (1860-1861), 464-67
LINCOLN, ABRAHAM, Presidential nominee (1860), 461-64
LINCOLN, ABRAHAM, secretaries (unidentified) write for: 484, 487, 489, 491, 493, 496, 499-501, 504, 509-11, 526, 537, 539-40, 545; *see also* Hay, John Milton; Neill, Edward Duffield; Nicolay, John George; *and* Stoddard, William Osborn
LINCOLN, ABRAHAM, surveyor, 431-33
Lincoln, Edward Baker (L.'s son "Eddie"), 442
Lincoln, Mary (Todd), 441-43, 477-78, 489, 497, 511, 517, 524, 527, 531, 550, 580-81, 588
Lincoln, Robert Todd: 442, 533, 571, 590; checks to, 458-62, 489, 580
Lincoln, Thomas ("Tad"), 476
Lincoln (Ill.), 451, 456, 466
Lincoln Among His Friends (Wilson), 588
Lincoln & Berry (New Salem, Ill.), 431
Lincoln and Ohio (Ryan), 459
Lincoln and the Civil War in the Diaries and Letters of John Hay (Dennett), 518, 524
Lincoln 1840-1846 (Pratt), 438
Lincoln 1854-1861 (Angle), 455-56, 463
Lincoln (Ill.) *Herald*, 458
Lincoln Herald (periodical), 530
"Lincoln in Coles County" (MS), 591
Lincoln Lore (periodical), 441
Lincoln the Politician (Seitz), 450, 591
Lincoln's First Years in Illinois (Ross), 436
Lincoln's Ottawa (Tisler) 442
Lincoln's Own Stories (Gross), 590
"Lincoln's Re-election" (art.), 566
Lincoln's Visit to Evanston (Currey), 461
Linder, Usher Ferguson, 434

Lindsay, William K., 445-46
Lindsey, John, 570
Lingenfelter, W. H., 471
Lintner, Amos, 552-53, 565
Lintner, John, 552-53, 565
Lippincott, Mrs., 506
Lippincott, Charles Elliott, 529
Lipscomb, W. C., 510
"Liquid Fire," 443
Liscombe, E. P., 486
Little, Robert, 533
Little, S., 457
Little, William, 551
Livermore, George, 507
Lives and Speeches of Abraham Lincoln and Hannibal Hamlin (Howells), 430, 462
Livingston, John, 458
Livingston, La Rhett Loralzo, 495
Livingston's United States Law Register, 458
Lloyd, Richard H., 458-59
Loami (Ill.), 435
Loan, Benjamin Franklin, 548, 572, 574
Lockport (Ill.), 438-39
Lockwood, Henry Clay, 488
Loewenthal, Philip, 508
Logan, John, 583
Logan, John Alexander, 521, 527, 552, 588
Logan, Stephen Trigg, 440, 447, 452, 590
Logan County (Ill.), 436, 445
London (England) *Times*, 548
Long, John F., 507
Long, Lee W., 525
"Looker-On, A" [pseud.], 436
Loomis, John S., 496, 538
López, Francisco Solano, 510
Lopinto, James, 587
Loree, John, 584
Loser, Henry, 564
Lossing, Benson John, 525
"Lost Townships" letters, 435
Loud, E. D., 464
Louden, Robert, 541
Loudon, John F., 582
Loughborough, James M., 450
Louisiana, 587
Louisville (Ky.), 551, 575
Lounsberry, John S., 530
Louttit, W. Easton, Jr., 475, 522

Love, Oscar, 437
Love, W. T., 568
Lovejoy, Owen, 455, 489
Loveland (Ohio), 467
Lowe, R. P., 575
Loyal Legion of the District of Columbia, 589-90
Lucas, George B., 566
Lucas, Josiah M., 446

Ludington, Elisha Harrison, 540
Luelson [?], see Suelson, James M.
Lufkin, Richard F., 579
Luhrs, Henry E., 463
Luiz I, King of Portugal, 483
Lynch, Thomas A., 544
Lynchburg (Va.), 564, 578
Lyons, Branton, 554

M

McAleer, H. M., 496
McBride, James, 512
McBride, John R., 584
McCalister, William H., 487
McCall, George Archibald, 492
McCallen, Andrew, 449
McCann, Thomas K., 520
McCarty, Ella C., 568
McCarty, William W., 568
McCauley, Abraham, 582
McClellan, George Brinton, 471, 476, 479, 481-85, 489, 491, 503, 550, 590
McClernand, John Alexander, 438, 498, 506
McClintock, John, 574
McClure, Alexander Kelly, 460, 462-63, 465, 549, 569
McClure, James E., 449
McClurg, Joseph Washington, 575
McCombs, Mrs. J. M., 537
McConnell, ———, 477
McCook, Daniel, 479
McCulloch, Benjamin, 583
McCulloch, Hugh, 521, 553
McDonald, Amos, 552
McDonald, David, 557, 559, 566
McDougall, J. F., 449
McDowell, Miss, 548
McDowell, Irvin, 489-90, 492
McEvers, T. L., 454
McFadden, Benjamin, 520
McFalls, Benjamin F., 483-84
McFalls, Thaddeus Banks, 483
McFarren, Samuel, 534
McFerran, John Courts, 557
McGee, Dennis, 525
McGill, George W., 540

McGill, John, 583
McGregor, Alexander, 556
McGunnegle, George Kennedy, 572
McIlvaine, Abraham Robinson, 447
McIlvaine, Charles Pettit, 506
McIndoe, Walter Duncan, 584
McIntosh, William H., 567
McKaye, James, 519
McKee, Abraham W., 556
McKee, Alexander R., 484
McKeever, Chauncey, 471
McKellup, ———, 501
Mackenzie, M. K., 558
Mackenzie, M. S., 463
Mackenzie, R. Shelton, 506
Mackenzie, Mrs. R. Shelton, 506
McKew, Michael, 516
Mackie, Charles, 484
Mackinac Island (Mich.), 489
Mackinaw (Ill.), 442
McKinley, James B., 455
McLaskey, ———, 549
McLean, W. E., 520
McLean County (Ill.), 444
McMahon, ———, 492
McMath, Jesse H., 490
McMillan, James Winning, 547
McMillen, William Linn, 573
McMullen, Warren, 517
McNabb, Robert, 432
McNamar [alias McNeil], John, 431
McNamee, Gertrude F., 489
McNeil, John, see McNamar, John
McPherson, Edward, 554; see also A Political History of the United States during the Great Rebellion
McRoberts, Josiah, 439

Macy, Jesse, 590
Madden, Samuel W., 568
Madigan, Thomas F., see *The Autograph Album;* and *A Catalogue of Lincolniana*
Madison (Ohio), 467
Madison (Wis.), 553
Magnolia (Ill.), 444
Maguire, John, 572, 577
Mahan, Asa, 482
Mahomet XVII, Sultan of Morocco, 478, 490
Main, H. P., 464
Maine, 467, 573
Mais, Lorenzo, 575
Mallison, Francis A., 553
Mallory, Robert, 482
Maloney, James D., 567
Manchester (N.H.) *Republican,* 461
Mangen, Jane, 503
Mangen, Michael, 503
Manly, John, 553
Manly, Uri, 481
Mann, William B., 502
Manning, J. W., *see* French, C. W.
Mapes, Henry, *see* Kelly, Nelson
March, William, 574
Marchant, Adeline, 515
Maring, Eugene, 578
Markbreit, Leopold, 557
Marples, George W., 501
"Mars & Neptune," 512
Marsh, George M., 432
Marsh, George Perkins, 470
Marsh, Joseph M., 565
Marsh, Matthew Sheafe, 432
Marsh, William, 509
Marshall, B. C., 435
Marshall, James F. B., 495
Marshall, Thomas A., 449, 454
Marshall, William H., 457
Marshall (Ill.), 438
Martin, Benjamin N., 510
Martin, George W., 571, 586
Martin, Nathaniel B., 437
Martin, Robert, 537, 555
Martin, Sarah, 437
Martínez, Tomás, 468-69, 505, 514
Maryland, 444, 504, 523, 538, 578
Masons, Ancient Free and Accepted, 440
Massachusetts, 444
Massett, Stephen C., 543
Matheny, ———, 456

Matheny, Charles Reynolds, 434-35
Matheny, Charles W., & Company (Springfield), 466
Mather, Peter S., 464
Mathews, R. Stockett, 570, 576
Matson, J. A., 568
Matteson, James T., 464
Matteson, Joel Aldrich, 452
Matthies, Katharine, 534
Mattoon (Ill.), 455
Maxwell, Edwin, 567
Maxwell, Lucinda, 587
Maxwell, William, 587
May, Caesar Rodney, 591
May, William Lewis, 435, 441
Maynard, George A., 583
Mayo, William L., 583
Meade, George Gordon, 499-500, 512, 514, 518, 523, 525, 533, 537, 547
Meade, Richard W., 443
Meagher, ———, 477
Mechanicsburg (Ill.), 433
Medill, Joseph Meharry, 454
Meehan, Michael, 519
Meek, James M., 583
Meigs, James L., 563
Meigs, Montgomery Cunningham: 475-76, 479, 486, 490-91, 496, 498, 500, 503-507, 510-11, 516-17, 519, 521, 524, 558, 566, 590; writes for L., 488, 492
Meigsville (Ohio), 568
Melloni, Macedonio, 448
Melvin, Mrs. Samuel Houston, 556
Memoirs of Gustave Koerner (McCormack), 452
Memoirs of William T. Sherman, 473
Memphis (Tenn.), 537, 569
Menard County (Ill.), 436, 439, 569
Mendota (Ill.), 451
Meredith, Joseph Dennie, 477
Meredith, Solomon, 567, 570-71, 581
Meredith, William M., 477
Meriden (Conn.), 461
Merrick, P. V., 576
Merrill, Charles W., 515
Merriman, Harry P., 450
Merritt, Abraham Clarkson, 573
Merwin Sales Company, 465
Metamora (Ill.), 444, 456
Metcalf, ———, 438, 534
Methodists, 532, 541
Metropolitan Art Association, catalogs

cited, 450, 487, 493, 508, 520, 564, 568
Metropolitan Bank (New York), 459-60, 462, 466
Metropolitan Railroad Company, 480
Mexican War, 442
Mexico, 469, 538, 587
Miamiville (Ohio), 467
Michigan, 467, 482
Middle Lick Creek (Ill.), 442
Milford (Ohio), 467
Military arrests, 491, 506
Military Bridges (Haupt), 547
Militia, 497, 538, 545-46, 569
Miller, B. C., 500
Miller, Charles, 500
Miller, Francis A., 497
Miller, George W., 462
Miller, John A., 503
Miller, John C., 585
Miller, R. L., 463
Mills, David D., 553
Millward, William, 470
Milroy, Robert Huston, 502, 513, 519, 521
Milton, George Fort, see *The Eve of Conflict*
Milwaukee (Wis.), 459
Milwaukee Sentinel, 459
Minnesota, 503-504, 511
Mint, U.S. (San Francisco), 528
Mission Sabbath School (Chicago), 464
Mississippi, 521
Mississippi River, 443-45
Missouri, 472, 479, 484, 492, 508, 532, 555, 560-61, 572, 580
Missouri Republican [St. Louis], 438
"Mr. Lincoln and the 'Crazy' Quaker" (art.), 501
Mitchel, Ormsby McKnight, 474, 477
Mitchell, James, 525
Mitchell, Louise M., 547
Mitchell, William, 557
Mitre, Bartolomé, 487-88
Mix, Charles E., 477
Mock, Caleb, 578
Moffat, Edward Stewart, 525
Moffett, Thomas, 437
Mohammed Saïd Pacha, Viceroy of Egypt, 470, 542
Monitor (ironclad), 487
Monroe, Thomas H. W., 501
Montana Territory, 550

Montgomery, ———, 485
Montgomery, Alexander, 542
Monticello (Ill.), 451, 455
Moody, Granville, 535
Moon, Squire, 483
Moore, Benjamin P., Jr., 527
Moore, Charles C., 544
Moore, Mrs. Charles C., 544
Moore, Clifton H., 455, 458
Moore, H. C., 535
Moore, Timothy C., 511
Moorhead, James Kennedy, 507, 571
Moorman, Sarah, 532
Moran, Daniel, 478
Moreno, Gabriel Garcia, 469
Morgan, David, 590
Morgan, Edwin Denison, 466, 471, 473, 488, 493, 504, 508, 585
Morgan, Mrs. Edwin Denison, 471
Morgan, George Washington, 469
Morgan, Manie, see *The New Stars*
Morgan, Morgan, 554
Morgan, William E., 499
Morgan County (Ill.), 443
Morganfield (Ky.), 438
Morley, William D., Inc., catalogs cited, 471, 477, 484, 519, 533, 536, 540, 542, 546, 571, 589
Morocco, 478, 490
Morrell, Daniel Johnson, 579
Morris, Charles, 472
Morris, Charles D., 479
Morris, Daniel, 536
Morris, Edward Joy, 475
Morris [alias Calahan], John, 534
Morris, John, Jr., 489
Morris, Martin Sims, 440, 453
Morris, Robert Y., Jr., 538
Morris, William Walton, 554
Morris (Ind.), 467
Morrison, Isaac L., 577
Morrison, Joseph Johnson, 547
Morrow, Robert, 585
Morrow (Ohio), 467
Morse, John H., 539
Morse, Samuel Finley Breese, 505
"Mortality" (poem), 590
Mortimore, John, 442
Morton, ———, 480
Morton, James, 523
Morton, Oliver Perry, 515, 557, 563, 571, 582
Moseley, Jourdan, 554-55
Moseley, Robert, 454

Moses, C. Lee, 545
Motley, John Lothrop, 474
Mott, Gordon Newell, 533
Mott, John Owen, 477
Mott, Samuel Rolla, 533
Mount Carmel (Ill.), 438
Mount Sterling (Ill.), 456
Mount Vernon (Ill.), 438
Mow, Jonathan, 587
Mudd, J. Henry Clay, 501
Mulfinger, C. L., 464
Muller, James N., 488
Mulligan, James Adelbert, 590
Mundy, Marcellus, 523
Munsell, Leander, 454
Murdoch, Alexander, 576
Murdoch, James E., 532

Murdock, James, 558
Murphy, Eugene Peter, 518
Murphy, Henry Cruse, 469
Murphy, John H., 439
Murphy, R. C., 517
Murray, ———, 447
Murray, Bronson, 472
Murrell, Samuel, 555
Mushir Mohammed El Sadar, Possessor of the Kingdom of Tunis, 491
"My Recollections of Abraham Lincoln" (art.), 438
Myers, ———, 560
Myers, A. H., 484
Mylacrain, Catharine, 585
Mylacrain, William, 585

N

Nagle, Patrick J., 453
Naglee, Henry Morris, 494, 505-506
Naglee, James, 500
Naples (Ill.), 456
Napoleon III, Emperor of the French, 468, 586
Nash, ———, 543
Nash, John F., 442
Nash, Michael, 525
Nashua (N.H.), 457
Nashville (Tenn.), 488, 554, 560, 583
Nassau (steamer), 496
Nathan, Clifford, 527
National Freedmen's Aid Society, 555
National Intelligencer [Washington], 444
National Republican [Washington], 470
Naval Academy, Annapolis, 508, 543
Naval Records, cited, 487
Naylor, Charles, 552
Neale, Samuel, Sr., 434
Neff, Henry K., 497
Negley, James Scott, 535
Negro troops, 500, 523, 533, 537, 541, 576
Negroes, 448, 487, 495, 505, 511, 515, 544, 576-77, 588
Neill, Edward Duffield, 547, 552, 554, 572

Neilson, George C., 513
Nelson, F. H., 517
Nelson, Thomas H., 473
Nelson, Thomas S., 480
Nelson, William (Ky.), 477
Nelson, William (N.Y.), 447
Nelson, Young, 557
Neptune, see "Mars and Neptune"
Nesmith, James Willis, 488
Netherlands, 469
Nevada Territory, 559, 561
Nevins, William R., 471
New Bedford (Mass.), 444
New Bedford Mercury, 444
New Bern (N.C.), 549
New Boston (Ill.), 432
New England Society (Springfield, Ill.), 452
New Hampshire, 461, 469, 573
New Haven (Conn.), 461
New Haven Palladium, 461
New Jersey, 502, 544, 551, 565, 585
New Kent Court House (Va.), 492
New Mexico Territory, 468-69, 472, 480, 484, 528, 538, 581, 589
New Orleans (La.), 511, 524, 534, 577
New Salem (Ill.), 431-33
New Stars, The (Morgan), 591
New Voice, The (periodical), 501
New York (city), 508, 577

New York (state), 471-73, 484, 499, 511, 554, 589
New York Agricultural Society Fair, 553
New York Chamber of Commerce, 506, 511
New York Herald, 466-67, 481, 524
New York Journal of Commerce, 528
New York Ladies' Educational Union, 483
New York Times, 467, 471, 553
New York Tribune, 442, 461, 466-67, 471, 474, 493, 506, 511, 576
New York Workingmen's Union, 552
Newby, W., 493
Newell, William Augustus, 480
Newhall House (Milwaukee), 459
Newkirk, Rodney B., 517
Newman, David A., 584
Newton, Isaac, 463, 497, 513
Niagara Falls, 550, 553
Nicaragua, 468-69, 505, 514
Nicholas, John C., 522
Nicholson, Francis, 510
Nicolay, John George, 469, 542, 574,

579; writes for L., 462-63, 466-67, 470-78, 480-81, 484-88, 490, 492-95, 499, 501, 503-14, 516-17, 525, 527-43, 547, 549-58, 559, 560, 562, 569-87, 591
Nielson, William, 590
Nininger, Alexander Ramsey, 490
Nixon, John Thompson, 511
Noble, Roland D., 500
Noell, John William, 509
Norfolk (Va.), 489-90, 501, 506, 543
North, ———, 574
North, John W. [M.], 559
North Carolina, 514, 548
Northrup, M. A., 459
Norton, Jesse Olds, 449, 562, 565
Norton, John W., 446
Norville, William T., 561
Norway, *see* Sweden and Norway
Norwich (Conn.), 461
Norwich Aurora, 461
Noyes, Benjamin, 583
Nutting, George S., 509
Nutting, Levi, 501

O

O'Beirne, Richard Fitzgerald, 514
O'Brien, John, 569
Odell, George C., 533
Odell, Moses Fowler, 569
Officer & Pusey, 460
Offutt, Denton, 430
Oglesby, Richard James, 579, 583
O'Grady, James, 476, 521
Ohio, 459, 467, 504, 553
Ohio, Department of the, 524
O'Kane, ———, 549
O'Kane, John, 549
Old Capitol Prison (Washington), 519, 522, 555, 570
"Old Settler, An" [pseud.], 434
Old Soldier, The [Springfield], 438
Olin, Abram Baldwin, 579
Oliphant, Ethelbert P., 445, 559
Oliver, Mordecai, 560
Olsen, Charles W., 509, 537, 590
Olympia (Wash.) Land Office, 587

Omberton, John F., 471
Onghetten, Alfred, 582
Onstot, Isaac, 447
Opdyke, George, 496, 524
Oquawka [Yellow Banks] (Ill.), 456
Oquawka Spectator, 456
Ord, Edward Otho Cresap, 534
Ordway, Otis O., 568
Oregon, 535
Oregon (Ill.), 451
O'Reilly, Miles, *see* Halpine, Charles G.
Orme, William Ward, 478
Osborn[e], Andrew L., 564, 571
Osborne, Thomas, 568
Oskaloosa (Iowa) *Saturday Globe,* 590
Otis, Ellen M., 483
Ottawa (Ill.), 451, 504
Ottawa Republican, 455
Otto, William T., 522, 552, 556
"Our Correspondent" [pseud.], 432-33

Outlook (periodical), 590
Owen, ———, 494
Owen, C. Norton, 485
Owen, John, 546
Owen, Joshua Thomas, 547

Owen, Richard Bently, 493
Owen, Robert Dale, 519
Owen, T. C., 540
Owens, Thornton, 558

P

Pace, ———, 578
Paddock, Algernon Sidney, 585
Paducah (Ky.), 516
Page, William T., 459
Paine, Eleazar A., 450, 456, 584
Paley, William, 433
Palmer, ———, 505
Palmer, Edwin A., Jr., 462
Palmer, Innis Newton, 549
Palmer, John McAuley, 481, 574
Palmer, Robert M., 469, 487
Pancoast, Samuel A., 477
Pantier, David M., 431
Pappsville (Ill.), 431
Paraguay, 510
Pardons, 472, 480, 489, 493-94, 501,
    503, 505, 508-509, 512-13, 516-19,
    522, 525-26, 528, 530-34, 538-41, 543,
    546, 549-51, 553-59, 562-63, 565, 567,
    570-73, 575-79, 581, 585-87, 590
Paris (France), 581
Parish, Francis D., 493
Parke-Bernet Galleries, catalogs cited,
    440, 444, 448, 450, 463, 470, 477,
    482-83, 491, 494, 500, 502, 505, 509,
    525, 531, 543, 547, 565, 567, 590
Parker, G. A., 507
Parker, Joel, 534, 565
Parker, John W., 540
Parker, Thomas M., 540
Parker, William B., 550
Parker, Wyman, 586
Parks, Samuel C., 449, 455, 461-62
Parmenter, E. A., 499
Paroles, 489, 508, 533, 555, 560, 575
Parsons, George M., 460
Parsons, Lewis Baldwin, 521
Partridge, James R., 485, 494, 514
Patrick, Mrs., 506
Patriotism in Poetry and Prose . . .
    from Lectures and Patriotic Read-

ings by James E. Murdoch . . . , 532
Patterson, Eli, see Barefoot, Sam
Patterson, George R., 501
Patterson, Helen H., 573
Patton, James, 451
Patton, William A., 536
Pavey, ———, 578
Payne, ———, 531
Payne, Mrs., 531
Payne, Fred A., 503, 524
Payson, Ira F., 498
Peacher, Cornelius E., 577
Peacher, John, Jr., 560
Pearson, John, 437
Peck, E. H., 447
Peck, Ebenezer, 441
Peck, J. A., 498
Pedro II, Emperor of Brazil, 471
Pedro V, King of Portugal, 469
Peirpoint, Francis Harrison, 474, 491,
    515
Pekin (Ill.), 440, 444, 448
Pelisan, Peter, 583
Pendleton, David J., 526
Pendleton, John S., 530
Pennal, J. J., 585
Pennsylvania, 467, 471, 502, 539, 576,
    585
Pensacola (Fla.), 581
Peoria, Baptiste, 587-88
Peoria (Ill.), 437, 439, 441, 444, 455
Peoria Democratic Press, 444
Peoria Record, 489
Peoria Register & North-Western Ga-
    zetteer, 437, 441
Perea, Francisco, 583
Pérez, José Joaquín, 473
Perkins, A. H. H., 445
"Perkins Steam Gun," 479
Perrince, William H., 476
Perry, Amos, 491

Perry, Horatio J., 503
Personal Notes and Reminiscences of Lincoln (Huidekoper), 590
Personal Recollections (Dodge), 589
Personal Recollections of Abraham Lincoln and the Civil War (Gilmore), 480
Personal Reminiscences 1840-1890 (Chittenden), 430
Peru, 479-80
Petersburg (Ill.), 433-34, 440-41, 443-44
Petersburg (Va.), 577
Pettijohn, Amos, 492
Pettis, Solomon Newton, 499
Pettus, John Jones, 468
Peyton, Bailie, 491
Phelps, John Smith, 499, 513
Phelps, William, 486
Philadelphia (Pa.), 472, 511, 536, 544, 550, 570
Philadelphia Press, 544
Philbrick, Charles H., 552
Philips, James M., 546
Phillips, David L., 518, 560
Phillips, Isaac Newton, see *Abraham Lincoln by Some Men Who Knew Him* and *Recollections*
Phillips, R. H., 573
Phillips, William A., 564
Piazza, ———, 512
Pickering, Henry M., 582
Pickett, George Edward, 439
Pickett, James B., 521
Pickett, Thomas Johnson, 441, 455, 457
Pierce, James F., 549
Pierce, Thornton S., 549
Pierce, William H., 537
"Pierce's Sub Marine Propellor," 490
Pikard, A. B., 458
Pike, James Stephen ("Particular Pike"), 469
Pike County Free Press [Pittsfield, Ill.], 452
Pine, Charles N., 484
Piper, Edward, Count, 528
Pitcher, Shadrach H., 556
Pitman, John T., Jr., 548
Pittsburgh (Pa.), 535
Pittsfield (Ill.), 452, 455
Pius IX, see Pope Pius IX
Platt, Edward Russell, 483
Pleasants, John H., 489

Pleasonton, Augustus, 573
Pleyel, Emmanuel J., 478
Pliny, Miles, 548
Plumb, A. V., 475
Point Lookout (Md.), 563
Poles, 510
Political Debates between . . . Lincoln and . . . Douglas . . . , 461, 463
Political History of the United States during the Great Rebellion . . . , A (McPherson), 481, 494, 502
Polk, Cornelia B., 530
Polk, James Knox, 443
Pollock, James, 447, 478
Pomeroy, Samuel Clarke, 490, 500, 503, 508, 588
Ponca Indian Agency, 470, 549
Pond, Fern (Nance), 431
Pond, Mrs. Henry E., see Pond, Fern (Nance)
Pond, Samuel G., 506
Pontiac (Ill.), 460
Pook, Samuel, 490
Pool, Henson, 572
Pope, John (1822-1892), 496, 514
Pope Pius IX, 469-70, 489, 502
Port Royal (S.C.), 481, 483, 487
Port Washington (Ohio), 467
Porter, David Dixon, 581, 588
Porter, Joseph K., 561
Porter, Maggie, 561
Porter, William, 472
Porter, William A., 575-76
Portsmouth (Va.), 558
Portugal, 469, 483
Post, Philip Sidney, 572
Post, Truman Augustus, 564
Post Office Department, 444
Potter, F. S., 454
Potter, H. L., 571
Potter, Joel A., 549
Potter, John Fox, 554
Potter, S. A., 505
Potts, John, 503, 505
Powell, Alexander, 569
Powell, Elihu N., 448
Powell, Lazarus Whitehead, 527
Powell, W. R., 529
Powell, William Henry (D.C.), 474-75
Prairie Beacon [Paris, Ill.], 450, 454
Prairie du Chien (Wis.), 512
Pratt, Mrs. C. W., 466

Pratt, Calvin Edward, 502
Pratt, Harry Edward, 436, 512; see also *Concerning Mr. Lincoln;* and *Lincoln 1840-1846*
Pratt, Thomas George, 575
Pratt, William H., 462
Prentice, George Denison, 482
Prentiss, Benjamin Mayberry, 507, 520
Presbyterians, 481, 493, 532
"President Lincoln's Entry into Richmond . . ." (art.), 588
President's orders, 486
Preston, Luther, 481
Preston, William C., 468
Price, Austin B., 556, 562
Price, James A., 559, 561
Price, John W., 506
Price, Mrs. L. J., 555
Price, Marion, 578
Price, Thomas Lawson, 484, 533
Price, William L., 520
Primm, Elizabeth (Wood), 568
Primm, Mrs. Ninian Edwards, *see* Primm, Elizabeth (Wood)
Prince, William Edgar, 489
Prisoners-of-war, 483, 485, 491, 493, 508, 523, 528, 531, 537, 547, 549-50, 553, 555, 558-70, 572-73, 575, 578-79, 581, 587
Pritchard, James T., 503
Private and Official Correspondence of Gen. Benjamin F. Butler, cited, 477
Proctor, Redfield, 475
Proctor, Thomas R., 462
Providence (R. I.) *Journal,* 461
Prussia, 468
Pruyn, Robert H., 480
Pryor, Roger Atkinson, 581
Pryor, Mrs. Roger Atkinson, *see* Pryor, Sara Agnes Rice
Pryor, Sara Agnes (Rice), 581
Pseudonymous letters, *see* LINCOLN, ABRAHAM, communications attributed to
Public lands, 435, 442, 444, 524
Pugh, Isaac C., 527
Pulliam, Lucy, 436
Pulliam, Martin G., 436
Pulliam, Mrs. Martin G., *see* Pulliam, Lucy
Purdy, Lovell, 478
Purkapile, John, 546
Purple, Norman Higgins, 439
Purviance, Samuel Anderson, 553
Pusey, Officer &, 460

Q

Quait, James L., 487
Quakers, 501, 504
Quincy (Ill.) *Whig,* 436, 440, 455

Quinlan, John, 466, 499
Quinlin, Michael, 533

R

Racey, John, 534
Racine (Wis.), 579
Rae, George W., 548
Rafael repeater gun, 515
Railroads, 443-45, 492, 538
Rainey, Josiah V., 556
Rains Gallery, catalog cited, 516
Ralph, ———, 463
Ramsay, George Douglas, 478, 525

Ramsay, Silas, 449
Ramsey, Alexander, 481, 490, 501, 503, 505
Randall, ———, 578
Randall, Alexander Williams, 489, 573
Randall, William Harrison, 537, 545
Randolph, William H., 449-50, 457
Rankin, Ira P., 482
Ranney, Nathan, 484

Rapp, Julius, 523
Rappahannock River, 490
Rauch, E. H., 464
Raybold, Augustus, 547
Raymond, Henry Jarvis, 508, 590
Reavis, Logan Uriah, 451
"Rebecca" letters, 440
Recollections of Abraham Lincoln
(Lamon), 590
Recollections of Rev. John Johnson,
438
Red River, 521
Red River of the North, 505
Redfield, Josiah C., 539
Redmond, Charles P., 558
Redwood, William H., Jr., 472
Redwood Falls (Calif.) Land Office,
587
Reece, J. E., 558-59
Reed, Benjamin N., 487
Reed, James H., 454
Reese, Henry Bickham, 582
Rehn, George F., 500
Reid, J. H., 458
Reiside, William, 576
Reitscher, August P., 569
Remann, Frederick, 446
Remington, Joseph, 496
Reminiscences of Abraham Lincoln
(Rice), 521, 528
Reminiscences of Peace and War
(Pryor), 581
*Reminiscences of Senator William M.
Stewart of Nevada*, 589
Remple, Ferdinand F., 487
*Report of the Committee of Arrange-
ments of the Common Council of
New York, of the Obsequies in
Memory of the Hon. Henry Clay*,
448
Republican clubs, 455, 457, 459
Reredel Corporation (New York),
463, 581
Revel, Emile, 541
Revel, Helen, 540-41
Reynolds, John, 457
Rhode Island, 461
Riblett, Henry, 449
Rice, Allen Thorndike, see *Reminis-
cences of Abraham Lincoln*
Rice, George, 546
Rice, Mrs. George, 546
Rice, James Clay, 516
Rice, John Hovey, 527, 542

Rich, D. A., 479
Richards, A. C., 506
Richards, Mrs. A. M., 577
Richards, John S., 488
Richards, P. D., 463
Richardson, B. H., 574
Richardson, F. A., 552
Richardson, J. A., 545
Richardson, James, 431
Richardson, John C., 463
Richmond, Thomas, 512
Richmond (Va.), 537-38, 569, 577,
580, 583, 588
Richstein, William F., 498
Rickard, Peter, 440
Ricketts, James Brewerton, 492
Ricks, J. W., 573
Riddle, Albert Gallatin, 541, 580
Ridlen, Samuel R., 567
Riley, Hugh F., 579
Rio Grande del Norte, 499, 511
Riotte, Charles N., 471
Ripley, Austin, 518
Ripley, James Wolfe, 479-80, 494, 497,
501, 514-16
Risley, David, 581
Risley, Jason P., 522
River and Harbor Convention (Chica-
go), 442
Rives, George W., 453, 456
Roaney, Thomas, 558
Roberts, Benjamin Stone, 534
Roberts, Charles, 464
Roberts, D. P., 454
Roberts, David M., 583
Robertson, Mrs., 526
Robinson, Christopher, 479
Robinson, G. J. F., 502
Robinson, William E., 584
Rochester (Ill.), 441
Rochester (N. Y.), 541
Rock Island (Ill.), 520-21, 531, 555,
565, 575, 578
Rock Island Register, 441
Rockford (Ill.), 519
Rockville (Md.), 444
Rockwell, Charles H., 506
Rockwell, John A., 447
Rodgers, John B., 515
Rodgers, Joshua H., 560
Rodgers, William H., 554
Rodriguez, ———, 491
Rodriguez, Mrs. A. C., 491
Rogan, L., 575

Rogers, ———, 525, 583
Rogers, Charles, 493
Rogers, Charles A., 562
Rogers, Mary D., 583
Rogers, R. B., 464
Rogers, Theodore, 545
Rollins, E. A., 530
Rome (Papal States), 469-70, 489, 502
Rompe, Eliza, 527
Root, Ira, 508
Rosamond [Ill.] Wide-Awake Club, 463
Rose, David G., 587, 589
Rosecrans, William Starke, 511, 516-18, 541, 548, 552-53, 560
Ross, Alexander Milton, 547
Ross, Harvey Lee, see *Lincoln's First Years in Illinois*
Ross, Leonard Fulton, 520
Ross, Wilkins, 579
Rossy, Alexander, 546
Rourke, Barney, 576
Row, Eli W., 583
Rowland, ———, 524

Rowley, George Augustus, 486
Royle Forum, The [Paterson, N. J.], 591
Royston, Mrs., 582
Ruckel, Jacob, 452
Rucker, William P., 555
Rucker, Mrs. William P., 555
Ruggles, James Monroe, 449
Rumsey, George D., 464
Ruppaner, Anthony, 576
Russell, Charles, 471
Russell, William H., 527
Russia, 470, 483, 489
Rutherford, Friend S., 453
Rutledge, Anna Mayes, 591
Rutledge, David Ham, 431
Rutledge, Robert, 463
Ryan, Daniel Joseph, see *Lincoln and Ohio*
Ryan, Edmund T., 522
Ryan, James, 518
Ryan, William, 451
Rynard, J. D., 474

S

St. Cecilia Society, 464
St. Clair County (Mich.), 587
St. Louis (Mo.), 476, 497, 508, 535, 563
St. Louis Globe-Democrat, 464
St. Louis Republic, 501
St. Marie Brass Band, 464
Sale, Thomas C. W., 457
Saline County (Ill.), 439
Salisbury (Ill.), 433
Salm-Salm, Félix, Prince de, 498
Salomon, Edward Selig, 512, 514
Salomon, Frederick, 520
Salter, G. H. Colton, 577
Samatano, Koedze, 486
"Sampson's Ghost" [pseud.], 434
Samuel, Edward M., 500, 555
Sanborn, Cyrus K., 486
Sandburg, Carl, see *Abraham Lincoln: The Prairie Years;* and *Abraham Lincoln: The War Years*
Sanders, Rufus K., 526
Sandford, Charles W., 554

Sands, Julia M., 476
Sandwich Islands, *see* Hawaiian Islands
Sanford, Henry S., 468
San Francisco (Calif.), 528
Sangamo Journal [Springfield], 432-42; see also *Illinois State Journal*
Sangamon County (Ill.), 434, 436, 445
Sangamon County Commissioners' Court, 432, 434-35
Sangamon County Temperance Union, 442
Sangamon River, 590
Sanger, L. P., 494
Sanitary Commission, 532, 536, 544
Santa Fe Railroad, 436
Santiago (Cuba), 586
Sapper, Mary, 552
Sargent, Henry A., 535
Sargent, Josiah M., 526
Saunders, Alvin, 582
Saunie, John, 515
Savannah (Ga.), 576, 585, 587-88

Savannah (Tenn.), 488
Savannah (ship), 472
Savitz, George F., 507
Sawyer, James, 522
Sayel, David A., 526
Saylor, Steward, 546
Scammon, Jonathan Young, 449, 576
Scates, Walter Bennet, 589
Schaase von Lex Ramp, Herman, 555
Schaeffer, George A., 474
Schenck, Robert Cumming, 468, 574, 583
Schindel, Jacob A., 510
Schoen, G., 500
Schofield, George Wheeler, 558
Schofield, John McAllister, 508, 532
Schools, land grants for, 436
Schurz, Carl, 460, 463, 469, 481, 490, 492, 494, 521, 549-50
Schurz, Mrs. Carl, see Schurz, Margarethe (Meyer)
Schurz, Margarethe (Meyer), 489
Schuylee, Henry, 528
Schwindler, William H., 567
Scott, A. W., 554
Scott, Thomas A., 479
Scott, Winfield, 448, 466, 474, 483
Scott County (Ill.), 443
Scott's Index, 542
Scovel, James M., 537
Scripps, John Locke, 564, 566
Searle, George W., 456
Sears, Charles, 570
Sears, James, 570
Secessionists, 499
Segar, Joseph Eggleston, 537
Seitz, Don Carlos, see Lincoln the Politician
Selden, James, 585
Sellers, Agnew, 567
Seminole Indians, 484
Senate, U. S., 469, 473, 484, 490, 494-95, 506, 512, 531, 535, 537, 541, 550, 576-78, 584
Seneca (Md.), 444
Servant, Richard B., 449
Sessler, Charles, 591
Seward, Frederick William, 484, 517, 579
Seward, William Henry, 468, 474, 477, 497, 502, 542; L. writes to, 465, 478-82, 484-87, 491, 493-95, 497, 501-502, 506-507, 509, 511, 515, 523, 527, 530, 535-36, 538, 541, 544-45,

550, 556, 568, 571-74, 576-82, 584-85, 587; writes for L., 469, 471, 481, 486, 493-94, 497, 502, 506, 576
Seymour, Horatio, 546
Seymour, Silas, 560
Shafer, ———, 514
Shaffer, Chauncey, 496
Shaler, Alexander, 570-71
Sharp, Edward Everett, 484
Sharpe, John, 560
Sharretts, Grayson W., 522
Shaver, A. G., 473
Shawneetown (Ill.), 438
Sheffield [England] Foreign Affairs Committee, 511
Shehan, James B., 535
Shelby, I., 447
Shelby Springs (Ky.), 582
Shelbyville (Ill.), 438
Shelbyville (Ind.), 466
Sheldon, Theodore, 465
Shellabarger, Samuel, 495, 585
Shepard, Elliott F., 464
Shepherd, Charles L., 566
Shepherd, Frank P., 566
Shepherd, Levin W., 498
Sheppard, Furman, see The Constitutional Text-Book
Sheppard House (Nashville, Tenn.), 583
Sheridan, Philip Henry, 555
Sherman, B. F., 477
Sherman, Charles E., 562
Sherman, John, 493, 585
Sherman, Thomas West [?], 478
Sherman, William Tecumseh, 473, 536, 557
Sherwood, Lorenzo, 546
Shick, G., 521
Shipley, Joshua H., 572
Shockey, A. H., 555
Shockley, Isaac, 579
Shoemaker, John H., 534
Shoemaker, T. F., 507
Shoup, Samuel N., 461
Shurtliff, R. N., 495
Sickles, Daniel Edgar, 477-78, 550
Sigel, Franz, 493, 540, 542
Silvey, James, 515
Simmons, Pollard, 434
Simms, George, 570
Simpson, Alexander, see Sympson, Alexander
Simpson, Alfred, 570

Simpson, Charles M., 584
Sioux Indians, 503-505, 511, 551
Skinner, Hestor, 551
Skinner, Ozias C., 457
Skinner, Thomas, 551
Skinner, W. I., 505
Slaght, James C., 558
Slaughter, Mary, 564
Slaughter, Mrs. John F., see Slaughter, Mary
Slavery, 434, 443, 445, 481-82, 513, 532, 535
Slingerland, John I., 444
Slingluff, Samuel, 518
Slipper, Joseph Augustus, 516
Sloan, Frank W., 522
Sloan, H. P., 454
Sloat, Ransom, 573
Slocum, Henry Warner, 533
Smead, Alexander Dallas Bache, 523
Smelt, Stephen, 588
Smelt, Thomas, 588
Smith, ———, 475
Smith, Mrs., 536
Smith, Aaron P., 560
Smith, Abraham, 454
Smith, Abraham D., 469
Smith, Andrew Jackson, 549, 573
Smith, Annie M., 519
Smith, Ben, 591
Smith, Caleb Blood, 470, 473, 478, 490, 505
Smith, Charles Ferguson, 483
Smith, Charles H., 493
Smith, C[lark] M[oulton] & S. (Springfield), 457
Smith, Daniel, 543
Smith, E. A., 526
Smith, E. Delafield, 519
Smith, E. O. [A.?], 447
Smith, Mrs. E. W. Easby, 530
Smith, Felix, 563
Smith, Fitzhugh, 513, 515
Smith, G. Rush, 522
Smith, George B., 509, 569
Smith, George F., 464, 469
Smith, George W., 438, 514
Smith, Green Clay, 529, 545
Smith, J. C. (N. Y.), 471
Smith, James, 553
Smith, James Youngs, 517, 548, 565
Smith, Job, 591
Smith, John C., 475, 479, 483

Smith, Joseph (naval construction commissioner), 490
Smith, Margaret, 543
Smith, Mrs. Melancthon, see Smith, Annie M.
Smith, P. Frazer, 545
Smith, Richard B., 562
Smith, Robert (Ill.), 473
Smith, Mrs. Thomas, 563
Smith, Thornton, 533
Smith, Truman, 524
Smith, Walton J., 487, 495
Smith, Willson G., 515
Smith Island (Va.), 557
Smithers, Nathaniel Barratt, 573
Snell, Jason D., 538
Snethen, Worthington G., 465, 476
Snider, Joseph, 529
Soldier vote, 538, 565
"Solidified Greek Fire" (weapon), 513
Somers, Claudius B., 585
Somers, Mathew, 510
Somers, William, 493
Sommers, Andrew J., 561
Sorby, Mary T., 513
Soulé, Frank, 528
South Carolina, 555, 577, 581-82
South Fork Schoolhouse [Sangamon Co., Ill.], 442
Southwick, John H., 485
Spain, 468-69, 498, 513
Spalding, Hillary C., 512
Spaulding, Annie, 562
Spaulding, Edward J., 562
Spaulding, Elbridge Gerry, 463
Spear, Isaac P., 433
Speed, Fanny (Henning), 439
Speed, James, 482, 504, 559, 564, 569-89
Speed, John J., 481
Speed, Joshua Fry, 439-40, 481
Speed, Mrs. Joshua Fry, see Speed, Fanny (Henning)
Speed Art Museum (Louisville), 442
Spence, William, 540
Spencer, J. A., 465-66
Spillman, Arabella, 574
Spinner, Francis Elias, 482
Sprague, William, 468, 475, 579
Spring, E., 465
Spring, Sydney, 455
Spring Creek [Ill.], 435
Springfield (Ill.), 431-42, 446, 448, 450-52, 457, 459-61, 463, 565, 590-91

Springfield & Alton Turnpike Road Company, 439
Springfield Land Office, 446
Springfield Mechanics' Union, 439
Sproul, ———, 492
Spurlock, ———, 565
Squier, Ephraim George, 511
Stackpole, Thomas, 478
Stanelsfield, E. C., 542
Stanford, Leland, 491
Stanifer, Simeon, 564
Stanley, Charles C., 562, 574
Stanly, Edward, 498
Stanton, Edwin McMasters: 471, 483-589, 591; writes for L., 485-86, 489-95, 509, 511, 515-16, 546
Stanton, Frederick Perry, 587
Staples, David K., 534
Starkweather, John Converse, 563
Starling, Lyne, 554
Starr, John Farson, 558
Staton, Daniel M., 561
Stealy, George J., 472
Stedman, J. O., 537
Steele, Frederick, 482, 551, 567
Steele, John, 546
Steever, Henry K., 550
Steiger, William, 479
Stein, Benjamin F., 465
Steinbach, Julia, see Stinbach, Julia
Steinburgh, Thomas, see Sternbergh
Stembel, A. G., 535
Stephens, Alexander Hamilton, 460
Stephens, Miss E. E., 515
Stephens, George, see Decker, Reuben
Stephens, James, Jr., 488
Stephens, William N., 516
Sterett, Samuel, 562, 565, 580
Sterling, A., 557
Sterling (Ill.), 450
Stern, Edward, 580
Sternbergh, Thomas, 543
Steuben County (N.Y.), 486
Stevens, Curtis, 561
Stevens, Henry, 435
Stevens, John A., Jr., 511
Stevens, John M., 522
Stevens, S., 550
Stevens, Thaddeus, 510, 552
Stewart, Alexander T[urney], & Company (New York), 474
Stewart, Andrew, 561
Stewart, J. A., 574
Stewart, James, 557

Stewart, Lorenzo C., 539
Stewart, William D., 518
Stewart, William Morris, 589
Stiger, Joseph L., 535
Stillwell, Thomas Neal, 587
Stinbach, Julia, 581
Stipp, George Winfield, 524-25
Stirling, Archibald, Jr., 571
Stirling, Douglas, 488
Stocionski, David, see Finks, Morris
Stockton, John P., 469
Stoddard, William Osborn, 523, 558
Stokes, William B., 568
Stone, ———, 486
Stone, Charles Pomroy, 490
Stone, James M., 586
Stone, Margaret (Ritchie), 517
Stone, Preston, 551
Stone, Robert K., 517
Stone, Mrs. Robert K., see Stone, Margaret (Ritchie)
Stone, W. F., 464
Storer, Bellamy, 567
Stormant, D. W., 571
Stoughton, Edwin Henry, 527-28
Stover, John Hubler, 559
Straat, John Nicholas, 501
Strachan, William R., 521
Stransky, John, 572
Stratton, John Leake Newbold, 564
Streeter, S. F., 504
Streeter, Thomas W., 541
Strickland, Edward P., 563
Stringer, A. P., 558
Stringham, Silas Horton, 583
Strobeck, Peter, 560
Strong, William Kerly, 479
Stuart, George Hay, 500, 513, 524
Stuart, John Todd, 432, 436, 527
Stuart, Mrs. John Todd, see Stuart, Mary Virginia
Stuart, Joseph G., 521
Stuart, Mary Virginia (Nash), 527
Stuart, W. E., 456
Stuart & Lincoln (Springfield), 439
Sturgis, Samuel Davis, 512
Sturtevant, Julian Monson, 443, 529
Sub-treasury system, 435-36
Suelson [Luelson?], James M., 578
Sugar Creek [Ill.], 433, 435
Sullivan, George M. [alias Michael Gardiner], 531
Sullivan, Henry V., 473
Sullivan, Jeremiah Cutler, 584

Sullivan, Thomas C., 537
Sullivan (Ill.), 455
Sumner, Charles, 467, 495, 497, 507, 518, 566, 570, 573-74
Supreme Court (Ill.), 439, 450
Supreme Court (U.S.), 471
Sutcliffe, John, 555
Sutin, A., 497
Sutton, Robert M., 580
Swangel, Benjamin F., 573
Swann Auction Galleries, catalogs cited, 455, 464
Swayne, Noah Haynes, 504, 557
Sweat, Peter, 489
Sweden and Norway, 468, 470, 528
Sweeney, Joseph, 557

Sweet, F. G., catalogs cited, 481, 483, 489
Sweet, Forest H., catalogs cited, 482-83, 502, 536
Sweitzer, Nelson Bowman, 479
Sweney, Thomas William, 481
Swenson, ——, 553
Swett, Leonard, 460, 478, 483, 558
Swift, Henry A., 575
Swift, John C., 534-35
Switzerland, 467
Sydenham, Moses H., 582
Sympson, Alexander, 579
Syntax of the Greek Language (Nielson), 590
Sypher [Syphus?], J. R., 522, 542

T

Taber, Thaddeus V., 492
Tackaberry, William G., 477
Taffe, John, 458
Taimer, Henry, 475
Talbott, Benjamin, 434
Talcott, Thomas B., 449
Tama County (Iowa), 458
Tappan, ——, 591
Tarbell, Ida Minerva, see *The Life of Abraham Lincoln*
Tariff, 441
Tarkington, John S., 503
Tatro, Peter, Jr., 570
Tatro, Talmer, 570
Taylor (Mrs.), 485
Taylor, Amos, 517
Taylor, Dick, 483
Taylor, Edmund Dick, 570
Taylor, Emaline (Johnson), 432
Taylor, Hawkins, 431, 455
Taylor, Joseph Pannel, 496, 498, 501, 540
Taylor, Robert F., 576
Taylor, Stuart M., 515
Taylor, William, 432
Taylor, Mrs. William, see Taylor, Emaline (Johnson)
Taylor, Zachary, 447
Tazewell County (Ill.), 441, 443, 445
Tazewell Whig [Tremont], 442
Teasa, Leander, 543

Temperance, 430, 435, 442
Temple, John B., 495
Ten Eyck, John Conover, 494, 512, 559, 576
"Ten Things You Cannot Do" (spurious), 591
Tennessee, 486, 498, 541, 583
Terre Haute (Ind.), 566
Terry, Alfred Howe, 523, 543
Terry, E. S., 566
Terwiliger, James H., 570
Tevis, Washington Carroll, 544
Texas, 506, 516, 534, 553, 577
Thanksgiving, spurious quotation on, 591
Thayer, Charles, 586
Thayer, Charles F., 485
Thayer, Mrs. Charles F., 485
Thayer, F. W., 482
Thayer, Martin Russell, 472, 583
Thayer, William H., 534
Thayer, William S., 470
Thirteenth Amendment to the Constitution, 579, 589
Thomas, C. M., 536-37
Thomas, Francis, 486
Thomas, Franklin, 543, 560
Thomas, George C., 480
Thomas, George Henry, 542
Thomas, J. W., 589
Thomas, Jesse Burgess, Jr., 438

Thomas, John Lewis, Jr., 571
Thomas, Lorenzo, 472, 474-75, 479-86, 488-89, 491-92, 494-95, 497, 502-503, 506, 508-509, 514, 516, 520, 522, 539-41, 545, 547-48, 550-51, 554, 557-60, 562, 568-69, 579, 581, 591
Thomas, William, 577, 579, 583
Thomas, William B., 513, 536
Thomasson, Charles L., 482
Thomasson, William Poindexter, 482
Thompson, Andrew, 526
Thompson, Egbert, 501
Thompson, Francis B., 443
Thompson, Horace B., 477
Thompson, James, 531
Thompson, James Kaster, 527
Thompson, Maria L., 575
Thompson, Philo Hale, 446
Thompson, Richard Wigginton, 462, 564, 566, 569
Thompson, Richard Wigginton, Jr., 549-50
Thompson, William, 510
Thornell, Thomas L., 463
Thornton, Anthony, 453
Thorpe, Thomas B., 590
Thurber, Mrs. H. A., 496
Thurber, W. H., 555, 557
Tillman, J. W., 466
Tisler, C. C., see *Lincoln's Ottawa*
Tod, David, 485
Todd, ———, 588
Todd, George W., 543
Todd, John Blair Smith, 470, 477, 511, 547, 549
Todd, Jonathan, 504
Todd, Robert Smith, 445
Todd, William A., 507
Todhunter, Lewis, 582
Tolono (Ill.), 455
Tolson, Betsy, 577
Tompkins, William Wright, 488
Toney, Lawrence, 519
Topeka (Kans.) Land Office, 571
Toplis, Fleetwood C., 561
Totten, James, 483
Totten, Joseph Gilbert, 472, 482, 485, 488, 502, 518, 528-29
Toulon (Ill.), 456
Townsend, Edward Davis, 509, 565, 572
Tracy, Frank W., 454
Tracy, Gilbert Avery, see *Uncollected Letters of Abraham Lincoln*

Tracy, William W., 527
Treat, Samuel Hubbel, 586
Tremont (Ill.), 444
Trenton (N. J.), 544
Tripoli, 472
Troops, specific cavalry units:
  Illinois
    15th Regt., 563
  Maryland
    3d Regt., 544
  New York
    8th Regt., 526, 569
    16th Regt., 564, 566
  Pennsylvania
    18th Regt., 563
  United States
    2d Regt., 484
    4th Regt., 482
    5th Regt., 484
Troops, specific infantry units:
  Delaware
    4th Regt., 502
  Illinois
    15th Regt., 510
    16th Regt., 584
    43d Regt., 565
    88th Regt., 565
    114th Regt., 563
  Indiana
    12th Regt., 491
    19th Regt., 514
    20th Regt., 491
  Massachusetts
    19th Regt., 515
  Missouri
    2d Regt., 478
  New York
    5th Regt., 522
    18th Regt., 476
    28th Regt., 571
    37th Regt., 484
    61st Regt., 504, 517
    86th Regt., 507
  Ohio
    5th Regt., 588
    12th Regt., 538
    42d Regt., 568
    147th Regt., 553
  Pennsylvania
    4th Regt., 501
    57th Regt., 563
    71st Regt., 507
    97th Regt., 504
    138th Regt., 527

187th Regt., 555
  Wisconsin
8th Regt., 517
  United States
2d Regt., 480
4th Regt., 484
Troops, specific units (other than cavalry and infantry):
  New York
Engineers, 15th Regt., 562, 563
Firemen's Zouave Regt., 475
  United States
Dragoons, 2d Regt., 571
Veteran Reserve Corps, 16th Regt., 571
Trowbridge, ———, 520
Troy, Thomas, 584
Troy (Kans.), 459
True Abraham Lincoln, The (Curtis), 591
Truett, Henry B., 435
Truex, William Snyder, 555
Trumbull, Benjamin M., 535, 585

Trumbull, Lyman, 450, 455, 465, 529, 542, 566
Tubman, Emily H., 530
Tucker, H. A., & Company, 457-58
Tuckerman, William S., 515
Tufts, Gardiner, 580
Tuller, H. W., 548
Tunis (Africa), 491
Turner, George, 559, 561
Turner, George Lemuel, 539
Turner, P., 516
Turner, Thomas Jefferson, 454
Turpin, Edward A., 478
Tuscarora Indians, 552
Tuscola County (Mich.), 473
Tuthill, Anna, 573
Tuthill, H. G., 573
Tyler, Daniel, 544
Tyler, Erastus Barnard, 525, 537
Tyler, Mrs. John, *see* Tyler, Julia (Gardiner)
Tyler, Julia (Gardiner), 552, 559

U

Ulbrich, Charles F., 462
Ulrici, Emil, 580
Uncollected Letters of Abraham Lincoln (Tracy), 447, 452, 457, 460, 517
Uncollected Works of Abraham Lincoln (Wilson), 436-38, 440
Underhill, Isaac, 438
Underwood, John C., 553
Underwood, Warner L., 493-94
Union Art Galleries, catalog cited, 529
Union League of America, 566, 574

Union Pacific Railroad, 526, 530
Union Place Hotel (New York), 540
Union Relief Association (Md.), 504
Upton, Charles Horace, 509-10
Upton, Henry, 569
Urbana (Ill.), 448, 450-51, 455
Urbana Union, 448, 450-52
Usher, A. G., 581
Usher, John Palmer, 503, 521-22, 526, 531, 534-35, 537, 539, 547, 549, 551, 556, 570-71, 573, 577, 584-88
Utah Territory, 472, 544

V

Vallandigham, Clement Laird, 516
Van Allen, C., 567
Van Buren, Martin, 432, 435
Van Buren County (Ill.) [proposed], 433

Vance, John P., 567
Vandalia (Ill.), 441
Vandalia Free Press, 435-36
Van de Leuf, Paul Petrément, 587
Vandervoort, C. M., 545

Vandeveer, Horatio Middleton, 459
Vandever, William, 584
Van Dyke, E. A., 582
Van Dyke, Mrs. E. A., 582
Van Horn, Benjamin, 533
Van Horn, Burt, 499
Van Ness & Company (Springfield, Ill.) 457
Van Winkle, J. H., 497
Van Wyck, W. E., 495
Varsell's [Vansell's?] farm, 433
Venable, Mrs. V. E., 577
Venezuela, 478, 497, 552
Vermilion County (Ill.), 439
Vermont, 467
Vermont (Ill.), 456

Vernon, J. M., 553
Vicksburg (Miss.), 496, 554, 562, 568
Victor Emmanuel II, King of Italy, 470
Victoria, Queen of Great Britain, 468
Viele, Egbert Ludovicus, 506
Vincent, John P., 499
Virginia, 527, 538, 541, 576
Virginia (Ill.), 443
"Virginia Republican, A" [pseud.], 558
Vogdes, Israel, 519
Volkmar, William Jefferson, 528
Von Horn, John, 520
Voullaire, Seymour, 474
Vrooman, ———, 580
Vrooman, Andrew, 580

W

Wade, Benjamin Franklin, 485, 509, 523, 531
Wadsworth, Daniel, 443
Wadsworth, James Samuel, 501
Wagener, William, 582
Wagener, Mrs. William, 582
Wagner, Gustave, 503
Waite, ——— (judge), 564
Wakeman, Abram, 525
Waldron, George P., 511
Walford, W. H., 550
Walker, Benjamin P., 502
Walker, Harvey, 544, 575
Walker, John M., 450
Walker, L. H., 485
Walker, Pinckney H., 487
Walker, Robert James, 480, 511, 591
Walker, Samuel, 560
Walker, William, 454
Wall, ———, 477
Wallace, Edward, 476, 502
Wallace, George A., 538
Wallace, John M., 539
Wallace, Lewis ("Lew"), 554
Wallace, William (Ind.), 523
Wallace, William S., 446
Wallach, Richard, 481
Waller, George, 571
Waller, Samuel, 571
Wallis, Thomas O., 540
Walpole Galleries, 490, 520

Walter, John S., 537
Walton, Frederick A., 549
Walton, S. R. B., 558
War of 1812, 443
War of the Rebellion, A Compilation of the Official Records of the Union and Confederate Armies, 476, 488, 496, 502, 503, 505, 517, 521, 529, 565
War Papers 71, a Non Commissioned Officer's Interview with President Lincoln, 589-90
Warburton, George, 431
Ward, Frederick B., 543
Ward, Marcus Lawrence, 586
Ward, William, 471, 563, 579
Warren, see Harren, W.
Warren, Fitz-Henry, 513
Warren, William Augustus, 488, 548
Washburn, ———, 591
Washburn, Charles Ames, 510
Washburn, Israel, Jr., 591
Washburne, Elihu Benjamin, 450, 453, 461-63, 498, 540, 563, 589
Washington, George, 544
Washington, Reade Macon, 583
Washington (D. C.), 444, 473, 480, 485, 513-14, 516-17, 525, 544, 550, 559, 568
Washington (Ill.), 444
Washington (Ind.), 441

Washington Arsenal, 588
Washington Chronicle, 525, 528
Washington Star, 467, 532
Washington Territory, 470, 527, 588
Wasp, Jim (Indian), 588
Waterloo (Ill.), 438
Waters, Levin L., 574
Waters' Camp Ground (Ill.), 435
Watkins, John, Sr., 431
Watkins, Joseph, 431
Watkins, Louis Douglas, 537
Watkins, Silas, 431
Watson, ——, 508
Watson, Benjamin Franklin, 474
Watson, Elmo Scott, see *Illinois Wesleyan Story*
Watson, Peter H., 487, 490, 501, 511-12
Watson, Philip L., 587
Watson, W[illiam] W., & Son (Springfield), 450
Watts, —— (major), 476
Watts, George D. H., 504, 517
Watts, John Sebrie, 468-69
Waugh, James A., 585
Waukegan (Ill.), 461
Weaver, Mrs. H. E. [nee Steever], 550
Weaver, W. H., 526
Webb, Mrs., 526
Webb, David, 476
Webb, James Watson, 471
Webb, L. E., 584
Webster, Daniel, 435
Webster, Edwin Hanson, 564
Webster, Francis, 440
Webster, J. S., 580
Weeden, Lizzie S., 464
Week by Week in Springfield, (periodical), 448
Weems, Kent, 529
Weir, William, 448
Weisel, D., 550
Weisenfeldt, Moses & Company, 571
Weit, Henry J., 531
Welker, Martin, 465
Weller, John B., 469
Welles, Gideon, 467, 470-71, 479, 487, 490, 501, 505, 507, 512-13, 515, 517, 524, 526, 528, 534-35, 543, 557, 579, 584, 591
Welles & Company, 486
Wells, Gabriel, 510, 533
Wells, James Madison, 587

Wells, Richard A., 514
Welsbank, S. B., 502
Wenck, George A., 460
Wentworth, John, 453, 460-61, 587
Werninger, Alstorphius, Jr., 567
Wert, Henry, 454
West Point, 472, 474, 477-78, 484-85, 488, 502, 510, 518, 521-22, 525, 529, 541-42, 544, 549, 556-57, 560, 564, 569
West Urbana (Ill.), see Champaign
Westbrook, Theodoric Romeyn, 574
Westcott, William, 541
Wetherill, John W., 516
Wetterstedt, Nicholas G., Baron de, 470
Whaley, Kellian Van Rensalear, 520
Wharton, James E., 473
Wharton, Oliver Perry, 546
Whary, David, 431
Wheeler, Clark R., 464
Wheeler, William Almon, 497
Whig Party, 435-36, 438, 440-41
Whipple, John, 551
Whipple, Lizzie A., 489
White, Charles, 510
White, Chilton Allen, 582
White, Horace, 461
White, John Chester, 506
White, Joseph Worthington, 534
White, Lesley, 507
White, Nelson L., 580
White, Peter A., 471
White, William W., 542
White, Zack, 562
White House (New Kent, Va.), 492
White House (Washington), 473, 487
Whitehead, J., 561
Whiting, Billington [Benjamin] C., 494
Whiting, George C., 570
Whiting, J. de W., 547
Whiting, Justin Rice, 556
Whiting, Riley, 581
Whiting, William, 527
Whitney, Daniel H., 449
Whitney, Henry Clay, 456, 458; see also *Life of Abraham Lincoln;* and *Life on the Circuit with Lincoln*
Whitney, Joshua, 542
Whittier, Mrs. S. A., 576
Whittlesey, Eliphalet, 527
Whittlesey, Elisha, 487
Wickizer, John H., 456

Wickliffe, D. C., 569
Wickliffe, Mrs. D. C., see Wickliffe, Virginia C.
Wickliffe, Rhoda, 564
Wickliffe, Virginia C., 569
Widney, Theodore J., 503
Wigginton, William H., 578
Wilber, H., 566
Wilbur, John E., 515
Wilbur, Julia A., 505
Wilcox, Nathaniel Green, 447
Wilder, Abel Carter, 543
Wilder, Daniel S., 569
Wilder, Mrs. Daniel S., 569
Wilder, David, Jr., 462
Wilderman, John L., 563
Wilderness, battle of the, 586
Wiley, Henry H., 517
Wiley, William L., 478
Wilgus, John B., 578
Wilkinson, Ira O., 461, 521
Willard, Joseph, 472
Willard, Moses T., 486
Willard, Nathan, 570
Willard's Hotel (Washington), 467
William, see Johnson, William
William III, King of the Netherlands, 469
William I, King of Prussia, 468
Williams, Archibald, 435, 472
Williams, Charles W., 499
Williams, John Benson, 513
William, John N., 586
Williams, John W., 587
Williams, Robert, 513
Williams, Mrs. Robert, 513
Williams, Rufus King, 536
Williams, Samuel, 583
Williams, Samuel S., 476
Williams, Thomas (Pa.), 483
Williams, Thomas I., 512
Williams, John, & Company (Springfield), 457, 460
Williamsburg (Va.), 524
Williamson, Alexander, 459
Williamson, Mrs. J. M., 531
Williamson, Oliver, 552
Williamson, W. H., 561
Willoughby, W., 562
Willoughby (Ohio), 467
Wilmington (N. C.), 548
Wilmot, David, 461, 463
Wilmot, William H., 441
Wilson, —— (chaplain), 543

Wilson, —— (deserter), 544
Wilson, Edwin C., 466
Wilson, G. W., 463
Wilson, Henry, 516, 576
Wilson, James Falconer, 488
Wilson, John Moulder, 466
Wilson, John P., 585
Wilson, Rufus Rockwell, see Lincoln Among His Friends; and Uncollected Works of Abraham Lincoln
Wilson, William (Ill.), 479
Wiltberger, Emily, 588
Wimmer, Boniface, 517
Winchester (Ill.), 455
Winchester (Va.), 491, 513
Winfield Scott: the Soldier and the Man (Elliott), 466
Winson, Harvey D., 554
Winters, Will A., 575
Wintersmith, Robert L., 576
Wisconsin, 470, 500, 546
Wise, Peter, 561
Wistar, Isaac Jones, 511
Witham, John T., 535
Withers, Allen, 444
Witt, Alvin R., 509
Wittig, Frederick, 562
Wolcott, Alexander, 550
Wolf, Edmund, 520
Wolf, Francis M., 508
Wood, Bradford Ripley, 470
Wood, Fernando, 470, 498
Wood, Jonathan Dayton, 510
Wood, L. S., 551
Wood, Seth G., 489
Wood, T. T., 528, 543
Wood, Thomas John, 480
Wood, William C., 501
Woodbridge, Frederick Enoch, 527
Woodhull, Phebe W., 577
Woodruff, William E., 524
Woods, John R., 565
Woodson, Silas, 561
Woodyard, H. M., 478
Wool, John Ellis, 477, 481, 485, 490, 494-95
Woonsocket (R. I.), 461
Wooster, Charles H., 573
Working Woman's Relief Association, 552
Works of William Paley, The, 433
Wright, Hendrick Bradley, 479
Wright, Horatio Gouverneur, 569, 588
Wright, John Montgomery, 541

Wright, Joseph Albert, 468, 536
Wright, P. C., 547
Wright, Robert L., 569
Wright, Weldon E., 547
Writings of Abraham Lincoln, The
 (Lapsley), 461, 467

"Wurtz Accelerator," 525
Wyckoff, P., 459
Wyman, L. B., 480
Wynne, ———, 486
Wynne, Lewis B., 569

X · Y · Z

Xenia (Ohio), 467

Yates, Edward, 511
Yates, Richard (1818-1873), 445, 448,
 453, 496, 498, 504, 520-21, 533, 538,
 544, 546, 559, 563, 586
Yeaman, George Helm, 532, 584
Yerby, G. W., 580
Yoder, O. B., 536
Yorke, Louis Eugene, 552
Young, ———, 527
Young, Mrs., 527

Young, E. M., 583
Young, Francis G., 541
Young, J. R., 557
Young, Otto, 544
"Young Lady No. 2," 464
Yurann, Jason, 463

Zane, William, 570
Zerman, Juan Napoleon, 486
Zimandy, A. P., 473
Zimmer, William G., 589
Zurich (Switzerland), 564

LOCATION OF LINCOLN DOCUMENTS

IN INSTITUTIONS

A

Abraham Lincoln Association, Springfield, Ill. (ISLA), references to photostats, facsimiles, and transcripts of documents in The Association files which were transferred to the Illinois State Historical Library on Dec. 31, 1952:

I: 15, 19 (2), 20, 37, 51, 93, 122, 143, 153, 195, 200, 233, 263 (2), 264, 267, 286, 307, 319, 328, 330, 336, 348, 352, 353, 355, 371, 380 (2), 391, 405, 451, 453 (2), 467, 477, 518

II: 18, 24, 45, 52, 56, 63, 77 (2), 94, 105, 110, 113, 114, 160, 193, 206, 210 (2), 219, 228, 234, 284, 286, 294, 307, 325 (2), 326, 330, 348, 358, 376, 379, 382, 383, 388, 389, 396, 410, 413, 414, 423, 424, 427 (2), 429, 431, 446, 456, 472, 482, 523, 524, 531, 532, 535 (2), 538 (2)

III: 85, 330, 332, 338, 341, 343 (2), 344, 347 (2), 348, 349, 381, 385, 388, 391, 399, 463, 491, 506, 554

IV: 37, 47, 52, 53, 54 (2), 57, 69, 73, 75, 78, 82, 93, 100, 103, 112, 115, 116, 117, 118, 120 (2), 122, 128, 156, 158, 178, 181, 231, 278, 288, 294, 297, 300, 301, 324, 326, 327, 329 (2), 333, 346, 349, 355, 356, 360, 376, 385, 390, 392, 399, 406, 409, 413, 442, 443, 447, 448, 456, 469, 471, 472, 476, 483, 494, 501, 515, 526, 535, 536, 543, 551, 556, 559

V: 9, 11, 21, 60, 65, 67, 68, 71, 88, 93, 108, 112, 115, 125, 129, 131, 143, 159, 171, 174, 202, 203, 217, 225 (2), 226, 253, 283, 326, 342, 348, 364, 380 (2), 386, 404, 429, 439, 449, 458, 480, 485, 489, 508, 538

VI: 20, 22, 28, 33, 44, 46, 49, 55 (2), 63, 70 (2), 75, 77, 78, 93, 94, 96, 99, 113, 115, 116, 128, 129, 134 (2), 140, 143, 146, 155, 165, 170, 175, 176, 185, 193, 196, 201, 219, 228, 236, 238, 239, 274, 276, 292, 293, 295, 312, 343, 355, 363, 380, 389, 397, 400, 427, 433, 438, 463, 472, 477, 488, 495, 507, 514, 520 (2), 531

VII: 3, 4, 11, 12, 23, 25, 28, 65, 77, 81, 88, 89, 92, 96, 103, 106, 127, 129, 136, 140, 151, 153, 174, 178 (2), 180, 185, 189, 194, 200, 212, 215, 230, 248, 251, 260, 265, 278, 280, 287, 305, 306, 315, 326 (2), 335, 366, 369, 400, 403, 421, 427, 430, 451, 457, 460 (2), 467, 489, 492, 494, 495, 511, 516, 519, 525, 543

VIII: 16, 17 (2), 26, 28, 32, 36, 37, 57, 76, 83, 89, 103, 110, 127, 131, 154, 161, 175, 178, 179, 183, 185, 189 (2), 204, 237, 294, 301, 302, 309, 321, 324, 331, 337, 340, 367, 368, 369, 375, 376, 377, 382, 384, 385, 399, 409 (3), 410, 412, 413, 419, 420 (2), 423 (2), 427, 431 (2), 433, 451, 452, (6), 453, 457 (6), 458 (4), 459 (2), 460 (6), 461 (2), 462 (5), 463 (2), 464 (5), 465 (2), 466 (6), 472, 475, 476, 481, 487, 488, 489, 492, 497, 501, 510, 514, 515, 517, 521, 523, 526, 528, 536, 541, 554, 556, 563, 566, 572, 575, 581, 593 (2), 594 (2), 595

Adams County Historical Society, *see* Quincy and Adams County, Historical Society of

Allegheny College, Meadville, Pa. (PMA), IV: 55; VI: 81

American Academy of Arts and Letters, New York City, II: 46
American Swedish Historical Museum, Philadelphia, V: 196
Annmary Brown Memorial Library,

Providence, R. I. (RPAB), V: 59, 93; VI: 361; VII: 295, 333
Aurora (Ill.) Historical Society, II: 314

B

Beloit (Wis.) Historical Society, VIII: 150
Berea (Ky.) College (KyBC), II: 107
Berkshire Museum, Pittsfield, Mass., VII: 491
Boston Public Library (MB), V: 268; VIII: 512
Brookline (Mass.) Public Library VIII: 548
Brown Memorial Library, see Annmary Brown Memorial Library
Brown University, Providence, R. I. (RPB), I: preceding page 1, 37, 152, 329, 355, 498; II: 15, 23, 50, 66, 72, 109, 161, 313, 327, 381, 413, 423, 456; III: 376, 383, 390, 492, 518, 519

IV: 31, 49, 68, 131, 134, 140, 145, 287, 298, 320, 326, 328, 348, 350, 381, 396, 399, 402, 403, 454, 459, 472, 493, 498, 503, 505, 511, 518, 527, 529, 552, 553

V: 20, 59, 64, 79, 83, 149, 156, 157, 159 (2), 172, 173, 174, 178 (2), 180 (2), 182, 184, 188, 189, 192, 195, 200, 202, 203, 207, 212, 216 (2), 217, 218, 225, 227, 231 (2), 232 (2), 233 (2), 234 (2), 235, 238 (2), 240 (2), 243, 244, 245 (2), 246 (2), 247 (2), 248 (3), 249 (2), 250 (2), 251 (2), 252 (3), 254, 255 (2), 256, 257, 258 (2), 259, 260, 261, 263 (2), 264 (3), 265, 268, 269, 274, 275, 276 (3), 277, 278, 279, 280, 288, 289 (2), 291, 293, 294, 295, 296, 301, 302 (2), 304, 305 (2), 313 (2), 315, 321 (2), 322, 323, 335, 347, 353, 357, 358, 364, 366, 367, 368, 369, 376 (2), 377 (3), 378, 379, 381, 384, 385, 386, 387, 392, 393, 394, 395, 397 (2), 398 (2), 400 (2), 401, 402, 408, 409 (3), 410,

412, 413, 415, 416, 417, 418, 419, 425, 426 (2), 427, 428 (3), 431, 452, 453, 454, 456, 457, 458, 459, 465 (3), 466, 471, 482, 484, 486, 487, 490, 497 (3), 499 (3), 514, 517, 544, 545, 546, 548

VI: 2, 6 (2), 7, 9 (2), 10, 20, 21, 26, 39, 43 (2), 48, 53, 82, 83, 84 (2), 86, 88, 90, 101, 103, 104, 111, 115, 117, 119, 126, 131, 137, 138, 142, 148 (2), 168, 170, 175, 185 (2), 186, 189, 191, 193, 194 (2), 195, 196, 200, 207, 210, 211, 215, 216, 218, 219, 224 (2), 225 (2), 226, 229 (2), 231, 232, 233, 234, 235, 236, 237, 238, 241, 244, 248, 252 (2), 254 (2), 255, 274, 275 (2), 279 (2), 283 (3), 285, 286, 287 (2), 289, 292, 293, 295 (2), 296, 298, 299 (3), 310, 311, 312, 314 (2), 317 (2), 319, 321 (2), 322 (2), 323 (2), 325, 326, 329 (2), 330, 331, 333, 337, 344, 346, 350, 353, 361, 362, 363, 366, 369, 370, 378, 382, 387, 388, 389, 392, 393, 394 (3), 395, 399 (2), 402, 403, 415, 417, 418 (2), 419, 420, 422, 423, 424 (2), 425, 427, 430, 434 (2), 435, 436, 439 (3), 442, 443, 444, 449, 450, 453, 459, 461, 462, 463, 464, 466, 470 (2), 472, 473 (2), 474 (2), 475, 476, 480, 482 (2), 483, 484, 485, 486, 488, 489, 491, 493, 494, 495 (2), 498 (2), 505, 511 (2), 512 (2), 513 (2), 514, 515 (2), 517, 518, 521, 522 (3), 524, 525 (3), 528, 529, 530, 531, 532, 537, 543, 545, 550, 552, 553 (2), 554 (2), 556, 562 (2)

VII: 4, 6, 7, 8, 9, 10 (2), 12, 13, 14 (2), 15, 26, 29 (3), 30, 34, 59 (2), 60, 61, 62, 67, 68, 75, 80, 82, 83, 87, 91, 93, 94, 96, 98 (2), 101, 103 (3),

106, 109, 112, 118, 121, 122 (2), 127,
130, 134, 137, 138 (2), 142, 143, 148,
150, 151, 153, 156, 157, 158, 160, 163,
167, 173, 175, 176, 177, 180, 182, 183,
185, 190, 191, 194 (2), 196 (2), 198,
199, 201, 203, 205, 206, 208, 212, 213,
219, 220, 221, 222, 226, 232, 261, 264,
275, 277, 281, 356, 399, 442, 444, 447,
473, 478, 496, 525, 533, 534
  VIII: 19, 24, 35, 51, 87, 103, 174,
175, 186, 214, 220, 225, 231, 241, 255,

266, 328, 340, 343, 416, 417, 418 (2),
423, 424, 442 (2), 462 (3), 463, 464,
466, 473 (3), 478, 479, 488, 500, 504
(2), 505, 507, 519, 520, 529 (2), 533,
536, 543 (2), 548, 563, 567, 573, 574,
580
Buffalo (N.Y.) Historical Society
  (NBuHi), IV: 326; V: 360, 385;
  VIII: 462
Bureau County (Ill.) Records, Princeton, III: 352

C

California, Archives and Central Record Depository, Sacramento, VII:
  215
Carnegie Institute Museum, Pittsburgh, IV: 340
Case Institute of Technology, Cleveland, Ohio (OCLCS), III: 513
Chase National Bank (NYC), VIII:
  489
Chicago, University of, see University
  of Chicago Library
Chicago Historical Society (ICHi), I:
  preceding page 1, 138, 139, 141 (2),
  146, 291, 305, 342, 345, 357, 360,
  416, 445; II: 100, 194, 211, 328, 436,
  473, 531; III: 381, 508, 514, 515;
  IV: 30, 144, 149, 159, 171, 184, 412;
  V: 193, 549; VI: 41, 107, 231, 246,
  279, 374, 376, 388; VII: 355, 513;
  VIII: 285, 292, 328, 392, 465, 592
Clark County Historical Society,
  Springfield, Ohio (OSHi), VIII: 27

Clements Library, see William L.
  Clements Library
Colorado, State Historical Society of,
  Boulder (CoHi), VIII: 356
Colorado, University of, see University
  of Colorado Library
Columbia University Library, New
  York City (NNC), I: preceding page
  1, VII: 74, 333, 495
Concord (Mass.), Free Public Library
  of (MCon), VIII: 95
Connecticut Historical Society, Hart-
  ford (CtHi), VII: 450; VIII: 170,
  479
Connecticut State Library, Hartford
  (Ct), IV: 338; VI: 212
Connecticut Valley Historical Society,
  Springfield, Mass. (MSHi), VIII:
  463, 465
Cornell University Library, Ithaca,
  N.Y. (NIC), I: 493; VII: 22, 440,
  521

D

Davenport (Iowa) Public Museum
  (IaDaM), I: 446; II: 348; VIII: 444
Delaware Historical Society, Wilming-
  ton (DeHi), V: 495

Detroit (Mich.) Public Library
  (MiD), II: 207
Dropsie College Library, Philadelphia
  (PPDrop), V: 212

E · F · G

Emerson Foundation, *see* Fred L. Emerson Foundation

Essex Institute, Salem, Mass., VIII: 515

Evansville (Ind.) Public Museum, IV: 131

Fayette County (Ky.) Records, II: 195, 204

Ford's Theatre, *see* Lincoln Museum

Fred L. Emerson Foundation, Auburn, N. Y. (NAuE), IV: 86, 127, 148, 149, 157, 164, 170, 173, 176, 183, 248, 273, 276 (2), 277, 280, 281, 283 (2), 285, 293, 297, 334, 337, 348, 353, 355, 359, 397 (2), 420, 475, 478, 494, 504, 521, 536, 538, 547, 551
    V: 5, 8, 62, 107, 147, 299, 383, 476; VI: 13, 174, 342, 388, 429,
459, 507; VII: 29, 188, 330, 334, 429, 434; VIII: 49, 102, 181, 195, 221, 243, 244, 251, 337, 412, 414, 426 (2)

Free Library of Philadelphia, *see* Philadelphia, Free Library of

Freeport (Ill.) Public Library (IFre), VIII: 415

Friends Library, Friends House, London, V: 92

Galesburg (Ill.) Public Library, II: 193

Grosvenor Library, Buffalo, N. Y. (NBuG), VII: 15

Guatemala, National Archives of, Guatemala City, VIII: 468

Guilford (N. C.) College Library (NcGu), VIII: 76

H

Hall of Records, *see* Maryland

Harvard University Library, Cambridge, Mass. (MH), I: 349, 351, 354, 356, 360, 366, 452, 497; II: 25, 53; IV: 178, 285; V: 28, 450, 488; VI: 232; VII: 35, 392; VIII: 53, 288, 334, 462, 464, 594

Haverford (Pa.) College Library (PHC), I: 422; II: 93; IV: 103, 485; VI: 433; VIII: 464, 482

Hawaii, Archives of, Honolulu, VIII: 408

Hayes Memorial Library, Fremont, Ohio (OFH), VI: 44; VII: 168; VIII: 50, 245

Hayner Library, *see* Jennie B. Hayner Memorial Library

Henry E. Huntington Library, San Marino, Calif. (CSmH), I: 44, 52, 78, 117, 154, 184, 228, 490, 498, 500; II: 16, 24, 46, 50, 67, 70, 109, 220, 317, 336, 343, 360, 386, 411, 427, 428, 430, 436, 459, 472; III: 327, 328, 345,
351, 356, 387, 391, 397, 495, 513, 521
    IV: 32, 34, 35, 38, 41, 46, 47, 56, 59, 68 (2), 70, 71, 74, 76, 77, 97 (2), 99, 102, 118, 122, 132, 136, 139, 146 (2), 150, 153, 160, 162, 184, 186, 292, 327, 348, 358, 366, 374, 386, 393, 395, 411, 416, 445, 454, 463, 496, 522, 542 (2)
    V: 2, 14, 30, 68, 72, 85 (2), 89, 104, 109, 127, 132, 139, 239, 247, 431, 472, 492, 500; VI: 44, 50, 58, 85, 104, 117, 120, 154, 158, 174, 180, 190, 256, 310, 386, 399, 466, 479, 542; VII: 2, 75, 80, 101, 142, 152, 189, 218, 261, 288, 324, 378, 415, 419, 461, 471, 530, 549
    VIII: 46, 75, 80, 82, 106, 123, 124, 131, 160, 193, 221, 248, 269, 317, 342, 347, 351, 354, 370, 375, 395, 419, 431, 436, 445, 448, 483, 506, 508, 513, 535

Hill School, Pottstown, Pa., II: 446; VI: 50

Illinois, University of, *see* University of Illinois

Illinois College Library, Jacksonville (IJI), VII: 388

Illinois State Auditor's Records, Springfield, III: 486

Illinois State Historical Library, Springfield (IHi), I: xxii, 3, 4, 13, 14, 17, 18, 21, 24, *facing* 25, 25, 26 (2), 47, 48, *facing* 48, *following* 48, 49, 51, 52, 54, 79, 80, 101, 107, 116 (2), 120, 121, 152, 153, 159, 209, 253, 264, 287, 288, 319, 327, 330, 340, 344, 346, 348, 350, 352, 381 (2), 395, 406, 418, 419, 420, 423, 430, 431, 446, 455, 458, 467, 478, 493, 500, 518
II: 22, 30, 31, 40, 42, 52, 53, 69, 73, 74, 75, 76 (2), 79, 101, 103, 104, 106, 107 (2), 110, 111, 159, 190, 191, 192, 194, 199 (2), 204, 205, 207, 209 (2), 217, 220, 287, 288, 292, 293 (2), 295, 304, 306, 308, 309, 312, 314, 328, 329, 330, 332, 340, 373, 380, 381, 388, 389, 412, 422, 426, 437, 444 (2), 447, 455, 458, 470 (2), 471, 475, 483, 502, 521, 523, 524, 532, 534, 536
III: 101, 144, 332, 333, 346, 348, 350, 374, 384, 385, 493, 510, 514, 516, 517, 518, 521
IV: 43, 77, 80, 86, 94, 95, 97, 99, 100, 103, 113, 121, 132, 133, 134, 136, 137, 142, 145, 146, 155, 159, 168, 175, 178, 184, 191, 217, 285, 296, 297, 302, 337, 345, 354, 355, 357, 362, 364, 370 (3), 372, 374, 381, 394, 396, 404, 406, 410, 418, 419, 442, 447, 457, 461 (2), 467, 472, 473, 480, 486, 490, 492 (2), 497, 498, 499, 501, 505, 507, 508, 515, 517, 522, 529, 530, 533, 535, 536, 539, 548, 549, 550, 555, 560, 562
V: 3, 7 (2), 11, 15, 23, 56 (2), 65, 66, 71, 76, 77, 79, 80, 85, 89, 92, 93, 103, 104, 111, 112, 117, 126, 130, 142, 148 (2), 154, 155, 162, 167, 169, 175, 179, 181, 183, 187, 191, 196, 206, 211, 219, 224, 253, 256, 257, 262, 263, 269, 277, 290, 297, 301, 303, 307, 317 (2), 320 (2), 322, 333, 334, 336, 347, 351, 364, 366, 367, 381, 390, 394, 396, 399, 402, 403, 405 (2), 408, 410, 411, 413, 426, 427, 430, 441, 447, 455, 457, 463, 465, 466, 469, 470, 472, 474 (2), 477, 479, 485, 491 (2), 495, 540 (2), 544, 547
VI: 5, 10, 19, 41, 56, 62, 63, 71, 72, 81, 83, 86, 90, 96, 98, 100, 107, 113, 118, 122, 126, 127, 129 (2), 130, 134, 136, 137, 144, 146, 149, 157, 161 (2), 169, 171, 187, 192, 194, 198, 199, 203, 212, 214, 219, 232, 235, 237, 238, 249, 253, 254, 255, 256, 260, 277, 283, 323, 325, 327, 339, 340, 352, 354, 362, 366, 383, 385, 386, 390, 403, 406, 414, 420 (2), 421, 423, 431, 434, 450, 452, 460, 465, 467, 469, 472, 474, 475, 477, 478, 482 (2), 483, 489, 504, 506 (2), 509, 510, 516, 537, 548, 550
VII: 11, 15, 16, 21, 32, 34 (2), 35 (3), 79, 89, 90, 94, 95, 97, 105 (2), 106, 109, 112, 114, 120, 123, 124, 131, 134, 138 (2), 141, 159 (3), 162, 167, 177, 186, 206, 217, 230, 245, 249, 253, 257, 276, 277, 289, 291, 293, 294, 299, 309, 314, 340, 353, 362, 363, 366, 367, 374, 378, 385, 386, 391, 401, 411, 418, 430 (2), 455, 470, 471, 486, 497, 513, 530, 537, 538, 547
VIII: 14, 30, 32, 35, 38, 74, 80, 81, 88, 92, 94, 95, 105, 106, 117, 121, 124, 128, 186, 192, 197 (2), 201, 203, 221, 224, 225, 238, 247, 252, 265, 290, 291, 300, 311, 322, 324, 326, 330 (2), 336, 349, 363, 366 (2), 385, 417, 429, 431 (2), 432 (2), 434, 440, 443, 450, 461, 462, 463, 472, 474 (2), 477, 479, 480, 481, 482, 483, 486, 487, 493, 494, 498 (2), 500 (2), 501, 503 (3), 504, 505, 507 (2), 509, 510 (2), 516, 520, 521 (2), 523 (3), 524, 525, 526 (2), 527 (2), 529, 530, 531, 532, 533 (2), 536, 542, 545, 554, 567, 569, 571, 577, 580, 595

The Library also has the originals of ,most of the Illinois newspapers cited; *see also* Abraham Lincoln Association.

Illinois State Library, Archives Division, Springfield (I-Ar), I: 26, 28

(3), 29, 30, 31 (2), 33 (2), 35 (2), 36, 39, 40 (2), 41, 42 (2), 43, 44 (2), 45, 46, 55, 57, 61, 70 (2), 71, 72 (2), 73 (2), 74, 76, 77, 80, 82 (2), 83, 84 (2), 86, 87 (2), 107, 122, 124, 125, 127, 137, 142, 145 (2), 147 (2), 155, 157 (2), 158, 180, 182, 183 (3), 185, 196, 197, 198 (2), 199, 200, 211, 213, 214, 218, 220, 232, 239 (2), 241, 284, 327, 343, 347, 349, 393, 394 II: 94, 161, 162, 188, 190, 326, 330, 394, 395, 414, 426, 436, 443; III: 335, 374; IV: 73, 92, 93; VIII: 437 (2), 439, 442
Illinois Supreme Court Clerk's Record, Springfield, VIII: 439

Indiana Historical Society, Indianapolis (InHi), IV: 410; VII: 144, 241, 277
Indiana State Library, Indianapolis (In), II: 63; IV: 534, 537, 541; VIII: 224, 334
Indiana University Library, Bloomington (InU), I: 151, 418, 448; V: 451; VII: 84
Iowa Masonic Library, Cedar Rapids (IaCrM), II: 414
Iowa State Department of History and Archives, Des Moines (IaHA), I: 322; III: 400; IV: 45, 93, 282 (2); V: 197, 352, 397; VI: 128, 547; VII: 440; VIII: 326

J · K

James Millikin University, Decatur, Ill. (IDecJ), II: 112
Jennie B. Hayner Memorial Library, Alton, Ill., I: 332
John Jermain Memorial Library, Sag Harbor, N. Y. (NSh), VIII: 53

John Scheide Library, Titusville, Pa., II: 349

Kalamazoo (Mich.) Public Library (MiK-M), II: 359
Kentucky, University of, *see* University of Kentucky Library

L

Library of Congress, Washington (DLC), I: xxii, 4, 259, 304, 367; II: 1, 38, 55, 57, 65, 66, 67, 93, 318, 336, 431, 443; III: 512

IV: 50, 83, 88, 95, 102, 115, 126, 127, 136 (2), 151, 155, 159, 165, 271, 282, 285, 286, 290, 298, 311, 327, 349, 350, 359, 372, 373, 388, 391, 400, 405, 408, 413, 448, 500, 504, 512

V: 10, 14, 35, 67, 71, 83, 106, 164, 176, 182, 185, 224, 228, 239, 286, 307, 309 (2), 327, 342, 348, 349, 350, 381, 382, 385, 407, 418 (2), 449, 451, 479, 492 (2), 493, 496, 510, 552; VI: 8, 22, 46, 67, 100, 153, 168, 198, 308, 313, 387, 490, 549

VII: 17, 18, 24, 59, 61, 192, 195, 205, 207, 208, 227, 229, 275, 292, 310, 321, 343, 347, 351, 354, 376, 428, 439, 486, 513, 514, 539; VIII: 3, 13, 74, 107, 118, 123, 125, 152, 179, 182, 208, 218, 229, 258, 310, 333, 351, 362, 366, 387, 389, 412, 413, 420 (2), 424, 425, 478, 479, 482, 505, 527 (2), 580, 591

Cameron Papers, III: 521; IV: 91, 168, 174, 273, 335, 369, 386, 392, 402, 407, 445, 446, 451, 462, 463, 467, 470, 480 (2), 486, 488, 489, 494, 495, 496, 500, 502, 504, 505, 509, 511, 514, 519, 525 (2), 530 (2), 555; V: 4, 8, 18, 19, 21, 23, 25, 28 (2), 55 (2), 61, 64 (2), 67, 80, 90, 96, 97; VII: 203, 289; VIII: 421

Herndon-Weik Collection, I: preceding page 1, 1, 21, 53, 150, 153, 285, 309, 319, 335, 455, 461, 479 (2), 498; II: 44, 119, 226, 331, 332, 374, 397, 469; III: 332, 355, 371, 374, 490 (2); IV: 32, 44, 81, 126, 281, 283; V: 379; VII: 258, 513; VIII: 166, 248, 431, 434 (2)

Robert Todd Lincoln Collection of the Papers of Abraham Lincoln, I: 24, facing 24, 301, 407, 431, 454, 473, 480, 501; II: 11, 25, 32, 37, 39, 40 (2), 41, 42, 44, 45 (2), 47, 53, 54, 221, 288, 299, 301, 388, 442, 445, 457, 522, 528; III: 203, 326, 328, 336, 337, 342, 363, 364, 377, 392, 425, 491, 506,

508, 509, 515, 517

IV: 34, 35, 49, 52 (2), 53, 60 (3), 101, 104, 108, 117, 119, 124, 129, 130, 131, 135, 137, 138 (2), 140, 144, 150, 153, 154, 163 (2), 167, 170, 172, 173, 175 (2), 177, 181, 182 (2), 186 (2), 187 (2), 188 (2), 191, 199, 201, 213, 246, 248, 249, 262, 277, 279, 285, 290, 291 (2), 292, 293, 295, 296, 299, 300, 301, 302, 304 (2), 309, 310 (2), 311 (2), 312, 313, 316, 317, 319, 322 (2), 324, 325 (2), 326, 327, 328 (2), 329, 331 (2), 333, 334, 335, 336, 338, 343, 344, 352, 354, 358, 365, 367, 368, 389, 394, 396, 404, 411, 413, 418 (2), 421, (2), 444, 446, 450, 452, 458, 464, 466, 477, 484, 486, 491, 497, 502, 506, 510, (2), 513 (3), 516, 518, 520 (2), 522, 524, 529, 533, 535 (2), 538, 542, 551, 553 (2), 556, 557, 558, 559, 561

V: 2, 3, 7, 9, 12, 13, 20, 23, 26, 31 (2), 32, 34, 54, 58 (2), 59, 60, 61, 64, 69, 75, 80, 81 (2), 82, 83, 86, 90, 92, 95, 96, 99, 106 (2), 108, 112, 113, 114, 116, 131, 132, 135, 146, 149, 153, 161 (2), 162, 163 (2), 164, 166, 168, 178, 180, 187, 196, 201, 203, 204, 206, 209, 223, 229, 237, 257, 273, 275, 285, 292, 296, 306, 309, 319, 320, 325, 328, 337, 340, 343, 346, 351, 352, 356, 362, 364, 365, 368, 370, 378, 382, 383 (2), 388, 391, 396, 400, 403 (2), 404, 405 (2), 437, 438, 439, 443, 444, 445, 448, 457, 458, 462, 463 (2), 467, 469, 470, 474, 477, 478, 491, 502, 503, 504, 505, 506, 507, 509, 512 (2), 515, 516 (2), 540, 548, 554

VI: 3, 13, 15 (2), 17, 18 (2), 20, 23, 24, 26, 30, 31, 32, 34, 37, 38 (2), 41, 42, 46, 49, 50, 52, 54, 56, 65, 66, 69 (2), 72 (2), 74, 76, 83, 85, 87, 94, 97, 99, 105, 108 (2), 109 (2), 113, 115, 118, 119, 120, 125, 126, 128, 130, 131, 137 (2), 139, 141, 145, 146 (2), 147, 149, 150, 151, 153, 154, 159, 161 (2), 163, 164, 165 (2), 167, 168, 170, 172, 177, 178, 182 (2), 183, 186, 187, 188, 189, 191, 192 (2), 195, 202, 208 (2), 217, 221 (2), 229, 234, 236, 238,

241, 243, 246, 251, 253, 257, 258 (2), 260, 270 (2), 276, 284, 286, 288, 289, 290, 291, 300, 307, 308, 313, 315, 328, 334, 338 (2), 340, 341, 344, 346, 348, 350, 351, 353, 354, 356, 359, 360, 366, 370, 372, 373, 374, 376, 378, 380, 382, 392, 396, 398, 399, 401, 402, 404, 406, 411, 413, 417, 423, 425, 426, 429, 432 (2), 438 (2), 440, 444, 463, 467, 468, 469, 471, 481, 485, 486, 493, 499, 505, 508, 514, 526, 527, 532, 533, 534, 538, 539, 542, 543, 544, 545, 552, 555, 557, 560

VII: 3, 5, 7, 9, 11, 14, 30, 32 (2), 36, 58, 62, 63 (2), 64 (2), 67, 71, 76, 81, 86, 97 (2), 107, 109, 110, 114, 117, 124, 126, 131, 135, 140, 146, 147, 161, 162, 168, 169, 174, 179, 181, 183, 185, 190, 191, 200, 204, 213, 214, 217, 218, 221, 223, 224, 227, 231, 235, 236 (2), 237, 242 (2), 243, 244, 247, 250, 251, 254, 260, 262, 264, 265, 266 (2), 268, 280, 282, 284, 285, 286, 287, 289, 295, 296, 299, 303, 318, 320, 324, 327, 328, 329, 330 (2), 333, 338, 339, 342 (2), 347, 350, 353, 354, 356, 360, 361, 368, 369, 372 (2), 374, 376, 380, 381, 386, 388, 399, 402 (2), 404 (2), 408 (2), 410, 413, 414, 417, 419, 420, 421, 431, 435, 440, 442, 443, 446 (2), 447, 451, 452, 453, 455, 457, 460, 461, 462, 479, 481, 482, 483, 486, 488, 490, 494, 496, 498, 501, 517, 519, 526, 527, 530, 535

VIII: 2 (2), 11 (2), 12 (2), 15 (2), 17, 18, 24, 26, 51, 73, 74, 77, 78 (2), 80, 90, 97, 104, 107, 114, 116, 121, 157 (2), 164, 174, 177, 178, 188, 190, 195, 197, 200, 202, 207, 212, 221 (2), 222, 227, 229, 231, 243, 251, 255, 261, 266, 267 (2), 271, 272, 274, 288, 295, 299, 306, 308, (2), 311, 318, 327, 339,

347, 348, 352, 354, 356, 364, 372, 381, 409, 445 (2), 446, (2), 452, 453 (2), 454, 457 (2), 458, 459 (2), 460, 461, 462 (2), 464, 466, 468 (2), 469, (3), 471 (2), 472 (2), 473, 478, 492, 507, 509 (2), 510, 512 (2), 513, 523, 527, 532, 534, 536, 541, 542, 554, 558, 563, 581

Stanton Papers, V: 99, 112, 119, 150, 151, 179, 207, 208, 209 (2), 236, 287, 313, 338, 349, 472, 488; VI: 100, 109, 130, 215, 335, 342, 382, 389; VII: 79, 104, 129, 179, 197, 199, 211, 254, 332, 393, 477, 482, 538; VIII: 91, 182, 307, 373, 513, 554, 555

Lincoln Memorial Shrine, Redlands, Calif., VI: 420

Lincoln Memorial University, Harrogate, Tenn. (THaroL), II: 23; IV: 85, 382, 416; V: 265, 368, 391, 447, 545; VI: 200, 370; VII: 25, 129, 164, 174, 203, 229; VIII: 82, 422, 424, 491

Lincoln Museum, Ford's Theatre, Washington (DLM), I: 53, 263; IV: 404; V: 369; VII: 325, 456, 489; VIII: 410

Lincoln National Life Foundation, Fort Wayne, Ind. (InFtwL), II: 92, 396; IV: 79, 83, 283, 475; VII: 344; VIII: 11, 36, 122, 342, 462, 464, 466, 478, 532

Litchfield (Conn.) Historical Society (CtLHi), VI: 163, 195

London, England, *see* Public Record Office

Long Island Historical Society, Brooklyn, N. Y. (NBLiHi), V: 102; VIII: 321

Los Angeles County (Calif.) Museum (CLCM), VII: 469

Louisiana State University Library, Baton Rouge (LU), VI: 368

M

Macalester College Library, St. Paul, Minn. (MnSM), VI: 426

McLean County Historical Society, Bloomington, Ill. (IBloHi), IV: 502; VIII: 451

Macon County (Ill.) Records, I: 2, 3

Maine Historical Society, Portland (MeHi), II: 29, 112; IV: 148, 512; V: 352; VI: 131, 405; VIII: 155

Marietta (Ohio) College Library

(OMC), III: 397

Marquette University, Milwaukee, Wis., I: 344

Maryland Hall of Records, Annapolis (MdAA), IV: 341; VI: 557

Maryland Historical Society, Baltimore (MdHi), VI: 141; VIII: 42

Mason County (Ill.) Plat Records, Havana, VIII: 433

Massachusetts Historical Society, Boston (MHi), I: 420, 516; II: 320; IV: 351; V: 26, 129, 361, 480; VI: 94; VII: 24, 168, 443

Michigan Historical Collection, University of Michigan, Ann Arbor (MiU-Hi), VII: 291

Millicent Library, Fairhaven, Mass. (MFai), I: 468

Millikin University, *see* James Millikin University

Minnesota Historical Society, St. Paul (MnHi), II: 286, 312; V: 173, 464, 541, 543; VI: 142; VII: 548

Missouri Historical Society, St. Louis (MoSHi), I: 181; II: 290, 332, 357, 425; III: 377, 515; IV: 281, 412, 479; V: 101, 502; VII: 528; VIII: 177

Missouri State Archives, Jefferson City, I: 88

Morgan County (Ill.) Commissioners' Records, Jacksonville, VIII: 433

Munson-Williams-Proctor Institute, Utica, N. Y., IV: 474; VII: 544; VIII: 462

N

National Archives, Washington:

Record Group 11, General Records of the United States Government, IV: 333, 339, 347, 354, 365, 402, 477, 483, 488, 540; V: 136, 186, 211, 223, 299, 341, 433, 437; VI: 30, 121, 157, 160, 179, 181, 204, 278, 333, 452, 479, 497, 524; VII: 73, 193, 270, 352, 427, 432, 434, 449, 504; VIII: 56, 84, 115, 172, 209, 253, 304, 350, 360, 397 (2), 398

Record Group 15A, Veterans' Administration, II: 108, 319

Record Group 26, United States Coast Guard, IV: 357

Record Group 45, Naval Records Collection, IV: 293, 321, 343, 389, 528, 548; V: 6, 341, 490, 496; VI: 36, 167, 183, 320, 349; VII: 532, 533; VIII: 182, 240

Record Group 46, United States Senate, IV: 288, 447, 464, 467, 470; V: 58, 73, 74 (2), 77, 88, 89, 102, 107, 109, 113, 115, 127, 132, 141, 146, 147, 161, 162, 176, 186, 189, 190, 191, 198, 219, 253, 260, 270, 282, 288, 299, 302, 307, 312, 315, 316, 325, 518, 539, 547 (2), 550 (2), 551, 552

VI: 10, 16, 19, 35, 36, 51, 62, 66, 69, 76, 79, 82, 92, 95, 96, 99, 102, 105, 109, 110, 116, 121, 122, 124; VII: 57 (2), 59, 70, 76, 77, 87, 88, 107, 123, 140, 143, 147, 160, 168, 169, 188, 198, 227, 228, 234, 241, 246, 247 (2), 266, 274, 311, 321, 323, 332, 339, 341, 365, 370, 380, 390, 394, 400, 415, 422

VIII: 135 (2), 136, 158, 204, 206, 250, 260, 271 (2), 286, 296, 297, 317, 329, 332, 346

Record Group 48, Interior Department, II: 47, 55; IV: 288, 297, 298, 303, 310, 311, 312, 320, 406, 456, 462, 498; V: 78, 262, 316, 354, 500; VI: 68, 69, 209, 232, 355; VII: 78, 225, 452, 465, 521; VIII: 34, 39, 89, 15, 193, 194, 225, 325, 338 (4), 339, 355, 356, 358 (4), 359 (2), 370, 446, 469, 470, 490, 496, 511, 534, 571 (2)

Record Group 49, General Land Office, II: 135, 223, 224

Record Group 56, Treasury Department, IV: 499, 558; V: 3, 32, 33, 139, 353; VI: 145, 369, 371, 432, 481; VII: 157, 472; VIII: 45, 159, 175, 210, 411, 473

Record Group 58, Bureau of Internal Revenue, VI: 453; VII: 99

Record Group 59, State Department, II: 30 (2), 31 (2), 37, 38 (2), 39, 48 (2), 61 (2), 62, 64 (2), 71, 78, 97, 103; IV: 278, 284 (2), 293 (2), 298, 311, 312 (2), 313, 360, 362, 445, 460, 466, 468, 471, 481 (2), 483 (2), 490, 491 (2), 493, 509 (2), 514, 527, 528, 540, 546, 547 (2), 551, 552

V: 7, 19, 27, 32, 56, 62, 66, 73, 75, 76 (2), 98, 103, 105 (2), 114, 118, 126, 133, 134, 158, 173, 178, 182, 187, 199, 339, 363, 367, 391, 392, 393, 440, 449, 451, 467, 483; VI: 19, 41, 45, 51 (2), 58, 77, 92, 95, 124, 136, 162, 171, 183, 213, 222, 260, 272, 358; VII: 110, 111, 119, 165, 216, 231, 238, 283, 297, 331, 337, 371, 373, 375, 403, 407, 475, 476, 477, 479, 494, 551

VIII: 53, 54, 57, 111, 132 (2), 157, 247, 343, 360, 415, 467, 468 (13), 469 (14), 470 (8), 471 (3), 472, 473 (2), 474, 475, 478 (4), 479 (2), 480 (4), 481, 483, 484, 485 (2), 486, 487 (2), 488, 489 (3), 490, 491 (2), 493 (2), 494 (2), 495, 497, 498, 502 (2), 505, 507, 508, 509, 510, 512, 514 (5), 515 (2), 518, 523, 527, 530, 538, 542, 552, 585, 586

Record Group 60, Justice Department, IV: 346, 366, 383, 392, 408, 448, 449, 543, 548, 554, 556; V: 163, 194, 195, 256, 267, 309, 386, 464; VI: 150, 202, 207, 223, 245, 284, 395, 495; VII: 15, 82, 128, 145, 215, 219, 220, 225, 270, 280, 292, 304, 355, 362, 428, 468, 480, 490, 497

VIII: 23, 98, 106, 122, 158, 160, 168, 190, 212, 222, 245, 268, 287, 349, 355, 368, 410, 412, 466, 475, 480, 483 (2), 488 (3), 489, 491, 492, 496, 509, 510, 524, 531, 542

Record Group 74, Bureau of Ordnance, VI: 3, 59, 272, 521, 530

Record Group 75, Office of Indian Affairs, IV: 391, 548; V: 346; VI: 164; VII: 300; VIII: 551

Record Group 77, Office of the Chief of Engineers, V: 58, 152, 177; VII: 468

Record Group 92, Office of the Quartermaster General, V: 230, 377, 390; VI: 59, 196, 476

Record Group 94, Office of the Adjutant General, I: 466; IV: 382, 387, 390, 392, 395, 398, 407, 417, 443, 448, 466, 473, 530; V: 9, 13, 33, 75, 104, 115, 139, 236, 296, 408, 456, 468, 473, 549; VI: 12, 60, 75, 88, 90, 110, 119, 132, 144, 162, 177, 216, 357, 362, 367, 403, 411, 413, 428, 433 (2), 443, 461, 463

VII: 26, 58, 106, 121, 139, 143, 154, 204, 210, 231, 240, 246, 278, 354, 367, 375, 454, 459, 471, 509, 511, 541, 545; VIII: 6, 13, 24, 31, 85, 156, 184, 185, 193, 233, 291, 334, 346, 474, 477 (2), 484, 507, 510, 513, 521, 522 (5), 523, 525, 529 (2), 536, 541, 542, 547, 549, 554, 560, 562, 564, 569, 571, 574

Record Group 107, Office of the Secretary of War, IV: 393, 405, 443, 493, 521, 526, 557; V: 94, 101, 138, 140, 171, 179, 183, 261, 503, 541; VI: 18, 60, 86, 114, 154, 184, 206, 309, 419, 490, 504, 528, 537, 545, 561

VII: 4, 27, 136, 166, 199, 204, 235, 239 (2), 240, 244, 248, 251 (2), 252 (2), 253, 257, 260, 265, 271, 272, 273, 275, 287, 289, 291, 294 (2), 297 (2), 298 (2), 304, 305, 306 (2), 308 (2), 310, 311, 316, 317, 318, 320, 322, 325, 330, 333, 335, 337, 340, 341, 343, 344, 347, 348, 350, 351 (2), 353, 354, 356 (2), 357, 358 (2), 359, 360, 362, 363, 364, 366, 367, 368, 370, 375, 379 (2), 390 (2), 391, 400, 401, 406, 407, 409, 416 (2), 417, 420, 422 (2), 424, 434, 436, 437, 438 (3), 440, 443, 444 (2), 445, 450, 453, 454, 456, 463, 465, 466 (2), 469 (2), 470, 472 (2), 473, 474, 476, 480, 481, 482 (2), 483, 484, 485 (2), 492, 493, 495, 499, 503, 508, 509, 511, 516, 519 (2), 520, 522 (2), 523, 524, 526, 529, 531, 534, 540, 541, 544 (3), 545, 546, 547

VIII: 3 (2), 4, 5, 6, 7, 8, 9 (3), 13, 19, 20, 22, 23 (2), 25 (2), 26, 27, 28 (3), 29 (3), 30, 34, 38, 41 (2), 43, 44 (2), 45, 46, 47 (2), 48, 49, 50, 57, 73, 74, 75, 76, 79 (2), 81, 82, 85,

86, 87 (2), 88 (2), 89, 91 (2), 93
(2), 94, 96, 97, 99 (2), 100, 102,
105, 110 (2), 111 (2), 116, 119, 120
(2), 121 (2), 122, 124, 125 (2), 126
(2), 136, 156, 159 (2), 166, 167 (2),
168, 169 (2), 173 (2), 174, 176, 177,
180, 182, 186, 187, 188, 190 (2),
192, 194, 198 (2), 203 (2), 206, 207,
211 (2), 212, 213, 215, 216 (2), 217,
223, 224, 226 (2), 229, 232 (2), 234,
235 (2), 237, 238, 239 (3), 240, 241,
243, 249, 250, 251, 252 (2), 255, 256
(3), 259 (2), 260, 263, 264 (2), 266,
269 (2), 273 (2), 274, 289 (2), 292,
293, 297, 298 (2), 299, 300, 301 (3),
302, 305 (2), 309, 310, 313, 314,
315, 316 (2), 319, 321, 325, 329, 337,
342, 344, 346, 348, 351, 357, 359,
365, 367, 368, 369 (2), 370, 371,
372 (2), 386, 392, 395, 405, 407, 473,
474, 475, 476, 478 (2), 479, 482,
484, 486 (2), 487, 490 (2), 491,
493, 495, 497 (2), 498 (2), 503 (3),
504, 505 (2), 506, 509 (2), 510, 511,
514, 517, 518, 520 (2), 521 (2), 523,
525 (2), 526, 544 (2), 547 (2), 563
(2), 572

*Record Group 108, Headquarters
of the Army*, V: 367, 506, 545; VI:
43, 77, 105, 210, 355 (2); VII: 100,
108, 158; VIII: 37, 379, 500, 543,
547

*Record Group 110, Provost Mar-
shall General's Bureau*, VI: 460

*Record Group 130, White House
Office*, VIII: 122, 229, 234, 236, 329,
357, 518, 531, 533, 546, 553

*Record Group 153, Office of the
Judge Advocate General (War)*, V:
15, 78, 103, 170 (2), 349, 362; VI:
211, 220, 241, 253, 280, 285, 287,
292, 293, 296 (3), 297 (4), 335 (3),
336 (5), 337 (3), 340, 347, 419, 421,
441, 442, 507, 562

VII: 2, 26, 33 (2), 65, 94, 99, 136,
161 (2), 167, 173, 175 (3), 176, 197,
219, 223, 227, 232, 276, 293, 298,
299, 307, 314, 322, 332, 357, 436, 447,
448 (2), 465, 474, 493, 497, 516, 531,
536, 543, 545, 546, 547

VIII: 8, 10, 17, 18, 24, 37, 39, 76,
90, 104 (2), 133, 180, 187, 210, 213,
219 (2), 229, 232, 233 (2), 246, 270,
309, 313, 326, 354, 357, 368, 405, 512,

513 (55), 515, 516, 517 (4), 518
(29), 519 (6), 522, 523, 525 (17),
529, 530, 531 (50), 532 (81), 533,
537, 539 (77), 540 (49), 542, 544,
545, 546 (31), 547 (2), 548, 549
(10), 550, 551 (23), 552, 554 (4),
555, 562 (3), 563 (2), 565, 567, 571
(2), 572 (2), 573, 575, 577 (14),
578 (15), 581, 585, 586

*Record Group 156, Office of the
Chief of Ordnance*, IV: 415; V: 430;
VII: 100; VIII: 480, 497

*Record Group 204, Office of the
Pardon Attorney*, IV: 299, 555; V:
57, 170, 202, 205, 211, 258 (2), 266
(3), 270, 300, 333, 336, 348, 352,
366, 390, 501; VI: 2, 55, 62, 65, 89,
98, 103, 106, 118, 133, 180, 194, 211,
240, 278, 294, 353, 385, 426, 477,
485, 488, 526, 551 (2); VII: 62, 67,
74, 77, 80, 91, 92, 105 (2), 148, 177,
195, 276, 286, 304 (2), 336, 391, 456,
463, 511; VIII: 5, 23, 32, 34, 45, 85,
112, 177, 196, 290, 298, 309, 324,
369, 370, 398, 473, 484, 494, 500 (2),
501, 508, 515, 519, 527, 535, 544,
555, 556, 562, 563, 572

*Record Group 217, General Ac-
counting Office*, IV: 407, 528; V:
394 (2); VIII: 472, 473, 474 (2),
497, 498

*Record Group 233, United States
House of Representatives*, I: 287,
420, 442, 444; II: 28; IV: 446, 450,
454, 469; V: 35, 55, 56, 61, 77, 88,
110, 132, 134, 140, 146, 162, 167,
181, 199, 229, 230, 259, 268, 270,
275, 299, 316, 539, 552; VI: 10, 39,
58, 62, 90; VII: 36, 88, 107, 113, 140,
187, 188, 198, 214, 247 (2), 274, 290,
311, 320, 327, 359, 380; VIII: 42,
135 (2), 199, 204, 271 (2), 274, 328,
414, 442, 443 (9), 444, 445 (6)

Record Group 241, Patent Office,
II: 32; V: 198

National Museum Library, Washington (DNM), IV: 460

New Salem State Park (Ill.) Museum,
I: *following* 48

New York Avenue Presbyterian
Church, Washington, V: 324; VI: 352

New-York Historical Society, New
York City (NHi), IV: 481; V: 87,
111, 200, 210, 261, 262, 263, 283,

332, 334, 339, 344, 360, 362, 365, 366, 370, 384 (2), 387, 411 (2), 416, 426, 430, 431, 432 (2), 453, 456, 483, 501; VI: 67, 74, 82, 97 (2), 106, 114, 134, 141, 166, 179, 180, 184, 197, 221, 223, 228, 285, 294, 298, 299, 312, 313, 324, 350, 352, 373, 381
VII: 11, 60, 95, 119, 121, 203, 225, 241, 250, 273, 279, 287, 308, 345, 374, 375, 389, 479, 484, 486, 510, 525; VIII: 25, 31, 158, 238, 247, 290, 427 (2), 492, 495, 511, 515 (2), 517, 520, 521, 526, 529, 530, 538, 544, 553

New York [City] Public Library (NN), III: 344, IV: 277, 337, 419, 489; V: 66, 298, 320, 352, 361, 389, 415; VI: 80, 93, 278, 282, 452, 465, 510; VII: 309, 312; VIII: 192, 468, 565
New York State Library, Albany (N), IV: 117, 185, 376, 384; V: 433; VI: 69; VII: 403; VIII: 38
Newberry Library, Chicago, VIII: 593
North Carolina State Archives, Raleigh, VIII: 468
North Shore Country Day School, Winnetka, Ill., II: 295

O · P · Q

Ohio, Historical and Philosophical Society of, Cincinnati (OCHP), III: 492; IV: 78; V: 156
Omaha (Nebr.) Public Library (NbO), IV: 511
Oregon Historical Society, Portland (OrHi), IV: 90, 101

Pennsylvania, University of, see University of Pennsylvania Library
Pennsylvania Historical Society, Philadelphia (PHi), I: 384; II: 19 (2), 205; III: 378, 384, 386; IV: 73, 98, 191, 362, 412, 416; V: 59, 118, 475; VI: 326, 344, 375, 397, 555; VII: 369, 390, 392, 468, 491, 535; VIII: 87, 424, 468
Pennsylvania State College Library, State College (PSt), IV: 70

Pequot Library, Southport, Conn. (CtSoP), VI: 368
Philadelphia, Free Library of (PP), V: 5, 341
Phillips Exeter Academy, Exeter, N. H. (NhExP), VII: 548
Pierpont Morgan Library, New York City (NNP), I: 386; II: 356, 448, 547; V: 22, 169, 471; VI: 150, 440, 468, 469; VII: 77, 132, 259; VIII: 287
Polish Roman Catholic Union, Chicago, IV: 480
Princeton (N. J.) University Library (NjP), VIII: 184
Public Record Office, London, England, IV: 417; V: 118

Quincy and Adams County (Ill.), Historical Society of, II: 118

R

Rhode Island State Archives, Providence, VIII: 468
Rochester (N. Y.), University of, see

University of Rochester (N. Y.) Library

S · T

Saddle and Sirloin Club, Union Stock-
yards, Chicago, VII: 279
St. John's Seminary Library, Cama-
rillo, Calif. (CCamStJ), IV: 109,
508; V: 156; VI: 53, 532; VII: 128,
331; VIII: 77, 489
Sangamon County (Ill.) Records,
Springfield, I: 16, 148; II: 114, 162,
201; VIII: 430, 431 (12), 432 (3),
433, 434 (5), 435 (2), 441, 452 (3)
Scheide Library, see John Scheide
Library
Sisters of Charity of Nazareth (Ky.),
VIII: 219
Skaneateles (N. Y.) Library Associa-
tion (NSk), II: 308; V: 31
South Dakota Historical Society,
Pierre, IV: 325

Southworth Library, Dryden, N. Y.
(NDry), VIII: 101
Speed Art Museum, Louisville, Ky.,
V: 61
Springfield (Ill.) City Council Min-
utes, VIII: 448
Springfield (Mass.) Library Associa-
tion (MS), VIII: 194
Springfield (Ill.) Marine Bank, IV:
189; VIII: 452

Tazewell County (Ill.) Records, Pekin,
VIII: 441
Tennessee Historical Society, Nash-
ville (THi), I: 211
Tippecanoe County Historical Associ-
ation, Lafayette, Ind. (InLTHi),
VI: 343

U

Union Bank of Commerce, Cleveland,
Ohio, VIII: 589
Union League Club, Philadelphia, VI:
534
Union Pacific Railroad Company,
Omaha, Nebr., VI: 491
United States District Court, South-
ern District of Illinois, Springfield,
VIII: 244
United States Military Academy Li-
brary, West Point, N. Y. (NWM),
IV: 369; VII: 74
United States Naval Academy Mu-
seum, Annapolis, Md., V: 154; VI:
562
University of Chicago Library (ICU),
I: 13, 496; II: 37, 52, 55, 71; III:

520; IV: 37, 179; VI: 51; VII:
294
University of Colorado Library,
Boulder (CoU), II: 14
University of Illinois, Urbana (IU),
I: 120; III: 37
University of Kentucky Library, Lex-
ington (KyU), VI: 141
University of Pennsylvania Library,
Philadelphia (PU), II: 117
University of Rochester (N. Y.) Li-
brary (NRU), IV: 98, 154, 186; V:
365; VI: 112; VII: 268; VIII: 356
University of Vermont Library, Bur-
lington (VtU), VIII: 207
University of Virginia Library, Char-
lottesville (ViU), VIII: 303

V

Vassar College, Poughkeepsie, N. Y., VIII: 463
Vermont, Secretary of State's Office, Montpelier, VIII: 468

Vermont, University of, *see* University of Vermont Library
Virginia, University of, *see* University of Virginia Library

W · Y

Wadsworth Atheneum, Hartford, Conn., V: 389
Warren County (Ill.) Deed Records, Monmouth, VIII: 432
Watertown (Conn.) Library Association (CtWat), II: 537
Watertown (Mass.) Town Clerk's Office, V: 407
West Virginia University Library, Morgantown (WvU), V: 166
Western Reserve Historical Society, Cleveland, Ohio (OClWHi), III: 494; IV: 30, 188, 520; V: 75, 221, 291, 447; VI: 360; VII: 93, 110, 354;

VIII: 345, 422, 464, 470, 553
William L. Clements Library, University of Michigan, Ann Arbor (MiU-C), II: 360; VII: 176; VIII: 461
Wilmington (Del.) Institute Free Library (DeWI), VI: 180; VIII: 4
Wisconsin, State Historical Society of, Madison (WHi), VI: 271; VII: 506

Yale University Library, New Haven, Conn. (CtY), III: 393; IV: 165, 549; V: 333; VIII: 374